SIXTH CANADIAN EDITION

personal finance

Jack R. Kapoor
College of DuPage

Les R. Dlabay
Lake Forest College

Robert J. Hughes
Dallas County Community Colleges

Arshad Ahmad
McMaster University

Jordan Fortino
McMaster University

McGraw-Hill Ryerson

Personal Finance
Sixth Canadian Edition

Statistics Canada information is used with the permission of Statistics Canada. Users are forbidden to copy this material and/or redisseminate the data, in an original or modified form, for commercial purposes, without the expressed permission of Statistic Canada. Information on the availability of the wide range of data from Statistics Canada can be obtained from Statistics Canada's Regional Offices, its World Wide Web site at http://www.statcan.ca and its toll-free access number 1-800-263-1136

The Internet addresses listed in the text were accurate at the time of publication. The inclusion of a Web site does not indicate an endorsement by the authors or McGraw-Hill Ryerson, nor does McGraw-Hill Ryerson guarantee the accuracy of information presented at these sites.

ISBN-13: 978-1-25-945314-4
ISBN-10: 1-25-945314-6

Care has been taken to trace ownership of copyright material contained in this text; however, the publisher will welcome any information that enables them to rectify any reference or credit for subsequent editions.

5 6 7 8 9 WEB 1 9 8 7 6

Director of product Management: Rhondda McNabb
Senior product Manager: Kimberley Veevers
Marketing Manager: Jeremy Guimond
Product Developer: Kamilah Reid-Burrell
Senior Product Team Associate: Marina Seguin
Permissions Editor: Tracy Leonard
Supervising Editor: Jessica Barnoski
Proofreader: Erin Moore
Plant Production Coordinator: Sheryl MacAdam
Cover and Interior Design: Valid Design & Layout/Dave Murphy
Cover Images: Woman on beach: Glow Images/Superstock; Smartphone: Gregor Schuster/Getty Images; Graph on smartphone:
Printer: Webcom
Brand X Pictures
Page Layout: Aptara®, Inc.

Printed in Canada

JACK KAPOOR

College of DuPage

Jack Kapoor is a Professor of Business and Economics in the Business and Technology Division. Dr. Kapoor has taught Business and Economics at College of DuPage since 1969. He received his B.A. and M.S. from San Francisco State College and his Ed.D. from Northern Illinois University. Professor Kapoor was awarded the Business and Services Division's Outstanding Professor Award for l999–2000.

Dr. Kapoor is known internationally as a co-author of several textbooks including *Business: A Practical Approach* (Rand McNally), *Business* (Houghton Mifflin), and *Focus on Personal Finance* (Richard D. Irwin/McGraw-Hill).

LES DLABAY

Lake Forest College

Les Dlabay teaches in the Department of Economics and Business at Lake Forest College, Lake Forest, Illinois. Over the past 25 years, he has taught more than 30 different courses in high school, community college, university, adult education, and teacher preparation programs. Dr. Dlabay has developed a wide variety of textbook materials, student activity guides, instructor manuals, testing programs, audio-visual materials, and software packages in the areas of Personal Finance, Consumer Economics, and International Business.

Dr. Dlabay has served as a consultant to corporations, educational institutions, and government agencies. He has presented more than 140 workshops and seminars in over 20 states to encourage teachers to actively involve students in the learning process with video presentations, newsletters, interviews, and Internet research activities.

ROBERT HUGHES

Dallas County Community Colleges

Robert Hughes teaches business, management, and finance courses at Dallas County Community Colleges. In addition to *Personal Finance*, he has written college texts for Introduction to Business, Small Business Management and Entrepreneurship, and Business Math and presently has five books in publication. Dr. Hughes received his bachelor's degree from Southern Nazarene University and his master's and doctorate degrees from the University of North Texas.

ARSHAD AHMAD

McMaster University

Arshad Ahmad is the Associate Vice President, Teaching & Learning at McMaster University in Hamilton, Ontario, Canada. He is also the Director of McMaster's Institute for Innovation and Excellence in Teaching and Learning. His current research interests are in Accelerated Learning Designs, Conceptual Change, and Teaching (Learning) Philosophies. Recently, he completed a 4-year term as the President of the National Society for Teaching and Learning in Higher Education.

Arshad received his MBA and Ph.D. in Educational Psychology at McGill University. He is the recipient of several Teaching and Professor-of-the-Year awards from local and international universities. In 1992, he was recognized for leadership in teaching with a lifetime 3M National Teaching Fellowship. In 1999, he designed and taught the first web-based course in Personal Finance at the John Molson School of Business at Concordia University, which continues to attract record numbers of students.

JORDAN FORTINO

McMaster University

Jordan Fortino is a lecturer at McMaster University, specializing in personal finance at the masters and undergraduate level. He also teaches several upper level courses in the department of finance including Real Estate Finance, Entrepreneurial Finance, Financial Management for Healthcare Professionals, and Financial Management for Sports Organizations.

Jordan received his MBA from DeGroote School of Business at McMaster University. After completing his MBA, Jordan worked in the financial services industry in several different Financial Advisory roles at a big-6 Canadian Bank, specializing in investments and credit analysis. In his current capacity, Jordan is working with DeGroote School of Business to develop the first online undergraduate course in Personal Finance. He also invests avidly in real estate and manages projects including the development and redevelopment of real estate.

Brief Contents

Contents

② MANAGING YOUR PERSONAL FINANCES

Chapter 4—The Banking Services of Financial Institutions   116

Chapter 5—Introduction to Consumer Credit   143

3 INSURING YOUR ASSETS

4 — INVESTING YOUR FINANCIAL RESOURCES

THE BOOK AND REALITY

In 2008, as we went to press, the world's stock exchanges were spiralling downward, stripping asset values in the trillions of dollars. It was a tumultuous period of anxiety and uncertainty. Today, while there is less drama in the equity markets, uncertainty remains as the number one issue on the minds of most people in the world. Although to a lesser degree than in 2008 and 2009, Governments continue to intervene and inject liquidity to keep markets functioning. A number of revered institutions continue to be revalued across industries. Additionally, numerous forecasters have continued to suggest that Canada is ripe for a real-estate correction, with some prognosticators suggesting adjustments in the magnitude of 30% in some Canadian markets.

While these extraordinary times are now the new normal, we recognize that the problem of excessive debt and the corrosive impact of borrowed money have not been resolved. In fact, with interest rates in Canada at a continued all-time low, some suggest the problem is only getting worse. To provide context to the economic woes that continue, we explore the implications of the world's financial crisis in two articles. First, the article *The Greatest Speculative Bubble in History?*, at the end of the preface, offers perspective on the continuing crisis by "myth-busting" some of the scenarios that led to the current economic mess. Second, *The Pillaging of America* introduces Part 4: Investing Your Financial Resources, and provides a context to the chapters within that section. While we do not pretend to have the right answers in this historic drama unfolding in economies around the world, we invite you to join us in asking difficult questions and helping each other adapt to the new emerging realities in the money, banking, consumer, and investment markets.

Families around the world are continuing to react in disbelief to the changes in the value of their savings and investments as pension, insurance, and retirement funds are implicated. It is in this climate of change when personal financial management is more important than ever. In the following sections, we share our pedagogical approach, content design, and learning resources to help you meet your challenges and to ensure an exciting journey of discovery in the world of personal finance.

VARIETY MAKES FOR A RICH LEARNING ENVIRONMENT

A mosaic emerges when its pieces fit together and when the whole exceeds the sum of its parts. We recognize that students have different learning styles and that a textbook can have features that appeal to these differences and help students understand and apply concepts. Beyond informing our readers, in writing this textbook we want to encourage students to raise important questions that require further investigation. As well, we decided to limit coverage to 15 chapters grouped within five sections so that we could provide sufficient depth without presuming to give the "last word" on each topic.

Thus, we took on the following triple challenge in revising each chapter for this edition. First, each chapter must qualify as being learner-centred and provide examples and situations students can easily relate to. Second, multiple perspectives must raise the bar of content so that the students begin to ask good questions and not simply accept material as prescription. Third, learning depends on the organization of material so that important concepts stand out and are reinforced in as many different contexts as possible.

UPDATED CONTENT

There are numerous changes, updates, and new exhibits in this edition. The reader might find the following highlights especially useful:

Chapter 1: Additional questions and examples on financial planning.

Chapter 2: Updated information on creating personal budgets and personal financial planning.

Chapter 3: Updated information on Tax-Free Savings Accounts, new information on the treatment of dividends for tax purposes, revised tax rates, tax scam warnings, and recent tax law changes for planning a tax strategy and filing an income tax return.

Chapter 4: Enhanced discussion on the higher costs of financial services, revised analysis of interest rates using current market conditions, and examples of using online banking features such as email money transfers.

Chapter 5: Details as to how the over-use of credit led to the Great Recession, more on credit card fraud, costs, features, and benefits; and policies for fraudulent charges, including Canadian scores equivalent to the U.S. FICO and VantageScore and details about newly enacted legislation to limit how much people can borrow against their homes.

Chapter 6: Update of information on bursaries and student loans such as the Ontario Student Assistance Program (OSAP) and a new article detailing how high interest rates are costing Canadians a lot of money.

Chapter 7: New information on additional types of mortgages and qualifications and changes to mortgage rules in Canada, do-it-yourself mortgages, prepayment options and penalties regarding refinancing, inclusion of a sample real estate purchase agreement, and an overview of renting versus buying.

Chapter 8: Updated information on errors and omissions in insurance and underlying factors affecting auto insurance and information on how recent natural disasters in Canada have impacted the insurance industry and policy holders.

Chapter 9: Revised information on life insurance fees and Canada's national health care expenditures.

Chapter 10: Update on new rules affecting income trusts and exemptions for REITs; an update on Canadian investment trends, a deeper understanding of risk related to lack of transparency, conflicts of interest with ratings agencies, boards of directors, and executive focus on short-term profits.

Chapter 11: Updated information on hedge funds and private equity, information about revised tax treatment of certain stock transactions, as well as links and exhibits that will help the reader evaluate a corporation's stocks and whether one should use a full-service or discount broker, including a revised fee guide associated with using online discount brokers.

Chapter 12: Updated information on sample bond transactions, current bond yields, real return bonds, details of the single-largest bond issuance in Canadian history, and why bond valuation is important for increasing the number of investors who buy bonds.

Chapter 13: Revised coverage of current mutual fund characteristics and mutual fund return rates through 2013.

Chapter 14: Revised information on types of pension plans, including details of recent changes to both CPP and OAS, defined benefit pension plans, pension adjustments (PA), pension adjustment reversals (PSPA), and past service pension adjustments (PAR).

Chapter 15: Updated information on the minimum requirements of a will and the characteristics of ethical wills, and more information on estate planning strategies.

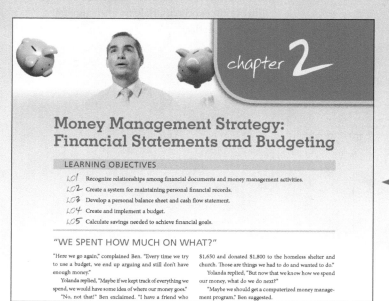

CHAPTER OPENING CASES describe a situation that the learner will face or is currently facing. A case begins each chapter's discussion by presenting a problem, dilemma, or circumstance that clearly needs immediate attention. The questions accompanying the case correspond to the sequence of the chapter's contents and link procedures that may otherwise seem unrelated.

LEARNING OBJECTIVES structure the chapter, and each objective is repeated in the margin at the appropriate point in the main body of the chapter. The Learning Objectives appear again in the summary at the end of the chapter and are used to organize end-of-chapter questions, problems, and exercises, as well as materials in the Instructor's Manual and the Test Bank.

LEARNING OBJECTIVES

LO1 Recognize relationships among financial documents and money management activities.
LO2 Create a system for maintaining personal financial records.
LO3 Develop a personal balance sheet and cash flow statement.
LO4 Create and implement a budget.
LO5 Calculate savings needed to achieve financial goals.

"WE SPENT HOW MUCH ON WHAT?"

"Here we go again," complained Ben. "Every time we try $1,650 and donated $1,800 to the homeless shelter and

SUMMARY OF LEARNING OBJECTIVES

LO1 **Recognize relationships among financial documents and money management activities.**
Successful money management requires effective coordination of personal financial records, personal financial statements, and budgeting activities.

LO2 **Create a system for maintaining personal financial records.**
An organized system of financial records and documents is the foundation of effective money management. This system should provide ease of access as well as security for financial documents that may be impossible to replace.

LO3 **Develop a personal balance sheet and cash flow statement.**
A personal balance sheet, also known as a net worth statement, is prepared by listing all items of value (assets) and all amounts owed to others (liabilities). The difference between your total assets and your total liabilities is your net worth. A cash flow statement, also called a personal income and expenditure statement, is a summary of cash receipts and payments for a given period, such as a month or a year. This report provides data on your income and spending patterns.

Financial Planning for Life's Situations

I Need $20,000 for My Education. Should I Borrow or Work Part-time?

Jim Stewarts is an accounting major at Concordia University; he takes five courses each semester and expects to graduate in three years. Jim came to the Financial Aid office for help in deciding whether he should borrow money or work part-time. Let's look at his situation:

Residential status: Jim lives with his parents and is free of food and board charges.

Potential number of hours allotted for part-time work: Assuming 35 weeks in a school year and that Jim will be unable to work for four weeks, Jim is left with 31 work weeks. Considering Jim's grades are of primary importance, we advise him to work for a maximum of 15 hours a week.

Potential number of hours allotted for full-time summer employment: Jim will have 17 weeks (52 less 35 weeks) during the summer, when he can work full-time for 40 hours a week. We suggest he work only 15 of these weeks so that some time is set aside for a vacation.

Jim's yearly gross income is $6,975 + $9,000 = $15,975.

Jim will not have use of the entire amount. His annual pay—net of taxes, Quebec Pension Plan, and Employment Insurance payments—is $14,485 (a total of $1,490 is deducted according to 2013 rates). However, when he files his income tax return, he should receive a refund of any taxes paid ($521 of the total $1,490 deducted).

IF JIM TAKES OUT A STUDENT LOAN FOR $20,000:

There are student loans offered by both the federal and provincial governments; these loans are of greater advantage because they offer lower interest rates than the banks and you are only required to pay them back once you graduate. If Jim were to take out a loan today for $20,000 from the Quebec Government's Aide Financiere aux Etudes program, he will pay an annual interest rate of 3.50 percent (afe.gouv.qc.ca/en/apresEtudes/tauxinteret.asp). Since he wants to pay the loan back in six years after graduation, using the present value formula he will make monthly payments of $308.37. (See Appendix 1B for PV of an annuity

STUDENT WORK has been incorporated into selected Financial Planning boxes and depicts how former students have approached a number of decisions relevant to them. These samples serve to model for the students' peers how they tackled difficult questions by highlighting methods of analysis and suggested courses of action.

FINANCIAL PLANNING FOR LIFE'S SITUATIONS offers information that encourages the learner to take action. This feature is based on the principle of active learning; it presents example situations to prompt learners to apply newly acquired concepts and make unique financial planning decisions.

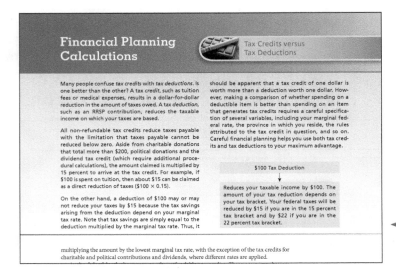

Financial Planning Calculations

Tax Credits versus Tax Deductions

Many people confuse *tax credits* with *tax deductions*. Is one better than the other? A tax *credit*, such as tuition fees or medical expenses, results in a dollar-for-dollar reduction in the amount of taxes owed. A tax *deduction*, such as an RRSP contribution, reduces the taxable income on which your taxes are based.

All non-refundable tax credits reduce taxes payable with the limitation that taxes payable cannot be reduced below zero. Aside from charitable donations that total more than $200, political donations and the dividend tax credit (which require additional procedural calculations), the amount claimed is multiplied by 15 percent to arrive at the tax credit. For example, if $100 is spent on tuition, then about $15 can be claimed as a direct reduction of taxes ($100 × 0.15).

On the other hand, a deduction of $100 may or may not reduce your taxes by $15 because the tax savings arising from the deduction depend on your marginal tax rate. Note that tax savings are simply equal to the deduction multiplied by the marginal tax rate. Thus, it

should be apparent that a tax credit of one dollar is worth more than a deduction worth one dollar. However, making a comparison of whether spending on a deductible item is better than spending on an item that generates a tax credit requires a careful specification of several variables, including your marginal federal rate, the province in which you reside, the rules attributed to the tax credit in question, and so on. Careful financial planning helps you use both tax credits and tax deductions to your maximum advantage.

$100 Tax Deduction

Reduces your taxable income by $100. The amount of your tax reduction depends on your tax bracket. Your federal taxes will be reduced by $15 if you are in the 15 percent tax bracket and by $22 if you are in the 22 percent tax bracket.

---

multiplying the amount by the lowest marginal tax rate, with the exception of the tax credits for charitable and political contributions and dividends, where different rates are applied.

FINANCIAL PLANNING CALCULATIONS features approximately 100 mathematical applications that the learner must master. All these calculations are situated in decisions that are typical of what learners encounter but may have shied away from due to the numbers behind these operations. The procedures illustrated in these calculations reinforce concepts introduced in the chapter in an applied setting. They are also tied to end-of-chapter questions and exercises.

ADVICE FROM A PRO is a great example of distributed expertise and multiple perspectives. In this box, industry professionals provide the kind of advice one can take home and internalize in order to make sense of the informational deluge that all of us face.

Advice from a Pro

A Pro Speaks on Tax Planning

Any attempt to calculate your investment return must include the least exciting, most annoying financial subject: taxes. Even the word makes me cringe!

The government will get their share of your money—no exceptions. Smart tax planning helps you pay less tax legally. The federal government isn't fooling around: Those who use illegitimate techniques to avoid paying taxes get socked with high-priced penalties or jail time. Pay your taxes on time.

Around the first of the year, you will begin to receive a series of statements from the jobs at which you have worked or financial institutions where you hold accounts. This includes brokerage firms, banks, mutual funds, and other intermediaries. Find the receipts from any charitable donations you've made and proof of any employment-related expenses you plan on writing off. Keep these materials together; lost forms waste time and money!

Your tax return has several sections of which you need to be aware. Generally, your income should be added up, including any losses. Figure your taxable income, factor in additional credits or taxes, and write a cheque. *You've just paid your taxes!*

For those with a home business, complicated returns, or sketchy paperwork, some professional tax guidance is highly recommended—*and worth it!* Spending some money on a tax preparer or CPA might seem daunting but will ensure that your return is filed accurately and rapidly.

Did you know?

Canadian households spent an average of $75,443 in 2012, including $56,000 on goods and services.

SOURCE: rcinet.ca/en/2014/01/29/ statistics-canada-canadian-household- spending.

The rate of inflation varies. During the late 1950s and early 1960s, the annual inflation rate was in the 1 to 3 percent range. During the late 1970s and early 1980s, the cost of living increased 10 to 12 percent annually.

More recently, the annual price increase for most goods and services as measured by the consumer price index has been in the 1 to 3 percent range. The *consumer price index* (CPI), published by Statistics Canada, is a measure of the average change in the prices urban consumers pay for a fixed "basket" of goods and services. For current CPI information, go to statcan.gc.ca.

CONSUMER SPENDING Total demand for goods and services in the economy influences employment opportunities and the potential for income. As consumer purchasing increases, the financial resources of current and prospective employees expand. This situation improves the financial condition of many households.

In contrast, reduced spending causes unemployment, since staff reduction commonly results from a company's reduced financial resources. The financial hardships of unemployment are a major concern of business, labour, and government. Retraining programs, income assistance, and job services can help people adjust.

INTEREST RATES In simple terms, interest rates represent the cost of money. Like everything else, money has a price. The forces of supply and demand influence interest rates. When consumer saving and investing increase the supply of money, interest rates tend to decrease. However, as consumer, business, government, and foreign borrowing increase the demand for money, interest rates tend to rise.

DID YOU KNOW? boxes contain up-to-date facts, figures, and answers to frequently asked questions. They are featured several times within each chapter and typically elicit an "a-ha!" from the learner. These are not just catchy but provide well-researched insights that are often quoted by students in discussion forums.

CONCEPT CHECKS are a valuable device to help learners digest conceptual chunks within a section before they proceed further into the chapter. These questions also serve to refocus the student's attention on the learning objective that applies to each section.

All other provinces and territories apply a Tax on Income (TONI) system that permits the province to decide its own tax rates to be applied to taxable income, as well as different non-refundable and refundable tax credits.

taxable income The net amount of income, after allowable deductions, on which income tax is computed.

employment income Remuneration received for personal effort.

CONCEPT CHECK 3–1

1. How should you consider taxes in your financial planning?
2. What types of taxes do people frequently overlook when making financial decisions?
3. Who must file an income tax return?

FINANCIAL PLANNING ACTIVITIES

1. *Researching Financial Services.* Using Web sites or library resources, obtain information about new developments in financial services. How have technology, changing economic conditions, and new legislation affected the types and availability of various saving and chequing financial services? LO1

2. *Monitoring Economic Conditions.* Research current economic conditions (interest rates, inflation) using *The Financial Post,* other library resources, or Web sites. Based on current economic conditions, what actions would you recommend to people who are saving and borrowing money? LO1

3. *Comparing Financial Institutions.* Collect advertisements and promotional information from several financial institutions, or go to financial institution Web sites, such as Bank of Montreal (bmo.com) and TD Canada Trust (tdcanadatrust. com). Create a list of factors that you might consider when comparing costs and benefits of various savings plans and chequing accounts. LO2

4. *Obtaining Opinions about Financial Services.* Survey several people to determine awareness and use of various financial services, such as online banking, "smart cards," and cheque-writing software. LO2

5. *Researching Credit Unions.* Using the Web site for the Credit Union Central of Canada (cucentral.ca) or other sources, obtain information about joining a credit union and the services this type of financial institution offers. LO2

6. *Comparing Savings Plans.* Collect advertisements from several financial institutions with information about the savings plans they offer. (You may do this using the Web sites of various financial institutions.) Compare the features and potential earnings of two or three savings plans. LO3, LO4

7. *Researching Current Savings Rates.* Using library resources (such as *The Financial Post* and other current business periodicals) or Web sites (such as money.canoe.ca), prepare a summary of current rates of return for various savings accounts, money market accounts, GICs and CSBs. LO3, LO4

8. *Analyzing Cheque-Writing Software.* Visit software retailers to obtain information about the features in various personal computer programs used for maintaining a chequing account. Information about such programs as Managing Your Money, Microsoft Money, and Quicken may be obtained on the Internet. LO5

138

FINANCIAL PLANNING ACTIVITIES provide an opportunity for students to translate learning objectives into research, which in turn feeds into decisions they may be ready to make. A "To Do" list includes various procedures, techniques, and sources of information.

LIFE SITUATION CASE

A Single Father's Tax Situation

Ever since his wife's death, Eric Armano has faced difficult personal and financial circumstances. His job provides him with a fairly good income but requires him to hire a caregiver for his daughters, ages 8 and 10, nearly 20 days a month. This requires him to use in-home child care services that consume a large portion of his income. Since the Armanos live in a small apartment, this arrangement has been very inconvenient.

Although Eric has created an investment fund for his daughters' education and for his retirement, he has not sought to select investments that offer tax benefits. Overall, he needs to look at several aspects of his tax-planning activities to find strategies that will best serve his current and future financial needs.

Eric has assembled the following information for the current tax year:

Earnings from wages	$47,500
Interest earned on GIC	$ 125
RRSP deduction	$ 2,000
Savings account interest	$ 65
Federal income tax deducted at source	$ 4,863

Total non-refundable tax credit amounts	$13,200
Child care deduction	$ 6,300
Filing status: Head of household	

Questions

1. What are Eric's major financial concerns in his current situation?
2. In what ways might Eric improve his tax-planning efforts?
3. Is Eric typical of many people in our society with regard to tax planning? Why, or why not?
4. What additional actions might Eric investigate regarding taxes and personal financial planning?
5. Calculate the following:
   a) What is Eric's 2007 federal taxable income? (Refer to Exhibit 3–1, page 75).
   b) What is his total 2007 federal tax liability? What is his average 2007 federal tax rate?
   c) Will Eric receive a tax refund or owe additional taxes to the federal government for 2007?

LIFE SITUATION CASES provide opportunities for the learner to understand real-life situations that individuals face. These cases allow the student to assume the role of a consultant who can identify underlying problems, establish a framework for analysis, clarify issues, and propose possible solutions.

THE CONTINUOUS CASE reinforces the benefits of case-based teaching by linking the major concepts presented in each of the five sections in the text. It provides an opportunity to identify and analyze a range of personal financial decisions about several topics in a given section. Students begin to appreciate the broad connections between chapters and sections.

CONTINUOUS CASE FOR PART 1

GETTING STARTED: PLANNING FOR THE FUTURE

Life Situation
Single; age 22; starting a career; no dependants

Financial Goals

- Evaluate current financial situation
- Establish a personal financial plan
- Develop a budgeting system for spending and savings

Financial Data

Monthly income	$2,400
Living expenses	1,980
Assets	6,200
Liabilities	1,270
Emergency fund	300

While in university, Pamela Jenkins worked part-time and was never concerned about long-term financial planning. Rather than creating a budget, she used her chequebook and savings account (which usually had a very low balance) to handle her financial needs.

After completing university, Pamela began her career as a sales representative for a clothing manufacturer located in Montreal. After one year, her assets consist of a 1995 Chevrolet, a television set, a stereo, and some clothing and other personal belongings, with a total value of $6,200.

Since a portion of her income is based on commissions, her monthly income varies from one month to the next. This situation has made it difficult for Pamela to establish a realistic budget. During lean months, she has had to resort to using her credit card to make ends meet. In fact, her credit card debt, $1,270, is her only liability at this time. Her only other source of income is a large tax refund. In the past, she has always used tax refunds to finance major purchases (a vacation or furniture) or pay off credit card debt.

Questions

1. What financial decisions should Pamela be thinking about at this point in her life?
2. What are some short-term, intermediate, and long-term financial goals that Pamela might want to develop?
3. How should Pamela budget for fluctuations in her income caused by commission earnings?
4. Assume Pamela's federal tax refund is $1,100. Given her current situation, what should she do with the refund?
5. Based on her life situation, what type of tax planning should Pamela consider?

COMPREHENSIVE TEACHING AND LEARNING PACKAGE

McGraw-Hill Connect™ is a web-based assignment and assessment platform that gives students the means to better connect with their coursework, with their instructors, and with the important concepts that they will need to know for success now and in the future. With Connect, instructors can deliver assignments, quizzes and tests easily online. Students can practice important skills at their own pace and on their own schedule. With Connect, students also get 24/7 online access to an eBook—an online edition of the text—to aid them in successfully completing their work, wherever and whenever they choose.

LEARNSMART

No two students are alike. Why should their learning paths be? LearnSmart uses revolutionary adaptive technology to build a learning experience unique to each student's individual needs. It starts by identifying the topics a student knows and does not know. As the student progresses, LearnSmart adapts and adjusts the content based on his or her individual strengths, weaknesses, and confidence, ensuring that every minute spent studying with LearnSmart is the most efficient and productive study time possible.

SMARTBOOK

As the first and only adaptive reading experience, SmartBook is changing the way students read and learn. SmartBook creates a personalized reading experience by highlighting the most important concepts a student needs to learn at that moment in time. As a student engages with SmartBook, the reading experience continuously adapts by highlighting content based on what each student knows and doesn't know. This ensures that he or she is focused on the content needed to close specific knowledge gaps, while it simultaneously promotes long-term learning.

INSTRUCTOR'S RESOURCES AVAILABLE ON CONNECT™

- **Instructor's Manual:** The Instructor's Manual is a course planning guide with instructional strategies, course projects, and supplementary resource lists. The Chapter Teaching Materials section of the Instructor's Manual provides a chapter overview, the chapter objectives with summaries, introductory activities, and detailed lecture outlines with teaching suggestions. This section also includes concluding activities, ready-to-duplicate quizzes, supplementary lecture materials and activities, and answers to Concept Checks, end-of-chapter questions, problems, and cases.
- **Computerized Test Bank:** Prepared by Glenn Davis of Red River College, the computerized test bank consists of over 1,000 true-false, multiple choice, and essay questions. The test bank is available in McGraw-Hill's EZ Test software, a user-friendly program for Windows that enables you to quickly create customized exams. You can sort questions by format, edit existing questions or add new ones, and scramble questions for multiple versions of the same test.
- **Microsoft® PowerPoint® Presentations:** Prepared by Cyndi Hornby of Fanshawe College, the PowerPoint lecture presentations may be edited and manipulated to fit a particular course format.

SUPERIOR SOLUTIONS AND SUPPORT

The McGraw-Hill Ryerson team is ready to help you assess and integrate any of our products, technology, and services into your course for optimal teaching and learning performance. Whether it's helping your students improve their grades, or putting your entire course online, the McGraw-Hill Ryerson team is here to help you do it. Contact your Learning Solutions Consultant today to learn how to maximize all of McGraw-Hill Ryerson's resources! For more information on the latest technology and Learning Solutions offered by McGraw-Hill Ryerson and its partners, please visit us online: **www.mheducation.ca/he/solutions**.

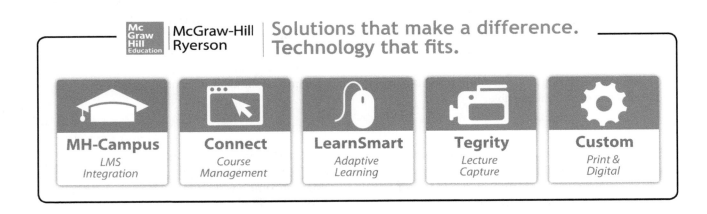

ACKNOWLEDGEMENTS

We express our deepest appreciation for the efforts of colleagues, contributors, and students for giving this textbook its own flavour and character. Thanks also go to the following reviewers whose constructive suggestions have been incorporated as much as possible. They are:

John Athanasiou, *KPMG LLP (Hamilton)*
Robert Foster, *Fanshawe College*
Jason Priest, *University of Toronto*
Vince Raso, *KPMG LLP (Hamilton)*
Barbara Rice, *Conestoga College*
Kamal Smimou, *University of Ontario Institute of Technology*
James Waring, *Vancouver Island University*

We would also like to acknowledge the professional contributions made by McGraw-Hill Higher Education and McGraw-Hill Ryerson. Thanks go to Kimberley Veevers, Senior Product Manager; Kamilah Reid-Burrell, Product Developer; Jessica Barnoski, Supervising Editor; and Erin Moore, Proofreader.

Finally, we look forward to your comments, suggestions, and questions. It is our hope that this textbook will make a difference in the lives of your students.

Arshad Ahmad
arshad@mcmaster.ca

Jordan Fortino
jordanfortino@gmail.com

THE GREATEST SPECULATIVE BUBBLE IN HISTORY?

Just as we talk about the great crash and Depression of 1929–1939, people will still talk about the great bubble, crash, and economic crisis of 2000–2013 a hundred years from now. In summary, what is common during both periods is a technological revolution financed by a speculative bubble that created record debt and illusory expectations of easy and instant wealth.

The previous paragraph was written for a previous edition of this text. However, we now revise these two comparative periods to 1929–1950 and 2000–2025. The U.S. crisis that started in 2008 evolved into a worldwide mess that still has not totally resolved itself, courtesy of our governments, central banks, financial institutions, Wall Street, voters, and consumers. All seem determined to spend above their means indefinitely. Choose your target for blame, but we are in it together.

IT IS NOT CYCLICAL, IT IS STRUCTURAL

What could have been a harmful cyclical financial crisis has turned into a distressing structural depression referred to as the Great Recession. Political and financial leaders have increased government and central bank interventions. In the process, they have created dangerous levels of debt and currency devaluation. Their interventions seem to treat the economic problems as if they were cyclical.

In a cyclical recession, providing access to debt and liquidity can be a good thing. Cheaper and more abundant money allows firms to clean up their balance sheets, reformulate business plans, and ultimately generate more revenues.

The current structural change includes a technological revolution spawned by the Internet, a speculative bubble, significant demographic changes, globalization, and the proliferation of derivative products. Combined, these factors have created conditions that require extreme adjustments in our economies and in our standard of living. Economic and investment principles have not changed, but the context certainly has. Point the finger where you may; as a society we have not yet adapted to the changes.

To help the reader to better understand what we believe is a continuing period of structural change, we revisit the "myths" that we outlined in a previous edition.

MYTH #1: STOCKS ALWAYS BEAT BONDS

Although the past forty years have clearly demonstrated that bonds do as well or better than stocks over many long periods, most investors still believe that stocks are better.

One of the reasons for this includes remuneration for the investment industry, including banks. Banks simply earn more by selling financial products that include stocks rather than bonds or money market investments.

Another reason for the preference for stocks is past market performance measures. A study by Franklin Templeton Institutional (presented at a conference of CFA Montreal) covering 1970 to 2005 showed the following: A Canadian Bond total return index had an annualized return of 9.6%, and Canadian stocks a return of 10.3%. After fees and commissions, that would make these two assets classes about equal. However, had you invested in a long-term bond index, you would have outperformed stocks over that time horizon.

MYTH #2: RISK IS VOLATILITY, WHICH CAN BE QUANTIFIED AND MANAGED

By clinging to statistical measures such as correlation, standard deviation, covariance, and the like, financial institutions thought they could manage risk quantitatively and continued to increase their leverage (debt). Two other underlying factors include:

1. A misunderstanding and misuse of the efficient market hypothesis and the Capital Asset Pricing Model (CAPM), which has been the hallmark of modern portfolio theory. First

introduced by Harry Markowitz in 1952, the misinterpretation of his work led to the definition of risk as volatility of expected returns. We feel that risk involves the chance that an asset will lose its ability to create future cash flows, and therefore permanently lose value. Volatility is only the market's expression of changes to the perception of risk.

2. Incredibly irresponsible deregulation, starting with the repeal of the Glass Steagall Act in 1999 and the consequent lack of regulation in derivative and swap markets, which continue to date.

A newsletter explaining the crisis used the following title: "The Dumbest Smart People in the World." The financial industry has recruited physicists, mathematicians, and statisticians at the expense of principled portfolio managers.

Since the turn of the century, it seems that at least two important questions were ignored. First, basic insurance and investment principles were overlooked. Notice that if everyone uses the same risk model based on volatility, it follows that at some point everyone will want to sell at the same time. Who in this situation will buy? Second, if most financial institutions, investors, and speculators protect their bonds and other leveraged investment risks with a few insurance firms who only insure those types of products, how will the insurance firms pay back when everyone has claims at the same time? This scenario occurred in 2008: firms were not able to pay back investors and subsequently went bankrupt.

MYTH #3: VALUATION AND FUNDAMENTALS DON'T MATTER

Over an extended bubble period, the principles of valuation are denounced as old-fashioned economic tools for ignorant and out-of-date investors. Speculators are busy praising momentum, short-term index weightings, and millisecond algorithm trading.

It is not uncommon that rigorous fundamental analysis and economic fundamentals on the value of businesses are dismissed during periods of speculative frenzy. Hand in hand, the investment horizons continue to shrink, even though these horizons do lengthen after the market collapses.

MYTH #4: SHORT-TERM SOLUTIONS CAN ADD UP TO ADDRESS LONG-TERM PROBLEMS

It is obvious that technology and globalization have increased the speed of communications. But the opposite is true with respect to the speed of policy, economic, and financial market reactions: these have become much slower.

One reason for this is the convergence of opinions to sustain the status quo as more people share more information more rapidly. The liquidity of a market comes not only from its size, but more importantly, from the diversity of opinions amongst market participants. Crisis scenarios are postponed again and again with short-term fixes, with information manipulated more subtly, even though fundamental deterioration is seemingly obvious.

The second reason is the access to and interplay of public and private funds, such as the trillion-plus social security funds. Add to this government-guaranteed or -sponsored entities, aggressive central banks, high value speculators, and investors who use derivatives, swaps, and carry trades, which can artificially create money for speculation. These have the effect of boosting asset prices. We end up in a synthetic and transient state of valuations, postponing the write-down of the mountains of debt created in the process. This crisis will almost surely end badly.

Using sound investment principles, prudent risk management, and risk avoidance do not provide a guarantee of success but can help the individual investor. In almost all financial crises since 1900, cash, Treasury bills, and deposits guaranteed by a major industrialized country have protected the investor from a loss of principal. More importantly, they have provided an opportunity to benefit from buying devalued assets toward the end of the crisis, when most people and corporations are selling assets to raise cash. Today, very few in the financial industry are recommending this strategy.

As a future financial advisor, saver, or investor, the complexity of financial markets is not about to simplify. This text has been written with great care to keep financial jargon at its minimum, and yet many experts ignore the ideas presented above. Mr. Market can become the Great Humbler, and investing should continue to be a perpetual learning process. We challenge you to use a principled approach, one that allows you to sleep well, rather than scrambling to eat well.

Arshad Ahmad
Associate VP, Teaching & Learning and 3M National Teaching Fellow
McMaster University

Paul Dontigny, Jr.
Gestionnaire de portefeuilles
Investissements, PDJ

part 1

Planning Your Personal Finances

chapter 1

Personal Financial Planning: An Introduction

LEARNING OBJECTIVES

LO1 Analyze the process for making personal financial decisions.

LO2 Develop personal financial goals.

LO3 Assess economic factors that influence personal financial planning.

LO4 Determine personal and financial opportunity costs associated with personal financial decisions.

LO5 Identify strategies for achieving personal financial goals for different life situations.

KAREN'S FINANCIAL PLAN

Karen Edwards, 23, completed her Bachelor of Science one year ago. The major cost of her tuition and books was covered by a scholarship. Through wise planning, she was able to save $15,000 from her part-time jobs. Acting on a suggestion from her parents, Karen met with a financial planner, who advised her to invest her money in low-risk bonds and saving certificates.

Karen works in an office in Toronto, Ontario, and she earns $35,000 a year. In approximately three years, she would like to return to school and start her master's degree. Then, she would like to buy a house. Karen wants to live on her salary and invest the $15,000 for her education and future home.

QUESTIONS

1. How did Karen benefit from her parents' advice and her own financial planning?

2. What decisions does Karen need to make regarding her future?

3. How could various personal and economic factors influence Karen's financial planning?

4. What would be the value of Karen's $15,000 in three years if it earned an annual interest rate of 7 percent?

5. Conduct a Web search to obtain information that Karen may find useful.

OVERVIEW

Personal financial planning has many important pieces. We begin with an overview of a six-step planning process, which will help you to review, revise, and align your goals with your changing circumstances. We then take a closer look at developing your financial goals by considering factors that may influence your goals and your changing life situation. We end this section by suggesting guidelines that can help you set realistic goals you can achieve.

Since financial planning does not occur in a vacuum, the next section considers the influence of prevailing economic factors including an overview of market forces, financial institutions, and global conditions that tend to have a major impact on your financial goals and plans.

Although opportunity costs are discussed in step 4 of the financial planning process, we emphasize the importance of financial opportunity costs—and, more specifically, the time value of money. Time value concepts and mechanics are key to understanding how future and present values take into account expectations of inflation and interest rates and how compounding and discounting translate monies over time.

Finally, the last section of this chapter identifies strategies that are consistent in achieving personal financial goals. In fact, all of the subsequent topics in this textbook are summarized to give you a preview of the important areas that will be explored in detail so that your financial plan considers all important aspects. This framework is the basis from which you can develop a way of thinking and, more importantly, implement practices and habits that will become the hallmark of effective personal financial decisions.

THE FINANCIAL PLANNING PROCESS

Everywhere you turn, someone is talking about money. When it comes to handling your finances, are you an *explorer*, someone who is always searching through uncharted areas? Are you a *passenger*, just along for the ride on the money decision-making trip of life? Or are you a *researcher*, seeking answers to the inevitable money questions of life?

LO1
Analyze the process for making personal financial decisions.

Most people want to handle their finances so that they get full satisfaction from each available dollar. Typical financial goals include such things as a new car, a larger home, advanced career training, extended travel, and self-sufficiency during working and retirement years. To achieve these and other goals, people need to identify and set priorities. Financial and personal satisfaction are the result of an organized process that is commonly referred to as *personal money management* or *personal financial planning*.

Personal financial planning is the process of managing your money to achieve personal economic satisfaction. This planning process allows you to control your financial situation. Every person, family, or household has a unique financial position, and therefore any financial activity must also be carefully planned to meet specific needs and goals.

personal financial planning The process of managing your money to achieve personal economic satisfaction.

A comprehensive financial plan can enhance the quality of your life and increase your satisfaction by reducing uncertainty about your future needs and resources. The specific advantages of personal financial planning include:

- Increased effectiveness in obtaining, using, and protecting your financial resources throughout your lifetime.
- Increased control of your financial affairs by avoiding excessive debt, bankruptcy, and dependence on others for economic security.
- Improved personal relationships resulting from well-planned and effectively communicated financial decisions.
- A sense of freedom from financial worries obtained by looking to the future, anticipating expenses, and achieving your personal economic goals.

We all make hundreds of decisions each day. Most of these decisions are simple and have few consequences. Some are complex and have long-term effects on our personal and financial situations. While everyone makes decisions, few people consider how to make better decisions. As Exhibit 1–1 shows, the financial planning process is a logical, six-step procedure:

1. Determining your current financial situation.
2. Developing financial goals.
3. Identifying alternative courses of action.
4. Evaluating alternatives.
5. Creating and implementing a financial action plan.
6. Re-evaluating and revising the plan.

STEP 1: DETERMINE YOUR CURRENT FINANCIAL SITUATION

In the first step of the financial planning process, you determine your current financial situation regarding income, savings, living expenses, and debts. Preparing a list of current asset and debt balances and amounts spent for various items gives you a foundation for financial planning activities. The personal financial statements discussed in Chapter 2 will provide the information you need to match your goals with your current income and potential earning power.

STEP 1 EXAMPLE   Within the next two months, Kent Mullins will complete his undergraduate studies with a major in international studies. He has worked part time in various sales jobs. He has a small savings fund ($1,700) and more than $8,500 in student loans. What additional information should Kent have available when planning his personal finances?

STEP 2: DEVELOP FINANCIAL GOALS

You should periodically analyze your financial values and attitude toward money. They will play a major role in shaping your financial goals.

Analyzing your **values** involves identifying what beliefs you hold with respect to money and how these beliefs lead you to act in certain ways. For example, you may believe that it is wrong to borrow in order to purchase consumer goods, such as expensive clothes. Because of this belief, you only shop for clothes once you save the money. You do not charge the clothes to a credit card when you know you won't have the funds to pay the bill once it arrives.

You should also be aware of your attitude toward money. Do you view money as a form of security? If so, you are likely a good saver. Do you view money as a means by which you can express your appreciation of others? If so, you probably enjoy giving lavish gifts to your friends and family and may risk overspending.

values Ideas and principles that a person considers correct, desirable, and important.

Exhibit 1–1

The Financial Planning Process

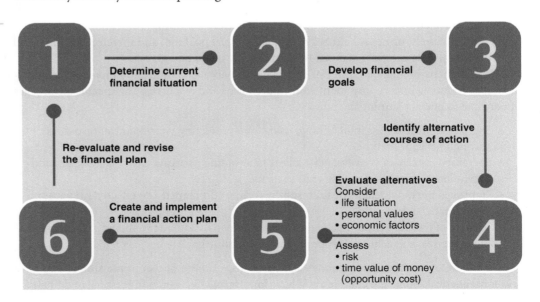

Finally, how are financial decisions made in your family? Is there one individual who makes all major financial decisions, such as how much to borrow to buy a home, and who leaves decisions of lesser importance to others? Or are financial decisions a joint effort and responsibility?

Being aware of your values, attitude toward money, and financial decision-making process will help you differentiate your needs from your wants and will lead you to a clearer definition of your financial goals. Financial goals represent what you hope to achieve with your money. They should be realistic, stated in specific dollar terms and time frames, and listed in order of priority. As discussed later in the chapter, they are also closely linked to your life situation and can be influenced by external economic factors as well.

STEP 2 EXAMPLE   Kent Mullins has several goals, including obtaining an advanced degree in global business management within five years, paying off his $8,500 student loan within 10 years, and working in Latin America for a multinational company once he completes his education.

STEP 3: IDENTIFY ALTERNATIVE COURSES OF ACTION

Developing alternatives is crucial for making good decisions. Although many factors will influence the available alternatives, possible courses of action usually fall into these categories:

- *Continue the same course of action.* For example, you may determine that the amount you saved each month is still appropriate.
- *Expand the current situation.* You may choose to save a larger amount each month.
- *Change the current situation.* You may decide to use a money market account instead of a regular savings account.
- *Take a new course of action.* You may decide to use your monthly savings budget to pay off credit card debts.

Not all of these categories will apply to every decision situation; however, they do represent possible courses of action. For example, if you want to stop working full time to go to school, you must generate alternatives under the category "Take a new course of action."

Creativity in decision making is vital to effective choices. Considering all of the possible alternatives will help you make more effective and satisfying decisions. For instance, most people believe they must own a car to get to work or school. However, they should consider alternatives such as public transportation, carpooling, renting a car, shared ownership of a car, or a company car.

Remember, when you decide not to take action, you elect to "do nothing," which can be a dangerous alternative.

STEP 3 EXAMPLE   Kent Mullins has several options available to obtain an advanced degree in global business management. He could go to graduate school full-time by taking out an additional loan, or he could go to school part-time and work part-time. What additional alternatives might he consider?

STEP 4: EVALUATE ALTERNATIVES

You need to evaluate possible courses of action, taking into consideration your life situation, personal values, and current economic conditions. How will the ages of dependants affect your saving goals? How do you like to spend leisure time? How will changes in interest rates affect your financial situation?

CONSEQUENCES OF CHOICES   Every decision closes off alternatives. For example, a decision to invest in stocks may mean you cannot take a vacation. A decision to go to school full-time may mean you cannot work full-time. **Opportunity cost** is what you give up by

opportunity cost
What a person gives up by making a choice.

making a choice. This cost, commonly referred to as the *trade-off* of a decision, cannot always be measured in dollars. It may refer to the money you forgo by attending school rather than working, but it may also refer to the time you spend shopping around to compare brands for a major purchase. In either case, the resources you give up (money or time) have a value that is lost.

In addition to time spent, personal opportunity costs include effort made and the effects on your health. For example, poor eating habits, lack of sleep, or avoiding exercise can result in illness, time away from school or work, increased health-care costs, and reduced financial security. Financial opportunity costs include interest, liquidity, and safety of investments. It is

time value of money
Increases in an amount of money as a result of interest earned.

measured in terms of the **time value of money**, the increases in an amount of money as a result of interest earned. Saving or investing a dollar today instead of spending it results in a future amount greater than a dollar. Every time you spend, save, invest, or borrow money you should consider the time value of money as an opportunity cost (see Exhibit 1–2).

Decision making is an ongoing part of your personal and financial situations. Therefore, you need to consider the lost opportunities that will result from your decisions. Since decisions vary based on each person's situation and values, opportunity costs differ for each person.

EVALUATING RISK   Uncertainty is a part of every decision. Selecting a college or university major and choosing a career field involve risk. What if you don't like working in that field or cannot obtain employment in it? Other decisions involve a low degree of risk, such as putting money in a savings account or purchasing items that cost only a few dollars. Your chances of losing something of great value are low in these situations.

In many financial decisions, identifying and evaluating risk is difficult. Some types of risk can affect everyone, such as interest rate risk or inflation risk. They arise from the financial and economic environment in which we live or from the products and services that we choose. Other risks are personal in nature, such as the risk of premature death or the risk of disability or loss of health. Some different types of risk are explained in Exhibit 1–3. The best way to consider risk is to gather information based on your experience and the experiences of others and to seek financial planning expertise by consulting various information sources.

FINANCIAL PLANNING INFORMATION SOURCES   When you travel, you often need a road map. Travelling the path of financial planning requires a different kind of map. Relevant information is required at each stage of the decision-making process. This book provides the foundation you need to make personal financial planning decisions. Changing personal, social, and economic conditions require that you continually supplement and update your knowledge. Exhibit 1–4 offers an overview of the informational resources available when making personal financial decisions. Appendix 1A provides additional information.

Exhibit 1–2

Opportunity Costs and Financial Results Should be Evaluated When Making Financial Decisions

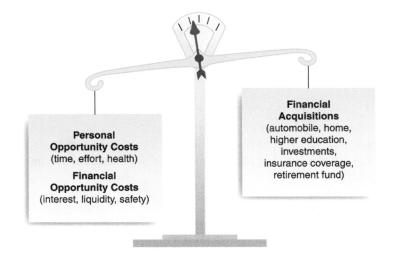

Economic and Product Risk	Personal Risk
Interest Rate Risk Changing interest rates affect your costs when you borrow, and your benefits when you invest.	*Risk of Death* Premature death may cause financial hardship to family members left behind.
Inflation Risk Rising prices cause lost buying power.	*Risk of Income Loss* Your income could stop as a result of job loss or because you fall ill or are hurt in an accident.
Liquidity Risk Some investments may be more difficult to convert to cash or to sell without significant loss in value.	*Health Risk* Poor heath may increase your medical costs. At the same time, it may reduce your working capacity or life expectancy.
Product Risk Products may be flawed or services may not meet your expectations. Retailers may not honour their obligations.	*Asset and Liability Risk* Your assets may be stolen or damaged. Others may sue you for negligence or for damages caused by your actions.

Exhibit 1–3

Types of Risk

STEP 4 EXAMPLE   As Kent Mullins evaluates his alternative courses of action, he must consider his income needs for both the short term and the long term. He should also assess career opportunities with his current skills and his potential with advanced training. What risks and trade-offs should Kent consider?

STEP 5: CREATE AND IMPLEMENT A FINANCIAL ACTION PLAN

In this step of the financial planning process, you develop an action plan. This requires choosing ways to achieve your goals. For example, you can increase your savings by reducing your spending or by increasing your income through extra time on the job. If you are concerned about year-end tax payments, you may increase the amount withheld from each

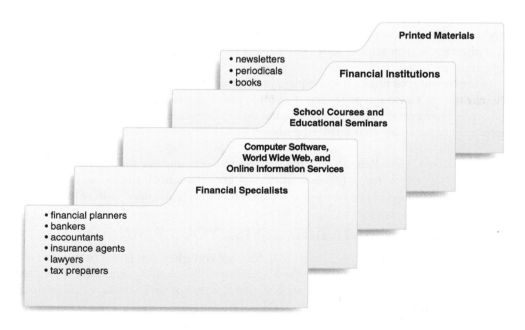

Exhibit 1–4

Financial Planning Information Sources

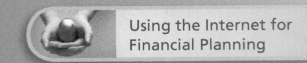
Web . . . email . . . URL . . . online banking!

Just a dozen years ago, these terms made no sense to most people. Even now, many people are still not quite sure about all this stuff. However, most know that good financial planning requires information, and the Internet is the most efficient source of information.

Throughout this book, the financial planning content presented can be expanded and updated using the Internet. The Web sites we suggest, along with others you locate yourself, allow you to quickly obtain information for making financial decisions appropriate to your life situation. In addition, at the end of each chapter, a feature called "Creating a Financial Plan" gives you an opportunity to use the Web to plan, research, and implement various components necessary for a comprehensive financial plan.

As you study the personal financial topics discussed in this book, the following Internet topic areas are especially useful:

- *Finding cyber-info for personal financial planning:* With thousands of personal finance Web sites available, where do you begin? Some useful ones include quicken.intuit.ca and advocis.ca.
- *Using online banking:* No more lines. No more overworked bank tellers. No more inhaling exhaust fumes while waiting in the drive-through lane. In addition to existing banks that are online, there are Web-only banks, such as tangerine.ca.

- *Getting online tax information and advice:* Tax planning should not happen only around April 30. For assistance, go to cra-arc.gc.ca or kpmg.ca.
- *Applying for a mortgage online:* Instead of waiting days or even weeks, prospective home buyers can now obtain financing online at sites such as scotiabank.ca.
- *Buying a car online:* Information that used to be difficult to get is now available to everyone. More than 70 percent of car buyers research their planned purchases online to get information about vehicle features and costs at such sites as ewheels.ca.
- *Selecting investments online:* As everyone knows, "information is power." This saying is especially true when investing. You can obtain company information and investment assistance at quicken .intuit.ca and mutualfundsnet.com/v2.
- *Being your own investment broker:* You already know which investments you want to buy? Then it's time to get into the market by going to bmoinvestorline.com.
- *Planning for retirement:* Whether you are 40 years or 40 minutes away from retiring, you can get lots of help at retirehappyblog.ca/.

Note: Refer to Appendix 1A for information on conducting Internet searches. Also, be aware that Web sites may change or no longer be in use after this book has published.

---

paycheque, file quarterly tax payments, or shelter current income in a tax-deferred retirement program. As you achieve your immediate or short-term goals, the goals next in priority will come into focus.

To implement your financial action plan, you may need assistance from others. For example, you may use the services of an insurance agent to purchase property insurance or the services of an investment broker to purchase stocks, bonds, or mutual funds. Your own efforts should be geared toward achieving your financial goals.

STEP 5 EXAMPLE   Kent Mullins has decided to work full-time for a few years while he (1) pays off his student loans, (2) saves money for graduate school, and (3) takes a couple of courses in the evenings and on weekends. What are the benefits and drawbacks of this choice?

STEP 6: RE-EVALUATE AND REVISE YOUR PLAN

Financial planning is a dynamic process that does not end when you take a particular action. You need to regularly assess your financial decisions. You should completely review your finances at least once a year. Changing personal, social, and economic factors may require more frequent assessments.

When life events affect your financial needs, this financial planning process provides a vehicle for adapting to those changes. Regularly reviewing this decision-making process helps you make priority adjustments that bring your financial goals and activities in line with your current life situation.

STEP 6 EXAMPLE   Over the next six to 12 months, Kent Mullins should reassess his financial, career, and personal situations. What employment opportunities or family circumstances might affect his need or desire to take a different course of action?

Did you know?

Sixty-two percent of those with comprehensive financial plans report that they have improved their ability to save in the last five years, versus 56 percent with limited planning and only 40 percent with no planning.

SOURCE: http://www.fpsc.ca/value-financial-planning.

CONCEPT CHECK 1–1

1. What steps should we take in developing our financial plan?
2. What are some risks associated with financial decisions?
3. What are some common sources of financial planning information?
4. Why should you re-evaluate your actions after making a personal financial decision?
5. What Web site feature of advocis.ca or canadianfinance.com would provide assistance with your financial decisions?

DEVELOPING PERSONAL FINANCIAL GOALS

Since Canada is among the richest countries in the world, it is difficult to understand why so many Canadians have money problems. The answer seems to be the result of two main factors. The first is poor planning and weak money management habits in areas such as spending and the use of credit. The other is extensive advertising, selling efforts, and product availability. Achieving personal financial satisfaction starts with clear financial goals.

LO2
Develop personal financial goals.

FACTORS THAT INFLUENCE YOUR FINANCIAL GOALS

Many factors influence your financial aspirations for the future. We have already discussed how your personal values and attitude toward money can shape your financial goals. Additional factors include the time frame in which you would like to achieve your goals, the type of financial need that drives your goals, and your life situation.

TIMING OF GOALS   What would you like to do tomorrow? Believe it or not, that question involves goal-setting. *Short-term goals* are goals to be achieved within the next year or so, such as saving for a vacation or paying off small debts. *Intermediate goals* have a time frame of two to five years. *Long-term goals* involve financial plans that are more than five years off, such as retirement savings, money for children's post-secondary education, or purchasing a vacation home.

Long-term goals should be planned in coordination with short- and medium-term ones. Setting and achieving short-term goals is commonly the basis for moving toward success of long-term goals. For example, saving for a down payment to buy a house is a short- or medium-term goal that can be the foundation for a long-term goal: owning your own home.

Goal frequency is another ingredient in the financial planning process. Some goals, such as vacations or money for gifts, may be set annually. Other goals, such as a higher education, a car, or a house, occur less frequently.

GOALS FOR DIFFERENT FINANCIAL NEEDS   A goal of obtaining increased career training is different from a goal of saving money to pay a semi-annual auto insurance premium. *Consumable-product goals* usually occur on a periodic basis and involve items that are used up quickly, such as food, clothing, and entertainment. Such purchases, if made unwisely, can have a negative effect on your financial situation.

Durable-product goals usually involve infrequently purchased, expensive items, such as appliances, cars, and sporting equipment; these consist of tangible items. In contrast, many people overlook *intangible-purchase goals*. These goals may relate to personal relationships, health, education, and leisure. Goal-setting for these life circumstances is also necessary for your overall well-being.

LIFE SITUATION

People in their 50s spend money differently from those in their 20s. Personal factors such as age, income, household size, and personal beliefs, influence your spending and saving patterns. Your life situation or lifestyle is created by a combination of factors.

As our society changes, different types of financial needs evolve. Today, people tend to get married at a later age, and more households have two incomes. Many households are headed by single parents. We are also living longer: more than 80 percent of all Canadians now living are expected to live past age 65. Past surveys indicate that approximately one-third of Canadians aged 45 to 64 not only are raising children, but also are caring for aging parents. Women form the large majority and, in response to these increased demands, report that they have had to reduce their working hours, change schedules, or forgo income.

adult life cycle The stages in the family situation and financial needs of an adult.

life cycle approach The idea that the average person goes through four basic stages in personal financial management.

As Exhibit 1–5 shows, the **adult life cycle**—the stages in the family situation and financial needs of an adult—is an important influence on your financial activities and decisions. The average person goes through four basic stages in personal financial management, referred to as the **life cycle approach** to financial planning. In the early years (until the mid-30s), the focus is on creating an emergency fund, saving for a down payment on a house or condo, and, if necessary, purchasing life insurance. This is also the time to start thinking about retirement, because the earlier you start the less money you have to save in later years to catch up. In the middle years (mid-30s to mid-50s), the focus is on building wealth by paying down the mortgage and increasing savings and investments. In middle age (50s+), when typically more disposable income is available, the focus is on providing an adequate

Exhibit 1–5

Life Situation Influences on Your Financial Decisions

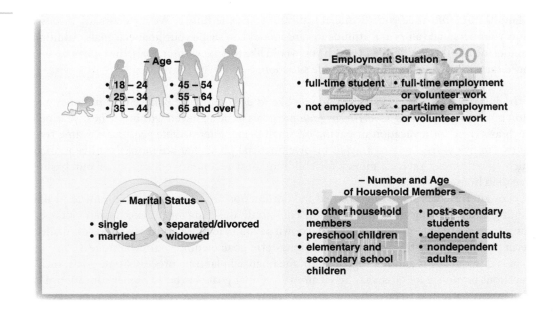

retirement fund. And, finally, in the retirement years the focus is on the efficient management of previously acquired wealth.

Your life situation is also affected by marital status, household size, and employment, as well as such events as:

- Graduation (at various levels of education).
- Engagement and marriage.
- The birth or adoption of a child.
- A career change or a move to a new area.
- Dependent children leaving home.
- Changes in health.
- Divorce.
- Retirement.
- The death of a spouse, family member, or other dependant.

Exhibit 1–6 offers typical goals and financial activities for various life situations.

GOAL-SETTING GUIDELINES

An old saying goes, "If you don't know where you're going, you might end up somewhere else and not even know it." Goal setting is central to financial decision making. Your financial goals are the basis for planning, implementing, and measuring the progress of your spending, saving, and investing activities.

Your financial goals should be stated to take the following factors into account:

1. *Financial goals should be realistic.* Financial goals should be based on your income and life situation. For example, it is probably not realistic to expect to buy a new car each year if you are a full-time student.
2. *Financial goals should be stated in specific, measurable terms.* Knowing exactly what your goals are help you create a plan designed to achieve them. For example, the goal of "accumulating $10,000 in an investment fund within three years" is a clearer guide to planning than the goal of "putting money into an investment fund."
3. *Financial goals should have a time frame.* In the preceding example, the goal is to be achieved in three years. A time frame helps you measure your progress toward your financial goals.
4. *Financial goals should indicate the type of action to be taken.* Your financial goals are the basis for the various financial activities you will undertake.

It is easier to achieve your financial objectives if your goals have meaning and value to you, and if they are SMART (specific, measurable, action-oriented, realistic, and timely). For example, "I want to save $3,600 for an emergency fund in the next 12 months by cutting back on entertainment expenses and working an extra 10 hours a week." The goal is specific and action-oriented. You can measure whether you reached it in exactly one year from today. If you are able to earn more money by working more hours, and are willing to cut down on expenses, your goal is realistic. And finally, it is timely: you have exactly 12 months to save the $3,600.

CONCEPT CHECK 1–2

1. What are examples of long-term goals?
2. What are the four main characteristics of useful financial goals?
3. How does your life situation affect your financial goals?

Exhibit 1–6 Financial Goals and Activities for Various Life Situations

Common Financial Goals and Activities

- Obtain appropriate career training.
- Create an effective financial record-keeping system.
- Develop a regular savings and investment program.

- Accumulate an appropriate emergency fund.
- Purchase appropriate types and amounts of insurance coverage.
- Create and implement a flexible budget.

- Evaluate and select appropriate investments.
- Establish and implement a plan for retirement goals.
- Make a will and develop an estate plan.

Life Situation	Specialized Financial Activities
Young, single (18–35)	• Establish financial independence. • Obtain disability insurance to replace income during prolonged illness. • Consider home purchase.
Young couple with children under 18	• Carefully manage the increased need for the use of credit. • Obtain an appropriate amount of life insurance for the care of dependants. • Use a will to name a guardian for children.
Single parent with children under 18	• Obtain adequate amounts of health, life, and disability insurances. • Contribute to savings and investment funds for children's higher education. • Name a guardian for children and make other estate plans.
Young dual-income couple, no children	• Coordinate insurance coverage and other benefits. • Develop savings and investment programs for changes in life situation (larger house, children). • Consider tax-deferred contributions to retirement fund.
Older couple (+50), no dependent children at home	• Consolidate financial assets and review estate plans. • Obtain health insurance for post-retirement period. • Plan retirement housing, living expenses, recreational activities, and part-time work.
Mixed-generation household (elderly individuals and children under 18)	• Obtain long-term health care insurance and life/disability income for care of younger dependants. • Use dependent care service, if needed. • Provide arrangements for handling finances of elderly if they become ill. • Consider splitting investment cost, with elderly getting income while alive and principal going to surviving relatives.
Older (+50), single	• Make arrangements for long-term health-care coverage. • Review will and estate plan. • Plan retirement living facilities, living expenses, and activities.

THE INFLUENCE OF ECONOMIC FACTORS ON PERSONAL FINANCIAL PLANNING

LO3

Assess economic factors that influence personal financial planning.

Daily economic activities are another important influence on financial planning. In our society, the forces of supply and demand play an important role in setting prices. **Economics** is the study of how wealth is created and distributed. The economic environment includes various institutions, principally business, labour, and government, that must work together to satisfy our needs and wants.

Financial Planning for Life's Situations

On the basis of your current situation or expectations for the future, identify two financial goals, one short-term and one long-term, using the following guidelines:

Step 1. Create realistic goals based on your life situation.

A. SHORT-TERM GOAL

_____
_____
_____
_____
_____

B. LONG-TERM GOAL

_____
_____
_____
_____

Step 2. State your goals in specific, measurable terms.

a. _____
_____

b. _____
_____

Step 3. Describe the time frame for accomplishing your goals.

a. _____
_____

b. _____
_____

Step 4. Indicate actions to be taken to achieve your goals.

a. _____
_____

b. _____
_____

MARKET FORCES

Prices of goods and services are generally determined by supply and demand. Just as a high demand for a consumer product forces its price up, a high demand for money pushes up interest rates. This price of money reflects the limited supply of money and the demand for it.

At times, the price of an item may seem to be unaffected by the forces of supply and demand but, in fact, at such times, other economic factors may also be influencing its price. Although such factors as production costs and competition influence prices, the market forces of supply and demand remain in operation.

economics The study of how wealth is created and distributed.

FINANCIAL INSTITUTIONS

Banks, trust companies, credit unions, insurance companies, and investment companies are the financial institutions with which most people do business. Financial institutions provide services that facilitate financial activities in our economy. They accept savings, handle chequing accounts, sell insurance, and make investments on behalf of others.

While various government agencies regulate financial activities, the Bank of Canada, our nation's central bank, has significant responsibility in our economy. The Bank of Canada is concerned with maintaining an adequate money supply. It achieves this by influencing borrowing, interest rates, and the buying or selling of government securities. The Bank of Canada attempts to make adequate funds available for consumer spending and business expansion while keeping interest rates and consumer prices at an appropriate level.

Did you know?

A basket of goods and services that cost $100 in 1914 cost $2,086.67 in 2014. And what you could buy for $100 in 2002 cost $125.83 in 2014.

SOURCE: bankofcanada.ca.

13

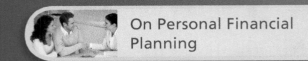

Advice from a Pro

On Personal Financial Planning

"Spend less than you earn" is the foundation of long-term financial security, according to financial planner Ellen Rogin.

Although it sounds simple, most people do not follow this basic requirement for financial planning success. Ms. Rogin has been advising people about their money for more than 12 years. While the typical clients of her company range in age from 30 to 50, some are younger or older. Most of her clients are professionals and executives who have a common concern: a secure retirement. But Ms. Rogin is quick to point out that she works with people with a variety of needs, life situations, and investment philosophies. She has even advised a lottery winner, although she doesn't recommend that expectation as a steady path to long-term financial security!

Ms. Rogin believes the availability of information is the most significant change in the financial planning marketplace in recent years. With the Internet, television programs, and an extensive number of magazines and books, people can be better informed regarding personal finance topics and investments. However, she warns that people must assess the validity of the information. She suggests "avoiding specific investment advice from magazines and other sources that may not be appropriate for your individual situation."

When planning your own financial direction, Ms. Rogin recommends three actions:

1. Set specific financial goals.
2. Reduce your debts.
3. Save for retirement.

Even if someone else is managing your finances, Ms. Rogin encourages you to "be involved." Be aware of your personal economic situation and the financial marketplace. Communicate your money views, risk acceptance, and financial priorities. Never let a financial planner, your spouse, or another family member have complete control.

GLOBAL INFLUENCES

The global marketplace also influences financial activities. Our economy is affected by both the financial activities of foreign investors and competition from foreign companies. Canadian businesses compete against foreign companies for the spending dollars of Canadian consumers.

When the export level of Canadian-made goods is lower than the level of imported goods, more Canadian dollars leave the country than the dollar value of foreign currency coming into Canada. This reduces the funds available for domestic spending and investment. Also, if foreign companies decide not to invest their dollars in Canada, the domestic money supply is reduced. This reduced money supply may cause higher interest rates.

ECONOMIC CONDITIONS

Newspapers and business periodicals regularly publish current economic statistics. Exhibit 1–7 provides an overview of some economic indicators that influence financial decisions. Your personal financial decisions are most heavily influenced by consumer prices, consumer spending, and interest rates.

inflation A rise in the general level of prices.

CONSUMER PRICES   **Inflation** is a rise in the general level of prices. In times of inflation, the buying power of the dollar decreases. For example, if prices increased 5 percent during the last year, items that cost $100 then would now cost $105. This means it now takes more money to buy the same amount of goods and services.

The main cause of inflation is an increase in demand without a comparable increase in supply. For example, if people have more money to spend because of pay increases or borrowing but the same amounts of goods and services are available, the increased demand can bid up prices for those goods and services.

Exhibit 1–7   Changing Economic Conditions and Financial Decisions

Economic Factor	What It Measures	How It Influences Financial Planning
Consumer prices	The value of the dollar; changes in inflation	If consumer prices increase faster than your income, you are unable to purchase the same amount of goods and services; higher consumer prices also cause higher interest rates.
Consumer spending	The demand for goods and services by individuals and households	Increased consumer spending is likely to create more jobs and higher wages; high levels of consumer spending and borrowing can also increase consumer prices and interest rates.
Interest rates	The cost of money; the cost of credit when you borrow; the return on your money when you save or invest	Higher interest rates make buying on credit more expensive; higher interest rates make saving and investing more attractive and discourage borrowing.
Money supply	The dollars available for spending in our economy	Interest rates tend to decline as more people save and invest; but higher saving (and lower spending) may reduce job opportunities.
Unemployment rate	The number of people without employment who are willing and able to work	People who are unemployed should reduce their debt level and have an emergency savings fund for living costs while out of work; high unemployment reduces consumer spending and job opportunities.
Housing starts	The number of new homes being built	Increased home building results in more job opportunities, higher wages, more consumer spending, and overall economic expansion.
Gross domestic product (GDP)	The total value of goods and services produced within a country's borders, including items produced with foreign resources	The GDP indicates a nation's economic viability resulting in employment and opportunities for personal financial wealth.
Trade balance	The difference between a country's exports and its imports	If a country exports more than it imports, interest rates may rise and foreign goods and foreign travel will cost more.
S&P/TSX composite index and other stock market indexes	The relative value of stocks represented by the index	These indexes provide an indication of the general movement of stock prices.

Inflation is most harmful to people living on fixed incomes. Due to inflation, retired people and others whose incomes do not change are able to afford smaller amounts of goods and services.

Inflation can also adversely affect lenders of money. Unless an adequate interest rate is charged, amounts repaid by borrowers in times of inflation have less buying power than the money they borrowed. If you pay 10 percent interest on a loan and the inflation rate is 12 percent, the dollars you pay the lender have lost buying power. For this reason, interest rates rise in periods of high inflation.

Did you know?

To find out how fast prices double, you can use the rule of 72. Just divide 72 by the annual inflation rate (or interest rate). For example, an annual inflation rate of 8 percent means prices will double in nine years (72 ÷ 8 = 9).

The rate of inflation varies. During the late 1950s and early 1960s, the annual inflation rate was in the 1 to 3 percent range. During the late 1970s and early 1980s, the cost of living increased 10 to 12 percent annually.

More recently, the annual price increase for most goods and services as measured by the consumer price index has been in the 1 to 3 percent range. The *consumer price index* (CPI), published by Statistics Canada, is a measure of the average change in the prices urban consumers pay for a fixed "basket" of goods and services. For current CPI information, go to statcan.gc.ca.

CONSUMER SPENDING   Total demand for goods and services in the economy influences employment opportunities and the potential for income. As consumer purchasing increases, the financial resources of current and prospective employees expand. This situation improves the financial condition of many households.

In contrast, reduced spending causes unemployment, since staff reduction commonly results from a company's reduced financial resources. The financial hardships of unemployment are a major concern of business, labour, and government. Retraining programs, income assistance, and job services can help people adjust.

INTEREST RATES   In simple terms, interest rates represent the cost of money. Like everything else, money has a price. The forces of supply and demand influence interest rates. When consumer saving and investing increase the supply of money, interest rates tend to decrease. However, as consumer, business, government, and foreign borrowing increase the demand for money, interest rates tend to rise.

Interest rates affect your financial planning. The earnings you receive as a saver or an investor reflect current interest rates as well as a *risk premium* based on such factors as the length of time your funds will be used by others, expected inflation, and the extent of uncertainty about getting your money back. Risk is also a factor in the interest rate you pay as a borrower. People with poor credit ratings pay a higher interest rate than people with good credit ratings. Finally, we must always take into consideration the role played by personal income taxes with respect to the interest income we earn and the interest expense we pay. Every dollar of interest we earn must be added to our taxable income. Therefore, if our income tax rate is 30 percent, we have only 70 cents of after-tax interest income. On the other hand, we can deduct the interest that we pay on certain types of loans. In that case, the true cost of one dollar of interest paid is only 70 cents. We will discuss the issue of before and after-tax investment income and borrowing costs in further detail in Chapter 3, Planning Your Tax Strategy.

CONCEPT CHECK 1–3

1.   How might the uncertainty of inflation make personal financial planning difficult?
2.   What factors influence the level of interest rates?

OPPORTUNITY COSTS AND THE TIME VALUE OF MONEY

LO4

Determine personal and financial opportunity costs associated with personal financial decisions.

Have you noticed that you always give up something when you make choices? In every financial decision, you sacrifice one thing to obtain another that you consider more desirable. For example, you might forgo current buying to invest funds for future purchases or long-term financial security. Or, you might gain the use of an expensive item now by making credit payments from future earnings. These *opportunity costs* may be viewed in terms of both personal and financial resources.

PERSONAL OPPORTUNITY COSTS

An important personal opportunity cost involves time that, when used for one activity, cannot be used for other activities. Time used for studying, working, or shopping will not be available for other uses. Allocating time should be viewed like any decision: select your use of time to meet your needs, achieve your goals, and satisfy personal values.

Other personal opportunity costs relate to health. Poor eating habits, lack of sleep, or avoiding exercise can result in illness, time away from school or work, increased health-care costs, and reduced financial security. Like financial resources, your personal resources (time, energy, health, abilities, knowledge) require careful management.

FINANCIAL OPPORTUNITY COSTS

You constantly making choices among various financial decisions. In making those choices, you must consider the time value of money, the increases in an amount of money as a result of interest earned. Saving or investing a dollar instead of spending it today results in a future amount greater than a dollar. Every time you spend, save, invest, or borrow money, you should consider the time value of that money as an opportunity cost. Spending money from your savings account means lost interest earnings; however, what you buy with that money may have a higher priority than those earnings. Borrowing to make a purchase involves the opportunity cost of paying interest on the loan, but your current needs may make this trade-off worthwhile.

The opportunity cost of the time value of money is also present in these financial decisions:

- Setting aside funds in a savings plan with little or no risk has the opportunity cost of potentially higher returns from an investment with greater risk.
- Having extra money withheld from your paycheque in order to receive a tax refund has the opportunity cost of the lost interest the money could earn in a savings account.
- Making annual deposits in a retirement account can help you avoid the opportunity cost of having inadequate funds later in life.
- Purchasing a new automobile or home appliance has the potential benefit of saving you money on future maintenance and energy costs.

INTEREST CALCULATIONS

Three amounts are used to calculate the time value of money for savings in the form of interest earned:

- The amount of the savings (commonly called the *principal*).
- The annual interest rate.
- The length of time the money is on deposit.

There are two methods of calculating interest: **simple interest** and compound interest. Simple interest is calculated as follows: $I = P \times R \times T$

simple interest
Interest computed on the principal, excluding previously earned interest.

(P) AMOUNT IN SAVINGS		(R) ANNUAL INTEREST RATE		(T) TIME PERIOD		(I) INTEREST
	$\times$		$\times$		$=$	

For example, $500 on deposit at a 2 percent annual interest rate for two years will earn $20 ($500 $\times$ 0.02 $\times$ 2).

compounding A process that calculates interest based on previously earned interest.

Compounding refers to interest that is earned on previously earned interest. Each time interest is added to the principal, the next interest amount is computed on the new balance. For example, the $500 on deposit at a 2 percent annual interest rate for two years will earn $20.20 ($500 × 0.02 = $10 the first year, and [$500 + $10] × 0.02 = $10.20 the second year—$10.20 + $10 = $20.20).

Since you are earning interest on the principal as well as accumulated interest, the total amount is greater than what you would earn under simple interest ($20.20 > $20).

You can calculate the increased value of your money from interest earned in two ways. You can calculate the total amount that will be available later (future value), or you can determine the current value of an amount desired in the future (present value).

FUTURE VALUE OF A SINGLE AMOUNT

future value The amount to which current savings will increase based on a certain interest rate and a certain time period; typically involves compounding.

Deposited money earns interest that increases over time. **Future value** is the amount to which current savings will increase on the basis of a certain interest rate and a certain time period. Future value computations typically involve *compounding*, since interest is earned on previously earned interest. Compounding allows the future value of a deposit to grow faster than it would if interest were paid only on the original deposit. For example, $100 deposited in a 2-percent account for two years will grow to $104.04. This amount is computed as follows:

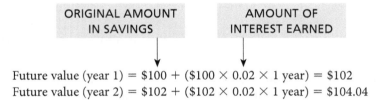

Future value (year 1) = $100 + ($100 × 0.02 × 1 year) = $102
Future value (year 2) = $102 + ($102 × 0.02 × 1 year) = $104.04

The same process can be continued for a third, fourth, and fifth year, but the computations are time-consuming. Future value tables simplify the process (see Exhibit 1–8). To use a future value table, multiply the amount deposited by the factor for the desired interest rate and time period. For example, $650 at 8 percent for 10 years has a future value of $1,403.35 ($650 × 2.159). The future value of an amount is always greater than the original amount. As Exhibit 1–8A shows, all the future value factors are greater than 1.

The sooner you make deposits, the greater the future value will be. Depositing $1,000 in a 5-percent account at age 40 will give you $3,387 at age 65. However, making the same deposit at age 25 will result in an account balance of $7,040 at age 65.

In the same manner, compounding more frequently than once a year results in a higher future value. In the above example, the compounding period was one year. However, most investment opportunities specify shorter compounding intervals. This is called *intra-period compounding*, which simply means that compounding frequency is more than once a year. Compounding can be semi-annually, quarterly, monthly, and so on.

Returning to the example of $100 deposited in a 2-percent account for two years, the amount is now compounded semi-annually:

m = number of compounding periods in a year = 2
i = interest rate per period = 2 ÷ 2 = 1%
Future value (after six months) = $100 + ($100 × 0.01 × 1 period) = $101
Future value (after 1 year) = $101 + ($101 × 0.01 × 1 period) = $102.01
Future value (after 1.5 years) = $102.01 + (102.01 × 0.01 × 1 period) = $103.03
Future value (after 2 years) = $103.03 + (103.03 × 0.01 × 1 period) = $104.04

The value of the investment grows to $104.06 instead of $104.04 due to the increased frequency in compounding per year. The difference in this example may seem negligible, but when you are investing for a long period of time or large sums of money the difference is significant.

A. FUTURE VALUE OF $1 (SINGLE AMOUNT)

Year	Percent				
	5%	6%	7%	8%	9%
5	1.276	1.338	1.403	1.469	1.539
6	1.340	1.419	1.501	1.587	1.677
7	1.407	1.504	1.606	1.714	1.828
8	1.477	1.594	1.718	1.851	1.993
9	1.551	1.689	1.838	1.999	2.172
10	1.629	1.791	1.967	2.159	2.367

B. FUTURE VALUE OF A SERIES OF ANNUAL DEPOSITS (ANNUITY)

Year	Percent				
	5%	6%	7%	8%	9%
5	5.526	5.637	5.751	5.867	5.985
6	6.802	6.975	7.153	7.336	7.523
7	8.142	8.394	8.654	8.923	9.200
8	9.549	9.897	10.260	10.637	11.028
9	11.027	11.491	11.978	12.488	13.021
10	12.578	13.181	13.816	14.487	15.193

C. PRESENT VALUE OF $1 (SINGLE AMOUNT)

Year	Percent				
	5%	6%	7%	8%	9%
5	0.784	0.747	0.713	0.681	0.650
6	0.746	0.705	0.666	0.630	0.596
7	0.711	0.665	0.623	0.583	0.547
8	0.677	0.627	0.582	0.540	0.502
9	0.645	0.592	0.544	0.500	0.460
10	0.614	0.558	0.508	0.463	0.422

D. PRESENT VALUE OF A SERIES OF ANNUAL DEPOSITS (ANNUITY)

Year	Percent				
	5%	6%	7%	8%	9%
5	4.329	4.212	4.100	3.993	3.890
6	5.076	4.917	4.767	4.623	4.486
7	5.786	5.582	5.389	5.206	5.033
8	6.463	6.210	5.971	5.747	5.535
9	7.108	6.802	6.515	6.247	5.995
10	7.722	7.360	7.024	6.710	6.418

Exhibit 1–8

The Value of Money Tables (condensed)

Note: See Appendix 1B at the end of this chapter for more complete future value and present value tables.

FUTURE VALUE OF A SERIES OF DEPOSITS

Quite often, savers and investors make regular deposits. An **annuity** is a series of equal amounts (deposits or withdrawals) made at regular time intervals. To determine the future value of equal yearly savings deposits, use Exhibit 1–8B. To use the table, the deposits must

annuity A series of equal amounts (deposits or withdrawals) made at regular time intervals.

earn a constant interest rate. If you deposit $50 a year at 7 percent for six years, starting at the end of the first year, you will have $357.65 immediately after the last deposit ($50 × 7.153). The Financial Planning Calculations box below presents examples of using future value to achieve financial goals.

PRESENT VALUE OF A SINGLE AMOUNT

present value The current value for a future amount based on a certain interest rate and a certain time period; also referred to as *discounting*.

Another aspect of the time value of money involves determining the current value of a desired amount for the future. **Present value** is the current value for a future amount based on a certain interest rate and a certain time period. Present value computations, also called *discounting*, allow you to determine how much to deposit now to reach a desired total in the future. Present value tables (Exhibit 1–8C) can be used to make the computations. If you want $1,000 five years from now and you earn 5 percent on your savings, you need to deposit $784 ($1,000 × 0.784).

Financial Planning Calculations

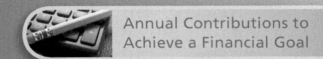

Annual Contributions to Achieve a Financial Goal

Achieving specific financial goals often requires regular deposits to a savings or investment account. By using time value of money calculations, you can determine the amount you should save or invest to achieve a specific goal for the future.

EXAMPLE 1

Jonie Emerson has two children who will start college in 10 years. She plans to set aside $1,500 a year for her children's college education during that period and estimates she will earn an annual interest rate of 5 percent on her savings. What amount can Jonie expect to have available for her children's college education when they start college?

Calculation from table:
    $1,500 × Future value of a series of deposits,
        5%, 10 years
    $1,500 × 12.578 = $18,867

With calculator:

    10   N

    5   I/Y

    0   PV

    1,500+/−   PMT

Then press   CPT   FV   and the answer
    = $18,866.84

EXAMPLE 2

Don Calder wants to accumulate $50,000 over the next 10 years as a reserve fund for his parents' retirement living expenses and health care. If he earns an average of 8 percent on his investments, what amount must he invest each year to achieve this goal?

Calculation from table:
    $50,000 ÷ Future value of a series of deposits,
        8%, 10 years
    $50,000 ÷ 14.487 = $3,451.37

Don needs to invest approximately $3,450 a year for 10 years at 8 percent to achieve the desired financial goal.

With calculator:

    10   N

    8   I/Y

    0   PV

    50,000   FV

Then press   CPT   PMT   and the answer
    = −$3,451.47

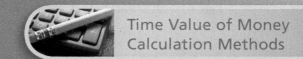
The time value of money may be calculated using a variety of techniques. When achieving specific financial goals requires regular deposits to a savings or investment account, the computation may occur in one of several ways. For example, Jonie Emerson plans to deposit $10,000 in an account for the next 10 years. She estimates these funds will earn an annual rate of 5 percent. What amount can Jonie expect to have available after 10 years?

Method	Process, Results
Formula Calculation The most basic method of calculating the time value of money involves using a formula. These are described in Appendix 1B at the end of this chapter.	For this situation, the formula is: $PV(1 = i)^n = FV$ The result is $\$10{,}000 \ (1 + 0.05)^{10} = \$16{,}288.95$
Time Value of Money Tables Instead of calculating with a formula, time value of money tables are available, and make the computations easier.	Using the future value table in Exhibit 1–8A: $\$10{,}000 \times$ Future value of $1, 5%, 10 years $\$10{,}000 \times 1.629 = \$16{,}290$
Financial Calculator A variety of handheld financial calculators are programmed with various financial functions. Both future value and present value calculations may be performed using the appropriate keystrokes.	Using a financial calculator, the keystrokes are: Amount −10000 PV Time periods 10 N Interest rate 5 I Result FV $16,288.95
Spreadsheet Software *Microsoft Excel* and other spreadsheet programs have built-in formulas for various financial computations, including time value of money.	When using a spreadsheet program, this type of calculation requires this format: = *FV*(rate, periods, amount per period, single amount) The results of this example are: = *FV*(0.05, 10, 0, −10000) = $16,288.95
Time Value of Money Web Sites Many time-value-of-money calculators are also available online. These Web-based programs perform calculations for the future value of savings as well as determining amounts for loan payments.	Some easy-to-use calculators for computing the time value of money and other financial computations are located at • grunderware.com • investopedia.com/calculator • ultimatecalculators.com • tvmcalcs.com

Note: The slight differences in answers are the result of rounding.

The present value of the amount you want in the future will always be less than the future value, since all of the factors in Exhibit 1–8C are less than 1 and interest earned will increase the present value amount to the desired future amount.

PRESENT VALUE OF A SERIES OF DEPOSITS

You can also use present value computations to determine how much you need to deposit so that you can withdraw a certain amount from the account for a desired number of years. For example, if you want to take $400 out of an investment account each year for nine years and your money is earning an annual rate of 8 percent, you can see from Exhibit 1–8D that you need to make a current deposit of $2,498.80 ($400 × 6.247).

Instructions on how to use a financial calculator, formulas for calculating future and present values, as well as tables covering a wider range of interest rates and time periods are presented in Appendix 1B. Computer programs for calculating time value of money are also available.

CONCEPT CHECK 1–4

1. How can you use future value and present value computations to measure the opportunity cost of a financial decision?

2. Use the time value of money tables in Exhibit 1–8 or a financial calculator to calculate the following:

   a. The future value of $100 at 7 percent in 10 years.

   b. The future value of $100 a year for six years earning 6 percent.

   c. The present value of $500 received in eight years with an interest rate of 8 percent.

ACHIEVING FINANCIAL GOALS

LO5

Identify strategies for achieving personal financial goals for different life situations.

Throughout life, our needs usually can be satisfied with the intelligent use of financial resources. Financial planning involves deciding how to obtain, protect, and use those resources. By using the eight major areas of personal financial planning to organize your financial activities, you can avoid many common money mistakes.

COMPONENTS OF PERSONAL FINANCIAL PLANNING

This book is designed to provide a framework for studying and planning personal financial decisions. Exhibit 1–9 presents an overview of the eight major personal financial planning areas. To achieve a successful financial situation, you must coordinate these components through an organized plan and wise decision making.

Exhibit 1–9

Components of Personal Financial Planning

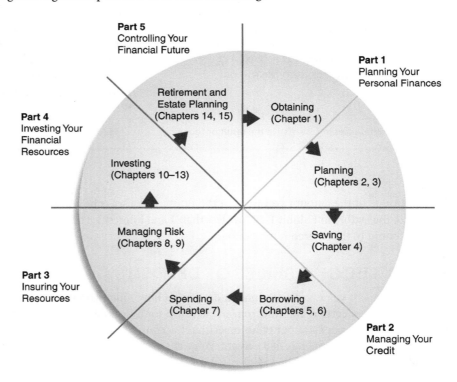

OBTAINING (CHAPTER 1)   You obtain financial resources from employment, investments, or ownership of a business. Obtaining financial resources is the foundation of financial planning, since these resources are used for all financial activities.

Key Web Sites for Obtaining: quicken.intuit.ca   monster.ca

PLANNING (CHAPTERS 2, 3)   Planned spending through budgeting is the key to achieving goals and future financial security. Efforts to anticipate expenses and financial decisions can also help reduce taxes. Paying no more than your fair share of taxes is vital to increasing your financial resources.

Key Web Sites for Planning: advocis.ca   quicken.intuit.ca

SAVING (CHAPTER 4)   Long-term financial security starts with a regular savings plan for emergencies, unexpected bills, replacing major items, and purchasing special goods and services, such as a higher education, a boat, or a vacation home. Once you establish a basic savings plan, you may use additional money for investments that offer greater financial growth.

An amount of savings must be available to meet current household needs. **Liquidity** refers to the ability to readily convert financial resources into cash without a loss in value. The need for liquidity varies, based on a person's age, health, and family situation. Savings plans, such as interest-earning chequing accounts, money market accounts, and money market funds, earn money on your savings while providing liquidity.

liquidity The ability to readily convert financial resources into cash without a loss in value.

Key Web Site for Saving: tangerine.ca

BORROWING (CHAPTERS 5, 6)   Maintaining control over your credit-buying habits contributes to your financial goals. Overusing and misusing credit may cause a situation in which your debts far exceed the resources available to pay those debts. **Bankruptcy** is a set of federal laws that allow you to either restructure your debts or remove certain debts. The people who declare bankruptcy each year might have avoided this trauma with wise spending and borrowing decisions. Chapter 6 discusses bankruptcy in detail.

bankruptcy A set of federal laws that allow you to either restructure your debts or remove certain debts.

Key Web Sites for Borrowing: cibc.ca   scotiabank.ca

SPENDING (CHAPTER 7)   Financial planning is designed not to prevent you from enjoying life but to help you obtain the things you want. Too often, however, people make purchases without considering the financial consequences. Some people shop compulsively, creating financial difficulties. You should detail your living expenses and your other financial obligations in a spending plan. Spending less than you earn is the only way to achieve long-term financial security.

Key Web Sites for Spending: consumerworld.org
consumer.ca

MANAGING RISK (CHAPTERS 8, 9)   Adequate insurance coverage is another component of personal financial planning. Certain types of insurance are commonly overlooked in financial plans. For example, the number of people who suffer disabling injuries or diseases at age 50 is greater than the number who die at that age, so people may need disability insurance more than they need life insurance. Yet surveys reveal that most people have adequate life insurance but few have disability insurance. The insurance industry is more aggressive in selling life insurance than in selling disability insurance, thus putting the burden of obtaining adequate disability insurance on you.

Did you know?

Personal bankruptcies in Canada in 2013 totalled 69,224. This level is 70 percent greater than that of 1990 and more than three times the level declared in 1980. Population growth between 1980 and 2013, on the other hand, was only 43 percent.

SOURCES: bankruptcycanada.com; statscan.gc.ca.

Financial Planning for Life's Situations

Jim Stewarts is an accounting major at Concordia University; he takes five courses each semester and expects to graduate in three years. Jim came to the Financial Aid office for help in deciding whether he should borrow money or work part-time. Let's look at his situation:

Residential status: Jim lives with his parents and is free of food and board charges.

Potential number of hours allotted for part-time work: Assuming 35 weeks in a school year and that Jim will be unable to work for four weeks, Jim is left with 31 work weeks. Considering Jim's grades are of primary importance, we advise him to work for a maximum of 15 hours a week.

Potential number of hours allotted for full-time summer employment: Jim will have 17 weeks (52 less 35 weeks) during the summer, when he can work full-time for 40 hours a week. We suggest he work only 15 of these weeks so that some time is set aside for a vacation.

Type of job: Assuming an entry-level job in his discipline, he will earn roughly $15 an hour.

Personal savings: It is common for students to have poor saving habits; therefore, we will assume that Jim currently has no savings.

IF JIM WORKS PART-TIME DURING SEMESTERS AND FULL-TIME DURING THE SUMMER:

During the school year, Jim can earn $6,975 ($15/hr × 15 hrs × 31 wks = $6,975).

During the summer he can earn $9,000 ($15/hr × 40 hrs × 15 wks = $9,000).

Jim's yearly gross income is $6,975 + $9,000 = $15,975.

Jim will not have use of the entire amount. His annual pay—net of taxes, Quebec Pension Plan, and Employment Insurance payments—is $14,485 (a total of $1,490 is deducted according to 2013 rates). However, when he files his income tax return, he should receive a refund of any taxes paid ($521 of the total $1,490 deducted).

IF JIM TAKES OUT A STUDENT LOAN FOR $20,000:

There are student loans offered by both the federal and provincial governments; these loans are of greater advantage because they offer lower interest rates than the banks and you are only required to pay them back once you graduate. If Jim were to take out a loan today for $20,000 from the Quebec Government's Aide Financiere aux Etudes program, he will pay an annual interest rate of 3.50 percent (afe.gouv. qc.ca/en/apresEtudes/tauxInteret.asp). Since he wants to pay the loan back in six years after graduation, using the present value formula he will make monthly payments of $308.37. (See Appendix 1B for PV of an annuity equation.)

$$PV = Payments \times \frac{1 - \frac{1}{(1 = i)^n}}{i}$$

Where PV = $20,000, i = Interest Rate = .0350/12, n = # of Monthly Payments = 72.

Solving for the payments, the result is $308.37. Jim will be able to make these monthly payments when he graduates, assuming he earns an accountant's average starting salary of $37,000 (talentegg.ca). Overall, this loan will cost Jim roughly $22,200 ($308.37 × 72 months).

Many households have excessive or overlapping insurance coverage. Insuring property for more than it is worth may be a waste of money, as is both partners having similar health insurance coverage.

Key Web Site for Managing Risk: canadalife.com

INVESTING (CHAPTERS 10–13) While many types of investment vehicles are available, people invest for two primary reasons. Those interested in current income select investments that pay regular dividends or interest. In contrast, investors who desire long-term growth choose stocks, mutual funds, real estate, and other investments with potential for increased value in the future.

RECOMMENDATION:

We recommend that Jim work part-time during the school year and full-time during the summer. We came to this conclusion on the basis of the following results:

As mentioned above, Jim's net pay after deductions at source will be $14,485. However, when he files his income tax return, all taxes that were deducted will be reimbursed ($521). He will therefore have use of $14,485 + $521 = $15,006. Furthermore, he will be considered his parents' dependant for Quebec tax purposes and can transfer unused education credits to his parents for federal tax purposes, which will lower their taxes in turn. They might consider this benefit and reimburse the remaining amounts deducted at source, $333 for Employment Insurance and $636 for the Quebec Pension Plan. With this strategy, Jim actually has full use of the $15,975 he earns. Since he needs $20,000 to finance his education (or $6,666.66 in each of his three years of university), will he still have enough money left over for his additional expenses? The following table suggests that he will:

By working part time, we recognize that Jim will forgo the additional time available for his studies. However, in our experience, students tend to squander additional time and procrastinate in completing their assigned work.

If Jim works instead of taking out a loan, he will earn enough money to finance his education, pay for additional personal expenses, and still save some money, which he can use toward such expenditures as a car or house. Although one advantage of credit is that you can enjoy a good or service now and only pay for it later, it may be more prudent to avoid loans, if possible. The advantage of working part-time is to avoid the cost of borrowed money as well as gain experience in the field. With our recommendation, Jim will be debt free upon graduation and with the money he has saved, he can start building a solid savings foundation (see Chapter 10).

SOURCE: Assignment was written by and reproduced with permission from the following students: Vikram Kotecha, Matthew Berry, Mili De Silva, and Rikesh Shah—Introductory Course in Personal Finance, JMSB, Concordia University, Winter 2002, updated for 2013 tax rates.

EXPENSES OF AN AVERAGE STUDENT WHO LIVES AT HOME

Expense	Amount (monthly) $	Amount (yearly) $
Clothing	50	600
Entertainment	80	960
Videos & CDs	35	420
Miscellaneous	20	240
Total	185	2,220

$15,975 − $6,666.66 = $9,308.34 (amount of money left over after paying for school)
$9,308.34 − $2,220 = $7,088.34 (balance left over for saving)

You can achieve investment diversification by including a variety of assets in your portfolio—for example, stocks, bond mutual funds, real estate, and collectibles, such as rare coins. Obtaining general investment advice is easy; however, it is more difficult to obtain specific investment advice to meet your individual needs and goals.

Key Web Site for Investing: canoe.ca/money

RETIREMENT AND ESTATE PLANNING (CHAPTERS 14, 15) Most people want financial security upon completion of full-time employment. But retirement planning also involves thinking about your housing situation, your recreational activities, and possible part-time or volunteer work.

Key Web Sites for Retirement and Estate Planning: estateplanning.ca
http://www.fcac-acfc.gc.ca/Eng/forConsumers/lifeEvents/planningRetirement/Pages/
home-accueil.aspx

Transferring money or property to others should be timed, if possible, to minimize the tax burden and maximize the benefits for those receiving the financial resources. A knowledge of property transfer methods can help you select the best course of action for funding current and future living costs, educational expenses, and retirement needs of dependants.

DEVELOPING A FLEXIBLE FINANCIAL PLAN

financial plan A formalized report that summarizes your current financial situation, analyzes your financial needs, and recommends future financial activities.

A **financial plan** is a formalized report that summarizes your current financial situation, analyzes your financial needs, and recommends future financial activities. You can create this document on your own, seek assistance from a financial planner, or use a money management software package (see Appendix 1A). Exhibit 1–10 offers a framework for developing and implementing a financial plan, along with examples for several life situations.

IMPLEMENTING YOUR FINANCIAL PLAN

You must have a plan before you can implement it. However, once you have clearly assessed your current situation and identified your financial goals, what do you do next?

Exhibit 1–10   Financial Planning in Action

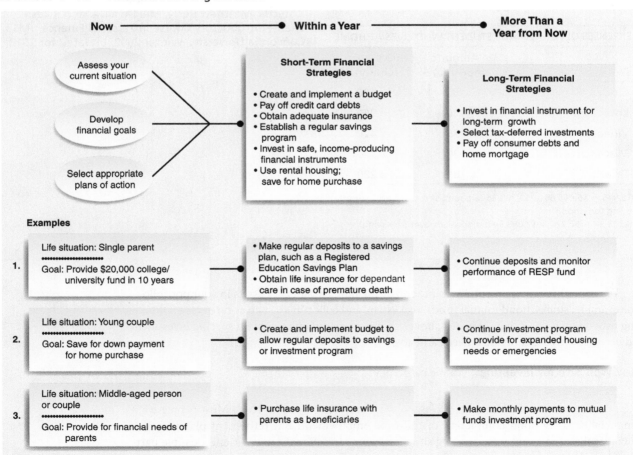

The most important strategy for success is the development of financial habits that contribute to both short-term satisfaction and long-term financial security, including the following:

1. Using a well-conceived spending plan helps you stay within your income while you save and invest for the future. The main source of financial difficulties is overspending.
2. Having appropriate insurance protection helps you prevent financial disasters.
3. Becoming informed about tax and investment alternatives helps you expand your financial resources.

Achieving your financial objectives requires two things: (1) commitment and a willingness to learn, and (2) appropriate information sources. You must provide the first element; the chapters that follow will provide the second. For successful financial planning, know where you are now, know where you want to be, and be persistent in your efforts to get there.

CONCEPT CHECK 1–5

1. What are the main components of personal financial planning?
2. What is the purpose of a financial plan?
3. Identify some common actions taken to achieve financial goals.

SUMMARY OF LEARNING OBJECTIVES

LO1 Analyze the process for making personal financial decisions.

Personal financial planning involves the following process: (1) determine your current financial situation; (2) develop financial goals; (3) identify alternative courses of action; (4) evaluate alternatives; (5) create and implement a financial action plan; and (6) re-evaluate and revise the financial plan.

LO2 Develop personal financial goals.

Financial goals should: (1) be realistic; (2) be stated in specific, measurable terms; (3) have a time frame; and (4) indicate the type of action to be taken. They are affected by a person's values, attitude toward money, and life situation.

LO3 Assess economic factors that influence personal financial planning.

Financial decisions are affected by economic factors such as consumer prices, interest rates, and employment opportunities.

LO4 Determine personal and financial opportunity costs associated with personal financial decisions.

Every decision involves a trade-off with things given up. Personal opportunity costs include time, effort, and health. Financial opportunity costs are based on the time value of money.

Future value and present value calculations enable you to measure the increased value (or lost interest) that results from a saving, investing, borrowing, or purchasing decision.

LO5 Identify strategies for achieving personal financial goals for different life situations.

Successful financial planning requires specific goals combined with spending, saving, investing, and borrowing strategies based on your personal situation and various social and economic factors.

KEY TERMS

adult life cycle 10

annuity 19

bankruptcy 23

compounding 18

economics 13

financial plan 26

future value 18

inflation 14

life cycle approach 10

liquidity 23

opportunity cost 5

personal financial planning 3

present value 20

simple interest 17

time value of money 6

values 4

KEY FORMULAS

Page	Topic	Formula
17	Simple Interest	$I = P \times R \times T$ $P =$ Amount in savings $R =$ Annual interest rate $T =$ Time period
18	Future Value (FV)	$FV = PV\,(1 + i)^n$ $PV =$ Present value $i =$ Interest rate $n =$ Number of time periods When compounding is more than once a year, $FV = PV\,(1 + i/m)^{nm}$ $i =$ Annual interest rate $m =$ Number of compounding periods per year $n =$ Number of years
39	Future Value of an Annuity	$FV = \left[\dfrac{(1 + i)^n - 1}{i}\right]$
39	Present Value (PV)	$FV \div (1 + i)^n$
40	Present Value of an Annuity	$PV = \left[\dfrac{1 - \left[1 \div (1 + i)^n\right]}{i}\right]$

FINANCIAL PLANNING PROBLEMS

 Practise and learn online with Connect.

(Note: Some of these problems require using the time value of money tables in Appendix 1B or a financial calculator.)

1. *Calculating Future Value of Property.* Ben Collins plans to buy a house for $65,000. If that real estate is expected to increase in value by 5 percent each year, what will its approximate value be seven years from now? LO3

2. *Using the Rule of 72.* Using the rule of 72, approximate the following amounts: LO3

   a. If land in an area is increasing 6 percent a year, how long will it take for property values to double?

   b. If you earn 10 percent on your investments, how long will it take for your money to double?

   c. At an annual interest rate of 5 percent, how long will it take for your savings to double?

3. *Determining the Average Price Increase.* A car that cost $12,000 in 1998 cost $16,000 10 years later. What was the rate of increase in the cost of the car over the 10-year period? LO3

4. *Determining the Required Deposit.* If you want to have $7,000 in five years, how much do you have to deposit today if your investment earns a rate of 3 percent per annum? LO3

5. *Determining Interest Rates.* The Benevolent Company has agreed to lend you funds to complete the last year of your degree. The Company will lend you $2,400 today, if you agree to repay a lump sum of $4,000 four years from now. What annual rate of interest is the Company charging you? LO3

6. *Calculating Future Value.* How long will it take to triple your money with a growth rate of 5 percent and 12 percent respectively? LO3

7. *Determining the Number of Years.* You discover $40,000 under your pillow, which can be invested at a rate of 18 percent per year. If you spend $11,435 per year, how long will the money last? LO3

8. *Calculating Annual Payments.* What annual payment is required to pay off a four year, $20,000 loan if the interest rate being charged is 7 percent? LO3

9. *Determining the Income Flow.* You have $100,000 to invest today. At 5 percent per year, what sum can you withdraw at the end of each year, for a period of 20 years, before your money is exhausted? LO4

10. *Exploring Other Time Value of Money Applications.* Using time value of money tables or a financial calculator, calculate the following: LO4

    a. The future value of $450 six years from now at 7 percent.

    b. The future value of $800 saved each year for 10 years at 8 percent.

    c. The amount you have to deposit today (present value) at a 6-percent interest rate to have $1,000 five years from now.

    d. The amount you have to deposit today to be able to take out $500 a year for 10 years from an account earning 8 percent.

11. *Calculating Future Value of a Series of Amounts.* Elaine Romberg prepares her own income tax return each year.

A tax preparer charges her $60 for this service. Over a period of 10 years, how much does Elaine gain from preparing her own tax return? Assume she can earn 6 percent with a savings certificate. LO4

12. *Calculating the Future Value of a Single Sum.* You have $800 in a savings account that earns 6 percent interest compounded annually. How much additional interest would you earn in two years if you moved the $800 to an account that earns 6 percent compounded semi-annually? LO4

13. *Calculating the Future Value of a Single Sum.* What is the future value of $20,000 received in 10 years if it is invested at 6 percent compounded annually for the next six years and at 5 percent compounded annually for the remaining four years? LO4

14. *Calculating the Present Value of a Single Sum.* Your parents have promised to give you a graduation present of $5,000 when you graduate in four years. If interest rates stay at 6 percent compounded annually for the next four years, how much is this money worth in today's dollars? LO4

FINANCIAL PLANNING ACTIVITIES

1. *Researching Personal Finance on the Internet.* Using Web sites, such as canadianfinance.com, advocis.ca, or quicken.intuit.ca, and search engines, obtain information about commonly suggested actions related to various personal financial planning decisions. What are some of the best sources of information on the Internet to assist you with financial planning? LO1

2. *Comparing Financial Planning Actions.* Survey friends, relatives, and others to determine the process they use when making financial decisions. How do these people measure risk when making financial decisions? LO1

3. *Using Financial Planning Experts.* Prepare a list of financial planning specialists (investment advisers, credit counsellors, insurance agents, real estate brokers, tax preparers) in your community who can assist people with personal financial planning. Prepare a list of questions that might be asked of these financial planning professionals by (a) a young person just starting out on his or her own, (b) a young couple planning for their children's education and for their own retirement, and (c) a person nearing retirement. LO1, LO3

4. *Setting Financial Goals.* Create one short-term goal and one long-term goal for people in these life situations: (a) a young single person, (b) a single parent with a child aged eight years, (c) a married person with no children, and (d) a retired person. LO2

5. *Analyzing Changing Life Situations.* Ask friends, relatives, and others how their spending, saving, and borrowing activities changed when they decided to continue their education, change careers, or have children. LO3

6. *Researching Economic Conditions.* Use library resources or Web sites to determine recent trends in interest rates, inflation, and other economic indicators. Information about the consumer price index (measuring changes in the cost of living) may be obtained at statcan.ca. Report how this economic information might affect your financial planning decisions. LO3

7. *Comparing Alternative Financial Actions.* What actions are necessary to compare a financial planner who advertises "One Low Fee Is Charged to Develop Your Personal Financial Plan" and one that advertises "You Are Not Charged a Fee, My Services Are Covered by the Investment Company for Which I Work"? LO4, LO5

8. *Determining Opportunity Costs.* What is the relationship between current interest rates and financial opportunity costs? Using time value of money calculations, state one or more goals in terms of an annual savings amount and the future value of this savings fund. LO2, LO4

9. *Researching Financial Planning Software.* Visit software retailers to obtain information about the features and costs of various personal financial planning activities. Information about such programs as Microsoft Money and Quicken may be obtained on the Internet. LO5

LIFE SITUATION CASE

Triple Trouble for the "Sandwich Generation"

Until recently, Fran and Ed Blake's personal finances ran smoothly. Both maintained well-paying jobs while raising two children. The Blakes have a daughter who is completing her first year of college and a son three years younger. Currently, they have $22,000 in various savings and investment funds set aside for the children's education. With education costs increasing faster than inflation, they are uncertain whether this amount is adequate.

In recent months, Fran's mother has required extensive medical attention and personal care assistance. Unable to live alone, she is now a resident of a long-term-care facility. The cost of this service is $2,050 a month, with annual increases of about 7 percent. While a major portion of the cost is covered by the Canada Pension Plan and Old Age Security, Fran's mother is unable to cover the entire cost. Their desire to help adds to the Blakes' financial burden.

The Blakes are like many other Canadians who have financial responsibilities for both dependent children and aging parents. Commonly referred to as the "sandwich generation," this group is squeezed on one side by the cost of raising and educating children and on the other side by the financial demands of caring for aging parents.

Finally, the Blakes, ages 47 and 43, are also concerned about saving for their own retirement. While they have consistently made annual deposits to a Registered Retirement Savings Plan (RRSP), various current financial demands may force them to tap into this money.

Questions

1. What actions have the Blakes taken that would be considered wise financial planning choices?

2. What areas of financial concern do the Blakes face? What actions might be appropriate to address these concerns?

3. Using time value of money calculations (tables in Appendix 1B or a financial calculator), compute the following:
    a. At 12 percent, what will be the value of the $22,000 education funds in three years?
    b. If the cost of long-term care is increasing at 7 percent a year, what will be the approximate monthly cost for Fran's mother eight years from now?
    c. Fran and Ed plan to deposit $1,500 a year to their RRSPs for 35 years. If they earn an average annual return of 9 percent, what will be the value of their RRSPs after 35 years?

Financial Planners and Other Financial Planning Information Sources

appendix 1A

"ATM fees rise."

"Global currency fluctuations may affect consumer prices."

"Mortgage interest rates remain constant."

These are just a few of the possible influences on personal financial decisions that occur each day. While this book offers the foundation for successful personal financial planning, changing social trends, economic conditions, and technology influence the decision-making environment. Your ability to continually supplement and update your knowledge is a skill that will serve you for a lifetime.

Various resources are available to assist you with personal financial decisions. These resources include printed materials, financial institutions, courses and seminars, the Internet, computer software, and financial planning specialists.

CURRENT PERIODICALS

As Exhibit 1A–1 shows, a variety of personal-finance periodicals are available to expand and update your knowledge. These periodicals, along with books on various personal-finance topics, can be found in libraries.

FINANCIAL INSTITUTIONS

Some financial advisers, such as insurance agents and investment brokers, are affiliated with companies that sell financial services. Through national marketing efforts or local promotions, banks, trust companies, credit unions, insurance companies, investment brokers, and real estate

---

Exhibit 1A–1   Personal Financial Planning Periodicals

The subject of personal finance is constantly changing. You can keep up with changes by reading the following periodicals. You can subscribe to them, read them at your school or community library, or access them on the Internet.

CPA Magazine 277 Wellington Street West Toronto, ON M5V 3H2 cpacanada.ca	**The Globe and Mail** 444 Front Street West Toronto, ON M5V 2S9 theglobeandmail.com	**MoneySense Magazine** 156 Front Street West Toronto, ON M5J 2L6 moneysense.ca
Canadian Business 777 Bay Street, Fifth Floor Toronto, ON M5W 1A7 canadianbusiness.com	**Maclean's** 777 Bay Street Toronto, ON M5W 1A7 macleans.ca	**National Post** 300–1450 Don Mills Road Don Mills, ON M3B 3R5 nationalpost.com
Canadian MoneySaver P.O. Box 370 Bath, ON K0H 1G0 canadianmoneysaver.ca		

offices offer suggestions on budgeting, saving, investing, and other aspects of financial planning. These organizations frequently offer booklets, financial planning worksheets, Web sites, and other materials and information.

COURSES AND SEMINARS

Colleges and universities offer courses in investments, real estate, insurance, taxation, and estate planning to enhance your knowledge of personal financial planning.

Civic clubs and community business organizations often schedule free or inexpensive programs featuring speakers and workshops on career planning, small-business management, budgeting, life insurance, tax return preparation, and investments. Financial institutions and financial service trade associations present seminars for current and prospective customers and members.

PERSONAL FINANCE SOFTWARE

Personal computer software is available to help you perform a variety of personal financial planning activities, from selecting a career to writing a will. These programs help you analyze your current financial situation and project your future financial position. Specialized computer programs are also available for conducting investment analyses, preparing tax returns, and determining the costs of financing and owning a home. Remember, a personal computer cannot change your saving, spending, and borrowing habits; only *you* can do that. However, your computer can provide fast and current analyses of your financial situation and progress. For information about the latest software, visit a computer store or read the articles and advertisements in magazines, such as *PC Magazine* and *MacLife*.

SPREADSHEETS

A spreadsheet program, such as Excel or Lotus 1-2-3, can assist with various financial planning tasks. Spreadsheet software can store, manipulate, create projections, and report data for such activities as:

- Creating budget categories and recording spending patterns.
- Maintaining tax records for different types of expenses, such as mileage, travel expenses, materials, and supplies, and business-related costs.
- Calculating the growth potential of savings accounts and investments.
- Monitoring changes in the market value of investments.
- Keeping records of the value of items for a home inventory.
- Projecting needed amounts of life insurance and retirement income.

MONEY MANAGEMENT AND FINANCIAL PLANNING PROGRAMS

Integrated financial planning programs can help you maintain home financial records, create a budget, observe spending patterns, write cheques, keep tax records, select and monitor investments, and project retirement needs. The most popular of these software packages are:

Microsoft Money
Microsoft
1-800-668-7975
(microsoft.com/money)

Quicken
Intuit
1-888-829-8684
(quicken.intuit.ca)

TAX SOFTWARE

Each year, the software available to prepare tax returns becomes more helpful. Besides preparing and printing the various forms and schedules, programs include tax-planning tips (with audio and video clips), audit warnings, and the ability to file your tax return electronically. The most readily available tax software includes:

Quicktax
Intuit
1-888-829-8684
(turbotax.intuit.ca)

INVESTMENT ANALYSIS PROGRAMS

Software designed for researching, trading, and monitoring an investment portfolio is also available. Most of these programs may be connected to online services to obtain current stock quotes and to buy and sell investments.

THE WEB AND PERSONAL FINANCIAL PLANNING

The Web makes it possible to access more information from your home or office than libraries offer. You may use the Web for a variety of personal financial planning activities, including: (1) researching current financial information; (2) obtaining programs to do financial planning calculations; (3) monitoring current stock and investment values; and (4) asking questions of experts and others through help lines, bulletin board services, and discussion forums. Some of the most useful Web sites providing current information on various personal finance topics include:

- *Canadian MoneySaver* magazine at canadianmoneysaver.ca; and *MoneySense* magazine at moneysense.ca.
- Current consumer price index and inflation information from Statistics Canada at statcan.gc.ca.
- The Quicken Web site at quicken.intuit.ca.
- Information on Bank of Canada activities and publications at bankofcanada.ca.
- Investing information at canoe.ca/money.

Additional Web sites are offered at the end of each chapter in the section "Creating a Financial Plan."

USING SEARCH ENGINES

A search engine is a Web site that allows you to locate information related to specific topics. Some of the most commonly used search engines include

bing.com	webcrawler.com
ask.com	yahoo.ca
searchaol.com	google.ca

Search engines operate in different ways and provide various features. Some search engines look for topic areas; others seek specific words. When conducting Web searches, be precise with your descriptive words. For example, use "mortgage rates" instead of "interest rates" to obtain information on the cost of borrowing to buy a home. Use "résumés" instead of "career planning" for assistance on developing a personal data sheet.

FINANCIAL PLANNING SPECIALISTS

Various specialists provide specific financial assistance and advice:

- *Accountants* specialize in tax matters and financial documents.
- *Bankers* assist with financial services and trusts.
- *Credit counsellors* suggest ways to reduce spending and eliminate credit problems.
- *Certified financial planners* coordinate financial decisions into a single plan.
- *Insurance agents* sell insurance coverage to protect your wealth and property.
- *Investment brokers* provide information and handle transactions for stocks, bonds, and other investments.
- *Lawyers* help with preparing wills, estate planning, tax problems, and other legal matters.
- *Real estate agents* assist with buying and selling a home or other real estate.
- *Tax preparers* specialize in the completion of income tax returns and other tax matters.

Many of these specialists offer services that include various aspects of financial planning. A financial planner's background or the company he or she represents is a good gauge of the financial planner's principal area of expertise. An accountant is likely to be most knowledgeable about tax laws, while an insurance company representative will probably emphasize how to use insurance for achieving financial goals.

WHO ARE THE FINANCIAL PLANNERS?

Many financial planners represent major insurance companies or investment businesses. Financial planners may also be individuals whose primary profession is tax accounting, real estate, or law. Financial planners are commonly categorized on the basis of three methods of compensation:

1. **Fee-only planners** charge an hourly rate that may range from $75 to $200, or may charge a fixed fee of between less than $500 and several thousand dollars. Other fee-only planners may charge an annual fee ranging from 0.04 percent to 1 percent of the value of your assets.
2. **Fee-and-commission planners** earn commissions from the investment and insurance products purchased and charge a fixed fee (ranging from $250 to $2,000) for a financial plan.
3. **Commission-only planners** receive their revenue from the commissions on sales of insurance, mutual funds, and other investments.

Consumers must be cautious about the fees charged and how these fees are communicated. A recent study revealed that more than half of financial planners who told "mystery shoppers" that they offer "fee-only" services actually earned commissions or other financial rewards for implementing the recommendations made to their clients.

DO YOU NEED A FINANCIAL PLANNER?

The two main factors that determine whether you need financial planning assistance are (1) your income, and (2) your willingness to make independent decisions. If you earn less than $40,000 a year, you probably do not need a financial planner. Income of less than this amount does not allow for many major financial decisions once you have allocated for the spending, savings, insurance, and tax elements of your personal financial planning.

Taking an active role in your financial affairs can reduce the need for a financial planner. Your willingness to keep up to date on developments related to investments, insurance, and taxes can reduce the amount you spend on financial advisers. This will require an ongoing investment of time and effort; however, it will enable you to control your own financial direction.

When deciding whether to use a financial planner, also consider the services he or she provides. First, the financial planner should help you assess your current financial position regarding spending, saving, insurance, taxes, and potential investments. Second, the financial planner should offer a clearly written plan with different courses of action. Third, the planner should take time to discuss the components of the plan and help you monitor your financial progress. Finally, the financial planner should guide you to other experts and sources of financial services as needed.

HOW SHOULD YOU SELECT A FINANCIAL PLANNER?

You can locate financial planners by using a telephone directory, contacting financial institutions, or obtaining references from friends, business associates, or professionals with whom you currently deal, such as insurance agents or real estate brokers.

When evaluating a financial planner, ask the following:

- Is financial planning your primary activity, or are other activities primary?
- Are you licensed as an investment broker or as a seller of life insurance?
- What is your educational background and formal training?
- What are your areas of expertise?
- Do you use experts in other areas, such as taxes, law, or insurance, to assist you with financial planning recommendations?
- What professional titles and certifications do you possess?
- Am I allowed a free initial consultation?
- How is the fee determined? (Is this an amount I can afford?)
- Do you have an independent practice, or are you affiliated with a major financial services company?
- What are sample insurance, tax, and investment recommendations you make for clients?
- My major concern is _____. What would you suggest?
- May I see a sample of a written financial plan?
- May I see the contract you use with clients?
- Who are some of your clients whom I might contact?

Also, make sure you are comfortable with the planner and that the planner can clearly communicate. This type of investigation takes time and effort; however, remember that you are considering placing your entire financial future in the hands of one person.

HOW ARE FINANCIAL PLANNERS CERTIFIED?

With the exception of the province of Quebec, there are currently few regulations governing financial planners in Canada.

Quebec adopted Bill 107 in December 2002 to authorize the creation of the Autorité des marches financiers (AMF) effective February 1, 2004. The AMF certifies and regulates the activities of financial planners, mutual funds representatives, and insurance agents, amongst others. The ongoing training and ethical conduct of financial planners is overseen by the Chambre de la sécurité financière (CSF), while those wishing to enter the profession must pass the licensing exam set by the Institut québécois de la planification financière (IQPF). In order to sit the exam, candidates are required to obtain a 450-hour personal financial planning certificate from one of four authorized educational institutions and two additional undergraduate certificates in a related field (e.g., commerce, law, or economics). In addition, candidates must successfully complete the 45-hour IQPF Professional Training course. Once they have successfully completed the IQPF exam, they are then allowed to use the title *financial planner*. Once certified, 60 hours of continuing education are required every two years.

The code of ethics governing Quebec's financial planners describes the duties and obligations of a financial planner toward the public, clients, and other members of the profession.

With respect to clients, a financial planner must act with integrity, objectivity, and independence; avoid conflicts of interest; and put the best interests of his or her client first. All client information must be kept confidential, and full disclosure of the planner's remuneration must be outlined in the service offer signed by the client and financial planner at the outset.

Elsewhere in Canada, a financial planner may be a professional lawyer, accountant, investment adviser, insurance salesperson, mutual fund specialist, or none of the above. Financial planners are bound by the same statutes and common law that apply to anyone selling services. They must perform their work with due care, and they cannot misrepresent their work or their qualifications. Financial planners should be willing and knowledgeable enough to call on an expert when advanced knowledge or licensing is required to meet the client's needs.

The Financial Planning Standards Council (FPSC) is a non-profit organization established in 1995 to guide the evolution of the financial planning profession across Canada. The FPSC is a self-regulated organization (SRO) and is the only body in Canada authorized to award the Certified Financial Planner (CFP) designation, recognized internationally (although insufficient in the province of Quebec). It also plays a leading role developing and enforcing ethical standards amongst financial planning professionals.

In order to sit the CFP exam held twice yearly (June and December), candidates must successfully complete an education program registered directly with the FPSC. Following is a partial list of colleges, universities, and organizations registered with the FPSC. For more information, visit the FPSC's Web site at cfp-ca.org.

Advocis	advocis.ca
B.C. Institute of Technology	bcit.ca
Canadian Institute of Financial Planners	cifps.ca
Canadian Securities Institute	csi.ca
George Brown College	gbrownc.ca
Institute of Canadian Bankers	csi.ca/icb
Ryerson University	ryerson.ca
University of Manitoba	umanitoba.ca
Wilfrid Laurier University	wlu.ca

The Time Value of Money: Future Value and Present Value Computations

"If I deposit $10,000 today, how much will I have for a down payment on a house in five years?"

"Will $2,000 saved a year give me enough money when I retire?"

"How much must I save today to have enough for my children's post-secondary education?"

As introduced in Chapter 1 and used to measure financial opportunity costs in other chapters, the *time value of money*, more commonly referred to as *interest*, is the cost of money that is borrowed or lent. Interest can be compared to rent, the cost of using an apartment or other item. The time value of money is based on the fact that a dollar received today is worth more than a dollar that will be received one year from today because the dollar received today can be saved or invested and will be worth more than a dollar a year from today. Similarly, a dollar that will be received one year from today is currently worth less than a dollar today.

The time value of money has two major components: future value and present value. *Future value* computations, which are also referred to as *compounding*, yield the amount to which a current sum will increase based on a certain interest rate and period of time. *Present value*, which is calculated through a process called *discounting*, is the current value of a future sum based on a certain interest rate and period of time.

In future value problems, you are given an amount to save or invest and you calculate the amount that will be available at some future date. With present value problems, you are given the amount that will be available at some future date and you calculate the current value of that amount. Both future value and present value computations are based on basic interest rate calculations.

FINANCIAL CALCULATORS

Currently, financial calculators, with time value of money functions built in, are widely used to calculate future value, present values, and annuities. For the following examples, we will use the Texas Instruments BA II Plus financial calculator, which is recommended by the Canadian Institute of Financial Planning.

When using the BA II Plus calculator to solve time value of money problems, you will be working with the TVM keys that include:

- `CPT` — Compute key used to initiate financial calculations once all values are inputted
- `N` — Number of periods
- `I/Y` — Interest rate per period
- `PV` — Present value
- `PMT` — Amount of payment, used only for annuities
- `FV` — Future value

Enter values for PV, PMT, and FV as negative if they represent cash outflows (e.g., investing a sum of money) or as positive if they represent cash inflows (e.g., receiving the proceeds of an investment). To convert a positive number to a negative number, enter the number and then press the $+/-$ key.

The examples that are shown in this chapter assume that interest is compounded annually and that there is only one cash flow per period. To reflect this, we must set the number of payments and compounding per period to 1 (the default setting is 12). To do this, press in turn the ⟨2ND⟩ button (yellow), the ⟨I/Y⟩ button (for the P/Y function shown above it), the number 1, the ⟨ENTER⟩ button, the ⟨2ND⟩ button again, and finally the ⟨CPT⟩ button (for the quit function above it). Before using any financial calculator, we strongly recommend that you consult the instruction manual that accompanies it and attempt the examples shown there.

Now let's try a problem. What is the future value of $100 after three years at a 10 percent annual interest rate? Remember that an investment of money is considered to be an outflow of cash; therefore, the present value of $100 should be entered as a negative number.

First, you must enter the data. Remember that an investment of money is considered to be an outflow of cash; therefore, the $100 should be entered as a negative number.

3	⟨N⟩
10	⟨I/Y⟩
100+/−	⟨PV⟩
0	⟨PMT⟩ (optional if registers are cleared)

To find the solution, the future value, press ⟨CPT⟩ ⟨FV⟩, and the future value of 133.1 is displayed.

FUTURE VALUE OF A SINGLE AMOUNT

The future value of an amount consists of the original amount plus compound interest. This calculation involves the following elements:

$$FV = \text{Future value}$$
$$PV = \text{Present value}$$
$$i = \text{Interest rate}$$
$$n = \text{Number of time periods}$$

The formula and financial calculator computations are as follows:
   (Note: These financial calculator notations may require slightly different keystrokes when using various brands and models.)

Future Value of a Single Amount		
Formula	**Table**	**Financial Calculator**
$FV = PV(1 + i)^n$	Using Exhibit 1B–1: FV = PV (Table Factor)	⟨PV⟩, ⟨I/Y⟩, ⟨N⟩, ⟨PMT⟩, ⟨CPT⟩ ⟨FV⟩
Example A: The future value of $1 at 10 percent after three years is $1.33. This amount is calculated as follows:		
$\$1.33 = \$(1.001 + 0.10)^3$	Using Exhibit 1B–1: $1.33 = $1.00(1.33)	1 ⟨PV⟩, 10 ⟨I/Y⟩, 3 ⟨N⟩, 0 ⟨PMT⟩, ⟨CPT⟩ ⟨FV⟩ 1.33

Future value tables are available to help you determine compounded interest amounts (see Exhibit 1B–1). Looking at Exhibit 1B–1 for 10 percent and three years, you can see that $1 is worth $1.33 at that time. For other amounts, multiply the table factor by the original amount. This process may be viewed as follows:

Formula	**Table**	**Financial Calculator**
Example B: If your savings of $400 earns 12 percent, compounded *monthly*, over a year and a half, use the table factor for 1 percent for 18 time periods; the future value is:		
$\$478.46 = \$400(1 + 0.01)^{18}$ $478.40 = $400(1.196)		400 ⟨PV⟩, 12/12 = 1 ⟨I/Y⟩, 1.5 × 12 = 18 ⟨N⟩, 0 ⟨PMT⟩ ⟨CPT⟩, ⟨FV⟩ 478.46

Sample Problem 1   What is the future value of $800 at 8 percent after six years?

Sample Problem 2   How much would you have in savings if you kept $200 on deposit for eight years at 8 percent, compounded *semi-annually*?

FUTURE VALUE OF A SERIES OF EQUAL AMOUNTS (AN ANNUITY)

Future value may also be calculated for a situation in which regular additions are made to savings. The formula and financial calculator computations are as follows:

Future Value of a Series of Payments		
Formula	Table	Financial Calculator
$FV = \text{Annuity} = \dfrac{(1 + i)^n - 1}{i}$	Using Exhibit 1B–2: FV = Annuity (Table Factor)	PMT , N , I/Y , PV , CPT FV

This calculation assumes that: (1) each deposit is for the same amount; (2) the interest rate is the same for each time period; and (3) the deposits are made at the end of each time period.

Example C: The future value of three $1 deposits made at the end of the next three years, earning 10 percent interest, is $3.31. This is calculated as follows:

$\$3.31 = \dfrac{(1 + 0.10)^3 - 1}{0.10}$	Using Exhibit 1B–2: $\$3.31 = \$1 \times 3.31$	-1 PMT , 3 N , 10 I/Y , 0 PV , CPT FV 3.31

This may be viewed as follows:

Example D: If you plan to deposit $40 a year for 10 years, earning 8 percent compounded annually, the future value of this amount is:

$\$579.46 = \dfrac{\$40(1 + 0.08)^{10} - 1}{0.08}$	Using Exhibit 1B–2: $\$579.48 = \$40(14.487)$	-40 PMT , 10 N , 10 I/Y , 0 PV , CPT FV 579.46

Sample Problem 3   What is the future value of an annual deposit of $230 earning 6 percent for 15 years?

Sample Problem 4   What amount would you have in a retirement account if you made annual deposits of $375 for 25 years earning 12 percent, compounded annually?

PRESENT VALUE OF A SINGLE AMOUNT

If you want to know how much you need to deposit now to receive a certain amount in the future, the formula and financial calculator computations are as follows:

Present Value of a Single Amount		
Formula	Table	Financial Calculator
$PV = \dfrac{FV}{(1 + i)^n}$	Using Exhibit 1B–3: PV = FV (Table Factor)	FV , N , I/Y , PMT , CPT PV

Example E: The present value of $1 to be received three years from now based on a 10 percent interest rate is calculated as follows:

$\$0.75 = \dfrac{\$1}{(1 + 0.10)^3}$	Using Exhibit 1B–3: $\$0.75 = \$1(0.751)$	1 FV , 3 N , 10 I/Y , 0 PMT , CPT PV $-$.75131

(*continued*)

This may be viewed as follows:
Present value tables are available to assist you in this process (see Exhibit 1B–3). Notice that $1 at 10 percent for three years has a present value of $0.75. For amounts other than $1, multiply the table factor by the amount involved.

Example F: If you want to have $300 seven years from now and your savings earn 10 percent, compounded *semi-annually* (5 percent for 14 time periods), finding how much you would have to deposit today is calculated as follows:

$$\$151.52 = \frac{\$300}{(1 + 0.05)^{14}}$$

Using Exhibit 1B–3:
$$\$151.50 = \$300(0.505)$$

300 [FV] , 7 × 2 = 14 [N] , 10/2 = 5 [I/Y] ,
0 [PMT] , [CPT] [PV] —151.52

Sample Problem 5   What is the present value of $2,200 earning 15 percent for eight years?

Sample Problem 6   To have $6,000 for a child's education in 10 years, what amount should a parent deposit in a savings account that earns 12 percent, compounded *quarterly*?

PRESENT VALUE OF A SERIES OF EQUAL AMOUNTS (AN ANNUITY)

The final time value of money situation allows you to receive an amount at the end of each time period for a certain number of periods. The formula and financial calculator computations are as follows:

Present Value of a Series of Payments		
Formula	Table	Financial Calculator
$$PV = \text{Annuity} \times \frac{1 - \dfrac{1}{(1 + i)^n}}{i}$$	Using Exhibit 1B–4: PV = Annuity (Table Factor)	[PMT] , [N] , [I/Y] , [FV] , [CPT] [PV]

Example G: The present value of a $1 withdrawal at the end of the next three years would be $2.49, for money earning 10 percent. This would be calculated as follows:

$$\$2.49 = \$1 \left[\frac{1 - \dfrac{1}{(1 + 0.10)^3}}{0.10} \right]$$

Using Exhibit 1B–4:
$$\$2.49 = \$1(2.487)$$

1 [PMT] , 3 [N] , 10 [I/Y] , 0 [FV] ,
[CPT] [PV] — 2.48685

This may be viewed as follows:
This same amount appears in Exhibit 1B–4 for 10 percent and three time periods. To use the table for other situations, multiply the table factor by the amount to be withdrawn each year.

Example H: If you wish to withdraw $100 at the end of each year for 10 years from an account that earns 14 percent, compounded annually, what amount must you deposit now?

$$\$521.61 = \$100 \left[\frac{1 - \dfrac{1}{(1 + 0.14)^{10}}}{0.14} \right]$$

Using Exhibit 1B–4:
$$\$521.60 = \$100(5.216)$$

100 [PMT] , 10 [N] , 14 [I/Y] , 0 [FV] ,
[CPT] [PV] 521.61156

Sample Problem 7   What is the present value of a withdrawal of $200 at the end of each year for 14 years with an interest rate of 7 percent?

Sample Problem 8   How much would you have to deposit now to be able to withdraw $650 at the end of each year for 20 years from an account that earns 11 percent?

Present value tables can also be used to determine instalment payments for a loan as follows:

USING PRESENT VALUE TO DETERMINE LOAN PAYMENTS

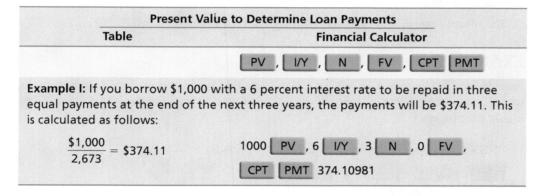

Present Value to Determine Loan Payments	
Table	Financial Calculator

PV , **I/Y** , **N** , **FV** , **CPT** **PMT**

Example I: If you borrow $1,000 with a 6 percent interest rate to be repaid in three equal payments at the end of the next three years, the payments will be $374.11. This is calculated as follows:

$$\frac{\$1,000}{2,673} = \$374.11$$

1000 **PV** , 6 **I/Y** , 3 **N** , 0 **FV** ,

CPT **PMT** 374.10981

Sample Problem 9 What would be the annual payment amount for a $20,000, 10-year loan at 7 percent?

ANSWERS TO SAMPLE PROBLEMS

[1] $800(1.587) = $1,269.60. (Use Exhibit 1B–1, 8%, 6 periods.)
[2] $200(1.873) = $374.60. (Use Exhibit 1B–1, 4%, 16 periods.)
[3] $230(23.276) = $5,353.48. (Use Exhibit 1B–2, 6%, 15 periods.)
[4] $375(133.33) = $49,998.75. (Use Exhibit 1B–2, 12%, 25 periods.)
[5] $2,200(0.327) = $719.40. (Use Exhibit 1B–3, 15%, 8 periods.)
[6] $6,000(0.307) = $1,842. (Use Exhibit 1B–3, 3%, 40 periods.)
[7] $200(8.745) = $1,749. (Use Exhibit 1B–4, 7%, 14 periods.)
[8] $650(7.963) = $5,175.95. (Use Exhibit 1B–4, 11%, 20 periods.)
[9] $20,000 ÷ 7.024 = $2,847.38. (Use Exhibit 1B–4, 7%, 10 periods.)

Calculator Solutions

[1] Calculator: 2ND CLRTVM; 6 N; 8 I/Y; 800 PV; CPT FV; Solution $1,269.50
[2] Calculator: 2ND CLRTVM; 16 N; 4 I/Y; 200 PV; CPT FV; Solution $374.60
[3] Calculator: 2ND CLRTVM; 15 N; 6 I/Y; 230 PMT; CPT FV; Solution $5353.47
[4] Calculator: 2ND CLRTVM; 25 N; 12 I/Y; 375 PMT; CPT FV; Solution $50,000.20
[5] Calculator: 2ND CLRTVM; 8 N; 15 I/Y; 2,200 FV; CPT PV; Solution $719.18
[6] Calculator: 2ND CLRTVM; 40 N; 3 I/Y; 6,000 FV; CPT PV; Solution $1839.34
[7] Calculator: 2ND CLRTVM; 14 N; 7 I/Y; 200 PMT; CPT PV; Solution $1749.09
[8] Calculator: 2ND CLRTVM; 20 N; 11 I/Y; 650 PMT; CPT PV; Solution $5176.16
[9] Calculator: 2ND CLRTVM; 10 N; 7 I/Y; 20,000 PV; CPT PMT; Solution $2,847.55

CALCULATING THE EFFECTIVE ANNUAL RATE (EAR) USING A FINANCIAL CALCULATOR (TEXAS INSTRUMENTS BA II PLUS)

The formula for calculating the effective annual rate, the return that takes compounding into effect, is as follows:

$$EAR = [(1 + APR/m)^m] - 1$$

Example from Chapter 4 (page 130): How much is your nominal EAR on a $100 loan at 12 percent yearly, compounded monthly? (There are 12 compounding periods in a year.)

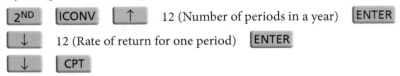

The effective rate of 12.68 percent is displayed on the screen.

EXAMPLE J

Assume your bank offers a 10 percent interest rate that is compounded every three months, while a competitor offers 10 percent compounded on a monthly basis. Which one offers a higher effective rate?

BANK (10% compounded every 3 months = 4 periods)

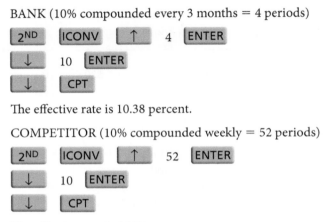

The effective rate is 10.38 percent.

COMPETITOR (10% compounded weekly = 52 periods)

2ND ICONV ↑ 52 ENTER
↓ 10 ENTER
↓ CPT

The effective rate is 10.51 percent.

As you can see, the competitor offers a higher return than your bank.

Exhibit 1B–1 Future Value (Compounded Sum) of $1 After a Given Number of Time Periods $FV = PV(1 + i)^n$

Period	1%	2%	3%	4%	5%	6%	7%	8%	9%	10%	11%
1	1.010	1.020	1.030	1.040	1.050	1.060	1.070	1.080	1.090	1.100	1.110
2	1.020	1.040	1.061	1.082	1.103	1.124	1.145	1.166	1.188	1.210	1.232
3	1.030	1.061	1.093	1.125	1.158	1.191	1.225	1.260	1.295	1.331	1.368
4	1.041	1.082	1.126	1.170	1.216	1.262	1.311	1.360	1.412	1.464	1.518
5	1.051	1.104	1.159	1.217	1.276	1.338	1.403	1.469	1.539	1.611	1.685
6	1.062	1.126	1.194	1.265	1.340	1.419	1.501	1.587	1.677	1.772	1.870
7	1.072	1.149	1.230	1.316	1.407	1.504	1.606	1.714	1.828	1.949	2.076
8	1.083	1.172	1.267	1.369	1.477	1.594	1.718	1.851	1.993	2.144	2.305
9	1.094	1.195	1.305	1.423	1.551	1.689	1.838	1.999	2.172	2.358	2.558
10	1.105	1.219	1.344	1.480	1.629	1.791	1.967	2.159	2.367	2.594	2.839
11	1.116	1.243	1.384	1.539	1.710	1.898	2.105	2.332	2.580	2.853	3.152
12	1.127	1.268	1.426	1.601	1.796	2.012	2.252	2.518	2.813	3.138	3.498
13	1.138	1.294	1.469	1.665	1.886	2.133	2.410	2.720	3.066	3.452	3.883
14	1.149	1.319	1.513	1.732	1.980	2.261	2.579	2.937	3.342	3.797	4.310
15	1.161	1.346	1.558	1.801	2.079	2.397	2.759	3.172	3.642	4.177	4.785
16	1.173	1.373	1.605	1.873	2.183	2.540	2.952	3.426	3.970	4.595	5.311
17	1.184	1.400	1.653	1.948	2.292	2.693	3.159	3.700	4.328	5.054	5.895
18	1.196	1.428	1.702	2.026	2.407	2.854	3.380	3.996	4.717	5.560	6.544
19	1.208	1.457	1.754	2.107	2.527	3.026	3.617	4.316	5.142	6.116	7.263
20	1.220	1.486	1.806	2.191	2.653	3.207	3.870	4.661	5.604	6.727	8.062
25	1.282	1.641	2.094	2.666	3.386	4.292	5.427	6.848	8.623	10.835	13.585
30	1.348	1.811	2.427	3.243	4.322	5.743	7.612	10.063	13.268	17.449	22.892
40	1.489	2.208	3.262	4.801	7.040	10.286	14.974	21.725	31.409	45.259	65.001
50	1.645	2.692	4.384	7.107	11.467	18.420	29.457	46.902	74.358	117.390	184.570

Exhibit 1B–1 (concluded)

Period	12%	13%	14%	15%	16%	17%	18%	19%	20%	25%	30%
1	1.120	1.130	1.140	1.150	1.160	1.170	1.180	1.190	1.200	1.250	1.300
2	1.254	1.277	1.300	1.323	1.346	1.369	1.392	1.416	1.440	1.563	1.690
3	1.405	1.443	1.482	1.521	1.561	1.602	1.643	1.685	1.728	1.953	2.197
4	1.574	1.630	1.689	1.749	1.811	1.874	1.939	2.005	2.074	2.441	2.856
5	1.762	1.842	1.925	2.011	2.100	2.192	2.288	2.386	2.488	3.052	3.713
6	1.974	2.082	2.195	2.313	2.436	2.565	2.700	2.840	2.986	3.815	4.827
7	2.211	2.353	2.502	2.660	2.826	3.001	3.185	3.379	3.583	4.768	6.276
8	2.476	2.658	2.853	3.059	3.278	3.511	3.759	4.021	4.300	5.960	8.157
9	2.773	3.004	3.252	3.518	3.803	4.108	4.435	4.785	5.160	7.451	10.604
10	3.106	3.395	3.707	4.046	4.411	4.807	5.234	5.696	6.192	9.313	13.786
11	3.479	3.836	4.226	4.652	5.117	5.624	6.176	6.777	7.430	11.642	17.922
12	3.896	4.335	4.818	5.350	5.936	6.580	7.288	8.064	8.916	14.552	23.298
13	4.363	4.898	5.492	6.153	6.886	7.699	8.599	9.596	10.699	18.190	30.288
14	4.887	5.535	6.261	7.076	7.988	9.007	10.147	11.420	12.839	22.737	39.374
15	5.474	6.254	7.138	8.137	9.266	10.539	11.974	13.590	15.407	28.422	51.186
16	6.130	7.067	8.137	9.358	10.748	12.330	14.129	16.172	18.488	35.527	66.542
17	6.866	7.986	9.276	10.761	12.468	14.426	16.672	19.244	22.186	44.409	86.504
18	7.690	9.024	10.575	12.375	14.463	16.879	19.673	22.091	26.623	55.511	112.460
19	8.613	10.197	12.056	14.232	16.777	19.748	23.214	27.252	31.948	69.389	146.190
20	9.646	11.523	13.743	16.367	19.461	23.106	27.393	32.429	38.338	86.736	190.050
25	17.000	21.231	26.462	32.919	40.874	50.658	62.669	77.388	95.396	264.700	705.640
30	29.960	39.116	50.950	66.212	85.850	111.070	143.370	184.680	237.380	807.790	2,620.000
40	93.051	132.780	188.880	267.860	378.720	533.870	750.380	1,051.700	1,469.800	7,523.200	36,119.000
50	289.000	450.740	700.230	1,083.700	1,670.700	2,566.200	3,927.400	5,988.900	9,100.400	70,065.000	497,929.000

Exhibit 1B–2   Future Value (Compounded Sum) of $1 Paid in at the End of Each Period for a Given Number of Time Periods (an Annuity) $FV = \dfrac{(1 + i)^n - 1}{i}$

Period	1%	2%	3%	4%	5%	6%	7%	8%	9%	10%	11%
1	1.000	1.000	1.000	1.000	1.000	1.000	1.000	1.000	1.000	1.000	1.000
2	2.010	2.020	2.030	2.040	2.050	2.060	2.070	2.080	2.090	2.100	2.110
3	3.030	3.060	3.091	3.122	3.153	3.184	3.215	3.246	3.278	3.310	3.342
4	4.060	4.122	4.184	4.246	4.310	4.375	4.440	4.506	4.573	4.641	4.710
5	5.101	5.204	5.309	5.416	5.526	5.637	5.751	5.867	5.985	6.105	6.228
6	6.152	6.308	6.468	6.633	6.802	6.975	7.153	7.336	7.523	7.716	7.913
7	7.214	7.434	7.662	7.898	8.142	8.394	8.654	8.923	9.200	9.487	9.783
8	8.286	8.583	8.892	9.214	9.549	9.897	10.260	10.637	11.028	11.436	11.859
9	9.369	9.755	10.159	10.583	11.027	11.491	11.978	12.488	13.021	13.579	14.164
10	10.462	10.950	11.464	12.006	12.578	13.181	13.816	14.487	15.193	15.937	16.722
11	11.567	12.169	12.808	13.486	14.207	14.972	15.784	16.645	17.560	18.531	19.561
12	12.683	13.412	14.192	15.026	15.917	16.870	17.888	18.977	20.141	21.384	22.713
13	13.809	14.680	15.618	16.627	17.713	18.882	20.141	21.495	22.953	24.523	26.212
14	14.947	15.974	17.086	18.292	19.599	21.015	22.550	24.215	26.019	27.975	30.095
15	16.097	17.293	18.599	20.024	21.579	23.276	25.129	27.152	29.361	31.772	34.405
16	17.258	18.639	20.157	21.825	23.657	25.673	27.888	30.324	33.003	35.950	39.190
17	18.430	20.012	21.762	23.698	25.840	20.213	30.840	33.750	36.974	40.545	44.501
18	19.615	21.412	23.414	25.645	28.132	30.906	33.999	37.450	41.301	45.599	50.396
19	20.811	22.841	25.117	27.671	30.539	33.760	37.379	41.446	46.018	51.159	56.939
20	22.019	24.297	26.870	29.778	33.066	36.786	40.995	45.762	51.160	57.275	64.203
25	28.243	32.030	36.459	41.646	47.727	54.865	63.249	73.106	84.701	98.347	114.410
30	34.785	40.588	47.575	56.085	66.439	79.058	94.461	113.280	136.310	164.490	199.020
40	48.886	60.402	75.401	95.026	120.800	154.760	199.640	259.060	337.890	442.590	581.830
50	64.463	84.579	112.800	152.670	209.350	290.340	406.530	573.770	815.080	1,163.900	1,668.800

Exhibit 1B–2   (concluded)

Period	12%	13%	14%	15%	16%	17%	18%	19%	20%	25%	30%
1	1.000	1.000	1.000	1.000	1.000	1.000	1.000	1.000	1.000	1.000	1.000
2	2.120	2.130	2.140	2.150	2.160	2.170	2.180	2.190	2.200	2.250	2.300
3	3.374	3.407	3.440	3.473	3.506	3.539	3.572	3.606	3.640	3.813	3.990
4	4.779	4.850	4.921	4.993	5.066	5.141	5.215	5.291	5.368	5.766	6.187
5	6.353	6.480	6.610	6.742	6.877	7.014	7.154	7.297	7.442	8.207	9.043
6	8.115	8.323	8.536	8.754	8.977	9.207	9.442	9.683	9.930	11.259	12.756
7	10.089	10.405	10.730	11.067	11.414	11.772	12.142	12.523	12.916	15.073	17.583
8	12.300	12.757	13.233	13.727	14.240	14.773	15.327	15.902	16.499	19.842	23.858
9	14.776	15.416	16.085	16.786	17.519	18.285	19.086	19.923	20.799	25.802	32.015
10	17.549	18.420	19.337	20.304	21.321	22.393	23.521	24.701	25.959	33.253	42.619
11	20.655	21.814	23.045	24.349	25.733	27.200	28.755	30.404	32.150	42.566	56.405
12	24.133	25.650	27.271	29.002	30.850	32.824	34.931	37.180	39.581	54.208	74.327
13	28.029	29.985	32.089	34.352	36.786	39.404	42.219	45.244	48.497	68.760	97.625
14	32.393	34.883	37.581	40.505	43.672	47.103	50.818	54.841	59.196	86.949	127.910
15	37.280	40.417	43.842	47.580	51.660	56.110	60.965	66.261	72.035	109.690	167.290
16	42.753	46.672	50.980	55.717	60.925	66.649	72.939	79.850	87.442	138.110	218.470
17	48.884	53.739	59.118	65.075	71.673	78.979	87.068	96.022	105.930	173.640	285.010
18	55.750	61.725	68.394	75.836	84.141	93.406	103.740	115.270	128.120	218.050	371.520
19	63.440	70.749	78.969	88.212	98.603	110.290	123.410	138.170	154.740	273.560	483.970
20	72.052	80.947	91.025	102.440	115.380	130.030	146.630	165.420	186.690	342.950	630.170
25	133.330	155.620	181.870	212.790	249.210	292.110	342.600	402.040	471.980	1,054.800	2,348.800
30	241.330	293.200	356.790	434.750	530.310	647.440	790.950	966.700	1,181.900	3,227.200	8,730.000
40	767.090	1,013.700	1,342.000	1,779.100	2,360.800	3,134.500	4,163.210	5,529.800	7,343.900	30,089.000	120,393.000
50	2,400.000	3,459.500	4,994.500	7,217.700	10,436.000	15,090.000	21,813.000	31,515.000	45,497.000	80,256.000	165,976.000

Exhibit 1B–3   Present Value of \$1 to Be Received at the End of a Given Number of Time Periods $PV = \dfrac{1}{(1+i)^n}$

Period	1%	2%	3%	4%	5%	6%	7%	8%	9%	10%	11%	12%
1	0.990	0.980	0.971	0.962	0.952	0.943	0.935	0.926	0.917	0.909	0.901	0.893
2	0.980	0.961	0.943	0.925	0.907	0.890	0.873	0.857	0.842	0.826	0.812	0.797
3	0.971	0.942	0.915	0.889	0.864	0.840	0.816	0.794	0.772	0.751	0.731	0.712
4	0.961	0.924	0.885	0.855	0.823	0.792	0.763	0.735	0.708	0.683	0.659	0.636
5	0.951	0.906	0.863	0.822	0.784	0.747	0.713	0.681	0.650	0.621	0.593	0.567
6	0.942	0.888	0.837	0.790	0.746	0.705	0.666	0.630	0.596	0.564	0.535	0.507
7	0.933	0.871	0.813	0.760	0.711	0.665	0.623	0.583	0.547	0.513	0.482	0.452
8	0.923	0.853	0.789	0.731	0.677	0.627	0.582	0.540	0.502	0.467	0.434	0.404
9	0.914	0.837	0.766	0.703	0.645	0.592	0.544	0.500	0.460	0.424	0.391	0.361
10	0.905	0.820	0.744	0.676	0.614	0.558	0.508	0.463	0.422	0.386	0.352	0.322
11	0.896	0.804	0.722	0.650	0.585	0.527	0.475	0.429	0.388	0.350	0.317	0.287
12	0.887	0.788	0.701	0.625	0.557	0.497	0.444	0.397	0.356	0.319	0.286	0.257
13	0.879	0.773	0.681	0.601	0.530	0.469	0.415	0.368	0.326	0.290	0.258	0.229
14	0.870	0.758	0.661	0.577	0.505	0.442	0.388	0.340	0.299	0.263	0.232	0.205
15	0.861	0.743	0.642	0.555	0.481	0.417	0.362	0.315	0.275	0.239	0.209	0.183
16	0.853	0.728	0.623	0.534	0.458	0.394	0.339	0.292	0.252	0.218	0.188	0.163
17	0.844	0.714	0.605	0.513	0.436	0.371	0.317	0.270	0.231	0.198	0.170	0.146
18	0.836	0.700	0.587	0.494	0.416	0.350	0.296	0.250	0.212	0.180	0.153	0.130
19	0.828	0.686	0.570	0.475	0.396	0.331	0.277	0.232	0.194	0.164	0.138	0.116
20	0.820	0.673	0.554	0.456	0.377	0.312	0.258	0.215	0.178	0.149	0.124	0.104
25	0.780	0.610	0.478	0.375	0.295	0.233	0.184	0.146	0.116	0.092	0.074	0.059
30	0.742	0.552	0.412	0.308	0.231	0.174	0.131	0.099	0.075	0.057	0.044	0.033
40	0.672	0.453	0.307	0.208	0.142	0.097	0.067	0.046	0.032	0.022	0.015	0.011
50	0.608	0.372	0.228	0.141	0.087	0.054	0.034	0.021	0.013	0.009	0.005	0.003

Exhibit 1B–3   (concluded)

Period	13%	14%	15%	16%	17%	18%	19%	20%	25%	30%	35%	40%	50%
1	0.885	0.877	0.870	0.862	0.855	0.847	0.840	0.833	0.800	0.769	0.741	0.714	0.667
2	0.783	0.769	0.756	0.743	0.731	0.718	0.706	0.694	0.640	0.592	0.549	0.510	0.444
3	0.693	0.675	0.658	0.641	0.624	0.609	0.593	0.579	0.512	0.455	0.406	0.364	0.296
4	0.613	0.592	0.572	0.552	0.534	0.515	0.499	0.482	0.410	0.350	0.301	0.260	0.198
5	0.543	0.519	0.497	0.476	0.456	0.437	0.419	0.402	0.320	0.269	0.223	0.186	0.132
6	0.480	0.456	0.432	0.410	0.390	0.370	0.352	0.335	0.262	0.207	0.165	0.133	0.088
7	0.425	0.400	0.376	0.354	0.333	0.314	0.296	0.279	0.210	0.159	0.122	0.095	0.059
8	0.376	0.351	0.327	0.305	0.285	0.266	0.249	0.233	0.168	0.123	0.091	0.068	0.039
9	0.333	0.300	0.284	0.263	0.243	0.225	0.209	0.194	0.134	0.094	0.067	0.048	0.026
10	0.295	0.270	0.247	0.227	0.208	0.191	0.176	0.162	0.107	0.073	0.050	0.035	0.017
11	0.261	0.237	0.215	0.195	0.178	0.162	0.148	0.135	0.086	0.056	0.037	0.025	0.012
12	0.231	0.208	0.187	0.168	0.152	0.137	0.124	0.112	0.069	0.043	0.027	0.018	0.008
13	0.204	0.182	0.163	0.145	0.130	0.116	0.104	0.093	0.055	0.033	0.020	0.013	0.005
14	0.181	0.160	0.141	0.125	0.111	0.099	0.088	0.078	0.044	0.025	0.015	0.009	0.003
15	0.160	0.140	0.123	0.108	0.095	0.084	0.074	0.065	0.035	0.020	0.011	0.006	0.002
16	0.141	0.123	0.107	0.093	0.081	0.071	0.062	0.054	0.028	0.015	0.008	0.005	0.002
17	0.125	0.108	0.093	0.080	0.069	0.060	0.052	0.045	0.023	0.012	0.006	0.003	0.001
18	0.111	0.095	0.081	0.069	0.059	0.051	0.044	0.038	0.018	0.009	0.005	0.002	0.001
19	0.098	0.083	0.070	0.060	0.051	0.043	0.037	0.031	0.014	0.007	0.003	0.002	0
20	0.087	0.073	0.061	0.051	0.043	0.037	0.031	0.026	0.012	0.005	0.002	0.001	0
25	0.047	0.038	0.030	0.024	0.020	0.016	0.013	0.010	0.004	0.001	0.001	0	0
30	0.026	0.020	0.015	0.012	0.009	0.007	0.005	0.004	0.001	0	0	0	0
40	0.008	0.005	0.004	0.003	0.002	0.001	0.001	0.001	0	0	0	0	0
50	0.002	0.001	0.001	0.001	0	0	0	0	0	0	0	0	0

Exhibit 1B–4   Present Value of $1 Received at the End of Each Period for a Given Number of Time Periods (an Annuity)

$$PV = \frac{1 - \frac{1}{(1 + i)^n}}{i}$$

Period	1%	2%	3%	4%	5%	6%	7%	8%	9%	10%	11%	12%
1	0.990	0.980	0.971	0.962	0.952	0.943	0.935	0.926	0.917	0.909	0.901	0.893
2	1.970	1.942	1.913	1.886	1.859	1.833	1.808	1.783	1.759	1.736	1.713	1.690
3	2.941	2.884	2.829	2.775	2.723	2.673	2.624	2.577	2.531	2.487	2.444	2.402
4	3.902	3.808	3.717	3.630	3.546	3.465	3.387	3.312	3.240	3.170	3.102	3.037
5	4.853	4.713	4.580	4.452	4.329	4.212	4.100	3.993	3.890	3.791	3.696	3.605
6	5.795	5.601	5.417	5.242	5.076	4.917	4.767	4.623	4.486	4.355	4.231	4.111
7	6.728	6.472	6.230	6.002	5.786	5.582	5.389	5.206	5.033	4.868	4.712	4.564
8	7.652	7.325	7.020	6.733	6.463	6.210	5.971	5.747	5.535	5.335	5.146	4.968
9	8.566	8.162	7.786	7.435	7.108	6.802	6.515	6.247	5.995	5.759	5.537	5.328
10	9.471	8.983	8.530	8.111	7.722	7.360	7.024	6.710	6.418	6.145	5.889	5.650
11	10.368	9.787	9.253	8.760	8.306	7.887	7.499	7.139	6.805	6.495	6.207	5.938
12	11.255	10.575	9.954	9.385	8.863	8.384	7.943	7.536	7.161	6.814	6.492	6.194
13	12.134	11.348	10.635	9.986	9.394	8.853	8.358	7.904	7.487	7.103	6.750	6.424
14	13.004	12.106	11.296	10.563	9.899	9.295	8.745	8.244	7.786	7.367	6.982	6.628
15	13.865	12.849	11.939	11.118	10.380	9.712	9.108	8.559	8.061	7.606	7.191	6.811
16	14.718	13.578	12.561	11.652	10.838	10.106	9.447	8.851	8.313	7.824	7.379	6.974
17	15.562	14.292	13.166	12.166	11.274	10.477	9.763	9.122	8.544	8.022	7.549	7.102
18	16.398	14.992	13.754	12.659	11.690	10.828	10.059	9.372	8.756	8.201	7.702	7.250
19	17.226	15.678	14.324	13.134	12.085	11.158	10.336	9.604	8.950	8.365	7.839	7.366
20	18.046	16.351	14.877	13.590	12.462	11.470	10.594	9.818	9.129	8.514	7.963	7.469
25	22.023	19.523	17.413	15.622	14.094	12.783	11.654	10.675	9.823	9.077	8.422	7.843
30	25.808	22.396	19.600	17.292	15.372	13.765	12.409	11.258	10.274	9.427	8.694	8.055
40	32.835	27.355	23.115	19.793	17.159	15.046	13.332	11.925	10.757	9.779	8.951	8.244
50	39.196	31.424	25.730	21.482	18.256	15.762	13.801	12.233	10.962	9.915	9.042	8.304

Exhibit 1B–4   (concluded)

Period	13%	14%	15%	16%	17%	18%	19%	20%	25%	30%	35%	40%	50%
1	0.885	0.877	0.870	0.862	0.855	0.847	0.840	0.833	0.800	0.769	0.741	0.714	0.667
2	1.668	1.647	1.626	1.605	1.585	1.566	1.547	1.528	1.440	1.361	1.289	1.224	1.111
3	2.361	2.322	2.283	2.246	2.210	2.174	2.140	2.106	1.952	1.816	1.696	1.589	1.407
4	2.974	2.914	2.855	2.798	2.743	2.690	2.639	2.589	2.362	2.166	1.997	1.849	1.605
5	3.517	3.433	3.352	3.274	3.199	3.127	3.058	2.991	2.689	2.436	2.220	2.035	1.737
6	3.998	3.889	3.784	3.685	3.589	3.498	3.410	3.326	2.951	2.643	2.385	2.168	1.824
7	4.423	4.288	4.160	4.039	3.922	3.812	3.706	3.605	3.161	2.802	2.508	2.263	1.883
8	4.799	4.639	4.487	4.344	4.207	4.078	3.954	3.837	3.329	2.925	2.598	2.331	1.922
9	5.132	4.946	4.772	4.607	4.451	4.303	4.163	4.031	3.463	3.019	2.665	2.379	1.948
10	5.426	5.216	5.019	4.833	4.659	4.494	4.339	4.192	3.571	3.092	2.715	2.414	1.965
11	5.687	5.453	5.234	5.029	4.836	4.656	4.486	4.327	3.656	3.147	2.752	2.438	1.977
12	5.918	5.660	5.421	5.197	4.988	4.793	4.611	4.439	3.725	3.190	2.779	2.456	1.985
13	6.122	5.842	5.583	5.342	5.118	4.910	4.715	4.533	3.780	3.223	2.799	2.469	1.990
14	6.302	6.002	5.724	5.468	5.229	5.008	4.802	4.611	3.824	3.249	2.814	2.478	1.993
15	6.462	6.142	5.847	5.575	5.324	5.092	4.876	4.675	3.859	3.268	2.825	2.484	1.995
16	6.604	6.265	5.954	5.668	5.405	5.162	4.938	4.730	3.887	3.283	2.834	2.489	1.997
17	6.729	6.373	6.047	5.749	5.475	5.222	4.988	4.775	3.910	3.295	2.840	2.492	1.998
18	6.840	6.467	6.128	5.818	5.534	5.273	5.033	4.812	3.928	3.304	2.844	2.494	1.999
19	6.938	6.550	6.198	5.877	5.584	5.316	5.070	4.843	3.942	3.311	2.848	2.496	1.999
20	7.025	6.623	6.259	5.929	5.628	5.353	5.101	4.870	3.954	3.316	2.850	2.497	1.999
25	7.330	6.873	6.464	6.097	5.766	5.467	5.195	4.948	3.985	3.329	2.856	2.499	2.000
30	7.496	7.003	6.566	6.177	5.829	5.517	5.235	4.979	3.995	3.332	2.857	2.500	2.000
40	7.634	7.105	6.642	6.233	5.871	5.548	5.258	4.997	3.999	3.333	2.857	2.500	2.000
50	7.675	7.133	6.661	6.246	5.880	5.554	5.262	4.999	4.000	3.333	2.857	2.500	2.000

chapter 2

Money Management Strategy: Financial Statements and Budgeting

LEARNING OBJECTIVES

LO1 Recognize relationships among financial documents and money management activities.

LO2 Create a system for maintaining personal financial records.

LO3 Develop a personal balance sheet and cash flow statement.

LO4 Create and implement a budget.

LO5 Calculate savings needed to achieve financial goals.

"WE SPENT HOW MUCH ON WHAT?"

"Here we go again," complained Ben. "Every time we try to use a budget, we end up arguing and still don't have enough money."

Yolanda replied, "Maybe if we kept track of everything we spend, we would have some idea of where our money goes."

"No, not that!" Ben exclaimed. "I have a friend who keeps a notebook and lists everything he spends. That would drive me crazy."

"Well, we can't keep going like we have," responded Yolanda. "A year ago, we owed $4,500 on the credit cards. Now it's up to $7,000. And we don't have anything in savings. How will we ever be able to have a down payment for a house?"

Ben and Yolanda decided to sort all their cheque stubs, receipts, and credit card statements to see where their money was going. Last year, they spent more than $2,000 in restaurants and charged more than $800 on their vacation.

"I didn't realize we spent that much on those things," commented Ben. "We also had auto maintenance costs of

$1,650 and donated $1,800 to the homeless shelter and church. Those are things we had to do and wanted to do."

Yolanda replied, "But now that we know how we spend our money, what do we do next?"

"Maybe we should get a computerized money management program," Ben suggested.

Yolanda countered, "Maybe we should just start with spending a few dollars on a notebook and file folders to record and sort our receipts."

QUESTIONS

1. What would Ben and Yolanda learn by sorting their expenses into various categories? What categories should they use?

2. How can knowing where their money goes help Ben and Yolanda plan their spending?

3. What financial goals might Ben and Yolanda consider to address some of their money management concerns?

4. Locate a Web site that would help Ben and Yolanda improve their money management skills.

PLANNING FOR SUCCESSFUL MONEY MANAGEMENT

LO1

Recognize relationships among financial documents and money management activities.

"Each month I have too much month and not enough money. If the month were only 20 days long, budgeting would be easy." Most of us have heard a comment like this when it comes to budgeting and money management.

Your daily spending and saving decisions are at the centre of financial planning. You must coordinate these decisions with your needs, goals, and personal situation. When people watch a baseball or football game, they usually know the score. In financial planning also, knowing the score is important. Maintaining financial records and planning your spending are essential to successful personal financial management. The time and effort you devote to these recordkeeping activities will yield benefits. **Money management** refers to the day-to-day financial activities necessary to manage current personal economic resources while working toward long-term financial security.

money management
Day-to-day financial activities necessary to manage current personal economic resources while working toward long-term financial security.

OPPORTUNITY COST AND MONEY MANAGEMENT

Consumers can choose from more than 25,000 items in a supermarket, from more than 11,000 periodicals, and from as many as 500 cable television stations. Daily decision making is a fact of life, and trade-offs are associated with each choice made. Selecting an alternative means you give up something else. In terms of money management decisions, examples of trade-off situations, or *opportunity costs*, include the following:

- Spending money on current living expenses reduces the amount you can use for saving and investing for long-term financial security.
- Saving and investing for the future reduces the amount you can spend now.
- Buying on credit results in payments later and a reduction in the amount of future income available for spending.
- Using savings for purchases results in lost interest earnings and an inability to use savings for other purposes.
- Comparison shopping can save you money and improve the quality of your purchases but uses up something of value you cannot replace: your time.

As you develop and implement various money management activities, you need to assess financial and personal costs and benefits associated with financial decisions.

COMPONENTS OF MONEY MANAGEMENT

As Exhibit 2–1 shows, the three major money management activities are interrelated. Personal financial records and documents are the foundation of systematic resource use. They provide written evidence of business transactions, property ownership, and legal matters. Personal

Exhibit 2–1

Money Management Activities

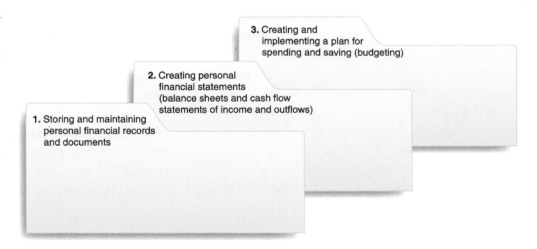

3. Creating and implementing a plan for spending and saving (budgeting)

2. Creating personal financial statements (balance sheets and cash flow statements of income and outflows)

1. Storing and maintaining personal financial records and documents

financial statements enable you to measure and assess your financial position and progress. Your spending plan, or budget, is the basis for effective money management.

CONCEPT CHECK 2–1

1. What opportunity costs are associated with money management activities?
2. What are the three major money management activities?

A SYSTEM FOR PERSONAL FINANCIAL RECORDS

Experts once predicted that computers would result in fewer paper documents. How wrong they were! Today, computers are generating more paperwork than ever. Much of that paperwork relates to financial matters. Invoices, credit card statements, insurance policies, and tax records are the basis of financial record keeping and personal economic choices.

LO2
Create a system for maintaining personal financial records.

An organized system of financial records provides a basis for:

- Handling daily business affairs, including paying bills on time.
- Planning and measuring financial progress.
- Completing required tax reports.
- Making effective investment decisions.
- Determining available resources for current and future buying.

As Exhibit 2–2 shows, most financial records are kept in one of three places: a home file, a safety deposit box, or a home computer. A home file should be used to keep records for current needs and documents with limited value. Your home file may be a series of folders, a cabinet with several drawers, or even a cardboard box. Whatever method you use, it is most important that your home file be organized to allow quick access to required documents and information.

Important financial records and valuable articles should be kept in a location that provides better security than a home file. A **safety deposit box** is a private storage area at a financial institution with maximum security for valuables and difficult-to-replace documents. Access to the contents of a safety deposit box requires two keys. One key is issued to you, the other is kept by the financial institution where the safety deposit box is located. Items commonly kept in a safety deposit box include stock certificates, contracts, a list of insurance policies, and valuables, such as rare coins and stamps.

safety deposit box A private storage area at a financial institution with maximum security for valuables.

The number of financial records and documents may seem overwhelming; however, they can easily be organized into 10 categories (see Exhibit 2–2). These groups correspond to the major topics covered in this book. You may not need to use all of these records and documents at present. As your financial situation changes, you will add others.

How long should you keep personal finance records? The answer to this question differs for various documents. Such records as birth certificates and wills should be kept permanently. Records on property and investments should be kept as long as you own these items. Federal tax laws dictate the length of time you should keep tax-related information. Copies of tax returns and supporting data should be saved for six years. Normally, an audit will go back only three years. However, under certain circumstances, the Canada Revenue Agency may request information from six years back. Financial experts recommend keeping documents related to the purchase and sale of real estate indefinitely.

Did you know?

In Canada, people keep various documents and valuables in safety deposit boxes in banks, trust companies, and credit unions. While these boxes are usually very safe, each year a few people lose the contents of their safety deposit boxes through theft, fire, or natural disasters. Such losses are usually, but not always, covered by the financial institution's insurance.

Exhibit 2–2   Where to Keep Financial Records

Home File

1. Personal and Employment Records (Chapter 2)
- Current résumé
- Employee benefit information
- Copy of birth certificates
- Social insurance number

2. Money Management Records (Chapter 2)
- Current budget
- Recent personal financial statements (balance sheet, income statement)
- List of financial goals
- List of safety deposit box contents

3. Tax Records (Chapter 3)
- Paycheque stubs, T4 slips
- Receipts for tax deductible items
- Records of taxable income
- Past income tax returns and documentation

4. Financial Services Records (Chapter 4)
- Chequebook, unused cheques
- Bank statements, cancelled cheques
- Location information and number of safety deposit box

5. Credit Records (Chapters 5, 6)
- Payment records
- Receipts, monthly statements
- List of credit account numbers and telephone numbers of issuers

6. Consumer Purchase & Automobile Records (Chapters 5, 6)
- Warranties
- Receipts for major purchases
- Owner's manuals for major appliances
- Automobile service and repair records
- Automobile registration
- Automobile owner's manual

7. Housing Records (Chapter 7)
- Lease (if renting)
- Property tax records
- Home repair receipts
- Copy of mortgage documents

8. Insurance Records (Chapters 8, 9)
- Original insurance policies
- List of insurance premium amounts and due dates
- Medical information (health history, prescription drug information)
- Claim reports

9. Investment Records (Chapters 10–13)
- Records of stock, bond, and mutual fund purchases and sales
- Brokerage statements
- Dividend records

10. Estate Planning and Retirement Records (Chapters 14–15)
- Will, power of attorney, and living will
- Company pension plan information
- Canada Pension Plan information
- RRSP information
- Trust agreements

Safety Deposit Box

- Birth, marriage, and death certificates
- Citizenship papers
- Adoption, custody papers
- Military papers
- Serial numbers of expensive items
- Photographs or video of valuable belongings

- Guaranteed Investment Certificates
- List of chequing and savings account numbers and financial institutions
- Credit contacts
- List of credit card numbers and telephone numbers of issuers

- Mortgage papers, title deed
- Automobile title
- List of insurance policy numbers and company names
- Stock and bond certificates
- Rare coins, stamps, gems, and other collectibles
- Copy of will

Personal Computer System (with back-up)

- Current and past budgets
- Summary of cheques written and other banking transactions
- Past income tax returns prepared with tax preparation software
- Account summaries and performance results of investments
- Computerized version of wills, estate plans, and other documents

CONCEPT CHECK 2–2

1. What are the benefits of an organized system of financial records and documents?
2. What suggestions would you give for creating a system for organizing and storing financial records and documents?
3. What influences the length of time you should keep financial records and documents?

PERSONAL FINANCIAL STATEMENTS FOR MEASURING FINANCIAL PROGRESS

Every journey starts somewhere. You need to know where you are before you can go somewhere else. Personal financial statements tell you the starting point of your financial journey.

Most of the financial documents we have discussed come from financial institutions, other business organizations, or the government. Two documents that you create yourself, the personal balance sheet and the cash flow statement, are called *personal financial statements*. These reports provide information about your current financial position and present a summary of your income and spending. The main purposes of personal financial statements are to:

LO3
Develop a personal balance sheet and cash flow statement.

- Summarize the value of the items that you own and the amounts that you owe.
- Track your cash inflows by source and your outflows by type.
- Identify strengths and weaknesses in your current financial situation.
- Measure progress toward your financial goals.
- Provide data for use in filing your income tax return or applying for credit.

THE PERSONAL BALANCE SHEET: WHERE ARE YOU NOW?

The current financial position of an individual or a family is a common starting point for financial planning. A **personal balance sheet**, also called a *net worth statement*, reports what you own and what you owe. You prepare a personal balance sheet to determine your current financial position using the following process:

personal balance sheet A financial statement that reports what an individual or a family owns and owes; also called a *net worth statement*.

ITEMS OF VALUE (WHAT YOU OWN)	−	AMOUNTS OWED (WHAT YOU OWE)	=	NET WORTH (YOUR WEALTH)

For example, if your possessions are worth $4,500 and you owe $800 to others, your net worth is $3,700.

STEP 1: LISTING ITEMS OF VALUE

Available cash and money in bank accounts combined with other items of value are the foundation of your current financial position. **Assets** are cash and other tangible property with a monetary value. The balance sheet for Rose and Edgar Gomez (see Exhibit 2–3) lists their assets under four categories:

assets Cash and other property with a monetary value.

liquid assets Cash and items of value that can easily be converted to cash.

1. **Liquid assets** are cash and items of value that can easily be converted to cash. Money in chequing and savings accounts is liquid and is available to the Gomez family for current spending. The cash value of their life insurance may be borrowed, if needed. While assets other than liquid assets can also be converted into cash, the process is not quite as easy.
2. *Real estate* includes a home, a condominium, vacation property, or other land that a person or family owns.
3. *Personal possessions* are a major portion of assets for most people. Included in this category are automobiles and other personal belongings. While these items have value, they may be difficult to convert to cash. You may decide to list your possessions on the balance sheet at their depreciated value (from original cost). However, these values probably need to be revised over time, since a five-year-old television set, for example, is worth less now than when it was new. Alternatively, you may wish to list your possessions at their current resale value (also referred to as *fair market value*). This method takes into account the fact that such things as a home or rare jewellery may increase in value over time, although most assets' resale value drops rapidly. You can estimate current value by looking at ads for the selling price of comparable automobiles, homes, or other possessions. Or you may use the services of an appraiser.

Exhibit 2–3   Creating a Personal Balance Sheet

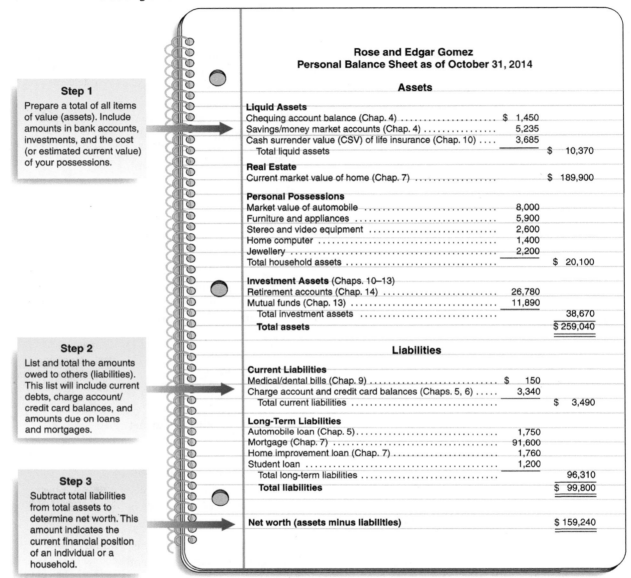

Step 1

Prepare a total of all items of value (assets). Include amounts in bank accounts, investments, and the cost (or estimated current value) of your possessions.

Step 2

List and total the amounts owed to others (liabilities). This list will include current debts, charge account/credit card balances, and amounts due on loans and mortgages.

Step 3

Subtract total liabilities from total assets to determine net worth. This amount indicates the current financial position of an individual or a household.

Rose and Edgar Gomez
Personal Balance Sheet as of October 31, 2014

Assets

Liquid Assets

Chequing account balance (Chap. 4)	$ 1,450	
Savings/money market accounts (Chap. 4)	5,235	
Cash surrender value (CSV) of life insurance (Chap. 10)	3,685	
Total liquid assets		$ 10,370

Real Estate

Current market value of home (Chap. 7)	$ 189,900

Personal Possessions

Market value of automobile	8,000	
Furniture and appliances	5,900	
Stereo and video equipment	2,600	
Home computer	1,400	
Jewellery	2,200	
Total household assets		$ 20,100

Investment Assets (Chaps. 10–13)

Retirement accounts (Chap. 14)	26,780	
Mutual funds (Chap. 13)	11,890	
Total investment assets		38,670
Total assets		**$ 259,040**

Liabilities

Current Liabilities

Medical/dental bills (Chap. 9)	$ 150	
Charge account and credit card balances (Chaps. 5, 6)	3,340	
Total current liabilities		$ 3,490

Long-Term Liabilities

Automobile loan (Chap. 5)	1,750	
Mortgage (Chap. 7)	91,600	
Home improvement loan (Chap. 7)	1,760	
Student loan	1,200	
Total long-term liabilities		96,310
Total liabilities		**$ 99,800**

Net worth (assets minus liabilities)	**$ 159,240**

4. *Investment assets* are funds set aside for long-term financial needs. The Gomez family will use their investments for such things as financing their children's education, purchasing a vacation home, and planning for retirement. Since investment assets usually fluctuate in value, the amounts listed should reflect their value at the time the balance sheet is prepared.

STEP 2: DETERMINING AMOUNTS OWED   Looking at the total assets of the Gomez family, you might conclude that they have a strong financial position. However, their debts must also be considered. **Liabilities** are amounts owed to others but do not include items not yet due, such as next month's rent. A liability is a debt you owe now, not something you may owe in the future. Liabilities fall into two categories:

liabilities Amounts owed to others.

current liabilities Debts that must be paid within a short time, usually less than a year.

1. **Current liabilities** are debts you must pay within a short time, usually less than a year. These liabilities include such things as medical bills, tax payments, instalment loans, lines of credit, mortgages, student loans, and charge accounts.

2. **Long-term liabilities** are debts you do not have to pay in full until more than a year from now. Common long-term liabilities include auto loans, educational loans, and mortgages. A *mortgage* is an amount borrowed to buy a house or other real estate that will be repaid over a period of 15, 20, or 25 years. Similarly, a home improvement loan may be repaid to the lender over the next five to 10 years.

long-term liabilities Debts that are not required to be paid in full until more than a year from now.

The debts listed in the liability section of a balance sheet represent the amount owed at the moment; they do not include future interest payments. However, each debt payment is likely to include a portion of interest. Chapters 5 and 6 discuss the cost of borrowing further.

STEP 3: COMPUTING NET WORTH   Your **net worth** is the difference between your total assets and your total liabilities. This relationship can be stated as:

net worth The difference between total assets and total liabilities.

$$\text{Assets} - \text{Liabilities} = \text{Net worth}$$

Net worth is the amount you would have if all assets were sold for the listed values and all debts were paid in full. Also, total assets equal total liabilities plus net worth. The balance sheet of a business is commonly expressed as:

$$\text{Assets} = \text{Liabilities} + \text{Net worth}$$

As Exhibit 2–3 shows, Rose and Edgar Gomez have a net worth of $159,240. Since very few people, if any, liquidate all assets, the amount of net worth has a more practical purpose: It provides a measurement of your current financial position.

A person may have a high net worth but still have financial difficulties. Having many assets with low liquidity means not having the cash available to pay current expenses. **Insolvency** is the inability to pay debts when they are due; it occurs when a person's liabilities far exceed available assets. Bankruptcy, discussed in Chapter 6, may be an alternative for a person in this position.

insolvency The inability to pay debts when they are due because liabilities far exceed the value of assets.

You can increase your net worth in various ways, including:

- Increasing your savings.
- Reducing spending.
- Increasing the value of investments and other possessions.
- Reducing the amounts you owe.

Remember, your net worth is *not* money available for use but an indication of your financial position on a given date.

THE CASH FLOW STATEMENT: WHERE DID YOUR MONEY GO?

Each day, financial events can affect your net worth. When you receive a paycheque or pay living expenses, your total assets and liabilities change. **Cash flow** is the actual inflow and outflow of cash during a given time period. Income from employment will probably represent your most important *cash inflow*; however, other income, such as interest earned on a savings account, should also be considered. In contrast, payments for such items as rent, food, and loans are *cash outflows*.

cash flow The actual inflow and outflow of cash during a given time period.

A **cash flow statement**, also called a *personal income and expenditure statement* (see Exhibit 2–4), is a summary of cash receipts and payments for a given period, such as a month or a year. This report provides data on your income and spending patterns, which will be helpful when preparing a budget. A chequing account can provide information for your cash flow statement. Deposits to the account are your *inflows*; cheques written are your *outflows*. Of course, in using this system, when you do not deposit the entire amounts received you must also note the spending of non-deposited amounts in your cash flow statement.

cash flow statement A financial statement that summarizes cash receipts and payments for a given period.

Exhibit 2–4   Creating a Cash Flow Statement of Inflows and Outflows

Step 1

For a set time period (such as a month), record your income from various sources, such as wages, salary, interest, or payments from government.

Step 2

Develop categories and record cash payments for the time period covered by the cash flow statement.

Step 3

Subtract the total outflows from the total inflows. A positive number (surplus) represents the amount available for saving and investing. A negative number (deficit) represents the amount that must be taken out of savings or borrowed.

Lin Ye
Cash Flow Statement for the Month Ended September 30, 2014

Income (cash inflows)

Salary (gross)		$4,350
Less deductions		
Federal income tax..................	$909	
Provincial income tax	359	
Canada Pension Plan	141	
Employment Insurance	104	
Total deductions	$1,513	$2,837
After-tax investment income		96
Total income		$2,933

Cash Outflows

Fixed Expenses

Rent	$1,150	
Loan payment	216	
Cable television	52	
Monthly train ticket (transit)	196	
Life insurance	32	
Apartment insurance	23	
Total fixed outflows		$1,669

Variable Expenses

Food at home	260	
Food away from home	168	
Clothing	150	
Telephone	52	
Electricity	48	
Personal care (dry cleaning,		
laundry, cosmetics)	66	
Medical expenses	85	
Recreation/entertainment	100	
Gifts................................	70	
Donations	80	
Total variable outflows	1,079	
Total outflows		$2,748
Cash surplus + (or deficit –)		+$185

Allocation of Surplus

Emergency fund savings	69
Savings for short-term/intermediate	
financial goals	33
Savings/investing for long-term	
financial security	83
Total surplus	$185

The process for preparing a cash flow statement is:

TOTAL CASH RECEIVED DURING THE TIME PERIOD	−	CASH OUTFLOWS DURING THE TIME PERIOD	=	CASH SURPLUS OR DEFICIT

STEP 1: RECORD INCOME   Creating a cash flow statement starts with identifying the cash received during the time period involved. **Income** is the inflow of cash to an individual or a household. For most people, the main source of income is money received from a job. Other common income sources include:

income Inflow of cash to an individual or a household.

- Wages, salaries, and commissions.
- Self-employment business income.

- Savings and investment income (interest, dividends, rent).
- Gifts, grants, scholarships, and educational loans.
- Government payments, such as Canada Pension Plan, welfare, and Employment Insurance benefits.
- Amounts received from pension and retirement programs.
- Alimony and child support payments.

In Exhibit 2–4, note that Lin Ye's monthly salary (or *gross income*) of $4,350 is her main source of income. However, she does not have use of the entire amount. **Take-home pay**, also called *net pay* or *net income*, is a person's earnings after deductions for taxes and other items. Lin's deductions for federal and provincial taxes, Canada Pension Plan contributions, and Employment Insurance are $1,513. Her take-home pay is $2,837. This amount, plus after-tax earnings from investments, is the income she has available for use during the current month.

Take-home pay is also called *disposable income*, the amount a person or household has available to spend. **Discretionary income** is money left over after paying for housing, food, and other necessities. Studies report that discretionary income ranges from less than 5 percent for people under age 25 to more than 40 percent for older people.

take-home pay
Earnings after deductions for taxes and other items; also called *disposable income*.

discretionary income
Money left over after paying for housing, food, and other necessities.

STEP 2: RECORD CASH OUTFLOWS   Cash payments for living expenses and other items make up the second component of a cash flow statement. Lin Ye divides her cash outflows into two major categories: fixed expenses and variable expenses. While every individual and household has different cash outflows, these main categories, along with the subgroupings Lin uses, can be adapted to most situations.

1. *Fixed expenses* are payments that do not vary from month to month. Rent or mortgage payments, instalment loan payments, cable television service fees, and a monthly train ticket for commuting to work are examples of constant or fixed cash outflows.

    For Lin, another type of fixed expense is the amount she sets aside each month for payments due once or twice a year. For example, Lin pays $384 every March for life insurance. Each month, she records a fixed outflow of $32 for deposit in a special savings account so that the money will be available when her insurance payment is due.

2. *Variable expenses* are flexible payments that change from month to month. Common examples of variable cash outflows are food, clothing, utilities (e.g., electricity, heating, and telephone), recreation, medical expenses, gifts, and donations. Using a chequebook or some other record keeping system is necessary for an accurate total of cash outflows.

Did you know?

The most common advice from financial planners?
- "Save more."
- "Save all you can."
- "Cut your spending so you can save more."

STEP 3: DETERMINE NET CASH FLOW   The difference between inflows and outflows can be either a positive (surplus) or a negative (deficit) cash flow. A deficit exists if more cash goes out than comes in during a given month. This amount must be made up by withdrawals from savings or by borrowing.

When you have a cash surplus, as Lin did (Exhibit 2–4), this amount is available for saving, investing, or paying off debts. Each month, Lin sets aside money for her emergency fund in a savings account that she can use for unexpected expenses or to pay living costs if she did not receive her salary. She deposits the rest of the surplus in savings and investment plans that have two purposes. The first is achieving short-term and intermediate financial goals, such as buying a new car, a vacation, or re-enrolling in school. The second is long-term financial security—her retirement.

A cash flow statement provides the foundation for preparing and implementing a spending, saving, and investment plan, discussed in this chapter's Budgeting for Skilled Money Management section.

People commonly prepare a balance sheet on a periodic basis, such as every three or six months. Between those times, use your budget and cash flow statement to plan and measure spending and saving activities. For example, during a certain calendar year, you might prepare a balance sheet on March 1, June 30, and December 31. Your budget serves to plan your spending and saving between these times, and your cash flow statement of inflows and outflows documents your actual spending and saving. This relationship is illustrated as shown below.

In part, changes in your net worth are the result of the relationship between cash inflows and outflows. In periods when your outflows exceed your inflows, you must draw on savings or borrow (buy on credit). When this happens, lower assets (savings) or higher liabilities (due to using credit) result in a lower net worth. When inflows exceed outflows, putting money into savings or paying off debts results in a higher net worth. In general, the relationship between the cash flow statement and the balance sheet may be expressed as follows:

Cash Flow Statement	Balance Sheet
If cash inflows (income) are greater than cash outflows . . .	Net worth increases
If cash outflows (payments) are greater than cash inflows (income)	Net worth decreases

Using a budget, creating a cash flow statement, and developing a balance sheet on a periodic basis can help you improve your financial situation.

ANALYZING YOUR CURRENT FINANCIAL SITUATION

YOUR BALANCE SHEET   Once you have completed a personal balance sheet and cash flow statement, you should sit back and assess your current financial situation. A personal balance sheet will permit you to

1. Measure your progress toward financial goals. Your goals will be achieved more rapidly if you are able to save and invest on a regular basis. For example, if you wish to retire early, you contribute regularly to a corporate pension plan or personal Registered Retirement Savings Plan (RRSP). With regular contributions and a sound investment plan, the value of these assets will increase over time. A global measure of your financial progress is the growth in your net worth.

2. Identify how your assets are distributed among the different categories. Each asset category has its purpose. Liquid assets are necessary to meet ongoing needs and to provide a cushion for emergencies. Whether or not you own a home, and the type of personal possessions you have acquired, are both aspects that define your lifestyle. Investment assets are the pool from which you will eventually draw the funds needed to attain certain financial goals, such as educating a child or retiring early.

However, while real estate and investment assets usually appreciate in value, personal possessions usually depreciate. It is normal to want a car, furniture, and other trappings of life, but care should be taken to implement a savings and investment plan early in life to build up liquid, real estate, and investment assets.

3.   Calculate your current asset allocation, defined as the percentage allocation of financial assets between cash, fixed income, and equity investments. Does this allocation match your investment risk tolerance and financial goals? For example, the higher your tolerance for risk and the longer the term of the financial goal, the greater should be the percentage of financial assets invested in equities.

4.   Identify whether your investments are tax efficient. This topic will be explored in Chapter 3, Planning Your Tax Strategy, and refers to planning your investments so that they provide you with the highest after-tax return for the amount of risk you are willing to assume. Interest-generating assets should be held in tax-sheltered registered accounts, such as RRSPs. Investments that generate dividends and capital gains are best held in non-registered investment accounts. Loans should be arranged such that the interest is tax deductible.

5.   Identify assets that may be lost, stolen, damaged, or destroyed. Such physical assets may require insurance coverage. This topic is discussed in Chapter 8, Home and Automobile Insurance.

6.   Summarize the types and extent of your indebtedness. Have you borrowed to finance depreciating assets such as a car, instead of an appreciating asset such as a house? Do you carry too many credit cards that inflate your debt ratios and reduce your access to future credit? Do you carry balances on your credit cards from month to month and, even worse, do you take a cash advance on one credit card to pay the minimum balance on another? Examining your debt level may reveal opportunities to pay down high-cost debt with low-yielding liquid assets or consolidate debt at a lower interest cost.

YOUR CASH FLOW STATEMENT(S)   Compiling your latest cash flow statements will:

1.   Highlight your sources of income. These may include direct employment income, employee benefits, investment income, or business and professional income. Some sources of income, such as dividends, receive better tax treatment, while other sources, such as business income, can be reduced by charging off permissible expenses.

2.   Reveal whether you are overspending. The only way to fund a cash flow deficit is to earn more, increase debt, or liquidate assets. However, taking on more debt or selling your assets will decrease your net worth over time.

3.   Help you assess your spending and saving patterns. Are you directing funds toward attaining your goals, or are you spending too much on discretionary items?

The relationship between various personal balance sheet and cash flow items can give an indication of your financial position. The next Financial Planning Calculations box explains several commonly used personal financial ratios. These financial ratios and other types of financial analysis provide insight into how well you are managing your cash flows and assets.

CONCEPT CHECK 2–3

1.   What are the main purposes of personal financial statements?
2.   What does a personal balance sheet tell about your financial situation?
3.   How can you use a balance sheet for personal financial planning?
4.   What information does a cash flow statement present?

Financial ratios provide guidelines for measuring changes in your financial situation. These relationships can indicate progress toward an improved financial position.

Ratio	Calculation	Example	Interpretation
Debt ratio	Liabilities divided by net worth	$25,000 ÷ $50,000 = 0.5	Shows relationship between debt and net worth. For many creditors. 0.5 is the maximum acceptable limit; a lower debt ratio would be better.
Current ratio	Liquid assets divided by current liabilities	$4,000 ÷ $2,000 = 2	Indicates $2 in liquid assets for every $1 of current liabilities. For many analysts, a ratio of 2 is considered good; a high current ratio is desirable to have cash available to pay bills.
Liquidity ratio	Liquid assets divided by monthly expenses	$10,000 ÷ $4,000 = 2.5	Indicates the number of months in which living expenses can be paid if an emergency arises. A high liquidity ratio is desirable.
Debt–payments* ratio	Monthly credit payments divided by take-home pay	$540 ÷ $3,600 = 0.15	Indicates how much of a person's earnings goes for debt payments (excluding a home mortgage). Most financial advisers recommend a debt–payment ratio of less than 20 percent.
Savings ratio	Amount saved each month divided by gross income	$648 ÷ $5,400 = 0.12	Financial experts recommend monthly savings of at least 10 percent.

*Unlike the gross debt service (GDS) and total debt service (TDS) ratios explained in Chapter 7, The Finances of Housing, the debt–payments ratio is based on take-home pay, not gross employment income.

BUDGETING FOR SKILLED MONEY MANAGEMENT

LO4

Create and implement a budget.

budget A specific plan for spending income.

A **budget**, or *spending plan*, is necessary for successful financial planning. The common financial problems of overusing credit, lacking a regular savings program, and failing to ensure future financial security can be minimized through budgeting. The main purposes of a budget are to help you:

- Live within your income.
- Spend your money wisely.
- Prioritize and attain your financial goals.
- Prepare for financial emergencies.
- Develop wise financial management habits.

STARTING THE BUDGETING PROCESS

The financial statements and documents discussed in the first sections of this chapter provide a starting point for your daily money management activities. Each day, you make decisions that communicate your *lifestyle* by indicating how you spend your time and money. The clothes you wear, the food you eat, and the interests you pursue contribute to your lifestyle. Some people spend time and money on automobiles or stereo equipment; other people travel, plant gardens, or engage in church or community activities. These actions reflect a lifestyle influenced by three factors:

- *Career.* Your job situation influences the amount of your income, the way you spend your leisure time, and even the people with whom you associate.
- *Family.* The size of your household and the ages of its members also affect your lifestyle. The spending priorities of a couple without children differ from those of a couple with several youngsters.
- *Values.* Ideas and beliefs you regard as important strongly influence your interests, activities, and purchasing habits.

These factors combine to create planned spending patterns that your financial goals reflect. Creating and implementing a budget can be achieved in seven steps:

1. Setting financial goals.
2. Estimating income.
3. Budgeting emergency fund and savings.
4. Budgeting fixed expenses.
5. Budgeting variable expenses.
6. Recording spending amounts.
7. Reviewing spending and saving patterns.

STEP 1: SETTING FINANCIAL GOALS   Future plans are an important dimension of your financial direction. Financial goals are plans for future activities that require you to plan your spending, saving, and investing. As discussed in Chapter 1, financial goals should be: realistic; be stated in specific, measurable terms; have a definite time frame; and imply the type of action to be taken. Your personal financial statements and budgeting allow you to achieve your financial goals with:

1. Your cash flow statement: telling you what you received and spent over the past month.
2. Your balance sheet: reporting your current financial position—where you are now.
3. Your budget: planning spending and saving to achieve financial goals.

STEP 2: ESTIMATING INCOME   You should first estimate available money for a given period. A common budgeting period is a month, since many payments, such as rent or mortgage, utilities, and credit cards, are due each month. In determining available income, include only money that you are sure you'll receive. Bonuses, gifts, or unexpected income should not be considered until the money is actually received.

If you get paid once a month, planning is easy since you will work with a single amount. But if you get paid weekly or twice a month, you need to plan how much of each paycheque will cover various expenses. If you get paid every two weeks, plan your spending based on the two paycheques you will receive each month. Then, during the two months each year that receive three paycheques, you can put additional amounts into savings, pay off some debts, or make a special purchase.

Budgeting income may be difficult if your earnings vary by season or your income is irregular, as with sales commissions. In these situations, attempt to estimate your income based on the past year and on your expectations for the current year. Estimating your income on the low side will help you avoid overspending and other financial difficulties.

STEP 3: BUDGETING EMERGENCY FUND AND SAVINGS   To set aside money for unexpected expenses as well as future financial security, the Fraziers budgeted several amounts for savings and investments (see Exhibit 2–5). Financial advisers suggest that an emergency fund representing three to six months of living expenses be established for use in periods of unexpected financial difficulty. This amount will vary based on a person's life situation and

Exhibit 2–5   The Fraziers Develop and Implement a Monthly Budget

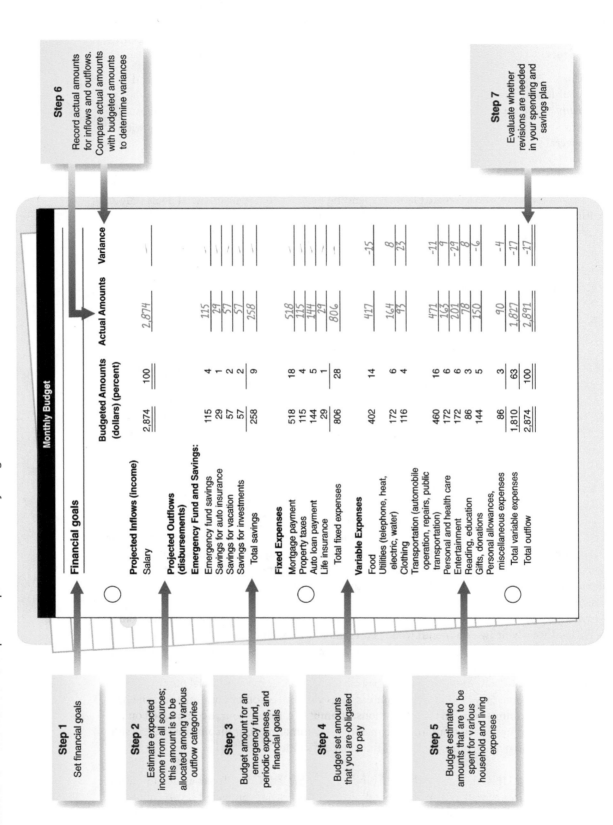

Step 1

Set financial goals

Step 2

Estimate expected income from all sources; this amount is to be allocated among various outflow categories

Step 3

Budget amount for an emergency fund, periodic expenses, and financial goals

Step 4

Budget set amounts that you are obligated to pay

Step 5

Budget estimated amounts that are to be spent for various household and living expenses

Step 6

Record actual amounts for inflows and outflows. Compare actual amounts with budgeted amounts to determine variances

Step 7

Evaluate whether revisions are needed in your spending and savings plan

Monthly Budget

	Budgeted Amounts (dollars)	(percent)	Actual Amounts	Variance
Financial goals				
Projected Inflows (income)				
Salary	2,874	100	2,874	—
Projected Outflows (disbursements)				
Emergency Fund and Savings:				
Emergency fund savings	115	4	115	—
Savings for auto insurance	29	1	29	—
Savings for vacation	57	2	57	—
Savings for investments	57	2	57	—
Total savings	258	9	258	—
Fixed Expenses				
Mortgage payment	518	18	518	—
Property taxes	115	4	115	—
Auto loan payment	144	5	144	—
Life insurance	29	1	29	—
Total fixed expenses	806	28	806	—
Variable Expenses				
Food	402	14	417	-15
Utilities (telephone, heat, electric, water)	172	6	164	8
Clothing	116	4	93	23
Transportation (automobile operation, repairs, public transportation)	460	16	471	-11
Personal and health care	172	6	163	9
Entertainment	172	6	201	-29
Reading, education	86	3	78	8
Gifts, donations	144	5	150	-6
Personal allowances, miscellaneous expenses	86	3	90	-4
Total variable expenses	1,810	63	1,827	-17
Total outflow	2,874	100	2,891	-17

employment stability. A three-month emergency fund is probably adequate for someone with a stable income or secure employment, while a person with erratic or seasonal income may need to set aside an emergency fund sufficient for six months or more of living expenses.

The Fraziers also set aside an amount each month for their automobile insurance payment, which is due every six months. Both this amount and the emergency fund are put into a savings account that earns interest. Savings methods for achieving financial goals are discussed later in this chapter.

A common budgeting mistake is to save the amount you have left at the end of the month. When you do that, you often have *nothing* left for savings. Since savings are vital to long-term financial security, advisers suggest that an amount be budgeted as a fixed expense.

STEP 4: BUDGETING FIXED EXPENSES   Definite obligations are the basis for this portion of a budget. As Exhibit 2–5 shows, the Fraziers have fixed expenses for housing, taxes, and loan payments. They make a monthly payment of $29 for life insurance. The budgeted total for the Fraziers' fixed expenses is $806, or 28 percent of estimated available income.

Assigning amounts to spending categories requires careful consideration. The amount you budget for various items will depend on your current needs and plans for the future. The following sources can help you plan your spending:

- Your cash flow statement.
- Consumer expenditure data (statcan.ca).
- Articles in magazines such as *MoneySaver*.
- Estimates of future income and expenses and anticipated changes in inflation rates.

Exhibit 2–6 provides suggested budget allocations for different life situations. Although this information is valuable when creating budget categories, most financial planners suggest you record and analyze your expenses over a period of one to three months to better understand how you spend your income. Use a simple system, such as a notebook or your chequebook. This "spending diary" will help you know where your money is going. Remember, a budget is an *estimate* for spending and saving intended to help you make better use of your money, not to reduce your enjoyment of life.

Did you know?

When withdrawing cash, use your own financial institution's ABMs whenever possible so that you won't be charged extra fees. It can cost more than $8 to use an ABM that is not owned by your financial institution.

SOURCE: "How to Save With the Way You Pay," Financial Consumer Agency of Canada, September 24, 2013, fcac-acfc.gc.ca/eng/about/downloads/Pages/Howtosav-Commentp.aspx, accessed June 6, 2014.

Exhibit 2–6   Budget Share of Major Spending Categories by Income Quintile, 2012

	Lowest Quintile	Second Quintile	Third Quintile	Fourth Quintile	Highest Quintile
			$		
Average household expenditures	29,921	43,507	64,008	88,061	151,506
Budget share for major spending categories			%		
Food	14.1	13.6	11.4	10.2	8.1
Shelter	32.5	26.9	22.6	20.8	16.4
Clothing	5.2	5.3	4.9	4.4	4.2
Transportation	13.8	16.0	17.2	16.0	13.1
Personal taxes	1.1	5.3	10.8	15.6	27.7

Based on data from the 2012 Survey of Household Spending (SHS). Note: Data from territories are not included.

SOURCE: "Budget share of major spending categories by income quintile, 2012." Adapted from the Statistics Canada website, statcan.gc.ca/daily-quotidien/140129/t140129a002-eng.htm.

STEP 5: BUDGETING VARIABLE EXPENSES
Planning for variable expenses is not as easy as budgeting for savings or fixed expenses. Some variable expenses are repeated every month, such as the cost of entertainment and recreation. Consider the variable cost of cellphones, which can dramatically change each week. Others occur only once a year or every few years, such as the cost of replacing appliances or home renovations. Variable expenses fluctuate by household situation, time of year, health, economic conditions, and a variety of other factors. A major portion of the Fraziers' planned spending—more than 60 percent of their budgeted income—is for variable living costs.

The Fraziers base their estimates on their needs and desires for the items listed and on expected changes in the cost of living. The *consumer price index (CPI)* is a measure of the general price level of consumer goods and services in Canada. This government statistic indicates changes in the buying power of a dollar. As consumer prices increase due to inflation, people must spend more to buy the same amount. Changes in the cost of living vary depending on where you live and what you buy.

STEP 6: RECORDING SPENDING AMOUNTS
After you establish your spending plan, you need to keep records of your actual income and expenses, similar to those you keep in preparing an income statement. In Exhibit 2–5, note that the Fraziers estimated specific amounts for income and expenses. These are presented under "Budgeted Amounts." The family's actual spending was not always the same as planned. A **budget variance** is the difference between the amount budgeted and the actual amount received or spent. The total variance for the Fraziers was a $17 **budget deficit**, since their actual spending exceeded their planned spending by this amount. The Fraziers would have had a **budget surplus** if their actual spending had been less than they had planned.

Variances for income should be viewed as the opposite of variances for expenses. Less income than expected is a deficit, while more income than expected is a surplus.

Spending more than planned for an item may be justified by reducing spending for another item or putting less into savings. However, it may be necessary to revise your budget and financial goals.

STEP 7: REVIEWING SPENDING AND SAVING PATTERNS
Like most decision-making activities, budgeting is a circular, ongoing process. You need to review and perhaps revise your spending plan on a regular basis.

Reviewing Your Financial Progress   The results of your budget may be obvious: having extra cash in chequing, falling behind in your bill payments, and so on. However, the results may not always be obvious. Occasionally, you will have to sit down (with other household members, if appropriate) and review areas where spending has been more or less than expected.

As Exhibit 2–7 shows, you can prepare an annual summary to compare actual spending with budgeted amounts. This type of summary may also be prepared every three or six months. A computer spreadsheet program is useful for this purpose. The summary will help you see areas where changes in your budget may be necessary. This review process is vital to both successful short-term money management and long-term financial security.

We encourage you to use a template for your annual budget summary, which can be found in Exhibit 2-8.

Revising Your Goals and Budget Allocations   What should you cut first when a budget shortage occurs? This question doesn't have easy answers, and the answers will vary for different household situations. The most common overspending areas

---

budget variance The difference between the amount budgeted and the actual amount received or spent.

budget deficit The amount by which actual spending exceeds planned spending.

budget surplus The amount by which actual spending is less than planned spending.

Did you know?

The percentage of Canadians who were classified as seriously delinquent on their non-mortgage loans reached an all-time low in 2012.

SOURCE: 2012 Equifax Canadian Consumer Credit Trends report, January 2013.

Exhibit 2–7   An Annual Budget Summary

Item	Monthly Budget	Jan.	Feb.	Mar.	Apr.	May	June	July	Aug.	Sept.	Oct.	Nov.	Dec.	Actual	Budgeted*
							Actual Spending (cash outflows)							Annual Totals	
Income	2,730	2,730	2,730	2,730	2,940	2,730	2,730	2,730	2,730	2,850	2,850	2,850	2,850	33,450	32,760
Savings	150	150	150	200	150	90	50	30	100	250	250	150	40	1,610	1,800
Mortgage/rent	826	826	826	826	826	826	826	826	826	826	826	826	826	9,912	9,912
Housing costs (insurance, utilities)	190	214	238	187	176	185	188	146	178	198	177	201	195	2,283	2,280
Telephone	50	43	45	67	56	54	52	65	45	43	52	49	47	618	600
Food (at home)	280	287	277	245	234	278	267	298	320	301	298	278	324	3,407	3,360
Food (away from home)	80	67	78	84	87	123	109	89	83	67	76	83	143	1,089	960
Clothing	100	98	78	123	156	86	76	111	124	87	95	123	111	1,268	1,200
Transportation (auto operation, public transportation)	340	302	312	333	345	297	287	390	373	299	301	267	301	3,807	4,080
Car loan payments	249	249	249	249	249	249	249	249	249	249	249	249	249	2,988	2,988
Insurance (life, health, other)	45	—	—	135	—	—	155	—	—	135	—	—	135	540	540
Health care	140	176	145	187	122	111	156	186	166	134	189	193	147	1,912	1,680
Recreation	80	67	98	123	98	67	45	87	98	65	87	87	111	1,033	960
Reading, education	40	32	54	44	34	39	54	12	38	54	34	76	45	516	480
Gifts, donations	100	102	110	94	87	123	89	95	94	113	87	99	134	1,227	1,200
Personal miscellaneous expense	60	89	45	67	54	98	59	54	49	71	65	90	56	797	720
Total	2,730	2,702	2,705	2,964	2,674	2,626	2,642	2,638	2,743	2,892	2,786	2,771	2,864	33,007	32,760
Surplus (deficit)		28	25	(234)	266	104	88	92	(13)	(42)	64	79	(14)	443	—

*Monthly budgeted spending times 12.

Exhibit 2–8   An Annual Budget Summary Template

Item	Monthly Budget	Actual Spending (cash outflows)												Annual Totals	
		Jan.	Feb.	Mar.	Apr.	May	June	July	Aug.	Sept.	Oct.	Nov.	Dec.	Actual	Budgeted*
Income															
Savings															
Mortgage/rent															
Housing costs (insurance, utilities)															
Telephone															
Food (at home)															
Food (away from home)															
Clothing															
Transportation (auto operation, public transportation)															
Car loan payments															
Insurance (life, health, other)															
Health care															
Recreation															
Reading, education															
Gifts, donations															
Personal miscellaneous expense															
Total															
Surplus (deficit)															

*Monthly budgeted spending times 12.

are entertainment and food, especially away-from-home meals. Purchasing less expensive brand items, buying quality used products, avoiding credit card purchases, and renting rather than buying are common budget adjustment techniques.

At this point in the budgeting process, you may also revise your financial goals. Are you making progress toward achieving your objectives? Have changes in personal or economic conditions affected the desirability of certain goals? Have new goals surfaced that should be given a higher priority than those that have been your major concern? Addressing these issues while creating an effective saving method will help ensure you accomplish your financial goals.

CHARACTERISTICS OF SUCCESSFUL BUDGETING

Having a spending plan will not eliminate financial worries. A budget works only if you follow it. Changes in income, expenses, and goals require changes in your spending plan. Money management experts advise that a successful budget should be:

- *Well planned.* A good budget takes time and effort to prepare. Planning a budget should involve everyone affected by it. Children can learn important money management lessons by helping to develop and use the family budget.
- *Realistic.* If you have a moderate income, don't immediately expect to save enough money for an expensive car or a lavish vacation. A budget is designed not to prevent you from enjoying life but to help you achieve what you want most.
- *Flexible.* Unexpected expenses and changes in your cost of living require a budget that you can easily revise. Also, special situations, such as two-income families or the arrival of a baby, may require increasing certain types of expenses.
- *Clearly communicated.* Unless you and others involved are aware of the spending plan, it will not work. The budget should be written and available to all household members. Many variations of written budgets are possible, including a notebook or a computerized system.

CONCEPT CHECK 2–4

1. What are the main purposes of a budget?
2. How does a person's life situation affect goal setting and amounts allocated for various budget categories?
3. What are the main steps in creating a budget?
4. What are commonly recommended qualities of a successful budget?
5. What actions might you take when evaluating your budgeting program?

SAVING TO ACHIEVE FINANCIAL GOALS

Saving current income (as well as investing, which is discussed in Part 4) is the basis for an improved financial position and long-term financial security. Common reasons for saving include:

LO5

Calculate savings needed to achieve financial goals.

- Setting aside money for irregular and unexpected expenses.
- Paying for the replacement of expensive items, such as appliances or an automobile, or to have money for a down payment on a house.
- Buying special items, such as home video or recreational equipment, or paying for a vacation.
- Providing for long-term expenses, such as children's education or retirement.
- Earning income from the interest on savings for use in paying living expenses.

SELECTING A SAVING TECHNIQUE

Traditionally, Canada ranks fairly low among industrial nations in savings rate. A low savings rate tends to slow economic growth with fewer funds available for business borrowing and for creation of new jobs. Low savings also affect the personal financial situations of people. Studies reveal that the majority of Canadians do not have an adequate amount set aside for emergencies.

Since most people find saving difficult, financial advisers suggest several methods to make it easier. One method is to arrange an automatic debit from your bank account and have the funds transferred periodically to an investment account. This savings deposit can be a percentage of income, such as 5 or 10 percent, or a specific dollar amount. Always "pay yourself first." To guarantee setting something aside for savings, view savings as a fixed expense in your spending plan.

Another method is *payroll deduction*, which is available at many places of employment. Under a *direct deposit* system, an amount is automatically deducted from your salary and deposited in a savings or investment account.

Finally, saving coins or spending less on certain items can help you save. Each day, put your change in a container. In a short time, you will have enough money to make a substantial deposit in a savings account. You can also increase your savings by taking a sandwich to work instead of buying lunch or refraining from buying snacks or magazines.

How you save is less important than making regular periodic savings deposits that will help you achieve financial goals. Small amounts of savings can grow faster than most people realize. For example, at a 5 percent rate of return, compounded daily, just $1 a day for 10 years will give you $4,700.

Did you know?

A report by BMO Economics suggests that young Canadians, specifically those between 25 and 34 years old, are on average richer than their parents were at that age. Using Statistics Canada data and other metrics, the study found that millennials today have more money than the generation preceding them at the same age. "Young people tend to be wealthier, have a little more spending power and enjoy better job opportunities than three decades ago" says BMO senior economist Sal Guatieri. Millennials had a median income of $34,700 in 2011, compared with $33,900 (when adjusted for inflation) among those in the same age bracket 30 years ago, says the report. "This means millennials can buy about two per cent more goods and services than their parents could in the mid-1980s," writes Guatieri. "That doesn't sound like much, but the difference adds up over time."

SOURCE: http://www.cbc.ca/news/world/millennials-have-more-spending-power-than-parents-did-but-also-more-debt-1.2644833.

CALCULATING SAVINGS AMOUNTS

To achieve your financial objectives, you should convert your savings goals into specific amounts. While certain saving methods involve keeping money at home, those funds should be deposited in an interest-earning savings plan on a regular basis. To earn interest, you must learn to "hide" money, not in your home but in an account at a financial institution or with an investment company.

Using a savings or investment plan is vital to the growth of your money. As Exhibit 2–9 shows, using the time value of money calculations introduced in Chapter 1 can help you achieve your financial goals.

TWO-INCOME HOUSEHOLDS

Since the 1970s, there has been a large shift in the financial structure of the family from single-earner households to dual-earner households. When women entered the workforce, budgeting strategies underwent a significant change. It was no longer reasonable for all resources to be pooled. Here are some suggestions for dual-income households.

1. *Pooled Income:* Both incomes are combined, and bills are paid from the pool. This method requires trust and shared goals and values.
2. *Sharing the Bills:* Each person is responsible for paying predetermined bills.
3. *50/50:* Each person contributes an equal amount into the pool to cover shared expenses.
4. *Proportionate Contributions:* This method is similar to the 50/50 method. However, each partner contributes a percentage of his or her income. This method is favourable when one partner earns a higher income than the other.

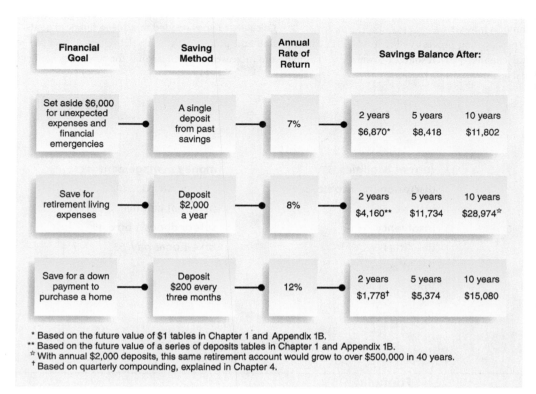

Exhibit 2–9

Using Savings to Achieve Financial Goals

Financial Goal	Saving Method	Annual Rate of Return	Savings Balance After:		
Set aside $6,000 for unexpected expenses and financial emergencies	A single deposit from past savings	7%	2 years $6,870*	5 years $8,418	10 years $11,802
Save for retirement living expenses	Deposit $2,000 a year	8%	2 years $4,160**	5 years $11,734	10 years $28,974☆
Save for a down payment to purchase a home	Deposit $200 every three months	12%	2 years $1,778†	5 years $5,374	10 years $15,080

* Based on the future value of $1 tables in Chapter 1 and Appendix 1B.
** Based on the future value of a series of deposits tables in Chapter 1 and Appendix 1B.
☆ With annual $2,000 deposits, this same retirement account would grow to over $500,000 in 40 years.
† Based on quarterly compounding, explained in Chapter 4.

Learning to share financial responsibilities is something many households must face these days. The best solution is to sit down and discuss goals and values in order to make the right decision.

CONCEPT CHECK 2–5

1. What are some suggested methods to make saving easy?
2. What methods are available to calculate amounts needed to reach savings goals?

SUMMARY OF LEARNING OBJECTIVES

LO1 Recognize relationships among financial documents and money management activities.

Successful money management requires effective coordination of personal financial records, personal financial statements, and budgeting activities.

LO2 Create a system for maintaining personal financial records.

An organized system of financial records and documents is the foundation of effective money management. This system should provide ease of access as well as security for financial documents that may be impossible to replace.

LO3 Develop a personal balance sheet and cash flow statement.

A personal balance sheet, also known as a net worth statement, is prepared by listing all items of value (assets) and all amounts owed to others (liabilities). The difference between your total assets and your total liabilities is your net worth. A cash flow statement, also called a personal income and expenditure statement, is a summary of cash receipts and payments for a given period, such as a month or a year. This report provides data on your income and spending patterns.

$LO4$ **Create and implement a budget.**
Implementing the seven-step budgeting process will help you live within your means and channel your resources toward attaining prioritized financial goals.

$LO5$ **Calculate savings needed to achieve financial goals.**
Future value and present value calculations may be used to compute the increased value of savings for achieving financial goals.

KEY TERMS

assets 51
budget 58
budget deficit 62
budget surplus 62
budget variance 62
cash flow 53
cash flow statement 53

current liabilities 52
discretionary income 55
income 54
insolvency 53
liabilities 52
liquid assets 51
long-term liabilities 53

money management 48
net worth 53
personal balance sheet 51
safety deposit box 49
take-home pay 55

KEY FORMULAS

Page	Topic	Formula
51	Net worth	Net worth = Total assets − Total liabilities
54	Cash surplus (or deficit)	Cash surplus (or deficit) = Total inflows − Total outflows
58	Debt ratio	Debt ratio = Liabilities ÷ Net worth
58	Current ratio	Current ratio = Liquid assets ÷ Current liabilities
58	Liquidity ratio	Liquidity ratio = Liquid assets ÷ Monthly expenses
58	Debt–payments ratio	Debt–payments ratio = Monthly credit payments ÷ Take-home pay
58	Savings ratio	Savings ratio = Amount saved per month ÷ Gross monthly income

FINANCIAL PLANNING PROBLEMS

 Practise and learn online with Connect.

1. *Creating Personal Financial Statements.* Using the procedures presented in the chapter, prepare your current personal balance sheet and a cash flow statement for the next month. $LO3$

2. *Calculating Balance Sheet Amounts.* Using the following data, compute the total assets, total liabilities, and net worth: $LO3$

    Liquid assets, $3,670
    Investment assets, $8,340
    Current liabilities, $2,670
    Household assets, $89,890
    Long-term liabilities, $76,230

3. *Preparing a Personal Balance Sheet.* Using the following data, calculate the total assets, total liabilities and the net worth. $LO3$

    Stock Investments = $1,800
    Credit card balance = $500
    Jewellery = $1,000
    House furniture = $800
    Consumer loan balance = $600
    Current value of automobile = $6,000
    Cash in chequing account = $1,200
    Balance in savings account = $3,500
    Other liabilities = $750

4. *Preparing a Personal Balance Sheet.* Use the following items to prepare a balance sheet and a cash flow statement. Determine the total assets, total liabilities, net worth, total cash inflows, and total cash outflows. LO3

> Rent for the month, $650
> Monthly take-home salary, $1,950
> Cash in chequing account, $450
> Savings account balance, $1,890
> Spending for food, $345
> Balance of educational loan, $2,160
> Current value of automobile, $7,800
> Telephone bill paid for month, $65
> Credit card balance, $235
> Loan payment, $80
> Auto insurance, $230
> Household possessions, $3,400
> Stereo equipment, $2,350
> Payment for electricity, $90
> Lunches/parking at work, $180
> Donations, $70
> Home computer, $1,500
> Value of stock investment, $860
> Clothing purchase, $110
> Restaurant spending, $130

5. *Computing Balance Sheet Amounts.* For each of the following situations, compute the missing amount: LO3
   a. Assets $45,000; liabilities $16,000; net worth $_____
   b. Assets $76,500; liabilities $_____; net worth $18,700
   c. Assets $34,280; liabilities $12,965; net worth $_____
   d. Assets $_____; liabilities $38,345; net worth $52,654

6. *Performing a ratio analysis.* Renée St. Clair is a 28-year-old occupational therapist living in the Annex district of Toronto. She recently graduated from the University of Toronto and now works as an independent contractor assessing the legitimacy of claims made by car accident victims. Like many students, Renée accumulated a large student debt during her years at university and plans to pay it off within the next five years.

   Perform a ratio analysis of Renée's financial statements. What does your analysis reveal? LO3

Cash Flow Statement
For the Year Just Ended

Income		
Professional billings	$ 58,205	
Less: Professional expenses		
and taxes	(23,890)	
Professional income net of		
expenses and taxes		$ 34,315
Dividends (after taxes)		130
Total Income		**$34,445**
Fixed Expenses		
Rent		9,600
Student loan payments		5,800
Total Fixed Expenses		**$15,400**

Variable Expenses		
Utilities, personal, food, clothing,		
and dental		$12,785
Moving expenses		225
Credit card interest		1,010
Recreation/entertainment		1,890
Vacations		6,200
Total Variable Expenses		**$22,110**
Total Expenses		**$37,510**
Surplus/(Deficit)		**($ 3,065)**

Personal Balance Sheet
As of Today

Assets		
Liquid Assets		
Bank account		$ 1,540
Personal Possessions		$ 10,280
Investment Assets		
BCE shares		$ 3,025
Total Assets		**$14,845**
Liabilities		
Current Liabilities		
Credit card balances		$ 7,855
Long-Term Liabilities		
Student loan		20,580
Total Liabilities		**$28,435**
Net Worth		**($13,590)**

7. *Determining Budget Variances.* Fran Bowen created the following budget:

   Food, $350
   Transportation, $320
   Housing, $950
   Clothing, $100
   Personal expenses and recreation, $275

   She actually spent $298 for food, $337 for transportation, $982 for housing, $134 for clothing, and $231 for personal expenses and recreation. Calculate the variance for each of these categories, and indicate whether it was a *budget deficit* or a *budget surplus.* LO4

8. *Calculating the Effect of Inflation.* Bill and Sally Kaplan have an annual spending plan that amounts to $36,000. If inflation is 5 percent a year for the next three years, what amount will the Kaplans need for their living expenses three years from now? LO4

9. *Computing Time Value of Money for Savings.* Use future value and present value calculations (see examples in Appendix 1B) to determine the following: LO5
   a. The future value of a $500 savings deposit after eight years at an annual interest rate of 7 percent.
   b. The future value of saving $1,500 a year for five years at an annual interest rate of 8 percent.
   c. The present value of a $2,000 savings account that will earn 6 percent interest for four years.

10. *Calculating Present Value of a Savings Fund.* Hal Thomas wants to establish a savings fund from which a community organization could draw $800 a year for 20 years. If the account earns 6 percent, what amount does he have to deposit now to achieve this goal? LO5

FINANCIAL PLANNING ACTIVITIES

1. *Researching Money Management Information.* Using Web sites, library sources, friends, relatives, and others, obtain information on common suggestions for successful money management. LO1

2. *Developing a Financial Document System.* Working with two or three others in your class, develop a system for filing and maintaining personal financial records. LO2

3. *Comparing Financial Record Systems.* Conduct a survey of people of various ages to determine the system they use to keep track of various financial documents and records. LO2

4. *Creating Personal Financial Statements.* Prepare a personal balance sheet and cash flow statement. LO3

5. *Creating a Student's Personal Budget.* Refer to Exhibit 2–5 and prepare a monthly budget to cover the next six months. Pay particular attention to variable but non-repetitive expenses, such as tuition fees, textbooks, and technology-related costs. LO3

6. *Researching Household Asset Information on the Internet.* Using the Web or library research, find information about the assets commonly held by households in Canada. How have the values of assets, liabilities, and net worth of Canadian consumers changed in recent years? LO3

7. *Researching Money Management Software.* Use the Web, store visits, or advertisements to determine the software a person might use to prepare personal financial statements, create a budget, and monitor spending, saving, and investing. LO3, LO4

8. *Analyzing Budgeting Situations.* Discuss with several people how the budget in Exhibit 2–5 might be changed based on various budget variances. If the household faced a decline in income, what spending areas might be reduced first? LO4

9. *Comparing Budgeting Systems.* Ask two or three friends or relatives about their budgeting systems. Obtain information on how they maintain their spending records. Create a visual presentation (video or slide presentation) that communicates wise budgeting techniques. LO4

10. *Analyzing Saving Habits.* Interview a young single person, a young couple, and a middle-aged person about their financial goals and saving habits. What actions do they take to determine and achieve various financial goals? LO5

LIFE SITUATION CASE

Out of Work but Not Out of Bills

Due to lower sales, the company for which Ed Weston works was cutting back on its workforce. Even though Ed had been with the company for seven years, most of his duties were being performed by new, automated equipment.

After getting the word about losing his job, Ed talked with his wife, Alice, and their two children (ages 12 and 9) about ways they could reduce spending. The Westons started by making up a list of three things: (1) bills they had to pay each month; (2) areas where they could reduce spending; and (3) sources of funds to help them pay current expenses. Each family member had several ideas to help them cope with the difficult financial burden that was likely to occur over the next few weeks and months.

Before Ed was unemployed, the Westons had a monthly take-home income of $3,165. Each month, the money went for the following items: $880 for rent, $180 for utilities, $560 for food, $480 for automobile expenses, $300 for clothing, $280 for insurance, $250 for savings, and $235 for personal and other items. After the loss of Ed's job, the household's monthly income is $1,550, from his wife's wages and his employment insurance (EI). The Westons also have savings accounts, investments, and retirement funds of $28,000.

Questions

1. What budget items might the Westons consider reducing to cope with their financial difficulties?

2. How should the Westons use their savings and retirement funds during this financial crisis? What additional sources of funds might be available to them during this period of unemployment?

3. What other current and future financial actions would you recommend to the Westons?

chapter 3

Planning Your Tax Strategy

LEARNING OBJECTIVES

LO1 Describe the importance of taxes for personal financial planning.

LO2 Illustrate how federal income taxes are computed by completing a federal income tax return.

LO3 Select appropriate tax strategies for different financial and personal situations.

LO4 Identify tax assistance sources.

I OWE HOW MUCH IN TAXES?

The year is 2014. Stephanie Seymour is employed full-time and earns an annual salary of $70,500. It has been a year since she graduated from university. However, she continues to take a few part-time courses in the evenings. Stephanie is paying off her student loan; she makes monthly contributions to her RRSP and has begun building an income-generating investment portfolio. She recently moved away from her parents' home and into her own apartment in downtown Toronto, which allows her to be 40 km closer to work and school. It should also be noted that Stephanie has made contributions to a few charities over the year. Stephanie is currently preparing to file her 2013 personal income taxes and has gathered the following information:

Income—$70,500 plus $1,500 bonus (T4 slip)

Federal tax paid on income—$10,481 (T4 slip)

Provincial tax paid on income—$4,916 (T4 slip)

Canada Pension Plan (CPP) contributions—$2,356.20 (T4 slip)

Employment Insurance premiums—$891.12 (T4 slip)

Tuition (2 semesters = 8 part-time months)—$1,100 (T2202A slip)

Interest portion of payments on student loan—$835

Rent—$15,000

Moving expenses—$1,200

Rent on safety deposit box—$30

Investment income (Eligible Dividends)—$125 (T5 slip)

RRSP contributions—$2,050

Charitable contributions—$173.33

We will follow Stephanie Seymour throughout the chapter as she completes her 2013 federal income tax return. All values are taken from this case as well as from Exhibits 3–6a and 3–6b (on pages 84–90) that present her *T1 General 2013—Income Tax and Benefit Return* and federal *Appendix 1*, respectively.

TAXES AND FINANCIAL PLANNING

LOl

Describe the importance of taxes for personal financial planning.

Taxes are an everyday financial fact of life. You pay some taxes every time you get a paycheque or make a purchase. However, most people concern themselves with taxes only in April. With about one-third of each dollar you earn going for income taxes, an effective tax strategy is vital for successful financial planning. Familiarity with the tax rules and regulations can help you to maximize your after-tax cash flows and net worth.

This financial obligation includes the many types of taxes discussed later in this section. To help you cope with these taxes, common goals related to tax planning include:

- Knowing the current tax laws and regulations that affect you.
- Maintaining complete and appropriate tax records.
- Making employment, purchase, and investment decisions that leave you with the greatest after-tax cash flows and net wealth.

Notice that the planning objective is *not* stated as minimizing taxes. While taxes are an important consideration in any financial decision, focusing solely on reducing taxes can lead to undesirable results. Consider, for example, the asset allocation decision. Deposits and other safe investments generate interest income that is 100 percent taxable. Common shares of growing companies often increase in value, resulting in a capital gain when the shares are eventually sold. However, only one-half of capital gains is taxable and so the tax treatment of capital gains is much more favourable than that of interest income. However, shifting your asset allocation toward high-risk common shares solely to reduce taxes may not match your financial goals and risk tolerance. A better approach, encompassing both investment and tax considerations, is to select an asset allocation based on your goals and risk tolerance and then decide in which account to hold the investments in order to maximize after-tax investment cash flows. This concept will be discussed later in the chapter under tax strategies.

The principal purpose of taxes is to finance government activities. As citizens, we expect the government to provide such services as police and fire protection, schools, road maintenance, parks and libraries, and safety inspection of food, drugs, and other products. Most people pay taxes in four major categories: taxes on purchases, property, wealth, and earnings.

Did you know?

Tax Freedom Day provides Canadians with a true picture of their tax burden. According to the Fraser Institute's annual calculations, income earned prior to June 10, 2013 was used to pay the total tax bill imposed by all levels of government. This means that, on the average, every dollar you earned in the first half of 2013 was not for you, but for the government.

SOURCES: C. Lammam and M. Palacios, "Canadians Celebrate Tax Freedom Day on June 10, 2013" (June 10, 2013); fraserinstitute.org.

TAXES ON PURCHASES

You probably pay sales tax on many of your purchases—for example, the 5 percent federal goods and services tax, commonly referred to as the GST. Provinces also charge an additional sales tax (with the exception of Alberta). In most provinces, federal and provincial sales taxes have been harmonized into a single tax, referred to as the Harmonized Sales Tax (HST). For example, Ontario has an HST rate of 13 percent while PEI has an HST rate of 14 percent. In order to reduce the economic burden of such taxes on the poor, certain goods and services—including most food items and prescription drugs—are exempt from sales taxes, and low-income individuals may be eligible for a refund of a portion of the HST/GST and provincial sales taxes they have paid.

excise tax A tax imposed on specific goods and services, such as gasoline, cigarettes, alcoholic beverages, tires, and air travel.

In addition to the sales tax, an **excise tax** may be imposed by the federal and provincial governments on specific goods and services, such as gasoline, cigarettes, alcoholic beverages, tires, air travel, and telephone service.

TAXES ON PROPERTY

Real estate property tax is a major source of revenue for local governments. This tax is based on the assessed value of land and buildings. The increasing amount of real estate property taxes is a major concern of homeowners. Retired people with fixed incomes may encounter financial difficulties when local property taxes increase rapidly.

Provincial and municipal governments may assess taxes on the value of automobiles, boats, furniture, and farm equipment.

TAXES ON WEALTH

Currently, the federal and provincial governments impose a tax on the increase in an individual's wealth, called a capital gains tax. With few exceptions, the increase in value of any capital asset that is realized at the time of sale or transfer is subject to capital gains tax. Most exceptions involve transfers to spouses and financially dependent or disabled children. Fifty percent of capital gains, net of any capital losses, are taxable in the year they are incurred.

The sale of an asset, such as a stock or bond, can trigger a capital gain (or loss). Transferring ownership of an asset through a gift or inheritance can also trigger capital gains and losses. Although the federal and provincial governments do not impose estate or inheritance taxes, there is a deemed disposition of all capital property by the deceased at the time of death, triggering any accrued capital gains. The executor of the estate must file a "terminal" income tax return for the deceased and include the deemed disposition of all assets. Thus, bequests and property passed on to heirs other than a spouse are received after-tax.

TAXES ON EARNINGS

Income taxes are used by the federal government to support a number of social benefit programs, such as the Old Age Security pension, Canada Pension Plan, and Employment Insurance. Income tax is a major financial planning factor for most people. Most workers are subject to federal and provincial income taxes.

Throughout the year, your employer withholds income tax amounts from your paycheque, and you may be required to make income tax instalments if you earn income from other sources, such as a business. Both types of payments are only estimates of your income taxes payable. You may need to pay an additional amount when you file your income tax return, or you may get a tax refund. The following sections will help you prepare your federal income tax return and plan your future tax strategies.

Did you know?

Personal taxes paid to the federal government in 2013 totalled $125.7 billion, $5.2 billion greater than 2012.

SOURCE: http://www.fin.gc.ca/afr-rfa/2013/report-rapport-eng.asp.

FILING YOUR FEDERAL AND PROVINCIAL INCOME TAX RETURN

As you stare at those piles of papers, you know it's time to do your taxes! Submitting your federal income tax return requires several decisions and actions. First, you must determine whether you are required to file a return. Next, you need to identify which basic form you need to complete, most often the *T1 General Income Tax and Benefit Return* for a particular province, and any necessary schedules or supplementary forms. Finally, you must decide whether to complete a paper return, file by telephone, or file electronically.

Each taxpayer is personally responsible for the information provided to the government in his or her income tax return. If any individual or firm has helped you to complete your return, take the time to review it before filing. There is no excuse for being ignorant of your tax situation.

WHO MUST FILE?

All residents of Canada must file a federal income tax return for any year in which they have a balance of taxes owing. A resident is considered to be anyone living in Canada, but also includes non-Canadians who are present 183 days (one-half of a year) or more. Canadian residents are taxed on their worldwide income. Usually, taxes paid to a foreign government can be offset by a foreign tax credit that alleviates potential double taxation of foreign income. In addition, the federal government will tax non-residents of Canada on certain income earned from Canadian sources, such as investment income. Even if you have no income to report, you may wish to file a tax return anyway in order to claim the HST/GST rebate.

Your province of residency as of December 31 of the taxation year determines which provincial income tax return you are required to file. Quebec is the only province that does not "piggyback" on the federal system of personal taxation and, as a result, its residents must file both a federal tax return and a separate Quebec tax return.

While the Quebec *Taxation Act* has a number of similarities with the federal *Income Tax Act*, there are still a number of differences. If you must file a return in the province of Quebec, it is imperative that you contact the Ministère du Revenu du Québec for further information. Quebec tax forms and guides are available in both French and English from the provincial government's Web site at gouv.qc.ca.

All other provinces and territories apply a Tax on Income (TONI) system that permits the province to decide its own tax rates to be applied to taxable income, as well as different non-refundable and refundable tax credits.

taxable income The net amount of income, after allowable deductions, on which income tax is computed.

employment income Remuneration received for personal effort.

CONCEPT CHECK 3–1

1. How should you consider taxes in your financial planning?
2. What types of taxes do people frequently overlook when making financial decisions?
3. Who must file an income tax return?

INCOME TAX FUNDAMENTALS

LO2

Illustrate how federal income taxes are computed by completing a federal income tax return.

Each year, millions of Canadians are required to pay their share of income taxes to the federal government. The process involves computing **taxable income**, determining the amount of income tax owed, and comparing this amount with the income tax payments withheld or made during the year. Exhibit 3–1 outlines the steps required in the calculation of your federal and provincial income tax due for all provinces other than Quebec.

STEP 1: DETERMINING TOTAL INCOME

net business income Net income from an activity that is carried out for profit, after expenses are deducted.

investment income Income from property, including income in the form of interest, dividends, and rents net of expenses.

taxable capital gains Net gains from the sale of capital assets such as stocks, bonds, and real estate. One-half of net capital gains are taxable.

TYPES OF INCOME   With minor exceptions, most income earned by Canadian residents is subject to federal and provincial income tax. Your total income consists of five main components:

1. **Employment income** is remuneration received for personal effort, including salaries, wages, commissions, tips, bonuses, and taxable employee benefits.
2. **Net business income** includes any income from an activity that is carried out for profit, including income from a sole proprietorship, partnership, corporation, or profession, after expenses are deducted.
3. **Investment income**, or income from property, includes income in the form of interest, dividends, and rental income net of expenses. Dividend income from eligible dividends is grossed-up by 45 percent to compute taxable dividends.
4. **Taxable capital gains**, although commonly referred to as investment income, is not defined as such by the *Income Tax Act*. As mentioned earlier, it is a tax on accumulated wealth. Capital gains are generated upon the sale of capital assets such as stocks, bonds, and real estate. Any capital losses incurred in the same calendar year are first subtracted from capital gains, and 50 percent of the resulting amount is taxable.

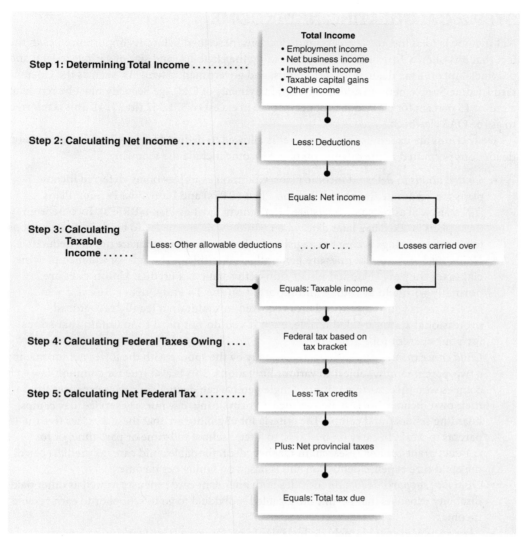

Step 1: Determining Total Income . . . .

Total Income
• Employment income
• Net business income
• Investment income
• Taxable capital gains
• Other income

Step 2: Calculating Net Income . . . .

Less: Deductions

Equals: Net income

Step 3: Calculating Taxable Income . . . . . .

Less: Other allowable deductions   . . . . or . . . .   Losses carried over

Equals: Taxable income

Step 4: Calculating Federal Taxes Owing . . . .

Federal tax based on tax bracket

Step 5: Calculating Net Federal Tax . . . .

Less: Tax credits

Plus: Net provincial taxes

Equals: Total tax due

Exhibit 3–1

Computing Taxable Income and Your Tax Liability

5. *Other income* includes retirement income from corporate pension plans and RRSPs; payments from government plans such as the Canada Pension Plan, Employment Insurance, or Old Age Security; and spousal and certain child support payments.

Income that is not subject to income tax includes lottery winnings, gifts, inheritances, certain child support payments, the GST/HST rebate, the Canada Child Tax Benefit, and scholarships, fellowships, and bursaries. As a student enrolled in a program that entitles you to claim the education amount, you do not need to report scholarships, fellowships, and bursaries as income. If you are not eligible for the education amount, however, you need to report the part of the scholarships, fellowships, or bursaries that is more than $500. If you do not have a court order or written agreement, there are no tax consequences for child support payments; the payments are not included in your income. If you have a court order or written agreement dated before May 1, 1997, child support payments are tax deductible for the payer and taxable for the recipient. Owning a home is one of the best tax shelters available in Canada, primarily because any capital gain realized upon its sale is exempt from capital gains tax as long as it qualifies as your principal residence. The residence can be a house, a condominium, a share in a co-operative housing corporation, or a summer cottage. The value of the land up to one-half hectare is also included.

STEP 2: CALCULATING NET INCOME

net income Total income reduced by certain deductions, such as contributions to an RRSP or RPP.

Net income is total income less certain deductions, described below. Its importance lies in the fact that it is often a critical factor in determining the eligibility and size of various federal and provincial income tax deductions, tax credits, and government payments, such as the Guaranteed Income Supplement. In addition, federal payments of Old Age Security must be repaid at a rate of 15 percent for every dollar of net income in excess of $71,562 (in 2014). This is referred to as the OAS clawback.

deductions Expenses that can be deducted from total income, such as child care expenses, union dues, disability support payments, investment counselling fees, and certain employment-related expenses.

Deductions are expenses that a taxpayer is allowed to deduct from total income. Common deductions permitted in the calculation of net income include the following:

- *Contributions* to deferred income plans. Common examples of tax-deferred income plans are corporate Registered Pension Plans (RPPs) and Individual Pension Plans (IPPs), as well as personal Registered Retirement Savings Plans (RRSPs). Income from these plans is taxed at a later date, when withdrawals are made. To be clear, contributions to a tax-free savings account or registered education savings plan are not tax deductible.

- *Union and professional dues* are generally deductible, although for Quebec provincial taxes they are included under non-refundable tax credits. Union dues are normally withheld at source and reported on the T4 and Québec Relevé 1 you receive from your employer. Dues required to maintain a legally recognized professional status are deductible, even if you do not need to maintain that status for your current job.

- *Child care expenses* can be deducted, usually by the spouse with the lower net income in a two-parent family, subject to various limitations. This is also true for common-law couples who meet certain criteria. Single parents can deduct child care expenses from their own income. These expenses include babysitting, day nursery service, day camps, boarding schools, and camps. The criteria for eligibility are that these services free the parents to work, to carry on business, to attend school full-time or part-time, or to conduct grant-funded research. In Quebec, the refundable child care tax credit replaces the child care expense deduction and is based on family net income.

- *Disability supports deduction* includes both attendant care expenses as well as other paid disability expenses that permit the disabled individual to go to school or to earn taxable income.

- *Moving expenses* are largely deductible if you move to start working at a new location or to start a business. The move must be to a home that is 40 km closer to your new work location than your old home. The 40-km distance is measured according to the shortest normal route of travel, not as a straight line between points. The deduction is not allowable if you are moving either to or from Canada. Moving expenses to go to school can be deducted only from that portion of scholarships, bursaries, fellowships, or grants reported as income. If you are eligible for the full education amount and do not need to report scholarships, bursaries, fellowships, or grants as income, then you cannot use moving expenses as a deduction to lower your net income.

- *Other deductions* that include:
  - Deductible business investment losses, defined as 50 percent of capital losses incurred on investments in Canadian-controlled private corporations.
  - Spousal and child support payments that are made under certain conditions.
  - Interest paid on loans, the proceeds of which are used to earn taxable investment income. This excludes loans for RRSP and RESP contributions. Other costs related to investing, referred to as carrying costs, are also deductible.
  - Employment expenses, if the employer requires the employee to pay for his or her own travel and/or other costs of employment by signing form T2200.

Your deductions are subtracted from total income to obtain your net income.

STEP 3: CALCULATING TAXABLE INCOME

Once net income has been determined, additional deductions and losses carried forward from prior years are permitted in determining taxable income. These include the following:

- *Security options deduction* that equals one-half of the stock option benefit included under employment income, if certain conditions are met. This deduction effectively renders the taxation of the benefit conferred by exercising a corporate stock option equivalent to that on a capital gain.
- *Capital gains deduction* equal to one-half of the eligible capital gains exemption. Current regulations entitle individuals to a $750,000 lifetime "capital gains exemption" on qualified small business corporation shares and eligible farm property. Taxable capital gains are included in net income, but then offset by this deduction in order to determine taxable income.
- *Net capital losses of prior years* can be carried forward indefinitely and used to offset any taxable capital gains reported under total income that are not eligible for the capital gains deduction discussed above.
- *Other deductions* that include the employee home relocation loan deduction, special deductions for Northern residents and those employed in the Canadian Forces, and the carry forward of non-capital losses from prior years.

You are required to maintain sufficient records to support tax deductions. Financial advisers recommend a home filing system (see Exhibit 3–2) for storing receipts and other tax documents. Travel expenses can be documented in a daily log with records of mileage, tolls, parking fees, and away-from-home costs.

Generally, you should keep tax records for three years from the date you receive your notice of assessment. However, you may be required to provide backup documentation for up to six years from filing. Certain records, such as housing documents, should be kept indefinitely.

Exhibit 3–2   A Tax Recordkeeping System

Tax Returns and Tax Filing Information

- Current tax returns and instruction booklets
- Reference books on current tax laws and tax-saving techniques
- Social insurance numbers of household members
- Copies of federal tax returns from previous years

Income Records

- T4 slips reporting salary and taxes withheld at source
- T4 slips reporting pension income
- T5 slips reporting interest, dividends, and capital gains and losses from savings and investments
- Other slips for Employment Insurance benefits, royalty income, retirement, and other support payments

Expense Records

- Receipts for medical, dependant care, charitable donations, and employment-related expenses
- Business, investment, and rental-property expense documents

STEP 4: CALCULATING FEDERAL TAXES OWING

Your taxable income is the basis for computing the amount of your income tax owing. Tax rates and the benefits of tax credits are the final phase of the tax computation process. This calculation is performed on Canada Revenue Agency (CRA) Schedule 1, not directly on the *T1 General Income Tax and Benefit Return*. The impact of non-refundable tax credits also appears on Schedule 1.

The four federal tax brackets and corresponding rates in 2013 were:

Taxable Income	Tax Rate
0–$43,561	15%
$43,561–$87,123	22%
$87,123–$135,054	26%
Over $135,054	29%

With the exception of Quebec, all provinces and territories have adopted the TONI system. TONI is a method of calculating provincial and territorial personal income tax that parallels the

Financial Planning for Life's Situations

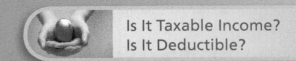

Certain financial benefits individuals receive are not subject to federal income tax. Indicate whether each of the following items is or is not included in taxable income when you compute your federal income tax.

	Yes	No
Is it taxable income . . . ?		
1. Lottery winnings	___	___
2. Child support received	___	___
3. Workers' compensation benefits	___	___
4. Life insurance death benefits	___	___
5. Provincial bond interest earnings	___	___
6. Bartering income	___	___
7. GST/HST credit	___	___

Note: These taxable income items and deductions are based on the 2013 tax year and may change due to changes in the *Income Tax Act*.

Indicate whether each of the following items is or is not deductible when you compute your federal income tax.

	Yes	No
Is it deductible . . . ?		
8. Life insurance premiums	___	___
9. Recurring spousal support payments	___	___
10. Fees for traffic violation tickets	___	___
11. Mileage for driving to volunteer work	___	___
12. A notary's fee for preparing a will	___	___
13. Income tax preparation fee	___	___

Answers: 5, 6, 9—yes; 1, 2, 3, 4, 7, 8, 10, 11, 12,13—no.

federal calculations with taxable income as the starting point. The TONI system replaces the tax on tax calculations. The province of Quebec continues to administer its own provincial income taxes.

marginal tax rate
The rate of tax paid on the next dollar of taxable income.

Your **marginal tax rate** is the rate you pay on the next dollar of taxable income earned. For example, suppose you earn $45,000 of taxable income. Your 2013 federal tax liability is calculated as 15 percent on the first $43,561, while the remaining $1,439 ($45,000 − $43,561) is taxed at 22 percent. In total, your federal taxes equal 15 percent of $43,561 = $6,534 and 22 percent of $1,439 = $317, for a total of $6,851 before the consideration of any tax credits. Your federal marginal tax rate is 22 percent, the rate applied to the next dollar of taxable income.

average tax rate
Total tax due divided by total income.

In contrast, the **average tax rate** is based on the total tax due divided by total taxable income. Except for taxpayers in the 15 percent tax bracket, this rate is less than a person's marginal tax rate. To continue our example, your average federal tax rate is calculated as your total tax bill of $6,851 divided by your taxable income of $45,000, resulting in an average federal tax rate of 15.22 percent.

Exhibit 3–3 shows the combined federal and provincial tax brackets for each province and territory for 2014.

Taxpayers who benefit from the special treatment given to certain income and receive special deductions may be subject to an additional tax. The *alternative minimum tax (AMT)* is designed to ensure that those who receive tax breaks also pay their fair share of taxes. Further discussion of the AMT is beyond the scope of this book; you may obtain information from the Canada Revenue Agency.

STEP 5: CALCULATING NET FEDERAL TAX

tax credit An amount subtracted directly from the amount of taxes owing.

There are two types of **tax credits** that can reduce the amount of tax you owe: non-refundable tax credits and refundable tax credits. The more common are non-refundable tax credits, which are subtracted from the amount of taxes owed but can never reduce net federal tax below zero. (See the Financial Planning Calculations feature on page 81.)

Province	Combined Income Tax Rate (2014)	
Newfoundland and Labrador	first $34,254	22.70%
	over $34,254 up to $43,953	27.50%
	over $43,953 up to $68,508	34.50%
	over $68,508 up to $87,907	35.30%
	over $87,907 up to $136,270	39.30%
	over $136,270	42.30%
Prince Edward Island	first $31,984	24.80%
	over $31,984 up to $43,953	28.80%
	over $43,953 up to $63,969	35.80%
	over $63,969 up to $87,907	38.70%
	over $87,907 up to $98,145	42.70%
	over $98,145 up to $136,270	44.37%
	over $136,270	47.37%
Nova Scotia	first $29,590	23.79%
	over $29,590 up to $43,953	29.95%
	over $43,953 up to $59,180	36.95%
	over $59,180 up to $87,907	38.67%
	over $87,907 up to $93,000	42.67%
	over $93,000 up to $136,270	43.50%
	over $136,270 up to $150,000	46.50%
	over $150,000	50.00%
New Brunswick	first $39,305	24.68%
	over $39,305 up to $43,953	29.82%
	over $43,953 up to $78,609	36.82%
	over $78,609 up to $87,907	38.52%
	over $87,907 up to $127,802	42.52%
	over $127,802 up to $136,270	43.84%
	over $136,270	46.84%
Quebec	first $41,495	28.53%
	over $41,495 up to $43,953	32.53%
	over $43,953 up to $82,985	38.37%
	over $82,985 up to $87,907	42.37%
	over $87,907 up to $100,970	45.71%
	over $100,970 up to $136,270	47.46%
	over $136,270	49.97%
Ontario	first $40,120	20.05%
	over $40,120 up to $43,953	24.15%
	over $43,953 up to $70,651	31.15%
	over $70,651 up to $80,242	32.98%
	over $80,242 up to $83,237	35.39%
	over $83,237 up to $87,907	39.41%
	over $87,907 up to $136,270	43.41%
	over $136,270 up to $514,090	46.41%
	over $514,090	49.53%
Manitoba	first $31,000	25.80%
	over $31,000 up to $43,953	27.75%
	over $43,953 up to $67,000	34.75%
	over $67,000 up to $87,907	39.40%
	over $87,907 up to $136,270	43.40%
	over $136,270	46.40%

Exhibit 3–3

(continued)

Exhibit 3–3
(concluded)

Province	Combined Income Tax Rate (2014)	
Saskatchewan	first $43,292	26.00%
	over $43,292 up to $43,953	28.00%
	over $43,953 up to $87,907	35.00%
	over $87,907 up to $123,692	39.00%
	over $123,692 up to $136,270	41.00%
	over $136,270	44.00%
Alberta	first $43,953	25.00%
	over $43,953 up to $87,907	32.00%
	over $87,907 up to $136,270	36.00%
	over $136,270	39.00%
British Columbia	first $37,606	20.06%
	over $37,606 up to $43,953	22.70%
	over $43,953 up to $75,213	29.70%
	over $75,213 up to $86,354	32.50%
	over $86,354 up to $87,907	34.29%
	over $87,907 up to $104,858	38.29%
	over $104,858 up to $136,270	40.70%
	over $136,270 up to $150,000	43.70%
	over $150,000	45.80%
Yukon	first $43,953	22.04%
	over $43,953 up to $82,073	31.68%
	over $82,073 up to $87,907	32.16%
	over $87,907 up to $136,270	38.01%
	over $136,270	42.40%
Northwest Territories	first $39,808	20.90%
	over $39,808 up to $43,953	23.60%
	over $43,953 up to $79,618	30.60%
	over $79,618 up to $87,907	34.20%
	over $87,907 up to $129,441	38.20%
	over $129,441 up to $136,270	40.05%
	over $136,270	43.05%
Nunavut	first $41,909	19.00%
	over $41,909 up to $43,953	22.00%
	over $43,953 up to $83,818	29.00%
	over $83,818 up to $87,907	31.00%
	over $87,907 up to $136,270	35.00%
	over $136,270	40.50%

SOURCE: taxtips.ca/tax_rates.htm.

Personal credits, such as the basic, spousal, dependants, age, and disability credits, reduce your payable income tax directly according to how each may apply to your situation. Some of the other credits that might also be claimed are for charitable or political donations, caregiver and medical expenses, Canada Employment amount, tuition fees, textbook amount, public transit passes, interest on student loans, and dividend tax credits.

The first step in calculating a non-refundable tax credit is to determine the maximum applicable amount. (See Exhibit 3–4 on page 82 for the maximum federal amounts in 2014.) Sometimes, the amount is pre-set by the government, as is the case for the basic personal amount set at $11,138 for 2014 federal tax purposes (this amount is indexed to inflation every year). In other cases, a calculation is required. The medical amount, for example, is calculated by subtracting 3 percent of your net income to a maximum of $2,171 in 2014 from eligible medical expenses. Once the maximum amounts are determined, the non-refundable tax credit is calculated by

Many people confuse *tax credits* with *tax deductions*. Is one better than the other? A tax *credit*, such as tuition fees or medical expenses, results in a dollar-for-dollar reduction in the amount of taxes owed. A tax *deduction*, such as an RRSP contribution, reduces the taxable income on which your taxes are based.

All non-refundable tax credits reduce taxes payable with the limitation that taxes payable cannot be reduced below zero. Aside from charitable donations that total more than $200, political donations and the dividend tax credit (which require additional procedural calculations), the amount claimed is multiplied by 15 percent to arrive at the tax credit. For example, if $100 is spent on tuition, then about $15 can be claimed as a direct reduction of taxes ($100 × 0.15).

On the other hand, a deduction of $100 may or may not reduce your taxes by $15 because the tax savings arising from the deduction depend on your marginal tax rate. Note that tax savings are simply equal to the deduction multiplied by the marginal tax rate. Thus, it

should be apparent that a tax credit of one dollar is worth more than a deduction worth one dollar. However, making a comparison of whether spending on a deductible item is better than spending on an item that generates tax credits requires a careful specification of several variables, including your marginal federal rate, the province in which you reside, the rules attributed to the tax credit in question, and so on. Careful financial planning helps you use both tax credits and tax deductions to your maximum advantage.

$100 Tax Deduction

↓

Reduces your taxable income by $100. The amount of your tax reduction depends on your tax bracket. Your federal taxes will be reduced by $15 if you are in the 15 percent tax bracket and by $22 if you are in the 22 percent tax bracket.

---

multiplying the amount by the lowest marginal tax rate, with the exception of the tax credits for charitable and political contributions and dividends, where different rates are applied.

At the federal level, there are very few refundable tax credits. These are sums that are refunded to individuals, if they qualify, even if their tax liability is zero. One such credit is the refundable medical expense supplement that can be claimed by individuals who have disproportionately high medical costs with respect to their net income. Another is the GST/HST credit.

Each province and territory has its own refundable and non-refundable tax credits. However, the maximum amounts, calculations, and percentage rates used to convert amounts to credits may be very different. Consult your provincial government's Web site for more details.

MAKING TAX PAYMENTS

SOURCE WITHHOLDING   Source withholding occurs as your employer and others are required to withhold tax at source and remit it to the CRA as well as the Ministère du Revenu du Québec if you live in Quebec. These withholdings are applied toward all forms of taxable income. Generally, there is no withholding of tax on interest, dividends, rent, or royalties paid to Canadian residents.

Tax withheld from a payment to you is considered to have been paid by you to the tax authorities, even if your employer never remits it. It is also considered to have been paid *to* you in the sense that it forms part of your total income.

After the end of the year, you will receive a federal T4 form (see Exhibit 3–5), which reports your annual earnings and the amounts that have been deducted for income tax, social benefits, and other taxes. A copy of the T4 form is filed with your tax return to document your earnings and the amount you have paid in taxes. The difference between the amount withheld and the tax owed is either the additional amount you must pay or the refund you will receive.

Many taxpayers view an annual tax refund as a "windfall," extra money they can count on each year. However, these taxpayers are forgetting the opportunity cost of withholding

Exhibit 3–4   2014 Federal Non-Refundable Tax Credit Amounts

Credit Type	Maximum 2014 Federal Base Amounts
Basic personal amount	11,138
Age amount (65 years of age or older)	6,916
—eliminated when taxpayer's net income exceeds	80,980
Spousal/common-law partner/dependant amount	11,138
—eliminated when dependant's net income exceeds	11,138
Infirm dependant amount (over 18 years of age)	6,589
—eliminated when dependant's net income exceeds	13,196
CPP/QPP contributions (employee)	2,425.50
CPP/QPP contributions (self-employed)	4,851
EI premiums	913.68
Canada employment amount	1,127
Pension income amount	2,000
Caregiver amount for in-home care of parent or grandparent over 65 years of age, or of infirm adult relative	4,530
—eliminated when relative's income exceeds	20,002
Disability amount	7,766
Disability amount supplement for taxpayers under 18 years of age	4,530
—eliminated when child/attendant care expenses exceed	7,184
Interest paid on student loan	Amount paid
Tuition and education amount	Tuition paid + $400 per month of full-time attendance
Textbook amount	$65 per month of full-time attendance
Medical amount	Amount paid in excess of 3% of net income or $2,171, whichever is less

SOURCE: Adapted from cra-arc.gc.ca. Reproduced with permission of the Canada Revenue Agency and the Minister of Public Works and Government Services Canada, 2014.

Exhibit 3–5

T4 Form

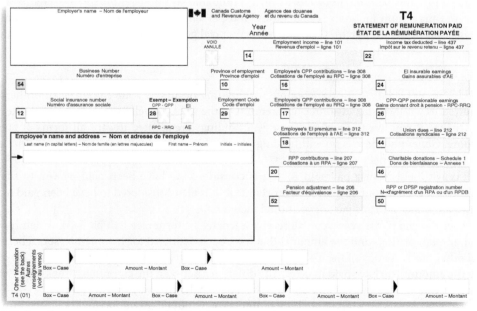

SOURCE: Canada Revenue Agency. Reproduced with permission of the Canada Revenue Agency and the Minister of Public Works and Government Services Canada, 2014.

excessive amounts. Others view their extra tax withholding as "forced savings." However, a payroll deduction plan for savings could serve the same purpose and would enable them to earn the interest instead of giving the government an interest-free loan.

REDUCTIONS OF SOURCE WITHHOLDINGS   It is possible to reduce source withholdings if you prove that you are paying more withholding tax than necessary. In any situation where you expect to receive a refund after filing your return, you can request to have your source withholdings reduced. This type of situation can arise due to personal tax credits, RRSP contributions, charitable donations, medical expenses, and spousal and child support payments. The CRA form used to request this is the TD-1, the Personal Tax Credit Return.

INSTALMENT PAYMENTS   Your tax payments must be paid in instalments if the difference between your payable taxes (including provincial tax) and the amount you have already had withheld at source is more than $2,000 in both the current year and either of the two preceding years. In Quebec, where the federal government does not collect the provincial tax, the threshold is $1,200 of provincial tax instead of $2,000. The payments, which must be made quarterly, are due on the 15th day of March, June, September, and December.

DEADLINES AND PENALTIES

Most people are required to file their federal and Quebec tax returns by April 30 each year. If you or your spouse (or common-law spouse) has business income, then you have until June 15 to file your return. Note, however, that even though the return is not due until June 15, you are required to pay any balance of tax owing by April 30. In cases where you have no tax to pay for the year, and neither the CRA nor the Ministère du Revenu du Québec has requested it, you have no obligation to file a return. Despite this, it is to your advantage to do so as it may affect your allowable RRSP contribution and other factors in future returns. Note that both parents must file a return to qualify for family support payments and GST/HST and QST refunds.

Your return must be postmarked or transmitted electronically by the due date. Failure to do this will incur an automatic 5 percent penalty on any balance owing. In addition, 1 percent of the unpaid balance will be added for each full month that your return is late, to a maximum of 12 months. If you repeatedly fail to file your returns on time, you may incur even higher penalties.

You should file your return on time even if you are unable to pay the balance owing since doing so will allow you to avoid the 5 percent automatic penalty. (Remember, though, that interest will continue to accrue on your unpaid balance.) Exhibit 3–6a on page 84 recaps the general section of your federal return.

CONCEPT CHECK 3–2

1. What are the five sections of the federal tax return?
2. What information is needed to compute net income?
3. What information is needed to compute taxable income?
4. What is the difference between your marginal tax rate and your average tax rate?
5. How does a tax credit affect the amount owed for federal and provincial income taxes?

Exhibit 3–6a   Stephanie Seymour's *T1 GENERAL Income Tax and Benefit Return for 2013*

Canada Revenue Agency   **Agence du revenu du Canada**

T1 GENERAL 2013

Income Tax and Benefit Return

Complete all the sections that apply to you in order to benefit from amounts to which you are entitled.

Identification

ON **8**

Attach your personal label here. Correct any wrong information.
If you are not attaching a label, print your name and address below.

First name and initial
Stephanie A.

Last name
Seymour

Mailing address: Apt No – Street No Street name
1414 King Street #6

PO Box | RR

City
Toronto

Prov./Terr.
O N

Postal code
M 6 J 3 B 1

Information about you

Enter your social insurance number (SIN) if you
are not attaching a label: 6 7 1 2 3 4 5 6 7

	Year	Month	Day
Enter your date of birth: 1 9 8 0 0 1 0 1

Your language of correspondence:
Votre langue de correspondance : English ☒ Français ☐

Check the box that applies to your marital status on December 31, 2013:
(see the "Marital status" section in the guide for details)

1 ☐ Married   2 ☐ Living common-law   3 ☐ Widowed
4 ☐ Divorced   5 ☐ Separated   6 ☒ Single

Information about your spouse or common-law partner (if you checked box 1 or 2 above)

Enter his or her SIN if it is not on the label, or if you
are not attaching a label:

Enter his or her first name:

Enter his or her net income for 2013 to claim certain credits:
(see the guide for details)

Enter the amount of Universal Child Care Benefit included in his or
her net income above (see the guide for details):

Enter the amount of Universal Child Care Benefit repayment
included on line 213 of his or her return:
(see the guide for details)

Check this box if he or she was self-employed in 2013: 1 ☐

Information about your residence

Enter your province or territory of
residence on **December 31, 2013:**   ONTARIO

Enter the province or territory where you **currently** reside if
it is not the same as that shown
above for your mailing address:

If you were self-employed in 2013,
enter the province or territory of
self-employment:

If you **became** or **ceased** to be a **resident of Canada in 2013**, give the date of:

	Month	Day			Month	Day
entry			or	departure		

Person deceased in 2013

	Year	Month	Day
If this **return** is for a **deceased** person, enter the date of death:			
Do not use this area			

Elections Canada

A) Are you a Canadian citizen?... Yes ☒ 1   No ☐ 2

Answer the following question **only if you are a Canadian citizen.**

B) As a Canadian citizen, do you authorize the Canada Revenue Agency to give your name,
address, date of birth, and citizenship to Elections Canada for the National Register of Electors?.......... Yes ☒ 1   No ☐ 2
Your authorization is valid until you file your next return. This information will be used only for
purposes permitted under the *Canada Elections Act.*

Goods and services tax/harmonized sales tax (GST/HST) credit application

See the guide for details.
Are you applying for the GST/HST credit?.. Yes ☒ 1   No ☐ 2

Do not use this area	172			171					

5006-R

SOURCE: Canada Revenue Agency. Reproduced with permission of the Canada Revenue Agency and the Minister of Public Works and Government Services Canada, 2014.

Exhibit 3–6a   Stephanie Seymour's *T1 GENERAL Income Tax and Benefit Return for 2013 (continued)*

2

Your guide contains valuable information to help you complete your return.
When you come to a line on the return that applies to you, look up the line number in the guide for more information.

Please answer the following question:

Did you own or hold foreign property at any time in 2013 with a total cost of more than CAN$100,000? (read the "Foreign income" section in the guide for details) .... **266** Yes ☐ 1   No ☒ 2
If *yes*, attach a completed Form T1135.

If you had dealings with a non-resident trust or corporation in 2013, see the "Foreign income" section in the guide.

As a Canadian resident, you have to report your income from all sources both inside and outside Canada.

Total income

Employment income (box 14 on all T4 slips)		101	72,000 00
Commissions included on line 101 (box 42 on all T4 slips)	102		
Other employment income		104 +	
Old Age Security pension (box 18 on the T4A(OAS) slip)		113 +	
CPP or QPP benefits (box 20 on the T4A(P) slip)		114 +	
Disability benefits included on line 114 (box 16 on the T4A(P) slip)	152		
Other pensions or superannuation		115 +	
Elected split-pension amount (see the guide and **attach** Form T1032)		116 +	
Universal Child Care Benefit (see the guide)		117 +	
Employment Insurance and other benefits (box 14 on the T4E slip)		119 +	
Taxable amount of dividends (eligible and other than eligible) from taxable Canadian corporations (see the guide and **attach** Schedule 4)		120 +	172 50
Taxable amount of dividends other than eligible dividends, included on line 120, from taxable Canadian corporations	180		
Interest and other investment income (**attach** Schedule 4)		121 +	
Net partnership income: limited or non-active partners only (**attach** Schedule 4)		122 +	
Rental income Gross 160 Net		126 +	
Taxable capital gains (**attach** Schedule 3)		127 +	
Support payments received Total 156 Taxable amount		128 +	
RRSP income (from all T4RSP slips)		129 +	
Other income Specify:		130 +	

Self-employment income (see lines 135 to 143 in the guide)

Business income	Gross 162	Net 135 +	
Professional income	Gross 164	Net 137 +	
Commission income	Gross 166	Net 139 +	
Farming income	Gross 168	Net 141 +	
Fishing income	Gross 170	Net 143 +	

Workers' compensation benefits (box 10 on the T5007 slip)	144		
Social assistance payments	145 +		
Net federal supplements (box 21 on the T4A(OAS) slip)	146 +		
Add lines 144, 145, and 146 (see line 250 in the guide). =		▶ 147 +	
Add lines 101, 104 to 143, and 147. This is your **total income**. 150 =			72,172 50

Exhibit 3–6a   Stephanie Seymour's *T1 GENERAL Income Tax and Benefit Return for 2013 (continued)*

3

↖ **Attach your Schedule 1 (federal tax) and Form 428 (provincial or territorial tax) here. Also attach here any other schedules, information slips, forms, receipts, and documents that you need to include with your return.**

Net income

Enter your **total income** from line 150.	150	72,172.50
Pension adjustment (box 52 on all T4 slips and box 34 on all T4A slips)	206	
Registered pension plan deduction (box 20 on all T4 slips and box 32 on all T4A slips)	207	
RRSP deduction (see Schedule 7 and **attach** receipts)	208 +	2,050 00
Saskatchewan Pension Plan deduction (maximum $600)	209 +	
Deduction for elected split-pension amount (see the guide and **attach** Form T1032)	210 +	
Annual union, professional, or like dues (box 44 on all T4 slips, and receipts)	212 +	
Universal Child Care Benefit repayment (box 12 on all RC62 slips)	213 +	
Child care expenses (**attach** Form T778)	214 +	
Disability supports deduction	215 +	
Business investment loss Gross **228** _____ Allowable deduction	217 +	
Moving expenses	219 +	1,200 00
Support payments made Total **230** _____ Allowable deduction	220 +	
Carrying charges and interest expenses (**attach** Schedule 4)	221 +	30 00
Deduction for CPP or QPP contributions on self-employment and other earnings (**attach** Schedule 8)	222 +	●
Exploration and development expenses (**attach** Form T1229)	224 +	
Other employment expenses	229 +	
Clergy residence deduction	231 +	
Other deductions Specify:	232 +	
Add lines 207 to 224, 229, 231, and 232.	233 =	3,280 00 ▶ – 3,280.00
Line 150 minus line 233 (if negative, enter "0"). This is your **net income before adjustments**.	234 =	
Social benefits repayment (if you reported income on line 113, 119, or 146, see line 235 in the guide) Use the federal worksheet to calculate your repayment.	235 –	●
Line 234 minus line 235 (if negative, enter "0"). If you have a spouse or common-law partner, see line 236 in the guide. This is your **net income**.	236 =	68,892.50

Taxable income

Canadian Forces personnel and police deduction (box 43 on all T4 slips)	244	
Employee home relocation loan deduction (box 37 on all T4 slips)	248 +	
Security options deductions	249 +	
Other payments deduction (if you reported income on line 147, see line 250 in the guide)	250 +	
Limited partnership losses of other years	251 +	
Non-capital losses of other years	252 +	
Net capital losses of other years	253 +	
Capital gains deduction	254 +	
Northern residents deductions (**attach** Form T2222)	255 +	
Additional deductions Specify:	256 +	
Add lines 244 to 256.	257 =	▶ –
Line 236 minus line 257 (if negative, enter "0"). This is your **taxable income**.	260 =	68,892.50

Use your taxable income to calculate your federal tax on Schedule 1 and your provincial or territorial tax on Form 428.

Exhibit 3–6a   Stephanie Seymour's *T1 GENERAL Income Tax and Benefit Return for 2013 (concluded)*

Refund or Balance owing   4

Net federal tax: enter the amount from line 52 of Schedule 1 (**attach** Schedule 1, even if the result is "0")	420	9,286.42
CPP contributions payable on self-employment and other earnings (**attach** Schedule 8)	421 +	
Social benefits repayment (enter the amount from line 235)	422 +	
Provincial or territorial tax (**attach** Form 428, even if the result is "0")	428 +	4,447.81

Add lines 420 to 428.
This is your **total payable**. 435 = 13,734.23 •

Total income tax deducted (see the guide)	437	15,397.00 •
Refundable Quebec abatement	440 +	•
CPP overpayment (enter your excess contributions)	448 +	•
Employment Insurance overpayment (enter your excess contributions)	450 +	•
Refundable medical expense supplement (use federal worksheet)	452 +	•
Working income tax benefit (**attach** Schedule 6)	453 +	•
Refund of investment tax credit (**attach** Form T2038(IND))	454 +	•
Part XII.2 trust tax credit (box 38 on all T3 slips)	456 +	•
Employee and partner GST/HST rebate (**attach** Form GST370)	457 +	•
Tax **paid** by instalments	476 +	•
Provincial or territorial credits (**attach** Form 479)	479 +	•

Add lines 437 to 479.
These are your **total credits**. 482 = 15,397.00 ▶ _ 15,397.00

Line 435 minus line 482   = −1,662.77

If the result is negative, you have a **refund**. If the result is positive, you have a **balance owing**.
⌐ Enter the amount below on whichever line applies.

Generally, we do not charge or refund a difference of $2 or less.

Refund 484 ____1,662.77__ •   **Balance owing** (see line 485 in the guide) 485 _____ •

Amount enclosed 486 [   ] •

⌐ Direct deposit – Start or change (**see line 484 in the guide**) ─────────

You do not have to complete this area every year. Do not complete it this year if your direct deposit information has not changed.
Refund and GST/HST credit – To start direct deposit or to change account information only, **attach** a "void" cheque or complete lines 460, 461, and 462.
Notes: To deposit your **CCTB** payments (including certain related provincial or territorial payments) into the **same** account, also check box 463.
To deposit your **UCCB** payments into the **same** account, also check box 491.

Branch number	Institution number	Account number	CCTB	UCCB
460 _____	461 _____	462 _____	463 ☐	491 ☐
(5 digits)	(3 digits)	(maximum 12 digits)		

Attach to page 1 a **cheque** or **money order** payable to the Receiver General. Your payment is due no later than April 30, 2014.

🏵 **Ontario Opportunities Fund**

You can help reduce Ontario's debt by completing this area to donate some or all of your 2013 refund to the Ontario Opportunities Fund. Please see the provincial pages for details.

Amount from line 484 above		1
Your donation to the Ontario Opportunities Fund	465 −	• 2
Net refund (line 1 minus line 2)	466 =	• 3

I certify that the information given on this return and in any documents attached is correct, complete, and fully discloses all my income.

Sign here _____
It is a serious offence to make a false return.

Telephone – –   Date

490 **For professional tax preparers only**	Name:
	Address:
	Telephone: – –

Do not use this area	487 ☐	488 ☐						•

STEPHANIE SEYMOUR'S 2013 FEDERAL TAX RETURN

IDENTIFICATION   Let's turn now to Stephanie Seymour's *T1 General 2013—Income Tax and Benefit Return*, shown on the preceding pages as Exhibit 3–6a. On the first page, Stephanie filled in the Identification section with her full name, address, province of residence as of December 31, social insurance number, date of birth, and marital status. She gave her consent to the CRA to provide basic personal information to the National Register of Electors. Stephanie also applied for the GST/HST credit and, at the top of the second page, indicated that she does not hold foreign property in the amount of $100,000 or more.

TOTAL INCOME   Box 14 of Stephanie's T4 slip, provided by her employer, shows that her employment income for the year 2013 was $72,000 ($70,500 salary plus $1,500 bonus). This amount is entered on line 101 on the second page of her federal return.

Stephanie received a T5 slip indicating that she was paid $125 in Eligible Canadian dividends. This amount is "grossed up" by 38 percent, and the amount of $125 × 1.38 = $172.50 is entered on line 120. See Chapter 10 for more details on the reasoning behind the dividend gross-up and offsetting dividend tax credit calculation.

Stephanie's total income, shown on line 150, is $72,172.50.

NET INCOME   Stephanie can deduct $2,050 from her total 2013 income on line 208 of the third page of her federal return because she invested this amount in an RRSP before the RRSP contribution deadline (60 days into the new year). This amount is deductible as long as it does not exceed the maximum deduction limit indicated on her *2012 Federal Notice of Assessment* or *Notice of Reassessment*.

Stephanie could not find her *2012 Federal Notice of Assessment*. Luckily, the CRA offers a service called "T.I.P.S." (Tax Information Phone Service), which can be reached by telephone at 1-800-267-6999 or online at cra-arc.gc.ca/tips. This service provides information on your RRSP deduction limit, as well as any unused contributions. It also allows you to track the status of your refund and offers other useful information. By calling T.I.P.S., Stephanie was able to confirm that the $2,050 RRSP contribution was fully deductible in 2013.

During 2013, Stephanie moved more than 40 km at a cost of $1,200 in order to start her new job. Stephanie completed Form T1-M (not included here) to determine that her moving expenses are fully deductible on line 219 of her federal return.

Finally, Stephanie is allowed to deduct her safety deposit box fees of $30.00 on line 221. She stores her stock certificate and other valuables in the safety deposit box.

After subtracting all eligible deductions, Stephanie calculates her net income on line 236 as $68,892.50.

TAXABLE INCOME   Stephanie's taxable income (line 260, page 3 of the federal return) is equal to her net income of $68,892.50 because she has no additional deductions to claim.

NET FEDERAL TAX   The federal Schedule 1 is used to determine an individual's net federal tax by first calculating her federal tax liability and then subtracting non-refundable tax credits. Stephanie's Schedule 1 is presented in Exhibit 3–6b. Her federal tax liability is calculated by multiplying her taxable income of $68,892.50 through the various federal tax brackets. Before subtracting any tax credits, Stephanie's federal tax liability is $12,106.93.

Under the section "federal non-refundable tax credits," Stephanie is eligible to claim the basic amount (line 300), her CPP contributions (line 308), her Employment Insurance premiums (line 312), the Canada Employment amount (line 363), the interest paid on her student loan (line 319), and the tuition and education amount (line 323) by completing Schedule 11 (not shown here). The amount of $2,220 entered on line 323 equals her tuition costs of $1,100 plus an amount of $120 for each month of part-time study (8 × $140 = $1,120). The total of all amounts to be converted into non-refundable tax credits at the 15 percent rate is $18,457.32 (line 335). Thus far, Stephanie's non-refundable tax credits equal $2,768.60 (line 338).

Exhibit 3–6b Stephanie Seymour's Federal Schedule 1 for 2013

T1-2013

Protected B when completed

Federal Tax

Schedule 1

Complete this schedule, and **attach** a copy to your return.
For more information, see the related line in the guide.

Step 1 – Federal non-refundable tax credits

Basic personal amount	claim $11,038	**300**	11,038 00	1
Age amount (if you were born in 1948 or earlier) (use the federal worksheet)	(maximum $6,854)	**301**		2
Spouse or common-law partner amount (**attach** Schedule 5)		**303**		3
Amount for an eligible dependant (**attach** Schedule 5)		**305**		4

Amount for children born in 1996 or later
Number of children for whom you **are not claiming**
the family caregiver amount **366** x $2,234 = _____ 5
Number of children for whom you **are claiming**
the family caregiver amount **352** x $4,274 = _____ 6

Add lines 5 and 6.	▶	**367**		7
Amount for infirm dependants age 18 or older (**attach** Schedule 5)		**306**		8

CPP or QPP contributions:

through employment from box 16 and box 17 of all T4 slips (**attach** Form RC381, if applicable)		**308**	2,356 20	● 9
on self-employment and other earnings (**attach** Schedule 8 or Form RC381, whichever applies)		**310**		● 10

Employment insurance premiums:

through employment from box 18 and box 55 of all T4 slips	(maximum $891.12)	**312**	891 12	● 11
on self-employment and other eligible earnings (**attach** Schedule 13)		**317**		● 12
Volunteer firefighters' amount		**362**		13
Canada employment amount (If you reported employment income on line 101 or line 104, see line 363 in the guide.)	(maximum $1,117)	**363**	1,117 00	14
Public transit amount		**364**		15
Children's fitness amount		**365**		16
Children's arts amount		**370**		17
Home buyers' amount		**369**		18
Adoption expenses		**313**		19
Pension income amount (use the federal worksheet)	(maximum $2,000)	**314**		20
Caregiver amount (**attach** Schedule 5)		**315**		21
Disability amount (for self) (Claim **$7,697** or, if you were under 18 years of age, use the federal worksheet)		**316**		22
Disability amount transferred from a dependant (use the federal worksheet)		**318**		23
Interest paid on your student loans		**319**	835 00	24
Your tuition, education, and textbook amounts (**attach** Schedule 11)		**323**	2,220 00	25
Tuition, education, and textbook amounts transferred from a child		**324**		26
Amounts transferred from your spouse or common-law partner (**attach** Schedule 2)		**326**		27

Medical expenses for **self, spouse or common-law partner, and your
dependent children born in 1996 or later** **330** _____ 28
  Enter $2,152 or 3% of line 236 of your return, whichever is **less.** _____ 29
  Line 28 minus line 29 (if negative, enter "0") _____ 30
Allowable amount of medical expenses for **other dependants**
(do the calculation at line 331 in the guide) **331** _____ 31

Add lines 30 and 31.	▶	**332**		32
Add lines 1 to 4, 7 to 27, and line 32.		**335**	18,457 32	33
Federal non-refundable tax credit rate			15 %	34
Multiply line 33 by line 34.		**338**	2,768 60	35
Donations and gifts (**attach** Schedule 9)		**349**	26 00	36
Add lines 35 and 36. Enter this amount on line 49 on the next page.	Total federal non-refundable tax credits	**350**	2,794 60	37

Go to Step 2 on the next page.

(continued)

Exhibit 3–6b   Stephanie Seymour's Federal Schedule 1 for 2013 *(concluded)*

Protected B when completed

Schedule 1 - Page 2

Step 2 – Federal tax on taxable income

Enter your **taxable income** from line 260 of your return.   68,892 50   **38**

Complete the appropriate column depending on the amount on line 38.	Line 38 is **$43,561** or less	Line 38 is more than **$43,561** but not more than **$87,123**	Line 38 is more than **$87,123** but not more than **$135,054**	Line 38 is more than **$135,054**	
Enter the amount from line 38.		68,892 50			**39**
	0 00	43,561 00	87,123 00	135,054 00	**40**
Line 39 minus line 40 (cannot be negative)		25,331 50			**41**
	15 %	22 %	26 %	29 %	**42**
Multiply line 41 by line 42.		5,572 93			**43**
	0 00	6,534 00	16,118 00	28,580 00	**44**
Add lines 43 and 44.		12,106 93			**45**
	Go to Step 3.	Go to Step 3.	Go to Step 3.	Go to Step 3.	

Step 3 – Net federal tax

Enter the amount from line 45.		12,106 93		**46**
Federal tax on split income (from line 5 of Form T1206)	424		● **47**	
Add lines 46 and 47.	404	12,106 93 ▶	12,106 93	**48**
Enter your total federal non-refundable tax credits from line 37 on the previous page.	350	2,794 60		**49**
Federal dividend tax credit	425	25 91	● **50**	
Overseas employment tax credit (**attach** Form T626)	426		**51**	
Minimum tax carryover (**attach** Form T691)	427		● **52**	
Add lines 49 to 52.		2,820 51 ▶	2,820 51	**53**
Line 48 minus line 53 (if negative, enter "0").	**Basic federal tax** 429		9,286 42	**54**

Federal foreign tax credit (**attach** Form T2209)	405		**55**
Line 54 minus line 55 (if negative, enter "0")	**Federal tax** 406	9,286 42	**56**

Total federal political contributions (**attach** receipts)	409		**57**	
Federal political contribution tax credit (use the federal worksheet) (maximum $650)	410		● **58**	
Investment tax credit (**attach** Form T2038(IND))	412		● **59**	
Labour-sponsored funds tax credit Net cost 413 Allowable credit 414			● **60**	
Add lines 58, 59, and 60.	416	▶		**61**
Line 56 minus line 61 (if negative, enter "0") If you have an amount on line 47 above, see Form T1206.	417	9,286 42		**62**
Working income tax benefit advance payments received (box 10 of the RC210 slip)	415		● **63**	
Special taxes (see line 418 in the guide)	418			**64**
Add lines 62, 63, and 64. Enter this amount on line 420 of your return.	**Net federal tax** 420	9,286 42		**65**

Privacy Act, Personal Information Bank number CRA PPU 005

The first $200 of charitable donations also generate a non-refundable tax credit at a rate of 15 percent. Amounts above $200 that are less than 75 percent of an individual's net income are converted into tax credits at a rate of 29 percent. In Stephanie's case, her charitable donation tax credit equals $26 ($173.33 × 0.15). The amount is calculated on federal Schedule 9 (not shown here) and entered on line 349 of Schedule 1.

Her final tax credit, the federal dividend tax credit, is calculated as 15.02 percent of the grossed-up dividends entered on line 120 in the income section of her federal return. Stephanie's dividend tax credit equals $25.91 ($172.50 × 0.1502). This amount is entered on line 425 of Schedule 1.

After subtracting her non-refundable tax credits, Stephanie's net federal tax is $9,286.42. This amount is carried forward to line 420 at the top of page 4 of her federal return (see page 87).

REFUND OWING   The calculation of Stephanie's Ontario tax of $4,447.81, entered on line 428, is presented in Appendix 3 on page 110 at the end of this chapter.

From box 22 on her 2013 T4 slip, Stephanie determines that the total amount of federal and provincial taxes deducted at source by her employer equals $15,397 ($10,481 for federal income taxes and $4,966 for Ontario provincial taxes). This amount is entered on line 437 of her federal return. As it exceeds her total taxes payable of $13,734.23 (line 435) by $1,662.77, this is the amount of her 2013 tax refund (line 484).

TAX-PLANNING STRATEGIES

Most people want to pay no more than their fair share of taxes. They do this by practising **tax planning**, the use of legitimate methods to reduce one's taxes. In contrast, **tax evasion** is the use of illegal actions to reduce one's taxes. To maximize after-tax cash flows, some simple strategies can be investigated:

1. Are you choosing the form of remuneration that is most advantageous to you?
2. Are you taking full advantage of all deductions and credits that are available to you? If you have a legal or common-law spouse, is the right person taking the deduction? Should amounts be accumulated and the tax credit taken only periodically?
3. Are you taking advantage of all possibilities to defer the payment of taxes to a later date?
4. Should you adopt "income-splitting" techniques that permit a lower-income member of your family to declare investment income and pay less tax on it?
5. Have you organized your investment portfolio so that it attracts the lightest tax liability?

We will explore each strategy in turn.

LO3

Select appropriate tax strategies for different financial and personal situations.

tax planning The use of legitimate methods to reduce one's taxes.

tax evasion The use of illegal actions to reduce one's taxes.

HOW SHOULD YOU RECEIVE INCOME?

If you are an employee, you may be able to arrange your compensation to improve your after-tax income. First, are you paid a salary or by commission? If you are a salaried employee, in most cases no employment-related deductions are available. If you earn commission income and are required by your employer to travel and/or absorb costs associated with your employment, then these costs may be deductible. This also applies to salaried employees who are required to absorb certain employment-related costs. (Form T-2200 must be signed by the employer.) Second, do you have a choice between receiving employment compensation in the form of a salary or via employee benefits? While most employee benefits are taxable, some, such as the benefit conferred by a stock option, receive more favourable tax treatment than regular income. Finally, if part of your remuneration involves a bonus, can the bonus be paid after December 31? The personal taxation year coincides with the calendar year, but some companies have a year-end that differs from December 31. They may be willing to pay your bonus in January of the following year if this still falls within their corporate fiscal year.

One question often asked of a financial planner is whether it is better for a small business owner to pay him- or herself a salary or receive remuneration in the form of dividends.

Co-ordinating personal and corporate taxation for small business owners earning less than $500,000 of taxable income means that, in effect, there is very little difference. In the first instance, the owner is taxed on his or her salary only. In the second instance, the business is required to pay corporate taxes before it could declare a dividend. The dividend paid out would then be grossed-up, taxed at the owner's personal tax rate and partially reduced by the dividend tax credit. The combined result of the corporate tax and personal tax on dividends is close to the tax levied on the salary alone.

What elements of the tax law would play a role in deciding the salary versus dividend dilemma for the small corporate business owner? First, salaries form part of "earned income" for purposes of calculating an individual's RRSP contribution limit, whereas dividends do not. In 2014, the RRSP contribution maximum is set as $24,270. If a person's maximum RRSP contribution equals 18 percent of his or her prior year's earned income, this implies that receiving a salary of $134,833 in 2013 ($24,270 ÷ 0.18) brings him or her to the maximum 2014 RRSP contribution. Second, if the business is a Canadian-controlled private corporation and meets certain qualifying criteria, any capital gain earned on the sale or transfer of the common shares in the business qualifies for the $750,000 capital gains exemption discussed on page 77. For the small entrepreneur who plans to grow his or her business by retaining earnings, the resulting increase in the value of the shares of the business, to a maximum of $750,000, could be sheltered from capital gains tax.

Self-employment income from a non-incorporated business or profession is reported on both a gross and net basis and is taxed at the individual's personal tax rate. Any reasonable expense incurred in order to generate taxable income is deducted from gross income to derive net income. This includes the cost of administrative support, leasing or buying an automobile and maintaining it for business purposes, office rent, equipment and supplies, advertising, and utilities. Only 50 percent of entertainment costs, however, are deductible. There are limits on automobile expense deductions from business income as well. Detailed information on this can be found under the subject Motor Vehicle Expenses Claimed by Self-Employed Individuals, on the Canada Revenue Agency Web site (cra.gc.ca). Of special interest are deductions permitted for maintaining a home office. If you have an office in your home, you can claim a portion of your home expenses as business expenses, subject to certain restrictions. The proportional expenses you can claim include rent or mortgage interest, utilities, maintenance, and home insurance. The portion you are allowed to claim will depend on the fraction of your home that is used for business purposes.

TAX-FREE SAVINGS ACCOUNT

An additional savings incentive in the form of Tax-Free Savings Accounts (TFSAs) was proposed by the federal government in their February 2008 budget. Starting in 2009 and continuing until 2012, Canadian residents aged 18 and older were eligible to contribute up to $5,000 annually to a TFSA, with any unused room carried forward. Beginning in 2013, the annual contribution limit was raised to $5,500. Investments in the TFSA grow on a tax-sheltered basis, and all amounts withdrawn from a TFSA are free of tax.

Investment gains within the TFSA, as well as any withdrawals, are not taken into consideration in determining the recipient's eligibility for federal income-tested benefits (such as OAS) or credits (such as the non-refundable tax credit for taxpayers 65 years and older). The attribution rules that normally apply between spouses are suspended for gains or income earned on contributions to a TFSA, made by one spouse on behalf of the other.

Withdrawals from a TFSA would create contribution room for future years. Neither contributions to a TFSA, nor the interest on monies borrowed to make contributions to a TFSA are tax deductible.

Some important facts about a TFSA:

- The current contribution limit is $5,500 per annum regardless of any amounts contributed to an RRSP/RPP.
- The current $5,500 limit is indexed to the CPI and increases in multiples of $500.

- Any unused room can be carried forward.
- Amounts can be withdrawn at any time and any amounts withdrawn can be re-contributed in the same year if one still has contribution room left over. If not, it can only be re-contributed the following year.
- If, at any time in a month, you have an excess TFSA amount, you are liable to a tax of 1 percent on your highest excess TFSA amount in that month. See cra-arc.gc.ca/tx/ndvdls/tpcs/tfsa-celi/txtn/txtn-eng.html for more information.
- TFSAs are subject to the same investment restrictions as RRSPs/RRPs.
- Neither the investment income earned in a TFSA nor the amounts received from a TFSA will trigger clawbacks of federal benefits such as the Guaranteed Income Supplement and/or Old Age Security.

TFSAs are particularly important to the following groups:

- Canadians with below-average incomes—TFSAs allow them to avoid the heavy clawback rates applicable to modest withdrawals from RRSPs and RPPs after the age of 65.
- Canadians with high incomes who need to save more than the current RRSP limit ($20,000), and who, until now, had no tax effective way to do so.
- Senior citizens, many of whom continue to save through their retirement years for medical emergencies, custodial care and/or to accumulate funds destined for charities or their children, and who, until now, had no tax-effective place to put these savings.
- Working Canadians who want to set money aside for post-retirement medical costs.
- Young Canadians who are trying to accumulate a down payment for their first home.
- Middle-aged Canadians who have paid off their mortgages and are looking for a flexible savings way to help them purchase a vacation/retirement home, pay for a "once in a lifetime" vacation, or supplement their post-retirement income.

EXAMPLE

Making Withdrawals from a TFSA:
In 2009, Carl was allowed to contribute $5,000. He contributed $2,000 for that year.

2009 TFSA dollar limit	$5,000
2009 contributions	−$2,000
Unused TFSA contribution room available for future years	$3,000

From 2010 through 2012, Carl did not contribute to his TFSA, but he made a $1,000 withdrawal from his account in 2013.

2009 unused TFSA contribution room	$3,000
2010 to 2013 TFSA dollar limit	+$20,500
2013 unused TFSA contribution room available for future years	$23,500
Carl's unused TFSA contribution room for 2014	
2013 unused TFSA contribution room	$23,500
2013 withdrawal	+$1,000
2014 TFSA dollar limit	+$5,500
Unused TFSA contribution room at the beginning of 2014	$30,000

Key Web Site for TFSAs: cra-arc.gc.ca

TFSA Q & A

1. Do contributions and withdrawals have any impact on taxes and income-tested benefits?

A. No, contributions to a TFSA are deductible in computing income for tax purposes, and no amount earned in or withdrawn from a TFSA is included in computing income for tax purposes.

2. How much can I contribute to a TFSA?

A. $5,000 per year with unused contributions carried over. Note: The TFSA dollar limit is indexed based on the inflation rate; details are available at the above Web site.

3. Do withdrawals from my TFSA affect my Old Age Security (OAS), Guaranteed Income Supplement (GIS), or any other federal credits?

A. Your Old Age Security (OAS) benefits, guaranteed income supplement (GIS), or Employment Insurance (EI) benefits are not reduced as a result of the income earned or the amounts withdrawn from a TFSA.

MAXIMIZING THE BENEFIT OF DEDUCTIONS AND TAX CREDITS

There are a multitude of tax deductions and credits available at both the federal and provincial level. Keeping up to date on the current tax laws and regulations is vital if you wish to ensure that you are taking full advantage of any deductions and credits available to you, your spouse, and your family.

The most common federal income tax deductions were described earlier in this chapter, in the section Income Tax Fundamentals. Contributions to corporate or personal retirement plans result in a tax deduction in the year of contribution, but their most important role is in deferring taxes on income until savings are withdrawn in retirement. With few exceptions, financial planners recommend that you contribute the maximum possible to your RRSP and contribute as early as possible in any taxation year. These plans are described in the following section, Tax-Deferral Techniques.

Other important facts to remember with respect to common deductions are as follows:

- Generally, the lower-income spouse is required to take the child care deduction, but there are exceptions to this rule, including situations where one spouse is a full- or part-time student.
- Before a ruling on May 1, 1997, alimony, child support, and spousal maintenance payments were deductible to the payer and taxable to the recipient. This is no longer the case. Under the new rules, child support payments are not deductible. Assess whether it is prudent to change any legal agreement reached prior to May 1, 1997, as it would then fall under the new tax legislation.
- All or part of the interest charged on funds invested to earn taxable investment income (interest and dividends) is tax deductible. Therefore, it makes better tax sense to use cash flows to acquire personal possessions, such as a car, and borrow to invest. However, as mentioned earlier in the chapter, the financial planning objective is not to *minimize taxes* but to *maximize after-tax cash flows*. Borrowing to invest (commonly referred to as leveraging) entails significant risk if the value of the investment declines, and this strategy should not be adopted merely to reduce your tax liability.
- If part of your employment remuneration involves a stock option plan, the taxable benefit incurred when the option is exercised must be included in taxable income, unless the shares belong to a Canadian-controlled private corporation (CCPC) or you elect to defer the taxable benefit until the shares are ultimately sold. An offsetting deduction, referred to as the security options deduction, can be taken if, at time of issue, the exercise price of the option did not exceed the fair market value of the share (i.e., the employee could not derive an immediate benefit from exercising the option)

or, in the case of a CCPC, the employee had owned the shares for two years prior to selling them. This deduction is equal to 50 percent of the taxable benefit included in total income. Care should be taken, therefore, in deciding when to exercise the option and when to sell the shares.

- Capital losses incurred in any year can be subtracted from capital gains earned in the same year to compute net capital gains. Fifty percent of net capital gains are taxable in the year they are incurred. If capital losses exceed capital gains in any year, then the net capital loss can be carried back three years to offset any capital gains already declared and taxed. However, the window of opportunity is only three years. Once the period of three years has elapsed, the tax paid on the net capital gains can no longer be reclaimed. However, net capital losses can also be carried forward and applied to reduce any capital gains earned at any time in the future. Special care should be taken to track, record, and report capital losses when filing your income tax return. Although they may not be of immediate value, they should not be overlooked in future years when capital gains must be reported.

- Each individual is eligible for a lifetime $750,000 capital gains exemption on shares of qualifying small businesses and eligible farm property. However, several conditions must be met. One of the qualifying criteria is a holding period of two years prior to sale or transfer of the shares. In addition, the firm itself must meet certain criteria over the two year holding period and at the moment of sale in order that any gain earned on the sale of its shares qualifies for the exemption. Verify that all conditions have been met before you sell shares in a small business.

In addition to various deductions, all individuals qualify for at least the basic personal amount and corresponding income tax credit. The following additional credits can be claimed:

- If you are single, widowed, divorced, or separated, and you support another family member (such as a minor or a disabled parent living with you), you are allowed to claim that person in calculating the amount for an eligible dependant.

- If you paid interest on a student loan made under the *Canada Student Loans Act* or equivalent provincial program, you can claim this credit for any interest paid in the current year and in the five preceding years (after 1997). This credit is not transferable, but it can be carried forward for up to five years.

- If you took post-secondary courses on a full- or part-time basis, your tuition fees and an education amount can be transformed into a tax credit in the current year; a maximum amount of $5,000 minus what you have used can be transferred to a supporting spouse, parent, or grandparent, or carried forward and used by you in the future. You can also claim a textbook amount of $20 per month of part-time study, or $65 per month of full-time study.

- If you had medical expenses, you can choose any 12-month period ending in the calendar year and combine expenses incurred by you, your spouse, and minor children. (A separate calculation can be made to claim the medical expenses of dependent adult children 25 years of age or less who are pursuing full-time studies.) The list of eligible expenses is extensive and is updated frequently, so all receipts for any health-related expense should be retained. All amounts in excess of 3 percent of the claimant's net income can be converted into a tax credit. It is best if the lower-income spouse claims the credit.

- If you are a first time home buyer, you can qualify for a non-refundable credit of up to $5,000. You will qualify for the HBTC if you or your spouse or common-law partner acquired a qualifying home; and you did not live in another home owned by you or your spouse or common-law partner in the year of acquisition or in any of the four preceding years. If you are a person with a disability or are buying a house for a related person with a disability, you do not have to be a first-time home buyer. However, the home must be acquired to enable the person with the disability to live in a more accessible dwelling or in an environment better suited to the personal needs and care of that person.

- If you have a severe and prolonged physical or mental impairment, you can claim the disability amount as a non-refundable tax credit to reduce your net income tax. You can claim this amount only if a qualified practitioner certifies on the disability tax credit certificate that you have a prolonged impairment, and the form is approved by the CRA. All or part of the disability amount can be transferred to your spouse or another supporting individual.

- If you use public transit regularly, you can claim the cost of monthly public transit passes or passes of longer duration such as an annual pass for travel within Canada on public transit.
- If you made charitable contributions, the first $200 of charitable contributions can be converted into a tax credit at the rate of 15 percent. Amounts in excess of $200 that do not exceed 75 percent of an individual's net income are converted at a rate of 29 percent. To maximize the credit, charitable donations for spouses should be taken by one individual. Charitable contributions may be carried forward five years, and it may be beneficial to wait and accumulate contributions before claiming them in order to benefit the most from the 29 percent rate.

Finally, certain unused non-refundable tax credits can be transferred between spouses. These include credits relating to the age amount, pension income amount, tuition and education amount, and disability amount. The transferring spouse must reduce his or her taxable income to zero before transferring any excess amounts.

TAX-DEFERRAL TECHNIQUES

Several techniques are available that permit taxpayers to defer the taxation of income until a later date when, presumably, their combined average income tax rate will be lower. Furthermore, during the deferral period, any investment income earned can be reinvested free of tax.

A major tax strategy of benefit to working people is the use of tax-deferred retirement plans, such as RRSPs, RPPs, IPPs, and Deferred Profit Sharing Plans (DPSPs).

RRSP   Registered Retirement Savings Plans are the quintessential tool in the Canadian taxpayer's toolbox. Virtually all taxpayers benefit from having these, and setting them up can be easily done at almost any bank or trust company or through a stockbroker or life insurance agent. The basic concept is simple: If you agree to put some of your salary away and not have immediate access to it, the tax system will tax that income and all proceeds from its investment when it is withdrawn from the RRSP, rather than when you earn it.

Contributions to an RRSP are deductible for any year in which they are made or for the prior year if made within the first 60 days of the year. The contribution that you are allowed to make depends on three factors. First, the most that can be contributed in any year has been set at $24,270 for 2014 and $24,930 for 2015. Second, you can contribute only up to 18 percent of your prior year's earned income, subject to the above limitations, plus any contribution room that you may have carried forward from prior years. Third is your pension adjustment, defined as the deemed value of your pension earned for the previous year. In other words, the amount you are allowed to contribute to your RRSP is diminished by the amount that you and your employer put aside for your retirement pension. The amount of your pension adjustment is shown on your T4 slip.

An additional advantage offered by RRSPs is that funds can be borrowed from the plan and paid back free of tax under the Home Buyers' Plan and Lifelong Learning Plan. Under the Home Buyers' Plan, you may withdraw up to $25,000 as a loan, if you qualify as a first-time buyer, without it counting as a withdrawal. You must then repay the loan over 15 years. The funds you withdraw must have been in the plan for at least 90 days. This plan is discussed more fully in later chapters.

The Lifelong Learning Plan permits a maximum tax-free withdrawal of $20,000 to permit you or your spouse to study full-time at a qualifying institution. Withdrawals must be repaid within 10 years, starting in the year after the last year of study. However, a disadvantage of withdrawals under both plans is that repayments are made without interest and the growth potential of your RRSP is less.

RPP   A Registered Pension Plan is set up for employees by their employers. Larger companies and many smaller ones have such plans, in which your employer contributes an annual amount on your behalf. Occasionally, you are required or allowed to contribute to the plan and you may deduct your contribution in the year that it is made.

In general, there are two types of registered pension plans: money-purchase and defined benefit. The former, also referred to as a Defined Contribution Pension Plan (DCPP), is much like an RRSP in that the amount of your pension depends on the contributions made and the growth achieved with those funds. Large corporations and public employers often provide the latter, defined benefit plans. Defined Benefit Pension Plans (DBPP) are becoming less common due to the high cost to the employer of administering them. With this type of plan, the amount you receive as a pension is known in advance and is usually based on a percentage of your actual salary over a specified number of years.

If you are allowed to contribute to a Defined Contribution Pension Plan, consider making your payment to an RRSP instead. Though the benefits in terms of taxes are the same, the amount you hold in your RPP is locked in and inaccessible.

When your pension benefits are *vested*, it means you are entitled to receive the benefits you have accrued under your pension plan as a result of satisfying an age or service requirement. If you leave a pension plan before your benefits are vested, you lose the right to any pension benefits under the plan. You are entitled to a taxable refund of any contributions you made, plus interest, but you are not entitled to any contributions made on your behalf by your employer.

If your pension benefits are vested at the time your employment terminates, but you are not yet eligible to receive pension income, you can leave your accrued benefits in the pension plan and receive your pension at time of retirement. You can also choose to transfer a lump-sum payment from your RPP to a locked-in RRSP or Registered Retirement Income Fund (RRIF). The amount allowed for transfer is limited, however, and you may be required to accept an immediate partial cash payment on which you will be taxed.

IPP   An individual pension plan is a defined-benefit registered pension plan designed and structured for one individual. IPP contributions are made according to the benefit payable at retirement. This type of plan may be to your advantage if you are already in your employer's group RPP but the benefits are not as high as you want. Generally, this type of plan is optimal for executives or owner-managers, people over 53, or those earning more than $100,000 as a base salary.

DPSP   Deferred Profit Sharing Plans are less common than RPPs but they operate in essentially the same way. Your employer makes contributions, and you are taxed only when you receive the funds. The contributions are based on current or accrued company profits but may have a defined minimum contribution amount. Further, they are limited to no more than 9 percent or one-half of the RPP contribution limits for the year. You are not allowed to contribute to this type of plan and the amounts contributed by your employer are reported as a pension adjustment on your T4, thereby reducing your RRSP contribution allowance.

Additional tax-deferral techniques include:

- Investing in capital assets, such as real estate or financial assets, that generate capital gains, as these gains become taxable only in the year of disposition.
- Opening a Registered Education Savings Plan (RESP) or an in-trust investment account to fund your child's higher education. These investment vehicles can be viewed as a means by which to defer taxes, as well as an opportunity to have investment income taxed in the hands of lower-income family members. They are described in the following section on Income-Splitting Techniques.

INCOME-SPLITTING TECHNIQUES

Given the Canadian tax system's use of progressive tax rates, with the marginal rate increasing with higher incomes, taxpayers may be tempted to invest in the name of their lower-income spouse or minor children in order to have any investment income taxed in their hands at a lower rate. However, this strategy is not permitted by law. The federal *Income Tax Act* contains a number of "attribution rules" to prevent income splitting in this fashion. In essence, these rules state that if a taxpayer transfers money or assets to a spouse or child under the age of 18, any investment income (interest, dividends, or rents) earned on the amount transferred will be taxed in the hands of the taxpayer, unless the spouse or minor child purchases the asset at its fair market value. In the case of a spouse, future capital gains on any assets transferred are also attributed back to the taxpayer. Attribution of capital gains does not apply in the situation of a minor.

The assets may be purchased outright with money, but can also be acquired through a swap of assets or loan. The loan can be extended by the taxpayer, as long as interest is charged at a rate at least equal to the CRA prescribed rate and paid by the borrowing spouse or minor by January 31 of the following year.

Other legal means of income splitting include:

- Making contributions to a spousal RRSP. Withdrawals are taxed in the hands of the recipient spouse as long as the funds are not withdrawn within two calendar years following the year of contribution.
- Splitting your Canada Pension Plan (CPP) or Quebec Pension Plan (QPP) benefits with your spouse. You may direct that 50 percent of your CPP/QPP benefits be paid to your spouse, provided that you are both over the age of 60.
- Since 2007, Canadian residents can also choose to split up to one-half of their eligible pension income with their spouse. The exact allocation amount is up to the individual but cannot exceed the prescribed limit. For this type of income splitting, Old Age Security and CPP or QPP payments do not qualify as eligible income.
- Having the high-income spouse pay living expenses, while the lower-income spouse invests income.
- Transferring assets that will be used to generate business income, as business income is not attributable.
- Opening a Registered Education Savings Plan (RESP) for your minor children. RESPs allow you to build an education fund for a child by earning tax-deferred investment income. The contributions are not tax deductible, but all income in the plan grows tax-free until withdrawn and taxed in the hands of the recipient. While there are no annual limits, the maximum lifetime contribution per beneficiary is $50,000. Contributions to an RESP can earn the Canada Education Savings Grant, formerly set at a maximum of $7,200 per beneficiary. However, the limit was increased in the federal budget of March 23, 2004, when it was proposed that the grant on the first $500 of annual contributions for minors be enriched for families with lower incomes. In 2013, on the first $500, the Canada Education Savings Grant amounts were up to $200 if your net family income was $43,561 or less; up to $150 if your net family income was between $43,561 and $87,123; or up to $100 if your net family income was more than $87,123. If you save more than $500 per year, the Canada Education Savings Grant can add up to $400 on the next $2,000.
- Opening a Registered Disability Savings Plan (RDSP) can help parents and others save for the long-term financial security of a person who is eligible for the Disability Tax Credit (disability amount). Contributions to an RDSP are not tax deductible and can be made until the end of the year in which the beneficiary turns 59 years of age. Contributions that are withdrawn are not to be included as income for the beneficiary when paid out of an RDSP. However, the Canada disability savings grant, Canada disability savings bond, and investment income earned in the plan are included in the beneficiary's income for tax purposes when paid out of the RDSP. For details, see cra-arc.gc.ca/tx/ndvdls/tpcs/rdsp-reei/menu-eng.html.
- Setting up an in-trust investment account for a minor to acquire capital gains–generating assets, as capital gains earned on funds invested for children under 18 years of age are not attributable.
- Investing the federal Child Tax Benefit in the child's name.

- Transfers of assets to adult children are not subject to the attribution rules as long as they are not made through a loan that charges interest at less than the prescribed rate.

It should be noted that second-generation investment income (i.e., investment income earned on a prior year's reinvested income) is not attributable.

ENSURING THAT YOUR PORTFOLIO IS TAX-EFFICIENT

While the taxation of investment income should not affect your choice of asset allocation or specific asset choices, it will play a role in the decision of which investment account should hold which type of asset. Some financial assets pay interest or generate income that is taxed in the same manner as interest—for example, the dividends paid on foreign stocks. Interest income is fully taxable at your marginal tax rate, and to minimize the tax burden such financial assets should be held in registered accounts, such as RRSPs, that defer taxes until withdrawals are made.

Other financial assets pay dividends or are expected to appreciate in value and generate a capital gain when sold. Both dividends on Canadian stocks and capital gains are taxed less heavily than interest income, and financial assets that pay dividends and/or generate capital gains should be held in non-registered investment accounts. Also, for high income earners, the dividend tax credit substantially reduces the effective tax rate on dividend income compared to other sources of investment income. Therefore, assuming that holding dividend-generating investments fits with the individual's risk tolerance (high) and financial objectives (long-term), it is better to hold non-registered investments in the form of dividend-generating assets to reduce the tax bill. For additional insights on tax efficient investments, see http://www.moneysense.ca/invest/asset-ocation-everything-in-its-place.

Tax efficiency also refers to whether the interest on a loan made for investment purposes can be deducted from taxable income. If the proceeds of a loan are invested in assets that generate taxable dividends, interest, or rents, then the interest paid on the loan is tax deductible, subject to certain conditions.

TAX ISSUES IMPORTANT TO STUDENTS

The CRA has issued a guide called *Students and Income Tax—P105*, which addresses tax issues of special importance to students. This guide can be accessed at the CRA's Web site at http://www.cra-arc.gc.ca/E/pub/tg/p105/p105-13e.pdf. In brief, the guide describes:

1. How to report income from scholarships, fellowships, bursaries, grants, and RESPs.
2. Common deductions, such as moving expenses, child care expenses, and interest paid on a student loan.
3. Non-refundable tax credits such as the tuition and education amount, and the textbook amount.
4. Other tax credits, such as the GST/HST credit and Canada Child Tax Benefit (CCTB).

In addition, most provinces offer tax deductions and credits designed to assist full- and part-time students. See Exhibit 3–7 for a summary of the general sections of the tax form.

CHANGING TAX STRATEGIES

Someone once said that "death and taxes are the only certainties of life." Changing tax laws seem to be another certainty. Each year, the CRA modifies the tax return and filing procedures. In addition, the government frequently passes legislation that changes the *Income Tax Act*. These changes require that you regularly determine how to best consider the tax laws for personal financial planning. Carefully consider changes in your personal situation and your income level. You should monitor your personal tax strategies to best serve your daily living needs and your long-term financial goals.

Exhibit 3–7

Five General Sections
of Your Federal Tax
Return Form

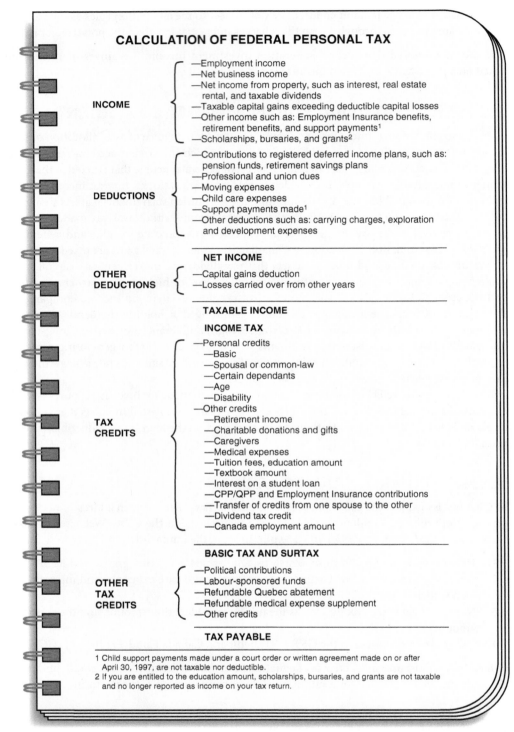

CALCULATION OF FEDERAL PERSONAL TAX

INCOME
—Employment income
—Net business income
—Net income from property, such as interest, real estate rental, and taxable dividends
—Taxable capital gains exceeding deductible capital losses
—Other income such as: Employment Insurance benefits, retirement benefits, and support payments[1]
—Scholarships, bursaries, and grants[2]

DEDUCTIONS
—Contributions to registered deferred income plans, such as: pension funds, retirement savings plans
—Professional and union dues
—Moving expenses
—Child care expenses
—Support payments made[1]
—Other deductions such as: carrying charges, exploration and development expenses

NET INCOME

OTHER DEDUCTIONS
—Capital gains deduction
—Losses carried over from other years

TAXABLE INCOME

INCOME TAX

TAX CREDITS
—Personal credits
—Basic
—Spousal or common-law
—Certain dependants
—Age
—Disability
—Other credits
—Retirement income
—Charitable donations and gifts
—Caregivers
—Medical expenses
—Tuition fees, education amount
—Textbook amount
—Interest on a student loan
—CPP/QPP and Employment Insurance contributions
—Transfer of credits from one spouse to the other
—Dividend tax credit
—Canada employment amount

BASIC TAX AND SURTAX

OTHER TAX CREDITS
—Political contributions
—Labour-sponsored funds
—Refundable Quebec abatement
—Refundable medical expense supplement
—Other credits

TAX PAYABLE

1 Child support payments made under a court order or written agreement made on or after April 30, 1997, are not taxable nor deductible.
2 If you are entitled to the education amount, scholarships, bursaries, and grants are not taxable and no longer reported as income on your tax return.

SOURCE: Five General Sections of Your Federal Tax Return Form. From "Things to Remember," Booklet published by CCH Canadian Tax Compliance Group © 2001. Reprinted with permission. Information updated using Canada Revenue Agency Web site, cra-arc.gc.ca. Reproduced with permission of the Canada Revenue Agency and the Minister of Public Works and Government Services, 2014.

CONCEPT CHECK 3–3

1. How does tax avoidance differ from tax evasion?
2. What common tax-planning strategies are available to most individuals and households?

TAX ASSISTANCE AND THE AUDIT PROCESS

In the process of completing your federal income tax return, you may seek additional information or assistance. After filing your return, you may be identified for a tax audit. If this happens, several policies and procedures protect your rights.

LO4
Identify tax assistance sources

TAX INFORMATION SOURCES

As with other aspects of personal financial planning, many resources are available to assist you with your taxes. Both the Canada Revenue Agency and the Ministère du Revenu du Québec offer comprehensive guides to help you plan and complete your tax return. Libraries and bookstores offer books and other publications that are updated yearly and that will help you create a strategy to effectively and legally maximize after-tax wealth and cash flows. In addition, most daily newspapers frequently contain articles related to personal taxes and their various effects. See Exhibit 3–8 for an example of a tax-planning system.

The fastest way to find information on the various rules and regulations for both the CRA and the Ministère du Revenu du Québec is by searching online at their respective Web sites. The CRA is available at cra-arc.gc.ca, while the Ministère du Revenu du Québec site can be found at revenu.gouv.qc.ca. Both can also be reached by telephone; you will find the telephone number for the closest service office in the blue pages of your local phone book.

TAX PUBLICATIONS   Each year, several personal tax guides are published. Most are available either directly from the issuers, in the case of various tax planning companies, or at a bookstore or library in the case of others. Some of the better-known publications from the financial-services sector include Ernst & Young's *Managing Your Personal Taxes*, KPMG's *Tax Planning for You and Your Family*, and CCH Canadian's *Preparing Your Income Tax Returns*. A free online publication from the Certified General Accountants of Ontario is available at cga-ontario.org; from the home page, click the link to Publications, then click through to Personal Tax Planning. In various bookstores, you may also find Evelyn Jacks's annual *Jacks on Tax Savings*, Prentice Hall Canada's annual *Canadian Guide to Personal Financial Management*, and a number of other books on the topic. Though current taxation rules often change, since the basics usually remain the same you will also find that many non-current-year tax advisory and information publications are relevant.

THE INTERNET   As with other personal finance topics, extensive information may be found on the Web. The Web sites for the CRA and the Ministère du Revenu du Québec are great places to start. Such sites as Canoe Money at canoe.ca/money, the Fraser Institute at fraserinstitute.org, CANTAX at cantax.com, and the Canadian Taxpayers Federation at taxpayer.com are all excellent sources of Canadian tax information. Two of Canada's largest accounting firms, Ernst & Young and KPMG, provide quality links to many other Internet resources and can be found at ey.com and kpmg.ca/tax, respectively. In addition, the Web sites of companies that sell tax software and tax-related organizations can be useful (see the Web sites suggested in the next section).

Exhibit 3–8

Tax-Planner Calendar

January	February	March
• Establish a recordkeeping system for your tax information • If you expect a refund, file your tax return for the previous year	• Deadline for RRSP contribution • Check to make sure you received T4 forms from all organizations from which you had income during the previous year; these should have been received by late February; if not, contact the organization	• Organize your records and tax information in preparation for filing your tax return; if you expect a refund, file as soon as possible • The first instalment for tax is due March 15 for income not covered by withholding

April	May	June
• April 30 is the deadline for filing your federal tax return if you have a balance owing; if it falls on a weekend, you have until the next business day (usually Monday)	• Review your tax return to determine whether any changes in withholding, exemptions, or marital status have not been reported to your employer	• The second instalment for tax is due June 15 for income not covered by withholding

July	August	September
• With the year half over, consider or implement plans for a personal retirement program, such as an RRSP or RPP or some other tax deferral plan	• Tax returns are due August 30 for those who received an extension	• The third instalment for tax is due September 15 for income not covered by withholding

October	November	December
• Determine the tax benefits of selling certain investments by year-end	• Make any last-minute changes in withholding by your employer to avoid penalties for too little withholding	• Make your final estimated quarterly instalment for income not covered by withholding • Determine if it would be to your advantage to make payments for next year before December 31 of the current year • Decide if you can defer income for the current year until the the following year

TAX PREPARATION SOFTWARE AND ELECTRONIC FILING

More and more taxpayers are using personal computers for tax record keeping and income tax preparation. A spreadsheet program is helpful in maintaining and updating tax data on various income and expense categories. There are also a number of different software packages that allow you to complete your return and then either file online or print the completed form for mailing. Popular choices are TurboTax and Ufile.ca. For more information on these programs, see turbotax.intuit.ca and ufile.ca, respectively.

ELECTRONIC FILING   Canadians have embraced CRA's push to file tax returns electronically—in 2012, over 75% of tax returns were filed with the CRA electronically. There are many advantages to filing your return electronically. Besides the obvious benefit to the environment, filing this way allows you to receive a refund within as little as two weeks, versus the six to eight weeks it might normally take. Also, you can keep all your records and are required to send them in only if expressly asked, thus reducing the paper burden.

The CRA has two systems to enable electronic filing of tax returns: EFILE and NETFILE. EFILE is a service that lets authorized service providers and discounters (a discounter is a tax preparer who calculates your refund, and immediately pays you part of your refund—called a discounted tax refund—before filing your income tax and benefit return with the CRA) send individual income tax return information to the CRA directly from the software used to prepare the tax return. Clients take their documents to a registered tax preparer that who, for a fee, will prepare their return and send it to the CRA electronically using EFILE. NETFILE is the "do-it-yourself" electronic filing option from the CRA. This transmission service allows you to file your personal income tax and benefit return directly to the CRA using the Internet; the only caveat is that tax returns filed via NETFILE must first be prepared using a NETFILE-certified product (like Turbo Tax or Ufile).

The Ministère du Revenu du Québec offers a similar service, the details of which are available at its Web site.

TAX PREPARATION SERVICES

Many Canadian taxpayers pay someone to prepare their income tax returns. The fee for this service can range from $50 to a tax preparer for a simple return to several thousand dollars to a chartered professional accountant (CPA) for a complicated return.

Many people prepare their own tax returns. This experience can help you improve your understanding of your financial situation. Doing your own taxes can be complicated, however, particularly if you have sources of income other than salary. The sources available for professional tax assistance include the following:

- Tax services ranging from local services to national firms with many offices, such as H&R Block and Liberty Tax Service.
- Many accountants who offer tax assistance along with other business services. CPAs (formally chartered accountants (CA), certified general accountants (CGA), and certified management accountants (CMA)) with special training in taxes can help with tax planning and preparing your annual tax return.
- Tax lawyers usually do not complete tax returns; however, you can use legal services when you are involved in a complicated tax-related transaction or when you have a difference of opinion with the government.

Even if you hire a professional tax preparer, you are responsible for supplying accurate and complete information and for the contents of your income tax return. Hiring a tax preparer will not guarantee that you pay the *correct* amount. A U.S. study conducted by *Money* magazine of 41 tax preparers reported fees ranging from $375 to $3,600, with taxes due ranging from $31,846 to $74,450 for the same fictional family. If you owe more tax because your return contains errors or you have made entries that are disallowed, it is your responsibility to pay that additional tax, plus any interest and penalties.

Be wary of tax preparers and other businesses that offer your refund in advance. These "refund anticipation loans" frequently charge high interest rates for this type of consumer credit. Studies reveal that interest rates sometimes exceed 300 percent (on an annualized basis).

WHAT IF YOUR RETURN IS AUDITED?

The CRA reviews all returns for completeness and accuracy. If you make an error, your tax is automatically recalculated and you receive either a bill or a refund. If you make an entry that is disallowed, you will be notified by mail. A **tax audit** is a detailed examination of your tax return by the CRA. In most audits, the revenue department requests more information to support the entries on your tax return. Be sure to keep accurate records to support your return. Keep receipts, cancelled cheques, and other evidence to support the amounts that you claim. Avoiding common filing mistakes (see Exhibit 3–9) helps to minimize your chances of an audit.

tax audit A detailed examination of your tax return by the Canada Revenue Agency.

Tax Scam Warnings

Alan Newell was attracted to the idea of reducing his taxes by running a business out of his home. However, the bogus home-based business promoted in an online advertisement did not qualify for a "home office" deduction. Vanessa Elliott liked the idea of increasing the refund she would receive from her federal income tax return. For a fee, she would be informed of additional tax deductions to lower her taxable income. Vanessa avoided the offer since the refund was promised without any knowledge of her tax situation. Ken Turner was informed that he had won a prize that required payment of the income tax on the item before it would be shipped to him. While taxes are usually due on large prizes, the amount would not be paid until later. Fortunately, Alan, Vanessa, and Ken did not fall for these deceptive offers. These three situations are some of the many common tax scams that cost consumers billions of dollars each year.

Other recently reported tax scams include:

- An official-looking, but phony, letter or email to trick a taxpayer into disclosing personal information and bank account numbers. Referred to as "phishing," the swindler uses the information to steal the person's identity and bank deposits. Impersonation scams can take the form of emails, tweets, phony Web sites, phone calls, or faxes to reach their victims. Scam artists mislead consumers by telling them they are entitled to a tax refund and that they must reveal personal information to claim the money.

- An offer to obtain a refund of contributions paid during a person's lifetime. The taxpayer is asked to pay a "paperwork" fee of $100. The law does not allow such a refund.

- A home visit by a con artist posing as a federal tax agent who tries to collect additional tax that the phony agent says is owed.

- A dishonest tax preparer may skim a portion of a client's refund or may promise a large refund. Remember, in the final analysis, the taxpayer is the one who is responsible for the accuracy of the return that is filed.

- Offers to overstate charitable donations and retirement plan contributions. Suggested actions to disguise business ownership, or financial activity to underreport income.

As with any fraud, consumers should be cautious. The opportunity to make fast money can end up being expensive. The Canada Revenue Agency has set up offices nationwide to deal with cases of suspected tax fraud.

SOURCE: Adapted from "Dirty Dozen Tax Scams," irs.gov.

Exhibit 3–9

Top Ten Filing Errors

1. Mathematical errors, such as adding or subtracting amounts incorrectly.

2. Forgetting to reduce income by identifying workers' compensation, social assistance payments, and net federal supplements.

3. Calculating and claiming provincial tax credits incorrectly.

4. Not including pension adjustments, which affect RRSP contribution room for the coming year.

5. Claiming GST/HST credits incorrectly by using incorrect spousal income amounts.

6. Entering the wrong amounts on lines referring to Canada Pension Plan, Quebec Pension Plan, and Employment Insurance contribution and overpayments.

7. Claiming incorrect amounts as RRSP contributions.

8. Forgetting to claim the basic personal amount.

9. Claiming the spousal amount incorrectly.

10. Forgetting to claim the age amount, or claiming it incorrectly.

Advice from a Pro

Any attempt to calculate your investment return must include the least exciting, most annoying financial subject: taxes. Even the word makes me cringe!

The government will get their share of your money—no exceptions. Smart tax planning helps you pay less tax legally. The federal government isn't fooling around: Those who use illegitimate techniques to avoid paying taxes get socked with high-priced penalties or jail time. Pay your taxes on time.

Around the first of the year, you will begin to receive a series of statements from the jobs at which you have worked or financial institutions where you hold accounts. This includes brokerage firms, banks, mutual funds, and other intermediaries. Find the receipts from any charitable donations you've made and proof of any employment-related expenses you plan on writing off. Keep these materials together; lost forms waste time and money!

Your tax return has several sections of which you need to be aware. Generally, your income should be added up, including any losses. Figure your taxable income, factor in additional credits or taxes, and write a cheque. *You've just paid your taxes!*

For those with a home business, complicated returns, or sketchy paperwork, some professional tax guidance is highly recommended—*and worth it!* Spending some money on a tax preparer or CPA might seem daunting but will ensure that your return is filed accurately and rapidly.

TYPES OF AUDITS   The simplest and most common type of audit is the *desk audit*. This mail inquiry requires you to clarify or document minor questions about your tax return. You usually have 30 days to provide the requested information.

The *field audit* is more complex. An auditing agent visits you at your home, your business, or the office of your accountant so you have access to records. A field audit may be done to verify whether an individual has an office in the home as claimed.

If you use EFILE, TELEFILE, or NETFILE you won't need to file receipts with your return. However, the CRA or the Ministère du Revenu du Québec may later ask to check certain claims, such as donations, RRSP contributions, or tuition fees. This is normally just a formality designed to maintain the integrity of the electronic filing system.

YOUR AUDIT RIGHTS   While most audits of individual taxpayers are desk audits, some are field audits. In either case, you should be aware of your rights. The auditor is not entitled to scrutinize all of your documents at will. He or she may request only specific information, and you have a right to ask why that information is needed. In any situation where you anticipate that you will have problems, you have the right to, and should, seek assistance from professional advisers. Generally, however, an audit is a simple verification and should not be cause for alarm if you have filed your return in good faith.

If either an audit of your return or an audit of another person's return gives an indication that your tax payable is not what you have calculated and declared, the CRA will issue a reassessment. In cases where this means that you need to pay more taxes, you will normally be contacted first and given the opportunity to make representations on your behalf. The reassessment cannot be issued if more than three years have passed from the last assessment, except in cases of fraud or misrepresentation stemming from "neglect, carelessness, or wilful default," whereby a reassessment can be issued at any time.

Another situation where the three-year limitation might not apply is where you have signed a waiver regarding a specific disputed issue, as asked by the CRA. You have the right to refuse to sign and can also revoke a signed waiver if you give six months' notice. Refusing to sign may be a sound strategy if the three-year limit is almost up, as it means that the reassessment may not be made if the revenue department does not have adequate time to complete its audit.

If you find yourself unable to pay your taxes or make a tax filing on time due to a natural or human-made disaster, serious illness, or accident, the *Income Tax Act*'s fairness rules give a degree of latitude to the CRA to waive penalties and interest on overdue payments. You should be aware, however, that your past compliance to taxation rules may be considered if you make a fairness-related request.

OBJECTIONS AND APPEALS   You have the right to file a Notice of Objection through your local Chief of Appeals in cases where you do not agree with an assessment. Doing so allows you to have your objection considered by the independent Appeals Officer, but you must file your notice within 90 days of the disputed assessment or one year after the due date of the return.

The Appeals Officer is normally your highest possible level of appeal within the CRA. The next step is to appeal to the Tax Court of Canada, at which point you are just two steps and extensive legal wrangling away from the Supreme Court of Canada.

Be aware that it is best to pay your full taxes, including items in dispute. Doing so avoids late charges if you lose your appeal, and interest on your payment will be returned to you if you win. Paying disputed amounts in advance of an appeals decision is not an admission of guilt, but rather a sound financial decision that should have no legal bearing on your dispute.

CONCEPT CHECK 3–4

1. What are the main sources available to help people prepare their taxes?
2. What actions can reduce the chances of an audit?
3. What appeal options do taxpayers have if they disagree with an audit decision?

SUMMARY OF LEARNING OBJECTIVES

LO1 **Describe the importance of taxes for personal financial planning.**

Tax planning can influence spending, saving, borrowing, and investing decisions. Knowing tax laws and maintaining accurate tax records allows you to take advantage of appropriate tax benefits. An awareness of income taxes, sales taxes, excise taxes, property taxes, estate taxes, and other taxes is vital for successful financial planning.

LO2 **Illustrate how federal income taxes are computed by completing a federal income tax return.**

The major sections of your tax return require you to calculate (1) your filing status, (2) income, (3) deductions, (4) other deductions, (5) tax credits, and (6) your refund or the additional amount you owe.

LO3 **Select appropriate tax strategies for different financial and personal situations.**

You may reduce your tax burden through careful planning and making financial decisions related to consumer purchasing, the use of debt, investments, and retirement planning.

LO4 **Identify tax assistance sources.**

The main sources of tax assistance are CRA services and publications, other publications, the Web, computer software, and professional tax preparers, such as commercial tax services, accountants, and attorneys.

KEY TERMS

average tax rate 78

deductions 76

employment income 74

excise tax 72

investment income 74

marginal tax rate 78

net business income 74

net income 76

tax audit 103

tax credit 78

tax evasion 91

tax planning 91

taxable capital gains 74

taxable income 74

FINANCIAL PLANNING PROBLEMS

 Practise and learn online with Connect.

1. *Computing Taxable Income.* Franklin Stewart arrived at the following tax information:

   Gross salary, $47,780
   Interest earnings, $225
   Dividend income, $80
   Basic personal amount, $9,600
   Deductions, $3,890
   Other losses, $1,150

   What amount will Franklin report as taxable income? LO1

2. *Calculating the Average Tax Rate.* What is the average tax rate for a person who paid taxes of $4,864.14 on a total taxable income of $39,870? LO2

3. *Tax Credits.* What is a tax credit? Distinguish between the two types of tax credits. LO2

4. *Determining a Refund or Taxes Owed.* Based on the following data, will Ann and Carl Wilton receive a federal tax refund or owe additional taxes in 2007? LO2

Net income, $48,190
Deductions to determine net income, $11,420
Federal income tax withheld, $6,784
Total non-refundable tax credit amounts, excluding medical expenses, $10,244
Medical expenses, $2,300

5. *Comparing Taxes on Investments.* Would you prefer a fully taxable investment earning 10.7 percent or a tax-exempt investment earning 8.1 percent? Why? Assume a combined 2007 marginal tax rate of 42 percent. LO3

6. *Future Value of a Tax Savings.* On December 30, you decide to make a $1,000 charitable donation. If you are in the 22-percent federal tax bracket, how much will you save in taxes for 2007? If you deposit that tax savings in a savings account for the next five years at 8 percent, what is the future value of that account? LO3

FINANCIAL PLANNING ACTIVITIES

1. *Searching the Web for Tax Information.* Using Web sites such as the Canadian Tax Foundation at ctf.ca, or Canoe Money at money.canoe.ca, or library resources, obtain information about the tax implications of various financial planning decisions. LO1

2. *Researching Tax-Exempt Income.* Using library resources or the Web, determine the types of income that are exempt from federal income tax. LO2

3. *Planning Your Tax Payment.* Survey several people about whether they get a federal tax refund or owe taxes each year. Obtain information about the following: LO2
   a) Do they usually get a refund or owe taxes when they file their federal tax return?

   b) Is their situation (refund or payment) planned?
   c) Why do they want to get a refund each year?
   d) Are there situations where getting a refund may not be a wise financial decision?

4. *Determining Tax Planning Activities.* Survey friends and relatives about their tax-planning strategies. LO3

5. *Researching Current Tax Forms.* Obtain samples of current tax forms you would use to file your federal income tax return. These may be ordered by mail, obtained at a local CRA office or post office, or obtained on the Web at cra-arc.gc.ca. LO4

6. *Researching Tax Questions.* Use CRA publications and other reference materials to answer a specific tax question. Contact a CRA office to obtain an answer for the same question. What differences, if any, exist between the information sources? *LO4*

7. *Analyzing Tax Preparation Software.* Visit a retailer that sells tax preparation software, such as intuit.com, or visit the software company Web sites to determine the costs and features of programs you may use to prepare and file your federal income tax return. *LO4*

8. *Reducing Tax Errors.* Create a visual presentation (video or slide presentation) that demonstrates actions a person might take to reduce errors when filing a federal tax return. *LO4*

LIFE SITUATION CASE

A Single Father's Tax Situation

Ever since his wife's death, Eric Armano has faced difficult personal and financial circumstances. His job provides him with a fairly good income but requires him to hire a caregiver for his daughters, ages 8 and 10, nearly 20 days a month. This requires him to use in-home child care services that consume a large portion of his income. Since the Armanos live in a small apartment, this arrangement has been very inconvenient.

Although Eric has created an investment fund for his daughters' education and for his retirement, he has not sought to select investments that offer tax benefits. Overall, he needs to look at several aspects of his tax-planning activities to find strategies that will best serve his current and future financial needs.

Eric has assembled the following information for the current tax year:

Earnings from wages	$47,500
Interest earned on GIC	$ 125
RRSP deduction	$ 2,000
Savings account interest	$ 65
Federal income tax deducted at source	$ 4,863

Total non-refundable tax credit amounts	$13,200
Child care deduction	$ 6,300
Filing status: Head of household	

Questions

1. What are Eric's major financial concerns in his current situation?

2. In what ways might Eric improve his tax-planning efforts?

3. Is Eric typical of many people in our society with regard to tax planning? Why, or why not?

4. What additional actions might Eric investigate regarding taxes and personal financial planning?

5. Calculate the following:
   a) What is Eric's 2007 federal taxable income? (Refer to Exhibit 3–1, page 75).
   b) What is his total 2007 federal tax liability? What is his average 2007 federal tax rate?
   c) Will Eric receive a tax refund or owe additional taxes to the federal government for 2007?

CONTINUOUS CASE FOR PART 1

GETTING STARTED: PLANNING FOR THE FUTURE

Life Situation
Single; age 22; starting a career; no dependants

Financial Goals

- Evaluate current financial situation
- Establish a personal financial plan
- Develop a budgeting system for spending and savings

Financial Data

Monthly income	$2,400
Living expenses	1,980
Assets	6,200
Liabilities	1,270
Emergency fund	300

While in university, Pamela Jenkins worked part-time and was never concerned about long-term financial planning. Rather than creating a budget, she used her chequebook and savings account (which usually had a very low balance) to handle her financial needs.

After completing university, Pamela began her career as a sales representative for a clothing manufacturer located in Montreal. After one year, her assets consist of a 1995 Chevrolet, a television set, a stereo, and some clothing and other personal belongings, with a total value of $6,200.

Since a portion of her income is based on commissions, her monthly income varies from one month to the next. This situation has made it difficult for Pamela to establish a realistic budget. During lean months, she has had to resort to using her credit card to make ends meet. In fact, her credit card debt, $1,270, is her only liability at this time. Her only other source of income is a large tax refund. In the past, she has always used tax refunds to finance major purchases (a vacation or furniture) or pay off credit card debt.

Questions

1. What financial decisions should Pamela be thinking about at this point in her life?

2. What are some short-term, intermediate, and long-term financial goals that Pamela might want to develop?

3. How should Pamela budget for fluctuations in her income caused by commission earnings?

4. Assume Pamela's federal tax refund is $1,100. Given her current situation, what should she do with the refund?

5. Based on her life situation, what type of tax planning should Pamela consider?

Stephanie's 2013 Ontario Tax T1 General Return

The following is Stephanie's three-page 2013 *Ontario Tax T1 General—2013* (ON428) return, along with Schedule ON(S11), *Provincial Tuition and Education Amounts*, upon which she calculated her Ontario tuition and education amount of $2,332. Stephanie's total Ontario tax of $4,453.28 (line 66) is transferred to line 428 of her Federal *T1 General 2013—Income Tax and Benefit Return*. Stephanie is not eligible to receive the Ontario property and sales tax credits.

 **Ontario**

Ontario Tax

ON428
T1 General – 2013

Complete this form and **attach a copy** to your return. For more information, see the related line in the forms book.

Step 1 – Ontario non-refundable tax credits

	For internal use only **5605**		
Basic personal amount	claim $9,574 **5804**	9,574 00	1
Age amount (if born in 1948 or earlier) (use *Provincial Worksheet*)	(maximum $4,674) **5808**		2
Spouse or common-law partner amount			
Base amount			
Minus: his or her net income from page 1 of your return			
Result: (if negative, enter "0")	(maximum $8,129) ▶ **5812**		3
Amount for an eligible dependant			
Base amount			
Minus: his or her net income from line 236 of his or her return			
Result: (if negative, enter "0")	(maximum $8,129) ▶ **5816**		4
Amount for infirm dependants age 18 or older (use *Provincial Worksheet*)	**5820**		5
CPP or QPP contributions:			
(amount from line 308 of your federal Schedule 1)	**5824**	2,356 20	•6
(amount from line 310 of your federal Schedule 1)	**5828**		•7
Employment insurance premiums:			
(amount from line 312 of your federal Schedule 1)	**5832**	891 12	•8
(amount from line 317 of your federal Schedule 1)	**5829**		•9
Adoption expenses	**5833**		10
Pension income amount	(maximum $1,324) **5836**		11
Caregiver amount (use *Provincial Worksheet*)	**5840**		12
Disability amount (for self) (Claim **$7,735** or, if you were under 18 years of age, use the *Provincial Worksheet*.)	**5844**		13
Disability amount transferred from a dependant (use *Provincial Worksheet*)	**5848**		14
Interest paid on your student loans (amount from line 319 of your federal Schedule 1)	**5852**	835 00	15
Your tuition and education amounts **[attach Schedule ON(S11)]**	**5856**	2,332 00	16
Tuition and education amounts transferred from a child	**5860**		17
Amounts transferred from your spouse or common-law partner **[attach Schedule ON(S2)]**	**5864**		18
Medical expenses:			
(Read line 5868 in the forms book.)	**5868**		19
Enter $2,167 **or** 3% of line 236 of your return, whichever is **less**.			20
Line 19 minus line 20 (if negative, enter "0")			21
Allowable amount of medical expenses for other dependants (use *Provincial Worksheet*)	**5872**		22
Add lines 21 and 22.	**5876**	▶	23
Add lines 1 to 18, and line 23.	**5880**	15,988 32	24
Ontario non-refundable tax credit rate		**5.05%**	25
Multiply line 24 by line 25.	**5884**	807 41	26
Donations and gifts:			
Amount from line 345 of your federal Schedule 9	177 33 x 5.05% = 8 75		27
Amount from line 347 of your federal Schedule 9	x 11.16% =		28
Add lines 27 and 28.	**5896** 8 75 ▶	8 75	29
Add lines 26 and 29. Enter this amount on line 42.	Ontario non-refundable tax credits **6150**	816 16	30

Go to Step 2 on the next page.

5006-C

ON428 – Page 2

Step 2 – Ontario tax on taxable income

Enter your **taxable income** from line 260 of your return.
If this amount is more than $20,000, you **must** complete **Step 6 – Ontario health premium**.   68,892 50 **31**

Complete the appropriate column depending on the amount on line 31.	Line 31 is **$39,723** or less	Line 31 is more than **$39,723** but not more than **$79,448**	Line 31 is more than **$79,448** but not more than **$509,000**	Line 31 is more than **$509,000**	
Enter the amount from line 31		68,892 50			**32**
	0 00	39,723 00	79,448 00	509,000 00	**33**
Line 32 minus line 33 (cannot be negative)		29,169 50			**34**
	5.05 %	9.15 %	11.16 %	13.16 %	**35**
Multiply line 34 by line 35.		2,669 01			**36**
	0 00	2,006 00	5,641 00	53,579 00	**37**
Add lines 36 and 37. **Ontario tax on taxable income**		4,675 01			**38**
	Go to step 3.	Go to step 3.	Go to step 3.	Go to step 3.	

Step 3 – Ontario tax

Enter your Ontario tax on taxable income from line 38.		4,675 01	**39**
Enter your Ontario tax on split income from Form T1206.	6151		• **40**
Add lines 39 and 40.		4,675 01	**41**

Enter your Ontario non-refundable tax credits from line 30.   816 16 **42**

Ontario dividend tax credit:
 If you entered an amount on line 120 of your return,
 complete line 6152 on the *Provincial Worksheet*.   **6152**   11 04 • **43**

Ontario overseas employment tax credit:
 Amount from line 426 of your federal Schedule 1   x 38.5% = **6153**   • **44**

Ontario minimum tax carryover:
 Amount from line 427 of your federal Schedule 1   x 33.67% = **6154**   • **45**

Add lines 42 to 45.	827 20 ▶	827 20	**46**
Line 41 minus line 46 (if negative, enter "0")		3,847 81	**47**

Ontario additional tax for minimum tax purposes:
Amount from line 95 of Form T691   x 33.67% =   **48**

Add lines 47 and 48.   3,847 81 **49**

Complete lines 50 to 52 only if the amount at line 49 is **more than $4,289**.
Otherwise, enter "0" on line 52 and continue completing the form.

Ontario surtax

(Line 49	3,853 28	minus $4,289) × 20% (if negative, enter "0")	=		**50**
(Line 49	3,853 28	minus $5,489) × 36% (if negative, enter "0")	=		**51**
Add lines 50 and 51.				▶	**52**
Add lines 49 and 52.				3,847 81	**53**

If you are not claiming an Ontario tax reduction or if the amount at line 53 is "0", enter the amount from line 53 on line 61,
and continue completing the form. Otherwise, complete lines 54 to 60 to calculate the Ontario tax reduction.

Step 4 – Ontario tax reduction

Basic reduction   221 00 **54**

If you had a spouse or common-law partner on December 31, 2013, **only** the
individual with the **higher net income** can claim the amounts on lines 55 and 56.

Reduction for dependent children born in 1995 or later
 Number of dependent children **6269**   × $409 =   **55**

Reduction for dependants with a mental or physical infirmity
 Number of dependants **6097**   × $409 =   **56**

Add lines 54, 55 and 56.   221 00 **57**

Enter the amount from line 57.	221 00 × 2 =	442 00	**58**
Enter the amount from line 53.		3,847 81	**59**
Line 58 minus line 59 (if negative, enter "0") **Ontario tax reduction claimed**		▶	**60**
Line 53 minus line 60 (if negative, enter "0")		3,847 81	**61**

Go to Step 5 on the next page.

5006-C

Protected B when completed
ON428 – Page 3

Enter the amount from line 61 on the previous page. _____ 3,847|81 **62**

Step 5 – Ontario foreign tax credit

Enter the Ontario foreign tax credit from Form T2036. _____ | **63**

Line 62 minus line 63 (if negative, enter "0") _____ 3,847|81 **64**

Go to Step 6.

Step 6 – Ontario health premium

If your taxable income (from line 31) is not more than $20,000, enter "0".
Otherwise, enter the amount calculated in the chart below.

Ontario health premium ▶ 600|00 **65**

Add lines 64 and 65.
Enter the result on line 428 of your return.

Ontario tax 4,447|81 **66**

Ontario Health Premium

Enter your **taxable income** from line 31. _____ 68,892|50 **1**

Go to the line that corresponds to your taxable income.

- If there is an Ontario health premium amount on that line, enter that amount on line 65 above.
- Otherwise, enter your taxable income in the first box, complete the calculation, and enter the result on line 65 above.

Taxable income				Ontario health premium
not more than **$20,000**	▶	▶	▶	$ 0
more than **$20,000**, but not more than **$25,000**	☐ − $ 20,000 = ☐	x 6 % = ☐		
more than **$25,000**, but not more than **$36,000**	▶	▶	▶	$ 300
more than **$36,000**, but not more than **$38,500**	☐ − $ 36,000 = ☐	x 6 % = ☐	+ $ 300 = ☐	
more than **$38,500**, but not more than **$48,000**	▶	▶	▶	$ 450
more than **$48,000**, but not more than **$48,600**	☐ − $ 48,000 = ☐	x 25 % = ☐	+ $ 450 = ☐	
more than **$48,600**, but not more than **$72,000**	▶	▶	▶	$ 600
more than **$72,000**, but not more than **$72,600**	☐ − $ 72,000 = ☐	x 25 % = ☐	+ $ 600 = ☐	
more than **$72,600**, but not more than **$200,000**	▶	▶	▶	$ 750
more than **$200,000**, but not more than **$200,600**	☐ − $ 200,000 = ☐	x 25 % = ☐	+ $ 750 = ☐	
more than **$200,600**	▶	▶	▶	$ 900

Privacy Act, Personal Information Bank number CRA PPU 005

Protected B when completed

 **Ontario**   **Provincial Tuition and Education Amounts**   Schedule ON(S11)
T1 General – 2013

Only the student must complete this schedule. Use it to:

- calculate your Ontario tuition and education amounts to claim on line 5856 of your Form ON428;
- determine the provincial amount available to transfer to a designated individual; and
- determine the unused Ontario amount, if any, available for you to carry forward to a future year.

Only the student attaches this schedule to his or her return.

Ontario tuition and education amounts claimed by the student for 2013

Ontario unused tuition and education amounts from your
2012 notice of assessment or notice of reassessment *   **1**

Eligible tuition fees paid for 2013   **5914**   1,100 00 **2**
Education amount for 2013: Use columns B and C of forms T2202A, TL11A,
TL11B, or TL11C. Only one claim per month (**maximum 12 months**)

Enter the number of months from column **B**
(do not include any month that is also included in column C).   8   × $154 = **5916**   1,232 00 **3**
Enter the number of months from column **C**.   × $515 = **5918**   **4**

Add lines 2, 3, and 4.   **Total 2013 tuition and education amounts**   2,332 00 ►   2,332 00 **5**
Add lines 1 and 5.   **Total available tuition and education amounts**   2,332 00 **6**

Enter the amount of your taxable income from line 260 of your return if it is $39,723
or less. If your taxable income is more than $39,723, enter instead the result of the
following calculation: amount from line 39 of your Form ON428 divided by 5.05%.   92,574 46 **7**
Total of lines 5804 to 5848 of your Form ON428   12,821 32 **8**
Line 7 minus line 8 (if negative, enter "0")   79,753 14 **9**
Unused Ontario tuition and education amounts claimed for 2013:
Enter the amount from line 1 or line 9, whichever is **less**.   ►   **10**
Line 9 minus line 10   79,753 14 **11**

2013 tuition and education amounts claimed for 2013:
Enter the amount from line 5 or line 11, whichever is **less**.   2,332 00 **12**
Add lines 10 and 12.   **Ontario tuition and education amounts**
Enter this amount on line 5856 of your Form ON428.   **claimed by the student for 2013**   2,332 00 **13**

Transfer/Carryforward of unused amount

Amount from line 6   2,332 00 **14**
Amount from line 13   2,332 00 **15**
Line 14 minus line 15   **Total unused amount**   **16**

If you are transferring an amount to another individual, continue on line 17.
Otherwise, enter the amount from line 16 on line 21.

Enter the amount from line 5.   (maximum $6,620)   2,332 00 **17**
Amount from line 12   2,332 00 **18**
Line 17 minus line 18 (if negative, enter "0")   **Maximum transferable**   **19**

You can transfer all or part of the amount on line 19 to your spouse or common-law partner, to his or her parent
or grandparent, or to your parent or grandparent. To do this, you have to **designate** the individual and **specify
the provincial amount** that you are transferring to him or her on Form T2202A, TL11A, TL11B, or TL11C.
Enter the amount on line 20 below.

Note: If you have a spouse or common-law partner, special rules may apply. Read line 5856 in the forms book.

Enter the amount you are transferring (cannot be more than line 19).   **Provincial amount transferred** **5920**   **20**

Line 16 minus line 20   **Unused provincial amount available to carry forward to a future year**   **21**

The person claiming the transfer should not attach this schedule to his or her return.

* If you resided in another province or territory on December 31, 2012, you must enter on line 1 your unused provincial or territorial tuition
and education amounts from your 2012 notice of assessment or notice of reassessment.
If you resided in Quebec on December 31, 2012, enter on line 1 your unused federal tuition, education, and textbook amounts.

part 2

Managing Your Personal Finances

chapter 4

The Banking Services of Financial Institutions

LEARNING OBJECTIVES

LO1 Analyze factors that affect selection and use of financial services.

LO2 Compare the types of financial institutions.

LO3 Compare the costs and benefits of various savings plans.

LO4 Identify the factors used to evaluate different savings plans.

LO5 Compare the costs and benefits of different types of chequing accounts.

PRESS 1 TO WITHDRAW CASH . . .
PRESS 2 TO DEPOSIT CASH . . .
PRESS 3 FOR HIGH BANKING FEES!

Chris Carter was visiting the cash machine near his place of work for the third time this week. "Wow! Another cash withdrawal," commented his friend Edwin. "You must have tons of money in that chequing account."

"Well, not really," Chris confessed. "I can use this ATM card to access either my chequing or savings account."

"You mean after you've used up everything in your chequing account, you start taking money out of your savings?" asked Edwin. "Doesn't this machine make it too easy for you to overspend?"

"It's just that I've been very busy at work the last few weeks. I've been eating at restaurants a lot, and my cash is used up quickly," replied Chris.

A couple of weeks later, Chris received his bank statement, which included a couple of surprises. "Oh no!" he exclaimed. "Withdrawing cash from my chequing account made me fall below the minimum balance for the account, so they charged me $8.50. My 11 cash withdrawals resulted in more fees. And what's this? Another charge for an overdraft! All those cash withdrawals and fees really hit me hard! And my savings account is down to $78!"

QUESTIONS

1. What benefits and costs are associated with automated teller machines?

2. How does using financial services like ATMs affect a person's overall financial plan?

3. What could Chris do to reduce his banking fees and manage his money more wisely?

4. Locate a Web site that provides information suggesting methods for reducing banking fees.

 **Connect** Practise and learn online with Connect.

A STRATEGY FOR MANAGING CASH

With 83 banks, 52 trust and loan companies, and over 360 credit unions and caisses populaires, an extensive Canadian financial services market exists. These organizations provide a variety of services for your daily payment and savings needs. Today, a trip to "the bank" may mean a visit to a credit union, an automated teller machine (or automatic banking machine), or checking an account balance on the Web. In recent years, financial services have expanded. A bank is not the only source of chequing accounts. Mortgages are available from several types of financial institutions.

LO1
Analyze factors that affect selection and use of financial services.

While some financial decisions relate directly to goals, your daily activities require using financial services for various business transactions. Exhibit 4–1 provides an overview of financial services for managing cash flows and moving toward financial goals. In simplest terms, you can increase current savings only by spending less than you take in.

MEETING DAILY MONEY NEEDS

Buying groceries, paying the rent, and other routine spending activities require a cash management plan.

MANAGING CASH   Cash, cheque, credit card, or automated teller machine (ATM) card (also known as *debit card*) are the common payment choices. While most people desire ease of payment, they must also consider fees and the potential for impulse buying and overspending. For example, in recent years ATM fees have risen from nothing to as high as $5 per transaction, depending upon the type of transaction, where it takes place, and whether or not ATM transactions are covered under the account's service package.

If you are charged two $1 transaction fees a week and could invest your money at 5 percent, this convenience will cost you more than $570 over a five-year period.

Common mistakes made when managing current cash needs include:

- Overspending as a result of impulse buying and using credit cards.
- Having insufficient liquid assets (cash, chequing account) to pay current bills.

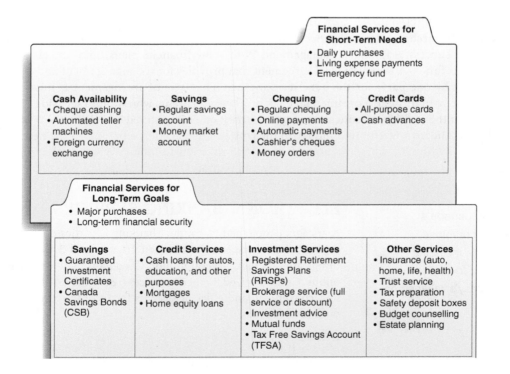

Exhibit 4–1

Financial Services for Managing Cash Flow

- Using savings or borrowing to pay for current expenses.
- Failing to put unneeded funds in an interest-earning savings account or investment plan to achieve long-term goals.

SOURCES OF QUICK CASH   No matter how carefully you manage your money, there may be times when you need more cash than you currently have available. To cope with that situation, you have two basic choices: liquidate savings or borrow. A savings account, redeemable Guaranteed Investment Certificate, mutual fund, or other investment may be raided when you need funds. Alternatively, a bank overdraft or credit card cash advance may supply funds quickly, but at a high cost. The best and most efficient source of quick cash is a personal line of credit, arranged before the need arises. Remember, however, that both using savings and increasing borrowing reduce your net worth and your potential to achieve long-term financial security.

TYPES OF FINANCIAL SERVICES

Banks and other financial institutions offer services to meet a variety of needs. These services fall into four main categories.

1. SAVINGS   Safe storage of funds for future use is a basic need for everyone. These services, commonly referred to as *time deposits*, include money in savings accounts and investment certificates. Selection of a savings plan is commonly based on the interest rate earned, liquidity, safety, and convenience. These factors are discussed later in the chapter.

2. PAYMENT SERVICES   The ability to transfer money to other parties is a necessary part of daily business activities. Chequing accounts and other payment methods, commonly called *demand deposits*, are also covered later in the chapter.

3. BORROWING   Most people use credit at some time during their lives. Credit alternatives range from short-term accounts, such as credit cards and cash loans, to long-term borrowing, such as a home mortgage. Chapters 5 and 6 discuss the types and costs of credit.

trust A legal agreement that provides for the management and control of assets by one party for the benefit of another.

4. OTHER FINANCIAL SERVICES   Insurance protection, investment for the future, real estate purchases, tax assistance, and financial planning are additional services you may need for successful financial management. With some financial plans, someone else manages your funds. A **trust** is a legal agreement that provides for the management and control of assets by one party for the benefit of another. This type of arrangement is most commonly created through a commercial bank or a lawyer. Parents who want to set aside certain funds for their children's education may use a trust or an Registered Education Savings Plan (RESP). The investments and money in the trust are managed by a bank, and the necessary amounts go to the children for their educational expenses. Trusts are covered in more detail in Chapter 15.

ELECTRONIC BANKING SERVICES

Years ago, people had to conduct banking activities only during set business hours, usually between 10 A.M. and 3 P.M. Today, things are different. Several million Canadians bank or pay bills online. Computerized financial services (see Exhibit 4–2) provide fast, convenient, and efficient systems for recording inflows and outflows of funds.

DIRECT DEPOSIT   Each year, more and more workers are receiving only a pay stub on payday. Their earnings are

Did you know?

Between 2002 and 2012, Canada's six largest banks spent a combined $60.4 billion on technology, including $7.7 billion in 2012 alone. Investing in technology is critical to today's reliance on electronic banking services.

SOURCE: Published by CBA, May 2014.

Exhibit 4–2
Electronic Banking Transactions

automatically deposited into chequing or savings accounts. This process saves time, effort, and money. Government agencies are also increasing their use of direct deposits to reduce costs. Provincial and federal government cheques going to contractors and to Canada Pension Plan, Old Age Security, and welfare recipients are deposited electronically into the payees' bank accounts.

AUTOMATIC PAYMENTS   Many utility companies, lenders, and other businesses allow customers to use an automatic payment system, with bills paid through direct withdrawal from a bank account. Experts recommend that you stagger your payments based on when paycheques are received. This allows you to pay bills in an orderly fashion while stabilizing your cash flow. Be sure to check bank statements regularly to ensure that the correct amounts have been deducted from your account. A minor error can result in an overdrawn account and expensive fees.

AUTOMATED TELLER MACHINES   **Automated teller machine (ATM)** convenience can be expensive. As the opening case points out, a person who uses an ATM several times a week can incur service charges of several hundred dollars a year.

To reduce ATM fees, experts suggest that you:

- Compare ATM fees at different financial institutions before opening an account. Get the fee schedule in writing.
- Use your own bank's ATM whenever possible to avoid surcharges imposed when using the ATM of another financial institution.
- Consider purchasing a monthly service package that includes ATM activity.
- Withdraw larger cash amounts, as needed, to avoid fees on several small transactions.
- Get cash back at the grocery store while paying with your debit card.
- Consider using personal cheques, traveller's cheques, credit cards, and prepaid cash cards when away from home if they are more cost effective.

automated teller machine (ATM)
A computer terminal used to conduct banking transactions.

Did you know?

Canada has the highest rate of debit transactions per inhabitant. There are now over 60,000 ATMs located across the country; 91 percent of Canadians hold a banking card. In 2012, Canadians used the Interac Direct Payment service 4.357 billion times. December 23, 2008, was the busiest day in the history of debit payments, logging 15.9 million transactions.

SOURCE: interac.org.

METHODS OF PAYMENT

1. POINT-OF-SALE TRANSACTIONS

Debit cards are routinely accepted in most retail stores and restaurants in major urban centres. Your personal identification number (PIN) is required and the amount is immediately debited from your bank account, reducing your available funds.

Credit cards are also used at the time of sale, but merchandise charges accumulate and appear on the following monthly statement. Credit card transactions used to require you to enter your PIN only for a cash advance but now most transactions require a PIN.

2. STORED-VALUE CARDS

Prepaid cards for buying telephone service, transit fares, laundry service, library fees, and school lunches are becoming common. While some of these access cards, such as phone cards, are disposable (or become collector's items), others are reloadable "stored-value" cards.

Did you know?

Generic ATMs are everywhere, with surcharges that are added to the regular transaction fees. These additional fees usually start at $1.50 and can climb much higher. Since the machines warn you about the service charge before your transaction is complete, however, you can cancel your transaction if you think the fee is excessive.

3. SMART CARDS

"Smart cards," sometimes called "electronic wallets," look like ATM cards; however, they also include a microchip. This minicomputer stores prepaid amounts for buying goods and services. In addition, the card stores data about your account balances, transaction records, insurance information, and medical history.

4. SOFTWARD-BASED PAYMENT SYSTEMS

Software-based payment solutions, such as Bitcoin, are often referred to as digital currencies. These currencies are electronically created and stored, and like traditional money, may be used to buy physical goods and services. Sometimes use of these currencies is restricted to certain communities, such as for use in certain online gaming communities or social networks. (Source: http://en.wikipedia.org/wiki/Digital_currency)

OPPORTUNITY COSTS OF FINANCIAL SERVICES

When making decisions about spending and saving, consider the trade-off between current satisfaction and long-term financial security. In a similar manner, you consider opportunity cost—what you give up—when you evaluate, select, and use financial services. The money you save by shopping around for a low-cost chequing account must be balanced against the value of the time you spend gathering information. Other common trade-offs related to financial services include the following:

- Higher returns of long-term savings and investment plans may be achieved at the cost of *low liquidity*, the inability to obtain your money quickly.
- The convenience of a 24-hour ATM or a bank branch office near your home or place of work must be weighed against service fees.
- The "no fee" chequing account that requires a non–interest-bearing $1,000 minimum balance means lost interest of nearly $220 at 2 percent compounded over 10 years. However, with interest rates being as low as they are today, in most cases maintaining a balance to avoid service fees outweighs the benefits of interest income.

You should evaluate costs and benefits in both monetary and personal terms to choose the financial services that best serve your needs.

FINANCIAL SERVICES AND ECONOMIC CONDITIONS

Changing interest rates, rising consumer prices, and other economic factors also influence financial services. For successful financial planning, be aware of the current trends and future

Exhibit 4–3

When interest rates are rising...

- Use long-term loans to take advantage of current low rates
- Select short-term savings instruments to take advantage of higher rates when they mature

- Use short-term loans to take advantage of lower rates when you refinance the loans
- Select long-term savings instruments to "lock in" earnings at current high rates

When interest rates are falling...

Changing Interest Rates and Decisions Related to Financial Services

prospects for interest rates (see Exhibit 4–3). You can learn about these trends and prospects by reading *The Financial Post* (financialpost.com), the business section of daily newspapers, and business periodicals such as *Business Week* (businessweek.com), and *Fortune* (fortune.com).

CONCEPT CHECK 4–1

1. What is the relationship between financial services and overall financial planning?
2. What are the major categories of financial services?
3. What financial services are available through electronic banking systems?
4. Why shouldn't you select financial services on the basis of only monetary factors?
5. How do changing economic conditions affect the use of financial services?

TYPES OF FINANCIAL INSTITUTIONS

Many types of businesses, such as insurance companies, investment brokers, and credit card companies, have become involved in financial services previously limited to banks. Such companies as Canadian Tire and The Hudson's Bay Company now issue or sponsor credit cards. Banks have also expanded their competitive efforts by opening offices that specialize in financial services, such as investments, insurance, or real estate. Increased competition has brought about the opening of many limited-service offices, sometimes called *non-banks*. These limited-service offices specialize in a particular banking activity, such as savings or personal loans.

Despite changes in the banking environment, many familiar financial institutions still serve your needs. Most of these institutions have expanded their services. As Exhibit 4–4 shows, financial institutions fall into two major categories: deposit-type institutions and non-deposit institutions.

LO2
Compare the types of financial institutions.

Deposit-Type Institutions

- Chartered banks
- Trust companies
- Credit unions/caisses populaires

Non-Deposit Institutions

- Life insurance companies
- Investment companies
- Mortgage and loan companies
- Pawnshops
- Cheque-cashing outlets

Exhibit 4–4

Types of Financial Institutions

Financial Planning for Life's Situations

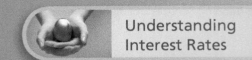

When people discuss higher or lower interest rates, they could be talking about one of many types of interest rates. Some interest rates refer to the cost of borrowing by a business; others refer to the cost of buying a home. Your awareness of various types of interest rates can help you plan your spending, saving, borrowing, and investing. The accompanying table describes the most commonly reported interest rates and gives their *annual average* for selected years.

Using the business section of a newspaper or other business information sources, obtain current numbers for some or all of these interest rates. How might the current trend in interest rates affect your financial decisions?

	1980	1985	1990	1995	2000	2005	2010	Current
Prime rate—the rate banks charge their most creditworthy corporate and retail clients	14.25	10.58	14.02	8.65	6.81	4.42	3.00	____%
Bank rate—the rate a central bank charges for loans to national banks (e.g., the rate the Bank of Canada charges the Bank of Montreal)	12.89	9.65	13.05	7.31	5.31	2.90	1.25	____
91-day T-bill rate—the yield on 91-day government treasury bills	12.79	9.43	12.81	6.89	5.21	5.45	0.97	____
30-yr T-bond rate—the yield on 30-year government treasury bonds	12.48	11.05	10.85	8.28	6.08	4.32	3.62	____
5-yr mortgage rate—the amount individuals pay to borrow for the purchase of a home	14.32	12.18	13.41	9.22	8.31	5.83	5.19	____
5-yr term deposit rate—the amount that individuals receive for 5-year term deposits	11.25	9.63	10.33	6.70	5.48	2.46	1.85	____
Savings deposit rate—the amount that individuals receive for regular savings deposits	11.15	6.08	8.77	0.50	0.10	0.05	0.05	____

DEPOSIT-TYPE INSTITUTIONS

For many years, government policies prohibited cross-ownership and foreign control of the four major types of businesses in financial services. This division, referred to as the "four pillars," separated banks, trust companies, insurance companies, and investment dealers, where rules were established to protect their core business (deposit taking and lending, fiduciary services, insurance protection and underwriting, and securities trading, respectively).

However, spurred by the deregulation efforts in the United States, since 1980, services provided by Canadian companies have broadened and overlapped, blurring the separation of the four pillars. Keeping up with international developments, the federal government passed legislation on June 1, 1992, permitting banks, trust and loan companies, and insurance companies to compete more directly with one another. In addition, the Bank of Canada, which is the country's central bank has four main areas of responsibility. These include: (1) monetary policy; (2) currency; (3) the financial system; and (4) funds management. These areas can be explored by visiting their Web site, bankofcanada.ca.

CHARTERED BANKS   Operating under the provisions of the *Bank Act*, the principal activity of the banks is to lend funds to businesses and consumers at interest rates that are higher than those the banks pay on deposits and other borrowings. **Chartered banks** own a range of other types of corporations, including brokerage firms, information service firms, and special financing corporations. This diversity enables banks to offer investment counselling and portfolio management services under one roof.

chartered bank A financial institution that offers a full range of financial services to individuals, businesses, and government agencies.

SCHEDULE I BANKS   These are full-service domestic banks, including the *big six* banks (RBC Financial, CIBC, Bank of Montreal, Scotiabank, TD Canada Trust, and the National Bank of Canada), smaller Canadian-owned banks, and other non-bank financial institutions.

SCHEDULE II BANKS   These are subsidiaries of foreign banks in Canada that have restrictions on asset growth as well as on lending activities that are a function of their local capital base rather than that of the parent bank. They tend to focus on commercial corporate loans rather than retail banking services to individuals. Some examples include HSBC Bank Canada, State Bank of India (Canada), and Bank of China (Canada).

SCHEDULE III BANKS   These are branches of foreign institutions that have been authorized under the *Bank Act* to do banking business in Canada, subject to certain restrictions. They specialize in niche financing and include Citibank, N.A., and Deutsche Bank, A.G.

TRUST COMPANIES   Trust companies offer a broad range of financial services similar to those provided by banks. In addition, they are the only corporations allowed to act as a trustee in charge of corporate or individual property, stocks, and bonds. Most trust companies are owned by banks, except the large independents, such as Sun Life, Manulife Financial, and Great-West Life.

CREDIT UNIONS AND CAISSES POPULAIRES   A **credit union** (or **caisse populaire** in Quebec) is a user-owned, non-profit, co-operative financial institution. Traditionally, credit union members had to have a common bond, such as work, church, or community affiliation. As the common bond restriction was loosened, the membership of credit unions increased.

credit union/caisse populaire A user-owned, non-profit co-operative financial institution that is organized for the benefit of its members.

Each year, surveys conducted by consumer organizations and others report lower fees for chequing accounts, lower loan rates, and higher levels of user satisfaction for credit unions compared with other financial institutions. Most credit unions offer credit cards, mortgages, home equity loans, direct deposit, cash machines, safety deposit boxes, and investment services.

NON-DEPOSIT INSTITUTIONS

Financial services are also available from such institutions as life insurance companies, investment companies, mortgage and loan companies, finance and leasing companies, pawnshops, and cheque-cashing outlets.

Did you know?

In comparing the various service fees payable at different financial institutions, you will generally find that credit unions or caisses populaires offer a better deal than chartered banks and trust companies.

LIFE INSURANCE COMPANIES   While the main purpose of life insurance is to provide financial security for dependants, many life insurance policies contain savings and investment features. Chapter 9 discusses these policies. In recent years, life insurance companies have expanded their financial services to include investment and retirement planning.

money market fund A savings investment plan offered by investment companies, with earnings based on investments in various short-term financial instruments.

INVESTMENT COMPANIES   Investment companies, also referred to as *mutual funds*, offer banking-type services. A common service of these organizations is the **money market fund**, a combination savings-investment plan in which the investment company uses your money to purchase a variety of short-term financial instruments. Your earnings are based on the interest the investment company receives. Unlike accounts at most banks, trust companies, and credit unions, investment company accounts are not covered by federal deposit insurance.

MORTGAGE AND LOAN COMPANIES   These companies provide real estate mortgage loans as well as financing opportunities for individuals and small businesses. In general, the loans provided have short and intermediate terms with higher rates than most other lenders charge. Some of these companies have expanded their activities to also offer other financial planning services.

FINANCE AND LEASING COMPANIES   Finance and leasing companies extend loans and leases to both individuals and businesses, and are categorized by the type of loan or lease they offer, or the sector they serve. Consumer loan companies offer cash lending services directly to individuals (e.g., Citi Financial Services Canada Ltd.), while finance companies that serve the corporate sector focus on loans or leases to small businesses or new, high-growth companies. Consumer loan companies tend to charge higher administrative fees and rates of interest than do banks, due to their smaller size, high cost of funding, and willingness to accept credit risks that other creditors might refuse.

PAWNSHOPS   Pawnshops, which often label themselves *cash converters*, make loans based on the value of tangible possessions, such as jewellery or other valuable items. Many low- and moderate-income families use these organizations to obtain cash loans quickly. Pawnshops charge higher fees than other financial institutions.

CHEQUE-CASHING OUTLETS   Most financial institutions will not cash a cheque unless the person has an account. Cheque-cashing outlets (CCOs) charge anywhere from 1 to 20 percent of the face value of a cheque; the average cost is between 2 and 3 percent. However, for a low-income family, that can be a significant portion of the total household budget.

CCOs offer a wide variety of services, including electronic tax filing, money orders, and private postal boxes. You can usually obtain most of these services for less expense at other locations.

ONLINE BANKING

Using online Web portals for personal banking has become common. Every major Canadian financial institution maintains a Web site where customers can log in and conduct everyday banking transactions, such as verifying account balances, transferring funds, and paying bills and credit card balances. The Web site also permits individuals to apply for loans and provides complete product information. The Bank of Montreal (bmo.com) and TD Canada Trust (tdcanadatrust.com) were among the first Canadian banks to do business on the Internet. Citizens Bank of Canada (citizensbank.ca) was one of the first Canadian financial institutions to operate exclusively on the Internet. Access to all accounts and transactions is available 24 hours a day, seven days a week. Not only is it always accessible, it is also offered free of charge to anyone who has a financial product with that institution.

One of the main deterrents to banking online is a lack of technical and computer expertise. Most banking transactions require specialized software for securely encrypting data. Do not worry; most financial Web sites show you how and where to download the required software free of charge.

Did you know?

The stark reality of services offered by cheque-cashing outlets is that the fees you pay are substantially higher than what you might be charged at other financial institutions. Studies reveal that poor consumers (who form the bulk of the outlets' clientele) can spend up to 10 times as much at a cheque-cashing outlet as they would with a basic account. Despite this fact, other studies have proposed that banks often poorly promote the availability of low-cost accounts.

FEATURES OF ONLINE BANKING

Electronic Bill Presentment and Payment (EBPP)   Electronic bill payment is a now-common feature of online banking, allowing a depositor to send money from his demand account to a creditor or vendor such as a public utility or a department store to be credited against a specific account. The payment is optimally executed electronically in real time, though some financial institutions or payment services will wait until the next business day to send out the payment.

Pre-authorized Debits and Recurring Transfers   This is an authorization set up in advance for a set amount of funds to be withdrawn from a bank account and be transferred to another account or be used to pay a bill. The former can either be a one-time transfer/payment or a recurring one, and the latter is a recurring pre-authorized debit.

Stop-payments   A stop-payment is put on either a cheque or a pre-authorized debit that has not gone through yet, and allows clients to cancel a pending payment. Generally certain information is required to be able to request this sort of service, such as details of the transaction such as the account to be debited, the payee, the payment amount, and the date of the payment.

Cheque Services   These can include ordering or re-ordering cheques as well as cheque imaging. This is used primarily by clients who for some reason need to know the details of a particular cheque or payment.

Email Money Transfer   Email Money Transfer (EMT) allows you to send money to and receive money from other financial institutions within Canada. The money transfer is sent quickly and securely between accounts using existing financial institution's electronic payment networks. The provider of this service is Interac, a division of Acxsys Corporation.

Downloadable Statements   Many banks allow customers to go virtually paperless with downloadable statements. Online banking services often archive up to two years of account activity, making it easy for customers to print statements and research potential payment disputes. By allowing customers to opt out of mailed, monthly statements, banks can pass savings along to account holders.

Synchronization with Quicken or Money   Customers who use software to manage their finances enjoy the ability to download transactions directly from a bank's Web site into Quicken or Microsoft Money. Most online banking services can export transaction lists in an industry standard format. However, some advanced online banking platforms interface directly with customers' desktop software packages, making account maintenance seamless.

Some online banking platforms support account aggregation to allow the customers to monitor all of their accounts in one place whether they are with their main bank or with other institutions.

Online Banking Benefits	Online Banking Concerns
• Time and money savings • Convenience for transactions, comparing rates • No paper trail for identity thieves • Transfer access for loans, investments • Email notices of due dates	• Potential privacy, security violations • ATM fees can become costly • Difficulty depositing cash, cheques • Overspending due to ease of access • Online scams, "phishing," and email spam

Would you pay $8 to cash a $100 cheque? Or pay $20 to borrow $100 for two weeks? Many people without ready access to financial services (especially low-income consumers) commonly use the services of cheque-cashing outlets, pawnshops, payday loan stores, and rent-to-own centres. Offers of "quick cash" and "low payments" attract consumers without a bank account or credit cards.

PAWNSHOPS

Despite a thriving economy in recent years, thousands of consumers are increasingly in need of small loans—usually $50 to $75, to be repaid in 30 to 45 days. Pawnshops have become the neighbourhood bankers and the local shopping malls, since they provide both lending and retail shopping services, selling items that owners do not redeem.

PAYDAY LOANS

Payday loans are also referred to as *cash advances*, *cheque advance loans*, *post-dated cheque loans*, and *delayed deposit loans*. Desperate borrowers pay annual interest rates of as much as 780 percent and more to obtain needed cash from payday loan companies. The most common users of payday loans are workers who have become trapped by debts run up by free spending or who have been driven into debt by misfortune.

In a typical payday loan, a consumer writes a personal cheque for $115 to borrow $100 for 14 days. The payday lender agrees to hold the cheque until the next payday. This $15 finance charge for the 14 days translates into an annual percentage rate of 391 percent. Some consumers "roll over" their loans, paying another $15 for the $100 loan for the next 14 days. After a few rollovers, the finance charge can exceed the amount borrowed.

RENT-TO-OWN CENTRES

Years ago, people who rented furniture and appliances found few deluxe items available. Today, rental businesses offer big-screen televisions, seven-piece cherry wood bedroom sets, and personal computers. The rental–purchase industry—defined as stores that lease products to consumers who can then own the item if they complete a certain number of monthly or weekly payments—is in rapid growth.

COMPARING FINANCIAL INSTITUTIONS

The basic concerns of a financial services customer are simple:

- Where can I get the best return on my savings?
- How can I minimize the cost of chequing and payments services?
- Will I be able to borrow money when I need it?

As you use financial services, decide what you want from the organization that will serve your needs. With the financial marketplace constantly changing, you must assess the various services and other factors before selecting an organization (see Exhibit 4–5).

Exhibit 4–5

How Should You Choose a Financial Institution?

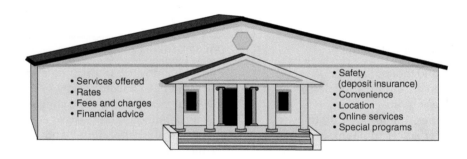

- Services offered
- Rates
- Fees and charges
- Financial advice

- Safety (deposit insurance)
- Convenience
- Location
- Online services
- Special programs

"We never close." "Highest savings rates anywhere." "Lowest chequing account fees ever."

These impressive banking services are now possible with the use of the Web. Banks, like other businesses and financial service companies, are now online with cyber-versions of their traditional activities.

COMPARING BANKING SERVICES

As you start or expand your use of online banking services, explore the several Web sites that provide a wide range of banking information. These include royalbank.ca and quicken.intuit.ca.

ONLINE BANK BRANCHES

Traditional banks are expanding to offer services online. Some examples include bmo.com and tdcanada-trust.com.

PAYING BILLS ONLINE

It is now possible to receive your bills online through email or by logging on to your bank's Web site. One mouse click can pay off your credit card, and another, your cellphone bill. Paperless billing is fast becoming the new way to settle accounts efficiently using the Internet. For information on paying bills online, go to quicken.intuit.ca, yahoo.ca, or canada.aol.com/home/index.adp.

VIRTUAL BANKS

Many of today's best chequing and savings deals come from branchless banks doing business solely on the Internet. Virtual or online banks usually require little or no minimum balance on chequing accounts. Many Internet banks also pay higher interest on chequing accounts than traditional banks. While ATMs are not readily available from Web banks, these online financial companies usually offer banking and customer service over the telephone. Some Internet banks include citizensbank.ca, President's Choice Financial (pcfinancial.ca), and Tangerine (tangerine.ca).

Be cautious! You can access the Web site of the Canadian Deposit Insurance Corporation (CDIC; cdic.ca) to obtain information on fraudulent cyber-banks. The CDIC can tell you if a Web bank has a legitimate charter to operate as a financial institution.

The services the financial institution offers are likely to be a major factor. Personal service is important to many customers. Convenience may be provided by business hours, branch offices, automated teller machines, and online services. Convenience and service have a cost, so be sure to compare fees and other charges at several financial institutions.

Finally, you should consider safety factors and interest rates. Obtain information about earnings you will receive on savings and chequing accounts and the rate you will pay for borrowed funds. Most financial institutions have deposit insurance to protect customers against losses; however, not all of them are insured by federal government programs. Investigate the type of protection you will have.

Your selection of a financial institution should be based on valid information. Never assume that one will provide a better interest rate or service than another. You need to compare banks, trust companies, and credit unions with other providers of financial services.

CONCEPT CHECK 4–2

1. What are examples of deposit-type financial institutions?
2. What factors do consumers usually consider when selecting a financial institution to meet their saving and chequing needs?

TYPES OF SAVINGS PLANS

LO3

Compare the costs and benefits of various savings plans.

As Chapter 2 emphasized, you need a savings program to attain financial goals. Evaluating various savings plans is the starting point of this process.

Changes in financial services have created a wide choice of savings alternatives (see Exhibit 4–6). While the number of savings plans may seem overwhelming, they can be grouped into these main categories: regular savings accounts, term deposits and GICs, interest-earning chequing accounts, and Canada Savings Bonds. Investment vehicles, such as Canadian treasury bills, are discussed in later chapters.

REGULAR SAVINGS ACCOUNTS

Regular savings accounts, traditionally called *passbook accounts*, usually involve a low or no minimum balance. Today, instead of a passbook showing deposits and withdrawals, savers may elect to receive a monthly or quarterly statement with a summary of transactions.

A regular savings account usually allows you to withdraw money as needed, but service fees may apply. However, *time deposits* may require a waiting period to obtain your funds.

TERM DEPOSITS AND GUARANTEED INVESTMENT CERTIFICATES (GICs)

Higher earnings are commonly available to savers when they leave money on deposit for a set time period.

Exhibit 4–6   Savings Alternatives

Type of Alternative	Benefits	Drawbacks
Regular savings accounts/ passbook accounts	Low minimum balance Ease of withdrawal Insured to $100,000 per financial institution	Low rate of return
Guaranteed Investment Certificates (GICs)	Guaranteed rate of return for time of GIC Insured	Possible penalty for early withdrawal Minimum deposit
Interest-earning chequing accounts	Chequing privileges Interest earned Insured to $100,000	Possible service charge for going below minimum balance Cost for printing cheques; other fees may apply
Money market accounts	Favourable rate of return (based on current interest rates) Allows some cheque writing	Higher minimum balance than regular savings accounts No interest or service charge, if below a certain balance
Money market funds	Favourable rate of return (based on current interest rates)	Minimum balance Not insured
Canada Savings Bonds (CSBs)	Rate of return varies with current interest rates Low minimum deposit Regular or compound interest Government guaranteed	No interest paid if redeemed before three months

TERM DEPOSITS   Contrary to a savings account, which does not have a guaranteed interest rate of return, **term deposits** guarantee a rate of interest for a specified term. The trade-off is that your money becomes less accessible for a time.

Some term deposits require a minimum deposit, and if you are willing to sacrifice some of the interest you might have earned you will usually be permitted to withdraw your funds before maturity. The amount of interest you will earn is inversely related to the term of the investment, which is typically between 30 and 364 days.

GUARANTEED INVESTMENT CERTIFICATES   **Guaranteed Investment Certificates (GICs)** are essentially term deposits with a longer term, ranging from one to five years. As is the case with term deposits, a minimum deposit is often required. Interest can be fixed-rate, variable, or *indexed-linked*—that is, based on a formula linked to stock market returns. Some GICs are redeemable prior to maturity, but will pay a lower rate of interest if redeemed than GICs of a similar term that are non-redeemable.

MANAGING YOUR TERM DEPOSITS AND GICs   When a term deposit or GIC reaches maturity, it is important to assess all earnings and costs. Do not allow your financial institution to automatically roll your money over into another deposit for the same term. If interest rates have dropped, you should consider investing in a term deposit for a shorter term in hopes that rates will rise. Alternatively, if you believe that rates are peaking and you do not think you will need your money for a time, then your best choice will be a longer-term GIC.

Deposit rates will often vary from one financial institution to the next. In addition, their personnel have some flexibility to offer rates higher than those advertised. It is wise to comparison-shop and negotiate the best rate available before locking in your money. Visit baystreet.ca/interest_rates/gic_rates.cfm to compare rates by institution and maturity.

term deposit A deposit that is made for a specified term in exchange for a higher rate of return. Can be redeemed before maturity by earning a reduced rate of interest (paying a penalty).

Guaranteed Investment Certificates (GICs) Term deposits made for a longer period, usually from one to five years.

INTEREST-EARNING CHEQUING ACCOUNTS

Chequing accounts can also be savings vehicles. These interest-earning accounts, which usually pay a very low interest rate, are discussed in the next section.

CANADA SAVINGS BONDS

Canada Savings Bonds (CSBs) developed from Victory bonds, which were offered between 1940 and 1944 in an effort to raise funds for the Canadian military action of the Second World War. Though crucial at the time and in the half century that followed, CSBs now have a declining role in the federal government's borrowing as the government's need for funds has diminished.

Unlike most investments, CSBs are sold only once a year, for the six-month period starting in October until the following April 1. They have a fixed rate of interest for the first year and, subject to a guaranteed minimum, rates can be adjusted according to market conditions in later years. Starting three months after purchase, CSBs are cashable at any time for their face value plus accrued interest. They are eligible investments for both Registered Retirement Savings Plans (RRSPs) and Registered Retirement Income Funds (RRIFs). Two types are available: the *regular interest bond* and the *compound interest bond*. The series numbering system indicates whether it is a "R" or "C" bond.

REGULAR INTEREST BOND   This bond pays regular annual interest by cheque or direct deposit to an investor's account on November 1 of each year. Denominations for this bond range from $300 to $10,000 and they must be purchased with cash.

COMPOUND INTEREST BOND   This bond reinvests earned interest automatically until redemption or maturity. It is available in denominations as low as $100 and up to $10,000. Compound interest bonds can be purchased by cash, by a monthly payment plan through a financial institution, or through a payroll savings plan.

The Government of Canada also offers the Canada Premium Bond (CPB). The CPB is sold during the same six-month period as the CSB, but offers a slightly higher rate of interest because it can be redeemed only on the anniversary of the issue date and during the 30 days that follow. More information concerning CSBs and CPBs can be found at csb.gc.ca.

CONCEPT CHECK 4–3

1. What are the main types of savings plans offered by financial institutions?
2. What are the benefits of Canada Savings Bonds?

EVALUATING SAVINGS PLANS

LO4

Identify the factors used to evaluate different savings plans.

Your selection of a savings plan will be influenced by the rate of return, inflation, tax considerations, liquidity, safety, and restrictions and fees.

RATE OF RETURN

rate of return The percentage of increase in the value of savings as a result of interest earned; also called *yield*.

Earnings on savings can be measured by the **rate of return**, or *yield*: the percentage of increase in the value of your savings from earned interest. For example, a $100 savings account that earned $2 after a year has a rate of return, or yield, of 2 percent. This rate of return was determined by dividing the interest earned ($2) by the amount in the savings account ($100).

COMPOUNDING   The yield on your savings usually will be greater than the stated interest rate. The more frequent the compounding, the higher your rate of return will be. For example, $100 in a savings account that earns 3 percent compounded annually will increase $3 after a year. But the same $100 in a 3 percent account compounded daily will earn $3.05 for the year. Although this difference may seem slight, large amounts held in savings for long periods of time will result in far higher differences (see Exhibit 4–7).

EFFECTIVE ANNUAL RATE (EAR)   To incorporate the compounding effect, the

effective annual rate (EAR) A formula that calculates the effective return, taking compounding into account.

effective annual rate (EAR) formula is used. Using the notation that m is the number of periods in a year and k is the rate of return quoted for the year,

$$EAR = \left[1 + \frac{k}{m}\right]^m - 1$$

Where: m = number of compounding periods in a year
k = rate of return quoted for a year.

Exhibit 4–7

Compounding Frequency Increases the Savings Yield

Shorter compounding periods result in higher yields. This chart shows the growth of $10,000, five-year GICs paying the same nominal rate of 4 percent, but with different compounding methods.

| End of Year | Compounding Method | | | |
	Daily	Monthly	Quarterly	Annually
1	$10,408.08	$10,407.42	$10,406.04	$10,400.00
2	10,832.82	10,831.43	10,828.57	10,816.00
3	11,274.89	11,272.72	11,268.25	11,248.64
4	11,735.01	11,731.99	11,725.79	11,698.59
5	12,213.89	12,209.97	12,201.90	12,166.53
Effective rate	4.08%	4.07%	4.06%	4.00%

It is important to note the effects of compounding. Imagine a simple case where you pay interest on a $100 loan at 6 percent yearly, compounded monthly. Not accounting for the compounding effect will lead you to conclude that you are paying 6 percent, or $6 per year in interest charges.

The reality is that you are paying more. Using the EAR formula, which allows for compounding, shows that you will actually pay 6.17 percent, or $6.17. EAR can also be calculated with a financial calculator; see Appendix 1B for examples.

INFLATION

The rate of return you earn on your savings should be compared with the inflation rate. When the inflation rate was more than 10 percent, people with money in savings accounts earning 5 or 6 percent were experiencing a real loss in the buying power of that money. The increase (or loss) in purchasing power of an investment is reflected in its *real* rate of return. We can approximate the real rate of return by subtracting the inflation rate from an investment's effective rate of return for the same period. For example, if a deposit pays 6 percent, compounded semi-annually, we have demonstrated that its effective annual interest rate is 6.09 percent, calculated as $(1 + 0.06 \div 2)^2 - 1$. If inflation over the same year were 3 percent, the investment's real rate of return would be approximately 3.09 percent (6.09 percent $-$ 3 percent). In general, as the inflation rate increases, the interest rates offered to savers must also increase to maintain the real rate of return.

TAX CONSIDERATIONS

Like inflation, taxes reduce interest earned on savings. For example, a 10 percent return for a saver in a 26 percent tax bracket means an after-tax return of 7.4 percent (the Financial Planning Calculations feature on the next page shows how to compute the after-tax savings rate of return). As discussed in Chapter 3 and discussed further in Part 4, several tax-exempt and tax-deferred savings plans and investments can increase your real rate of return.

LIQUIDITY

Liquidity refers to the ease with which you can access cash or convert investments to cash with a minimal loss of principal. Some savings plans impose penalties for early withdrawal or have other restrictions. With certain types of savings certificates and accounts, early withdrawal may be penalized by a loss of interest or a lower earnings rate.

You should consider the degree of liquidity you desire in relation to your savings goals. To achieve long-term financial goals, many people trade off liquidity for a higher return.

SAFETY

Most savings plans at banks, trust companies, and credit unions or caisses populaires are insured by agencies affiliated with the federal government. This protection prevents loss of money due to the failure of the insured institution.

The CDIC protects eligible deposits up to a maximum of $100,000 per person, including principal and interest, for each different member institution involved. Eligible deposits include savings and chequing accounts, term deposits, GICs, debentures, and other obligations issued by institutions that are members of the CDIC.

In the event that a member institution becomes insolvent, your insured funds are secure up to $100,000. In the case of a joint deposit, the funds insured will be $100,000 divided among all the names in the account.

Be aware that deposits in different branches of the same institution are counted as a single account and are insured only to $100,000. If you have more than this amount to deposit, it is wise to spread your money among different members of the CDIC, although chartered banks

The taxability of interest on your savings reduces your after-tax rate of return. In other words, you lose some portion of your interest to taxes. This calculation consists of the following steps:

1. Determine your top tax bracket for federal income taxes.
2. Subtract this rate, expressed as a decimal, from 1.0.
3. Multiply the result by the yield on your savings account.
4. The result, expressed as a percentage, is your after-tax rate of return.

For example,

1. You are in the 26 percent tax bracket (federally).
2. $1.0 - 0.26 = 0.74$.
3. If the yield on your savings account is 6.25 percent, $0.0625 \times 0.74 = 0.046$.
4. Your after-tax rate of return is 4.6 percent.

But what if inflation over the same period is 3 percent? What is your real, after-tax rate of return? It is approximately 4.6 percent less 3 percent, or only 1.6 percent!

offer a variety of products that may be insured separately. To find out more about eligible deposits and an updated list of member institutions, visit the CDIC Web site at cdic.ca.

Since not all financial institutions have federal deposit insurance, investigate this matter when you are selecting a savings plan.

RESTRICTIONS AND FEES

Other limitations can affect your choice of a savings program. For example, there may be a delay between the time interest is earned and the time it is added to your account. This means it will not be available for your immediate use. Also, some institutions charge a transaction fee for each deposit or withdrawal and pay interest only if you maintain a minimum monthly balance.

In the past, some financial institutions had promotions offering a "free gift" when a certain savings amount was deposited. To receive this gift, you had to leave your money on deposit for a certain time period or you may have received less interest, since some of the earnings were used to cover the cost of the "free" items. Economists tell us that "there is no such thing as a free lunch." The same holds true for toasters and television sets.

CONCEPT CHECK 4–4

1. When would you prefer a savings plan with high liquidity over one with a high rate of return?
2. What is the relationship between compounding and the future value of an amount?
3. How do inflation and taxes affect earnings on savings?

SELECTING PAYMENT METHODS

LO5

Compare the costs and benefits of different types of chequing accounts.

Although the use of physical cheques is declining as electronic payment methods gain in popularity, a chequing account is still a necessity for most people.

TYPES OF CHEQUING ACCOUNTS

Chequing accounts fall into three major categories: regular chequing accounts, activity accounts, and interest-earning chequing accounts.

REGULAR CHEQUING ACCOUNTS   usually have a monthly service charge that you may avoid by keeping a minimum balance in the account. Some financial institutions will waive the monthly fee if you keep a certain amount in savings. Avoiding the monthly service charge is beneficial. For example, a monthly fee of $7.50 results in $90 a year. However, you lose interest on the minimum-balance amount in a non–interest-earning account.

ACTIVITY ACCOUNTS   charge a fee for each cheque written or electronic payment processed and sometimes a fee for each deposit, in addition to a monthly service charge. However, you do not have to maintain a minimum balance. An activity account is most appropriate for people who write only a few cheques or electronic payments each month and are unable to maintain the required minimum balance.

INTEREST-EARNING CHEQUING ACCOUNTS   usually require a minimum balance. If the account balance goes below this amount, you may not earn interest and will likely incur a service charge.

EVALUATING CHEQUING ACCOUNTS

Would you rather have a chequing account that pays interest and requires a $1,000 minimum balance or an account that doesn't pay interest and requires a $300 minimum balance? This decision requires evaluating such factors as restrictions, fees and charges, interest, and special services (see Exhibit 4–8).

RESTRICTIONS   The most common limitation on chequing accounts is the amount you must keep on deposit to earn interest or avoid a service charge.

Did you know?

Non-sufficient funds (NSF) cheques mean big money for the banking industry. Every year, banks make billion-dollar profits from bounced-cheque fees. Studies show that some institutions charge up to 32 times what it actually costs them to process a cheque that is issued with insufficient funds.

Exhibit 4–8

Chequing Account Selection Factors

CHEQUING ACCOUNT SELECTION FACTORS

Restrictions	Fees and Charges
• Minimum balance	• Monthly fee
• Deposit insurance	• Fees for each cheque or deposit
• Hours and location of branch offices	• Printing of cheques
• Holding period for deposited cheques	• Fee to obtain cancelled cheque copy
	• Overdraft, stop-payment order, certified cheque fee
	• Fees for preauthorized bill payment, fund transfer, or home banking activity

Special Services	Interest
• Direct deposit of payroll and government cheques	• Interest rate
• Automated teller machines	• Minimum deposit to earn interest
• Overdraft protection	• Method of compounding
• Banking-at-home	• Portion of balance used to compute interest
• Discounts or free chequing for certain groups (students, senior citizens, employees of certain companies)	• Fee charged for falling below necessary balance to earn interest
• Free or discounted services, such as traveller's cheques	

FEES AND CHARGES   Nearly all financial institutions require a minimum balance or impose service charges for chequing accounts. When using an interest-bearing chequing account, compare your earnings with any service charge or fee. Also, consider the cost of lost or reduced interest due to the need to maintain the minimum balance.

Chequing account fees have increased in recent years. Such items as cheque printing, overdraft fees, and stop-payment orders have doubled or tripled in price at some financial institutions. Some institutions will try to entice you with fancy cheques at a low price and then charge a much higher price when you reorder. You may be able to purchase cheques at a lower cost from a mail-order company that advertises in magazines or the Sunday newspaper.

INTEREST   As discussed earlier, the interest rate, the frequency of compounding, and the interest computation method affect the earnings on your chequing account.

SPECIAL SERVICES   Financial institutions commonly offer chequing account customers services such as 24-hour ATM and home banking services. Financial institutions are also attempting to reduce the paper and postage costs associated with chequing accounts. One solution is to not return cancelled cheques to customers. The financial institution then uses microfilm to store cheques and provides customers with detailed statements summarizing the cheques written. If a customer requests a copy of a cancelled cheque, the institution reproduces the copy from its microfilm file for a fee.

overdraft protection
An automatic loan made to chequing account customers to cover the amount of cheques written in excess of the available balance in the account.

Overdraft protection is an automatic loan made to chequing account customers for cheques written in excess of the available balance. This service is convenient but costly. Most overdraft plans make loans based on $50 or $100 increments. An overdraft of just $1 might trigger a $50 loan and corresponding finance charges of perhaps 18 percent or some minimum fee such as $5 per overdraft. But overdraft protection can be less costly than the fee charged for a cheque you write when you do not have enough money on deposit to cover it. That fee may be $20 or more. Many financial institutions allow you to cover chequing account overdrafts with an automatic transfer from a savings account for a nominal fee.

Beware of chequing accounts that offer several services (safety deposit box, traveller's cheques, low-rate loans, and travel insurance) for a single monthly fee. This may sound like a good value; however, financial experts observe that such accounts benefit only a small group of people who make constant use of the services offered.

The Financial Planning Calculations box on page 136 offers a method for comparing the costs of various types of chequing accounts.

OTHER PAYMENT METHODS

In addition to personal cheques, other forms of payment are also available. A *certified cheque* is a personal cheque with guaranteed payment. The amount of the cheque is deducted from your balance when the financial institution certifies the cheque. You may purchase a *money order* in a similar manner from financial institutions, post offices, and stores. Certified cheques, cashier's cheques, and money orders allow you to make a payment that the recipient knows is valid.

Traveller's cheques allow you to make payments when you are away from home. This payment form requires you to sign each cheque twice. First, you sign the traveller's cheques when you purchase them. Then, to identify you as the authorized person, you sign them again as you cash them.

Prepaid travel cards are becoming more common. The card allows travellers visiting other nations to get local currency from an ATM.

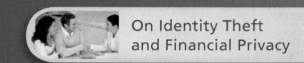
People who put their social insurance and driver's licence numbers on their cheques are making identity theft fairly easy, according to the pros. With one cheque, a con artist knows your social insurance, driver's licence, and bank account numbers as well as your address, phone number, and even has a sample of your signature.

Identity fraud ranges from passing bad cheques and using stolen credit cards to theft of another person's total financial existence. While situations as portrayed in the movie *The Net* are rare, people need to be aware that they can easily become a victim.

Pros also suggest that you not mail your bills from your home mailbox, especially if the box is out by the street. This gives a potential scam artist easy access to a variety of financial and personal information.

The ease of obtaining social insurance numbers and more than three billion credit solicitations a year make identity theft a fairly simple scam. Each day, more than a thousand people have their identities stolen by a con artist applying for credit in the victim's name. After obtaining a loan or racking up credit card charges, the thief disappears, leaving a ruined credit rating that may take years to correct.

Banks and other financial institutions work to protect the identities and privacy of their depositors. The pros remind bank customers that the slight inconvenience of being asked for identification or having an account balance checked protects you and others from financial losses.

Other recommendations to protect yourself from identity fraud include the following:

- Shred or burn financial information containing account or social insurance numbers.
- Use passwords other than maiden names.
- Don't put your social insurance number on any document unless it is legally required.
- Check your credit report once or twice a year to make sure it is correct.
- Have your name removed from mailing lists operated by credit agencies and companies offering credit promotions.
- If you become a victim, notify the credit card company and other businesses with specific details. Also, file a police report to provide documentation of the scam.

You can find out more about financial privacy and identity theft online. Industry Canada's Consumer Measures Committee Internet site (cmcweb.ic.gc.ca) offers access to innovative products and to consumer information on a range of topics.

The Canadian Bankers Association describes, step by step, how to protect yourself against identify theft, at cba.ca/en/consumer-information/42-safeguarding-your-money.

The Public Interest Advocacy Centre (PIAC) provides legal and research services on behalf of consumer interests concerning the provision of public services, especially telecommunications, broadcasting, energy, and banking, and with regard to privacy and competition. Access its Web site at piac.ca.

CONCEPT CHECK 4–5

1. What factors are commonly considered when selecting a chequing account?
2. Are chequing accounts that earn interest preferable to regular chequing accounts? Why, or why not?

Financial Planning Calculations

Comparing interest earned and service charges and fees for chequing accounts can be confusing. To assist with this analysis, use the following calculation.

Remember: Not all items listed here will apply to every type of chequing account.

Inflows
Step 1.
Multiply average monthly balance $ _____ by average rate of return _____ percent to determine annual earnings
Total estimated annual inflow $ _____

Outflows	
Step 2.	
Monthly service charge $ _____ × 12	$ _____
Average number of cheques written per month _____ × charge per cheque × 12	$ _____
Average number of deposits per month _____ × charge per deposit × 12	$ _____
Fee for dropping below minimum balance $ _____ × number of times below minimum	$ _____
Lost interest: Opportunity cost _____ percent × required minimum balance $ _____	$ _____
Total estimated annual outflow	$ _____

Step 3.		
Estimated annual inflows less annual outflows =		
	+ Net earnings for account (Step 1)	$ _____
	− Net cost for account (Step 2)	$ _____
		+/− $ _____

NOTE: This calculation does not take into account charges and fees for such services as overdrafts, stop-payments, ATM use, and cheque printing. Be sure to consider these costs when selecting a chequing account.

SUMMARY OF LEARNING OBJECTIVES

LO1 **Analyze factors that affect selection and use of financial services.**

Financial products such as savings plans, chequing accounts, loans, and trust services are used for managing daily financial activities. Technology, opportunity costs, and economic conditions affect the selection and use of financial services.

LO2 **Compare the types of financial institutions.**

Chartered banks, trust companies, credit unions and caisses populaires, life insurance companies, investment companies, mortgage and loan companies, finance and leasing companies, pawnshops, and cheque-cashing outlets may be compared on the basis of services offered, rates and fees, safety, convenience, and special programs available to customers.

LO3 **Compare the costs and benefits of various savings plans.**

Commonly used savings plans include regular savings accounts, term deposits and Guaranteed Investment Certificates, interest-earning chequing accounts, and Canada Savings Bonds.

LO4 **Identify the factors used to evaluate different savings plans.**

Savings plans may be evaluated on the basis of rate of return, inflation, tax considerations, liquidity, safety, and restrictions and fees.

LO5 **Compare the costs and benefits of different types of chequing accounts.**

Regular chequing accounts, activity accounts, and interest-earning chequing accounts can be compared with regard to restrictions (such as a minimum balance), fees and charges, interest, and special services.

KEY TERMS

automated teller machine (ATM) 119

chartered bank 123

credit union/caisse populaire 123

effective annual rate (EAR) 130

Guaranteed Investment Certificates (GICs) 129

money market fund 123

overdraft protection 134

rate of return 130

term deposit 129

trust 118

KEY FORMULAS

Page	Topic	Formula
130	Effective annual rate (EAR)	$\text{EAR} = \left[1 + \dfrac{k}{m}\right]^{m} - 1$ m = the number of compounding periods in a year k = the rate of return quoted for a year
132	After-tax rate of return	Interest rate $\times$ (1 − Tax rate)

FINANCIAL PLANNING PROBLEMS

connect Practise and learn online with Connect.

1. *Determining Savings Goals.* What are common savings goals for a person who buys a five-year GIC paying 4.75 percent instead of an 18-month savings certificate paying 3.5 percent? *LO4*

2. *Evaluating a Savings Plan.* Compute the earnings for the year, for a $15,000 savings account that earns 12 percent compounded (a) annually, (b) quarterly, (c) monthly, and (d) daily. *LO4*

3. *Computing Future Value.* What is the value of a savings account started with $500, earning 3 percent (compounded annually) after 10 years? *LO5*

4. *Calculating Present Value.* Brenda Young wants to have $10,000 eight years from now for her daughter's college fund. If she earns 7 percent (compounded annually) on her money, what amount should she deposit now? Use the present value of a single amount calculation. *LO5*

5. *Computing Future Value of Annual Deposits.* What amount would you have if you deposited $1,500 a year for 30 years at 8 percent (compounded annually)? (Use Appendix 1B.) *LO5*

6. *Comparing Taxable and Tax-Free Yields.* With a 26 percent marginal tax rate, would a tax-free yield of 7 percent or a taxable yield of 9.5 percent give you a better return on your savings? Why? *LO5*

7. *Calculating Opportunity Cost.* What is the annual opportunity cost of a chequing account that requires a $350 minimum balance to avoid service charges? Assume an interest rate of 6.5 percent. *LO5*

8. *Comparing Costs of Chequing Accounts.* What is the net annual cost of the following chequing accounts? *LO5*
   a. Monthly fee, $3.75; processing fee, 25 cents per cheque; cheques written, an average of 22 a month.
   b. Interest earnings of 6 percent with a $500 minimum balance; average monthly balance, $600; monthly service charge of $15 for falling below the minimum balance, which occurs three times a year (no interest earned in these months).

9. *Reconciling Your Chequing Account.* Based on the following information, determine the true balance in your chequing account. (Use Appendix 4.)

   Balance in your chequebook, $356
   Balance on bank statement, $472
   Service charge and other fees, $15
   Interest earned on the account, $4
   Total of outstanding cheques, $187
   Deposits in transit, $60

FINANCIAL PLANNING ACTIVITIES

1. *Researching Financial Services.* Using Web sites or library resources, obtain information about new developments in financial services. How have technology, changing economic conditions, and new legislation affected the types and availability of various saving and chequing financial services? *LO1*

2. *Monitoring Economic Conditions.* Research current economic conditions (interest rates, inflation) using *The Financial Post*, other library resources, or Web sites. Based on current economic conditions, what actions would you recommend to people who are saving and borrowing money? *LO1*

3. *Comparing Financial Institutions.* Collect advertisements and promotional information from several financial institutions, or go to financial institution Web sites, such as Bank of Montreal (bmo.com) and TD Canada Trust (tdcanadatrust.com). Create a list of factors that you might consider when comparing costs and benefits of various savings plans and chequing accounts. *LO2*

4. *Obtaining Opinions about Financial Services.* Survey several people to determine awareness and use of various financial services, such as online banking, "smart cards," and cheque-writing software. *LO2*

5. *Researching Credit Unions.* Using the Web site for the Credit Union Central of Canada (cucentral.ca) or other sources, obtain information about joining a credit union and the services this type of financial institution offers. *LO2*

6. *Comparing Savings Plans.* Collect advertisements from several financial institutions with information about the savings plans they offer. (You may do this using the Web sites of various financial institutions.) Compare the features and potential earnings of two or three savings plans. *LO3, LO4*

7. *Researching Current Savings Rates.* Using library resources (such as *The Financial Post* and other current business periodicals) or Web sites (such as money.canoe.ca), prepare a summary of current rates of return for various savings accounts, money market accounts, GICs, and CSBs. *LO3, LO4*

8. *Analyzing Cheque-Writing Software.* Visit software retailers to obtain information about the features in various personal computer programs used for maintaining a chequing account. Information about such programs as Managing Your Money, Microsoft Money, and Quicken may be obtained on the Internet. *LO5*

LIFE SITUATION CASE 1

Checking Out Financial Services

Carla and Ed Johnson have separate chequing accounts. Each pays part of the household and living expenses. Carla pays the mortgage and telephone bill, while Ed pays for food and utilities and makes the insurance and car payments. This arrangement allows them the freedom to spend whatever extra money they have each month without needing to explain their actions to each other. Carla and Ed believe their separate accounts have minimized disagreements about money. Since both spend most of their money each month, they have low balances in their chequing accounts, resulting in a monthly charge totalling $15.

In the same financial institution where Carla has her chequing account, the Johnsons have $600 in a passbook savings account that earns 2.2 percent interest. If the savings account balance exceeded $1,000, they would earn 3.15 percent. If the balance stayed above $1,000, they would not have to pay the monthly service charge on Carla's chequing account. The financial institution has a program that moves money from chequing to savings. This program would allow the Johnsons to increase their savings and work toward a secure financial future.

Ed has his chequing account at a bank that offers an electronic banking system, allowing customers to obtain cash at many locations 24 hours a day. Ed believes this feature is valuable when cash is needed to cover business expenses and

personal spending. For an additional monthly fee, the bank would also provide Ed with a credit card, a safety deposit box, and a single monthly statement summarizing all transactions.

While most people plan their spending for living expenses, few plan their use of financial services. Therefore, many people are charged high fees for chequing accounts and earn low interest on their savings. Despite a wide choice of financial institutions and services, you can learn to compare their costs and benefits. Your awareness of financial services and your ability to evaluate them are vital skills for a healthy personal economic future.

Questions

1. Which financial services are most important to Carla and Ed Johnson?

2. What efforts are the Johnsons currently making to assess their use of financial services in relation to their other financial activities?

3. How should the Johnsons assess their needs for financial services? On what basis should they compare financial services?

4. What should the Johnsons do to improve their use of financial services?

LIFE SITUATION CASE 2

Selecting Online Financial Services

Each month, Margo Bostrom becomes more frustrated with the fees she pays for financial services. Recently, her chequing account and ATM fees were over $15 a month. In addition, Margo is frustrated by the lower quality of customer service.

Margo is considering a Web-only bank that offers continuous access to account information along with electronic bill-paying service. She would earn 6 percent interest on funds in her chequing account, which is about three times higher than what she currently earns. But since the Web-only bank doesn't have its own ATMs, she could incur significant fees when obtaining cash. On the positive side, she would have access to low-cost, online investment trading.

The Web-only bank requires direct deposit of paycheques. Cash deposits would have to be handled through an ATM or through an electronic transfer at a traditional bank.

Margo's current bank is expanding its services to include 24-hour access to account balances and electronic bill paying through its Web site. This added service might entice her to continue doing business with the bank. She is also concerned about deposit insurance with the Web-only bank.

Questions

1. What factors should Margo consider when comparing a Web-only bank and online banking with her current financial institution?

2. Locate Web sites that Margo might use while considering online banking.

3. What actions would you recommend for Margo?

Using a Chequing Account

OPENING A CHEQUING ACCOUNT

Deciding who the owner of the account will be is your starting point for opening a chequing account. Only one person is allowed to write cheques on an *individual account*. A *joint account* has two or more owners, with any authorized person allowed to write cheques if it is specified as an "or" account. In contrast, an "and" account with two owners requires the signatures of both owners on cheques. This arrangement is commonly used by businesses and other organizations.

Both an individual account and a joint account require a signature card. This document is a record of the official signatures of the person or persons authorized to write cheques on the account.

MAKING DEPOSITS

A *deposit form* is used for adding money to your chequing account (see Exhibit 4–A). On this document, you list the amounts of the cash and cheques being deposited. Each cheque you deposit requires an *endorsement*—your signature on the back of the cheque—to authorize the transfer of the funds into your account. The following are three common endorsement forms:

- A *blank endorsement* is your signature. Use this endorsement form only when you are actually depositing or cashing a cheque, since a cheque could be cashed by anyone once its back has been signed.
- A *restrictive endorsement* consists of the words *for deposit only*, followed by your signature. This endorsement form is especially useful when you are depositing cheques by mail.
- A *special endorsement* allows you to transfer a cheque to an organization or another person. On this endorsement form, the words *pay to the order of* are followed by the name of the organization or person and then by your signature.

WRITING CHEQUES

Before writing a cheque, record the information in your cheque register and deduct the amount of the cheque from your balance; otherwise, you will think you have more money available than you really do. Many chequing account customers use duplicate cheques to maintain a record of their current balance.

Exhibit 4–A

Deposit Slip

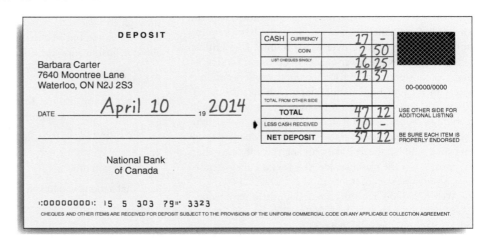

The procedure for proper cheque writing, displayed in Exhibit 4–B, consists of the following steps:

1. Record the current date.
2. Write the name of the person or organization receiving the payment.
3. Record the amount of the cheque in figures.
4. Write the amount of the cheque in words; cheques for less than a dollar should be written as "only 79 cents," for example, with the word *dollars* on the cheque crossed out.
5. Sign the cheque in the same way you signed the signature card when you opened your account.
6. Make a note of the reason for payment to assist with budget and tax preparation.

Cheque-writing software is available as a separate program or as part of a financial planning package, such as Quicken (quicken.intuit.ca). These programs can easily prepare cheques while maintaining your financial records, such as the cheque register, personal financial statements, and a budget.

A *stop-payment order* may be necessary if a cheque is lost or stolen or if a business transaction was not completed in a satisfactory manner. The fee for a stop-payment commonly ranges from $0 to $20. If several cheques are missing or you lose your chequebook, the bank may suggest closing that account and opening a new one. This action is likely to be less costly than paying several stop-payment fees.

MAINTAINING A CHEQUING ACCOUNT

Each month you can receive a *bank statement*, a summary of the transactions for a chequing account. This document reports deposits made, cheques paid, interest earned, and fees for such items as service charges and printing of cheques. The balance reported on the bank statement probably will differ from the balance in your chequebook. Reasons for a difference are cheques that you have written but have not yet cleared, deposits you have made since the bank statement was prepared, interest added to your account, and deductions for fees and charges.

To determine your true balance, you should prepare a *bank reconciliation*. This report accounts for differences between the bank statement and your chequebook balance. The steps you take in this process, shown in the Financial Planning Calculations box on page 142, are as follows:

1. Compare the cheques you wrote over the past month with those reported as paid on your bank statement. Use the cancelled cheques from the financial institution, or compare your cheque register with the cheque numbers reported on the bank statement (many financial institutions no longer return cancelled cheques to customers). *Subtract* from the *bank statement balance* the total of the cheques written but not yet cleared.

Exhibit 4–B

A Personal Cheque

Financial Planning Calculations

The process of comparing your chequebook balance to the bank statement is vital for determining any errors that may have occurred. Use the following steps to reconcile your account:

The Bank Statement		
Balance on current bank statement	$	643.96

Step 1.

	Date	Amount
Add up outstanding cheques (cheques that you have written but have not yet cleared the banking system) and withdrawals still outstanding.	10-4	70.00
	10-6	130.00
	10-7	111.62
Subtract the total.	$	−311.62

Step 2.

	Date	Amount
Add up deposits in transit (deposits that have been made but are not reported on the current statement).	10-2	60.00
	10-5	90.00
Add the total.	$	+150.00
Adjusted bank balance	$	482.34

Your Chequebook		
Current balance in your chequebook	$	295.91

Step 3.

Subtract total of fees or other charges listed on bank statement.	$	−15.75
Subtract ATM withdrawals.	$	−100.00

Step 4.

Add interest earned.	$	+2.18
Add direct deposits.	$	+300.00
Adjusted chequebook balance	$	482.34

2. Determine whether any recent deposits are not on the bank statement. If so, *add* the amount of the outstanding deposits to the *bank statement balance*.
3. *Subtract* any fees or charges on the bank statement and ATM withdrawals from your *chequebook balance*.
4. *Add* any interest earned to your *chequebook balance*.

At this point, the revised balances for both your chequebook and the bank statement should be the same. If the two do not match, check your math, making sure every cheque and deposit was recorded correctly in your chequebook and on the bank statement.

Many people do not take the time to reconcile their accounts; however, failure to do this could cost you money. If the bank subtracts more for a cheque than the amount for which you wrote it and you don't complain within a year, the bank may not be liable for correcting the error.

chapter 5

Introduction to Consumer Credit

LEARNING OBJECTIVES

LO1 Define consumer credit and analyze its advantages and disadvantages.

LO2 Differentiate among various types of credit.

LO3 Assess your credit capacity and build your credit rating.

LO4 Describe the information creditors look for when you apply for credit.

LO5 Identify the steps you can take to avoid and correct credit mistakes.

A RISING HOUSE OF CARDS? POORER BORROWERS USE MORE PLASTIC

The strong economy of the mid-2000s was, for the most part, a result of the significant availability of credit. However, mid-2007 marked the beginning of a downturn. The "Great Recession" was different from those in the past; it was primarily driven by a "credit-crunch" that saw most banks and financial institutions drastically reduce the amount of credit available to consumers and businesses. The recession resulted in increases in both personal and corporate bankruptcies and even resulted in some governments declaring bankruptcy. The U.S. Financial Crisis Inquiry Commission determined that the financial crisis that led to the Great Recession "was avoidable and was caused by: Widespread failures in financial regulation; dramatic breakdowns in corporate governance including too many financial firms acting recklessly and taking on too much risk; an explosive mix of excessive borrowing and risk by households and Wall Street that put the financial system on a collision course with crisis; key policy makers ill prepared for the crisis, lacking a full understanding of the financial system they oversaw; and systemic breaches in accountability and ethics at all levels."

As noted, one cause of the Great Recession was excessive household debt. Recent trend analyses have shown that as credit card debt has risen, a new class of borrowers has come to the fore. The growing use and convenience of credit cards has facilitated the process of borrowing, and even those who can't really afford to borrow still do. Where at one time credit cards might have been reserved for those with the capacity to handle credit appropriately, they are now available to all.

Recent studies have shown that as ownership of cards has risen, the proportion of cards held by people with lower incomes has gone up. In addition, debt due to credit cards has also increased over the years.

According to Bankruptcy Canada (bankruptcy-canada.ca), personal debt is the ticking time bomb. The reason is rooted in a more than 100 percent increase in the amount of household debt compared to levels a decade ago. Some consumers are heading for the precipice, perhaps without realizing how close the danger actually is or how sharp the drop might be.

Poorer, riskier borrowers joined the credit card ranks in the 1990s and were approved for mortgages throughout the mid-2000s and apparently took on a lot of debt in the process. This group, which includes both white and blue collar workers, is highly vulnerable to even a modest cyclical slowdown or change in interest rates.

QUESTIONS

1. Why are today's consumers spending and borrowing heavily?
2. Why do some experts suggest that a new class of borrowers may be especially at risk if economic growth slows down?

WHAT IS CONSUMER CREDIT?

LO1

Define consumer credit and analyze its advantages and disadvantages.

credit An arrangement to receive cash, goods, or services now and pay for them in the future.

consumer credit The use of credit for personal needs (except a home mortgage).

"Charge it!" "Cash or credit?" "Put it on my account." As these phrases indicate, the use of credit is a fact of life in personal and family financial planning. When you use credit, you satisfy needs today and pay for this satisfaction in the future. While the use of credit is often necessary and even advantageous, responsibilities and disadvantages are associated with its use.

Credit is an arrangement to receive cash, goods, or services now and pay for them in the future. **Consumer credit** refers to the use of credit for personal needs (except a home mortgage) by individuals and families, in contrast to credit used for business purposes.

Although Polonius, in Shakespeare's *Hamlet* cautioned, "Neither a borrower nor a lender be," using and providing credit have become a way of life for many people and businesses in today's economy. In January, you pay a bill for electricity that you used in December. You write a cheque for $120, a minimum payment on a $1,400 credit card bill. With a bank loan, you purchase a new car. These are all examples of using credit: paying later for goods and services obtained now.

Most consumers have three alternatives in financing current purchases: they can draw on their savings, use their present earnings, or borrow against their expected future income. Each of these alternatives has trade-offs. If you continually deplete your savings, little will be left for emergencies or retirement income. If you spend your current income on luxuries instead of necessities, your well-being will eventually suffer. And if you pledge your future income to make current credit purchases, you will have little or no spendable income in the future.

Consumer credit is based on trust in people's ability and willingness to pay bills when due. It works because people, by and large, are honest and responsible. But how does consumer credit affect our economy, and how is it affected by our economy?

CONSUMER CREDIT IN OUR ECONOMY

Consumer credit dates back to colonial times. While credit was originally a privilege of the affluent, farmers came to use it extensively. No direct finance charges were imposed; instead, the cost of credit was added to the prices of goods. With the advent of the automobile in the early 1900s, instalment credit, in which the debt is repaid in equal instalments over a specified period of time, exploded on the North American scene.

All economists now recognize consumer credit as a major force in the North American economy. Any forecast or evaluation of the economy includes consumer spending trends and consumer credit as a sustaining force. To paraphrase an old political expression, as the consumer goes, so goes the economy.

The aging of the baby boom generation has added to the growth of consumer credit. This generation currently represents almost 30 percent of the population but holds nearly 60 percent of the outstanding debt. The people in this age group have always been disproportionate users of credit, since consumption is highest as families are formed and homes are purchased and furnished. Thus, while the extensive use of debt by this generation is nothing new, the fact that it has grown rapidly has added to overall debt use.

USES AND MISUSES OF CREDIT

Using credit to purchase goods and services may allow consumers to be more efficient or more productive or to lead more satisfying lives. There are many valid reasons for using credit. A medical emergency may leave a person strapped for funds. A homemaker returning to the workforce may need a car. It may be possible to buy an item now for less money than it will cost later. Borrowing for a higher education is another valid reason. But it probably is not reasonable to borrow for everyday living expenses or to finance a Corvette on credit when a Ford Escort is all your budget allows.

"Shopaholics" and young adults are most vulnerable to misusing credit. Post-secondary students are a prime target for credit card issuers, and issuers make it easy for students to get credit cards. Tanya Svetlana, a 25-year-old teacher in Victoria, knows this all too well. As a university first-year student, she applied for and got seven credit cards, all bearing at least an 18.9 percent interest rate and a $20 annual fee. Although unemployed, she used the cards freely, buying expensive clothes for herself, extravagant presents for friends and family, and even a one-week vacation in the Bahamas. "It got to a point where I didn't even look at the price tag," she said. By her senior year, Tanya had amassed $9,000 in credit card debt and couldn't make the monthly payments of nearly $200. She eventually turned to her parents to bail her out. "Until my mother sat me down and showed me how much interest I had to pay, I hadn't even given it a thought. I was shocked," Tanya said. "I would have had to pay it off for years."

Using credit increases the amount of money a person can spend to purchase goods and services now. But the trade-off is that it decreases the amount of money that will be available to spend in the future. However, many people expect their incomes to increase and therefore expect to be able to make payments on past credit purchases and still make new purchases.

Here are some questions you should consider before you decide how and when to make a major purchase, for example, a car:

- Do I have the cash I need for the down payment?
- Do I want to use my savings for this purchase?
- Does the purchase fit my budget?
- Could I use the credit I need for this purchase in some better way?
- Could I postpone the purchase?
- What are the opportunity costs of postponing the purchase? (Alternative transportation costs, a possible increase in the price of the car.)
- What are the dollar costs and the psychological costs of using credit? (Interest, other finance charges, being in debt and responsible for making a monthly payment.)

If you decide to use credit, make sure the benefits of making the purchase now (increased efficiency or productivity, a more satisfying life, etc.) outweigh the costs (financial and psychological) of using credit. Thus, credit, when effectively used, can help you have more and enjoy more. When misused, credit can result in default, bankruptcy, and loss of creditworthiness.

ADVANTAGES OF CREDIT

Consumer credit enables people to enjoy goods and services now—a car, a home, an education, help in emergencies—and pay for them through payment plans based on future income.

Credit cards permit you to purchase goods even when funds are low. Customers with previously approved credit may receive other extras, such as advance notice of sales and the right to order by phone or to buy on approval. In addition, many shoppers believe it is easier to return merchandise they have purchased on account. Credit cards also provide shopping convenience and the efficiency of paying for several purchases with one monthly payment.

> *Did you know?*
>
> The Canadian household debt to disposable income (income after taxes, EI contributions, etc.) ratio reached the highest on record for Q3 2013 at 164.2 percent, which is a 10.9 percent increase over the previous year. This level of debt continues to exceed the level of U.S. household debt.
>
> SOURCE: http://www.bnn.ca/News/2014/3/14/Household-debt-to-income-ratio-slips-from-record-high.aspx.

Credit is more than a substitute for cash. Many of the services it provides are taken for granted. Every time you flick the light switch or telephone a friend, you are using credit.

It is safer to use credit, since charge accounts and credit cards let you shop and travel without carrying a large amount of cash. You need a credit card to make a hotel reservation, rent a car, and shop by phone. You may also use credit cards for identification when cashing cheques, and using credit provides you with a record of expenses.

Using credit cards can provide up to a 30-day "float," the time lag between when you make the purchase and when the lender deducts the balance from your chequing account when the payment is due. This float, offered by many credit card issuers, includes a grace period of 21 to 30 days. During the grace period, no finance charges are assessed on current purchases if the balance is paid in full each month.

Some large corporations, such as WestJet and Canadian Tire, issue either co-branded (also known as affinity or value-added) cards or their own Visa or MasterCard and offer rebates on purchases. For example, shopping with a WestJet RBC Mastercard allows you to earn 1.0 to 1.5 percent of every purchase to be applied to future flights or vacation packages booked through WestJet. A Canadian Tire Options MasterCard allows you to earn 20 percent more Canadian Tire money per dollar spent at Canadian Tire, and 1 percent earned per dollar spent outside of Canadian Tire. Points can be redeemed instantly at the point of sale in Canadian Tire on all merchandise in the store. Similarly, a CIBC, TD, or American Express Aeroplan Miles card lets you earn Aeroplan miles with each and every purchase.

Platinum credit cards offered by American Express provide emergency medical evacuation for travellers. In 1994, Nathan Aman of Winnipeg was vacationing in a tiny, isolated town in Brazil. He ate something that made him gravely ill. With no doctor nearby, a friend frantically called Aman's credit card company about its guarantee to arrange emergency medical evacuation and treatment for card users. The company moved fast: It lined up a car to rush Aman to the nearest large town, managed to book a room in a sold-out hotel, and sent a doctor there to make a house call. The physician even accompanied Aman's travel partner, Carlos Piet, to a local pharmacy for medicine. "When we went home to see our doctor, he told us she had saved Nathan's life," recalls Piet. "For the last five years we have been indebted to the company."

Finally, credit indicates stability. The fact that lenders consider you a good risk usually means you are a responsible individual. However, if you do not repay your debts in a timely manner, you will find that credit has many disadvantages.

DISADVANTAGES OF CREDIT

Perhaps the greatest disadvantage of using credit is the temptation to overspend, especially during periods of inflation. It seems easy to buy today and pay tomorrow using cheaper dollars. But continual overspending can lead to serious trouble.

Whether or not credit involves security (something of value to back the loan), failure to repay a loan may result in loss of income, valuable property, and your good reputation. It can even lead to court action and bankruptcy. Misusing credit can create serious long-term financial problems, damage to family relationships, and a slowing of progress toward financial goals. Therefore, you should approach credit with caution and avoid using it more extensively than your budget permits.

Although credit allows more immediate satisfaction of needs and desires, it does not increase total purchasing power. Credit purchases must be paid for out of future income; therefore, credit ties up the use of future income. Furthermore, if your income does not increase to cover rising costs, your ability to repay credit commitments will diminish. Before buying goods and services on credit, consider whether they will have lasting value, whether they will increase your personal satisfaction during present and future income periods, and whether your current income will continue or increase.

Finally, credit costs money. It is a service for which you must pay. Paying for purchases over a period of time is more costly than paying for them with cash. Purchasing with credit, rather than cash, involves one obvious trade-off: the fact that it will cost more due to monthly finance charges and the compounding effect of interest on interest.

SUMMARY: ADVANTAGES AND DISADVANTAGES OF CREDIT

Using credit provides immediate access to goods and services, flexibility in money management, safety and convenience, a cushion in emergencies, a means of increasing resources, and a good credit rating if you repay your debts in a timely manner. But remember, using credit is a two-sided coin. An intelligent decision about its use demands careful evaluation of your current debt, your future income, the added cost, and the consequences of overspending.

CONCEPT CHECK 5–1

1. How might consumers with credit card debt fare if a cyclical slowdown occurs?
2. What is consumer credit?
3. Why is consumer credit important to our economy?
4. What are the uses and misuses of credit?
5. What are the advantages and disadvantages of credit?

TYPES OF CREDIT

Two basic types of consumer credit exist: consumer loans and revolving credit. With **consumer loans** (also known as instalment loans), you repay one-time loans in a specified period of time with a pre-determined payment schedule. With **revolving credit**, loans are made on a continuous basis and you are billed periodically for at least partial payment. Exhibit 5–1 shows examples of consumer loans and revolving credit.

LO2
Differentiate among various types of credit.

consumer loan One-time loans that the borrower repays in a specified period of time with a pre-determined payment schedule.

CONSUMER LOANS

A consumer loan is used for a specific purpose and involves a specified amount. Home mortgages and consumer instalment loans to purchase an automobile or household furnishings are all types of consumer loans. Demand loans, where the lender can demand full repayment of the loan at any time, are also classified as consumer or instalment loans.

A written agreement, or contract, lists the repayment terms of consumer loans for each credit purchase: the number of payments, the payment amount, and whether the loan rate is floating or fixed. For consumer purchases, a down payment or trade-in may be required, with the remaining cost financed by an instalment loan that requires equal periodic payments over a period of time. Demand loans, however, may be interest-only for a set period of time. If the loan is secured, the lender will have a legal claim against the security pledged until the loan has been completely paid off.

Exhibit 5–2 shows that consumer loans reached over $513 billion in 2013.

revolving credit A line of credit in which loans are made on a continuous basis and the borrower is billed periodically for at least partial payment.

REVOLVING CREDIT

Using a credit card issued by a department store, using a bank credit card (Visa, MasterCard) to make purchases at different stores, charging a meal at a restaurant, and using overdraft protection are examples of revolving credit. As you will soon see, you do not apply for revolving credit to make a single purchase, as you do with consumer loans. Rather, you can use revolving credit to make any

Consumer Loans	Revolving Credit
• Home mortgages • Automobile loans • Other consumer instalment loans • Demand loans	• Credit cards issued by banks (Visa) or stores (Canadian Tire) • Charge cards or Travel and Entertainment cards (Diners Club) • Lines of credit • Overdraft protection

Exhibit 5–1

Examples of Consumer Loans and Revolving Credit

Exhibit 5–2   Consumer Credit, Excluding Mortgages

	2009	**2010**	**2011**	**2012**	**2013**
			$ millions		
Total outstanding balances	**430,074**	**463,491**	**438,413**	**503,153**	**512,844**
Chartered banks	314,362	350,151	322,790	421,754	435,686
Trust and mortgage loans companies	656	2,081	656	3,125	947
Life insurance company policy loans	5,933	6,185	5,933	6,480	6,599
Credit unions and caisses populaires	25,810	28,729	25,810	30,704	31,293
Special purpose corporations (securitization)	48,323	41,028	48,320	12,259	13,148

NOTE: Figure may not add to totals because of rounding.
SOURCES: Statistics Canada CANSIM Table 176-0027 and Bank of Canada. Last modified June 6, 2014.

Did you know?

Signs of Financial Trouble

- Not paying your bills on time
- Struggling to make minimum payments
- Making payments using credit cards
- Taking cash advances out on your credit cards
- Reaching or going beyond the limit on your credit cards
- Getting refused for credit
- Spending more than you earn
- Dipping into savings or retirement
- Paying late fees
- Juggling bills
- Counting on a future windfall
- Fighting with your partner over finances
- You're worried
- Regularly paying overdraft fees
- You have a savings rate of zero
- Treating your home like a piggy bank

SOURCE: http://www.consumercredit.com/about-us/media-mentions/17-signs-you-might-be-flirting-with-financial-disaster.aspx, accessed June 6, 2014.

credit limit The dollar amount, which may or may not be borrowed, that a lender makes available to a borrower.

purchases you wish if you do not exceed your **credit limit**, the maximum dollar amount of credit the lender has made available to you. You may have to pay **interest**, a periodic charge for using credit, or other finance charges. Some creditors allow you a grace period to pay a bill in full before you incur any interest charges.

You may have had an appointment with a dentist or chiropractor that you did not pay for until later. Professionals and small businesses often do not demand immediate payment but will charge interest if you do not pay the bill in full within 30 days. *Incidental credit* is a credit arrangement that has no extra costs and no specific repayment plan.

Many retailers issue retail cards. Customers can purchase goods or services up to a fixed dollar limit at any time. Usually, you have the option to pay the bill in full within 30 days without interest charges or to make set monthly instalments based on the account balance plus interest.

Many banks extend a **personal line of credit**, a pre-arranged loan for a specified amount that you can use by writing a special cheque. Repayment is made in instalments over a set period. The finance charges are based on the amount of credit used during the month and on the outstanding balance.

CREDIT CARDS   Credit cards are extremely popular: 91 percent of Canadian adults carry one or more credit cards.

Seventy percent of all credit card users generally pay off their balances in full each month. These cardholders are often known as *convenience users*. Others are borrowers; they carry balances beyond the grace period and pay finance charges. In Canada, consumers use more than 76.3 million credit cards to buy clothing, meals, vacations, gasoline, groceries, and other goods and services on credit.

While cash advances on credit cards can look attractive, remember that interest usually accrues from the moment you accept the cash, and you must also pay a transaction fee. One cash advance could cost you the money you were saving for a birthday gift for that special someone.

Most financial institutions participate in the credit card business, and the vast majority of them are affiliated with Visa International or the Interbank Card Association, which issues

MasterCard. The Financial Planning for Life's Situations box on page 152 provides a few helpful hints for choosing a credit card.

Affinity marketing or *co-branding* is the linking of a credit card with a business trade name offering "points" or premiums toward the purchase of a product or service. Affinity or value-added cards have become increasingly popular since the success of General Motors Corporation's credit card. Co-branded credit cards offer rebates on products and services, such as health clubs, tax preparation services, and gasoline purchases. Banks are realizing that affinity credit cards help build customer loyalty.

Smart cards, the ultimate plastic, embedded with a computer chip that can store 500 times the data of a credit card, have been introduced into the market. A smart card is a plastic card embedded with a computer chip that stores and transacts data between users. The card data is transacted via a reader that is part of a computing system. A single smart card, for example, can be used to buy an airline ticket, store it digitally, and track frequent-flyer miles. In 1997, Visa Canada and Scotiabank launched Canada's first field trial of a reloadable chip-based Visa Cash card in Barrie, Ontario. Although the trial was a success, smart cards have failed to make the impact on the Canadian consumer market that was initially envisioned when developed.

It is also important to consider the impact of the financial crisis that has helped politicians to enact new regulations that provide greater protection to credit card users. According to the Department of Finance Canada (fin.gc.ca) these regulations are summarized in Exhibit 5-3 below.

Did you know?

As of 2013, there are 76.3 million MasterCard and Visa credit cards in circulation in Canada that are accepted in more than 30 million locations worldwide. In 2013, Canadians charged $341.62 billion to Visa and MasterCard for retail purchases and conducted more than three billion transactions.

SOURCE: Canadian Bankers Association, cba.ca/contents/files/statistics/stat_cc_db038_en.pdf, accessed June 6, 2014.

interest A periodic charge for the use of credit.

personal line of credit A pre-arranged loan from a bank for a maximum specified amount.

Exhibit 5–3
New Regulations Protecting Canadian Credit Card Users

Originally announced in September, 2009, the new regulations:

- Mandate an effective minimum 21-day, interest-free grace period on all new credit card purchases when a customer pays the outstanding balance in full.
- Lower interest costs by mandating allocations of payment in favour of the consumer. For example, any payment made in excess of the required minimum must either be allocated to the balance with the highest interest rate first or distributed proportionally to each type of balance (cash advances, purchases, etc).
- Provide information on the cardholder's monthly statement on the time it would take to fully repay the balance, if only the minimum payment is made every month. For example, a balance of $1,000 on a credit card that charges 18 percent could take more than 10 years to pay off.
- Mandate advance disclosure of interest rate increases prior to their taking effect, even if this information was included in the credit contract.
- The regulations apply to credit cards issued by federally regulated institutions. Some provisions in the regulations have broader application to other financial products, such as fixed- and variable-rate loans and lines of credit.

These new credit card regulations are in addition to those that came into effect earlier in 2009, which include:

- Providing a summary box on credit contracts and application forms that sets out key features, such as interest rates and fees.
- Requiring express consent for credit limit increases.
- Limiting debt collection practices used by financial institutions.

SOURCES: "Regulations Come into Force to Protect Canadian Credit Card Users," September 1, 2010, fin.gc.ca/n10/10-076-eng.asp. Reproduced with the permission of the Minister of Public Works and Government Services Canada, 2012.

COSTS ASSOCIATED WITH CREDIT CARDS

The major fees charged to customers are for:

- Late or overdue payments.
- Charges that result in exceeding the credit limit on the card (whether done deliberately or by mistake), called over limit fees.
- Returned cheque fees or payment processing fees (e.g., phone payment fee).
- Cash advances and convenience cheques (often 3 percent of the amount).
- Transactions in a foreign currency (as much as 3 percent of the amount). (A few financial institutions do not charge a fee for this.)
- Membership fees (annual or monthly), sometimes a percentage of the credit limit.
- Exchange rate loading fees (sometimes these might not be reported on the customer's statement, even when applied). The variation of exchange rates applied by different credit cards can be substantial, as much as 10 percent according to a Lonely Planet report in 2009.

BENEFITS OF CREDIT CARDS

If you use the right credit card, and use it responsibly, there are a number of benefits you can enjoy:

- You get a short-term no-interest loan when making a purchase if you pay off the balance each month.
- There are several reward credit cards that let you earn different types of rewards, rebates, or points.
- Insurance that covers purchases made by a credit card. A purchase made with a credit card is a form of insurance. The credit card issuer can help you in disputes with a dishonest merchant if you run into problems with incorrect charges. You should note that this is not the case with debit cards. In many cases your credit card might insure you against damages to or thefts of purchased goods within 90 days of the purchase. A purchase with a credit card may even extend the manufacturer's warranty.
- Federal law states that you are only responsible for the first $50 of unauthorized charges on your credit card.
- The availability of a credit card in case of an emergency.

STEPS TO FOLLOW WHEN A CREDIT CARD IS STOLEN

- Find the toll-free number to call on your credit card statement and call your credit card issuer to tell them your card was stolen.
- Have the stolen card cancelled immediately.
- Ask for a new account number and a new card to be sent to you (it can take a couple of weeks to get your new card).
- Carefully check your future credit card statements for any purchases you didn't make.
- If you find any charges that aren't yours, call the toll-free number again, and inform them.

PROTECTING YOURSELF AGAINST DEBIT/ CREDIT CARD FRAUD

Credit fraud losses, when compared against the total debt owed by consumers on their credit cards, represents less than one-hundredth of 1 percent of the total owed. As a result, fraud losses related to credit may not seem terrible. But it *is* terrible for fraud victims. Though they may be protected financially, they are forced to endure major inconvenience. Many fraud victims are devastated emotionally; the negative effects can linger for years. Moreover, all of us pay the costs of credit card fraud through higher prices, higher interest rates, and increased inconvenience.

CREDIT CARD THEFT, LOSS, AND FRAUDULENT CHARGES   By federal law, your credit card agreement must explain your maximum liability (no more than $50) in the case of a lost or stolen credit card, or the unauthorized use of your credit card number.

In the case of loss or theft, review your credit card statements carefully. If unauthorized charges appear on your statement, it is a good idea to send a letter to the card issuer describing each questionable charge.

FRAUD PROTECTION   Visa, MasterCard, and American Express cardholders are also provided with protection beyond the maximum liability indicated in their credit card agreements. This is done through a public commitment that Visa and Master-Card call the "zero-liability policy." American Express has also made a public commitment through its Fraud Protection Guarantee: If your credit card is lost or stolen, or if someone uses your credit card number to make transactions you didn't authorize, you can usually be reimbursed.

How can you protect yourself against credit card fraud? You can take several measures:

- Sign your new card as soon as it arrives.
- Treat your card like money. Store it in a secure place.
- Shred anything with your account number before throwing it away.
- Don't give your card number over the phone or online unless you initiate the call.
- Don't write your card number on a postcard or on the outside of an envelope.
- Remember to get your card and receipt after a transaction, and double-check to be sure it's yours.
- Advise the card issuer of any upcoming changes in spending patterns (e.g., while on holiday in a foreign country) to avoid having your transactions refused.
- If your billing statement is incorrect or your credit cards are lost or stolen, notify your card issuers immediately.
- If you don't receive your billing statement, notify the company immediately.
- If you are a victim of credit card fraud, call your lender immediately.
- Request a copy of your credit report every few years. Reviewing your report will tell you if anyone has applied for credit in your name and whether any accounts are being used without your knowledge, with the billing statement being sent to a different address.[1]

> **Did you know?**
>
> A 2013 survey by Abacas Data found that 70 percent of Canadian households pay off the monthly credit card balance each month, which means that these Canadians pay no interest. 55 percent of Canadians who do carry a balance pay more than the minimum amount due each month.
>
> SOURCE: "Credit Cards: Statistics and Facts," May 2014, cba.ca.

The Internet has joined the telephone and television as an important part of our lives. Every day, more consumers use the Internet for financial activities, such as investing, banking, and shopping. When you make purchases online, make sure your transactions are secure, your personal information is protected, and your fraud sensors are sharpened. Although you can't control fraud or deception on the Internet, you can take steps to recognize it, avoid it, and report it if it does occur. Here's how:

- *Use a secure browser*, software that encrypts or scrambles the purchase information you send over the Internet, to guard the security of your online transactions. Most computers come with a secure browser already installed. You can also download some browsers for free over the Internet.
- *Keep records of your online transactions*. Read your email. Merchants may send you important information about your purchases.

---

[1] Experian Consumer Education Department, *Reports on Credit*, 1997.

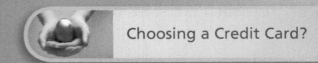
When choosing a credit card, it pays to shop around. Follow these suggestions to select the card that best meets your needs.

1. Department stores and gasoline companies are good places to obtain your first credit card. Pay your bills in full and on time to avoid interest charges of 28 percent and higher, and you will begin to establish a good credit history.

2. Bank cards are offered through banks and credit unions. Fees and finance charges vary considerably (from 8 to 21.6 percent), so shop around.

3. If you usually pay your bill in full, try to deal with a financial institution with an interest-free grace period, which is the time after a purchase has been made and before a finance charge is imposed, typically 21 to 30 days.

4. If you're used to paying monthly instalments, look for a card with a low monthly finance charge. Be sure you understand how that finance charge is calculated.

5. Consider obtaining a card from an out-of-province financial institution if it offers better terms than those offered locally.

6. Be aware of some credit cards that offer "no fee" or low interest but start charging interest from the day you purchase an item.

7. Watch out for credit cards that do not charge annual fees but instead charge a "transaction fee" each time you use the card.

8. If you're paying only the minimum amounts on your monthly statement, you need to plan your budget more carefully. The longer it takes for you to pay off a bill, the more interest you pay.

The finance charges you pay on an item could end up being more than the item is worth.

9. With a grace period of 25 days, you actually get a free loan when you pay bills in full each month.

10. To avoid delays that may result in finance charges, follow the card issuer's instructions as to where, how, and when to make bill payments.

11. Beware of offers of easy credit. No one can guarantee to get you credit.

12. Be aware of credit cards offered by "credit repair" companies or "credit clinics." These firms may also offer to clean up your credit history for a fee. But remember, only time and good credit habits will repair your credit report if you have a poor credit history.

13. If you don't have a list of your credit issuers' telephone numbers, you will be able to obtain them online.

14. Travel and entertainment (T&E) cards often charge higher annual fees than most credit cards. Usually, you must make payment in full within 30 days of receiving your bill or typically no further purchases will be approved on the account.

15. Often, additional credit cards on your account for a spouse or child (over 18) are available with a minimum additional fee or no fee at all.

16. Be aware that debit cards are not credit cards but simply a substitute for a cheque or cash. The amount of the sale is subtracted from your chequing account.

SOURCES: American Institute of Certified Public Accountants; U.S. Office of Consumer Affairs; Federal Trade Commission.

- *Review your monthly bank and credit card statements* for any billing errors or unauthorized purchases. Notify your credit card issuer or bank immediately if your credit card or chequebook is lost or stolen.
- *Read the policies of Web sites you visit*, especially the disclosures about a site's security, its refund policies, and its privacy policy on collecting and using your personal information. Some Web sites' disclosures are easier to find than others; look at the bottom of the home page, on order forms, or in the "About" or "FAQ" section of a site. If you can't find a privacy policy, consider shopping elsewhere.
- *Keep your personal information private.* Don't disclose personal information—your address, telephone number, social insurance number, or email address—unless you know who's collecting the information, why they're collecting it, and how they'll use it.
- *Give payment information only to businesses you know and trust*, and only in appropriate places, such as electronic order forms.

Advice from a Pro

A Pro's Views on Credit Chaos

According to Jonathan Hoenig, a radio show host and a columnist, "the bubonic plague of personal finance comes in the form of a 17 percent or higher interest rate on your credit card. You'll have to do a lot of bargain shopping and coupon clipping to compensate for your constantly compounding finance charges. Bummer? *Yes*. Your fault? *Yes*. Just because you have access to credit doesn't mean you should necessarily partake of the plastic." He cautions that credit cards can be a useful part of personal finance or a painful experience. A good rule to live by: *Don't buy things you can't afford.*

Thankfully, most young people seem to be following the rules these days. Compared with the majority of cardholders, most of whom carry a balance, young people are demonstrating their financial savvy in record numbers.

Paying cash? You'll still deal with debt. Certain types, like student loans, car payments, and mortgages, are designed to be paid over longer periods of time. This is reflected in a lower interest rate. A credit card bill, and other types of "unsecured" debt, however, should be paid as soon as possible, advises Hoenig.

Various surveys suggest young people are headed in the right direction. Most college/university students recognize the importance of establishing and maintaining a good credit history.

- *Never give your password to anyone online*, even your Internet service provider.
- *Do not download files sent to you by strangers or click on hyperlinks from people you don't know*. Opening a file could expose your computer system to a virus.[2]

TRAVEL AND ENTERTAINMENT (T&E) CARDS
T&E cards are really not credit cards but charge cards because the monthly balance is due in full. However, most people think of Diners/En Route or American Express cards as credit cards because they don't pay the moment they purchase goods or services.

PERSONAL LINES OF CREDIT
A personal line of credit is usually set up as a *revolving line of credit*, typically with a variable interest rate linked to the lender's prime rate. A specified credit limit is established and funds can be withdrawn at the borrower's convenience by using a debit card or by writing a cheque. Payments to reduce the line of credit can be interest only or the lender may specify a minimum payment to be applied against the outstanding loan balance. The lender will advise the borrower in writing of the required monthly minimum payment.

If the line of credit is secured by a pledge of assets, such as a Guaranteed Investment Certificate (GIC), the interest rate charged on funds borrowed will be reduced. In the event the borrower defaults, the lender can sell the collateral and recover the outstanding loan balance.

In a **home equity line of credit**, the limit on the line of credit is based on the difference between the current market value of your home and the amount you still owe on your mortgage. Generally, you can borrow up to 65 percent of the appraised value of your home, less your mortgage loan balance. Compared to an unsecured personal line of credit, most borrowers can obtain a higher credit limit at a lower interest rate with a home equity line of credit because of the pledge of the equity in their home as collateral. Interest paid on a home equity line of credit

home equity line of credit A personal line of credit based on the current market value of your home less the amount still owed on the mortgage.

---

[2] Adapted from Guide to Online Payments, Federal Trade Commission, March 1999 (ftc.gov).

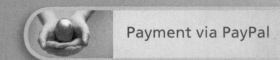
With the emergence of online auction sites such as eBay, shoppers have been looking for a fast and easy way to pay for their purchases without having to mail a cheque or provide personal financial information. By visiting the Web site paypal.com, buyers and sellers can open a password-protected account that registers information concerning their personal payment options (credit card and bank account numbers, etc.). Following an online purchase, the buyer then logs on to the PayPal site and requests that funds be transferred to the seller, who also has a PayPal account, and indicates the mode of payment (credit card, bank account), the timing of the transfer, and the desired currency. This process permits buyers and sellers to send and receive money online in a secure fashion, without having to reveal their credit card number or other financial information to the other party. PayPal is an international service that can transfer funds in any currency to anyone in almost any country. The service charges a small annual fee allowing for unlimited annual transactions. Currently, there are over 150 million PayPal account holders worldwide.

SOURCE: paypal.com.

can be tax deductible if the loan proceeds are used to generate taxable investment income. As with a personal line of credit, some lenders permit interest-only payments. A professional real estate appraiser is required to determine the house's fair market value. The cost of the appraisal, along with other application and legal fees that must be paid at the outset, are a major disadvantage of using a home equity line of credit.

Your home is your largest asset. You should use the home equity line of credit only for major items, such as education, home improvements, or medical bills, and not for daily expenses. If you miss payments on a home equity loan, you can lose your home. Furthermore, when you sell your home, you probably will be required to pay off your home equity line of credit in full. If you plan to sell your house in the near future, consider whether annual fees to maintain the account and other costs of setting up an equity credit line make sense. See the Financial Planning Calculations box for an example of a home equity line of credit.

CONSUMER LOANS

MORTGAGE LOANS   A home mortgage is probably the biggest single debt most individual Canadians will incur. For this reason, we have devoted all of Chapter 7, The Finances of Housing, to this topic.

CAR LOANS   Buying a vehicle is the second largest investment you will probably make after buying a house. Before acquiring a vehicle, be sure to comparison shop with reference to the Canadian Red Book (canadianredbook.com) or the Canadian Black Book (canadianblackbook.com). Both sources are updated regularly and offer a wealth of information concerning wholesale and retail prices, major options, and other information. There are many options available for financing your purchase. Here is a brief description of the financing available.

Financing at a Bank   Most financial institutions offer consumer instalment loans to purchase an automobile. The purchaser may be required to make a minimum down payment against the cost of the vehicle, with the remaining cost financed by an instalment loan, at a fixed or variable interest rate, for terms ranging from one to five years. Payment frequency can be arranged to suit the borrower's needs. The loan has an open prepayment clause, unlike a home mortgage, and the borrower suffers no penalty for early repayment. The lender may offer additional terms, such as the ability to skip a regular payment without penalty.

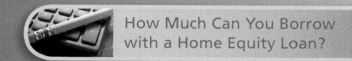
Depending on your income and the equity in your home, you can apply for a line of credit for anywhere from $10,000 to $250,000 or more.

In Canada, you can access up to 65 percent of the value of your home through a home equity line of credit. However, it's also important to remember that your outstanding mortgage loan balance + your home equity line of credit cannot equal more than 80 percent of the value of your home. To determine how much equity is at your disposal, start by taking your home's current market value and multiplying it by 80 percent. Next, subtract the balance of your mortgage. The remaining figure is how much you can access through a home equity line of credit—so long as the amount is not worth more than 65 percent of the value of your home. To be sure, simply divide the home equity line of credit amount by your home's market value. (Source: RateHub.ca)

Use the following chart to calculate your home loan value, which is the approximate amount of your home equity line of credit.

In this example, your home loan value (the amount for which you could establish your account) is $30,000.

Once your account is established, you can write a cheque for any amount you need up to $30,000.

In choosing a home equity loan,

1. Find out if your lending institution protects you against rising interest rates.
2. Compare the size of your lender's fee with those of other institutions.
3. Find out if your lender charges an inactivity fee.
4. Be wary of interest-only payments on home equity loans.
5. Find out whether your lender has the right to change the terms and conditions of your plan or to terminate your plan.
6. Carefully evaluate your reasons for using the equity in your home for loans.
7. Know the full costs and risks of home equity loans before you make a commitment to a lending institution.

	Example	Your Home
Approximate market value of your home	$300,000	$_____
Multiply by 0.80	× 0.80	× 0.80
Approximate loan value	240,000	_____
Subtract balance due on mortgage(s)	210,000	_____
Approximate credit limit available	$ 30,000	$_____

Financing at the Dealership   Most car dealers offer financing in affiliation with car manufacturers (also referred to as factory financing) or financial institutions (via a conditional sales contract). Factory financing enables you to get a loan directly from the car manufacturer, and you can expect to pay significantly lower interest rates and no down payment on the models they are trying to move. If you choose bank financing in the form of a conditional sales contract, you will receive a loan from a bank, which normally has a lower interest rate or some other incentive, and the dealer takes care of all the paper work.

Leasing   Lower monthly payments associated with car leasing have resulted in its increased popularity during the last decade of rising car costs. There are two types of leases: closed-end leases and open-end leases. The Royal Bank of Canada Web site (royalbank.ca) describes the two as follows:

Closed-end lease: The leasing company is responsible for the residual value of the vehicle at lease-end. You can choose to buy the vehicle for that price and any other charges or fees stipulated in the contract, or return it to the leasing company.

Open-end lease: You are responsible for the residual value of the vehicle and must pay that amount and any other charges or fees stipulated in the lease at lease-end.

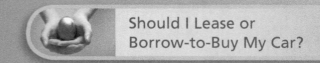

The decision whether to buy or lease a car is one that requires a lot of thought and financial consideration. Besides monetary discrepancies, personal preferences also come into the decision process. Many drivers prefer to own their automobiles, while many drivers must lease the cars they cannot currently afford. In addition, many people lease because they would rather switch cars every few years for added variety.

To compare the pure financial cost of buying a car versus that of leasing a car, we will first compute the monthly payment, then the present value of all the cash flows under each scenario.

Borrow-to-buy

Retail price	$26,995
Cost with taxes at 14.975%[1]	$31,037
Down payment	$ 8,000
Loan amount	$23,037
Resale value in 4 years	$13,500
Financing rate (APR, compounded monthly)	5.25%, or 0.4375% per month
Loan term	48 months

The monthly loan payment is calculated as:

2ND	CLRTVM
23,037	PV
48	N

0.4375	I/Y
CPT PMT	−$533.14

(Refer to Appendix 1B on the time value of money for an explanation of the time value of money calculations and calculator keystrokes. Ensure the I/Y button is set to 1.)

The present value of all cash flows of the purchase decision equals:

2ND	CLRTVM
−533.14	PMT
13,500	FV
0.4375	I/Y
48	N
CPT PV	$12,089 + $8,000 = $20,089

Leasing

Capital cost reduction[2] ($8,000 ÷ 1.14975) ($8,000 − $6,958 = $1,042 to pay the associated sales tax)	$ 6,958
Net capitalized value ($26,995 − $6,958)	$20,037
Residual value[3]	$13,500
Lease term	48 months
Dealer interest rate (APR, compounded monthly)	5.25%

While low monthly payments and, occasionally, a zero down payment have been the most visible attractions of leasing a car, this method also appeals to individuals who prefer to trade in their car for a new model on a regular basis or those who use their automobile infrequently and wish to avoid the responsibilities of ownership. Companies often lease vehicles for their employees because it results in a lower taxable benefit to them.

Remember, however, that leasing a car is a contractual arrangement that cannot easily be broken. While you lease the car, you are still responsible for all maintenance and repairs. Mileage restrictions and charges for excess wear and use may result in additional charges coming due at the end of the lease.

Refer to the Financial Planning for Life's Situations box above for a description of the calculations involved in the lease-versus-buy decision for a car.

The following are some words of advice in negotiating a lease:

1. Ensure that the price of the car is identical under the lease and purchase option and that any discounts, trade-ins, and credits are identical.
2. Ensure that the financing rate is identical under both options.
3. Lease cars that maintain their value so that the residual value used in the lease calculation is high. This will result in a lower monthly lease payment.

Lease payments are made at the beginning of the month and equal:

2ND	CLRTVM
BGN	
20,037	PV
13,500+/−	FV
0.4375	I/Y
48	N
CPT PMT	$210.35

Taxes at 14.975 percent (in Quebec) are added to the lease payment for a total of $241.85.

The present value of all cash flows of the leasing decision equal:

2ND	CLRTVM
BGN	
241.85+/−	PMT
48	N
0.4375	I/Y
CPT PV	$10,450

$10,450 + $8,000 = $18,450

There is a small financial advantage to leasing the car, largely the result of the fact that taxes are not paid on the residual value[3] in a lease, whereas taxes on the full listed price are charged if the vehicle is purchased, but are not recovered at time of resale.

For more information concerning the buy-versus-lease decision with respect to automobiles, visit canadabusiness.ca.

Notes:
[1] Taxes in Quebec: $1 - [(1.05)(1.095)] = 0.14975$ or 14.975%
[2] Capital cost reduction is the down payment (if any) to reduce the capital cost and monthly payments. Most leases require a down payment and the amount is taxable.
[3] Residual value is the established value for the vehicle at the end of the lease. Typically, the residual value is a percentage of the Manufacturer Suggested Retail Price (MSRP) for the vehicle that is being leased. In an open-end lease, the lessee is responsible for the residual value of the lease. In a closed-end lease, the lessee is not responsible for the residual value.

4. Assess any mileage restrictions and additional front-end or back-end charges under a lease.
5. New cars offer a three- to five-year warranty. Keep the lease term within this time frame.

Paying Cash   This is the least expensive method to pay for your new or used vehicle because you avoid the cost of borrowed money (interest charges). Of course, if you are able to place the amount in an investment that earns a higher rate of return than the cost of borrowing the money, it is better to invest it. For example, if you were faced with the choice of financing a car at 1.7 percent interest or investing your available funds to earn 6 percent interest, the better solution is to invest, even considering that your investment returns will be taxed and the interest on the car loan is not deductible unless the car is used for business purposes. The after-tax interest earned on the investment would permit you to pay the interest cost of the car loan and pocket the difference.

CONCEPT CHECK 5–2

1. What are the two main types of consumer credit?
2. What is a home equity loan?

MEASURING YOUR CREDIT CAPACITY

LO3

Assess your credit capacity and build your credit rating.

The only way to determine how much credit you can assume is to first learn how to make an accurate and sensible personal or family budget. Budgets, as you learned in Chapter 2, are simple, carefully considered spending plans. With budgets, you first provide for basic necessities, such as rent or mortgage, food, and clothing. Then you provide for such items as home furnishings and other heavy, more durable goods.

CAN YOU AFFORD A LOAN?

Before you take out a loan, ask yourself whether you can meet all of your essential expenses and still afford the monthly loan payments. You can make this calculation in two ways. One is to add up all of your basic monthly expenses and then subtract this total from your take-home pay. If the difference will not cover the monthly payment and still leave funds for other expenses, you cannot afford the loan.

A second and more reliable method is to ask yourself what you plan to give up to make the monthly loan payment. If you currently save a portion of your income that is greater than the monthly payment, you can use these savings to pay off the loan. But if you do not, you will have to forgo spending on entertainment, new appliances, or perhaps even necessities. Are you prepared to make this trade-off? Although it is difficult to precisely measure your credit capacity, you can follow certain guidelines.

GENERAL RULES OF CREDIT CAPACITY

DEBT-PAYMENTS-TO-INCOME RATIO   The debt-payments-to-income ratio is calculated by dividing your monthly debt payments (not including house payment, which is a long-term liability) by your net monthly income. Experts suggest that you spend no more than 20 percent of your net (after-tax) income on consumer credit payments. Thus, as Exhibit 5–4 shows, a person making $1,068 per month after taxes should spend no more than $213 on credit payments per month.

The 20 percent estimate is the maximum; however, 15 percent is much better. The 20 percent estimate is based on the average family, with average expenses; it does not take major emergencies into account. If you are just beginning to use credit, you should not consider yourself safe if you are spending 20 percent of your net income on credit payments.

Exhibit 5–4

How to Calculate Debt-Payments-to-Income Ratio

Spend no more than 20 percent of your net (after-tax) income on credit payments.

Monthly gross income	$1,500
Less:	
All taxes	270
Canada Pension Plan contribution	112
Monthly RRSP contribution	50
Monthly net income	$1,068
Monthly instalment credit payments:	
Visa	25
MasterCard	20
Diners/En Route card	15
Education loan	—
Personal bank loan	—
Auto loan	153
Total monthly payments	$ 213
Debt-payments-to-income ratio ($213 ÷ $1,068)	19.94%

Some financial institutions do not take the actual monthly credit card or personal line of credit payment into account when calculating the debt-payments-to-income ratio. Instead, they factor in the minimum payment on the card or line assuming that the balance had reached the maximum. This implies that even if a card or personal line of credit is not used, the credit potential that it provides is factored into the ratio. For this reason, some financial planners will recommend that an individual carry, at most, two credit cards.

GDS AND TDS RATIOS

When it comes to mortgage loans, most lenders use the gross debt service (GDS) ratio or the total debt service (TDS) ratio to determine whether you can afford the loan. The GDS is your monthly mortgage payment, including principal, interest, heating, and taxes, as a percentage of your gross monthly income. The lender will not allow you to spend more than 30 to 32 percent of your gross income on shelter costs. The TDS ratio is your monthly mortgage payment, including payments on any outstanding debt as a percentage of your gross monthly income. The amount the lender will allow you to spend on shelter and non-shelter financial obligations combined should not exceed 40 percent of gross monthly income. The combined incomes of both spouses are usually considered, but excluding rental income. More details on GDS and TDS are provided in Chapter 7.

CO-SIGNING A LOAN

What would you do if a friend or a relative asked you to co-sign a loan? Before you give your answer, make sure you understand what co-signing involves.

You are being asked to guarantee a debt. Think carefully before you do. If the borrower doesn't pay the debt, you will have to. Be sure you can afford to pay if you have to and that you want to accept this responsibility.

You may have to pay up to the full amount of the debt if the borrower does not pay. You may also have to pay late fees or collection costs, which increase this amount.

The creditor can use the same collection methods against you that can be used against the borrower, such as suing you, garnishing your wages, and so on. If this debt is ever in default, that fact may become a part of your credit record.[3]

CO-SIGNERS OFTEN PAY Some studies of certain types of lenders show that as many as three of four co-signers are asked to wholly or partially repay the loan. That statistic should not surprise you. When you are asked to co-sign, you are being asked to take a risk that a professional lender will not take. The lender would not require a co-signer if the borrower met the lender's criteria for making a loan.

If you do co-sign and your friend or relative misses a payment, the lender can collect the entire debt from you immediately without pursuing the borrower first. Also, the amount you owe may increase if the lender decides to sue to collect. If the lender wins the case, it may be able to take your wages and property.

IF YOU DO CO-SIGN Remember that if the payments are missed by the principal borrower, your credit rating can be affected. Despite the risks, at times you may decide to co-sign. Perhaps your child needs a first loan or a close friend needs help. Here are a few things to consider before you co-sign:

1. Be sure you can afford to pay the loan. If you are asked to pay and cannot, you could be sued or your credit rating could be damaged.

---

[3] https://www.consumer.ftc.gov/articles/0215-co-signing-loan

2. Consider that even if you are not asked to repay the debt, your liability for this loan may keep you from getting other credit you want.

3. Before you pledge property, such as your automobile or furniture, to secure the loan, make sure you understand the consequences. If the borrower defaults, you could lose the property you pledge.

4. Check your provincial law. Some provinces have laws giving you additional rights as a co-signer.

5. Request that a copy of overdue-payment notices be sent to you so that you can take action to protect your credit history.

BUILDING AND MAINTAINING YOUR CREDIT RATING

If you apply for a charge account, credit card, car loan, personal loan, or mortgage, your credit experience, or lack of it, will be a major consideration for the creditor. Your credit experience may even affect your ability to get a job or buy life insurance. A good credit rating is a valuable asset that should be nurtured and protected. If you want a good rating, you must use credit with discretion: Limit your borrowing to your capacity to repay, and live up to the terms of your contracts. The quality of your credit rating is entirely up to you.

In reviewing your creditworthiness, a creditor seeks information from a credit bureau. Most creditors rely heavily on credit reports in considering loan applications.

credit bureau A reporting agency that assembles credit and other information about consumers.

CREDIT BUREAUS   **Credit bureaus** collect credit and other information about consumers. There are two main credit bureaus in Canada: Equifax Canada (equifax.ca, 1-800-465-7166) and TransUnion Canada (transunion.ca, 1-800-663-9980). In addition, several thousand regional credit bureaus collect credit information about consumers. These firms sell the data to creditors that evaluate credit applications.

WHO PROVIDES DATA TO CREDIT BUREAUS?   Credit bureaus obtain their data from banks, finance companies, merchants, credit card companies, and other creditors. These sources regularly send reports to credit bureaus containing information about the kinds of credit they extend to customers, the amounts and terms of that credit, and customers' paying habits. Credit bureaus also collect some information from other sources, such as court records.

WHAT IS IN YOUR CREDIT FILES?   As the sample credit report in Exhibit 5–5a shows, the credit bureau file contains your name, address, social insurance number, and birthdate. It may also include the following information:

- Your employer and position.
- Your former address.
- Your former employer.
- Your spouse's name, social insurance number, and employer.
- Public records and information.
- Cheques returned for insufficient funds.

Your credit file may also contain detailed credit information. Each time you buy from a reporting store on credit or take out a loan at a bank, a finance company, or some other reporting creditor, a credit bureau is informed of your account number and the date, amount, terms, and type of credit. As you make payments, your file is updated to show the outstanding balance, the number and amounts of payments past due, and the frequency of 30-, 60-, or 90-day delinquencies. Any suits, judgments, or tax liens against you may appear as well. However, provincial laws protect your rights if the information in your credit file is erroneous. Exhibit 5–5b shows the consumer update form; you can use this form to make changes or inquiries to your credit report.

EQUIFAX
Consumer Services Canada

Equifax Credit Report

Personal Information

Personal Data

Name:	RICHARD DENTON	**Other Names**	
SIN:	899XXX157	Also Known as: C RICHARD DENTON	
Date of Birth:	1967-04-XX		

Current Address

		Previous Address	
Address:	11TH AVE WILLOW ST TORONTO, ON	Address:	WILLOW ST TORONTO, ON
Date Reported:	2013-12	Date Reported:	2000-12
		Address:	WESTMARR RD REGINA, SK
		Date Reported:	2011-06

Current Employment

		Previous Employment	
Employer:	MCDOUGLAS HAULAGE	Employer:	PRIORITY TRUCKING
Occupation:	SUPERVISOR	Occupation:	DRIVER
		Employer:	MIDTOWN CATERING
		Occupation:	SUPERVISOR

Consumer Statement

Date Reported:	2014-02	Date to Be Removed: 2021-09	
Statement:	CONSUMER STATES SLOW PAYMENTS ON ACCOUNT ARE DUE TO BEING UNEMPLOYED		

Credit Information

This section contains information on each account that you've opened in the past. It is retained in our database for not more than 6 years from the date of last activity.

An installment loan is a fixed-payment loan in which the monthly payment does not change from month to month. Examples of such loans are a mortgage, car loan or a student loan. A revolving loan is a loan in which the balance or amount owed changes from month to month, such as a credit card.

Note: The account numbers have been partially masked for your security.

HUDSONS BAY

Phone Number:	Not Available	High Credit/Credit Limit:	$4,500.00
Account Number:	XXX...890	Payment Amount:	$910.00
Association to Account:	Individual account	Balance:	$6,700.00
Type of Account:	Revolving	Past Due:	$6,700.00
Date Opened:	2011-01	Date of Last Activity:	2014-03
Status:		Date Reported:	2014-05
Months Reviewed:	36		
Payment History:	No payment 30 days late		
	No payment 60 days late		
	No payment 90 days late		
Prior Paying History:	Meaning two payments past due(2014-05)		
	Meaning one payment past due(2014-02)		
	Meaning at least 120 days past due(2013-12)		
Comments:	Subject disputes this account		
	Employee account		

Banking Information

Bank Account Information

Date Reported:	2014-03	Account Number:	423156
Financial Institution:	BQE NATIONALE	Account Type:	Savings Account
Date Opened:	2012-01	Balance:	$5,255.00
Telephone Number:	Not Available	# of NSF:	2 NSF IN 2013
Status:			
Comments:	Overdraft		

Public Records and Other Information

This section includes bankruptcies, judgments, voluntary repayment programs and secured loans. Public record information is retained in our database for a maximum of 7 years from the date filed, except in the case of multiple bankruptcies, which results in retention of bankruptcy information for 14 years. P.E.I is an exception to this and displays Public Records for 7 to 10 years and Bankruptcies for 14 years.

SOURCE: Sample Credit Report. Used with permission of Equifax Canada Inc.

(continued)

Exhibit 5–5a

Sample Credit Report

All credit reports contain your name, address, social insurance number, and birthdate.

Exhibit 5–5a

(concluded)

Bankruptcy

Date Filed:	2010-03
Name of Court:	MIN OF ATTORNEY GEN
Case Number and Trustee:	456789 ABC ASSOCIATES
Assets:	$1,500.00
Liabilities:	$55,000.00
Type:	Individual
Filer:	Subject
Date Discharged:	2011-12
Comments:	

Legal Item

Date Filed:	2010-12	Legal Item Status:	
Case Number:	321245	Date Verified:	
Court Name:	COLL MTL	Satisfied Date:	2010-12
Amount:	$255.00	Lawyer:	
Plaintiff:	CITY OF TORONTO		
Defendant:	RICHARD DENTON		
Comments:			

Secured Loans

Court Name:	COLL MTL	Date Filed:	2010-09
Industry Class:	Credit Unions	Creditor's Name and Amount:	TRANS CANADA CREDIT 9 ELLIS AVE TOR 3600
Maturity Date:	2014-04		
Comments:			

Collections

The following accounts have been turned over to an agency for collection. Collection information stays on file for a maximum period of 6 years from date of last payment to the creditor, or if none, 5 years from the date assigned to the collection agency.

32145 TIM HORTON

Date Assigned:	2010-05	Account Number:	32415678
Collection Agency:	COLL MTL	Reason:	Unknown
Amount:	$1,260.00	Balance:	$1,260.00
Date of Last Payment:	2010-12	Date Paid:	
Date Verified:			
Comments:			

Credit Inquiries

The following inquiries were generated because the listed company requested a copy of your credit report.

2014-02-15	FIRST DATA RESOURCES (402)777-9729
2013-04-27	FUTURE MORTGAGE CORP (416)783-1808
2013-03-24	BANK OF MONTREAL (Phone Number Not Available)

The following "soft" inquiries were also generated. These soft inquiries do not appear when lenders look at your file; they are only displayed to you and do not affect your credit score.

2014-06-11	EQUIFAX CONS SERV CP (Phone Number Not Available)
2014-06-10	EQUIFAX CONS SERV CP (Phone Number Not Available)
2014-06-07	EQUIFAX CONS SERV CP (Phone Number Not Available)

Investigate your File

Your confirmation number is 0010627347. Please keep this number in your records for future communication with us.

To launch an investigation of information contained in your credit report, you will need to complete a Consumer Credit Report Update Form.

credit reporting legislation

Fair Credit Reporting Act—Applicable in British Columbia, Ontario, Nova Scotia, and Prince Edward Island

CREDIT BUREAU REGULATION IN CANADA   Besides Alberta, New Brunswick, and the territories, each province has legislation regarding consumer reporting agencies, such as credit bureaus. The principal concerns of these regulations are the protection of consumer privacy with respect to credit information and the consumer's right not to suffer from false credit and personal information.

In addition, **credit reporting legislation** stipulates the nature of the information that can be used in a credit report; a distinction is made between consumer information and personal data.

Consumer Credit Report Update Form

Upon review of your personal credit report should you wish to make corrections you will need to complete the form below. All required fields are in bold.

Personal Identification

First Name [   ]   Middle Name [   ]

Last Name [   ]   Suffix [▾]

Month Day Year
Date of Birth [▾][▾][   ]

Social Insurance Number [   ]–[   ]–[   ]

Current Address
Street Address [   ]

City [   ]   Province [▾]

Postal Code [   ]–[   ]

Previous Address
Street Address [   ]

City [   ]   Province [▾]

Postal Code [   ]–[   ]

Current Employment [   ]

E-mail Address [   ]

Please note: Equifax will not provide the personal information you supply to any non-affiliated third party.

Public Record Items, Bankruptcy and Collections Information

Courthouse Name or Agency   Case # / Account / Plaintiff
[   ]   [   ]

Reason for Investigation
[▾]

If other, please explain
[   ]

Credit Account Information

Company Name   Account Number
[   ]   [   ]

Reason for Investigation
[▾]

If other, please explain
[   ]

SOURCE: Consumer Credit Report Update Form. Used with permission of Equifax Canada Inc.

Exhibit 5–5b

Consumer Update Form

Form used to make changes or inquiries to your credit report.

While the former might include such details as your name, address, occupation, income, paying habits, and a number of other pertinent issues, personal information, such as character, reputation, and other characteristics, may not be included in a credit report.

ACCESS TO CREDIT REPORTS   While you have a right to know the contents of your credit bureau file at any time, others may view your file only if you have given written consent or if you have been sent a written notice that your report has been obtained. Generally, you will find that a request for permission to access your report is included in a credit application.

In the event that you do not apply for credit but a request for information is made, the credit bureau must inform you of the request and provide you with the name and address of the requestor.

Though access to information is well legislated and despite the claims to the contrary by credit bureaus, many consumer organizations have expressed concerns that credit bureau files are less than secure. The relatively recent shift to electronic files has created a whole new level of vulnerability in terms of privacy and consumer groups are worried that anyone with a computer and a modem will be able to access confidential files.

Credit Reporting Agencies Act—Applicable in Saskatchewan and Newfoundland and Labrador

Personal Investigations Act—Applicable in Manitoba

Consumer Protection Act—Applicable in Quebec

TIME LIMITS ON ADVERSE DATA

There are limitations to the inclusion of detrimental information in a credit report. As an example, in Ontario, a first bankruptcy can be reported only within seven years of its occurrence. In the event of a second bankruptcy, both bankruptcies will remain on the file for a total of 14 years after the second bankruptcy is discharged. In Saskatchewan, the limit is 14 years for bankruptcy and seven years for any other adverse data. The actual limits may vary slightly from province to province, but the common goal is to limit the credit-damaging effect of past events.

There are also rules in place to protect the consumer's privacy, including restrictions on the situations in which a credit report agency may make a report. Your data can be divulged only in the event of a court order or a legitimate request from a person or organization concerned with extending credit, employment, or insurance to you.

INCORRECT INFORMATION IN YOUR CREDIT FILE   Credit bureaus are required to follow reasonable procedures to ensure that subscribing creditors report information accurately. However, mistakes may occur. Your file may contain erroneous data or records of someone with a name similar to yours. When you notify the credit bureau that you dispute the accuracy of its information, it must reinvestigate and modify or remove inaccurate data. You should give the credit bureau any pertinent data you have concerning an error. If you contest an item on your credit report, the reporting agency must remove the item unless the creditor verifies that the information is accurate (see Exhibit 5–6).

You should review your credit files annually even if you are not planning to apply for a big loan. Married women and young adults should make sure that all accounts for which they are individually and jointly liable are listed in their credit files.

CREDIT SCORING   Credit scoring is a system used by lenders and others to assess the credit risk of prospective borrowers, most often when they apply for credit cards, automobile loans, and, more recently, home mortgages. Information about the applicant and his or her credit history is collected from the credit application and the individual's credit bureau report. Data contained in the credit report is summarized in a credit score, such as a *FICO* score (derived from statistical models developed by Fair Isaac Corporation), which awards points for each factor that helps predict the applicant's creditworthiness. The higher the score, the more likely the individual is to pay his or her bills on time. FICO scores range between 300 and 900, and scores of 600 and above are considered very good.

FICO scores assign different weightings, or importance, to five categories of data contained in a credit report: payment history, length of credit history, amounts owed, types of credit used, and number of recent applications for credit. However, they do not consider such factors as age, race, colour, religion, nationality, sex, marital status, or employment data.

Date
Your Name
Your Address
Your City, Province, Postal Code

Complaint Department
Name of Credit Reporting Agency
Address
City, Province, Postal Code

Dear Sir or Madam:

I am writing to dispute the following information in my file. The items I dispute are also encircled on the attached copy of the report I received. (Identify item(s) disputed by name of source, such as creditor or tax court, and identify type of item, such as credit account, judgment, etc.)

This item is (inaccurate or incomplete) because (describe what is inaccurate or incomplete and why). I am requesting that the item be deleted (or request another specific change) to correct the information.

Enclosed are copies of (use this sentence if applicable and describe any enclosed documentation, such as payment records, court documents) supporting my position. Please reinvestigate this (these) matter(s) and (delete or correct) the disputed item(s) as soon as possible.

Sincerely,
Your name

Enclosures: (List what you are enclosing)

Exhibit 5–6

Sample Dispute Letter

The law requires credit card companies to correct inaccurate or incomplete information in your credit report.

SOURCE: This information is provided by Fair Isaac Corporation, and is used with permission. Copyright © Fair Isaac Corporation. All rights reserved. Further use, reproduction, or distribution is governed by the FICO Copyright Usage Requirements, which can be found at www.fico.com.

A strong credit score will enable you to obtain credit faster and at more advantageous rates. So how can you improve your credit score? The answer is simple: by managing your debt responsibly. Establish a credit history as soon as possible, pay your bills on time, limit the amount of credit you use or have access to, and avoid certain types of credit, such as loans from finance companies. Don't apply for too much new credit at one time—frequent applications will have a negative impact on your credit score.

OBTAINING YOUR CREDIT REPORT   To obtain a copy of your credit report, credit score, and score analysis online in Canada, you can visit the Equifax Canada Web site at equifax. ca, or the TransUnion Web site at transunion.ca. From Equifax you can purchase a basic online credit report, a package including an online credit report, credit score, and analysis, and other packages and services. TransUnion also charges a fee for an online credit report; you can pay additional amounts to include your credit score and/or your score analysis. You can also receive your credit report by mail, free of charge, by downloading a credit report request form from either Web site, completing the form, and sending it by mail to the relevant company.

CONCEPT CHECK 5–3

1. What are the general rules for measuring credit capacity?
2. What can happen if you co-sign a loan?
3. What can you do to build and maintain your credit rating?
4. How do you correct erroneous information in your credit file?
5. What is credit scoring?

APPLYING FOR CREDIT

LO4

Describe the information creditors look for when you apply for credit.

A SCENARIO FROM THE PAST

Marie and Jerome Mangan have a joint income that is more than enough for them to make payments on their dream house, yet they are turned down for a mortgage loan. The lender says Marie might become pregnant and leave her job.

In fact, however, it is illegal for a creditor to ask or assume anything about a woman's child-bearing plans. It is even illegal to discourage the Mangans from applying for a loan because Marie is of child-bearing age. Also, the lender must fully acknowledge Marie's income.

When you are ready to apply for credit, you should know what creditors think is important in deciding whether you are creditworthy. You should also know what they cannot legally consider in their decisions. By law, race, colour, age, gender, marital status, sexual orientation, and certain other factors may not be used to discriminate against you in any part of a credit dealing. All individuals should build and protect their own credit histories.

WHAT CREDITORS LOOK FOR: THE FIVE Cs OF CREDIT MANAGEMENT[4]

When a lender extends credit to its customers, it recognizes that some customers will be unable or unwilling to pay for their purchases. Therefore, lenders must establish policies for determining who will receive credit. Most lenders build their credit policies around the five Cs of credit: character, capacity, capital, collateral, and conditions, but this can vary from one financial institution to another.

character The borrower's attitude toward credit obligations.

Character is the borrower's attitude toward credit obligations. Most credit managers consider character the most important factor in predicting whether you will make timely payments and ultimately repay your loan. Character is assessed by your credit score, credit report, and credit rating.

capacity The borrower's financial ability to meet credit obligations.

Capacity is your financial ability to meet credit obligations—that is, to make regular loan payments as scheduled in the credit agreement. Therefore, the lender checks your salary statements and other sources of income, such as dividends and interest. Your other financial obligations and monthly expenses are also considered before credit is approved. Typically, the gross debt service (GDS) ratio is approximately 30 percent and the total debt service (TDS) ratio 40 percent. See Chapter 7 for more information on GDS and TDS ratios.

capital The borrower's assets or net worth.

Capital refers to your assets or net worth. Generally, the greater your capital, the greater your ability to repay a loan. The lender determines your net worth by requiring you to complete a credit application (see Exhibit 5–7). You must authorize your employer and financial institutions to release information to confirm the claims made in the credit application.

collateral A valuable asset that is pledged to ensure loan payments.

Collateral is an asset that you pledge to a financial institution to obtain a loan. If you fail to honour the terms of the credit agreement, the lender can repossess the collateral and then sell it to satisfy the debt.

conditions The general economic conditions that can affect a borrower's ability to repay a loan.

Conditions refer to general economic conditions that can affect your ability to repay a loan. The basic question focuses on security—of both your job and the firm that employs you.

Creditors use different combinations of the five Cs to reach their decisions. Some creditors set unusually high standards, and others simply do not make certain kinds of loans. Creditors also use different kinds of rating systems. Some rely strictly on their own instinct and experience. Others use a credit-scoring or statistical system to predict whether an applicant is a good credit risk. They assign a certain number of points to each characteristic that has proven to be a reliable sign that a borrower will repay. Then they rate the applicant on this scale.

---

[4] Adapted from William M. Pride, Robert J. Hughes, and Jack R. Kapoor, *Business*, 6th ed. (Boston: Houghton Mifflin, 1999), pp. 498–500.

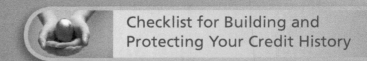
It is simple and sensible to build and protect your own credit history. Here are some steps to get you started.

If you are single:
- Open a chequing or savings account, or both.
- Apply for a local department store card.
- Take out a small loan from your bank. Make timely payments.

If you are married:
- Establish credit in your own name.
- Open your own accounts.
- Try to have separate credit card accounts in your own name.
- Review your joint accounts.
- Make sure that creditors report your credit history to credit bureaus in both names.

If you are getting married:
- Write to your creditors and ask them to continue maintaining your credit file separately.

If you have recently been separated or divorced:
- Close all of your joint accounts. Your credit record could suffer if your ex-partner is delinquent.
- Meet with your creditors and clear your credit record if your ex-partner has hurt your credit rating.

If you are widowed:
- Notify all creditors and tell them whether you or the executor of the estate will handle payment.
- Transfer all existing joint loans to your name alone. You may also want to renegotiate repayment terms.

- Transfer joint credit card accounts to your name alone or reapply for new accounts.
- Seek professional advice, if needed.

And remember that a creditor *cannot:*
- Refuse you individual credit in your own name if you are creditworthy.
- Require a spouse to co-sign a loan. Any credit-worthy person can be your co-signer if one is required.
- Ask about your birth control practices or family plans or assume that your income will be interrupted to have children.
- Consider whether you have a telephone listing in your own name.

A creditor *must:*
- Evaluate women on the same basis as male applicants.
- Consider income from part-time employment.
- Consider reliable alimony, child support, or separate-maintenance payments.
- Consider the payment history of all joint accounts that accurately reflects your credit history.
- Report the payment history on an account if you use the account jointly with your spouse.
- Disregard information on accounts if you can prove that it does not reflect your ability or willingness to repay.

SOURCE: Reprinted and adapted courtesy of the Office of Public Information, Federal Reserve Bank of Minneapolis, Minneapolis, MN 55480.

- Amount of loan requested
- Proposed use of the loan
- Your name and birthdate
- Social insurance number and driver's licence number
- Present and previous street addresses
- Present and previous employers and their addresses
- Present salary
- Number and ages of dependants
- Other income and sources of other income
- Have you ever received credit from us?

- If so, when and at which office?
- Chequing account number, institution, and branch
- Savings account number, institution, and branch
- Name of nearest relative not living with you
- Relative's address and telephone number
- Your marital status
- Information regarding joint applicant: same questions as above

Exhibit 5–7

Sample Credit Application Questions

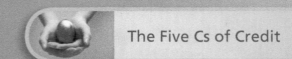
Here is what lenders look for in determining your creditworthiness.

CREDIT HISTORY

	Yes	No
1. Character: Will you repay the loan?	___	___
Do you have a good attitude toward credit obligations?	___	___
Have you used credit before?	___	___
Do you pay your bills on time?	___	___
Have you ever filed for bankruptcy?	___	___
Do you live within your means?	___	___

STABILITY

How long have you lived at your present address? _____ yrs.

Do you own your home? ___ ___

How long have you been employed by your present employer? _____ yrs.

INCOME

2. Capacity: Can you repay the loan?

Your salary and occupation? $_____ ; _____

Place of occupation? _____

Is your income reliable? ___ ___

Any other sources of income? $ _____

EXPENSES

Number of dependants? _____

Do you pay any alimony or child support? ___ ___

Current debts? $ _____

NET WORTH

3. Capital: What are your assets and net worth?

What are your assets? $ _____

What are your liabilities? $ _____

What is your net worth? $ _____

LOAN SECURITY

4. Collateral: What if you don't repay the loan?

What assets do you have to secure the loan? (Car, home, furniture?) _____

What sources do you have besides income? (Savings, stocks, bonds, insurance?) _____

JOB SECURITY

5. Conditions: What general economic conditions can affect your repayment of the loan?

How secure is your job? Secure ___ Not secure ___

How secure is the firm you work for? Secure ___ Not secure ___

SOURCE: Adapted from William M. Pride, Robert J. Hughes, and Jack R. Kapoor, *Business*, 6th ed. (Boston: Houghton Mifflin, 1999), pp. 498–500.

FICO AND VANTAGESCORE

Typical questions in a credit application appear in Exhibit 5–7. Exhibit 5–8 shows how your credit application might be scored. In addition, during the loan application process, the lender may evaluate many of the following criteria to determine whether you are a good credit risk.

FICO This is a type of credit score that makes up a substantial portion of the credit report that lenders use to assess an applicant's credit risk and whether to extend a loan. The FICO score is calculated based on the information contained in your Equifax credit history—a number generally between 300 and 900 that rates how risky a borrower is. The higher the score, the less risk you pose to creditors.

The largest percentage of the FICO score (35 percent) is based on payment history. Payment history indicates whether payments to creditors were made and made on time. If a consumer is past due or has paid on time, it is reflected in the FICO score. The next largest factor in a FICO score is the total of amounts owed on outstanding credit. This component makes up 30 percent. The amounts owed on all credit as well as the amount of available credit are included in this group. The amount of time that credit has been maintained makes up 15 percent of the credit score.

Your FICO score is available from equifax.com for a fee. Free credit reports do not contain your credit score.

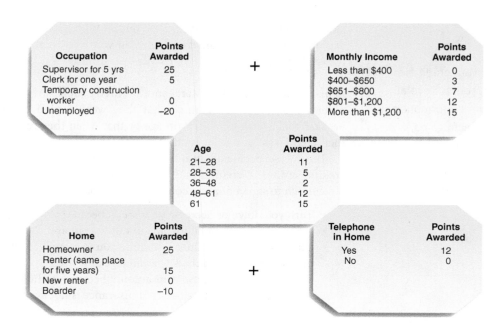

Exhibit 5–8

How a Consumer's
Application Is Scored

VantageScores   This is a credit rating product that is offered by the two major credit bureaus operating in Canada (Equifax and TransUnion) and a third minor one (Experian). The product was unveiled by the three bureaus in March 2006. Like the FICO score, VantageScore uses the information contained in your credit reports from each of the three credit reporting companies and calculates it into a three digit score. The model used to calculate your credit score is different than the FICO scoring model. VantageScores range from 501 to 990 with the higher score representing the lowest risk to the creditor. The VantageScore is calculated primarily on the past 24 month's activity on your credit reports from each of the three credit bureaus. The Vantage-Score model does not take authorized user accounts into consideration when calculating your score, whether or not they are in good standing.

Several factors influence your VantageScore:

Recent credit	30 percent
Payment history	28 percent
Credit use	23 percent
Credit balances	9 percent
Depth of credit	9 percent
Available credit	1 percent

VantageScore assigns a letter grade to each consumer's credit score. The letter grade takes the guesswork out of figuring out what's a good credit score. Based on US Data,

901–990 = A, Super Prime; 16% of consumers are Super Prime
801–900 = B, Prime Plus; 20% of consumers are Prime Plus
701–800 = C, Prime; 20% of consumers are Prime
601–700 = D, Non-Prime; 25% of consumers are Non-Prime
501–600 = F, High Risk; 19% of consumers are High Risk

HOW CAN I IMPROVE MY CREDIT SCORE?

A credit score is a snapshot of the contents of your credit report at the time it is calculated. The first step in improving your score is to review your credit report to ensure it is accurate. Long-term, responsible credit behaviour is the most effective way to improve future scores. Always

Did you know?

Most of the information in your credit file may be reported for seven years. Several Web sites can provide current information about credit files. Visit fcac-acfc.gc.ca, equifax.ca, or transunion.ca for more information.

SOURCE: Visit fcac-acfc.gc.ca, equifax.ca, or transunion.ca for more information.

pay your bills on time, pay at least the minimum payment by the due date, don't go over the credit limit on your credit card, and use credit wisely to improve your score over time.

AGE   Gene and Melissa Marchand, a retired couple, and many older people have complained that they were denied credit because they were over a certain age or that when they retired, their credit was suddenly cut off or reduced.

The law is specific about how a person's age may be used in credit decisions. A creditor may ask about your age, but if you're old enough to sign a binding contract, a creditor may not:

- Turn you down or decrease your credit because of your age.
- Ignore your retirement income in rating your application.
- Close your credit account or require you to reapply for it because you have reached a certain age or retired.
- Deny you credit or close your account because credit life insurance or other credit-related insurance is not available to people of your age.

PUBLIC ASSISTANCE   You may not be denied credit because you receive Old Age Security or public assistance. But, as with age, certain information related to this source of income could have a bearing on your creditworthiness.

HOUSING LOANS   Federal laws ban discrimination due to such characteristics as your race, colour, sexual orientation, or gender, or to the race or national origin of the people in the neighbourhood where you live or want to buy your home. Creditors may not use any appraisal of the value of your property that considers the race of the people in your neighbourhood.

WHAT IF YOUR APPLICATION IS DENIED?

ASK QUESTIONS IF YOUR APPLICATION IS DENIED   If you receive a notice that your application has been denied, you should ask to know the specific reasons for denial. If the denial is based on a credit report, you should enquire about the specific information in the credit report that led to it. After you receive this information from the creditor, you should contact the local credit bureau to find out what information it reported. You may ask the bureau to investigate any inaccurate or incomplete information and correct its records.

CONCEPT CHECK 5–4

1. What are the five Cs of credit?
2. What can you do if your credit application is denied?

AVOIDING AND CORRECTING CREDIT MISTAKES

LO5

Identify the steps you can take to avoid and correct credit mistakes.

Has a department store's computer ever billed you for merchandise that you returned to the store or never received? Has a credit company ever charged you for the same item twice or failed to properly credit a payment on your account?

The best way to maintain your credit standing is to repay your debts on time. But complications may still occur. To protect your credit and save your time, money, and future credit rating, you should learn how to correct any mistakes and misunderstandings that crop up in your credit accounts. If a snag occurs, first try to deal directly with the creditor.

IN CASE OF A BILLING ERROR

First, notify the creditor. Give the creditor your name and account number, say that you believe the bill contains an error, and explain what you believe the error to be. State the suspected amount of the error or the item you want explained.

Lending institutions in general will review all contested material within a stated time frame, and will specify the grace period they allow for any complaints or requests for changes. They will usually ask that you pay all amounts in full pending the results of their investigation of your complaint, with the agreement that they will refund any erroneous billing amounts.

While billing errors are generally rare, it is important to work with your creditor to set things right if they do happen. Most companies will investigate and address errors if they occur, but it is your responsibility to verify every billing for accuracy (see Exhibit 5–9). In most cases, the source of the error will be with the seller, not the creditor.

IDENTITY CRISIS: WHAT TO DO IF YOUR IDENTITY IS STOLEN

"I don't remember charging those items. I've never even been in that store."

Maybe you never charged those goods and services, but someone else did—someone who used your name and personal information to commit fraud. When impostors take your name, social insurance number, credit card number, or some other piece of your personal information for their use, they are committing a crime.

The biggest problem is that you may not know your identity has been stolen until you notice that something is amiss: You may get bills for a credit card account you never opened, your credit report may include debts you never knew you had, a billing cycle may pass without you receiving a statement, or you may see charges on your bills that you didn't sign for, didn't authorize, and know nothing about.

If someone has stolen your identity, you should:

1. *Contact the fraud departments of each of the two major credit bureaus* (see the table that follows). Tell them to flag your file with a fraud alert, including a statement that creditors should call you for permission before they open any new accounts in your name.

	To Report Fraud or To Order Credit Report	Web Site
Equifax	1-800-465-7166	equifax.ca
TransUnion	1-800-663-9980	transunion.ca

2. *Contact the creditors for any accounts that have been tampered with or opened fraudulently.* Ask to speak with someone in the security or fraud department, and follow up in writing.
3. *File a police report.* Keep a copy in case your creditors need proof of the crime.

To prevent an identity thief from picking up your trash to capture your personal information, tear or shred your charge receipts, copies of credit applications, insurance forms, bank cheques and statements, expired charge cards, and credit offers you get in the mail.

If you believe an unauthorized person has accessed your bank accounts, chequing account, or ATM card, close the accounts immediately. When you open new accounts, insist on password-only access. If your cheques have been stolen or misused, stop payment. If your ATM card has been lost, stolen, or otherwise compromised, cancel the card and get another with a new personal identification number (PIN). Reviewing this information could uncover that your identity has been compromised.

Exhibit 5–9

Steps for Resolving a Billing Dispute

The Consumers' Association of Canada (consumer.ca) offers advice about effective billing dispute resolution.

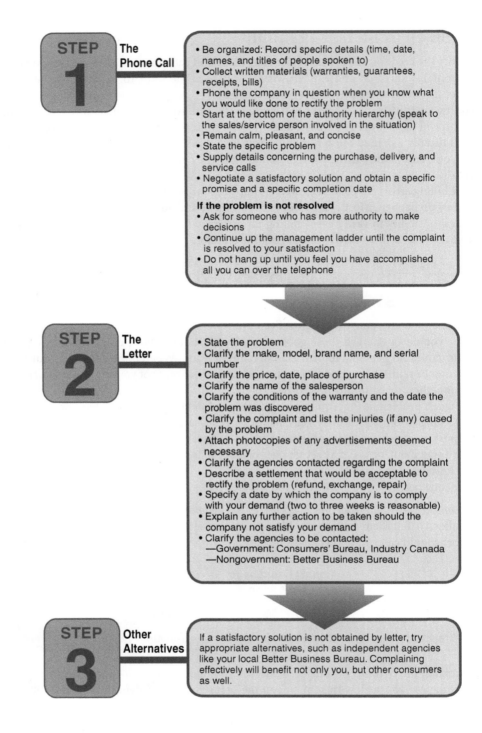

STEP 1 The Phone Call

- Be organized: Record specific details (time, date, names, and titles of people spoken to)
- Collect written materials (warranties, guarantees, receipts, bills)
- Phone the company in question when you know what you would like done to rectify the problem
- Start at the bottom of the authority hierarchy (speak to the sales/service person involved in the situation)
- Remain calm, pleasant, and concise
- State the specific problem
- Supply details concerning the purchase, delivery, and service calls
- Negotiate a satisfactory solution and obtain a specific promise and a specific completion date

If the problem is not resolved
- Ask for someone who has more authority to make decisions
- Continue up the management ladder until the complaint is resolved to your satisfaction
- Do not hang up until you feel you have accomplished all you can over the telephone

STEP 2 The Letter

- State the problem
- Clarify the make, model, brand name, and serial number
- Clarify the price, date, place of purchase
- Clarify the name of the salesperson
- Clarify the conditions of the warranty and the date the problem was discovered
- Clarify the complaint and list the injuries (if any) caused by the problem
- Attach photocopies of any advertisements deemed necessary
- Clarify the agencies contacted regarding the complaint
- Describe a settlement that would be acceptable to rectify the problem (refund, exchange, repair)
- Specify a date by which the company is to comply with your demand (two to three weeks is reasonable)
- Explain any further action to be taken should the company not satisfy your demand
- Clarify the agencies to be contacted:
  —Government: Consumers' Bureau, Industry Canada
  —Nongovernment: Better Business Bureau

STEP 3 Other Alternatives

If a satisfactory solution is not obtained by letter, try appropriate alternatives, such as independent agencies like your local Better Business Bureau. Complaining effectively will benefit not only you, but other consumers as well.

If, after taking all these steps, you are still having identity problems, stay alert to new instances of identity theft. Notify the company or creditor immediately and follow up in writing.

CONCEPT CHECK 5–5

1. What should you do to protect your rights if a billing error occurs?
2. What can you do if your identity is stolen?

SUMMARY OF LEARNING OBJECTIVES

LO1 **Define consumer credit and analyze its advantages and disadvantages.**

Consumer credit is borrowing money to obtain goods or services by individuals and families for personal needs. Among the advantages of using credit are the ability to purchase goods when needed and pay for them gradually, the ability to deal with financial emergencies, convenience in shopping, and establishing a credit rating. Disadvantages are that credit costs money, encourages overspending, and ties up future income.

LO2 **Differentiate among various types of credit.**

Consumer loans and revolving credit are two types of consumer credit. With consumer loans, the borrower pays back a one-time loan in a stated period of time and with a specified number of payments. With revolving credit, the borrower is permitted to take loans on a continuous basis and is billed for partial payments periodically.

LO3 **Assess your credit capacity and build your credit rating.**

General rules for measuring credit capacity are the debt-payments-to-income ratio and the GDS and TDS ratios. In reviewing your creditworthiness, a creditor seeks information from one of the two national credit bureaus or a regional credit bureau.

LO4 **Describe the information creditors look for when you apply for credit.**

Creditors determine creditworthiness on the basis of the five Cs: character, capacity, capital, collateral, and conditions.

LO5 **Identify the steps you can take to avoid and correct credit mistakes.**

If a billing error occurs on your account, notify the creditor in writing within 60 days. If the dispute is not settled in your favour, you can place your version of it in your credit file. You may also withhold payment on any defective goods or services you have purchased with a credit card as long as you have attempted to resolve the problem with the merchant.

KEY TERMS

capacity 166	consumer credit 144	credit reporting legislation 162
capital 166	consumer loan 147	home equity line of credit 153
character 166	credit 144	interest 149
collateral 166	credit bureau 160	personal line of credit 149
conditions 166	credit limit 148	revolving credit 147

FINANCIAL PLANNING PROBLEMS

 Practise and learn online with Connect.

1. *Types of Credit.* What are the two basic types of credit? Describe and distinguish between them. **LO1**

2. *Calculating the Amount for a Home Equity Loan.* A few years ago, Misha Azim purchased a home for $100,000. Today, the home is worth $150,000. His remaining mortgage balance is $50,000. Assuming Misha can borrow up to 80 percent of the market value of his home, what is the maximum amount he can borrow? **LO2**

3. *Determining the Debt-Payments-to-Income Ratio.* Louise Gendron's monthly gross income is $2,000. Her employer withholds $400 in federal and provincial income taxes and $160 in Canada Pension Plan contributions per month. Louise contributes $80 per month to her RRSP. Her monthly credit payments for Visa, MasterCard, and Diners/En Route cards are $35, $30, and $20, respectively. Her monthly payment on an automobile loan is $285. What is Louise's debt-payments-to-income ratio? Is Louise living within her means? Explain. **LO3**

4. *Calculating Net Worth and Determining a Safe Credit Limit.* LO3
   a. Calculate your net worth on the basis of your present assets and liabilities.
   b. Refer to your net worth statement and determine your safe credit limit. Use the debt-payments-to-income formula.

5. *Using Credit Cards as Identification.* Dinesh Dani flew to Toronto to attend his brother's wedding. Knowing that his family would be busy, he did not ask anyone to meet him at the airport. Instead, he planned to rent a car to use while in Toronto. He has no nationally known credit cards but is prepared to pay cash for the rental car. The car rental agency refuses to rent him a car, even though it has several cars available. Why do you think Dinesh is unable to rent a car? LO4

6. *Determining What Creditors Look for in Approving Loans.* Juan Villavera, a recent teachers' college graduate, has accepted a teaching position at Brockville High School. Jim moved to Brockville and applied for a car loan at the Royal Bank. He had never used credit or obtained a loan. The bank notified him that it will not approve the loan unless he has a co-signer. On what basis has the bank denied Juan credit? LO4

7. *Analyzing Feasibility of a Loan.* Friedrich Reine has had a student loan, two auto loans, and three credit cards. He has always made timely payments on all obligations. He has a savings account of $2,400 and an annual income of $25,000. His current payments for rent, insurance, and utilities are about $1,100 per month. Friedrich has accumulated $12,800 in an individual retirement account. Friedrich's loan application asks for $10,000 to start up a small restaurant with some friends. Friedrich will not be an active manager; his partner will run the restaurant. Will he get the loan? Explain your answer. LO4

FINANCIAL PLANNING ACTIVITIES

1. *Determining Whether or Not to Use Credit.* Survey friends and relatives to determine the process they used in deciding whether or not to use credit to purchase an automobile or a major appliance. What risks and opportunity costs did they consider? LO1

2. *Analyzing Opportunity Costs of Using Credit.* Think about the last three major purchases you made. LO1
   a. Did you pay cash? If so, why?
   b. If you paid cash, what opportunity costs were associated with the purchase?
   c. Did you use credit? If so, why?
   d. What were the financial and psychological opportunity costs of using credit?

3. *Comparing Reasons for Using Credit.* Prepare a list of similarities and differences in the reasons the following individuals might have for using credit. LO2
   a. A teenager.
   b. A young adult.
   c. A growing family of four.
   d. A retired couple.

4. *Using the Internet to Obtain Information about Credit Cards.* Choose one of the following organizations and visit its Web site. Then prepare a report that summarizes the information the organization provides. How could this information help you in choosing your credit card? LO2
   a. Canoe Money provides information on credit card rates. (money.canoe.ca)
   b. The Canadian Broadcasting Corporation provides information on how to regain financial health, uses and misuses of credit cards, and many other related topics. (cbc.ca/consumers)

5. *Using Your Home Equity to Obtain a Loan.* Visit your local financial institutions, such as banks, trust companies, and credit unions, to obtain information about getting a home equity loan. Compare their requirements for the loan. LO2

6. *Determining Whether to Co-sign a Loan.* Talk to a person who has co-signed a loan or to a representative from a financial institution. What experiences did this person have as a co-signer? LO3

7. *Determining Net Worth and Credit Capacity.* What changes might take place in your personal net worth during different stages of your life? How might these changes affect your credit capacity? LO4

8. *Assessing How Lenders Determine Creditworthiness.* Survey credit representatives, such as bankers, managers of credit departments in retail stores, managers of finance companies, credit union officers, managers of credit bureaus, and loan officers. Ask what procedures they follow in granting or refusing a loan. Write a report of your survey. LO4

9. *Analyzing Credit-Related Problems.* Bring to class examples of credit-related problems of individuals or families. Suggest ways in which these problems might be solved. LO5

10. *Evaluating Creditors and Seeking Help with Credit-Related Problems.* Compile a list of places a person can call to report dishonest credit practices, get advice and help with credit problems, and check out a creditor's reputation before signing a contract. LO6

LIFE SITUATION CASE

A Hard Lesson on Credit Cards

Parents of post-secondary students, beware: The empty-nest syndrome you're experiencing may end up as empty-wallet syndrome. The moment your kids step on campus, they become highly-sought-after credit card customers. To establish relationships they hope will extend well beyond the post-secondary years, card marketers offer students everything from free T-shirts to chances to win airline tickets as enticements to sign up. As a result, some students have heavy credit card debts.

"Students who have no history with credit are being handed it on a silver platter," say Gina Orente, education adviser for a consumer advocacy group in Hull, Quebec. As long as they are over 18, students can get a card without asking mom or dad to co-sign. But when they get into trouble, they often go running to their folks for help. Huan Kwo did—and then some. Now 21 and in his final year at McGill University in Montreal, Kwo racked up $21,000 in debt on 16 cards over four years. "When I first started, my attitude was: 'I'll get a job after university to pay off all my debt,'" he says. He realized he dug himself into a hole when he couldn't meet the minimum monthly payments. Now he works three part-time jobs, and his parents are helping him pay his tuition and loans.

Questions

1. Why should parents of students be wary?

2. How do credit card marketers entice students?

3. Where do students turn for help when they get into debt trouble?

chapter 6

Choosing a Source of Credit: The Costs of Credit Alternatives

LEARNING OBJECTIVES

LO1 Analyze the major sources of consumer credit.

LO2 Determine the effective cost of borrowing by considering the quoted rate, the number of compounding periods, the timing of the interest payments, and any other service charges.

LO3 Develop a plan to manage your debts.

LO4 Evaluate various private and governmental sources that assist consumers with debt problems.

LO5 Assess the choices in declaring personal bankruptcy.

THE PERILS OF TEASER RATES

Remember Huan Kwo from the previous chapter, who racked up $21,000 in credit card debt? Having educated himself on the pitfalls of credit, Kwo now speaks to student groups on the issue. Since card issuers' pitches may be confusing, he and other experts offer this advice: Beware of teaser rates. Credit card marketers may advertise a low annual percentage rate (APR), but it often jumps substantially after three to nine months. One group that is often targeted by marketers is the student population. The incentive offered is a discounted rate for the first few months, which then leaps upward afterwards. Many students, eager for credit and receptive to the notion of "fast cash," will sign up without fully understanding the risks involved.

Because students move often and may not get their mail forwarded quickly, bills can get lost. Then, the students fall prey to late-payment fees. Some cards have late fees as high as $30. If one or two payments are overdue, many cards' interest rates increase.

Students are often unaware that rates on cash advances are much higher than those on card balances.

Some cards impose a fee of as much as 4 percent of the advance.

The moral? *Don't ask for extra credit.* Instead, find a card that has a restrictive credit line. Another option: Get a secured credit card. Its credit limit depends on your savings at the issuing bank. Debt advisers say students should hold only a credit card on which they can carry a small balance and a charge card they must pay off monthly. They should pay more than the minimum on credit cards. And they should not charge purchases they can pay for in cash, such as pizza and gas, unless one is trying to establish a credit rating by promptly paying for items they can pay for.

If you are a parent, talk to your kids about responsible credit card use. Make sure your kids know a card isn't a way of getting items they can't afford.

QUESTIONS

1. What is Huan Kwo's advice to student groups?
2. Are teaser rates unique to student credit cards?
3. Should you get a secured credit card? Why, or why not?

SOURCES OF CONSUMER CREDIT

Credit costs got you down? Well, you are not alone. Credit costs money; therefore, always weigh the benefits of buying an item on credit now versus waiting until you have saved enough money to pay using cash. We can all get into credit difficulties if we do not understand how and when to use credit.

LO1
Analyze the major sources of consumer credit.

Financial and other institutions, the sources of credit, come in all shapes and sizes. They play an important role in our economy, and they offer a broad range of financial services. By evaluating your credit options, you can reduce your finance charges. You can reconsider your decision to borrow money, discover a less expensive type of loan, or find a lender that charges a lower interest rate.

Before deciding whether to borrow money, ask yourself these three questions: Do I need a loan? Can I afford a loan? Can I qualify for a loan? We discussed the affordability of loans and the qualifications required to obtain loans in the last chapter. Here we wrestle with the first question.

You should avoid credit in two situations. The first situation is one in which you do not need or really want a product that requires financing. Easy access to instalment loans or possessing credit cards sometimes encourages consumers to make expensive purchases they later regret. The solution to this problem is simple: After you select a product, resist any sales pressure to buy immediately and take a day to think it over.

The second situation is one in which you can afford to pay cash. Consider the trade-offs and opportunity costs involved. Paying cash is almost always cheaper than using credit. In fact, some stores offer a discount for payment in cash.

WHAT KIND OF LOAN SHOULD YOU SEEK?

As discussed in the last chapter, two types of credit exist: consumer loans and revolving credit. Because instalment loans may carry a lower interest rate, they are the less expensive credit option for loans that are repaid over a period of many months or years. However, because credit cards usually provide a float period—a certain number of days during which no interest is charged—they represent the cheaper way to make credit purchases that are paid off in a month or two. Also, once you have a credit card, using it is always easier than taking out an instalment loan. An alternative to a credit card is a travel and entertainment (T&E) card, such as an American Express or Diners/En Route card. A T&E card usually requires full payment of the balance due each month and does not impose a finance charge, although some cards, such as American Express, offer the option to pay over time. Annual fees on T&E cards can be high.

In seeking an instalment loan, you may think first of borrowing from a bank or a credit union. However, less expensive credit sources are available.

INEXPENSIVE LOANS   Parents or family members are often the source of the least expensive loans. They may charge you only the interest they would have earned had they not made the loan—as little as the percentage they would have earned on a passbook account. In order to avoid the income tax attribution rules described in Chapter 3, family members should charge a rate equal to or greater than the CRA's prescribed rate, set quarterly. However, such loans can complicate family relationships. All loans to or from family members should be in writing and state the interest rate, if any, repayment schedule, and the final payment date.

Also relatively inexpensive is money borrowed on financial assets held by a lending institution—for example, a bank Guaranteed Investment Certificate (GIC) or the cash value of a whole life insurance policy. The interest rate on such loans typically ranges from 4 to 7 percent. But the trade-off is that your assets are tied up until you repay the loan.

MEDIUM-PRICED LOANS   Often, you can obtain medium-priced loans from banks, trust companies, and credit unions. New-car loans, for example, may cost 5 to 9 percent; used-car loans and home improvement loans may cost slightly more.

Borrowing from credit unions has several advantages. These institutions provide credit life insurance, are generally sympathetic to borrowers with legitimate payment problems, and provide personalized service. Credit unions can now offer the same range of consumer loans that banks and other financial institutions do. More than 10 million Canadians belong to credit unions, and the number of credit union members has been growing steadily. About 360 credit unions exist in Canada today.

EXPENSIVE LOANS   Though convenient to obtain, the most expensive loans available are from finance companies, retailers, and banks through credit cards. Finance companies often lend to people who cannot obtain credit from banks or credit unions. Typically, the interest ranges from 12 to 25 percent, although a card from The Bay or Canadian Tire can cost up to 29 percent. Other organizations, such as Money Mart, provide cheque cashing and related financing services that can cost up to 1 percent per week. By law, no lender in Canada can charge a rate higher than 60 percent per annum. If you are denied credit by a bank or a credit union, you should question your ability to afford the higher rate a loan company charges.

Borrowing from used car dealers, appliance stores, department stores, and other retailers is also relatively expensive. The interest rates retailers charge are usually similar to those charged by finance companies, frequently 20 percent or more.

Banks lend funds not only through instalment loans but also through cash advances on MasterCard or Visa cards. Credit card co-branding has become increasingly popular with banks and industries. Co-branded credit cards, such as the Target-RBC Mastercard, make shopping at Target even more economical. Target designates the Target-RBC Mastercard as its "preferred card" and promotes the card throughout its stores and online and offers customers an additional 5 percent discount each time the card is used at a Target location.

One type of loan from finance companies is currently less expensive than most other credit forms discussed. Loans of this kind, which often can be obtained at a rate of under 5 percent, are available from the finance companies of major automakers. But a car dealer that offers you such a rate may be less willing to discount the price of the car or throw in free options.

STUDENT LOANS   Inexpensive loans to finance education beyond high school are available from the Government of Canada. The interest charged on these types of loans is lower than commercial rates because these rates are subsidized by the federal government. Moreover, you don't have to begin to repay your loans until you complete your education. Exhibit 6-1 presents a summary of various loan programs and their important features.

Student loans, unlike grants and work-study, are borrowed money that must be repaid, with interest, just like car loans and mortgages. You cannot have these loans cancelled because you were dissatisfied with your education, didn't get a job in your field of study, or because you are in financial difficulty. Loans are legal obligations, so before you take out a student loan, think about the amount you'll have to repay over the years.

GOVERNMENT STUDENT LOAN PROGRAMS   The Government of Canada offers loans to full- and part-time post-secondary students who demonstrate financial need in most provinces and territories across Canada.

In Canada, there are two main student loan programs, one federal and the other provincial. The federal program is called the Canada Student Loans Program (CSLP) and is open to both full-time and part-time students. There are also provincial and territorial programs; however, in five provinces these two programs have been integrated. This essentially means that students apply only to their province of residence. In addition, the repayment and management of the loan is done through one entity, the National Student Loans Service Centre. The five provinces offering the integrated loans are Ontario, British Columbia, New Brunswick, Newfoundland and Labrador, and Saskatchewan.

All other provinces and territories, with the exception of Yukon, offer stand-alone loans. This means that although students apply to only one place for assistance, they must manage and repay two separate loans. For information on student financial aid from individual provinces, visit canlearn.ca/eng/loans-grants/loans/provincial.shtml.

In addition to the CSLP, the government of Canada also offers grants through the Canada Student Grants Program (CSGP) by offering additional assistance to those who demonstrate greater need. The main difference between grants and loans is that grants do not have to be paid back.

Exhibit 6–1   Student Loan Comparison Chart

Loan Program	Eligibility	Award Amounts	Interest Rates	Links
Ontario Student Assistance Program (OSAP)	Graduate and undergraduate students	The federal government funds 60 percent of a student's loan, up to a maximum of $210 per week of study, which is provided to students in September. The provincial government funds the remaining 40 percent, up to $150 per week, which is provided in January.	On the provincial part of the loan, the interest rate is the prime rate of interest plus 1 percent. The interest rate on Canada Student Loan portion is prime plus 2.5 percent and you have the option of a one-time lock in at prime plus 5 percent.	https://osap.gov .on.ca/OSAPPortal
Newfoundland and Labrador Student Financial Assistance	Post-secondary education	Full-time students: provincial loan—$140 per week. Full-time students: federal loan—$210 per week. Part-time students: federal loan—maximum of $10,000	No interest will accumulate on the Newfoundland and Labrador portion of your student loan. The interest rate on Canada Student Loan payments is prime plus 2.5 percent and you have the option of a one-time lock in at prime plus 5 percent.	http://www.aes .gov.nl.ca/ studentaid/
Saskatchewan Student Financial Assistance	Post-secondary education	Full-time students: provincial loan—$198 per week. Full-time students: federal loan—$210 per week. Part-time students: federal loan—maximum of $10,000	On the provincial part of the loan, the variable interest rate is the prime rate of interest and the fixed interest rate is the prime rate plus 2.5 percent. The variable interest rate on Canada Student Loan portion is prime plus 2.5 percent and you have the option of a one-time lock in at prime plus 5 percent.	http://ae.gov.sk.ca/ student-loan- handbook-2014-15
Canada Student Loan and New Brunswick Student Loan	Post-secondary education, full-time students	The Government of Canada provides 60 percent of assessed need in the form of Canada Student Loan funding, up to a maximum of $210 per week of study. The Government of New Brunswick provides 40 percent of assessed need in the form of New Brunswick Student Loan funding, up to $140 per week of study.	Same as above	studentaid.gnb.ca

According to the CSLP and CSGP Web site (hrsdc.gc.ca/eng/learning/canada_student_loan/index.shtml), the Government of Canada provides 60 percent of the assessed need, up to a maximum of $210 in loans per week of study. The remaining 40 percent may be provided in the form of provincial or territorial student loans.

An estimated 4.3 million students have received almost $32 billion in Canada student loans since the CSLP was created in 1964. In 2011–2012, the CSLP provided over $2.4 billion in full- and part-time student loans to approximately 345,000 students and awarded $647 million in non-repayable Canada Study Grants and Canada Access Grants (336,000 grants).

CONCEPT CHECK 6–1

1. Why do students fall prey to late-payment fees?

2. What are the major sources of consumer credit?

3. What are some advantages and disadvantages of securing a loan from a credit union? From a finance company?

4. The CLSP has agreed to lend you funds to complete your 3-year bachelors' degree. The government will lend you $2,400 if you agree to repay the loan five years from now with a lump-sum payment of $5,000. What annual interest rate is the CLSP charging you?

THE COST OF CREDIT

LO2

Determine the effective cost of borrowing by considering the quoted rate, the number of compounding periods, the timing of the interest payments, and any other service charges.

If you are thinking of borrowing money or opening a credit account, your first step should be to figure out how much it will cost you and whether you can afford it. Then, you should shop for the best terms. Two key concepts that you should remember are the finance charge and the annual percentage rate.

THE EFFECTIVE COST OF BORROWING

Credit costs vary. The effective annual interest rate charged on a loan depends upon the quoted annual percentage rate, how frequently interest is compounded, whether interest is charged on a discount basis (up front), and whether any other charges are incurred, such as service charges, credit-related insurance premiums, or appraisal fees.

annual percentage rate (APR) The yearly interest rate quoted by a financial institution on a loan. The APR may be compounded more frequently than once a year, in which case the effective annual rate on the loan will be higher than the APR.

The **annual percentage rate (APR)** is the yearly interest rate quoted by the financial institution on a loan. However, interest may be charged more frequently than once a year—for example, on a monthly basis. In this case, we say that the loan is compounded monthly. The higher the compounding frequency, the higher is the effective annual rate (EAR) of the loan, as demonstrated in the table below. Effective annual rates were discussed in Chapter 4, The Banking Services of Financial Institutions, on page 116. Financial institutions are obliged to disclose both the APR and the EAR to the borrower at the time the loan contract is signed.

Quoted APR	EAR If Compounding Frequency Is			
	Semi-annually	**Monthly**	**Weekly**	**Daily**
5	5.0625	5.1162	5.1246	5.1267
6	6.0900	6.1678	6.1800	6.1831
7	7.1225	7.2290	7.2458	7.2501
8	8.1600	8.3000	8.3220	8.3278
9	9.2025	9.3807	9.4089	9.4162
10	10.2500	10.4713	10.5065	10.5156

Let's look at an example. Suppose you wish to borrow $100 from an unsecured personal line of credit for a year and your bank quotes you an annual interest rate of 6 percent, compounded semi-annually. The quoted rate of 6 percent is the APR. Compounding semi-annually means that the bank will charge you 3 percent interest on the loan after six months (6 percent ÷ 2) and another 3 percent after the remaining six months. When you repay the loan after one year, you will owe $3 of interest for the first semi-annual period ($100 × 3 percent) and, as this interest is not actually paid but added to the amount you owe, the interest charged for the second six months of the year will be $3.09 ($103 × 3 percent). The total interest charge will equal $6.09 ($3 + $3.09) and the effective annual interest rate of your loan will be 6.09 percent ($6.09 ÷ $100 × 100).

We can calculate the effective annual interest rate on the loan using the following formula, where m equals the number of times a year the interest is compounded:

$$EAR = (1 + APR/m)^m - 1$$

$$EAR = (1 + 0.06/2)^2 - 1 = 0.0609 \times 100 = 6.09\%$$

If the financial institution charges interest up front, we say that the loan is made on a discount basis. Interest that is prepaid increases the effective annual cost of the loan. For example, assume that a bank quotes a loan rate of 5 percent, compounded monthly. We can see from the previous table that the EAR charged on the loan is 5.1162 percent. This is the effective annual cost of the loan if the interest and principal are repaid after one year. However, if you pay the $5.1162 in interest up front, the actual dollar amount you are able to use over the year equals $94.8838. This means that the effective annual cost of borrowing is 5.3921 percent [($5.1162 ÷ $94.8838) × 100]. Discounting interest results in a higher annual cost of borrowing.

What if the financial institution charges you an upfront administrative fee of $5 on your loan, but interest is repaid after one year? At an APR of 5 percent, compounded monthly, the effective annual interest rate on the loan is 5.1162 percent. However, the $5 fee reduces the funds available to you over the year. You would pay $5.1162 for the use of $95 ($100 − $5). As is the case with discount interest, the administrative fee increases the effective annual cost of your loan, this time to 5.3855 percent [($5.1162 ÷ $95) × 100].

TACKLING THE TRADE-OFFS

When you choose your financing, there are trade-offs between the features you prefer (term, size of payments, fixed or variable interest, or payment plan) and the cost of your loan. Here are some of the major trade-offs you should consider.

TERM VERSUS INTEREST COSTS   Many people choose longer-term financing because they want smaller monthly payments. But the longer the term for a loan at a given interest rate, the greater is the amount you must pay in interest charges. Consider the following analysis of the relationship between the term and interest costs.

Even when you understand the terms a creditor offers, it's easy to underestimate the difference in dollars that different terms can make. Suppose you're buying a $7,500 used car. You put down $1,500, and you need to borrow $6,000. Compare the following three credit arrangements:

	APR, Compounded Monthly	Term of Loan	Monthly Payment	Total Amount Repaid	Total Interest Cost
Creditor A	6%	36 months	$182.53	$6,571.14	$571.14
Creditor B	6%	48 months	$140.91	$6,763.73	$763.73
Creditor C	7%	48 months	$146.48	$7,030.91	$1,030.91

Financial Planning for Life's Situations

In Canada, from 1980 to 1995, credit card interest rates generally moved up and down with the bank rate, with a time lag. However, this trend has not been evident in the past few years. Generally, the interest rates on standard cards have not moved along with the bank rate since 1995, and low-rate cards have not followed suit since 1999. Moreover, retail credit card rates have not changed in the last 25 years (see the following chart, which shows that the rate has not changed significantly for the past two decades even though the general level of interest rates has).

THE BANK OF CANADA RATE AND CREDIT CARD INTEREST RATES

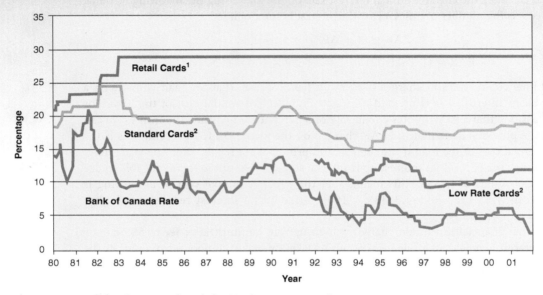

[1] Based on the average of the Sears card and the Hudson's Bay card
[2] Based on the average of the six major banks (for purchases)

SOURCE: Federal Consumer Agency of Canada (FCAC), "Credit Cards and You." *Quarterly Credit Card Cost Report*, December 2001, fcac-acfc.gc.ca.

How do these choices compare? The answer depends partly on what you need. The lowest-cost loan is available from creditor A. If you are looking for lower monthly payments, you could repay the loan over a longer period of time. However, you would have to pay more in total costs. A loan from creditor B—also at a 6 percent APR, but for four years—adds about $193 to your finance charge.

If that four-year loan were available only from creditor C, the APR of 7 percent would add another $267 to your total interest cost. Other terms, such as the size of the down payment, will also make a difference. Be sure to look at all the terms before you make your choice.

LENDER RISK VERSUS INTEREST RATE   You may prefer financing that requires low fixed payments with a large final payment or only a minimum of upfront cash. But both of these requirements can increase your cost of borrowing because they create more risk for your lender.

If you want to minimize your borrowing costs, you may need to accept conditions that reduce your lender's risk. Here are a few possibilities.

VARIABLE INTEREST RATE   A variable interest rate is based on fluctuating rates in the banking system, such as the prime rate. With this type of loan, you share the interest rate risks with the lender. Therefore, the lender may offer you a lower initial interest rate than it would with a fixed-rate loan.

A SECURED LOAN   If you pledge property or other assets as collateral, you'll probably receive a lower interest rate on your loan.

UPFRONT CASH   Many lenders believe you have a higher stake in repaying a loan if you pay cash for a large portion of what you are financing. Doing so may give you a better chance of getting the other terms you want. Of course, by making a large down payment, you forgo interest that you might earn in a savings account.

A SHORTER TERM   As you have learned, the shorter the period of time for which you borrow, the smaller the chance that something will prevent you from repaying and the lower the risk to the lender. Therefore, you may be able to borrow at a lower interest rate if you accept a shorter-term loan, but your payments will be higher.

   In the next section, you will see how the above-mentioned trade-offs can affect the cost of consumer loans and revolving credit.

CALCULATING YOUR LOAN PAYMENTS

In this section, we examine how your loan payments are determined for two typical forms of consumer credit—a fixed-rate instalment loan and a floating-rate personal line of credit—and highlight the advantages and disadvantages of each.

FIXED-RATE INSTALMENT LOAN   Peter MacLellan wants to buy a used car. The car's list price is $10,000 and a sales tax of 15 percent applies, bringing the total cost of the car to $11,500 ($10,000 $\times$ 1.15). Peter has $6,500 for a down payment and approaches his bank for a $5,000 loan to be repaid in equal monthly instalments over one year. The bank quotes a fixed rate of 6 percent, compounded monthly, meaning that Peter's monthly interest rate is 0.50 percent (6 percent $\div$ 12). The monthly payment on Peter's car loan is fixed over the term of the loan and is calculated as follows (refer to the time value of money discussion in Chapter 1 and the formula given in Exhibit 1B–4 on page 46):

$$\$5,000 = \text{PMT} \left[\frac{1 - [1 \div (1.0050)^{12}]}{0.0050} \right]$$

$$\$5,000 = \text{PMT} \,[11.619]$$

$$\text{PMT} = \$5,000 \div 11.619 = \$430.33$$

or by using the BAII calculator as follows (remember to set the I/Y button to 1, as explained in Chapter 1):

2ND	F	CLRTVM
5,000 +/−		PV
12		N
0.50		I/Y
CPT	PMT	$430.33

   Peter's loan is amortized over 12 months; this means that the monthly payments he makes will gradually reduce the loan balance. Each payment is composed of interest and principal repayments, with the interest component higher in the earlier payments and reducing over time. As his loan approaches maturity, more of the monthly payment will be used to pay off the principal than to pay the interest. See the following loan amortization chart.

Month	Beginning Loan Balance	Payment	Interest	Principal Reduction	Remaining Balance
1	$5,000.00	$430.33	$25.00	$405.33	$4,594.67
2	$4,594.67	$430.33	$22.97	$407.36	$4,187.31
3	$4,187.31	$430.33	$20.94	$409.39	$3,777.92
4	$3,777.92	$430.33	$18.89	$411.44	$3,366.48
5	$3,366.48	$430.33	$16.83	$413.50	$2,952.98
6	$2,952.98	$430.33	$14.76	$415.57	$2,537.41
7	$2,537.41	$430.33	$12.69	$417.64	$2,119.77
8	$2,119.77	$430.33	$10.60	$419.73	$1,700.04
9	$1,700.04	$430.33	$8.50	$421.83	$1,278.21
10	$1,278.21	$430.33	$6.39	$423.94	$854.27
11	$854.27	$430.33	$4.27	$426.06	$428.21
12	$428.21	$430.35	$2.14	$428.21	$0.00

Instalment loans impose financial responsibility as they are designed to pay off the loan over a pre-determined period of time. Each payment represents a blend of interest and principal. With blended payments, interest owing is satisfied first and the remaining portion of the payment is applied to the principal.

FLOATING-RATE PERSONAL LINE OF CREDIT   Had Peter made arrangements with his bank to set up a personal line of credit, he could have drawn down the required $5,000 loan when he purchased the car. Lines of credit usually charge a variable interest rate tied to the lender's prime rate. Interest is compounded daily. In view of Peter's credit risk, let's assume that his bank charges him a rate of prime plus 2 percent. The line of credit payment may be interest only, but borrowers are often required to repay a minimum 3 to 5 percent of the outstanding loan balance on a periodic basis. We will assume that Peter must pay at least 5 percent of the outstanding loan balance each month.

If the prime rate is 3 percent and he pays 2 percent above prime, then the daily interest rate charged on Peter's line of credit is 0.01369863 percent (5 percent ÷ 365). Assuming 30 days in each month, his first three loan payments are:

Month	Beginning Loan Balance	Interest Charge	Principal Reduction	Total Payment	Ending Loan Balance
1	$5,000.00	$20.55*	$250.00	$270.55	$4,750.00
2	$4,750.00	$19.52	$237.50	$257.02	$4,512.50
3	$4,512.50	$18.54	$225.63	$244.17	$4,286.87

*Calculated as: $5,000 × 0.0001369863 × 30

If the prime rate rises to 5 percent, the interest rate on Peter's loan will rise to 7 percent (5 percent + 2 percent). His daily interest rate will be 0.0191781 percent (7 percent ÷ 365) and his fourth loan payment is:

| 4 | $4,286.87 | $24.66 | $214.34 | $239.00 | $4,072.53 |

Notice that Peter's total loan payment drops to $239 from $244.17 because he is required to pay a lesser amount against the principal each month. However, the interest component of his fourth payment has risen because the bank's prime rate rose 2 percent. Peter's loan payments are not fixed and are subject to the risk that interest rates could rise (unless he has the option to lock in the current rate). However, if interest rates fall, the interest component of his total payment will fall as well. In this way, a floating interest rate can be either an advantage or a disadvantage to the borrower.

The principal disadvantage of using an interest-only line of credit, or one with a very low minimum principal repayment, is the considerably longer time it takes to repay the loan compared to a traditional consumer instalment loan. If Peter makes only the minimum required principal payment each month, it will take him almost eight years to reimburse the principal of $5,000 on his line of credit!

FINANCIAL PLANNING CALCULATIONS

When you apply to a financial institution for a consumer instalment loan, the loan officer can provide you with a complete amortization schedule, as described above. However, there is a shorter way to determine your loan balance at any point in time, or what the interest and principal components of any payment might be.

The balance of a loan equals the present value of the remaining payments. Referring to Peter's automobile loan, what is his loan balance after three payments?

2ND	F	CLRTVM
$430.33		PMT
12 − 3 =		N
0.50		I/Y
CPT	PMT	$3,777.92

Once we determine his loan balance at any point in time, we can then calculate the interest and principal components of the next payment, in this instance the fourth payment:

$$\text{Interest} \quad \$3{,}777.92 \times 0.50 \div 100 \quad = \$18.89$$

$$\text{Principal} \quad \$430.33 - \$18.89 \quad = \$411.44$$

COST OF CARRYING CREDIT CARD BALANCES Revolving credit includes not only personal lines of credit, but also credit cards, store cards, and overdraft protection. During the month, all purchases made with a credit card are tallied and appear on the bill issued on the card's billing date. This delay in billing can be viewed as a period during which you benefit from an interest-free loan. In addition, creditors must tell you when finance charges on your credit account begin so that you know how much time you have to pay your bills before a finance charge is added. Some creditors, for example, give you a 20- to 25-day grace period, from the billing date, to pay your balance in full before imposing a finance charge. But in most cases, the grace period applies only if you have no outstanding balance on your card.

When you do not pay off the balance on your bank or store credit card each month, an interest charge will appear on your following monthly statement. Creditors use various methods to calculate the balance on which they will apply interest charges. Some creditors add interest after subtracting payments made during the billing period; this is called the **adjusted balance method**. Other creditors give you no credit for payments made during the billing period; this is called the **previous balance method**. Under the third—and the fairest—method, the **average daily balance method**, creditors add your balances for each day in the billing period and then divide by the number of days in the period. The average daily balance may include or exclude new purchases during the billing period.

adjusted balance method The assessment of finance charges after payments made during the billing period have been subtracted.

previous balance method A method of computing finance charges that gives no credit for payments made during the billing period.

average daily balance method A method of computing finance charges that uses a weighted average of the account balance throughout the current billing period.

Here is how these different methods of calculating the interest on unpaid credit card balances affect the cost of credit:

	Average Daily Balance (including new purchases)	Average Daily Balance (excluding new purchases)
Monthly rate	1½%	1½%
APR	18%	18%
Previous balance	$400	$400
New purchases	$50 on 18th day	$50 on 18th day
Payments	$300 on 15th day (new balance = $100)	$300 on 15th day (new balance = $100)
Average daily balance	$270*	$250**
Finance charge	$4.05 (1½% × $270)	$3.75 (1½% × $250)

*To figure average daily balance (*including* new purchases):
        ($400 × 15 days) + ($100 × 3 days) + ($150 × 12 days) ÷ 30 days
        = ($6,000 + $300 + $1,800) ÷ 30 = $8,100 ÷ 30 days = $270
**To figure average daily balance (*excluding* new purchases):
        [($400 × 15 days) + ($100 × 15 days)] ÷ 30 days = $7,500 ÷ 30 days = $250

	Adjusted Balance	Previous Balance
Monthly rate	1½%	1½%
APR	18%	18%
Previous balance	$400	$400
Payments	$300	$300
Average daily balance	N/A	N/A
Finance charge	$1.50 (1½% × $100)	$6 (1½% × $400)

As the example shows, the interest charge varies for the same pattern of purchases and payments. Therefore, you benefit from an interest-free period on your card only if you pay the bill in full every month.

The following table shows how much you would save by using a low-rate credit card or a line of credit instead of a credit card with a higher rate of interest.

	Regular-Rate Credit Card	Low-Rate Credit Card	Line of Credit
Average monthly balance	$2,500	$2,500	$2,500
Annual interest rate[1]	× 18%	× 12%	× 7.0%
Annual interest charges	= $450	= $300	= $175
Annual fee[1]	+ $0	+ $20	+ $0
Total annual cost	= $450	= $320	= $175
Total annual savings[2]	—	$130	$275

[1] Based on the average of the six major banks, caisses, and credit unions listed in the comparison tables of this kit for both regular-rate and low-rate cards. For lines of credit, the annual interest rate approximates the June 2014 industry average and varies between institutions and with your credit rating.

[2] This example assumes you carry a constant balance of $2,500 and that you make all minimum payments on time. Otherwise, your interest rate may increase, or you may be subject to additional fees that will increase your overall costs. If you compare the low-rate card with a retail card for the same outstanding balance, the savings are even higher.

SOURCE: "Saving Money with a Low-Rate Credit Card or Line of Credit," fcac-acfc.gc.ca/eng/publications/CreditCardsYou/PDFs/Money-e.pdf, Financial Consumer Agency of Canada, 2004. Reproduced with the permission of the Minister of Public Works and Government Services Canada, 2008.

COST OF CREDIT AND EXPECTED INFLATION   As you have seen, interest rates dictate when you must pay future dollars to receive current dollars. However, borrowers and lenders, are less concerned about dollars, present or future, than about the goods and services those dollars can buy—that is, their purchasing power.

Inflation erodes the purchasing power of money. Each percentage point increase in inflation means a decrease of approximately 1 percent in the quantity of goods and services you can purchase with a given quantity of dollars. As a result, lenders, seeking to protect their purchasing power, add the expected rate of inflation to the interest rate they charge. You are willing to pay this higher rate because you expect inflation to enable you to repay the loan with cheaper dollars.

For example, if a lender expects a 4 percent inflation rate for the coming year and wants an 8 percent return on a loan, you will probably be charged a 12 percent nominal or stated rate (a 4 percent inflation premium plus an 8 percent "real" rate).

For another example, assume you borrowed $1,000 from your relative at the bargain rate of 5 percent for one year. If the inflation rate was 4 percent during that year, your relative's real rate of return was only 1 percent (5 percent stated interest − 4 percent inflation rate) and your "real" cost was not $50 but only $10 ($50 − $40 inflation premium).

AVOID THE MINIMUM MONTHLY PAYMENT TRAP   The "minimum monthly payment" is the smallest amount you can pay and still be a cardholder in good standing. Banks often encourage you to make the minimum payment, such as 3–5 percent of your outstanding balance or a minimum of $10. Some statements refer to the minimum as the "cardholder amount due." But that is not the total amount you owe. To help consumers understand the "trap" associated with minimum rates, credit card issuers must assist consumers manage their credit card obligations by providing information on the time it would take to fully repay the balance, if only the minimum payment is made every month.

Consider the following examples. In each example, the minimum payment is based on $1/36$ of the outstanding balance or $20, whichever is greater.

Example 1   You are buying new books for your courses. If you spend $500 on textbooks using a credit card charging 19.8 percent interest and make only the minimum payment, it will take you more than 2½ years to pay off the loan, adding $150 in interest charges to the cost of your purchase. The same purchase on a credit card charging 12 percent interest costs $78 extra.

Example 2   You purchase a $2,000 3-D television using a credit card with 19 percent interest and a 2 percent minimum payment. If you pay just the minimum every month, it will take you 265 months—more than 22 years—to pay off the debt and cost you nearly $4,800 in interest payments. Doubling the amount paid each month to 4 percent of the balance owed allows you to shorten the payment time to 88 months from 265 months—or 7 years as opposed to 22 years—and save you about $3,680.

Example 3   You charge $2,000 in tuition and fees on a credit card charging 18.5 percent interest. If you pay off the balance by making the minimum payment each month, it will take you more than 11 years to repay the debt. By the time you pay off the loan, you will have spent an extra $1,934 in interest alone—almost the actual cost of your tuition and fees. Again, to be prudent, pay off the balance as quickly as possible.

CREDIT INSURANCE

Credit insurance ensures the repayment of your loan in the event of death, disability, or loss of property. The lender is named the beneficiary and directly receives any payments made on submitted claims.

There are three types of credit insurance: credit life, credit accident and health, and credit property. The most commonly purchased type of credit insurance is credit life insurance, which provides for the repayment of the loan if the borrower dies. According to many consumer organizations, most borrowers don't need credit life insurance. Those who don't have life insurance can buy term life insurance for less. Term life insurance is discussed in Chapter 9.

credit insurance Any type of insurance that ensures repayment of a loan in the event the borrower is unable to repay it.

Credit accident and health insurance, also called *credit disability insurance*, repays your loan in the event of a loss of income due to illness or injury. Credit property insurance provides coverage for personal property purchased with a loan. It may also insure collateral property, such as a car or furniture. However, premiums for such coverage are quite high and the coverage may be substandard.

CONCEPT CHECK 6–2

1. Distinguish between the APR and the EAR.
2. What can you learn from a loan amortization schedule?
3. Distinguish among the adjusted balance, previous balance, and average daily balance methods of calculating the cost of revolving credit.

MANAGING YOUR DEBTS

LO3

Develop a plan to manage your debts.

A sudden illness or the loss of your job may make it impossible for you to pay your bills on time. If you find you cannot make your payments, contact your creditors at once and try to work out a modified payment plan with them. If you have paid your bills promptly in the past, they may be willing to work with you. Do not wait until your account is turned over to a debt collector. At that point, the creditor has given up on you.

Automobile loans present special problems. Most automobile financing agreements permit your creditor to repossess your car anytime you are in default on your payments. No advance notice is required. If your car is repossessed and sold, you will still owe the difference between the selling price and the unpaid debt, plus any legal, towing, and storage charges. Try to solve the problem with your creditor when you realize you will not be able to meet your payments. It may be better to sell the car yourself and pay off your debt than to incur the added costs of repossession.

If you are having trouble paying your bills, you may be tempted to turn to a company that claims to offer assistance in solving debt problems. Such companies may offer debt consolidation loans, debt counselling, or debt reorganization plans that are "guaranteed" to stop creditors' collection efforts. Before signing with such a company, investigate it. Be sure you understand what services the company provides and what they will cost you. Do not rely on verbal promises that do not appear in your contract. Also, check with the Better Business Bureau and your provincial or local consumer protection office. It may be able to tell you whether other consumers have registered complaints about the company.

Did you know?

The Royal Bank of Canada offers a number of online tools aimed at helping consumers manage their money. Visit http://www.rbcroyalbank.com/personal-loans/budget/budget-calculator.html to view a sample tool and explore the RBC Web site to view all the tools available.

WARNING SIGNS OF DEBT PROBLEMS

Jerome Olsen, in his early 30s, has a steady job with a $55,000 annual income. Jerome, his wife, and their two children enjoy a comfortable life. A new car is parked in the driveway of their home, which is furnished with such modern conveniences as a new induction oven, a new built-in freezer, an Apple in-home automation system, a fully automatic espresso machine, and a 90″ 3-D television.

However, Jerome Olsen is in debt. He is drowning in a sea of bills, with most of his income tied up in repaying debts. Foreclosure proceedings on his home have been instituted, and several stores have court orders to repossess practically every major appliance in it. His current car payment is overdue, and three charge accounts at local stores are several months delinquent.

This case is neither exaggerated nor isolated. Unfortunately, a large number of people are in the same floundering state. These people's problem is immaturity. Mature consumers have certain information; they demonstrate self-discipline, control their impulses, and use sound judgment; they accept responsibility for money management; and they are able to postpone and govern expenditures when overextension of credit appears likely.

Referring to overindebtedness as one of the nation's main family financial problems, an expert on consumer affairs lists the following as frequent reasons for indebtedness:[1]

1. *Emotional problems,* such as the need for instant gratification, as in the case of a man who can't resist buying a costly suit or a woman who impulsively purchases an expensive dress in a trendy department store.
2. *The use of money to punish,* such as a husband who buys a new car without consulting his wife, who, in turn, buys a diamond watch to get even.
3. *The expectation of instant comfort* among those who assume that by use of the instalment plan they can immediately have the possessions their parents acquired after years of work.
4. *Keeping up with the Joneses,* which is more apparent than ever, not only among prosperous families but also among limited-income families.
5. *Overindulgence of children,* often because of the parents' own emotional needs, competition with each other, or inadequate communication regarding expenditures for the children.
6. *Misunderstanding or lack of communication among family members.* For example, a salesperson visited a Calgary family to sell them an expensive freezer. Although the freezer was beyond the means of this already overindebted family and too large for their needs anyway, the husband thought his wife wanted it. Not until later, in an interview with a debt counsellor, did the wife relate her concern when she signed the contract; she had wanted her husband to say no.
7. *The amount of the finance charges,* which can push a family over the edge of their ability to pay, especially when they borrow from one company to pay another and these charges pyramid.

Did you know?

Visa International offers the guide *Practical Money Skills for Consumers,* with worksheets that calculate budgets, loans, mortgages, etc. Visit practicalmoneyskills.ca for more information.

Exhibit 6–2 lists some danger signals of potential debt problems.

THE SERIOUS CONSEQUENCES OF DEBT

Just as the causes of indebtedness vary, so too does a mixture of other personal and family problems that frequently result from overextending credit.

There are a number of warning signs that tell you when you are too far in debt and need to make changes in order to avoid bankruptcy. You are too far in debt if you:

- continually go over your spending limit or use your credit cards as a necessity rather than a convenience;
- borrow money to make it from one payday to the next;
- have had your wages garnished to pay for outstanding debts;
- pay only interest or service charges monthly and do not reduce your total debt over many months;
- have creditors pressuring you for payment, threatening to sue or repossess your car, furniture, or television, or hire a collection agency to recover the money for them; or
- have your utility companies cut off service because your bills have gone unpaid.

Depending on your personal circumstances and the extent of the problem, several options are available to help you reduce your debt.

SOURCE: "Dealing with Debt: A Consumer's Guide," Industry Canada, Office of the Superintendent of Bankruptcy Canada, http://www.ic.gc.ca/eic/site/bsf-osb.nsf/eng/br01861.html, accessed June 16, 2014.

Exhibit 6–2

Warning Signs of Debt

Seek help from a consumer credit counselling service if you experience any of these warning signs.

---

[1] Judy Hammond, "Consumer Credit Counselors Say Debt Recovery Can Take Three to Five Years," *Knight-Ridder/Tribune Business News,* February 16, 1999.

Losing a job because of garnishment proceedings may occur in a family that has a disproportionate amount of income tied up in debts. Another possibility is that such a family is forced to neglect vital areas. In the frantic effort to rob Peter to pay Paul, scrimping may seriously affect the family's health and neglect the educational needs of children. Excessive indebtedness may also result in heavy drinking, neglect of children, marital difficulties, and drug abuse. But help is available to those debtors who seek it.

CONCEPT CHECK 6–3

1. What are the most frequent reasons for indebtedness?
2. What are common danger signals of potential debt problems?

CONSUMER CREDIT COUNSELLING SERVICES

LO4

Evaluate various private and governmental sources that assist consumers with debt problems.

If you are having problems paying your bills and need help, you have several options. You can contact your creditors and try to work out an adjusted repayment plan yourself, or you can check your telephone directory for a non-profit financial counselling program to get help.

Various provincial authorities provide debt counselling services for families and individuals with financial problems. For example, the Government of Alberta's Web site provides a consumer tip sheet at http://www.servicealberta.ca/ConsumerTipsheets.cfm#credit. Links to the federal government's various consumer tip sheets and services can be found at http://www.fcac-acfc.gc.ca/Eng/resources/publications/creditLoans/Pages/home-accueil.aspx.

Credit counsellors are aware that most people who are in debt over their heads are basically honest people who want to clear up their indebtedness. Too often, the problems of such people arise from a lack of planning or a miscalculation of what they earn. Therefore, the counsellor is as concerned with preventing the problems as with solving them. As a result, credit counselling activities are divided into two parts:

1. Aiding people with serious debt problems by helping them manage their money better and setting up a realistic budget and plan for expenditures.
2. Helping people prevent debt problems by teaching them the necessity of family budget planning, providing education to people of all ages regarding the pitfalls of unwise credit buying, suggesting techniques for family budgeting, and encouraging credit institutions to provide full information about the costs and terms of credit and to withhold credit from those who cannot afford to repay it.

Universities, military bases, credit unions, some employers, and provincial and federal housing authorities sometimes provide non-profit counselling services. These organizations usually charge little or nothing for such assistance. You can also check with your local bank or consumer protection office to see whether it has a listing of reputable, low-cost financial counselling services.

But what if a debtor suffers from an extreme case of financial woes? Is there any relief? The answer is yes: bankruptcy proceedings.

CONCEPT CHECK 6–4

1. What is a credit counselling service?
2. What are the two major activities of credit counselling services?
3. What options do consumers have for financial counselling?

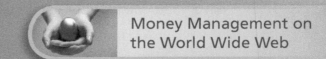
Whether you're developing a plan for reaching your financial goals or searching for a low-interest credit card, you can look to the Internet for a world of free information. Many Web sites provide interactive worksheets that allow you to plug in personal information and obtain customized reports. Here are some suggestions.

Leadfusion, at leadfusion.com, provides nifty payment calculators that help you figure out the actual dollars paid in interest over the period of a credit card debt or the maximum amount you should borrow at your current income. If your payments have been piling up, take a deep breath before travelling here.

Canoe Money, at money.canoe.ca, provides you with everything you need to successfully manage your personal finances. News and reference materials allow you stay up to date on money matters. You can also use analytical tools to track your investments and plan your finances, and there are discussion groups and real-time chats with experts.

The Canadian Association of Financial Planners, at cafp.org, offers consumer information on what to expect from a financial planner, as well as how and why to choose one. A handy search tool lets you pinpoint an adviser close to home.

The Quicken Financial Network, at quicken.intuit.ca, is the developer of the popular software programs Quicken and TurboTax, which encompass a financial fitness test, expert advice, investment tracking, and other financial help.

Credit Counselling Canada at creditcounsellingcanada.ca, is a non-profit organization that provides consumer credit education and services throughout Canada.

DECLARING PERSONAL BANKRUPTCY

Janine Leclaire typifies the new face of bankruptcy. A 50-year-old freelance commercial photographer from Victoria, British Columbia, she was never in serious financial trouble until she began incurring big dental costs last year and reached for her credit cards to pay the bills. Since Janine didn't have dental insurance, her debt quickly mounted. It was too much for her to pay off with her $25,000-a-year freelance income. Her solution: Declare personal bankruptcy for the immediate freedom it would bring from creditors' demands.

LO5
Assess the choices in declaring personal bankruptcy.

Ms. Leclaire's move put her in familiar company, demographically speaking. An increasing number of bankruptcy filers are well-educated, middle-class baby boomers with an overwhelming level of credit card debt. A recent report by the Vanier Institute notes that "Over the last 20 years, the number of Canadians over 65 who have declared bankruptcy has gone up by an incredible seventeen hundred percent. The insolvency rate increase for the population as a whole rose by only 139% over the same period. These numbers underline the precarious economic situation of many seniors, particularly those living alone or unattached." (Source: http://www.vanierinstitute.ca/modules/news/newsitem.php?ItemId=423)

Unfortunately for some debtors, bankruptcy has become an acceptable tool of credit management. In the years 1997–2012, consumer bankruptcies and proposals increased by 86.5 percent (see Exhibit 6–3).

FENDING OFF BANKRUPTCY: CONSOLIDATION LOANS

Sometimes it may be possible to avoid declaring bankruptcy. If you are under an excessive debt load and would like to regularize and control your payments, you may be able to obtain a consolidation loan. This is a new loan that is used to discharge a collection of existing debts and has various advantages and disadvantages.

The advantages of a consolidation loan are that it will have a single interest rate on the full amount of your selected debts, and you may be able to extend the term of the loan beyond that of your initial debts, allowing you to make smaller payments as you repay your loan.

The disadvantages of this type of loan are twofold: cost and term. In general, you will be asked to pay a higher interest rate because you are considered to be a higher risk for the lender.

Exhibit 6–3

Canadian Bankruptcies and Proposals 1997–2012

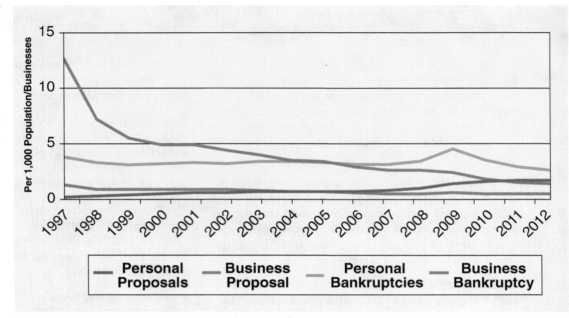

SOURCES: Reproduced from the Office of the Superintendent of Bankruptcy Canada Web site at https://www.ic.gc.ca/eic/site/bsf-osb.nsf/eng/br01819.html. Reproduced with permission of the Minister of Public Works and Government Services, 2008.

Did you know?

Declaring bankruptcy does not eliminate all of your obligations. For example, alimony or support payments, debts incurred through fraud, and court costs must still be paid. Student loans are only discharged once the individual has been out of school for more than 7 years.

In addition, as you extend the term of the loan you will find that the total of what you pay might be considerably higher than the sum of your debt load.

If you do decide to use a consolidation loan, it is best to limit it to paying off only your highest interest debts. It is unwise to use this option to pay off any debt that is low– or non–interest-bearing.

BANKRUPTCY AND INSOLVENCY ACT

The decision to declare bankruptcy is a hard one, but each year sees at least 100,000 Canadian consumers choosing this route when all else fails. The *Bankruptcy and Insolvency Act*, a commercial statute that is reviewed and amended on a regular basis and regulates bankruptcy (a straight declaration of insolvency) and proposal (a plan of arrangement) proceedings in Canada. It falls under the responsibility of the Office of the Superintendent of Bankruptcy at Industry Canada. By this Act you are allowed to declare insolvency either through a consumer proposal or through an assignment in bankruptcy.

consumer proposal
A maximum five-year plan for paying creditors all or a portion of a debt owed.

CONSUMER PROPOSALS   A **consumer proposal** is a maximum five-year plan for paying creditors all or a portion of the total debt owed. To be eligible for this type of insolvency protection application, you must be insolvent and be less than $250,000 in debt (excluding a mortgage on your principal residence). Initiating the process involves applying to an administrator of consumer proposals, who may be a trustee in bankruptcy or another person appointed by the Office of the Superintendent of Bankruptcy to the task. The administrator will provide you with counselling and guidance and will disburse paid funds to your creditors.

Both the court and your creditors must approve a consumer proposal. Once approved, it becomes binding for both you and your creditors. While, in general, this type of agreement will not release you from certain obligations, such as court imposed fines, alimony, or co-signer responsibilities, it does protect you from a number of types of harassment or abuse. Your creditors will be restricted from demanding accelerated payments; any pre-existing wage-garnishment arrangements will be annulled; and your employer cannot subject you to any type of disciplinary action resulting from your consumer proposal. When all the conditions of your consumer proposal have been met, you will be issued a "Certificate of Full Performance of Proposal."

The advantage of a consumer proposal is that it will save you from bankruptcy if it is approved. If it is not approved, either by the court or by your creditors, you may then need to seek a trustee in bankruptcy. This person is a federally licensed individual who administers bankruptcies.

BANKRUPTCY   Approximately 90 percent of all bankruptcies in Canada are by consumers, rather than businesses. If you are forced to take this choice, the first step is assigning your assets to a licensed trustee. From this time until you are released from your debt by the courts, you are considered an un-discharged bankrupt.

In some cases, a meeting will then be held with your creditors, who need to prove their claim against your estate. Your secured creditors, such as your mortgage and your car-loan lenders, will generally be paid first, as their claims are against specific assets. After that, your remaining assets are distributed by specified order with the costs of the bankruptcy administration taking precedence over all other claims. Once this process is complete, the court can grant you a discharge. This document frees you from all claims from creditors, with some exceptions, such as court imposed costs, alimony or support payments, and certain debts incurred through fraud.

PROTECTED ASSETS   It is important to realize that not all of your assets are seized or considered in a bankruptcy proceeding. Some of your property are protected from creditors by provincial law. Typically, items that you may require to live and earn a living are exempt from the tally of your assets.

CHANGES TO THE BANKRUPTCY AND INSOLVENCY ACT   Proposed changes to the *Bankruptcy and Insolvency Act* came into force as of July 7, 2008. Some of the major changes affecting consumer bankruptcy were made to income tax debt, Registered Retirement Savings Plans (RRSPs), consumer proposals, and student loans. Bankrupt individuals owing more than $200,000 in personal income tax, representing 75 percent or more of their total unsecured liabilities, are no longer eligible for an automatic discharge—they have to prove their case in court. This is intended to prevent high-income individuals from using bankruptcy to avoid paying large income tax debt.

RRSPs and RRIFs continue to be exempt from seizure in accordance with the laws of the provinces that have such exemptions—Saskatchewan, Manitoba, Quebec, Prince Edward Island, and Newfoundland and Labrador. For provinces without RRSP exemption laws, amounts held in RRSP funds are also exempt. A one-year clawback is in effect, but the court has no jurisdiction to extend the clawback period. This means that only RRSP contributions made in the 12 months prior to bankruptcy (in provinces without exemption laws) are taken into the bankruptcy estate.

The dollar threshold for consumer proposals has been raised to $250,000 per person or $500,000 per couple. Student loans are eligible for discharge in bankruptcy cases if seven years (down from the current 10 years) have passed since the completion of studies.

For more details, read the Summary of Key Issues in Chapter 47 of the *Statutes of Canada, 2005,* and Chapter 36 of the *Statutes of Canada, 2007,* available on the Office of the Superintendent of Bankruptcy Canada Web site at strategis.gc.ca/epic/site/bsf-osb.nsf/en/br01782e.html.

EFFECTS OF BANKRUPTCY ON FUTURE CREDIT

Different people have different experiences in obtaining credit after they file bankruptcy. Some find obtaining credit more difficult. Others find obtaining credit easier because they have relieved themselves of their prior debts or because creditors know they cannot file another bankruptcy case for a period of time. Obtaining credit may be easier for people who file a consumer proposal and repay some of their debts than for people who file a straight bankruptcy and make no effort to repay. The bankruptcy law prohibits your employer from discharging you simply because you have filed a bankruptcy case.

WHAT ARE THE COSTS?   According to the Bankruptcy and Insolvency General Rules issued by the Department of Justice Canada (laws.justice.gc.ca/en/ShowFullDoc/cr/C.R.C.-c.368///en), the costs for submitting a consumer proposal are a basic fee of $1,500, a filing fee of $100, plus an additional 20 percent of the amount of your assets that are distributed to creditors. In addition, there is a fee of $170 for budget counselling. In the case of bankruptcy, the trustee may charge 100 percent of the first $975 of receipts, plus to a maximum of $15,000 of receipts, 35 percent of receipts between $975 and $2,000, plus 50 percent of receipts in excess of $2,000. The filing fee is $75, and there is a fee of $170 for budget counselling.

There are also intangible costs to bankruptcy. For example, obtaining credit in the future may be difficult, since bankruptcy reports are retained in credit bureaus for six years. Therefore, you should take the extreme step of declaring personal bankruptcy only when no other options for solving your financial problems exist.

CONCEPT CHECK 6–5

1. What is the purpose of a consumer proposal?
2. What is the difference between a consumer proposal and bankruptcy?
3. How does bankruptcy affect your job and future credit?
4. What are the costs of declaring bankruptcy?

SUMMARY OF LEARNING OBJECTIVES

LO1   Analyze the major sources of consumer credit.
The major sources of consumer credit are banks, trust companies, credit unions, finance companies, life insurance companies, and family and friends. Each of these sources has unique advantages and disadvantages.

Parents or family members are often the source of the least expensive loans. They may charge you only the interest they would have earned had they not made the loan. Such loans, however, can complicate family relationships.

LO2   Determine the effective cost of borrowing by considering the quoted rate, the number of compounding periods, the timing of the interest payments, and any other service charges.
Financial institutions quote an annual percentage rate (APR) on instalment loans and lines of credit, but the effective cost of borrowing rises if this rate is compounded more frequently than once a year, or if the loan is made on a discount basis with service fees added.

LO3   Develop a plan to manage your debts.
Debt has serious consequences if a proper plan for managing it is not implemented.

Most experts agree that emotional problems, using money to punish, expecting instant comfort, keeping up with the Joneses, overindulging children, misunderstanding or lack of communication among family members, and the amount of finance charges are common reasons for indebtedness.

LO4   Evaluate various private and governmental sources that assist consumers with debt problems.
If you cannot meet your obligations, contact your creditors immediately. Before signing up with a debt consolidation company, investigate it thoroughly. Better yet, contact a credit counselling service or other debt counselling organization.

Such organizations help people manage their money better by setting up a realistic budget and planning for expenditures. These organizations also help people prevent debt problems by teaching them the necessity of family budget planning and providing education to people of all ages.

LO5   Assess the choices in declaring personal bankruptcy.
A debtor's last resort is to declare bankruptcy. Consider the financial and other costs of bankruptcy before taking this extreme step. A debtor can declare insolvency either through a consumer proposal or through an assignment in bankruptcy.

Some people find obtaining credit more difficult after filing bankruptcy. Others find obtaining credit easier because they have relieved themselves of their prior debts or because creditors know they cannot file another bankruptcy case for a period of time.

KEY TERMS

adjusted balance method 185   **average daily balance method** 185   **credit insurance** 187

annual percentage rate (APR) 180   **consumer proposal** 192   **previous balance method** 185

KEY FORMULAS

Page	Topic	Formula
181	Calculating the EAR	$(1 + APR/m)^m - 1$ *Example:* APR = 6% m = 4, for quarterly compounding EAR = $(1 + 0.06 \div 4)^4 - 1 = 0.06136.$ or 6.14%
183	Calculating an instalment loan payment	$PMT = PV \div \left[\dfrac{1 - [1 \div (1 + i)^n]}{i} \right]$ *Example:* PV = $10,000 (loan amount) n = 48 months i = 0.5% per month $PMT = \$10,000 \div \left[\dfrac{1 - [1 \div (1.005)^{48}]}{0.005} \right]$ PMT = $10,000 ÷ 42.58 = $234.85
185	Calculating monthly interest on a line of credit	Interest = $B \times APR \times (N \div 365)$ *Example:* B = $10,000 (loan balance) APR = 9% N = 30 days Interest = $10,000 × 0.09 × (30 ÷ 365) = $73.97

FINANCIAL PLANNING PROBLEMS

 Practise and learn online with Connect.

1. *Calculating the Effective Cost of Borrowing.* Dave borrowed $500 and paid $50 in interest when he repaid the principal after one year. The bank also charged him a $5 service fee on a discount basis. What was the effective cost of his loan? *LO2*

2. *Calculating the Effective Annual Interest Rate.* If the 5 percent interest rate quoted on Dave's loan had been compounded monthly, what would have been the effective annual interest rate charged on the loan? *LO2*

3. *Calculating the Annual Interest Charged.* The CLSP has agreed to lend you funds to complete your 3-year bachelors' degree. The government will lend you $2,400 today, if you agree to repay the loan five years from now with a lump sum payment of $5,000. What annual interest is CLSP charging you? *LO2*

4. *Calculating Instalment Loan Payments, Interest, and Principal.* If Dave had borrowed the $500 for one year at an APR of 5 percent, compounded monthly, what would have been his monthly loan payment? What would have been the breakdown between interest and principal of the fifth payment? LO2

5. *Calculating the Payment on a Line of Credit.* Assume Dave borrowed the $500 on his personal line of credit. Interest is charged at a rate of 5 percent, but calculated on a daily basis. Dave is required to pay a minimum of 5 percent of the remaining loan balance every month. What is Dave's first monthly loan payment? Assume a 30-day month. LO2

6. *Comparing the Costs of Credit Cards.* Bobby is trying to decide between two credit cards. One has no annual fee and an 18 percent interest rate, and the other has a $40 annual fee and an 8.9 percent interest rate. Should he take the card that's free or the one that costs $40? LO2

7. *Calculating Cash Advance Fees and the Dollar Amount of Interest.* Sidney took a $200 cash advance by using cheques linked to her credit card account. The bank charges a 2 percent cash advance fee on the amount borrowed and offers no grace period on cash advances. Sidney paid the balance in full when the bill arrived. What was the cash advance fee? What was the interest for one month at an 18 percent APR? What was the total amount she paid? What if she had made the purchase with her credit card (assuming no over-credit limit) and paid off the bill in full promptly? LO2

8. *Comparing the Cost of Credit during Inflationary Periods.* Dorothy lacks cash to pay for a $600 dishwasher. She could buy it from the store on credit by making 12 monthly payments of $52.74. The total cost would then be $632.88. Instead, Dorothy decides to deposit $50 a month in the bank until she has saved enough money to pay cash for the dishwasher. One year later, she has saved $642; $600 in deposits plus interest. When she goes back to the store, she finds the dishwasher now costs $660. Its price has gone up 10 percent, the current rate of inflation. Was postponing her purchase a good trade-off for Dorothy? LO2

9. *Comparing Costs of Credit Using Three Calculation Methods.* You have been pricing a compact disc player in several stores. Three stores have the identical price of $300. Each store charges 18 percent APR, has a 30-day grace period, and sends out bills on the first of the month. On further investigation, you find that store A calculates the finance charge by using the average daily balance method, store B uses the adjusted balance method, and store C uses the previous balance method. Assume you purchased the disc player on May 5 and made a $100 payment on June 15. What is the finance charge if you purchased from store A? from store B? from store C? LO2

10. *Determining Interest Cost Using the Simple Interest Formula.* What are the interest cost and the total amount due on a six-month loan of $1,500 at 13.2 percent simple annual interest? LO2

FINANCIAL PLANNING ACTIVITIES

1. *Determining Criteria to Establish if a Loan Is Needed.* Survey friends and relatives to find out what criteria they have used to determine the need for credit. LO1

2. *Comparing Costs of Loans from Various Lenders.* Prepare a list of sources of inexpensive loans, medium-priced loans, and expensive loans in your area. What are the trade-offs in obtaining a loan from an "easy" lender? LO1

3. *Using the Internet to Obtain Information about the Costs of Credit.* As pointed out at the beginning of this chapter, credit costs money; therefore, you must conduct a cost/benefit analysis before making any major purchase. While most people consider credit costs, others simply ignore them and eventually find themselves in financial difficulties. To help consumers avoid this problem, each of the following organizations provides information on a Web site:
   - The Quicken Financial Network, at quicken.intuit.ca, helps consumers save money when purchasing, financing, or refinancing by keeping them up to date on news, views, and rates.
   - CCC Consumer Credit Counselling, at iamdebtfree.com, offers financial counselling and debt consolidation services.

   - Canoe Money, at money.canoe.ca, brings you the latest rates for mortgages, credit cards, auto loans, home equity loans, and personal loans, as well as a slew of financial advice.

   Choose one of the above organizations and visit its Web site. Then, prepare a report that summarizes the information the organization provides. Finally, decide how this information could help you better manage your credit and its costs. LO2

4. *Choosing between the Features and Costs of a Loan.* When you choose financing, what are the trade-offs between the features you prefer (term, size of payments, fixed or variable interest, or payment plan) and the cost of your loan? LO2

5. *Calculating the Cost of Credit Using Two APR Formulas.* How are the simple interest and simple interest on the declining balance formulas used in determining the cost of credit? LO2

6. *Handling Contacts from Debt Collection Agencies.* Your friend is drowning in a sea of overdue bills and is being harassed by a debt collection agency. Prepare a list of the steps your friend should take if the harassment continues. LO3

7. *Seeking Assistance from Consumer Credit Counselling Services.* Visit a local office of a credit counselling service. What assistance can debtors obtain from this office? What is the cost of this assistance, if any? LO4

8. *Assessing the Choices in Declaring Personal Bankruptcy.* What factors would you consider in assessing the choices in declaring personal bankruptcy? Why should personal bankruptcy be the choice of last resort? LO4

LIFE SITUATION CASE

Financing Sophie's Geo Metro

After shopping around, Sophie Aman decided on the car of her choice, a used Geo Metro. The dealer quoted her a total price of $8,000. Sophie decided to use $2,000 of her savings as a down payment and borrow $6,000. The salesperson wrote this information on a sales contract that Sophie took with her when she set out to find financing.

When Sophie applied for a loan, she discussed loan terms with the bank lending officer. The officer told her that the bank's policy was to lend only 80 percent of the total price of a used car.

Sophie showed the officer her copy of the sales contract, indicating that she had agreed to make a $2,000, or 25 percent, down payment on the $8,000 car, so this requirement caused her no problem. Although the bank was willing to make 48-month loans at an annual percentage rate of 15 percent on used cars, Sophie chose a 36-month repayment schedule. She believed she could afford the higher payments, and she knew she would not have to pay as much interest if she paid off the loan at a faster rate. The bank lending officer provided Sophie with a copy of the statement shown here.

Statement (Loans)

Annual Percentage Rate	Finance Charge	Amount Financed	Total of Payments 36
The cost of your credit as a yearly rate.	The dollar amount the credit will cost you.	The amount of credit provided to you or on your behalf.	The amount you will have paid after you have made all payments as scheduled.
15%	$1,487.64	$6,000.00	$7,487.64

You have the right to receive at this time an itemization of the Amount Financed.

☒ I want an itemization.   ☐ I do not want an itemization.

Your payment schedule will be:

Number of Payments	Amount of Payments	When Payments Are Due
36	$207.99	1st of each month

Sophie decided to compare the APR she had been offered with the APR offered by another bank, but the 20 percent APR of the second bank (bank B) was more expensive than the 15 percent APR of the first bank (bank A). Here is her comparison of the two loans:

	Bank A 15% APR	Bank B 20% APR
Amount of financed	$6,000.00	$6,000.00
Finance charge	$1,487.64	$2,027.28
Total of payments	$7,487.64	$8,027.28
Monthly payments	$ 207.99	$ 222.98

The 5 percent difference in the APRs of the two banks meant Sophie would have to pay $15 extra every month if she got her loan from the second bank. Of course, she got the loan from the first bank.

Questions

1. What is perhaps the most important item shown on the statement? Why?

2. What is included in the finance charge?

3. What amount will Sophie receive from the bank?

4. Should Sophie borrow from bank A or bank B? Why?

CONTINUOUS CASE FOR PART 2 (A)

USING FINANCIAL SERVICES: SAVINGS, CHEQUING, AND CREDIT

Life Situation

Recently married couple: Pamela, 26; Isaac, 28; renting an apartment

Financial Goals

- Develop a savings fund for emergencies and long-term financial security
- Reduce monthly debt payments

Financial Data

Monthly income	$ 5,840
Living expenses	3,900
Assets	13,500
Liabilities	7,800
Emergency fund	1,000

Pamela Wall recently married Isaac Mortimer. Pamela continues to work as a sales representative for a clothing manufacturer, and her monthly income has averaged $2,840 a month over the past year. Isaac is employed as a computer programmer and earns $3,000 a month.

The Mortimers' combined monthly income, $5,840, allows them to enjoy a comfortable lifestyle. Yet, they have been unable to save any money for emergencies. According to Isaac, "It's hard to believe, but we don't even have a savings account because we spend everything we make each month." Every month, they deposit each of their paycheques in separate chequing accounts. Isaac pays the rent and makes the car payment. Pamela buys the groceries and pays the monthly utilities. They use the money left over to purchase new clothes and the other "necessities" of life that they both want. To make matters worse, they often resort to using their seven credit cards for everyday purchases when they both run out of money at the end of the month. As a result, they have credit card debts totalling $2,800.

Questions

1. What is the minimum amount that the Mortimers should have in an emergency fund?

2. What should the Mortimers do to increase the amount of money they set aside for emergencies?

3. Pamela and Isaac have separate chequing accounts. Do you think they should give up their separate chequing accounts and open a joint chequing account?

4. If you were Pamela or Isaac, how would you go about paying off your credit card debts and other liabilities?

5. What would you recommend to the Mortimers regarding their future use of credit?

chapter 7

The Finances of Housing

LEARNING OBJECTIVES

LO1 Evaluate available housing alternatives.

LO2 Analyze the costs and benefits associated with renting.

LO3 Implement the home-buying process.

LO4 Obtain mortgage financing.

LO5 Develop a strategy for selling a home.

TWO CAN BUY MORE CHEAPLY THAN ONE

During a time when mortgage rates were fairly high, Ana Chen and her sister, Yvonne, were unable to buy the house they wanted. Their parents had given them $4,000 for a down payment, but that was not enough for the type of house they wanted.

After finishing university, Ana rented an apartment for seven years. During that time, she was able to save $8,000 for a down payment on a home. She now earns enough money to afford the monthly costs of a home.

During the past eight months, mortgage rates in their area of the country have declined 1.5 percentage points. Ana and Yvonne have decided to combine their resources to purchase a home. The *co-ownership* arrangement allows them to buy a home valued at $15,000 more than they could have afforded a year ago.

However, Ana and Yvonne should ask themselves a few questions before buying the house. What happens to the house if one of them marries or accepts a job transfer to another city? What if one of them can no longer meet the financial requirements of the home? How will they share maintenance responsibilities and costs?

Ana and Yvonne need to answer these and other questions before entering a co-ownership housing arrangement.

QUESTIONS

1. What factors affect a person's ability to buy a house?

2. What are common sources for a down payment? Why should home buyers not use all of their savings to make the down payment on a home?

3. What problems could arise in a co-ownership housing arrangement?

4. Locate Web sites that provide housing information that would be of value to Ana and Yvonne during their home-buying activities.

 Practise and learn online with Connect.

EVALUATING HOUSING ALTERNATIVES

As you walk around various neighbourhoods, you are likely to see a variety of housing types. When you assess housing alternatives, you need to identify the factors that will influence your choice.

YOUR LIFESTYLE AND YOUR CHOICE OF HOUSING

While the concept of lifestyle—how you spend your time and money—may seem intangible, it materializes in consumer purchases. Every buying decision is a statement about your lifestyle. Your lifestyle, needs, desires, and attitudes are reflected in your choice of a place to live. For example, some people want a kitchen large enough for family gatherings. Career-oriented people may want a lavish bathroom or a home spa where they can escape the pressures of work. As you select housing, you might consider the alternatives in Exhibit 7–1.

While personal preferences are the foundation of a housing decision, financial factors may modify the final choice. Traditional financial guidelines suggest that "you should spend no more than 25 or 30 percent of your take-home pay on housing" or "your home should cost about 2½ times your annual income." While changes in our economy and our society no longer make these guidelines completely valid, you need some sort of financial guideline to determine the amount to spend on housing. A budget and other financial records discussed in Chapter 2 can help you evaluate your income, living costs, and other financial obligations to determine an appropriate amount for your housing expenses.

OPPORTUNITY COSTS OF HOUSING CHOICES

Although the selection of housing is usually based on life situations and financial factors, you should also consider what you might have to give up. While the opportunity costs of your housing decision vary, some common trade-offs include:

- The interest earnings lost on the money used for a down payment on a home or the security deposit for an apartment.

Exhibit 7–1

Possible Housing
for Different Life
Situations

Life Situation	Possible Housing Types
Young single	Rental housing requires limited maintenance activities and offers mobility in the event of a job transfer Purchase a home or a condominium for potential financial benefits
Single parent	Rental housing provides a suitable environment for children and some degree of home security Purchase low-maintenance housing that meets the financial and social needs of family members
Young couple, no children	Rental housing offers convenience and flexibility of lifestyle Purchase housing for financial benefits and to build long-term financial security
Couple, young children	Rental housing can provide appropriate facilities for children in a family-oriented area Purchase a home to meet financial and other family needs
Couple, children no longer at home	Rental housing offers convenience and flexibility for changing needs and financial situations Purchase housing that requires minimal maintenance and meets lifestyle needs
Retired person	Rental housing can meet financial, social, and physical needs Purchase housing that requires minimal maintenance, offers convenience, and provides needed services

- The time and cost of commuting to work when you live in an area that offers less expensive housing or more living space.
- The loss of equity growth when you rent a city apartment to be close to your work.
- The time and money you spend when you repair and improve a lower-priced home.
- The time and effort involved when you have a home built to your personal specifications.

Like every other financial choice, a housing decision requires consideration of what you give up in time, effort, and money.

RENTING VERSUS BUYING HOUSING

The choice between renting and buying your residence should be analyzed based on lifestyle and financial factors. Exhibit 7–2 can help you assess renting and buying alternatives. Mobility is a primary motivator of renters, while buyers usually want permanence.

EVALUATING HOUSING ALTERNATIVES

Renting
Apartment

Advantages	Disadvantages
• Easy to move	• Limitations regarding remodelling
• Fewer responsibilities for maintenance	• May have restrictions regarding pets, other activities
• Minimal financial commitment	• More frequent moves may be costly

Renting
House

Advantages	Disadvantages
• Easy to move; less maintenance	• Higher utility expenses than apartment
• More room than apartment	• Limitations regarding remodelling
• Minimal financial commitment	

Owning
New house

Advantages	Disadvantages
• No previous owner	• Financial commitment
• Pride of ownership	• Higher living expenses than renting
• Capital gains exemption on sale, if principal residence	• Limited mobility
• Warranty in some provinces if builder is registered	• Pay HST/GST

Owning
Previously owned house

Advantages	Disadvantages
• Pride of ownership	• Financial commitment
• Established neighbourhood	• Possibility of repairs or replacements
• Capital gains exemption on sale, if principal residence	• Limited mobility

Owning
Condominium

Advantages	Disadvantages
• Fewer maintenance responsibilities than house	• Less privacy than house
• Usually good accessibility to recreation and business districts	• Financial commitment
	• Uncertain demand affecting property value
• Capital gains exemption on sale, if principal residence	• Potential disagreements with condominium association regarding rules
	• Monthly condominium fees

Owning
Co-operative

Advantages	Disadvantages
• Ownership in form of nonprofit organization	• Frequently difficult to sell
	• Potential disagreements among members
	• Other members may have to cover costs of unrented units

Owning
Manufactured home (mobile home)

Advantages	Disadvantages
• Less expensive than other ownership options	• May be difficult to sell in future
	• Financing may be difficult to obtain
• Flexibility in selection of home features and appliances	• Construction quality may be poor
	• Asset depreciates in value

Exhibit 7–2

Evaluating Housing Alternatives

Financial Planning Calculations

Renting versus Buying
Your Place of Residence

Comparing the costs of renting and buying involves considering a variety of factors. The following framework and example provides a basis for assessing these two housing alternatives. The apartment in the example has a monthly rent of $1,300, and the home costs $325,000, with a $250,000 mortgage at 3.5 percent over a 25-year amortization period. A 29 percent tax rate is assumed.

Although the numbers in this example favour renting, the most important point to remember is that calculations provide only part of the answer. You should also consider your needs and values and assess the opportunity costs associated with renting and buying. Also, in making any real estate decision, you must factor overall market conditions before making any decision.

	Example	Your Figures
RENTAL COSTS		
Annual rent payments	$ 15,600	$ _____
Renter's insurance	400	_____
Interest lost on security deposit (amount of security deposit × after-tax GIC interest rate)	36	
Total annual cost of renting	$ 16,036	_____
BUYING COSTS		
Annual mortgage payments	$ 15,852	_____
Property taxes (annual costs)	5,000	_____
Homeowner's insurance (annual premium)	1,000	_____
Estimated maintenance and repairs (2%)	6,500	_____
After-tax interest lost on down payment and closing costs	750	_____
Less (financial benefits of home ownership):		
Growth in equity	−6,264	_____
Estimated annual appreciation (2.0%)*	−6,500	_____
Total annual cost of buying	$ 16,338	_____

*This is a Canadian estimated long-term average; actual appreciation of property varies by geographic area and economic conditions.

As you can see in the Financial Planning Calculations feature above, the choice between renting and buying usually is not clear-cut. In general, renting costs less in the short run, but home ownership usually has long-term financial advantages.

HOUSING INFORMATION SOURCES

As with other consumer purchases, housing information is available. Start your data search with basic resources, such as this book and books available in libraries. Consult the real estate section of your newspaper for articles about renting, buying, financing, remodelling, and other housing topics. Other helpful information sources are friends, real estate agents, and government agencies.

The World Wide Web has become an important source of housing information. Canada's Mortgage & Housing Corporation (cmhc.ca) or the Financial Consumer Agency of Canada (fcac-acfc.gc.ca) are valuable sources. In addition to providing home-buying tips and mortgage rates, several other online sites can be used to access available housing in an area.

CONCEPT CHECK 7–1

1. How does a person's employment and household situation influence the selection of housing?
2. What are some common opportunity costs associated with the selection of housing?

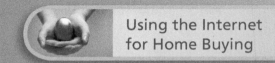
RENTING

Are you interested in a "2-bd garden apt, a/c, crptg, mod bath, lndry"? Not sure? Translated, this means a two-bedroom garden apartment (at or below ground level) with air conditioning, carpeting, a modern bath, and laundry facilities.

At some point in your life, you are likely to rent your place of residence. You may rent when you are first on your own or later in life when you want to avoid the activities required to maintain your own home.

As a tenant, you pay for the right to live in a residence owned by someone else. Exhibit 7–3 presents the activities involved in finding and living in a rental unit.

LO2

Analyze the costs and benefits associated with renting.

SELECTING A RENTAL UNIT

An apartment is the most common type of rental housing. Apartments range from modern, luxury units with extensive recreational facilities to simple one- and two-bedroom units in quiet neighbourhoods.

If you need more room, you should consider renting a house. The increased space will cost more, and you will probably have some responsibility for maintaining the property. If you need less space, you may rent a room in a private house.

The main sources of information on available rental units are newspaper ads, real estate and rental offices, and people you know. When comparing rental units, consider the factors presented in Exhibit 7–4.

ADVANTAGES OF RENTING

The three main advantages of renting are mobility, fewer responsibilities, and lower initial costs.

203

Exhibit 7–3   Housing Rental Activities

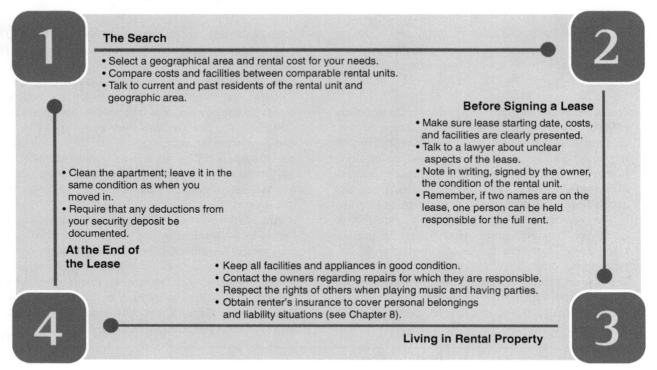

MOBILITY   Renting offers mobility when a location change is necessary or desirable. A new job, a rent increase, the need for a larger apartment, or the desire to live in a different community can make relocation necessary. It is easier to move when you are renting than when you own a home. After you have completed school and started your career, renting makes it easier for job transfers.

FEWER RESPONSIBILITIES   Renters have fewer responsibilities than homeowners since they usually do not have to be concerned with maintenance and repairs. However, they are

Exhibit 7–4

Selecting an Apartment

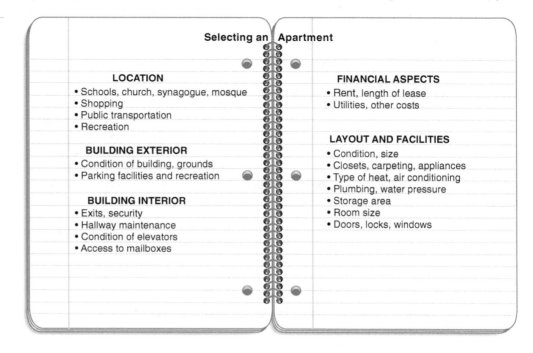

expected to do regular household cleaning. Renters also have fewer financial concerns. Their main housing costs are rent and utilities, while homeowners incur expenses related to property taxes, property insurance, and upkeep.

LOWER INITIAL COSTS   It is less expensive to take possession of a rental unit than to buy a home. While new tenants have only the first month's rent to pay, a new home buyer is likely to have a down payment and closing costs of several thousand dollars.

DISADVANTAGES OF RENTING

Renting has few financial benefits, may impose a restricted lifestyle, and involves legal details.

FEW FINANCIAL BENEFITS   Renters are subject to rent increases, over which they have little control, and do not share in any increase in the value of the property. Also, money spent on rent could be used to build equity through home ownership instead.

RESTRICTED LIFESTYLE   Renters in multi-unit dwellings are generally limited in the types of activities they can pursue in their place of residence. Noise from a sound system or parties may be monitored closely. Tenants in some provinces may be subject to restrictions regarding pets and decorating the property.

LEGAL DETAILS   Most tenants sign a **lease**, a legal document that defines the conditions of a rental agreement. This document provides the following information:

lease A legal document that defines the conditions of a rental agreement.

- A description of the property, including the address.
- The name and address of the owner/landlord (the *lessor*).
- The name of the tenant (the *lessee*).
- The effective date of the lease.
- The length of the lease.
- The amount and due date of the monthly rent.
- The location at which the rent must be paid.
- The date and amount due of charges for late rent payments.
- A list of the utilities, appliances, furniture, or other facilities that are included in the rental amount.
- The restrictions regarding certain activities (pets, remodelling).
- The tenant's right to sublet the rental unit.
- The charges for damages or for moving out of the rental unit later (or earlier) than the lease expiration date.
- The conditions under which the landlord may enter the apartment.

It is important to remember that each province has its own *Residential Tenancies Act* (RTA) that sets out the rights and obligations of tenants and landlords. Even if your lease does not cover all the details listed here, your rights as a tenant or landlord will still be protected under your province's RTA.

Standard lease forms include conditions you may not want to accept. The fact that a lease is printed does not mean you must accept it as is. Negotiate with the landlord about lease terms you consider unacceptable.

Some leases give you the right to *sublet* the rental unit. Subletting may be necessary if you must vacate the premises before the lease expires. Subletting allows you to have another person take over rent payments and live in the rental unit.

Most leases are written, but oral leases are also valid. With an oral lease, one party must give a 30-day written notice to the other party before terminating the lease or imposing a rent increase.

A lease provides protection to both landlord and tenant. The tenant is protected from rent increases during the lease term, unless the lease contains a provision allowing an increase. In most

Did you know?

Renter's insurance is one of the most overlooked expenses of apartment dwellers. Damage or theft of personal property (clothing, furniture, sound system, jewellery) usually is not covered by the landlord's insurance policy.

Did you know?

As a tenant, when you sign a lease you are assured of: (a) *habitability*—a building with minimum health and safety standards that is free of serious defects and has running water, heat, and electricity; (b) prompt return of your security deposit, including interest when required by law; and (c) advance notice of rent increases and eviction, as prescribed in the lease. For additional information on tenant rights, check your lease or conduct a Web search.

provinces, the tenant cannot be locked out or evicted without a court hearing. The lease gives the landlord the right to take legal action against a tenant for non-payment of rent or destruction of property and, under certain circumstances, to repossess the premises. To view a sample lease agreement, visit the Ontario Real Estate Association (OREA) Web site at orea.com.

COSTS OF RENTING

As a renter, you will incur other living expenses besides monthly rent. For many apartments, water is covered by the rent; however, other utilities may not be covered. If you rent a house, you will probably pay for heat, electricity, water, and telephone. When you rent, you should obtain insurance coverage for your personal property. Renter's insurance is discussed in Chapter 8.

RENTING RIGHTS

The Canadian Charter of Human Rights recognizes and protects your rights to rent any apartment without discrimination based on race, colour, gender, pregnancy, sexual orientation, civil status, age, religion, political conviction, language, ethnic or national origin, social condition, or handicap. Renting is not hassle-free; problems can arise between tenants and landlords and/or room-mates. The World Wide Web contains many helpful resources on how to deal with problems. See apartments.about.com. Visit your provincial and municipal government Web sites to find out the rules, regulations, and rights for renting that apply to you.

CONCEPT CHECK 7–2

1. What are the main benefits and drawbacks of renting a place of residence?
2. Which components of a lease are likely to be most negotiable?

THE HOME-BUYING PROCESS

LO3

Implement the home-buying process.

Many people dream of having a place of residence they can call their own. Home ownership is a common financial goal. Exhibit 7–5 presents the process for achieving this goal.

STEP 1: DETERMINE HOME OWNERSHIP NEEDS

In the first phase of the home-buying process, you should consider the benefits and drawbacks of this major financial commitment. Also, evaluate different types of housing units and forms of ownership, and determine the amount you can afford.

EVALUATE OWNING YOUR PLACE OF RESIDENCE

What Are the Benefits of Home Ownership?   Whether you purchase a house, a condominium, or a manufactured home, you can enjoy the pride of ownership, financial benefits, and lifestyle flexibility of home ownership.

1. *Pride of ownership.* Having a place to call one's own is a primary motive of many home buyers. Stability of residence and a personalized living location can be important.

Exhibit 7–5   The Home-Buying Process

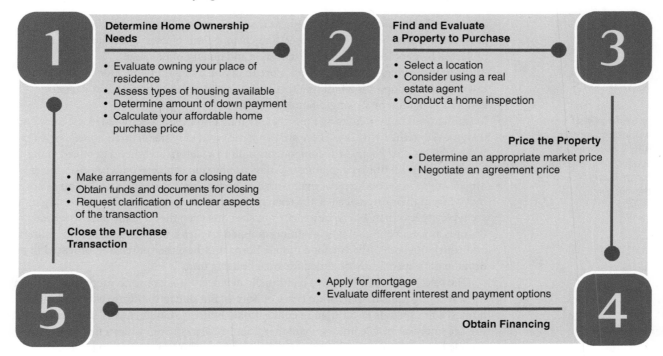

2. *Financial benefits.* A potential benefit is increases in the value of the property. If the dwelling is your principal residence, there is no tax on any realized capital gain when you sell it. Finally, homeowners may be able to borrow against the equity in their homes. *Equity* is the home value less the amount owed on the mortgage.
3. *Lifestyle flexibility.* While renting gives you mobility, home ownership gives you more opportunity to express individuality. Homeowners have greater freedom than renters in decorating their dwellings and entertaining guests.

What Are the Drawbacks of Home Ownership?   Buying one's own home does not guarantee a glamorous existence. This investment can result in financial uncertainty, limited mobility, higher living costs, and higher property taxes.

1. *Financial uncertainty.* Among the challenges associated with buying a home is saving enough to cover the down payment. Other uncertainties include home prices that escalate as you save, and obtaining mortgage financing if your personal or economic situation is unfavourable at the time you are ready to purchase. Finally, changing property values in an area can affect your financial investment.
2. *Limited mobility.* Home ownership does not provide ease of changing living location as does renting. If changes in your situation make it necessary to sell your home, doing so may be difficult. High interest rates and other factors can result in a weak demand for housing.
3. *Higher living costs.* Owning your place of residence can be expensive. The homeowner is responsible for maintenance and costs of repainting, repairs, and home improvements.
4. *Higher property taxes.* Even for homeowners who no longer have mortgage payments, higher property values and higher tax rates mean higher real estate taxes. Higher taxes affect homeowners more directly than renters, who pay them in the form of higher rent. It is harder for homeowners to counter the effects of high taxes by moving to less expensive housing.

ASSESS TYPES OF HOUSING AVAILABLE   Some common options available to home buyers are:

- *Single-family dwellings*, the most popular form of housing. These residences include previously owned houses, new houses, and custom-built houses. Older houses may be preferred by people who want a certain style and quality of housing.
- *Multi-unit dwellings*—dwellings with more than one living unit—include duplexes and townhouses. A duplex is a building that contains two separate homes. A *townhouse* contains two, four, or six single-family living units.
- **Manufactured homes**, housing units that are fully or partially assembled in a factory and then moved to the living site. There are two basic types of manufactured homes. One type is the *prefabricated home*, with components built in a factory and then assembled at the housing site. With this type of housing, mass production can keep building costs lower.
- *Mobile homes*, a second type of manufactured home. Since very few mobile homes are moved from their original sites, the term is not completely accurate. These housing units are typically less than 100 square metres in size; however, they usually offer the same features as a conventional house—fully equipped kitchens, fireplaces, cathedral ceilings, and whirlpool baths. The site for a mobile home may be either purchased or leased in a development specifically designed for such housing units.

    The safety of mobile homes is continually debated. Fires occur no more frequently in these housing units than in other types of homes. But due to the construction of mobile homes, a fire spreads faster than in conventional houses. Manufacturers' standards for the fire safety of mobile homes are higher than in the past. Still, when a fire occurs in a mobile home, the unit is often completely destroyed. This type of housing is also vulnerable to wind forces.

    Another common concern about mobile homes is their tendency to depreciate in value. When this occurs, an important benefit of home ownership is eliminated. Depreciation may make it difficult to obtain financing to purchase a mobile home.

- *Building a home.* Some people want a home built to their specifications. Before you begin such a project, be sure you possess the necessary knowledge, money, and perseverance. When choosing a contractor to coordinate the project, consider the following:
  - Does the contractor have the experience needed to handle the type of building project you require?
  - Does the contractor have a good working relationship with the architect, materials suppliers, electricians, plumbers, carpenters, and other personnel needed to complete the project?
  - What assurance do you have about the quality of materials?
  - What arrangements must be made for payments during construction?
  - What delays in the construction process will be considered legitimate?
  - Is the contractor licensed and insured?
  - Is the contractor willing to provide names, addresses, and phone numbers of satisfied customers?
  - Have local consumer agencies received any complaints about this contractor?

Your written contract should include a time schedule, cost estimates, a description of the work, and a payment schedule.

You can save as much as 25 percent of the cost of a new house by supervising its construction. Home-building suppliers and owners of homes under construction can suggest quality tradespeople.

CONSIDER FORMS OF HOME OWNERSHIP   The most common form of home ownership is one in which an individual or a couple is the sole owner of an entire property. Most people mistakenly think condominiums and co-operative housing are types of housing. They are, in fact, legal forms of home ownership.

---

manufactured home
A housing unit that is fully or partially assembled in a factory before being moved to the living site.

Condominium   Condominiums, often referred to as "condos," consist of two parts: a collection of private housing called *units,* and the shared areas of the building such as lobbies, hallways, elevators, recreational facilities, gardens, and so on. Each unit is owned by the purchaser of that unit and the common areas are jointly owned by these individual unit owners, who are jointly responsible for the operational costs, maintenance, and repairs. Ownership percentage in shared areas varies depending on the proportion of the value of a particular unit in relation to the total value of all the units. Each unit holder must pay monthly condo fees (for maintenance and renewal) based on this proportion.

Although they are often thought of as being high-rise residential buildings, this form of ownership can also be applied to low-rise residential buildings, townhouse complexes, and individual homes. In British Columbia they are known as *strata,* and in Quebec they are called *syndicates of co-ownership.*

condominium An individually owned housing unit in a building with several such units.

Co-operative Housing   Housing co-operatives, often referred to as "co-ops," are member-owned communities where residents make decisions on how the co-op operates. A co-op is governed by directors and members of the co-op. Each member has a vote and a say in its overall direction.

There are two main types of housing co-operatives: **non-profit** and **for-profit**. Many provinces require that housing co-ops operate on a non-profit basis because the main purpose is to provide affordable housing. In a non-profit co-op, members cannot sell their shares. In a for-profit co-op, members own a share of the co-op but not the individual unit in which they live.

Co-ops come in many different shapes and sizes, ranging from collections of single-unit townhouses and small buildings with a few units, to large apartment-size buildings with hundreds of units. As long as a members abide by the rules of the co-op and pay their housing charge on time, they can live in a co-op for as long as they like. Further information on housing co-operatives is available online or at your local library.

co-operative housing A type of subsidized housing in which half the units have geared-to-income rental prices.

non-profit co-operative housing Rental housing owned by a community group, religious group, or non-profit organization to provide affordable housing.

DETERMINE AMOUNT OF DOWN PAYMENT   Before shopping for a home, you should analyze your financial capacity to make a down payment and, thereafter, to assume the cost of the ongoing mortgage payments. The amount of cash available for a down payment affects the size of the mortgage loan you require. A large down payment, such as 20 percent or more, makes it easier for you to obtain a mortgage even though a minimum 5 percent is required.

Personal savings, pension plan funds, sales of investments or other assets, and assistance from relatives are the most common sources of a down payment. Parents can help their children purchase a home by giving them a cash gift or a loan, depositing money with the lender to reduce the interest rate on the loan, co-signing the loan, or acting as co-mortgagors.

If you are a first-time buyer, you can use up to $25,000 of your RRSP holdings to help make a down payment, or double this amount for a couple. As an incentive, you will not be charged taxes on this withdrawal, provided that you pay back the money within a stated time period (generally 15 years).

The RRSP Home Buyers' Plan requires minimum annual payments of 1/15th of the borrowed funds until the full amount is repaid to your RRSP. If a payment is missed, it must be included as taxable income. For more information on this plan, go to http://www.cra-arc.gc.ca/tx/ndvdls/tpcs/rrsp-reer/hbp-rap/menu-eng.html on the Canada Revenue Agency Web site.

Making an immediate down payment of at least 20 percent of the purchase price allows you to qualify for a conventional mortgage. Alternatively, you may qualify for what is known as a high-ratio mortgage if you make no down payment or any amount less than 20 percent of the house's appraised value.

Federal law requires that you have mortgage insurance if your mortgage represents 80 percent or more of the total price you pay for your home. This coverage protects the lender from financial

for-profit co-operative housing Rental housing for which members own shares although they do not own the units in which they live.

Did you know?

According to various surveys, the following housing features are most popular: modern kitchens; finished basements; big, modern bathrooms; fresh-looking and fresh-smelling living areas; large closets; fireplaces; and curb appeal created by plants and walkways.

loss due to default, while at the same time enabling the borrower to get a competitive interest rate and can be obtained through the Canada Mortgage and Housing Corporation (CMHC), a federal Crown corporation, or Genworth Financial, a private company. The charge for this insurance varies with the *loan-to-value* ratio of your mortgage, which is the amount of your loan as a percentage of the total purchase price you will pay. Typically, the premium is between 0.60 and 3.35 percent of your total loan in addition to an application fee, which may also be called an *underwriting fee*.

CALCULATE YOUR AFFORDABLE HOME PURCHASE PRICE   Do you have funds for a down payment? Do you earn enough to make mortgage payments while covering other living expenses? Do you have a good credit rating? Unless you pay cash for a home, a favourable response to these questions is necessary. A **mortgage** is a personal loan used to purchase a property. The property being purchased is pledged as security for the loan. Payments on a mortgage are usually made over 15, 20, or 25 years. Banks, trust companies, credit unions, and mortgage companies are the most common home financing sources. Mortgage brokers can help home buyers obtain financing, since they are in contact with several financial institutions. A mortgage broker may charge higher fees than a lending institution with which you deal directly.

To qualify for a mortgage, you must meet criteria similar to those for other loans. The home you buy serves as security, or *collateral*, for the mortgage. The major factors that affect the affordability of your mortgage are your income, other debts, the amount available for a down payment, the length of the loan, and current mortgage rates. When looking at income, lenders use two ratios, the **gross debt service (GDS) ratio** and the **total debt service (TDS) ratio**. The GDS ratio is your monthly shelter costs as a percentage of your gross monthly income. Shelter costs typically include your monthly mortgage payment principal and interest, property taxes, and heating costs. If applicable, 50 percent of condominium fees may be included in shelter costs as well. Most lenders recommend you spend no more than 30 to 32 percent of your gross income on shelter costs.

The TDS ratio is your monthly shelter costs plus any outstanding debt payments and obligations (such as credit card bills, car payments, personal loans, alimony, and other monthly expenses) as a percentage of your gross monthly income. Most lenders recommend you spend no more than 40 percent of your gross income on shelter and non-shelter financial obligations.

The ratios are calculated as follows:

$$\text{Gross debt service (GDS)} = \frac{PI + T + H}{GI} \times 100\%$$

$$\text{Total debt service (TDS)} = \frac{PI + T + H + D}{GI} \times 100\%$$

where,

PI = monthly principal and interest payments on your mortgage
T = monthly property taxes
H = monthly heating costs
D = monthly debt service payments
GI = monthly gross income

The combined incomes of both spouses are usually considered, excluding rental income. The results calculated in Exhibit 7–6 are (a) the maximum monthly mortgage payment you can afford, (b) the maximum mortgage amount you can afford, and (c) the maximum home purchase price you can afford.

The procedures in Exhibit 7–6 include the following:

1. Indicate your monthly gross income.
2. Multiply your monthly gross income by 0.30 (or 0.40 if you have other debts, such as an auto loan). Lenders commonly use 30 percent (from the GDS ratio) and 40 percent (from the TDS ratio). These guidelines help determine the maximum amount most people can afford for housing.

mortgage A personal loan used to purchase a property.

gross debt service (GDS) ratio Your monthly shelter costs as a percentage of your gross monthly income; a ratio used to determine the maximum affordable mortgage payment, mortgage amount, and home purchase price.

total debt service (TDS) ratio Your monthly shelter costs plus any outstanding debt payments and obligations as a percentage of your gross monthly income; a ratio used to determine the maximum affordable mortgage payment, mortgage amount, and home purchase price.

Exhibit 7–6   Housing Affordability and Mortgage Qualification Amounts

			Example A	Example B
Step 1:	Determine your monthly gross income (annual income divided by 12).		$ 72,000 ÷ 12	
Step 2:	With a down payment of at least 10 percent, lenders use 30 percent of monthly gross income as a guideline for the GDS ratio, and 40 percent of monthly gross income as a guideline for the TDS ratio.		$ 6,000 × 0.40 $ 2,400	$ 6,000 × 0.30 $ 1,800
Step 3:	Subtract other debt payments (e.g., payments on an auto loan) and an estimate of the monthly costs of property taxes, heating, homeowner's insurance, mortgage insurance, and condo fees if applicable.		− 500 − 600	— − 600
(a) *Affordable monthly mortgage payment*			$ 1,300	$ 1,200
Step 4:	Divide this amount by the monthly mortgage payment based on current mortgage rates—a 4 percent, 25-year loan, for example (see Exhibit 7–7) and multiply by $1,000.		÷ $ 5.26 × $ 1,000	÷ $ 5.26 × $ 1,000
(b) *Affordable mortgage amount*			$247,148	$228,137
Step 5:	Divide your affordable mortgage amount by 1 minus the fractional portion of your down payment (e.g., a 10 percent down payment).		÷ 0.9	÷ 0.9
(c) *Affordable home purchase price*			$274,609	$253,485

Note: The two ratios lending institutions use (step 2) and other loan requirements may vary based on a variety of factors, including the type of mortgage, the amount of the down payment, your income level, and current interest rates.

3. After subtracting the monthly debt payments and an estimate of the monthly cost for property taxes, heating, homeowner's insurance, and mortgage insurance (as this is a high-ratio mortgage), and condo fees if applicable, you arrive at your maximum *affordable monthly mortgage payment* (a).

4. Divide (a) by the factor from Exhibit 7–7, based on your mortgage term (in years) and rate. Then multiply your answer by $1,000 to convert your figure to thousands of dollars. This gives you your maximum *affordable mortgage amount* (b). Exhibit 7–7 provides the amount you need to pay back per $1,000 over 15, 20, or 25 years based on various interest rates.

5. To obtain your maximum *affordable home purchase price* (c), divide (b) by the amount you will be financing, such as 0.9 when you make a 10 percent down payment.

The affordable home purchase price in the example is $274,609 using the TDS ratio, and $253,485 using the GDS ratio.

These sample calculations are typical of those most financial institutions use; the actual qualifications for a mortgage may vary by lender and by the type of mortgage. In addition, current mortgage interest rates affect the amount of the mortgage loan for which you qualify. It is important to remember that these are maximum amounts. In reality, it is wise to stay below these limits. Purchasing a home and acquiring a mortgage is a long-term responsibility. Not leaving enough room to be able to meet unexpected expenses, or even to enjoy a night out or take a vacation once in a while, can put serious strain on individuals and on marriages.

The mortgage loan for which you can qualify is larger when interest rates are low than when they are high. For example, a person who can afford a monthly mortgage payment of $700 will qualify for a 25-year loan of $100,000 at 7 percent.

If you think back to the 1980s when mortgage rates exceeded 20 percent, you get a broader perspective in terms of why the last decade has been one of significantly lower rates. As interest

Exhibit 7–7

Mortgage Payment Factors (principal and interest factors per $1,000 of loan amount)

Term Rate	25 Years	20 Years	15 Years
4.0%	$5.26	$6.04	$ 7.38
4.5%	5.53	6.30	7.63
5.0%	5.83	6.57	7.88
5.5%	6.10	6.84	8.14
6.0%	6.40	7.12	8.40
6.5%	6.70	7.41	8.66
7.0%	7.00	7.69	8.93
7.5%	7.32	7.99	9.21
8.0%	7.63	8.28	9.48
8.5%	7.95	8.59	9.76
9.0%	8.28	8.89	10.05
9.5%	8.61	9.20	10.33
10.0%	8.94	9.52	10.62

rates rise, fewer people are able to afford the cost of an average-priced home. See Exhibit 7–8 for recent mortgage rates in Canada. A great wealth of information on mortgages can be found online at most banks' Web sites, such as royalbank.ca, mortgageforless.com, or ratehub.ca.

To determine how much you can afford to spend on a home, ask a loan officer at a mortgage company or other financial institution to pre-qualify you. This service is usually provided without charge. Being pre-approved for a mortgage can make your offer of purchase more credible to a seller. According to the CMHC, bring the following information to get pre-approval: (1) your personal information, such as your driver's licence; (2) proof of salary and your other sources of income; (3) details on all bank accounts, loans, and other debts; (4) proof of financial assets; (5) source and amount of down payment and deposits; and (6) source of funds to cover the closing costs, which can be from 1.5 to 4 percent of the purchase price.

Exhibit 7–8

Mortgage and Prime Rates Through the Years (5-year conventional mortgage rates)

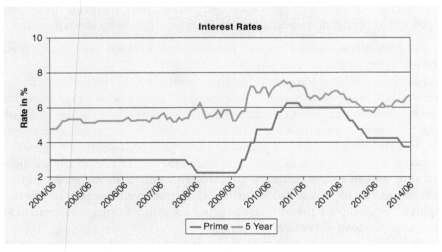

SOURCE: http://www.bankofcanada.ca/rates/interest-rates/canadian-interest-rates/.

However, being pre-approved does not mean you should not shop around and negotiate a better rate.

Finally, keep in mind that you will most likely require an additional budget of 1.5 to 4 percent of the price of your home to cover the extra costs associated with the purchase of a house, such as survey fees, inspection costs, fire insurance, legal fees, land transfer tax, and closing costs.

STEP 2: FIND AND EVALUATE A PROPERTY TO PURCHASE

Next, you should select a location, consider using the services of a real estate agent, and conduct a home inspection.

SELECTING A LOCATION   An old adage among real estate people is that the three most important factors to consider when buying a home are location, location, and location! Do you prefer an urban, a suburban, or a rural setting? Do you want to live in a small town or in a resort area? In selecting a neighbourhood, compare your values and lifestyle with those of current residents. Also, TV shows like *Holmes Inspection* and *Property Virgins*, which appear on HGTV, might provide additional insights.

Be aware of **zoning laws**, restrictions on how the property in an area can be used. The location of businesses and the anticipated construction of industrial buildings or a highway may influence your buying decision.

zoning laws
Restrictions on how the property in an area can be used.

If you have or plan to have a family, you should assess the school system. Educators recommend that schools be evaluated on program variety, achievement level of students, percentage of students who go on to post-secondary education, dedication of faculty members, facilities, school funding, and involvement of parents. Homeowners without children also benefit from strong schools, since the educational advantages of a community help maintain property values.

USING A REAL ESTATE AGENT   A real estate agent can help you assess your housing needs and determine the amount you can afford to spend. Real estate agents have information about areas of interest to you and housing available to buy.

The main services a real estate agent provides include: (1) presenting your offer to the seller; (2) negotiating a settlement price; (3) assisting you in obtaining financing; and (4) representing you at the closing. A real estate agent will also recommend lawyers, notaries (in Quebec), insurance agents, home inspectors, and mortgage companies to serve your needs.

Since the seller of the home usually pays the real estate agent's commission, the buyer may not incur a direct cost. However, this expense may be reflected in the price paid for the home. In some cases, the agent is working for the seller. In others, the agent may work for the buyer or may be a *dual agent*, working for both the buyer and the seller. As a buyer, you are better off using an exclusive *buyer's agent*, an agent who looks out only for the interests of the buyer and gets him or her the lowest possible price.

CONDUCTING A HOME INSPECTION   Before reaching your decision about a specific home, conduct a complete evaluation of the property. An evaluation by a trained home inspector can minimize future problems. Do not assume everything is in proper working condition because someone lives there now. Being cautious and determined will save you headaches and unplanned expenses.

Some provinces, cities, and lenders require inspection documents. The mortgage company will usually conduct an *appraisal* to determine the fair market value of the property; although the appraisal is not a detailed inspection, it does help to assess the condition of the home. Exhibit 7–9 presents a detailed format for inspecting a home. A home purchase agreement may include the right to have a contractor or several professionals (roofer, plumber, electrician) inspect the property.

Exhibit 7–9   Conducting a Home Inspection

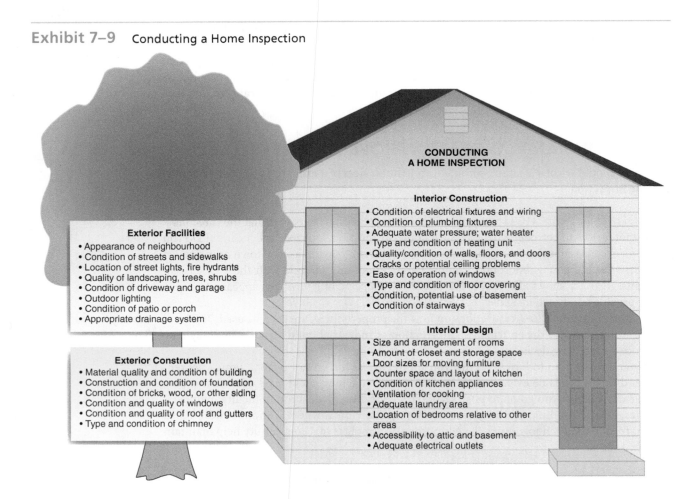

CONDUCTING A HOME INSPECTION

Interior Construction
- Condition of electrical fixtures and wiring
- Condition of plumbing fixtures
- Adequate water pressure; water heater
- Type and condition of heating unit
- Quality/condition of walls, floors, and doors
- Cracks or potential ceiling problems
- Ease of operation of windows
- Type and condition of floor covering
- Condition, potential use of basement
- Condition of stairways

Exterior Facilities
- Appearance of neighbourhood
- Condition of streets and sidewalks
- Location of street lights, fire hydrants
- Quality of landscaping, trees, shrubs
- Condition of driveway and garage
- Outdoor lighting
- Condition of patio or porch
- Appropriate drainage system

Interior Design
- Size and arrangement of rooms
- Amount of closet and storage space
- Door sizes for moving furniture
- Counter space and layout of kitchen
- Condition of kitchen appliances
- Ventilation for cooking
- Adequate laundry area
- Location of bedrooms relative to other areas
- Accessibility to attic and basement
- Adequate electrical outlets

Exterior Construction
- Material quality and condition of building
- Construction and condition of foundation
- Condition of bricks, wood, or other siding
- Condition and quality of windows
- Condition and quality of roof and gutters
- Type and condition of chimney

STEP 3: PRICE THE PROPERTY

After you select a home, determine an offer price and negotiate a final buying price.

DETERMINING THE HOME PRICE   What price should you offer for the home? The main factors to consider are recent selling prices in the area, current demand for housing, the length of time the home has been on the market, the owner's need to sell, financing options, and features and condition of the home. Each of these factors can affect your offer price. For example, you will have to offer a higher price in times of low interest rates and high demand for homes. On the other hand, a home that has been on the market for over a year could mean an opportunity to offer a lower price. The services of a real estate agent or an appraiser can assist you in assessing the current value of the home.

Your offer will be in the form of an *offer to purchase*, or contract (see Exhibit 7–10). This document constitutes your legal offer to purchase the home. Your first offer price usually will not be accepted.

NEGOTIATING THE PURCHASE PRICE   If your initial offer is accepted, you have a valid contract. If your offer is rejected, you have several options, depending on the seller. A counter-offer from the owner indicates a willingness to negotiate a price settlement. If the counter-offer is only slightly lower than the asking price, you are expected to move closer to that price with your next offer. If the counter-offer is quite a bit off the asking price, you are closer to the point where you might split the difference to arrive at the purchase price. If no counter-offer is forthcoming, you may wish to make another offer to see whether the seller is willing to do any negotiating. Be cautious in your negotiations if the seller is using a dual agent. Remember, in that situation, the agent represents the interests of the seller.

Components of an Offer to Purchase

In a real estate transaction, the contract between buyer and seller contains the following information:

- ❏ A description of the property
- ❏ The proposed price of the property
- ❏ The amount of the mortgage that will be needed
- ❏ The amount of the earnest money deposit
- ❏ The date and time of the closing
- ❏ Where the closing will take place
- ❏ A provision for extension of the closing date
- ❏ Time period for which the offer is in effect

- ❏ A provision for disposition of the deposit money if something goes wrong
- ❏ Adjustments to be made at the closing
- ❏ Details of what is included in the sale—home appliances, drapes, carpeting, and other items
- ❏ Special conditions of the sale
- ❏ Inspections the buyer can make before the closing

Exhibit 7–10

The Components of an Offer to Purchase

SOURCE: *Homeownership: Guidelines for Buying and Owning a Home* (Richmond, VA: Federal Reserve Bank of Richmond).

In times of high demand for housing, negotiating may be minimized; this situation is referred to as a *seller's market*, since the current homeowner is likely to have several offers for the property. In such a situation, the final sales price may even exceed the seller's original asking price. In contrast, when home sales are slow, a *buyer's market* exists and a lower price is likely.

When you buy a previously owned home, your negotiating power is based on current market demand and the current owner's need to sell. When you buy a new home, a slow market may mean lower prices or an opportunity to obtain various amenities (fireplace, higher-quality carpeting) from the builder at a lower cost.

Once a price has been agreed on, the purchase contract becomes the basis for the real estate transaction. As part of the offer, the buyer must present a portion of the purchase price deposited as evidence of good faith to show that the purchase offer is serious. At the closing of the home purchase, this earnest money is applied toward the down payment. The money is usually returned if the sale cannot be completed due to circumstances beyond the buyer's control.

Home purchase agreements often contain a *contingency clause*. This contract condition states that the agreement is binding only if a certain event occurs. For example, a real estate contract may stipulate that the contract will not be valid unless the buyer obtains financing for the purchase within a certain period of time, or it may make the purchase of a home contingent on the sale of the buyer's current home.

CONCEPT CHECK 7–3

1. What are the drawbacks of home ownership?
2. What type of individual might prefer a condominium over a single-family dwelling?
3. What are the main sources of funding for a down payment?
4. What is the TDS ratio?
5. How do changing interest rates affect the amount of mortgage a person can afford?
6. How can the quality of a school system in a community benefit even homeowners who do not have school-age children?
7. What services are available to home buyers from real estate agents?
8. How does a *seller's* market differ from a *buyer's* market?

THE FINANCES OF HOME BUYING

LO4

Obtain mortgage
financing.

After you decide to purchase a specific home and have agreed on a price, you will probably apply for a loan. Financing a home purchase requires obtaining a mortgage, developing an awareness of types of mortgages, and settling the real estate transaction.

STEP 4: OBTAIN FINANCING

In Step 1, you determined the most you could save to make a down payment on a home and your most affordable home price, given your income and using lenders' debt service guidelines. Now you must start the application process to obtain mortgage financing.

THE APPLICATION PROCESS   Applying for a mortgage involves three main phases:

1. After completing the mortgage application, a meeting between lender and borrower is scheduled. The borrower presents evidence of employment, income, ownership of assets, and amounts of existing debts.
2. The lender obtains a credit report and verifies other aspects of the borrower's application and financial status.
3. The mortgage is either approved or denied. The decision is based on the potential borrower's credit and financial history and an evaluation of the home, including its location, condition, and value. This process indicates the maximum mortgage for which you qualify. This amount may not be lent on every house you are considering.

The loan commitment is the financial institution's decision to provide the funds needed to purchase a specific property. At this point, the purchase contract for the home becomes legally binding. The approved mortgage application usually *locks in* an interest rate for a certain period.

Sub-Prime Crisis   The term "sub-prime mortgage crisis" refers to the financial crisis precipitated in 2007 after a sharp increase in mortgage foreclosures, mainly sub-prime, collapsed numerous mortgage lenders and hedge funds. Unlike prime rate loans that are given to the lenders' best clients who are most likely to pay back, sub-prime loans are given to less creditworthy customers and in many cases to those who did not have any ability to pay back!

According to investopedia, "The meltdown spilled over into the global credit market as risk premiums increased rapidly and capital liquidity was reduced. The sharp increase in foreclosures and the problems in the sub-prime mortgage market were largely blamed on loose lending practices, low interest rates, a housing bubble and excessive risk taking by lenders and investors" (investopedia.com/terms/s/subprime-meltdown.asp).

Approximately 80 percent of U.S. mortgages issued in recent years to sub-prime borrowers were adjustable-rate mortgages. After U.S. house prices peaked in mid-2006 and began their steep decline thereafter, refinancing became more difficult. As adjustable-rate mortgages began to reset at higher rates, mortgage delinquencies soared. Securities backed with sub-prime mortgages, widely held by financial firms, lost most of their value. The result has been a large decline in the capital of many banks and U.S. government-sponsored enterprises, tightening credit around the world.

EVALUATING DIFFERENT INTEREST AND PAYMENT OPTIONS   The interest rate charged on mortgages can be fixed for a specific term, or can be variable or floating.

amortization The
reduction of a loan
balance through
payments made over
a period of time.

Fixed-Rate Mortgages   Fixed-rate mortgages offer the home buyer the opportunity to lock in a mortgage rate for a specific term, usually one, three, or five years, and occasionally longer. At the end of the term, the rate on the mortgage is renegotiated. The term of a mortgage should not be confused with its amortization period. The **amortization** period is the period chosen by the borrower to repay the entire loan. In Canada, effective July 2012, the maximum amortization period was reduced from 30 years to 25 years, and the maximum amount Canadians can borrow in refinancing their mortgages was reduced from 85 percent to 80 percent of the value of their homes. These, amongst other changes, will help Canadians to pay off their mortgages earlier and promote saving through home ownership as well as limit the repackaging of consumer debt into mortgages guaranteed by taxpayers.

These types of mortgages are also referred to as *closed mortgages*. They are *closed* inasmuch as borrowers must pay a penalty, or a prepayment fee, if they wish to pay down the loan before the end of the term. However, most Canadian mortgages do offer the opportunity to prepay a portion of the capital (e.g., 10 percent of the outstanding balance on the anniversary date) without penalty. If the borrower chooses an *open mortgage*, then the mortgage balance can be paid at any time without penalty. However, as the risk is greater to the lender, the rates charged on open mortgages are higher than those for closed mortgages of similar terms. The term of most open mortgages does not exceed three years.

Since the amount borrowed is large, the payments made during the early years of the mortgage are applied mainly to interest, with only small reductions in the principal of the loan. As the amount owed declines, the monthly payments have an increasing impact on the loan balance. Near the end of the mortgage term, nearly all of each payment is applied to the balance.

> **Did you know?**
>
> Among different lenders, interest rates on a 25-year mortgage may vary up to a full percentage point within a single geographic region—so shop around before you sign the mortgage loan agreement.

For example, a $150,000, 25-year, 5 percent mortgage has monthly payments of $872.41. The breakdown of the first two payments is as follows:

Month	Payment	Interest	Principal	Remaining Balance
1st	$872.41	$618.59	$253.82	$149,746.18
2nd	$872.41	$617.54	$254.87	$149,491.31

In Canada, fixed-rate mortgages are compounded semi-annually. However, payments are usually made monthly, weekly, or bi-weekly. In the above example, we have assumed monthly payments. With a quoted mortgage rate of 5 percent, the effective annual rate, assuming semi-annual compounding, is 5.06 percent $[(1.025)^2 - 1]$. The effective monthly rate is 0.4124 percent $[(1.0506)^{1/12} - 1]$. Using the effective rate and a financial calculator, we can calculate the monthly mortgage payment amount:

2ND	CLRTVM	
150,000	PV	
300	N	(25 years × 12 periods per year)
0.4124	I/Y	(effective monthly rate as shown above)
0	FV	
CPT	PMT	

The solution of $872.41 is displayed.

The interest portion of the first month's payment is $150,000 × 0.4124 = $618.59, and the principal amount paid back is $872.41 − $618.59 = $253.82—leaving a balance remaining of $149,746.18. (Refer to Chapter 6 for a discussion of loan amortization schedules.)

As explained earlier, if the loan-to-value ratio of the mortgage is 80 percent or less, it is called a conventional mortgage.

In the past, many conventional mortgages were *assumable*. This feature allowed a home buyer to continue with the seller's original agreement. Assumable mortgages were especially attractive if the mortgage rate was lower than market interest rates at the time of the sale. Today, due to volatile interest rates, few assumable mortgages are offered.

variable-rate mortgage (VRM) A home loan with an interest rate that can change during the mortgage term due to changes in market interest rates; also called a *flexible-rate mortgage*.

rate cap A limit on the increases and decreases in the interest rate charged on an adjustable-rate mortgage.

Variable-Rate Mortgages   Variable-rate mortgages are a second major category of financing available to home buyers. The **variable-rate mortgage** (VRM), also referred to as a flexible-rate mortgage, has an interest rate that increases or decreases during the life of the loan. When mortgage rates were at record highs, many people took out variable-rate home loans, expecting rates would eventually go down. VRMs usually have a lower initial interest rate than fixed-rate mortgages; however, the borrower, not the lender, bears the risk of future interest rate increases.

A **rate cap** may restrict the amount by which the interest rate can increase or decrease during the VRM term. This limit prevents the borrower from having to pay an interest rate significantly higher than the one in the original agreement. Most rate cap limits increase (or decrease) in the mortgage rate to one or two percentage points in a year and to no more than five points over the life of the loan. Most lenders charge a premium for this.

The monthly amount you pay remains the same, regardless of the direction that interest rates may be going. What can change is the proportion of your payment that goes toward paying off your principal relative to the interest on the loan. If interest rates rise, then more of your money is used against the interest than the principal, which increases the total amount payable. This effect is called *negative amortization*, and it extends the number of payments to be made to pay off the mortgage.

Consider several factors when you evaluate variable-rate mortgages: (1) determine the frequency of and restrictions on allowed changes in interest rates; (2) consider the frequency of and restrictions on changes in the monthly payment; (3) investigate the possibility that the loan will be extended due to negative amortization, and find out whether the mortgage agreement limits the amount of negative amortization; and (4) find out what index the lending institution will use to set the mortgage interest rate over the term of the loan.

The rate for a variable- or flexible-rate mortgage fluctuates from month to month according to the prime rate. If you believe that the prime rate will decline then a variable-rate mortgage is advisable, as this translates to more of your principal being paid down. Studies have also shown that a variable-rate mortgage can be less costly over the life of a mortgage as long as interest rates remain fairly stable.

Most institutions will allow you to convert your variable-rate mortgage to a fixed rate. If rates are rising, or if you do not wish to or are unable to keep track of rates, this is a good strategy.

Did you know?

The main reason to opt for a shorter than standard amortization period is so that you become mortgage-free sooner. And since you are agreeing to pay off your mortgage in a shorter period of time, the interest you pay over the life of the mortgage is therefore greatly reduced. On the same $100,000 mortgage, by taking out a 15-year instead of a 25-year mortgage, a home buyer can save approximately $41,000.

SOURCE: http://mortgage.rbc.com/pdfs/longer-or-shorter-amortization-e.pdf.

Split or Multi-Rate Mortgages   This type of mortgage allows you to split the borrowed amount into three to five parts, each of a different maturity and interest rate. For example, a $200,000 mortgage can be split into four parts of $50,000 each, with terms of six months, one year, three years, and five years, respectively. The total mortgage payment is the sum of the payments required under each part. The advantage to the borrower is the reduction in interest rate risk, as different parts of the mortgage are renewed at different times and, presumably, under different interest rate conditions.

Options for Paying Back Your Mortgage   Most mortgage lenders offer options to your payment plan that will allow you to speed up your payment schedule. These include the option to switch to accelerated mortgage payments, double up on monthly payments, or make lump-sum deposits that directly reduce the outstanding principal. Alternatively, and subject to conditional rules, some institutions will also allow you to miss the occasional payment. In both cases, the details of the available options should be verified with the lender.

Other Financing Methods   To assist first-time home buyers, builders and financial institutions offer financing plans to make the purchase easier.

Second Mortgages   A second mortgage, more commonly called a home equity loan, allows a homeowner to borrow on the paid-up value of the property. Traditional second mortgages allow a homeowner to borrow a lump sum against the equity and repay it in monthly instalments. Recently, lending institutions have offered a variety of home equity loans, including a line of credit program that allows the borrower to obtain additional funds. You need to be careful when using a home equity line of credit. This revolving credit plan can keep you continually in debt as you request new cash advances.

Home Equity Loan   A home equity loan makes it possible to deduct the interest on consumer purchases on your federal income tax return. However, it creates the risk of losing the home if required payments on both the first and second mortgages are not made. To help prevent financial difficulties, home equity loans for amounts that exceed 65 percent of your equity in the home are usually not allowed.

Reverse Mortgage   A *reverse mortgage* is a mortgage designed specifically for the changing financial needs of Canadian seniors. You must be 60 or older and own a home or condo to qualify for a reverse mortgage in Canada. Unlike a traditional mortgage, a reverse mortgage does not require a set payment schedule. You can make monthly interest payments if you want to, but most people choose to pay back the mortgage when they sell their home. The flexibility of never having to make monthly payments is why reverse mortgages are such an attractive option for thousands of Canadian homeowners.

Parent-Backed Mortgages   Obtaining funds for a home purchase from parents can reduce the mortgage rate and increase the value of the home you can afford. With shared-equity financing, parents or other relatives who provide part of the down payment share in the appreciation of the property. A contract among the parties should detail (a) who makes the mortgage payments and gets the tax deduction, (b) how much each person will pay of the real estate taxes, and (c) how and when the equity will be shared. This arrangement allows parents to invest in real estate without having to buy a property on their own.

Do-it-Yourself Mortgages   Self-employed people may find it difficult to obtain a mortgage since their income is often uncertain. The mortgage applicant has two options: (a) *stated-income loans* are based on the amount of income the borrower reports, which makes for a riskier loan unless the applicant has a high credit score or a large down payment, and (b) *regular loans with income documentation,* in which one or two year's of tax returns are required. Recommended in both situations are efforts to improve your credit score by paying off debts and making payments on time. Detailed financial records will also provide evidence of your creditworthiness.

Refinancing   During the term of your mortgage, you may want to **refinance** your home—that is, obtain a new mortgage on your current home at a lower interest rate. Before taking this action, be sure the costs of refinancing do not offset the savings of a lower interest rate. Refinancing is most advantageous when you can get a rate 2 or 3 percent lower than your current rate and when you plan to own your present home for at least two more years. Divide the costs of refinancing by the amount saved each month to determine the time you need to cover your costs.

> **refinancing** The process of obtaining a new mortgage on a home to get a lower interest rate.

Most closed fixed-rate mortgages have a **prepayment penalty** that is the higher of three month's interest or the interest rate differential (IRD). The IRD is based on the interest rate that is the difference between the original mortgage rate and the interest rate the lender can charge you today if you borrowed for the remaining term of the mortgage. This IRD is applied to the amount you are prepaying. The cost may be thousands of dollars. The Financial Consumer Agency of Canada has information on mortgage penalties (http://www.fcac-acfc.gc.ca/eng/forConsumers/topics/mortgages/Pages/Renegoti-Reneacut.aspx).

> **prepayment penalty** A charge imposed by the lender if the borrower pays off the loan early.

Prime borrowers can usually negotiate a lower interest rate in exchange for accepting a prepayment penalty. Investors who buy loans from lenders in the secondary market are willing to accept a lower rate in exchange for a prepayment penalty. The benefit of the penalty to them is that it discourages refinancing if interest rates decline in the future. Lenders will then pass the benefit on to knowledgeable borrowers who ask for it. Whether it is a good deal depends on the rate reduction, and the size and scope of the penalty.

Penalties on Loans to Sub-Prime Borrowers   In contrast to prime loans, where penalties are an option, penalties are required on most sub-prime loans. Lenders demand them because the risk of refinancing is higher on sub-prime loans than on prime loans. Sub-prime borrowers profit from refinancing if their credit rating improves, even when the general level of mortgage rates does not change. Because of high origination costs and high default costs, sub-prime lending is not profitable if the good loans walk out the door after only two years.

STEP 5: CLOSE THE PURCHASE TRANSACTION

Before finalizing the transaction, do a *walk-through* to inspect the conditions and facilities of the home you plan to buy. You can use a digital or video camera to collect evidence for any last-minute items you may need to negotiate.

The *closing* involves a meeting among the buyer, seller, and notary, or representatives of each party, to complete the transaction. Documents are signed, last-minute details are settled, and appropriate amounts are paid. A number of expenses are incurred at the closing. The **closing costs**, also referred to as settlement costs, are the fees and charges paid when a real estate transaction is completed (see Exhibit 7–11).

Title insurance is one closing cost. Title insurance protects your ownership of the property and protects you against errors in surveys or other official records, zoning infractions, future defects, and unforeseen claims that could result in a financial loss. Unlike home insurance, you pay a one-time premium with no deductible. First Canadian Title is Canada's leading provider of title insurance for residential and commercial real estate transactions.

Also due at closing time is the deed recording fee. The **deed** (or **title**) is the document that transfers ownership of property from one party to another. This document certifies that the seller is the true owner of the property, there are no claims against the title, and the seller has the right to sell the property.

Mortgage insurance can also be a closing cost, if it is not included in your monthly mortgage payments. If required, mortgage insurance protects the lender from loss resulting from a mortgage default.

At the closing and when you make your monthly payments, you will probably deposit money to be used for home expenses. For example, the lender will require that you have property insurance. An **escrow account** is money, usually deposited with the lending institution, for the payment of property taxes and homeowner's insurance. This account protects the lender from financial loss due to unpaid real estate taxes or damage from fire or other hazards.

As a new-home buyer, you might also consider purchasing an agreement that gives you protection against defects in the home. *Implied warranties* created by federal and provincial laws may cover some problem areas; other repair costs can occur. Home builders and real estate sales companies offer warranties to buyers. Coverage offered commonly provides protection against structural, wiring, plumbing, heating, and other mechanical defects. Most home warranty programs have many limitations.

closing costs Fees and charges paid when a real estate transaction is completed; also called *settlement costs.*

title insurance Insurance that, during the mortgage term, protects the owner or the lender against financial loss resulting from future defects in the title and from other unforeseen property claims not excluded by the policy.

deed (or **title**) A document that transfers ownership of property from one party to another.

escrow account Money, usually deposited with the lending institution, for the payment of property taxes and homeowner's insurance.

Did you know?

The Home Buyers' Plan allows you to withdraw up to $25,000 from your RRSP to use as a down payment on your first home (or double this amount for couples). For more information go to cra-arc.gc.ca.

Exhibit 7–11   Common Additional Costs

When looking toward buying a home, it is important to prepare for other costs so there are no surprises. The following is a list of the most common costs of home purchasing, with an estimated price. Not all of these fees will apply to every situation or every province.

Item	Cost	Comments
Appraisal	$200–$300	Determines the value of your property; may be covered by your lender.
Home Inspection	$300–$500	Can tell you what condition your home is in, and estimate the cost of repairs. It's a good idea to make your offer conditional on a home inspection.
Property Survey	$750–$1,000	A recent legal written/mapped description of your home, including its location and dimensions, is usually required by your mortgage lender (typically paid for by the seller).
Insurance for High-Ratio Mortgages	Varies	Typically between 0.60 and 3.35 percent of your mortgage amount.
Home Insurance	$750	Your lender will require that you adequately insure to protect the investment.
Land Transfer Tax	$2,000+	Tax levied by some provinces whenever property changes hands.
Interest Adjustment	$100–$1,000	In the event that your home purchase closing date does not coincide with the date when your mortgage payments start, you may be required to pay interest for this period. It is worthwhile to arrange for your mortgage payments to begin exactly one payment period after your closing date. You may also be able to negotiate to have your lender waive or reduce this payment.
Prepaid Property Tax and Utility Adjustments	$400–$1,500	If the previous owners prepaid property taxes and/or other utilities you will have to reimburse them, starting at the date your house sale closes.
Legal Fees	$500–$2,500	A real estate lawyer (a notary in Quebec) will bill you for conducting a title search, drafting the title deed, and preparing the mortgage. Registration fees and other disbursements are extra.
Moving Expenses	$500–$2,000	The cost of moving into your new home will vary, depending on whether you rent a truck and do it yourself or hire movers.
Service Charges	$150–$200	There may be additional charges for hooking up your gas, hydro, phone, cable, and so on.
HST/GST	For new homes only	HST/GST is charged on newly built homes. The builder often pays this tax and/or a rebate is available depending on the price of the home, therefore it's a good idea to ask and clarify this prior to closing.
Life Insurance	Optional	This is optional, but it serves to cover your mortgage in the event of the insured's death.
Mortgage Application Fee	Varies	This amount varies from one institution to the next and is usually waived for prime borrowers.

There are many ways to reduce the amortization period on your mortgage and, ultimately, the total interest that you will pay. One way involves switching from a regular to an *accelerated* payment. Let's look at an example.

If you take out a $100,000, 25-year mortgage at a rate of 4.0 percent, compounded semi-annually, your monthly mortgage payment is $526. Total interest costs on the mortgage amount to approximately $57,800, in addition to repaying the $100,000 in principal. We calculate this as follows:

$526 × 300 payments = $157,800 in total payments

$157,800 − $100,000 principal = $57,800 in interest charges

If you were offered the opportunity to make accelerated weekly payments, your financial institution would calculate the weekly payment as one-quarter of the monthly payment. In this case, the weekly payment is $131.50 ($526 ÷ 4). But because there are more than four weeks in each month (except February), the result of paying $131.50 every week means that you are accelerating the repayment of your mortgage.

Given the same mortgage rate of 4.0 percent compounded semi-annually, and weekly payments of $131.50, the reduced amortization period on your mortgage is 21 years and 10 months (1,139 weeks). This means you pay:

$131.50 × 1,139 payments = $149,779 in total payments

$149,779 − $100,000 principal = $49,779 in interest charges

Switching from a monthly to an accelerated weekly mortgage results in a reduction of three years and one month in your amortization period and a saving of approximately $8,021 ($57,800 − $49,779) in interest charges!

To explore other options to reduce your mortgage amortization period and interest charges, visit http://mortgage.rbc.com/pdfs/longer-or-shorter-amortization-e.pdf.

HOME BUYING: A FINAL WORD

For most people, buying a home is the most expensive decision they will undertake. As a reminder, Exhibit 7–12 provides an overview of the major elements to consider when making this critical financial decision.

Exhibit 7–12

The Main Elements of Buying a Home

- **Location.** Consider the community and geographic region. A $350,000 home in one area may be an average-priced house, while in another part of the country it may be fairly expensive real estate. The demand for homes is largely affected by the economy and the availability of jobs.

- **Down payment.** While making a large down payment reduces your mortgage payments, you will also need funds for closing costs, moving expenses, repairs, or furniture.

- **Mortgage application.** When applying for a home loan, you will usually be required to provide copies of recent tax returns, a residence and employment history, information about bank and investment accounts, a listing of debts, and evidence of auto and any real estate ownership.

- **Closing costs.** Settlement costs can range from 1 to 4 percent of the loan amount. This means you could need as much as $12,000 to finalize a $300,000 home purchase; this amount is in addition to your down payment.

- **PIT.** Your monthly payment for principal, interest, and taxes is an important budget item. Beware of buying "too much house" and not having enough for other living expenses.

- **Maintenance costs.** As any homeowner will tell you, owning a home can be expensive. Set aside funds for repair and remodelling expenses.

CONCEPT CHECK 7–4

1. Under what conditions might a variable-rate mortgage be more appropriate than a fixed-rate mortgage?
2. When might refinancing a mortgage be advisable?
3. How do closing costs affect a person's ability to afford a home purchase?

SELLING YOUR HOME

Most people who buy a home will eventually be on the other side of a real estate transaction. Selling your home requires preparing it for selling, setting a price, and deciding whether to sell it yourself or use a real estate agent.

LO5
Develop a strategy for selling a home.

PREPARING YOUR HOME FOR SELLING

The effective presentation of your home can result in a fast and financially favourable sale. Real estate salespeople recommend that you make needed repairs and paint worn exterior and interior areas. Clear the garage and exterior areas of toys, debris, and old vehicles, and keep the lawn cut and the leaves raked. Keep the kitchen and bathroom clean. Avoid offensive odours by removing garbage and keeping pets and their areas clean. Remove excess furniture and dispose of unneeded items to make the house, closets, and storage areas look larger. When showing your home, open drapes and turn on lights to give it a pleasant atmosphere. This effort will give your property a positive image and make it attractive to potential buyers.

DETERMINING THE SELLING PRICE

Putting a price on your home can be difficult. You risk not selling it immediately if the price is too high, and you may not get a fair amount if the price is too low. An **appraisal**, an estimate of the current value of the property, can provide a good indication of the price you should set. An asking price is influenced by recent selling prices of comparable homes in your area, demand in the housing market, and available financing based on current mortgage rates.

appraisal An estimate of the current value of a property.

The home improvements you have made may or may not increase the selling price. A hot tub or an exercise room may have no value for potential buyers. Among the most desirable improvements are energy-efficient features, a remodelled kitchen, an additional or remodelled bathroom, added rooms and storage space, a converted basement, a fireplace, and an outdoor deck or patio.

The time to think about selling your home is when you buy it and every day you live there. Daily maintenance, timely repairs, and home improvements will increase the future sales price.

SALE BY OWNER

If you decide to sell your home without using a real estate professional, price the home and advertise it through local newspapers or by listing it on Web sites designed for this purpose (such as ComFree). Obtain a listing sheet from a real estate office as an example of the information to include on your flier. Put up a "For Sale" sign to attract those shopping for homes in your neighbourhood and, if possible, create a virtual tour on the Web to attract prospective buyers who live farther away. Recent changes even allow you to place your home for sale on MLS if you are selling it yourself.

When selling your home on your own, obtain information about the availability of financing and financing requirements. This information will help you and potential buyers to determine whether a sale is possible. Use the services of a lawyer or title company to assist you with the contract, the closing, and other legal matters.

Require potential buyers to provide their names, addresses, telephone numbers, and background information, and show your home only by appointment. As a security measure, show it only when two or more adults are at home. Selling your own home can save you several thousand dollars in commission, but it requires an investment of time and effort.

LISTING WITH A REAL ESTATE AGENT

You may decide to sell your home with the assistance of a real estate agent. These businesses range from firms owned by one person to nationally franchised companies. Primary selection factors should be the real estate agent's knowledge of the community and the agent's willingness to actively market your home.

Your real estate agent will provide you with various services for a fee, usually in the area of 6 percent of the home's sale price. These services include suggesting a selling price, making potential buyers and other agents aware of your home, providing advice on features to highlight, conducting showings of your home, and handling the financial aspects of the sale. A real estate agent can also help screen potential buyers to determine whether they will qualify for a mortgage.

Discount real estate brokers are available to assist sellers who are willing to take on certain duties and want to reduce selling costs.

CONCEPT CHECK 7–5

1. What actions are recommended when planning to sell your home?
2. What factors affect the selling price of a home?
3. What should you consider when deciding whether to sell your home on your own or use the services of a real estate agent?

SUMMARY OF LEARNING OBJECTIVES

LO1 Evaluate available housing alternatives.
Your needs, life situation, and financial resources are the major factors that influence your selection of housing. Assess renting and buying alternatives in terms of their financial and opportunity costs.

LO2 Analyze the costs and benefits associated with renting.
The main advantages of renting are mobility, fewer responsibilities, and lower initial costs. The main disadvantages of renting are few financial benefits, a restricted lifestyle, and legal concerns.

LO3 Implement the home-buying process.
Home buying involves five major stages: (1) determining home ownership needs; (2) finding and evaluating a property to purchase; (3) pricing the property; (4) financing the purchase; and (5) closing the real estate transaction.

LO4 Obtain mortgage financing.
Financing a home purchase requires obtaining a mortgage, as well as an awareness of types of mortgages and how to settle the real estate transaction.

LO5 Develop a strategy for selling a home.
When selling a home, you must decide whether to make certain repairs and improvements, determine a selling price, and choose between selling the home yourself and using the services of a real estate agent.

KEY TERMS

amortization 216

appraisal 223

closing costs 220

condominium 209

co-operative housing 209

deed (or title) 220

escrow account 220

for-profit co-operative housing 209

gross debt service (GDS) ratio 210

lease 205

manufactured home 208

mortgage 210

non-profit co-operative housing 209

prepayment penalty 219

rate cap 218

refinancing 219

title insurance 220

total debt service (TDS) ratio 210

variable-rate mortgage (VRM) 218

zoning laws 213

KEY FORMULAS

Page	Topic	Formula
210	Gross debt service (GDS) ratio	$= \dfrac{\text{Principal and interest payment} + \text{Taxes} + \text{Heating}}{\text{Gross monthly income}} \times 100\%$
210	Total debt service (TDS) ratio	$= \dfrac{\text{Principal and interest payment} + \text{Taxes} + \text{Heating} + \text{Debt payment}}{\text{Gross monthly income}} \times 100\%$

FINANCIAL PLANNING PROBLEMS

 Practise and learn online with Connect.

1. *Determining Appropriate Housing.* What type of housing would you suggest for people in the following life situations? LO1
   a. A single parent with two school-age children.
   b. A two-income couple without children.
   c. A person with both dependent children and a dependent parent.
   d. A couple near retirement with grown children.

2. *Comparing Renting and Buying.* Based on the following data, would you recommend buying or renting? Assume an after-tax savings interest rate of 6 percent and a tax rate of 28 percent. LO2

Rental Costs	Buying Costs
Annual rent, $7,380	Annual mortgage payments,
Insurance, $145	$9,800 ($9,575 is interest)
Security deposit, $650	Property taxes, $1,780
	Insurance/maintenance, $1,050
	Down payment/closing costs, $4,500
	Growth in equity, $225
	Estimated annual appreciation, $1,700

3. *Analyzing the Buy-versus-Rent Decision.* Use the buy-versus-rent analysis on page 202 to compare two residences you might consider. LO2

4. *Calculating the GDS and TDS Ratios.* Calculate the gross debt service (GDS) and the total debt service (TDS) ratios for the following data. LO3

   Monthly mortgage payment = $2,100
   Property taxes = $200
   Heating costs = $115
   Other housing costs = $70
   Personal loan payment = $150
   Car loan payment = $200
   Credit card payment = $150
   Gross monthly household income = $7,800

5. *Estimating a Monthly Mortgage Payment.* Estimate the affordable monthly mortgage payment, the affordable mortgage amount, and the affordable home purchase price for the following situation (see Exhibit 7–6). LO3

   Monthly gross income, $2,950
   Down payment to be made, 15 percent of purchase price
   Other debt (monthly payment), $160
   Monthly estimate for property taxes and insurance, $210
   25-year loan at 6.5 percent.
   Factor of 6.7

6. *Calculating Monthly Mortgage Payments.* Based on Exhibit 7–7, page 212, what are the monthly mortgage payments for each of the following situations?
   a. A $40,000, 15-year loan at 7.5 percent.
   b. A $76,000, 25-year loan at 9 percent.
   c. A $65,000, 20-year loan at 10 percent.

   What relationship exists between the length of the loan and the monthly payment? How does the mortgage rate affect the monthly payment? *LO3*

7. *Comparing Total Mortgage Payments.* Which mortgage would result in higher total payments? *LO3*

   Mortgage A: $985 a month for 25 years
   Mortgage B: $780 a month for 5 years and $1,056 for 25 years

8. *Evaluating a Refinance Decision.* Kelly and Tim Johnson plan to refinance their mortgage to obtain a lower interest rate. They will reduce their mortgage payments by $56 a month. Their closing costs for refinancing will be $1,670. How long will it take them to cover the cost of refinancing? *LO4*

9. *Future Value of an Amount Saved.* You estimate that you can save $3,800 by selling your home yourself, rather than using a real estate agent. What is the future value of that amount if invested for five years at 7 percent? *LO5*

FINANCIAL PLANNING ACTIVITIES

1. *Comparing Housing Alternatives.* Interview several people about the factors that influenced their current residence. *LO1*

2. *Comparing Rental Situations.* Compare the costs, facilities, and features of apartments and other rental housing in your area. You may obtain this information through newspaper advertisements, rental offices, or online searches. *LO2*

3. *Researching Rental Agreements.* Interview a tenant and a landlord to obtain their views about potential problems associated with renting. How do their views on tenant–landlord relations differ? *LO2*

4. *Comparing Home-Buying Alternatives.* Visit the sales office for a condominium, a new home, and a mobile home. Based on the information obtained, prepare a written or an oral presentation comparing the benefits and potential concerns of these housing alternatives. *LO3*

5. *Using a Real Estate Agent.* Interview a real estate agent about the process involved in selecting and buying a home. Ask about housing prices in your area and the services the agent provides. Also, find out the agent's opinion as to what will happen to housing prices and interest rates over the next six months. *LO3*

6. *Comparing Types of Mortgages.* Talk with people who have different types of mortgages. What suggestions do they offer about obtaining home financing? What were their experiences with closing costs when they purchased their homes? *LO4*

7. *Comparing Types of Mortgage Financing.* Visit bank Web sites, such as royalbank.ca, to learn how fixed-rate and variable-rate mortgages differ. What are the advantages and disadvantages of each? Which would a first-time home buyer likely prefer, and why? *LO4*

8. *Comparing Mortgage Companies.* Contact several mortgage companies and other financial institutions to obtain information about current mortgage rates, application fees, and the process for obtaining a mortgage. *LO4*

9. *Searching the Web for Mortgage Rates.* Using Web sites such as canadamortgage.com, cannex.com, or money.canoe.ca, obtain information on current mortgage rates available in different parts of the country. *LO4*

10. *Analyzing Homes for Sale.* Visit a couple of homes for sale. What features do you believe would appeal to potential buyers? What efforts were made to attract potential buyers to the open houses? *LO5*

LIFE SITUATION CASE 1

Housing Decisions

When Marcel and Vanya St. Onge first saw the house, they didn't like it. However, it was a dark, rainy day. They viewed the house more favourably on their second visit, which they had expected to be a waste of time. Despite cracked ceilings, the need for a paint job, and a kitchen built in the 1950s, the St. Onges saw the potential to create a place they could call their own.

Brigitte Lavoie purchased her condominium four years ago. She obtained a mortgage rate of 9.75 percent, a very good rate then. Recently, when interest rates dropped, Brigitte was considering refinancing her mortgage at a lower rate.

Matthew and Petra Steward had been married for five years and were still living in an apartment. Several of the Stewards' friends had recently purchased homes. However, Matthew and Petra were not sure they wanted to follow this example.

Although they liked their friends' homes and had viewed photographs of homes currently on the market, they also liked the freedom from maintenance responsibility they enjoyed as renters.

Questions

1. How could the St. Onges have benefited from buying a home that needed improvements?

2. How might Brigitte Lavoie have found out when mortgage rates were at a level that would make refinancing her condominium more affordable?

3. Although the Stewards had good reasons for continuing to rent, what factors might make it desirable for an individual or a family to buy a home?

LIFE SITUATION CASE 2

Mortgage Affordability

Jose and Maria Dias bought their first home in Milton, Ontario, two years ago. The purchase price was $200,000. They were determined to get a conventional mortgage and were able to come up with a down payment of $50,000 by combining $15,000 in gifts received from their parents, saving another $15,000, and borrowing $20,000 from their RRSPs. They were approved for a 6.5 percent 25-year mortgage for $150,000 with monthly payments of $1,004.74. In addition, they chose to pay the lender another $310 per month for property taxes.

So far everything has been going well. They both have good jobs. Jose makes $49,000 a year and has a take-home pay of $2,045. Maria earns $35,000 and has a take-home pay of $1,550. They have no credit card debts but pay $600 per month for an auto loan and RRSP loan repayment. Other monthly expenses are as follows: home insurance $60, auto insurance $90, utilities $240, food $400, and transportation $150. What is left is either used for entertainment or put into a savings account.

Maria is now six months' pregnant with the couple's first child and she is worried about whether they will be able to meet their living and financial expenses while she is on maternity

leave. She is also wondering whether, in the event her mother is unable to look after the child, they can afford child care expenses of $600 or more for the baby when Maria returns to work.

Questions

1. While on maternity leave, Maria will receive only 55 percent of her salary. Taking this and some of the additional baby costs (such as diapers and formula) into account, will the Diases be able to make ends meet? Will they be eligible for any tax credits and benefits that would increase their cash inflow? Are there any expenses they can reduce to help meet their obligations?

2. Calculate the maximum monthly mortgage payment, the maximum mortgage amount, and the maximum home purchase price Maria and Jose could have afforded based on the GDS ratio and TDS ratio guidelines? Would this have been wise?

3. When her maternity leave ends, can Maria afford to go back to work?

CONTINUOUS CASE FOR PART 2 (B)

SPENDING PATTERNS FOR FINANCIAL SECURITY

Life Situation

Young married couple: Pamela, 30; Isaac, 32; two children, ages 1 and 3

Financial Goals

- Improve daily spending habits
- Purchase a new home
- Acquire a second motor vehicle

Financial Data

Monthly income	$ 3,600
Living expenses	3,125
Assets	33,850
Liabilities	1,520

The Mortimers now have two preschool-age children. Their household income has declined because Pamela has "retired" for a while to care for the children. To compensate for their lower monthly income, Pamela and Isaac have cut back to the basics and purchase only the necessities each month. Still, their expenses total $3,125 a month. However, the Mortimers have managed to pay down their liabilities over the past four years; now their liabilities total $1,520.

Housing needs are also changing for the Mortimers as their family increases in size. At present, they pay $750 in rent for a two-bedroom apartment. To purchase a home for a comparable monthly payment, the Mortimers would have to relocate farther from Isaac's place of employment.

In addition to buying a home, the Mortimers need to purchase a second automobile. Currently, Pamela must drive Isaac to the train station (creating many inconveniences for her and the children) if she wants to use the car for various business and education activities. If they move to the suburbs, the situation will only get worse.

Questions

1. What major factors are affecting the Mortimers' spending habits?

2. Based on a monthly income of $3,600, an estimated $240 per month for property taxes and homeowner's insurance, current mortgage interest rates of 9 percent, and a down payment of at least 10 percent, what would it cost the Mortimers to purchase a home?

3. What tax advantages will the Mortimers realize by purchasing a home, rather than renting?

4. What transportation alternatives should the Mortimers consider? If they decide that they need a second motor vehicle, how should they finance it?

part 3

Insuring Your Assets

CHAPTER 8

Home and Automobile Insurance

CHAPTER 9

Life, Health, and Disability Insurance

chapter 8

Home and Automobile Insurance

LEARNING OBJECTIVES

LO1 Develop a risk management plan using insurance.

LO2 Discuss the importance of property and liability insurance.

LO3 Explain the insurance coverages and policy types available to homeowners and renters.

LO4 Analyze factors that influence the amount of coverage and cost of home insurance.

LO5 Identify the important types of automobile insurance coverages.

LO6 Evaluate factors that affect the cost of automobile insurance.

SHOPPING FOR A CAR? HAVE YOU CONSIDERED THE INSURANCE PREMIUMS?

Justin Kirby was getting ready to begin his final year of studies at the University of Toronto's Mississauga campus. After years of taking the bus to commute to school and his part-time job, Justin was finally going to have his own car! For his belated 20th birthday gift, Justin's dad had offered to buy him a car. There was only one condition attached to this generous offer: Justin would have to pay for gas and the monthly auto insurance premiums.

After searching for quotes on kanetix.ca, Justin quickly realized that his age, gender, and driving experience made the insurance premiums on a brand-new Toyota Matrix unaffordable. Taking into account his father's budget of $20,000 and his own after-tax monthly income of $900—which seemed to disappear as quickly as he earned it—Justin wondered what his dad would say to buying a used car.

His girlfriend suggested he do some more research on automobile insurance before wasting his time with car dealers.

The Insurance Bureau of Canada Web site (ibc.ca) was eye-opening. Justin learned that in addition to his personal driving record several other factors—such as the safety and theft records of the area he lived in; the year, make, and model of the car; the intended use of the car; the annual mileage; and the extent of coverage desired—would affect his insurance premiums.

After looking over the lists of "Top 10 Most Stolen Cars" and "How Cars Measure Up," he decided to purchase a 2010 silver Toyota Yaris two-door hatchback. His monthly auto insurance premiums turned out to be $315.

QUESTIONS

1. What are some additional factors that would influence the cost of auto insurance for Justin?

2. What are some measures Justin can take to maintain or reduce existing auto insurance premiums?

 Practise and learn online with Connect.

INSURANCE AND RISK MANAGEMENT: AN INTRODUCTION

You purchase insurance to control the effects of uncontrollable financial risk inherent to life and living (and for that matter even death). The idea is that certain bad things will happen, but you have no idea when or what, so your best bet is to be ready for them at all times. You do this by buying insurance, and the amount of insurance you buy should reflect the potential financial impact of the loss or partial loss of what you are insuring.

LO1
Develop a risk management plan using insurance.

WHAT IS INSURANCE?

Insurance is protection against possible financial loss. Although many types of insurance exist, they all have one thing in common: They give you the peace of mind that comes from knowing that money will be available to meet the needs of your survivors, pay medical expenses, protect your home and belongings, and cover personal or property damage.

Life insurance replaces income that is lost if the policyholder dies. Health insurance helps meet medical expenses when the policyholder becomes ill. Automobile insurance helps cover property and personal damage caused by the policyholder's car. Home insurance covers the policyholder's place of residence and its associated financial risks, such as damage to personal property and injuries to others.

An **insurance company**, or **insurer**, is a risk-sharing firm that agrees to assume financial responsibility for losses that may result from an insured risk. A person joins the risk-sharing group (the insurance company) by purchasing a **policy** (a contract). Under the policy, the insurance company agrees to assume the risk for a fee (the **premium**) that the person (the **insured**, or the **policyholder**) pays periodically.

Insurance mitigates the risks of financial uncertainty and unexpected losses. The financial consequences of failing to obtain the right amount and type of insurance can be disastrous.

insurance Protection against possible financial loss.

insurance company A risk-sharing firm that assumes financial responsibility for losses that may result from an insured risk.

insurer An insurance company.

policy A written contract for insurance.

premium The amount of money a policyholder is charged for an insurance policy.

insured A person covered by an insurance policy.

policyholder A person who owns an insurance policy.

risk Chance or uncertainty of loss; may also mean "the insured."

peril The cause of a possible loss.

hazard A factor that increases the likelihood of loss through some peril.

TYPES OF RISKS

You face risks every day. You can't cross the street without some danger that you'll be hit by a car. You can't own property without taking the chance that it will be lost, stolen, damaged, or destroyed. Insurance companies offer financial protection against such dangers and losses by promising to compensate the insured for a relatively large loss in return for the payment of a much smaller but certain expense called the *premium*.

Risk, *peril*, and *hazard* are important terms in insurance. Each has a distinct, technical meaning in insurance terminology.

Risk is the chance that something may be lost. When people buy insurance, they assume that even if the associated risk happens, they will not be overly affected. For example, many people insure their car for loss and damage because they know the odds are good that risk may occur, and they know that repair or replacement costs could be high. By buying insurance, they minimize the potential impact of a risk.

Peril is the cause of a possible loss. It is the event that causes someone to take out insurance. People buy policies for financial protection against such perils as fire, windstorms, explosions, robbery, accidents, and premature death.

Hazard increases the likelihood of loss through some peril. For example, defective house wiring is a hazard that increases the likelihood of the peril of fire.

The most common risks are classified as personal risks, property risks, and liability risks. *Personal risks* are the uncertainties surrounding loss of income or life due to premature death, illness, disability, old age, or unemployment. *Property risks* are the uncertainties of direct or indirect losses to property due to fire, windstorms, accidents, theft, and other hazards. *Liability risks* are loss possibilities due to negligence resulting in bodily harm or property damage to others. Such harm or damage could be caused by an automobile, professional misconduct, injury suffered on one's property, and so on.

pure risk A risk in which there is only a chance of loss; also called insurable risk.

speculative risk A risk in which there is a chance of either loss or gain.

Personal risks, property risks, and liability risks are types of **pure risk**, or *insurable risk*, since there is a chance of loss only if the specified events occurred. Pure risks are accidental and unintentional risks for which the nature and financial cost of the loss can be predicted.

A **speculative risk** is a risk that carries a chance of either loss or gain. Starting a small business that may or may not succeed is an example of speculative risk. So is gambling. Speculative risks are legally defined as uninsurable.

RISK MANAGEMENT METHODS

Risk management is an organized strategy for protecting assets and people. It controls financial losses caused by destructive events. Risk management is a long-range planning process. People's risk management needs change at various points in their lives. If you understand risks and how to manage them, you can provide better protection for yourself and your family. You can reduce your financial losses and thereby improve your chances for economic, social, physical, and emotional well-being. Since you will probably be unable to afford to cover all risks, you need to understand how to obtain the best protection you can afford.

Most people think of risk management as buying insurance. However, insurance is not the only method of dealing with risk; in certain situations, other methods may be less costly. Four general risk management techniques are commonly used.

Did you know?

Alien abduction protection, haunted house insurance, and coverage if you have an immaculate conception are some of the strange but real-life policies available for a price. Contest insurance pays for prizes such as a new car, a trip, or $10,000 in cash when someone hits a hole-in-one at a golf tournament. Some insurance companies allow people to insure their body parts, including letting Bette Davis insure her waist, Julia Roberts her smile, Bruce Springstein his voice, and an Australian cricket player his moustache.

SOURCE: Caterina Pontoriero, "Unusual Insurance Coverages," www.propertycasualty360.com, September 14, 2012, accessed, June 10, 2014.

RISK AVOIDANCE   You can avoid the risk of an automobile accident by not driving to work. General Motors can avoid the risk of product failure by not introducing new cars. Risk avoidance is practised in both instances, but at a high cost. You might have to give up your job, and General Motors might lose out to competitors that introduce new models.

In some situations, however, risk avoidance is practical. At the personal level, people avoid risks by not smoking or by not walking through high-crime neighbourhoods. At the business level, jewellery stores avoid losses through robbery by locking their merchandise in vaults. Obviously, no person or business can avoid all risks.

RISK REDUCTION   While avoiding risks completely may not be possible, reducing risks may be a cause of action. You can reduce the risk of injury in an auto accident by wearing a seat belt. You can install smoke alarms and fire extinguishers to protect life and reduce potential fire damage. You can reduce the risk of illness by eating a balanced diet and exercising.

RISK ASSUMPTION   Risk assumption means taking on responsibility for the loss or injury that may result from a risk. Generally, it makes sense to assume a risk when the potential loss is small, when risk management has reduced the risk, when insurance coverage is expensive, and when there is no other way to obtain protection. For instance, you might decide not to purchase collision insurance on an older car. Then, if an accident occurs, you will bear the costs of fixing the car.

self-insurance The process of establishing a monetary fund to cover the cost of a loss.

Self-insurance is the process of establishing a monetary fund to cover the cost of a loss. Self-insurance does not eliminate risks, it only provides means for covering losses. Many people self-insure by default, not by choice. Others take on as much insurance as they can afford and then self-insure the rest.

RISK SHIFTING   The most common method of dealing with risk is to shift, or transfer, it to an insurance company or some other organization. Insurance is the protection against loss afforded by the purchase of an insurance policy from an insurance company. Insurers, in their turn, usually insure themselves through what is known as re-insuring. By re-insuring the risks they have assumed by insuring your risk, they are acting very much like you: they are controlling the potential effects should risks actualize.

Exhibit 8–1 summarizes various risks and appropriate strategies for managing them.

PLANNING AN INSURANCE PROGRAM

Because all people have their own needs and goals, many of which change over the years, a personal insurance program should be tailored to those changes. In the early years of marriage, when the family is growing, most families need certain kinds of insurance protection. This protection may include property insurance on an apartment or a house, life and disability insurance for wage earners and caretakers of dependants, and adequate health insurance for the whole family.

Did you know?

Deductibles are a combination of risk assumption and risk shifting. The insured person assumes part of the risk, paying the first $100, $250, $500, or $1,000 of a claim. The majority of the risk for a large claim is shifted to another party, the insurance company.

Exhibit 8–1   Examples of Risks and Risk Management Strategies

Risks		Strategies for Reducing Financial Impact		
Personal Events	**Financial Impact**	**Personal Resources**	**Private Sector**	**Public Sector**
Disability	Loss of one income Loss of services Increased expenses	Savings, investments Family observing safety precautions	Disability insurance	Disability insurance
Illness	Loss of one income Medical expenses	Health-enhancing behaviour	Health insurance	Medicare

Death	Loss of one income
	Loss of services
	Funeral expenses
		Estate planning
		Risk reduction
			Life insurance	Veteran's life
				  insurance
				Government
				  programs; e.g.,
				  survivor's
				  benefits

Retirement	Decreased income
	Unplanned living
	  expenses
		Savings
		Investments
		Hobbies, skills
			Retirement and/or
			  pensions
				Public pensions
				Pension plan for
				  government
				  employees

Property loss	Catastrophic storm
	  damage to property
	Repair or replacement
	  cost of theft
		Property repair
		  and upkeep
		Security plans
			Automobile
			  insurance
			Homeowner's
			  insurance
			Tenant's insurance
				Basic disaster
				  relief

Liability	Claims and settlement
	  costs
	Lawsuits and legal
	  expenses
	Loss of personal assets
	  and income
		Observing safety
		  precautions
		Maintaining
		  property
			Homeowner's
			  insurance
			Automobile
			  insurance	

Later, when the family has a higher income and a different financial situation, protection needs change. There might be a long-range provision for the children's education, more life insurance to match higher income and living standards, and revised health insurance protection. Still later, when the children have grown and are on their own, retirement and health coverage benefits are a consideration, further changing the family's personal insurance program.

Exhibit 8–2 outlines the steps in developing a personal insurance program.

STEP 1: SET INSURANCE GOALS   In managing risks, your goal is to minimize personal, property, and liability risks. Your insurance goals should define what to do to cover the basic risks present in your life situation. Covering the basic risks means providing a financial resource to cover costs resulting from a loss.

Suppose your goal is to buy a new car. You must plan to make the purchase and to protect yourself against financial losses from accidents. Auto insurance on the car lets you enjoy the car without worrying that an auto accident might leave you worse off, financially, than before.

Each individual has unique goals. Income, age, family size, lifestyle, experience, and responsibilities influence the goals you set, and the insurance you buy must reflect those goals. In general, financial advisers say that a basic risk management plan must set goals to reduce the impact of the following events:

- Potential loss of income due to the premature death, illness, accident, or unemployment of a wage earner.
- Potential loss of income and extra expense resulting from the illness, disability, or death of a spouse.
- Additional expenses due to the injury, illness, or death of other family members.
- Potential loss of real or personal property due to fire, theft, or other hazards.
- Potential loss of income, savings, and property due to personal liability.

STEP 2: DEVELOP A PLAN TO REACH YOUR GOALS   Planning is a sign of maturity, a way of taking control of life instead of letting life happen to you. What risks do you face? Which risks can you afford to take without having to back away from your goals? What resources— public programs, personal assets, or private risk-sharing plans—are available to you?

Exhibit 8–2

Creating a Personal Insurance Program

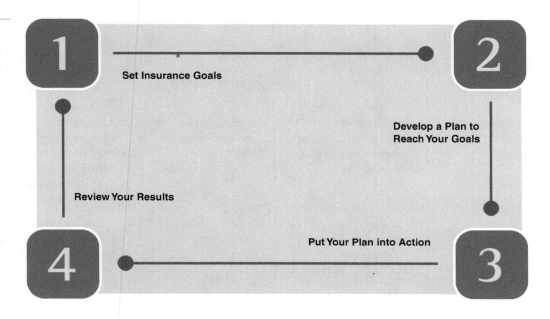

1 Set Insurance Goals

2 Develop a Plan to Reach Your Goals

3 Put Your Plan into Action

4 Review Your Results

Following are some key questions to ask your insurance provider BEFORE you purchase your home insurance.

(Questions supplied by the *Insurance Bureau of Canada*)

- Who is covered under this policy?
- What property is covered?
- What "perils" are covered? (A peril is an event that can cause damage, such as fire, theft, or wind.)
- What is NOT covered? (This is called an "exclusion." Exclusions may apply to the persons who are covered, the property covered, the perils insured against, or the location where the coverage applies. Not every circumstance can be covered by an insurance policy. Normal wear-and-tear and deterioration of property are not insurable; you should check your policy for other exclusions.)

- What extensions of coverage are available? (Often called "riders," "forms," or "endorsements," some policy extensions are automatic, while others are optional and/or conditional.)
- What are the conditions of coverage, and what do you have to do to make sure that coverage continues?
- What do you do if there's a loss? How do you make a claim to recover a loss?

The preceding questions are intended as a guideline only and are not meant to be exhaustive.

SOURCE: insurance-canada.ca/.

To understand and use the resources at your command, you need good information. In terms of insurance, this means a clear picture of the available insurance, the reliability of different insurers, and the comparative costs of the coverage needed.

STEP 3: PUT YOUR PLAN INTO ACTION   As you carry out your plan, obtain financial and personal resources, budget them, and use them to reach your risk management goals. If, for example, you find the insurance protection you have is not enough to cover your basic risks, you may purchase additional coverage, change the kind of insurance coverage, restructure your budget to cover additional insurance costs, and strengthen your savings or investment programs to reduce long-term risk.

The best risk management plans have flexibility. Savings accounts or other cash, for example, should be available as emergency funds for unexpected financial problems. The best plans are also flexible enough to allow you to respond to changing life situations. Your goal should be an insurance program that expands (or contracts) with changing protection needs.

To put your risk management plan to work, you must answer four basic questions: (1) what should I insure, (2) for how much, (3) what kind of insurance should I buy, and (4) from whom?

STEP 4: REVIEW YOUR RESULTS   Evaluate your insurance plan periodically, at least every two or three years or whenever your family circumstances change. Among the questions you should ask yourself are, "Does it work?" and "Does it adequately protect my plans and goals?" An effective risk manager consistently checks decision outcomes and is alert to changes that may reduce the effectiveness of the current risk management plan.

A young working couple may be entirely happy with their life and health insurance coverage. When they add an infant to the family, however, a review of protection is appropriate. Suddenly the risk of financial catastrophe to the family (should one or both parents die or become disabled) is much greater.

The needs of a single person differ from those of a family, a single parent, a couple, or a group of unrelated adults living in the same household. While these people face similar risks, their financial responsibility to others differs greatly. In each case, the vital question is, "Have I provided the financial resources and risk management strategy needed to take care of my basic responsibilities for my own well-being and the well-being of others?"

> ### CONCEPT CHECK 8–1
>
> 1. What is the purpose of insurance?
> 2. How are the most common risks classified?
> 3. What is the difference between pure risk and speculative risk?
> 4. What are the methods of managing risk?
> 5. What are the steps in planning your personal insurance coverage?

PROPERTY AND LIABILITY INSURANCE

LO2

Discuss the importance of property and liability insurance.

Major disasters have caused catastrophic amounts of property loss. Some recent examples of these types of disasters are when heavy rain caused catastrophic flooding in areas along Alberta's Bow and South Saskatchewan rivers, including severe damage in Calgary; the ice storm of 2013 that devastated parts of Ontario, Quebec, and Atlantic Canada; and the forest fires in British Columbia and elsewhere that frequently spring up in dry seasons and threaten to envelop entire villages.

Since most people invest large amounts of money in their homes and motor vehicles, protecting these assets from loss is a great concern. The cost of injuries and property damage caused by automobiles is also great. Most people use insurance to reduce their chances of economic loss from these risks.

The price you pay for home and automobile insurance may be viewed as an investment in financial protection against these losses. Although the costs of home and automobile insurance may seem high, the financial losses from which insurance protects you are much higher. Property and liability insurance offer protection from financial losses that may arise from a wide variety of situations.

The main risks related to homes and automobiles are property damage or loss, and your responsibility for injuries to others or damage to the property of others.

POTENTIAL PROPERTY LOSSES

Houses, automobiles, furniture, clothing, and other personal belongings represent a substantial financial commitment. Property owners face two basic types of risks. The first is *physical damage* caused by such hazards as fire, wind, water, and smoke. These hazards can cause destruction of your property or temporary loss of its use. For example, if a windstorm causes a large tree branch to break your windshield, you lose the use of the vehicle while it is being repaired. The second risk property owners face is *loss of use* due to robbery, burglary, vandalism, or arson.

LIABILITY PROTECTION

liability Legal responsibility for the financial cost of another person's losses or injuries.

negligence Failure to take ordinary or reasonable care in a situation.

strict liability A situation in which a person is held responsible for intentional or unintentional actions.

vicarious liability A situation in which one person is held legally responsible for the actions of another person.

In many circumstances, you may be judged legally responsible for injuries or damages. For example, if a child walks across your property, falls, and sustains severe injuries, the child's family may be able to recover damages from you as a result of the injuries. If you accidentally damage a rare painting while assisting a friend with home repairs, the friend may take legal action against you to recover the cost of the painting.

Liability is legal responsibility for the financial cost of another person's losses or injuries. Your legal responsibility is commonly caused by **negligence**, failure to take ordinary or reasonable care. Doing something in a careless manner, such as improperly supervising children at a swimming pool or failing to remove items from a frequently used staircase, may be ruled as negligence in a liability lawsuit.

Despite taking great care, you may still be held liable in a situation. **Strict liability** is present when a person is held responsible for intentional or unintentional actions. **Vicarious liability** occurs when one person is held responsible for the actions of another person. If a child's behaviour causes financial or physical harm to others, the parent may be held responsible; if an employee's activities cause damage, the employer may be held responsible.

CONCEPT CHECK 8–2

1. What property and liability risks might some people overlook?
2. How could a person's life situation influence the need for certain types of property and liability insurance?

PRINCIPLES OF HOME AND PROPERTY INSURANCE

Your home and personal belongings are probably a major portion of your assets. Whether you rent your dwelling or own a home, property insurance is vital. **Homeowner's insurance** is coverage for your place of residence and its associated financial risks, such as damage to personal property and injuries to others (see Exhibit 8–3).

LO3
Explain the insurance coverages and policy types available to homeowners and renters.

HOMEOWNER'S INSURANCE COVERAGES

A homeowner's policy provides coverages for the building and other structures, additional living expenses, personal property, replacement value of your home, personal liability and related coverages, and specialized coverages.

homeowner's insurance Coverage for a place of residence and its associated financial risks.

BUILDING AND OTHER STRUCTURES   The main component of homeowner's insurance is protection against financial loss due to damage or destruction to a house or other structures. Your dwelling and attached structures are covered for fire and other damages. Detached structures on the property, such as a garage, tool shed, or gazebo, are also protected. The coverage may also include trees, shrubs, and plants.

ADDITIONAL LIVING EXPENSES   If damage from a fire or other event prevents the use of your home, additional living expense coverage pays for the cost of living in a temporary location while your home is being repaired. Some policies limit additional living expense coverage to 10 to 20 percent of the home's coverage and limit payments to a maximum of six to nine months; other policies pay the full cost incurred for up to a year.

Exhibit 8–3   Home Insurance Coverage

| Building and other structures | Personal property | Loss of use/additional living expenses while home is uninhabitable | Personal liability and related coverages |

PERSONAL PROPERTY   Typically, a home insurance policy covers damage or destruction of the contents of your home—clothes, furniture, appliances, and similar items. The total value of the contents of your home may be calculated in one of two ways: as a percentage of the total value of your insurance coverage, or on an itemized basis that lists and values all the contents of your home. The limit coverage on your personal contents is usually an amount equal to 70 to 80 percent of the limit of insurance on the dwelling. This amount can be increased for an additional premium. However, this method could be inadequate at times, as it might understate the value of certain items.

The itemizing method, an approach generally recommended by insurance agents and companies, allows you to list and value all the items that you wish to protect and ensures adequate coverage. This method allows you to fully insure as much or as little as you wish within your home. It is recommended that you keep your list of items in a safety deposit box or some other location away from the insured property.

Personal property coverage commonly has limits for the theft of certain items, such as $1,000 for jewellery, $2,000 for firearms, and $2,500 for silverware. Items with a value exceeding these limits, such as fine jewellery and coin or stamp collections, can be protected with a **personal articles endorsement**, which covers the damage or loss of a specific item of high value. An endorsement requires a detailed description of the item and periodic appraisals to verify the current value. This coverage protects the item, regardless of location; thus, the item is insured while you are travelling or transporting it. Endorsements to protect home computers and other expensive equipment are recommended.

Personal property coverage usually provides protection against the loss or damage of articles taken with you when away from home as well as for contents of your vehicle. For example, possessions taken on vacation or used while at school are usually covered up to a policy limit. Although personal items of value that you take with you when you travel remain insured, depending on how long you are away from your home your insurer may no longer provide coverage for your home. Be sure to contact your home insurance provider to find out exactly what you need to do to maintain coverage. Many insurance companies require they be notified if you are going to be away for more than 30 days, and you will most likely need to get a special permit. You will still need to have a reliable person check on your home regularly (a good idea even if you are leaving your home empty for shorter durations). Property that you rent, such as some power tools or a rug shampoo machine, is insured while in your possession.

In the event of damage or loss of property, you must be able to prove both ownership and value. A **household inventory** is a list or other documentation of personal belongings, with purchase dates and cost information. You can get a form for such an inventory from an insurance agent. Exhibit 8–4 provides a reminder of the items you should include in the inventory. For items of special value, you should have receipts, serial numbers, brand names, model names, and written appraisals of value.

Your household inventory can include photographs or a video recording of your home and contents. Make sure the closet and storage area doors are photographed open. On the backs of the photographs, indicate the date and the value of the objects. Regularly update your inventory, photos, and appraisal documents. Keep a copy of each document in a secure location, such as a safety deposit box or a fire proof safe.

REPLACEMENT VALUE OF YOUR HOME   Contrary to popular belief, the replacement value of your home for insurance purposes is not its current market value, principally because that type of valuation includes the value of the land and foundation, which are unlikely to be affected by typical disasters. As a result, the home insurance that you purchase will be based on the replacement value of your home's structure, which is the cost of rebuilding or otherwise replacing the structure of your home.

A professional appraisal will usually give you both the **depreciated value** and the replacement value of the structure of your home. Your broker or agent, or your insurance company, can arrange an inspection of your property to help you calculate the rebuilding value of your home. Some insurance companies automatically set the amount of home insurance to the amount of the mortgage on the house. You should note, however, that insurance set at this amount protects

---

personal articles endorsement
Additional property insurance to cover the damage or loss of a specific item of high value.

household inventory
A list or other documentation of personal belongings, with purchase dates and cost information.

depreciated value
A reduction in the value of an object, based upon its age and the percentage it has decreased each year.

Exhibit 8–4   Household Inventory Contents

Attic
• Luggage, trunks
• Holiday items
• Items in storage
• Sports equipment
• Seasonal clothing

Bathroom
• Carpets, curtains
• Medications
• Electrical appliances
• Linens, towels, shower curtain

Bedrooms
• Beds, bedding
• Books, bookcases
• Bureaus, contents
• Chests, contents
• Closets, contents
• Desks, contents
• Dressers, contents
• Electrical appliances
• Clocks
• Curtains
• Lamps
• Carpets
• Pictures
• Mirrors
• Radios, television
• Tables
• Computers/tablets

Personal Belongings
• Coats, hats
• Suits, slacks
• Sweaters, jackets
• Shirts, skirts
• Underwear, ties
• Shoes, socks
• Jewellery, gloves
• Furs, rainwear

Family Room
• Bar, equipment
• Books, bookcases
• Cabinets, contents
• Carpets, pictures
• Chairs, couches
• Desks, contents
• Lamps, tables
• Musical equipment
• Television, stereo

Garage
• Lawn mower
• Lawn furniture
• Garden tools
• Shelving
• Workbench
• Bicycles
• Camping equipment
• Sports equipment
• Power tools

Living Room
• Air conditioner
• Books, bookcases
• Cabinets, contents
• Carpets, chairs
• Clocks, couches
• Desks, contents
• Curtains, shades
• Fireplace equipment
• Lamps, mirrors
• Pictures, piano
• Radio, television, gaming devices
• Tables, wall hangings

Hallway
• Cabinets
• Carpets
• Chairs
• Clocks
• Closet, contents
• Curtains
• Lamps
• Mirrors
• Pictures
• Tables

Kitchen
• Cabinets, contents
• Chairs, tables
• Dishes, pans
• Silverware
• Clocks, tables
• Radio, lamps
• Electrical appliances
• Floor coverings
• Wall hangings
• Cookbooks
• Curtains

Dining Room
• Buffet
• Cabinets
• Carpets
• Candlesticks
• Chairs
• China
• Clocks
• Dinnerware
• Linens
• Lamps
• Table
• Glassware

Basement
• Washing machine
• Dryer
• Shelves
• Workbench
• Power tools
• Ironing board

the mortgage lender's interests and is not meant to cover your own interests in the structure as its owner.

While replacement value offers you better protection than depreciated value coverage, you are required to rebuild the house in order to receive a settlement from the insurance company. With depreciated value coverage, your compensation is in the form of cash and you can decide whether or not to rebuild.

PERSONAL LIABILITY AND RELATED COVERAGES   Each day, you face the risk of financial loss due to injuries to others or damage to property for which you are responsible. The following are examples of this risk:

• A neighbour or guest falls on your property, resulting in permanent disability.
• A spark from burning leaves on your property starts a fire that damages a neighbour's roof.
• A member of your family accidentally breaks an expensive glass statue while at another person's house.

In each of these situations, you could be held responsible for the costs incurred. The personal liability component of a homeowner's policy protects you from financial losses resulting from legal action or claims against you or family members due to damages to the property of others. This coverage includes the cost of legal defence.

Not all individuals who come to your property are covered by your liability insurance. While a babysitter or others who assist you occasionally are probably covered, regular employees, such as a housekeeper or a gardener, may require worker's compensation coverage.

umbrella policy
Supplementary personal liability coverage; also called a personal catastrophe policy.

Most homeowner's policies provide a basic personal liability coverage of a minimum of $1,000,000, but additional amounts are frequently recommended. An **umbrella policy**, also called a *personal catastrophe policy*, supplements your basic personal liability coverage. This added protection covers you for personal injury claims, such as libel, slander, defamation of character, and invasion of property. Extended liability policies are sold in amounts of $1 million or more and are useful for individuals with substantial net worth. If you are a business owner, you may need other types of liability coverage.

voluntary medical payments Home insurance that pays the cost of minor accidental injuries on one's property.

Voluntary medical payments pay the costs of minor accidental injuries on your property and minor injuries caused by you, family members, or pets away from home. Settlements under voluntary medical payments are made without determining fault. This protection allows fast processing of small claims, generally up to $5,000. Suits for more severe personal injuries are covered by the personal liability portion of the homeowner's policy. Voluntary medical payments coverage does not cover the people who live in the home being insured.

rider An addition of coverage to a standard insurance policy.

Should you or a family member accidentally damage another person's property, the voluntary property damages of homeowner's insurance will pay for these minor mishaps. This protection is usually limited to $500 or $1,000. Again, payments are made regardless of fault. Any property damage claims for greater amounts would require action under the personal liability coverage.

Did you know?

Landlords have relatively few legal obligations to compensate tenants for damage to or loss of their tenants' personal possessions. Tenants, on the other hand, are responsible for harm they may cause to any part of the building in which they live, or to others who live or visit there. A fire ignited by a tenant's defective toaster could, for example, gut an entire apartment complex. That's a lot of liability!

SOURCE: ibc.ca/homeauto_hominsure_tenant.asp.

SPECIALIZED COVERAGES   Homeowner's insurance and, in fact, most common insurance, is general. It won't cover special risks automatically. Area-specific risks include earthquakes, flooding, and brush-fires. Those with a need for that kind of assurance need a related **rider**, or addition of coverage, added to their policies. In Canada, the only insurance coverage available for flooding is that caused by sewer backup.

Insurance riders and policies can be purchased to cover just about anything, but something to keep in mind is that the costs of insurance are bound to rise wherever risks increase. Policy buyers must ensure that the risks of loss outweigh the costs of insurance at all times.

TENANT'S INSURANCE

For people who rent, home insurance coverages include personal property protection, additional living expenses coverage, and personal liability and related coverages. Protection against financial loss due to damage or loss of personal property is the main component of tenant's insurance. Often, tenants believe they are covered under the insurance policy of the building owner. In fact, the building owner's property insurance does not cover tenants' personal property unless the building owner can be proven liable. If faulty wiring causes a fire and damages a tenant's property, the renter may be able to collect for damages from the building owner. Tenant's insurance is relatively inexpensive and provides protection from financial loss due to many of the same risks covered in homeowner's policies. Your tenant's insurance should include third-party liability coverage. As with the contents of your rented space, the building owner's property insurance coverage is not applicable if someone is hurt in your apartment and has sustained a significant injury, unless the building owner can be proven liable. Most importantly, the liability section of your tenant's package policy covers you for your Tenant's Legal Liability. Under any liability policy, you are not protected for loss to property in your care or control. If you cause damage to your apartment or unit because of fire, smoke, explosion, or water damage, you can be held liable for it. The Tenant's Legal Liability portion of your policy responds to this type of loss.

HOME INSURANCE TYPES

To provide consumers with the coverage best suited to their individual needs, insurance companies offer a number of policy forms. Each form differs in the number of perils, or events that could cause a loss, that it provides protection against. Essentially, there are two types of policies. The first is called a **named perils** policy. Only those perils that are specifically listed in the policy are covered should a loss occur. If you suffer a loss to your property, you must show that the cause of the loss was one of the perils named in order for the loss to be covered. The second type is known as an **all risk** policy. Any event that causes physical loss or damage to the insured property is covered unless it is specifically excluded. Most personal property policies do not cover, for example, damage to business or agricultural property, damage caused by wars, floods, or earthquakes, or intentional damage (see Exhibit 8–5). If you suffer a loss to your property it is the responsibility of the insurance company to show that the cause of the loss is excluded, and if the company cannot do so, the loss is covered. Before purchasing insurance you should be aware of the types of losses or property that are not covered by your policy.

Insurance companies combine different types of coverage together in package policies so that you can choose the one that best suits your needs and your budget. A good guideline is, the

named perils A policy in which only those perils that are specifically listed will be covered should a loss occur.

all risk A policy in which any event that causes loss or damage to the insured property is covered unless it is specifically excluded.

Certain personal property is specifically excluded from the coverage provided by homeowner's insurance:

- Articles separately described and specifically insured, such as jewellery, furs, boats, or expensive electronic equipment.

- Animals, birds, or fish.

- Motorized land vehicles, except those used to service an insured's residence, that are not licensed for road use.

- Any device or instrument for the transmission and recording of sound, including any accessories or antennas, while in or on motor vehicles.

- Aircraft and parts.

- Property of roomers, boarders, and other tenants who are not related to any insured.

- Property contained in an apartment regularly rented or held for rental to others by any insured.

- Property rented or held for rental to others away from the residence premises.

- Business property in storage, or held as a sample, or for sale, or for delivery after sale.

- Business property pertaining to business actually conducted on the residence premises.

- Business property away from the residence premises.

Exhibit 8–5

Not Everything Is Covered

more extensive the coverage, the higher the premium you will pay. The following chart shows the common combinations of coverage:

Policy Form	Building	Contents
Standard form	Named perils	Named perils
Broad form	All risk	Named perils
Comprehensive form	All risk	All risk

Manufactured housing units and mobile homes usually qualify for insurance coverage with conventional policies. However, certain mobile homes may require a special arrangement and higher rates since their construction makes them more prone to fire and wind damage. The cost of mobile home insurance coverage is most heavily affected by location and by the method used to attach the housing unit to the ground. This type of property insurance is quite expensive; a $60,000 mobile home can cost as much to insure as a $250,000 house.

In addition to the property and liability risks previously discussed, home insurance policies include coverage for:

- Identity theft, credit card fraud, cheque forgery, and counterfeit money.
- The cost of removing damaged property.
- Emergency removal of property to protect it from damage.
- Temporary repairs after a loss to prevent further damage.
- Fire department charges in areas with such fees.

EXCLUSIONS

Exclusions are like small print. Pay attention to them because they are part of what defines your insurance policy. Insurance companies use exclusions to help limit the risks they assume for the policyholder. In the wake of the terrorist attacks on the United States on September 11, 2001, for example, many insurers began including a terrorism exclusion in virtually any type of property insurance policy. To the average Canadian landowner, that may be no big deal, but you can be sure it caused concern for the owners of the CN Tower!

CONCEPT CHECK 8–3

1. What main coverages are included in home insurance policies?
2. What is the purpose of personal liability coverage?
3. How does tenant's insurance differ from other home insurance policies?

HOME INSURANCE COST FACTORS

LO4

Analyze factors that influence the amount of coverage and cost of home insurance.

Financial losses caused by fire, theft, wind, and other risks amount to billions of dollars each year. Since most homeowners have a mortgage on their property, their lending institutions usually require insurance. When purchasing insurance, you can get the best value by selecting the appropriate coverage amount and being aware of factors that affect insurance costs.

DEDUCTIBLES

Before an insurance company pays you any amount of your claim, it will ask that you pay a *deductible*, a fixed sum of money that is stipulated by your policy. The amount of your deductible is often $100, $250, $500, or $1,000, and your insurance company will subtract that amount from your claim. For example, if you have a $2,000 claim resulting from a fire in your home and your policy stipulates that your deductible is $500, then the insurance company will pay you only $1,500, and you will pay the first $500. If, on the other hand, your insurable loss is $500 or less, then the insurance company will pay nothing.

In general, the higher a deductible you agree to pay, the lower your policy premium. The insurance company does this for three reasons. First, since you share more of your risk with the insurance company, it needs to pay less. Second, it is generally agreed that people are more careful if the costs of being careless are higher. Finally, a higher deductible means that the insurance company deals with fewer claims, thus saving administration fees.

A higher deductible can also be to your personal advantage as the effect of a higher deductible is to lower the premium cost per dollar of insurance and, thus, raise the amount of coverage. The ultimate result is that your financial resources will be more secure.

There is a general rule that many financial experts use as a means to determine what an acceptable level of deductible is for a given individual. The rule is that your deductible should total no more than 3 percent of your net worth. Accordingly, if your net worth is $25,000, your acceptable deductible on insurance should be no more than $750.

HOW MUCH COVERAGE DO YOU NEED?

Several factors affect the insurance coverage needed for your home and property (see Exhibit 8–6). Your insurance protection should be based on the amount needed to rebuild or repair your house, not the amount you paid for it. As construction costs rise, you should increase the amount of coverage. In recent years, most insurance policies have included an inflation clause that increases coverage as property values increase.

In the past, most homeowner's policies contained a provision requiring that the building be insured for at least 80 percent of the replacement value. This is referred to as the 80-percent rule. Under this **co-insurance clause**, the homeowner has to pay for part of the losses if the property is not insured for the specified percentage of the replacement value. As an example, suppose that you bought a $280,000 home insurance policy on your $400,000 home (keeping in mind that this is the replacement value of the house, not including its foundation or the land it stands upon).

co-insurance clause
A policy provision that requires a homeowner to pay for part of the losses if the property is not insured for the specified percentage of the replacement value.

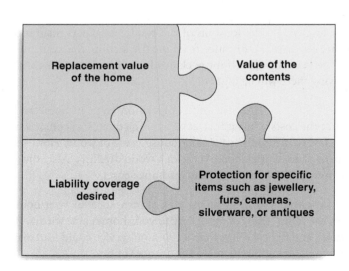

Exhibit 8–6

Determining the Amount of Home Insurance You Need

actual cash value (ACV) A claim settlement method in which the insured receives payment based on the current replacement cost of a damaged or lost item, less depreciation.

replacement value A claim settlement method in which the insured receives the full cost of repairing or replacing a damaged or lost item.

If you then suffered a fire loss of $120,000, the insurance company would pay you only $105,000 (which is $280,000 ÷ $320,000 × $120,000). Had you bought insurance on at least 80 percent of your home's structural value, or $320,000 in this example, you would have received the full reimbursement from the insurance company. While a few companies still use a co-insurance clause, most companies today suggest full coverage.

If you are financing a home, the lending institution will require you to have property insurance in an amount that covers its financial investment. Remember, too, that the amount of insurance on your home determines the coverage on the contents. Personal belongings are generally covered up to an amount ranging from 55 to 75 percent of the insurance amount on the dwelling.

If you own a business running out of your home, your employees are not covered under your homeowner's plan and you need to purchase separate business liability coverage.

Insurance companies base claim settlements on one of two methods. Under the **actual cash value (ACV)** method, the payment you receive is based on the current replacement cost of a damaged or lost item less depreciation. This means you would receive $180 for a five-year-old bar fridge that cost you $400 and had an estimated life of eight years if the same fridge now costs $480. Your settlement amount is determined by taking the current cost of $480 and subtracting five years of depreciation from it—$300 for five years at $60 a year.

Under the **replacement value** method for settling claims, you receive the full cost of repairing or replacing a damaged or lost item; depreciation is not considered. In order to receive the replacement value, the item lost must be replaced with an item of like kind and quality and for the same use. Certain items, such as antiques or memorabilia, do not qualify for replacement value. If the item is not replaced the insurance company will pay you the item's actual cash value at the time the loss occurred.

FACTORS THAT AFFECT HOME INSURANCE COSTS

The main influences on the premium paid for home and property insurance are the location of the home, the type of structure, the coverage amount and policy type, discounts, and differences among insurance companies.

LOCATION OF HOME   The location of the residence affects insurance rates. So do the efficiency of the fire department, distance from the fire station, the available water supply, and the frequency of thefts in the area. If more claims have been filed in an area, home insurance rates for people living there will be higher.

REPLACEMENT COSTS   The size and composition (type of home and the construction materials) influence the costs of insurance coverage. The quality of construction, a brick house, for example, costs less to insure than a similar house made of wood. However, earthquake coverage is more expensive for a brick home than for a wood dwelling. Also, the age and style of the house can create potential risks and increase insurance costs.

ELECTRICITY   Some factors affecting the cost of insurance for your home are the presence of breaks or fuses, the "amp" (flow of electricity to your home) and wiring. Breakers are generally better than fuses, and typically, less than a 100-amp service could lead to overloading or fire. In addition, aluminum wiring can increase the chances of fire.

HEATING   The source of heat, especially auxiliary heating sources such as a wood stove or a fireplace, affect the premium charged for your home. The chances of house fires and carbon monoxide poisoning increase with these appliances, so an insurance company may want an inspection performed.

PIPES   If you have an older home, it is important that the utilities, such as the wiring and plumbing, be updated regularly and meet current building codes. Lead piping could mean an older piping system, and a higher chance of cracking, leaking, or other problems. Upgrading to copper or plastic piping is preferred.

AGE OF ROOF   Your roof should also be in good condition to ensure the best price on your insurance. Generally, a roof that has been renovated or replaced in the last 20 years is deemed acceptable. Some insurers will only pay the depreciated value or a percentage of the replacement cost for roofs that are near the end of their life.

OTHER FACTORS   Insurers are often concerned with the presence of a security or fire alarm, and the presence of other structures (such as pools, sheds, guesthouses) on your property that are worth 10 percent of the insured value of your home.

COVERAGE AMOUNT AND POLICY TYPE   The policy you select and the financial limits of coverage affect the premium you pay. It costs more to insure a $500,000 home than a $350,000 home. The comprehensive form of homeowner's policy costs more than a tenant's policy.

As discussed, the *deductible* amount in your policy also affects the cost of your insurance. If you increase the amount of your deductible, your premium will be lower since the company will pay out less in claims. According to the insurance regulator in Ontario, Increasing your automobile insurance deductible from $300 to $500 can reduce your auto insurance premium 10 percent or more.

REDUCING HOME INSURANCE COSTS

HOME INSURANCE DISCOUNTS   Most companies offer incentives that reduce home insurance costs. Your premium may be lower if you have smoke detectors that are monitored remotely by a third-party alarm company. Deterrents to burglars, such as deadbolt locks or an alarm system, can also save you money. Some companies offer home insurance discounts to policyholders who are non-smokers or may give a discount for being "claim free" for a certain number of years.

COMPANY DIFFERENCES   Studies show that you can save up to 25 percent on homeowner's insurance by comparing companies. Contact insurance agents who work for one company and independent brokers who represent several. The information you obtain will enable you to compare rates. Home insurance rates may be compared using information from such Web sites as kanetix.ca/home-insurance.

Don't select a company based on price alone. Also consider service and coverage. Not all companies settle claims in the same way. For example, a number of homeowners had two sides of their houses dented by hail. Since the type of siding used in these houses was no longer available, all of the siding had to be replaced. Some insurance companies paid for complete replacement of the siding, while others paid only for replacement of the damaged areas. Provincial insurance commissions, other government agencies, and consumer organizations can provide information about the reputations of insurance companies.

CONCEPT CHECK 8–4

1. What major factors influence the cost of home insurance?
2. What actions can a person take to reduce the cost of home insurance?

AUTOMOBILE INSURANCE COVERAGES

LO5

Identify the important types of automobile insurance coverages.

The potential damages associated with the risks of owning and operating an automobile can be great, so much so that they may prove to be disastrous for your wealth and financial future. As a result, all provinces and territories require a minimum automobile insurance coverage if you own and/or operate an automobile. Your policy protects you from three major financial risks (see Exhibit 8–7). The first is the risk of injury or death to you, as owner, and your passengers. The second is the possibility of damages, destruction, or theft. Finally, and perhaps most importantly, the third risk that an automobile insurance policy protects you against is third-party liability, the possibility that you will be held financially liable if you and your car injure someone else.

While the exact details of minimum coverage vary widely depending on the province or territory in which you live, the following information is intended to provide you with an understanding of the basic principles and concepts involved in automobile insurance. Every jurisdiction has minimum insurance laws because of the tremendous social and financial risks that are associated with automobiles. In fact, the risks are so significant that it is generally agreed that society cannot simply leave the task of automobile insurance protection to people's personal discretion.

To this effect, British Columbia, Manitoba, and Saskatchewan each provide basic automobile insurance coverage, with extra coverage available from private insurers. In Quebec, auto insurance coverage is split between the provincial government and private insurers. In all the other provinces and territories, providing auto insurance is left to private insurers.

You should note that in areas where your insurance is publicly provided, you can expect to pay just one price for coverage and to get it in just one place. Conversely, if the insurance is provided privately through an insurance company, you will find a number of competing suppliers and the price you will be asked to pay may vary.

From the fourth quarter of 2011 to the fourth quarter of 2012, auto insurance rates increased in the province of Quebec while decreasing in both Ontario and Alberta. In Q4 of 2012 rates in Quebec were 6.8 percent higher than those in Q4 of 2011. According to Kanetix, this indicates that consumers may not be aware of or taking advantage of discounts that they are entitled to. Rates in Alberta and Ontario decreased by 8.1 percent and 3.3 percent from Q4 of 2011 to Q4 of 2012, respectively. The decline in auto insurance rates in these provinces are said to be a result more drivers taking advantage of winter tire discounts, roadside assistance discounts, group discounts, as well as online comparison services.*

no-fault insurance
An automobile insurance program in which drivers involved in accidents collect medical expenses, lost wages, and related injury costs from their own insurance companies.

It is difficult to compare auto insurance among provinces because of the differences in cost structures and benefit levels between tort-based and no-fault systems. In a tort-based system, as in British Columbia, injured parties are allowed to take the at-fault party to court for the full amount of their damages. But as the cost to settle bodily injury claims accelerated relative to the premiums the insuring company had to pay, many provinces decided to implement no-fault insurance. **No-fault insurance** is widely misunderstood by the general public. Most people think it has to do with whether their premium will go up following a claim, when, in fact, fault is determined in every incident for the purpose of premium calculation. No-fault insurance

*SOURCE: http://www.insurance-canada.ca/consinfoauto/infonews/2013/Kanetix-study-falling-auto-rates-1301.php.

Exhibit 8–7

The Major Risks Assumed by Automobile Owners, and the Protective Insurance Coverage Available

Risk	Insurance Coverage
Injury to or death of yourself or your passengers	Accident benefits
Damage to your vehicle	Physical damage insurance, such as comprehensive or collision coverage
Liability to others for injury, death, or property damage	Third-party liability coverage

allows you to collect payment from your own insurance company for bodily injury, and to claim for damage to your own automobile no matter who is at fault in an accident. Despite its name, if you are at fault, your insurance premiums may increase. The system is intended to provide faster claims settlements and reduce the cost associated with taking legal action against the at-fault third party. Manitoba, Saskatchewan, Quebec, and Ontario have all implemented variations of the no-fault system. In Quebec, the right to sue the at-fault party for your bodily injury losses has been removed, as the government pays injured parties. Ontario has a partial no-fault system that still allows suits in situations involving serious injury or death.

MOTOR VEHICLE COVERAGES

Most of the money automobile insurance companies pay in claims is spent on legal expenses of injury lawsuits, medical expenses, and related costs. The main bodily injury coverages are bodily injury liability, accident benefits, and uninsured motorist's protection (see Exhibit 8–8). The main property damage coverages are property damage liability, collision, and comprehensive physical damage.

BODILY INJURY LIABILITY
Bodily injury liability covers the risk of financial loss due to legal expenses, medical expenses, lost wages, and other expenses associated with injuries caused by an automobile accident for which you were responsible. This insurance protects you from extensive financial losses.

The automobile owner's policy covers both the owner and people who drive the vehicle with the owner's permission. As a result, if you are driving someone else's vehicle with their permission and have an accident causing bodily injury to other people, the automobile owner's policy will cover any liability claim. In cases where the owner is uninsured, your own policy will be needed to settle the claim.

ACCIDENT BENEFITS
While bodily injury liability pays for the costs of injuries to persons who were not in your automobile, **accident benefits** cover income replacement, medical, rehabilitation and attendant care expenses, and death and funeral costs for people who were injured in your automobile, including yourself. This protection covers friends, carpool members, and others who ride in your vehicle. These benefits are available if the related costs are the result of an automobile accident, regardless of fault.

bodily injury liability
Coverage for the risk of financial loss due to legal expenses, medical costs, lost wages, and other expenses associated with injuries caused by an automobile accident for which the insured was responsible.

accident benefits
Automobile insurance that covers medical expenses for people injured in one's car.

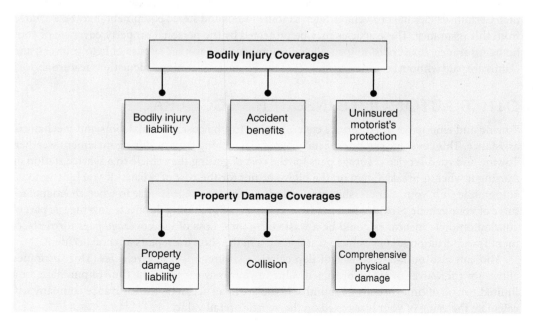

Exhibit 8–8

Two Major Categories of Automobile Insurance

Financial Planning Calculations

Both collision and comprehensive coverages are commonly sold with a deductible to help reduce insurance costs. If a broken windshield costs $250 to replace and you have a $100 deductible on your comprehensive coverage, the insurance company will pay $150 of the damages.

Deductibles keep insurance premiums lower by reducing the number of small claims companies pay. Going from full-coverage comprehensive insurance to a $100 deductible may reduce the cost of that coverage by as much as 40 percent.

---

uninsured motorist coverage Automobile insurance coverage for the cost of injuries to a person and members of his or her family caused by a driver with inadequate insurance or by a hit-and-run driver.

property damage Insurance that covers damage to another's property, as by an automobile accident.

collision Automobile insurance that pays for damage to the insured's car when it is involved in an accident.

comprehensive physical damage Automobile insurance that covers financial loss from damage to a vehicle caused by a risk other than a collision, such as fire, theft, glass breakage, hail, or vandalism.

UNINSURED MOTORIST'S PROTECTION   If you are in an accident caused by an unidentified (unknown) or uninsured person, the **uninsured motorist coverage** protects the insured against the financial burden of injuries to you and your family up to $200,000. Protection is provided for bodily injury claims if the driver is unidentified or uninsured but covers only damage to your vehicle if the driver is identified but uninsured.

PROPERTY DAMAGE   When your automobile is involved in an accident, **property damage** coverage insures you against damage to your own vehicle, typically through collision and comprehensive damage. Your property damage liability covers any damage you may cause to the vehicle and/or property of others.

COLLISION   When your automobile is involved in an accident, **collision** insurance pays for the damage to the automobile, regardless of fault. However, if another driver caused the accident, your insurance company may try to recover the repair costs for your vehicle through the other driver's property damage liability. The insurance company's right to recover the amount it pays for the loss from the person responsible for the loss is called *subrogation*.

The amount you can collect with collision insurance is limited to the actual cash value of the automobile at the time of the accident.

COMPREHENSIVE PHYSICAL DAMAGE   Another protection for your automobile involves financial losses from damage caused by a risk other than a collision. **Comprehensive physical damage** covers you for such risks as fire, theft, glass breakage, falling objects, vandalism, wind, hail, flood, tornado, lightning, earthquake, avalanche, or damage caused by hitting an animal. Certain articles in your vehicle, such as some radios and stereo equipment, may be excluded from this insurance. These articles may be protected by the personal property coverage of your home insurance. Like collision insurance, comprehensive coverage applies only to your car, and claims are paid without considering fault. (See the Financial Planning Calculations feature above.)

OTHER AUTOMOBILE INSURANCE COVERAGES

Towing and emergency road service coverage pays for the cost of breakdowns and mechanical assistance. This coverage can be especially beneficial on long trips or during inclement weather. Towing and road service coverage pays for the cost of getting the vehicle to a service station or starting it when it breaks down on the highway, not for the cost of repairs. If you belong to an automobile club, your membership may include towing coverage similar to when the manufacturer of your vehicle provides free roadside assistance. Purchasing duplicate coverage as part of your automobile insurance could be a waste of money. Loss of use coverage pays for replacement transportation if your vehicle is stolen or is in the shop for repairs after an accident.

You can also purchase waiver of depreciation coverage for new vehicles. This insurance allows for the waiver of any depreciated value in your new car from the time of purchase for a limited period of time, usually 24 months. If you are in an accident, the insurance company will calculate the value of your loss based on the vehicle's retail value.

1. What are the main coverages included in most automobile insurance policies?
2. What is no-fault insurance?
3. How does collision coverage differ from comprehensive physical damage coverage?

AUTOMOBILE INSURANCE COSTS

Automobile insurance premiums reflect the amounts insurance companies pay for injury and property damage claims. Your automobile insurance is directly related to coverage amounts and such factors as the vehicle, your place of residence, and your driving record.

LO6
Evaluate factors that affect the cost of automobile insurance.

The years 2001 and 2002 were an age of awakening for the automobile insurance industry in Canada. Costs related to insurance claims skyrocketed, and insurers scrambled to raise their prices quickly enough to cover the damage. Ontario and the Maritimes were the hardest hit by rising claims costs, but the resulting increases in insurance premiums were felt throughout the country.

AMOUNT OF COVERAGE

"How much coverage do I need?" This question affects the amount you pay for insurance. Our legal environment and increasing property values influence coverage amounts.

LEGAL CONCERNS   As discussed earlier, every province has laws that mandate automobile liability insurance coverage.

Third-party liability (with a minimum limit by law of $200,000 in most provinces), accident benefits, and uninsured motorist coverage are mandatory in order to operate a motor vehicle in Canada. Driving without insurance can result in fines and criminal charges. Physical damage coverage is optional, but if your vehicle is being used as security for a loan, your lending contract may insist upon this coverage in order to protect the interests of the financial institution.

How much is enough? This, of course, depends on you. The minimum liability coverage required by all provinces except Quebec is $200,000. In Quebec, the minimum liability coverage is $50,000 for property damage, and as a Quebec resident you are compensated for injury without regard to fault.

You may prefer to carry more insurance. Further, if you feel that your net worth is large enough for the liability risk of losing it to be too great, you will want to get more coverage. The prudent amount of coverage that is now commonly sought by Canadian drivers is $1,000,000. Additional coverage can be added for a very modest cost and is recommended if you plan to travel to the United States.

AUTOMOBILE INSURANCE PREMIUM FACTORS

Several factors influence the premium you pay for automobile insurance. The main factors are vehicle type, type of use, rating territory, driver classification, and provincial differences.

WHERE YOU LIVE   If you live in an urban area, the probability of accidents and car burglary are higher, most likely increasing the amount of your premium.

Did you know?

A common myth expressed by many is their belief that the colour of a vehicle being insured increases the premiums. The Canadian Insurance industry makes no distinction between colours for premium purposes. This misconception is due to the underlying characteristic of the vehicle being insured. Muscle cars, convertibles, sports cars often are more colourful than the traditional family sedan. The increased premium is due to the underlying characteristic of the vehicle, and not its colour.

MAKE AND STYLE OF CAR   The type of car you drive generally does not affect the premium you pay for third-party liability insurance. It does, however, affect the cost of coverage for physical damage to your car. Insurance companies rate vehicles according to their safety record and cost to repair or replace them. The Canadian Loss Experience Automobile Rating (CLEAR) system rewards car owners with lower premiums for buying vehicles that experience fewer and smaller losses. For example, some vehicles may be more susceptible to theft than others; some may be better designed and less easily damaged; some are less expensive to repair; some protect their occupants better than others. The CLEAR system was developed by the non-profit Vehicle Information Centre of Canada (VICC), which was sponsored by the automobile insurance industry and is now a division of the Insurance Bureau of Canada. It also makes available pamphlets that you should check before buying your next vehicle: Choosing Your Car, How Cars Measure Up, and Car Theft. Checking before you buy could save you substantial insurance premium dollars. See ibc.ca or call your insurance agent.

USE OF THE VEHICLE   What you use your vehicle for has an impact on your premium. Insurance companies differ with regard to vehicles used for pleasure, business, or farming, the distance driven to work each day, and if you use the vehicle for deliveries or carrying passengers.

rating territory The place of residence used to determine a person's automobile insurance premium.

RATING TERRITORY   Your **rating territory** is the place of residence used to determine your automobile insurance premium. Various geographic locations have different costs due to differences in the number of claims made. For example, fewer accidents and less vandalism occur in rural areas than in large cities.

driver classification A category based on the driver's age, gender, marital status, driving record, and driving habits; used to determine automobile insurance rates.

DRIVER CLASSIFICATION   You are compared with other drivers to set your automobile insurance premium. **Driver classification** is a category based on the driver's age, gender, marital status, driving record, and driving habits; drivers' categories are used to determine automobile insurance rates. In general, young drivers (under age 25) and those over 70 years of age have more frequent and severe accidents. As a result, they pay higher premiums.

Accidents and traffic violations influence your driver classification. Usually, the more incidents (speeding tickets, drinking and driving, and other moving violations) on your record, the higher the premium you pay. Finally, you pay less for insurance if you do not drive to work than if you use your automobile for business.

The number of claims you file with your insurance company also affects your premiums. If you have many expensive claims or a poor driving record, your company may cancel your policy, making it difficult for you to obtain coverage from another company.

PROVINCIAL DIFFERENCES   The factors used for determining the rate of your insurance premium varies among provinces. In Quebec, you pay a set premium that is established for a given class of vehicle, rather than depending on your qualifications as the driver. In Manitoba, the rates depend on the make and model of your automobile, its use, geographical location, and your driving record, with no discrimination based on your age, gender, or marital status. In British Columbia, you pay premiums determined by the value of your automobile, its use, geography, and your history of claims.

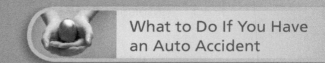
No one plans to have an auto accident; nevertheless, thousands of accidents occur each year. If you are involved in an auto accident, you should take the following actions:

- Stop your vehicle, turn off your ignition, and remain at the scene of the accident.
- Seek medical assistance for anyone who is injured. Do not move an injured person; that should be done by medical personnel.

- Obtain the names and addresses of other drivers, passengers, and witnesses; make notes regarding the circumstances of the accident.
- Assist in preparing a police report, if required, by providing your name, address, licence number, and vehicle and insurance information. Do not admit fault.
- Obtain a copy of the police accident report, if any; file the necessary accident documents with your insurance company and provincial or local government agencies.

HIGH-RISK-DRIVER INSURANCE

Some drivers have accident records or other characteristics that make them high-risk and therefore unacceptable to standard insurance companies. Nonetheless, some form of coverage must be made available to them if they are required by law to be insured. The insurance industry has solved this problem by creating an insurance pool that assigns high-risk cases to companies in proportion to their share of automobile insurance in each province. The result is that no company receives more than its fair share of bad risks and insurance is available to all drivers.

To address this problem, every province has an assigned risk pool consisting of people who are unable to obtain automobile insurance. Some of these people are assigned to each insurance company operating in the province. They pay several times the normal rates, but they do get coverage. Once they establish a good driving record, they can reapply for insurance at regular rates.

Having your policy assigned to the **high-risk pool** will not change any of the details of your application for insurance or of your claim. Both processes are the same as for other drivers, with the principal difference being that your premium will be considerably higher.

high-risk pool
Consists of people who are unable to obtain automobile insurance due to poor driving or accident records and must obtain coverage at high rates.

REDUCING AUTOMOBILE INSURANCE PREMIUMS

Methods for lowering automobile insurance costs include comparing companies and taking advantage of commonly offered discounts.

COMPARING COMPANIES   Rates and service vary among automobile insurance companies. Among companies in the same area, premiums can vary as much as 100 percent. If you relocate, don't assume your present company will offer the best rates in your new living area.

Also consider the service the local insurance agent or broker provides. Will this company representative be available to answer questions, change coverages, and handle claims as needed?

PREMIUM DISCOUNTS   The best way to keep your rates down is to establish and maintain a safe driving record. Taking steps to avoid accidents and traffic violations will mean lower automobile insurance premiums. In addition, most insurance companies offer various discounts.

Installing security devices such as a fuel shutoff switch, a second ignition switch, or an alarm system will decrease your chances of theft and lower your insurance costs. Being a non-smoker can qualify you for lower automobile insurance premiums. Discounts may also be offered for insuring two or more vehicles with the same company. Ask your insurance agent about other methods for lowering your automobile insurance rates.

Increasing the amount of deductibles will result in a lower premium. Also, some people believe old cars are not worth the amount paid for collision and comprehensive coverages and therefore dispense with them. However, before doing this, be sure to compare the value of your car for getting you to school or work with the cost of these coverages. Finally, it is wise not to make small claims to your insurance company. Your insurance company keeps track of the number of claims you make per year and if you make too many you may very well be placed in a higher-risk category. The resulting increased premiums you would have to pay would far outweigh the compensation you would receive from making small claims.

If you change your driving habits, get married, or alter your driving status in other ways, be sure to notify the insurance company. Premium savings can result. Also, some employers make group automobile insurance available to workers. And, before you buy a motor vehicle, find out which makes and models have the lowest insurance costs. This information can result in a purchasing decision with many financial benefits.

CONCEPT CHECK 8–6

1. What factors influence how much a person pays for automobile insurance?
2. What actions can a person take to reduce the cost of automobile insurance?

SUMMARY OF LEARNING OBJECTIVES

LO1 Develop a risk management plan using insurance.

The four general risk management techniques are risk avoidance, risk reduction, risk assumption, and risk shifting. In planning a personal insurance program, set your goals, make a plan to reach your goals, put your plan into action, and review your results.

LO2 Discuss the importance of property and liability insurance.

Owners of homes and automobiles face the risks of (1) property damage or loss, and (2) legal actions by others for the costs of injuries or property damage. Property and liability insurance offer protection from financial losses that may arise from a wide variety of situations faced by owners of homes and users of automobiles.

LO3 Explain the insurance coverages and policy types available to homeowners and renters.

Homeowner's insurance includes protection for the building and other structures, additional living expenses, personal property, replacement value of your home, and personal liability. Tenant's insurance includes the same coverages excluding protection for the building and other structures, which is the concern of the building owner. The main types of home insurance policies are the named perils and all risk policy forms. These policies differ in the risks and property they cover.

LO4 Analyze factors that influence the amount of coverage and cost of home insurance.

The amount of home insurance coverage is determined by the replacement cost of your dwelling and personal belongings. The cost of home insurance is influenced by the location of the home, the type of structure, the coverage amount, the policy type, discounts, and insurance company differences.

LO5 Identify the important types of automobile insurance coverages.

Automobile insurance is used to meet provincial minimum insurance laws and to protect drivers against financial losses associated with bodily injury and property damage. The major types of automobile insurance coverages are bodily injury liability, accident benefits, uninsured motorist's, property damage liability, collision, and comprehensive physical damage.

LO6 Evaluate factors that affect the cost of automobile insurance.

The cost of automobile insurance is affected by the amount of coverage, automobile type, use of vehicle, rating territory, driver classification, provincial differences, and premium discounts.

KEY TERMS

accident benefits 247

actual cash value (ACV) 244

all risk 241

bodily injury liability 247

co-insurance clause 243

collision 248

comprehensive physical
    damage 248

depreciated value 238

driver classification 250

hazard 231

high-risk pool 251

homeowner's insurance 237

household inventory 238

insurance 231

insurance company 231

insured 231

insurer 231

liability 236

named perils 241

negligence 236

no-fault insurance 246

peril 231

personal articles
    endorsement 238

policy 231

policyholder 231

premium 231

property damage 248

pure risk 232

rating territory 250

replacement value 244

rider 240

risk 231

self-insurance 232

speculative risk 232

strict liability 236

umbrella policy 240

uninsured motorist
    coverage 248

vicarious liability 236

voluntary medical
    payments 240

FINANCIAL PLANNING PROBLEMS

 Practise and learn online with Connect.

1. *Calculating Property Loss Claim Coverage.* Most home insurance policies cover jewellery and silverware for a limited amount unless items are covered with additional insurance. If $3,500 worth of jewellery and $3,800 worth of silverware were stolen from a family, what amount of the claim would not be covered by insurance? *LO3*

2. *Computing Actual Cash Value Coverage.* What amount would a person with actual cash value (ACV) coverage receive for two-year-old furniture destroyed by a fire? The furniture would cost $1,000 to replace today and had an estimated life of five years. *LO3*

3. *Determining Replacement Cost.* What would it cost an insurance company to replace a family's personal property that originally cost $18,000? The replacement costs for the items have increased 15 percent. *LO3*

4. *Calculating a Co-insurance Claim.* If Carissa Dalton has a $130,000 home insured for $100,000, based on the 80-percent co-insurance provision how much would the insurance company pay on a $5,000 claim? *LO3*

5. *Determining the Claim Amount (with Deductibles).* For each of the following situations, what amount would the insurance company pay? *LO3*

a. Wind damage of $785; the insured has a $500 deductible.
b. Theft of a stereo system worth $1,300; the insured has a $250 deductible.
c. Vandalism that does $375 of damage to a home; the insured has a $500 deductible.

6. *Calculating Future Value of Insurance Savings.* Beverly and Kyle Nelson currently insure their cars with separate companies, paying $450 and $375 a year. If they insured both cars with the same company, they would save 10 percent on the annual premiums. What would be the future value of the annual savings over 10 years on the basis of an annual interest rate of 6 percent? *LO5*

7. *Determining the Benefits of Premium Discounts.* Kate Austin currently pays $300 per month for car insurance. When the time arrives to renew her policy, her insurance agent informs her that she could save an additional 15 percent in premium costs if she had a car alarm installed in her car. If the cost of the device is $150 with taxes, what would her net savings be for the year, assuming a monthly interest rate of 0.5 percent? *LO6*

FINANCIAL PLANNING ACTIVITIES

1. *Determining Insurance Coverages.* Survey friends and relatives to determine the types of insurance coverages they have. Also, obtain information about the process used to select these coverages. LO1

2. *Researching Insurance on the Internet.* Locate Web sites that provide useful information for selecting and comparing various insurance coverages. LO1

3. *Developing a Personal Insurance Plan.* Outline a personal insurance plan with the following phases: (a) identify personal, financial, and property risks; (b) set goals you might achieve when obtaining needed insurance coverages; and (c) describe actions you might take to achieve these insurance goals. LO1

4. *Analyzing Insurance Coverages.* Talk to a financial planner or an insurance agent about the financial difficulties faced by people who lack adequate home and auto insurance. What common coverages do many people overlook? LO2

5. *Maintaining a Household Inventory.* Survey several people about their household inventory records. In the event of damage or loss, would they be able to prove the value of their personal property and other belongings? LO3

6. *Comparing Home Insurance Costs.* Contact two or three insurance agents to obtain information about home or tenant's insurance. Compare the coverage and costs. LO3

7. *Analyzing Home Insurance Policies.* Examine a homeowner's or tenant's insurance policy. What coverages does the policy include? Does the policy contain unclear conditions or wording? LO3

8. *Reducing Home Insurance Costs.* Talk to several homeowners about the actions they take to reduce the cost of their home insurance. Locate Web sites that offer information about reducing home insurance costs. Prepare a video or other visual presentation to communicate your findings. LO4

9. *Determining Auto Insurance Coverages.* Survey several people to determine the types and amounts of automobile insurance coverage they have. Do most of them have adequate coverage? LO5

10. *Comparing Auto Insurance Costs.* Contact two or three insurance agents to obtain information about automobile insurance. Compare the coverage and costs. LO6

11. *Reducing Auto Insurance Costs.* Search the World Wide Web or talk to an insurance agent to obtain suggestions for reducing automobile insurance costs. LO6

CREATING A FINANCIAL PLAN

Obtaining Home and Auto Insurance

Creating an insurance plan that includes appropriate coverage for your home, personal property, and motor vehicles helps to avoid financial difficulties.

Web Sites for Home and Auto Insurance

- The Insurance Bureau of Canada, at **ibc.ca**, has a useful resource page containing information on insurance regulations, safe driving, and related Ontario-specific advice.

- Insurance Canada, at **insurance-canada.ca**, offers insurance-related consumer information.

- The Insurance Institute of Canada, at **iic-iac.org**, is the professional education arm of Canada's property and casualty insurance industry.

- Thompson's World Insurance News, at **thompsonsnews .com**, lays claim to being the Internet home of Canada's only independent news weekly for insurance professionals. It also provides a useful and extensive list of links.

- Kanetix Inc., **kanetix.ca**, is Canada's leader in online insurance quoting. Receive free insurance quotes on auto, property, life, and more from some of Canada's most recognized and trusted insurance companies.

(Note: Web site addresses and content change, and new sites are created daily. Use search engines to update and locate Web sites for your current financial planning needs.)

Short-Term Financial Planning Activities

1. List your current and needed insurance coverages.

2. (a) Prepare an inventory of personal belongings. (b) Compare the cost of homeowner's or tenant's insurance from two or more companies.

3. Compare the cost of auto insurance from two or more companies.

Long-Term Financial Planning Activities

1. Identify buying decisions that could reduce your future home and auto insurance costs.

2. Develop a plan to monitor changes in your life situation that would affect the need to change home or auto insurance coverages.

LIFE SITUATION CASE

We Rent, So Why Do We Need Insurance?

"Have you been down in the basement?" Nathan asked his wife, Erin, as he entered their apartment.

"No, what's up?" responded Erin.

"It's flooded because of all that rain we got last weekend!" he exclaimed.

"Oh no! We have the extra furniture my mom gave us stored down there. Is everything ruined?" Erin asked.

"The couch and coffee table are in a foot of water; the loveseat was the only thing that looked okay. Boy, I didn't realize the basement of this building wasn't waterproof. I'm going to call our landlady to complain."

As Erin thought about the situation, she remembered that when they moved in last fall, Kathy, their landlady, had informed them that her insurance policy covered the building but not the property belonging to each tenant. Because of this, they had purchased renter's insurance. "Nathan, I think our renter's insurance will cover the damage. Let me give our agent a call."

When Erin and Nathan purchased their insurance, they had to decide whether they wanted to be insured for cash value or for replacement costs. Replacement was more expensive, but it meant they would collect enough to go out and buy new household items at today's prices. If they had opted for cash value, the couch Erin's mother had paid $1,000 for five years ago would be worth less than $500 today.

Erin made the call and found out their insurance did cover the furniture in the basement, and at replacement value after they paid the deductible. The $300 they had invested in renter's insurance last year was well worth it!

Not every renter has as much foresight as Erin and Nathan. Fewer than 4 in 10 renters have tenant's insurance. Some aren't even aware they need it. They may assume they are covered by the landlord's insurance, but they aren't. This mistake can be costly.

Think about how much you have invested in your possessions and how much it would cost to replace them. Start with your stereo equipment or the colour television and DVD player that you bought last year. Experts suggest that people who rent start thinking about these things as soon as they move into their first apartment. Your policy should cover your personal belongings and provide funds for living expenses if you are dispossessed by a fire or other disaster.

Questions

1. Why is it important for people who rent to have insurance?

2. Does the building owner's property insurance ever cover the tenant's personal property?

3. What is the difference between cash value and replacement value?

4. When shopping for renter's insurance, what coverage features should you look for?

chapter 9

Life, Health, and Disability Insurance

LEARNING OBJECTIVES

LO1 Define *life insurance* and describe its purpose and principle.

LO2 Determine your life insurance needs.

LO3 Distinguish between the two types of life insurance policies and analyze various types of life insurance.

LO4 Select important provisions in life insurance contracts.

LO5 Create a plan to buy life insurance.

LO6 Define *health insurance* and explain its importance in financial planning.

LO7 Recognize the need for disability income insurance.

LO8 Understand the value of supplemental health insurance.

STAYING AFLOAT WHEN YOUR HEALTH SINKS

Harry Mills had just bought a second dental practice when he was stricken with plasma cell cancer. For two years, he battled to make payments on his new office. At this point, debilitated by both illness and intensive treatments, the dentist had fallen far behind.

But the Mills' still had one big asset: a $250,000 life insurance policy. So, the following year, Harry tapped it for $100,000. By the time he died in July of that year, all his debts were paid off. "He didn't have to think he was a failure," says his widow Shirley, "He was able to die with dignity."

As the Mills' learned, it is not easy to raise cash once you're diagnosed with a terminal illness. But there are ways to stay financially afloat in your final months. "Look at where the dollars are," says Herbert Daroff, a financial planner. "The value of your house, your life insurance, and

your retirement assets." If you get a terminal diagnosis, give yourself time to absorb the doctor's words. Then, get in touch with a financial expert—a planner, broker, or lawyer you trust. The choices you make will depend on your family, resources, and life expectancy. If you have young children, holding on to assets may be a key goal. But if you have three years to live and can no longer work, you may need steady income to pay medical costs and living expenses.

An often overlooked source of income is life insurance. You can tap policies that have cash value, such as whole or universal life, in several ways. The simplest: Take a loan. Most are at near-market rates. And ask about accelerated death benefit riders. If you have fewer than six months to live, such policies will pay up to half their value before you die. These options are not available if you have more common term insurance. But you can sell any policy to investors at a discount to its face value, an arrangement called a *viatical settlement.*

Check out the company; make sure it is regulated by an insurance commission. Shop around. Contact several different companies to get the best offer. Instead of selling a permanent life insurance policy, you can borrow using the policy as a collateral.

Some companies will lend up to 85 percent of a policy's value, depending on your life expectancy, and will pay your premiums. You repay nothing while you live, but your interest obligations will be compounding all the while. After you die, the company deducts interest and fees, and returns to your heirs any of the policy's remaining value. You may be charged an application fee of 2 or 3 percent of the total loan. Shirley Mills says her loan cost about $16,000. None of these alternatives is easy. And scrambling for money in the face of terminal illness may be the toughest financial decision you'll ever have to make.

QUESTIONS

1. How can the Internet help you create a life insurance program?
2. What was Harry Mills' biggest asset? Were all his debts paid off when he died?
3. What is an overlooked source of income for terminally ill people?

SOURCE: Adapted from "Staying Afloat When Your Health Sinks," *Business Week*, June 28, 1999, p. 134.

LIFE INSURANCE: AN INTRODUCTION

Canadians are among the most life-insured people in the world. By year-end 2012, we owned $3,903 billion in life insurance, we received $66.4 billion in payments from life and health insurance companies, and there were 90 active life insurance companies operating in Canada. In that year alone, Canadians paid a total of $83.3 billion in premiums on existing and new policies. About 21 million Canadians now have life insurance, and the average amount per insured individual in 2012 was about $183,600. The average size of new individual policies in 2012 was $334,200.

LOl

Define *life insurance* and describe its purpose and principle.

The problem is that despite these figures, many families are still not adequately covered. All too often, either too little or too much insurance is purchased, or the wrong kind of coverage is sought for the wrong people. The consequence is that when a crisis situation arises, many find that their insurance coverage is inadequate, too stringent in its criteria for claims admissibility, or both.

The following chapter will introduce you to life insurance and will help you determine the level of your need for it as well as help you decide between different types of life insurance policies. It describes what life insurance is and how it works, as well as how you can use it to protect your family.

WHAT IS LIFE INSURANCE?

Life insurance is neither mysterious nor difficult to understand. It works in the following manner: A person joins a risk-sharing group (an insurance company) by purchasing a contract (a policy). Under the policy, the insurance company promises to pay a sum of money at the time of the policyholder's death to the person or persons selected by him or her (the beneficiaries). In the case of an endowment policy, the money is paid to the policyholder (the insured) if he or she is alive on the future date (the maturity date) named in the policy. The insurance company makes this promise in return for the insured's agreement to pay it a sum of money (the premium) periodically.

Advice from a Pro

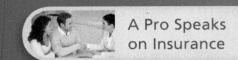

A Pro Speaks on Insurance

Ever been to a casino? Ever made a bet?

Buying insurance is essentially making a bet that you *don't* want to win. While you can't *plan* on experiencing many of life's calamities, you *should* plan for them. Without the appropriate insurance, a single event, such as a major accident, can completely destroy the value of your hard-earned assets.

Never smoked? Healthy as a horse? It doesn't matter! Insurance is specifically designed for those situations you hope will never occur. When those situations do occur, however, you'll find that savvy spending on appropriate insurance was money well spent.

Life insurance takes care of your dependants after you die. If you have a spouse, children, or other loved ones who are directly dependent on your income, life insurance is a *must*. Young people generally find they don't need life insurance.

In Canada, government health insurance plans cover most of your medical bills if you get sick. However, if you have ever paid full price for a medical prescription, you are probably aware that health-care costs have skyrocketed. In recent years, the government has cut back substantially on the type and amount of health care it will cover. Fortunately, many employers offer group insurance at reasonable rates that can provide you with supplemental health insurance coverage. Be sure to inquire about health insurance when applying for a job; the level of insurance offered might affect your interest in working for a particular company. Self-employed? Individuals who purchase private policies will pay more for equivalent coverage.

Keep in mind that there are insurance products available for any number of scenarios, so do your homework and evaluate your needs. As always, read everything and ask questions.

THE PURPOSE OF LIFE INSURANCE

Most people buy life insurance to protect someone who depends on them from financial losses caused by their death. That someone might be the non-working spouse and children of a single-income family. It can be the wife or husband of a two-income family. It can be an aging parent. It might be a business partner or a corporation.

Life insurance proceeds may be used to:

- Pay off a home mortgage or other debts at the time of death.
- Provide lump-sum payments through an endowment to children when they reach a specified age.
- Provide an education or income for children.
- Make charitable bequests after death.
- Provide a retirement income.
- Accumulate savings.
- Establish a regular income for survivors.
- Set up an estate plan.
- Make estate and death tax payments.

Life insurance is one of the few ways to provide liquidity at the time of death.

THE PRINCIPLE OF LIFE INSURANCE

The principle of home insurance, discussed in Chapter 8, can be applied to the lives of people. From records covering many years and including millions of lives, mortality tables have been prepared to show the number of deaths among various age groups during any year. A standard mortality table is shown in Exhibit 9–1. A 30-year-old man has a 0.001 probability of dying before his next birthday. If he wishes to buy a $200,000 term insurance policy for one year, the premium he will pay is close to $200, or $0.001 \times \$200,000$, since this is the average amount of money the insurance company expects to need to pay out for every $200,000 of coverage for all of its male clients aged 30.

Age	Alive at Start of Year	Days During Year of Survival	Probability of Survival	Probability of Death
0 year	100,000	533	0.99467	0.00533
1 year	99,467	29	0.99971	0.00029
2 years	99,438	22	0.99978	0.00022
3 years	99,416	18	0.99982	0.00018
4 years	99,398	15	0.99985	0.00015
5 years	99,383	13	0.99987	0.00013
6 years	99,371	11	0.99989	0.00011
7 years	99,360	10	0.9999	0.0001
8 years	99,349	10	0.9999	0.0001
9 years	99,340	10	0.9999	0.0001
10 years	99,330	10	0.9999	0.0001
11 years	99,320	11	0.99989	0.00011
12 years	99,309	13	0.99987	0.00013
13 years	99,296	16	0.99984	0.00016
14 years	99,279	21	0.99978	0.00022
15 years	99,258	30	0.9997	0.0003
16 years	99,228	42	0.99958	0.00042
17 years	99,186	53	0.99946	0.00054
18 years	99,133	63	0.99936	0.00064
19 years	99,069	71	0.99929	0.00071
20 years	98,999	77	0.99922	0.00078
21 years	98,922	81	0.99918	0.00082
22 years	98,841	82	0.99917	0.00083
23 years	98,759	81	0.99918	0.00082
24 years	98,677	78	0.99921	0.00079
25 years	98,599	74	0.99925	0.00075
26 years	98,525	72	0.99927	0.00073
27 years	98,453	71	0.99928	0.00072
28 years	98,381	71	0.99927	0.00073
29 years	98,310	73	0.99926	0.00074
30 years	98,237	76	0.99923	0.00077
65 years	86,010	1,152	0.9866	0.0134

As the table indicates, by age 65, 13.4% of the cohort has died.

Age	Alive at Start of Year	Days During Year of Survival	Probability of Survival	Probability of Death
66 years	84,857	1,252	0.98525	0.01475
67 years	83,606	1,358	0.98376	0.01624
68 years	82,248	1,470	0.98212	0.01788
69 years	80,778	1,590	0.98031	0.01969
70 years	79,188	1,717	0.97832	0.02168
71 years	77,471	1,850	0.97612	0.02388
72 years	75,621	1,989	0.9737	0.0263
73 years	73,632	2,134	0.97102	0.02898
74 years	71,498	2,283	0.96807	0.03193
75 years	69,215	2,435	0.96482	0.03518
76 years	66,780	2,589	0.96123	0.03877
77 years	64,191	2,743	0.95727	0.04273
78 years	61,448	2,895	0.95289	0.04711
79 years	58,553	3,041	0.94807	0.05193
80 years	55,513	3,179	0.94274	0.05726
81 years	52,334	3,304	0.93686	0.06314
82 years	49,030	3,414	0.93037	0.06963
83 years	45,616	3,503	0.9232	0.0768

Exhibit 9–1

Mortality Table for Canadian Males

The table provides the number of deaths expected during any year of life for a hypothetical cohort of 100,000 Canadian males.

SOURCE: Adapted from Statistics Canada, Life Tables, Canada, Provinces and Territories 2007 to 2009, http://www.statcan.gc.ca/pub/84-537-x/2013003/tbl/tbl1a-eng.htm.

(continued)

Exhibit 9–1
(concluded)

Age	Alive at Start of Year	Days During Year of Survival	Probability of Survival	Probability of Death
84 years	42,113	3,567	0.91529	0.08471
108 years	27	13	0.52438	0.47562
109 years	14	7	0.5088	0.4912
110 years and over	7	7	0	1

Column 1, Age, is the starting age for the given year.

Column 2, Alive at Start of Year, shows how many of the cohort were alive at the start of the year at the age shown in column 1. For example, we see that in the third year, 99,416 of the original cohort were expected to be living.

Column 3, Deaths During Year of Survival, records the number of deaths expected to occur during the year starting on the birthday in Column 1. We see that, on average, 18 of the 99,416 alive on their third birthday are expected to die before their fourth birthday. In the entry for Column 2, Alive at Start of Year, Age 4 is equal to Column 2 minus Column 3 from the previous line, Age 3.

Column 4, Probability of Survival, is calculated as (Column 2 − Column 3) ÷ Column 2, rounded to five decimal places. Thus, a three-year-old boy has a 0.99982 probability of surviving to his next birthday.

Column 5, Probability of Death, is calculated as Column 3 ÷ Column 2, rounded to five decimal places.

Of course, this amount may be adjusted for a number of factors, including particular characteristics that may put a person at higher or lower risk, the various administrative fees that each company must pay, and other factors. In general, it is best to look for a company that manages its resources efficiently, as this lower company cost may translate to a lower premium for you.

CONCEPT CHECK 9–1

1. How can the Internet help you create a life insurance plan?
2. What is the meaning of life insurance?
3. What is the purpose of life insurance?
4. What is the principle of life insurance?
5. What do mortality tables indicate?

DETERMINING YOUR LIFE INSURANCE NEEDS

LO2

Determine your life insurance needs.

You should consider a number of factors before you buy life insurance. These factors include your present and future sources of income, other savings and income protection, group life insurance, group annuities (or other pension benefits), net worth, and government benefits. First, however, you should determine whether you need life insurance.

DO YOU NEED LIFE INSURANCE?

If your death would cause financial stress for your spouse, children, parents, or anyone else you want to protect, you should consider purchasing life insurance. Your stage in the life cycle and the type of household you live in will influence this decision. Single persons living alone or with their parents usually have little or no need for life insurance. Consider Brian Brickman, 28, a bachelor who does not smoke, is in excellent health, and has no dependants. Brian owns a $300,000 condominium with a $270,000 mortgage. Since his employer provides a $300,000 group term life policy, he needs no additional life insurance. Larry Lucas, 32, and his wife, Liz, 30, are professionals, each earning $85,000 a year. The Lucas' have no dependants. This two-earner couple may have a moderate need for life insurance, especially if they have a mortgage or other large debts. Parents with small children usually have the greatest need for life insurance.

DETERMINING YOUR LIFE INSURANCE OBJECTIVES

Before you consider types of life insurance policies, you must decide what you want your life insurance to do for you and your dependants.

First, how much money do you want to leave to your dependants should you die today? Will you require more or less insurance protection to meet their needs as time goes on?

Second, do you wish to leave your dependants debt-free? Are there any special expenses beyond daily living, such as an education fund for your children, that you wish to ensure are met? Do you want your funeral expenses to be covered?

Finally, how much will you be able to pay for your insurance program? Are the demands on your family budget for other living expenses likely to be greater or lower as time goes on?

When you have considered these questions and developed some approximate answers, you are ready to select the types and amounts of life insurance policies that will help you accomplish your objectives.

Once you have decided what you want your life insurance to accomplish, the next important decision is how much to buy.

ESTIMATING YOUR LIFE INSURANCE REQUIREMENTS

How much life insurance should you carry? This question is important for every person who owns or intends to buy life insurance. Because of the various factors involved, the question cannot be answered by mathematics alone. Nevertheless, an insurance policy puts a price on the life of the insured person, and therefore methods are needed to estimate what that price should be.

Two methods for determining the amount of insurance you may need are the income replacement method and the family need method, both discussed below.

THE INCOME REPLACEMENT METHOD   Simple as this method is, it is remarkably useful. It is based on the insurance agent's general rule that a typical family will need approximately 70 percent of your salary for seven years before they adjust to the financial consequences of your death. In other words, for a simple estimate of your life insurance needs, just multiply your current gross income by 7 (7 years) and 0.70 (70 percent).

Example:

$$\$70,000 \text{ current income} \times 7 = \$490,000$$

$$\$490,000 \times 0.70 = \$343,000$$

Your figures:

$\$$_____ current income $\times$ 7 = $\$$_____ $\times$ 0.70 = $\$$_____

This method assumes your family is "typical" and that you do not have any liquid assets available for dependants which would otherwise reduce your life insurance needs. You may need more insurance if you have four or more children, if you have above-average family debt, if any member of your family suffers from poor health, or if your spouse has poor employment potential. On the other hand, you may need less insurance if your family is smaller.

THE FAMILY NEED METHOD   The income replacement method assumes you and your family are "typical" and ignores important factors such as government benefits and your liquid assets. Exhibit 9–2 provides a detailed worksheet for making a thorough estimate of your life insurance needs. You can also visit Web sites such as Life Events Planner (lifeevents planner. cuis.com) and calculate the amount of life insurance you need by using a life insurance calculator. The calculator allows you to enter detailed information regarding your assets, expenses at death, and income and living expenses, and determines your insurance needs based on the inflation rate and your expected rate of return.

Although this method is quite thorough, you may believe it does not address all of your special needs. If so, you should obtain further advice from an insurance expert or a financial planner.

Exhibit 9–2

A Worksheet to Calculate Your Life Insurance Needs

SOURCES: *About Life Insurance*, Metropolitan Life Insurance Company, February 1997, p. 3; *The TIAA Guide to Life Insurance Planning for People in Education* (New York: Teachers Insurance and Annuity Association, January 1997), p. 3.

1. Five times your personal yearly income _____ (1)

2. Total approximate expenses above and beyond your daily living costs for you and your dependants (e.g., tuition, care for a disabled child or parent)   + _____ (2)

3. Your emergency fund (three to six months of living expenses)   + _____ (3)

4. Estimated amount for your funeral expenses (average is $6,000)   + _____ (4)

5. Total estimate of your family's financial needs (add lines 1 through 4)   = _____ (5)

6. Your total liquid assets (e.g., savings accounts, GICs, money market funds, existing life insurance both individual and group, pension plan death benefits, and government benefits)   − _____ (6)

7. Subtract line 6 from line 5 and enter the difference here.   = _____ (7)

The net result (line 7) is an estimate of the shortfall your family would face upon your death. Remember, these are just guidelines. For a complete analysis of your needs, consult a professional.

As you determine your life insurance needs, don't forget to consider the life insurance you may already have. You may have ample coverage through your employer and through any mortgage and credit life insurance you have purchased.

CONCEPT CHECK 9–2

1. How do you determine the need for life insurance?
2. What determines your life insurance objectives?
3. What are the two methods of estimating your life insurance requirements?

TYPES OF LIFE INSURANCE

LO3

Distinguish between the two types of life insurance policies and analyze various types of life insurance.

New insurance products are introduced to the market regularly, and there are many different types of life insurance available. However, they all fall into two basic types: term life and permanent life. Term insurance provides insurance coverage for a specific number of years. Permanent insurance provides protection for life. Both types pay a death benefit if you should die with the policy still in force. Exhibit 9–3 shows the types of policies issued in Canada recently.

TERM LIFE INSURANCE

term insurance Life insurance protection for a specified period of time; sometimes called *temporary life insurance.*

Term insurance is like fire or auto insurance in that it provides protection against a specified financial risk for a finite period of time, often 10 or 20 years. It is pure insurance with no frills, and after the end of the specified term, you will not be eligible to collect any sum from the insurance company. A term insurance policy pays a benefit only if you die during the period it covers. If you stop paying the premiums, the insurance stops. Term insurance is, therefore, sometimes called *temporary life insurance.*

Term insurance is a basic, "no frills" form of life insurance and is the best value for most consumers. The premiums for people in their 20s and 30s are lower than those for whole life insurance, discussed in the next section.

Exhibit 9–3

Types of Life
Insurance Policies
Issued

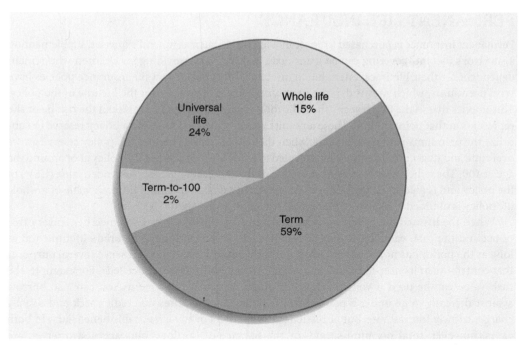

SOURCE: Reprinted from "A Guide to Life Insurance," 2002, with the permission of the Canadian Life and Health Insurance Association Inc., clhia.ca.

You need insurance coverage most while you are raising young children. Although term life insurance premiums increase as you get older, you can reduce your coverage as your children grow up and your assets (the value of your savings, investments, home, autos, etc.) increase.

Various options for term insurance are outlined below. Each affects the premium charged for the policy.

RENEWABILITY OPTION   The coverage of term insurance ends at the conclusion of the term, but you can continue it for another term if you have a renewability option.

CONVERSION OPTION   If you have convertible term insurance, you can exchange it for a whole life policy without a medical examination and at a higher premium. The premium for the whole life policy stays the same for the rest of your life. Consider this option if you want cash-value life insurance and can't afford it now but expect to be able to in the future.

TERM-TO-100   An alternative to paying for the option to convert term insurance to more costly permanent insurance is to opt for term insurance coverage that remains in effect to the age of 100. Term-to-100 insurance charges a level premium to the end of the contract (death or age 100), but at a cost significantly less than traditional permanent insurance because the policy holder does not have any right to cash value if the policy is cancelled during the insured's lifetime. Refer to the discussion of cash values under the topic of whole life insurance, which follows.

DECREASING TERM INSURANCE   Term insurance is also available in a form that pays less to the beneficiary as time passes. The insurance period you select might depend on your age or on how long you decide you will need the coverage. For example, a decreasing term contract for 25 years might be appropriate as coverage of a mortgage loan balance on a house because the coverage decreases as the mortgage balance decreases. You could get the same result by purchasing annual renewable term policies of diminishing amounts during the period of the mortgage loan. An annual renewable policy offers more flexibility to change coverage if you sell or remortgage the house. Mortgage insurance, therefore, is a form of decreasing term insurance, decreasing to keep pace with the principal balance on your mortgage loan.

PERMANENT LIFE INSURANCE

Permanent insurance is purchased to cover lifelong needs, such as funeral expenses, supplementing a survivor's income, covering capital gains taxes at death, and providing for children who remain dependent for their lifetimes, often due to disability. Most permanent life insurance policies have **level premiums**, which means that the premiums remain the same over the lifetime of the policy. This implies that in the initial years, the policyholder pays higher premiums than the risk he or she represents at that point in time. These amounts are then invested to create a policy reserve to subsidize the premiums paid in later years, when the risk of death is higher. The policy reserve grows over time and its accumulated value is expected to equal the face value of the policy at or around the age of 100. The policy reserve is also referred to as the **cash value** or cash surrender value (CSV) of the policy and is paid out if the policy is cancelled. The dollar amount of the cash value of a whole life policy is outlined in a table of guaranteed values up to the age of 100.

When the insured dies, the face value of the policy is paid out to the named beneficiary free of tax and the cash value or reserve terminates. However, during the insured's lifetime and as long as the policy has not been cancelled, the cash value of the policy can serve several purposes that contribute to its non-forfeiture value (value if the policy is not cancelled). For example, the cash value can be used if you are unable to make a premium payment. You can also borrow against the cash value under a policy loan. A policy loan requires no credit check and usually charges a lower interest rate, but necessitates the approval of any irrevocable beneficiary. In both cases, however, total premiums paid, or the balance of the loan plus accrued interest, are deducted from the proceeds of the policy paid to the beneficiary should the insured die.

Full or partial withdrawals of the cash value can also take place. Partial withdrawals of the cash value without surrendering the policy reduce the face value of the policy on a pro rata basis. Full withdrawal of the cash value cancels the insurance contract. Full and partial withdrawals are subject to income tax, but the cash value grows tax-free as long as it remains untouched. Insurance salespeople often emphasize the "forced savings" aspect of whole life policies and their tax deferral potential, but they offer a dubious benefit for individuals who have a proper personal financial plan. These types of policies are often particularly expensive, and administrative costs eat into the cash value's investment return, making it less competitive as a savings vehicle.

Permanent life insurance comes in the following variations: whole life, universal life, variable life, and endowment life. Exhibit 9–4 compares some important features of the most common types of life insurance; Exhibit 9–5 compares the costs of term and permanent life insurance.

level premiums Insurance premiums that remain the same over the lifetime of a policy.

cash value The amount received after giving up a life insurance policy.

WHOLE LIFE INSURANCE   The **whole life policy** is an insurance plan for which the policyholder pays a specified premium each year for as long as he or she lives; also called a *straight life policy, cash-value life policy,* or an *ordinary life policy*. In return, the insurance company promises to pay a stipulated sum to the beneficiary when you die. The amount of your premium depends primarily on the age at which you purchase the insurance.

One important feature of the whole life policy is its cash value. Cash value (or *cash surrender value*) is an amount, which increases each year, that you receive if you give up the insurance. Hence, cash-value policies provide a death benefit *and* a savings benefit. Insurance salespeople often emphasize the "forced savings" aspect of cash-value insurance.

Cash-value policies may make sense for people who intend to keep the policies for the long term or for people who must be forced to save. But you should not have too low a death benefit just because you would like the savings component of a cash-value life policy. Experts suggest that you explore other savings and investment strategies before investing your money in a permanent life insurance policy.

The insurance company accumulates a substantial reserve during the early years of the whole life policy to pay the benefits in the later years, when your chances of dying are greater. At first, the annual premium for whole life insurance is higher than that for term insurance. However, the premium for a whole life policy remains constant throughout your lifetime, whereas the premium for a term policy increases with each renewal.

whole life policy An insurance plan for which the policyholder pays a specified premium each year for as long as he or she lives; also called a *straight life policy,* a *cash-value life policy,* or an *ordinary life policy*.

Exhibit 9–4   Types of Insurance

| Policy Type | Permanent | | Term to 100 | Term |
	Whole Life	Universal Life		
Period of coverage	Life	Life	To age 100	Depends on term in contract. Often renewable for additional terms but usually not past age 70 or 75.
Premiums	Guaranteed. Usually remain level.	Flexible. Can be increased or decreased by policyholder within certain limits.	Guaranteed. Usually remain level.	Guaranteed and remain level for term or policy (e.g., 1 year, 5 years, 10 years, etc.). Increase with each new term.
Death benefits	Guaranteed in contract. Remain level. Dividends may be used to enhance death benefits in participating policies.	Flexible. May increase or decrease according to fluctuations in cash value fund.	Guaranteed in contract. Remain level.	Guaranteed in contract.
Cash values	Guaranteed in contract.	Flexible. May increase or decrease according to investment returns and level of policyholder deposits.	Usually none. (Some policies have a small cash value or other non-forfeiture value after a long period, say, 20 years.)	Usually none. (Some long-term policies have a small cash value or other non-forfeiture value.)
Other Non-forfeiture Options	Guaranteed in contract.	Guaranteed in contract.	See above.	See above.
Dividends	Payable on "participating" policies. Not guaranteed.	Most policies are "non-participating" and do not pay dividends.	Most policies are "non-participating" and do not pay dividends.	Most policies are "non-participating" and do not pay dividends.
Advantages	• Provides protection for your entire lifetime—if kept in force. • Premium cost usually stays level, regardless of age or health problems. • Has cash values that can be borrowed, used to continue protection if premiums are missed, or withdrawn if the policy is no longer required. • Other non-forfeiture options allow the policyholder various possibilities of continuing coverage if premiums are missed or discontinued. • If the policy is participating, it receives dividends that can be taken in cash, left to accumulate at interest, or used to purchase additional insurance.		• Provides protection to age 100—if kept in force. • Premium cost usually stays level, regardless of age or health problems. • Premium cost is lower relative to traditional permanent policies.	• Suitable for short term insurance needs, or specific liabilities, such as a mortgage. • Provides more immediate protection because initially it is less expensive than permanent insurance. • Can be converted to permanent insurance without medical evidence if it has a convertibility option, often up to ages 65 or 70.
Disadvantages	• Initial cost may be too high for a sufficient amount of protection for your current needs. • May be an inefficient means of covering short-term needs. • Cash values tend to be small in the early years. You have to hold the policy for a long time, say over 10 years, before the cash values become sizable.		• Usually no cash values and no or limited non-forfeiture values.	• If renewed, premiums increase with age and at some point higher premium costs may make it difficult or impossible to continue coverage. • Renewability of coverage will terminate at some point, commonly age 65 or age 75. • If premium is not paid, the policy terminates after 30 days and may not be reinstated if health is poor. • Usually no cash values and no non-forfeiture options.

SOURCE: clhia.ca/, Canadian Life and Health Insurance Association Inc.

Exhibit 9–5

Cost Comparison of Term Life Insurance and Permanent Life Insurance

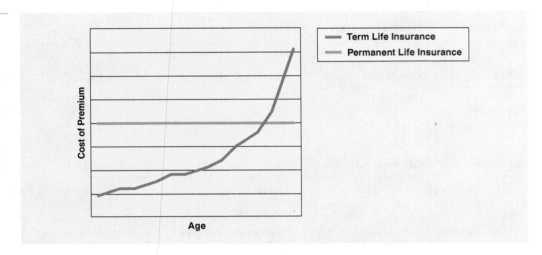

universal life   A permanent life insurance policy that combines term insurance and investment elements.

UNIVERSAL LIFE INSURANCE   Unlike whole life policies, which use long-term interest rate assumptions, the **universal life** insurance policy uses current interest rates that can be adjusted periodically. This is an advantage when rates rise, but makes universal policies more vulnerable when rates decline, although some policies guarantee a minimum investment return.

Universal life policies consist of two parts: life insurance and an investment account. The policyholder decides what to do with each part of the policy, within certain limitations.

Premiums are flexible but not guaranteed, although at a minimum they should cover the pure cost of insurance and administrative costs. A maximum is set relative to the policy face value to ensure that the tax-exempt status of the investment account is maintained. This is important because the savings component of a permanent life insurance policy can grow free of tax as long as the policy is viewed primarily as an insurance product and not a tax-sheltered investment vehicle. This opportunity to defer taxes is especially attractive to affluent investors who have exhausted other tax deferral strategies, such as contributing the maximum amount to their registered retirement savings plan (RRSP) or their tax-free savings account (TFSA). Premiums that the policyholder chooses to pay in excess of this stated maximum are tracked in a side fund, often invested in segregated funds offered by the insurer, with investment income taxed annually.

What are the differences between universal life and whole life insurance? While both policy types have cash value, universal life gives you more direct control. With universal life, you control your outlay and can change your premium without changing your coverage. Whole life, in contrast, requires you to pay a specific premium every year, or the policy will lapse. Universal life allows you access to your cash value by a policy loan or withdrawal. Whole life allows only for policy loans.

Since your primary reason for buying a life insurance policy is the insurance component, the cost of that component should be your main consideration. Thus, universal life policies that offer a high rate of return on the cash value but charge a high price for the insurance element generally should be avoided.

VARIABLE INSURANCE   *Variable life insurance* is another type of policy that is sensitive to interest rates. Premiums are usually guaranteed in these policies; however, the cash values vary based on the performance of an investment fund or other index. A minimum death benefit is guaranteed, but the death benefit can rise above the minimum, depending on the earnings of the dollars invested in the separate fund. When you purchase a variable life policy, you assume the risk of poor investment performance.

There are a number of things that affect life insurance fees. The following are some of the factors considered when pricing life insurance premiums:

- **The Amount of Insurance**: The higher the amount one is insured for, the higher the premium.

- **Your Health Class:** This factor attempts to determine your mental and physical health using questions regarding family medical history (genetics), blood pressure and cholesterol problems, smoking habits and other health concerns. Typically, the better the health of the applicant, the lower the premium.
- **Age:** The younger a person is when first applying for life insurance, the better his or her chances are of getting a lower premium. This is consistent with the fact that your age may indicate how much longer you might live, and may bring on ailments and medical problems.
- **Gender:** It is said that women live longer than men, and therefore their life insurance premiums are generally less expensive. However, because of this very fact, their health insurance premiums are typically higher.
- **Marital Status:** Statistics show that married people tend to live longer than their unmarried counterparts. Though this may not drastically change the price you pay for your insurance, it certainly is something insurance companies consider when fixing premiums.
- **Occupation:** Since some jobs can be more dangerous than others, insurance companies are concerned with an applicant's occupation to determine the likelihood that they will have to pay out benefits to them. Generally speaking, the riskier the job, the higher the premium.
- **Recreation:** Extreme sports are one example of a leisure activity that may put you on an insurance company's risky candidate list. Statistically, the chances of such a candidate cashing in his or her policy are greater than a candidate who enjoys quieter, less adventurous extracurricular activities.*

ENDOWMENT LIFE INSURANCE   *Endowment life insurance* provides coverage from the beginning of the contract to maturity and guarantees payment of a specified sum to the insured, even if he or she is still living at the end of the endowment period. The face value of the policy is paid to beneficiaries upon the death of the insured. The endowment period typically has a duration of 10 to 20 years or the attainment of a specified age.

OTHER TYPES OF LIFE INSURANCE POLICIES

GROUP LIFE INSURANCE   A group insurance plan insures a large number of persons under the terms of a single policy without requiring medical examinations. In general, the principles that apply to other forms of insurance also apply to group insurance.

Fundamentally, group insurance is term insurance, which was described earlier. Usually, the cost of group insurance is split between the employer and the employees so that the cost of insurance per $1,000 is the same for each employee, regardless of age. For older employees, the employer pays a larger portion of the costs of the group policy. Group insurance is an important part of a person's total insurance coverage, but it is important to remember that the coverage ends if the member leaves the group.

CREDIT LIFE INSURANCE   *Credit life insurance* is a specialized version of group insurance that is purchased by creditors to cover the lives of a group of borrowers. The insurer agrees to reimburse to the creditor any outstanding debt in the event of the debtor's death. Ultimately, the cost for this coverage is borne by the borrower in the form of higher premiums.

Mortgage insurance, frequently purchased by homeowners as a requirement for obtaining a mortgage, is, in fact, a form of group insurance. Like credit life insurance, it protects the lender, in this case the institution providing your mortgage, from the possibility of your death.

CONCEPT CHECK 9–3

1. What are the major types and sub-types of life insurance?

_____

*SOURCES: lifeinsurancequote.com/; lifeinsurancerate.com/66-factors-affecting-your-life-insurance-rate.html.

One pro, a fee-only insurance consultant, states that North Americans make thousands of costly decisions about life insurance. He advises that when you are in doubt about which life insurance to purchase, buy term. It is the least expensive, easy to understand, and a good start. If you want a whole life policy, buy a low-load cash-value policy. These policies are sold directly to the public or through fee-for-service advisers. Ask your agent to explain plausible risk in writing. Review annual statements and ask your agent for an in-force illustration every few years to determine whether the current premium is still adequate.

IMPORTANT PROVISIONS IN A LIFE INSURANCE CONTRACT

LO4

Select important provisions in life insurance contracts.

Modern life insurance policies contain numerous provisions whose terminology can be confusing. Therefore, understanding these provisions is important for the insurance buyer.

In our dynamic economy, inflation and interest rates change often. Therefore, experts recommend that you re-evaluate your insurance coverage every two years. Be sure to update your insurance whenever your situation changes substantially. For example, the birth of a child or an increase in your home mortgage can boost your insurance needs.

Your life insurance policy is valuable only if it meets your objectives. When your objectives change, it may not be necessary to give up the policy. Instead, study the policy carefully and discuss its provisions with your agent. Following are some of the most common provisions. Exhibit 9–6 shows the effects of inflation on a $100,000 policy.

NAMING YOUR BENEFICIARY

beneficiary A person designated to receive something, such as life insurance proceeds, from the insured.

An important provision in every life insurance policy is the right to name your beneficiary. A **beneficiary** is a person who is designated to receive something, such as life insurance proceeds, from the insured. In your policy, you can name one or more persons as contingent beneficiaries who will receive your policy proceeds if the primary beneficiary dies before you do. It is essential to name a beneficiary of your life insurance policy if you do not wish the death benefit of the policy to form part of your estate and be subject to a probate fee that is often calculated as a percentage of your estate's value.

THE GRACE PERIOD

When you buy a life insurance policy, the insurance company agrees to pay a certain sum of money under specified circumstances and you agree to pay a certain premium regularly. The *grace period* applies in situations where the premium is due but not yet paid. It allows 28 to 31 days to elapse, during which time you may pay the premium without penalty. After that time, the policy lapses if you have not paid the premium.

POLICY REINSTATEMENT

A lapsed policy can be put back in force, or reinstated, if it has not been turned in for cash. To reinstate the policy, you must again qualify as an acceptable risk, and you must pay overdue premiums with interest. There is a time limit on reinstatement, usually one or two years.

NON-FORFEITURE CLAUSE

non-forfeiture clause A provision that allows the insured not to forfeit all accrued benefits.

One important feature of the whole life policy is the **non-forfeiture clause**, which prevents the forfeiture of accrued benefits if you choose to drop the policy. For example, if you decide not to continue paying premiums, you can exercise specified options with your cash value.

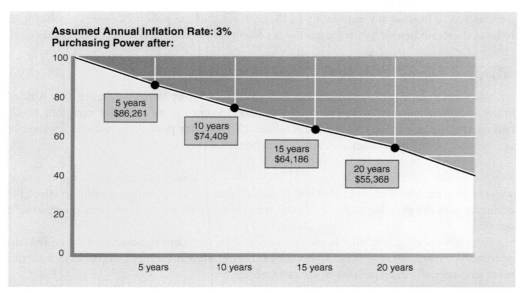

Assumed Annual Inflation Rate: 3%
Purchasing Power after:

5 years
$86,261

10 years
$74,409

15 years
$64,186

20 years
$55,368

Exhibit 9–6

Effects of Inflation on a $100,000 Life Insurance Policy

SOURCE: *The TIAA Guide to Life Insurance Planning for People in Education* (New York: Teachers' Insurance and Annuity Association, January 1997), p. 8.

INCONTESTABILITY CLAUSE

The **incontestability clause** stipulates that after the policy has been in force for a specified period (usually two years), the insurance company cannot dispute its validity during the lifetime of the insured for any reason, including fraud. One reason for this provision is that the beneficiaries, who cannot defend the company's contesting of the claim, should not be forced to suffer because of the acts of the insured.

incontestability clause A provision stating that the insurer cannot dispute the validity of a policy after a specified period.

SUICIDE CLAUSE

The **suicide clause** provides that if the insured dies by suicide during the first two years the policy is in force, the death benefit equals the amount of the premium paid. Generally, after two years, the suicide becomes a risk covered by the policy and the beneficiaries of a suicide receive the same benefit that is payable for death from any other cause.

suicide clause A provision stating that if the insured dies by suicide during the first two years the policy is in force, the death benefit equals the amount of the premium paid.

AUTOMATIC PREMIUM LOANS

With an automatic premium loan option, if you do not pay the premium within the grace period, the insurance company automatically pays it out of the policy's cash value if that cash value is sufficient in your whole life policy. This prevents you from inadvertently allowing the policy to lapse.

MISSTATEMENT OF AGE PROVISION

The misstatement of age provision says that if the company finds out that your age was incorrectly stated, it will pay the benefits your premiums would have bought if your age had been correctly stated. The provision sets forth a simple procedure to resolve what could otherwise be a complicated legal matter.

POLICY LOAN PROVISION

A loan from the insurance company is available on a whole life policy after the policy has been in force for a time as stated in the policy. This feature, known as the *policy loan provision*, permits you to borrow any amount up to the cash value of the policy. However, a policy loan reduces the death benefit by the amount of the loan plus interest if the loan is not repaid.

RIDERS TO LIFE INSURANCE POLICIES

rider A document attached to a policy that modifies its coverage.

An insurance company can change the provisions of a policy by attaching a rider to it. A **rider** is any document attached to the policy that modifies its coverage by adding or excluding specified conditions or altering its benefits. A whole life insurance policy may include a waiver of premium disability benefit, an accidental death benefit, or both.

WAIVER OF PREMIUM DISABILITY BENEFIT

Under this provision, the company waives any premiums that are due after the onset of total and permanent disability. In effect, the company pays the premiums. The disability must occur before you reach a certain age, usually age 60.

The waiver of premium rider is sometimes desirable. Don't buy it, however, if the added cost prevents you from carrying needed basic life insurance. Some insurance companies include this rider automatically in all policies issued through age 55.

ACCIDENTAL DEATH BENEFIT

double indemnity A benefit under which the company pays twice the face value of the policy if the insured's death results from an accident.

Under this provision, the insurance company pays twice the face amount of the policy if the insured's death results from an accident. The accidental death benefit is often called **double indemnity**. Accidental death must occur within a certain time period after the injury, usually 90 days, and before the insured reaches a certain age, usually age 60 or 65.

The accidental death benefit is expensive. Moreover, your chances of dying in the exact manner stated in the policy are small, as are the chances that your beneficiary will collect the double payment.

GUARANTEED INSURABILITY OPTION

This option, also referred to as *future increase option*, allows you to buy additional amounts of life insurance without proof of insurability. Therefore, even if you do not remain in good health, you can increase the amount of your insurance as your income rises. This option is desirable if you anticipate the need for additional life insurance in the future.

CRITICAL ILLNESS

Critical illness benefits are life insurance policy proceeds paid to a terminally ill policyholder *before* he or she dies. The benefits may be provided for directly in the policies, but more often, they are added by riders or attachments to new or existing policies.

JOINT, LAST TO DIE

A *joint, last to die life insurance* policy, also called *survivorship life*, insures two lives, usually husband and wife. The death benefit is paid when the second spouse dies. Usually, a second-to-die policy is intended to pay estate taxes when both spouses die. However, some attorneys claim that with the right legal advice, you can minimize or avoid estate taxes completely.

Now that you know the various types of life insurance policies and the major provisions of and riders to such policies, you are ready to make your buying decisions.

CONCEPT CHECK 9–4

1. What are the most common provisions in life insurance contracts?
2. What is a beneficiary?
3. What is a rider?
4. What is the concept of double indemnity?

BUYING LIFE INSURANCE

You should consider a number of factors before buying life insurance. As discussed earlier in this chapter, these factors include your present and future sources of income, other savings and income protection, group life insurance, group annuities (or other pension benefits), government benefits, and, of course, the financial strength of the company.

LO5
Create a plan to buy life insurance.

FROM WHOM TO BUY?

Look for insurance coverage from financially strong companies with professionally qualified representatives. It is not unusual for a relationship with an insurance company to extend over a period of 20, 30, or even 50 years. For that reason alone, you should choose carefully when deciding on an insurance company or an insurance agent. Fortunately, you have a choice of sources.

SOURCES   Protection is available from a wide range of private and public sources, including: insurance companies and their representatives; private groups, such as employers, labour unions, and professional or fraternal organizations; and financial institutions and manufacturers offering credit insurance.

> ### Did you know?
>
> In 2012, Canadians purchased:
>
> | | |
> |---|---|
> | Individual life insurance | $227.8 billion |
> | Group life insurance | 93.9 billion |
> | Total life insurance | $321.7 billion |
>
> SOURCE: http://www.clhia.ca/domino/html/clhia/clhia_lp4w_lnd_webstation.nsf/resources/The+Industry/$file/KeyStats2013_EN.pdf.

RATING INSURANCE COMPANIES   Some of the strongest, most reputable insurance companies in the nation provide excellent insurance coverage at reasonable costs. In fact, the financial strength of an insurance company may be a major factor in holding down premium costs for consumers.

Locate an insurance company by checking the reputations of local agencies. Ask members of your family, friends, or colleagues about the insurers they prefer.

CHOOSING YOUR INSURANCE PROVIDER   Before you purchase your insurance, you need to consider whether you want to buy through a direct insurer, an agent, a broker, or a group plan. Agents and direct insurers represent one insurance company and offer only the products of that company. If that company has a range of products, then your needs will likely be met. It does, however, require that you have some knowledge of the products available in the marketplace so you can compare.

A broker, considered by most to be the better option, contracts with a limited number of insurance companies and can offer the products of those companies with which the broker has a contract.

A group plan can function either through an agent or a broker system. In some cases, while the plan may be serviced by a broker, the broker may use one insurance company almost exclusively for that plan. In this sense, the broker is really functioning more as an agent. Group plans may be offered through an employer, an alumni association, or another group affiliation.

Once you find a provider, you must decide which policy is right for you. The best way to do this is to talk to your agent, which does not obligate you to buy insurance.

The Canadian Life and Health Insurance Association (clhia.ca) suggests you ask about the professional qualifications and training the agent has had. Agents with a CLU (Chartered Life Underwriter) or C.H.F.C. (Chartered Financial Consultant) demonstrate commitment to their profession. These programs require several years of study and examinations.

COMPARING POLICY COSTS

Each life insurance company designs the policies it sells to make them attractive and useful to many policyholders. One policy may have features another policy doesn't; one company may be more selective than another company; one company may get better returns on its investments than another company. These and other factors affect the prices of life insurance policies.

In determining the cost of insurance, don't overlook the time value of money. You must include as part of that cost the interest (opportunity cost) you would earn on money if you did not use it to pay insurance premiums. For many years, insurers did not assign a time value to money in making their sales presentations. Only recently has the insurance industry widely adopted interest-adjusted cost estimates.

If you fail to consider the time value of money, you may get the false impression that the insurance company is giving you something for nothing. Here is an example. Suppose you are 35 years old and have a $10,000 face amount, 20 year, limited-payment, participating policy. Your annual premium is $210, or $4,200 over the 20-year period. Your dividends over the 20 year payment period total $1,700, so your total net premium is $2,500 ($4,200 − $1,700). Yet the cash value of your policy at the end of 20 years is $4,600. If you disregard the interest your premiums could otherwise have earned, you might get the impression that the insurance company is giving you $2,100 more than you paid ($4,600 − $2,500). If you consider the time value of money (or its opportunity cost), the insurance company is not giving you $2,100. What if you had invested the annual premiums in a conservative-stock mutual fund? At an 8 percent annual yield, your account would have accumulated to $6,180 in 20 years. Therefore, instead of receiving $2,100 from the insurance company, you have paid the company $1,580 for 20 years of insurance protection:

Premiums you paid over 20 years	$4,200
Time value of money	$1,980 ($6,180 − $4,200)
Total cost	$6,180
Cash value	$4,600
Net cost of insurance	$1,580 ($6,180 − $4,600)

Be sure to request interest-adjusted indexes from your agent; if he or she doesn't give them to you, look for another agent. As you have seen in the example, you can compare the costs among insurance companies by combining premium payments, dividends, cash value buildup, and present value analysis into an index number.

In brief, five factors affect the price a company charges for a life insurance policy: the company's cost of doing business, the returns on its investments, the mortality rate it expects among its policyholders, the features the policy contains, and competition among companies with comparable policies.

The prices of life insurance policies vary considerably among life insurance companies. Moreover, a particular company will not be equally competitive for all policies. One company might have a competitively priced policy for 24-year-olds but not for 35-year-olds.

interest-adjusted index A method of evaluating the cost of life insurance by taking into account the time value of money.

Ask your agent to give you interest-adjusted indexes. An **interest-adjusted index** is a method of evaluating the cost of life insurance by taking into account the time value of money. Highly complex mathematical calculations and formulas combine premium payments, dividends, cash-value buildup, and present value analysis into an index number that makes possible a fairly accurate cost comparison among insurance companies. The lower the index number, the lower the cost of the policy. The Financial Planning Calculations feature above shows how to use an interest-adjusted index to compare the costs of insurance.

OBTAINING A POLICY

A life insurance policy is issued after you submit an application for insurance and the insurance company accepts the application. The application usually has two parts. In the first part, you state your name, age, and gender, what type of policy you desire, how much insurance you want, your occupation, and so forth. In the second part, you give your medical history. While a medical examination is frequently required for ordinary policies, usually no examination is required for group insurance.

The company determines your insurability by means of the information on your application, the results of the medical examination, and the inspection report. Of all applicants, 98 percent are found to be insurable, though some may have to pay higher premiums because of an existing medical condition.

EXAMINING A POLICY

BEFORE THE PURCHASE   When you buy a life insurance policy, read every word of the contract and, if necessary, ask your agent for a point-by-point explanation of the language. Many insurance companies have rewritten their contracts to make them more understandable. These are legal documents, and you should be familiar with what they promise, even though they use technical terms. Above all, ensure that your policy stipulates that your insurance provider will allow you some time to examine the policy properly and will allow you to cancel it without cost within a certain time limit, usually 10 days.

AFTER THE PURCHASE   After you buy new life insurance, you have a 10-day "free-look" period during which you can change your mind. If you do so, the company will return your premium without penalty.

It's a good idea to give your beneficiaries and your lawyer a photocopy of your policy. Your beneficiaries should know where the policy is kept because to obtain the insurance proceeds, they will have to send it to the company upon your death, along with a copy of the death certificate.

CHOOSING SETTLEMENT OPTIONS

A well-planned life insurance program should cover the immediate expenses resulting from the death of the insured. However, that is only one of its purposes. In most instances, the primary purpose of life insurance is to protect dependants against a loss of income resulting from the premature death of the primary wage earner. Thus, selecting the appropriate settlement option is an important part of designing a life insurance program. The most common settlement options are lump-sum payment, limited instalment payment, life income option, and proceeds left with the company.

LUMP-SUM PAYMENT   The insurance company pays the face amount of the policy in one instalment to the beneficiary or to the estate of the insured. This form of settlement is the most widely used option.

LIMITED INSTALMENT PAYMENT   This option provides for payment of the life insurance proceeds in equal periodic instalments for a specified number of years after your death.

LIFE INCOME OPTION   Under the life income option, payments are made to the beneficiary for as long as she or he lives. The amount of each payment is based primarily on the gender and attained age of the beneficiary at the time of the insured's death.

PROCEEDS LEFT WITH THE COMPANY   The life insurance proceeds are left with the insurance company at a specified rate of interest. The company acts as trustee and pays the interest to the beneficiary. The guaranteed minimum interest rate paid on the proceeds varies among companies.

SWITCHING POLICIES

Think twice if your agent suggests that you replace the whole life or universal life insurance you already own. Consumers lose millions of dollars each year because they don't hold on to their cash life insurance policies long enough or because they purchase the wrong policies. Half of those who buy whole or universal life policies drop them within 10 years.

Before you give up this protection, make sure you are still insurable (check medical and any other qualification requirements). Remember that you are now older than you were when you purchased your policy, and a new policy will cost more. Moreover, the older policy may have provisions that are not duplicated in some of the new policies. This does not mean you should reject the idea of replacing your present policy; rather, you should proceed with caution. We recommend that you ask your agent or company for an opinion about the new proposal to get both sides of the argument.

CONCEPT CHECK 9–5

1. How do insurance companies price their products?
2. How do insurance companies determine your insurability?
3. What should you do in examining a policy before and after the purchase?
4. What are the four most common settlement options?
5. Should you switch life insurance policies?

HEALTH INSURANCE AND FINANCIAL PLANNING

LO6

Define *health insurance* and explain its importance in financial planning.

In Canada, most basic medical procedures are provided for under provincial government health-care plans. This publicly financed health-care system is usually referred to as Medicare (derived from "Medical Care Act"). You are assured of proper treatment that will not affect your financial situation to an overly large extent.

Because such items as semi-private or private hospital rooms, prescription drugs, eyeglasses, and dental care are either not covered or only partially covered by provincial insurance plans, you may want to supplement your health insurance through private medical insurance companies, such as Blue Cross, Green Shield Canada, or CoverMe [Canada].

When travelling outside Canada, it is important to remember that health-care costs outside the country can be very high and may not be fully covered by provincial health-care plans. In such cases, it is imperative to have adequate insurance protection.

WHAT IS HEALTH INSURANCE?

Health insurance, like other forms of insurance, reduces the financial burden of risk by dividing losses among many individuals. It works in the same way as life insurance, homeowner's insurance, and automobile insurance. You pay the insurance company a specified premium, and the company guarantees you some degree of financial protection. Like the premiums and benefits of other types of insurance, the premiums and benefits of health insurance are calculated based on average experience. To establish rates and benefits, insurance company actuaries rely on general statistics that tell them how many people in a certain population group will become ill and how much their illnesses will cost.

Medical expense insurance and disability income insurance, discussed in the next section, are an important part of your financial planning. To safeguard your family's economic security, both protections should be a part of your overall insurance program.

THE NEED FOR SUPPLEMENTAL HEALTH INSURANCE

While the bulk of financial risks related to medical costs are minimized by the various provincial health-care insurance programs, these programs do not provide coverage for *all* health-care needs. The provincial governments do not provide coverage for the following: private rooms in hospitals, private nursing care, cosmetic surgery, and physician testimony in court. If you should fall ill and require hospitalization, basic provincial coverage provides you with a room that holds three other beds besides your own. This means that—at a time when you may be feeling less than sociable—you will be required to make concessions to the noise and occasional indiscretions of your roommates and their visitors. If this proposition is unappealing, you will want to request a private or at the least a semi-private room. Financially, this is where a problem can arise.

If provincial medical coverage does not pay for the additional costs of a semi-private or private room, you will be asked to defray these costs yourself. For extended stays, this could translate to thousands of dollars. Similarly, once you leave the hospital, you will be required to assume either some or all of the costs for your medications. Again, this could prove costly.

Having thought out a few scenarios in which you might incur similar charges, you may choose to purchase supplemental medical coverage. Especially in cases where your personal wealth is small and might possibly be rapidly exhausted by the incidental costs of ill health, dental maintenance, and vision correction, buying supplemental medical coverage can be a sound financial planning decision.

GROUP HEALTH INSURANCE

Supplemental health insurance coverage is most commonly available under group insurance plans. Group plans comprise about 65 percent of all the health insurance issued by health and life insurance companies. Most of these plans are employer sponsored, and the employer often pays part or most of the cost. Group insurance will cover you and your immediate family. Group insurance seldom requires evidence that you are insurable if you enrol when you first become eligible for coverage.

The protection group insurance provides varies from plan to plan. The plan may not cover all of your health insurance needs; therefore, you will have to consider supplementing it with individual health insurance. Most universities offer health insurance coverage to full-time students. One of the leading providers for student health and dental plans in Canada is studentcare.net/works (aseq.com in Quebec).

Two factors to examine with group insurance are transferability and how the coverage is paid for. Many group plans do not allow for transfer of an insurance policy to the individual when an employee leaves the group. This is because underwriting for a group policy does not transfer well to individuals, but the consequence is that the departing employee loses both the benefits and coverage. He or she will need to replace the coverage privately and may find such factors as being older or having a degraded health status leading to heavy costs.

In the case of premium payments in a group plan, it matters who pays for what. Tax consequences vary, depending on payment source. For example, with disability insurance, if the premium is paid for by the employer, then the benefit received is taxed. If the employee makes the payments, then the benefit is not taxed. Be sure to discuss this with your plan administrator.

> *Did you know?*
>
> In 2012, Canadians paid $30.9 billion for health and disability insurance products.
>
> SOURCE: clhia.ca.

INDIVIDUAL HEALTH INSURANCE

Individual health insurance covers either one person or a family. If the kind of health insurance you need is not available through a group or if you need coverage in addition to the coverage a group provides, you should obtain an individual policy—a policy tailored to your particular needs—from the company of your choice. This requires careful shopping because coverage and cost vary from company to company.

Find out what your group insurance will pay for and what it won't. Make sure you have enough insurance, but don't waste money by over insuring.

SUPPLEMENTING YOUR GROUP INSURANCE

A sign that your group coverage needs supplementing would be its failure to provide benefits for the major portion of your medical care bills. For example, if your group policy pays only $50 per day toward a hospital room and the cost in your area is $100, you should look for an individual policy that covers most of the remaining amount. In supplementing your group health insurance, also consider the health insurance benefits your employer-sponsored plan provides for family members.

If you have any questions about your group plan, you should be able to get answers from your employer, union, or association. If you have questions about an individual policy, talk with your insurance company representative.

CONCEPT CHECK 9–6

1. What is health insurance, and what is its purpose?

DISABILITY INCOME INSURANCE

LO7

Recognize the need for disability income insurance.

disability income insurance Provides payments to replace income when an insured person is unable to work.

Because you feel healthy, you may overlook the very real need for disability income insurance. Disability income insurance protects your most valuable asset: your ability to earn income. Most people are more likely to lose their incomes due to disability than to death. The fact is that for all age groups, disability is more likely than death.

Disability income insurance provides regular cash earnings lost by individuals as the result of an accident or illness. Disability income insurance is probably the most neglected form of insurance protection. Many people who insure their houses, cars, and other property fail to insure their earning power. Disability can cause much greater financial problems than death. In fact, disability is often called "the living death." Disabled persons lose earning power while expenses continue to rise. They often face huge expenses for the medical treatment and special care their disabilities require.

A survey conducted by Statistics Canada in 2006 confirms that the disability rate gradually increases with age. Among children aged 0 to 14 the disability rate was 3.7 percent. Among adults aged 25 to 44 the rate was 8 percent, and among adults aged 75 and over the rate was more than 56 percent. Across Canada, 8.6 percent of people experience mild to moderate disabilities while another 5.7 percent of the population experience severe to very severe disabilities. The results also confirm that in general the disability rate is higher for women.*

DEFINITION OF DISABILITY

Disability has several definitions. The *own occupation* definition refers to the inability to perform the duties of your ordinary occupation, and full benefits are provided even if you return to work in some other capacity. Under a *regular occupation* definition, you are insured if you cannot perform the duties of your ordinary occupation, but benefits are reduced if you return to an alternative occupation. Under an *any occupation* definition, full benefits are paid only if you cannot perform the duties of any occupation for which your experience or education qualifies you. *Total disability* occurs if you are unable to work at all, while *residual or partial disability* benefits apply if you are able to work, but at a reduced workload.

---

*SOURCE: *Profile of Disability in Canada, 2006.* Statistics Canada, 2011, http://publications.gc.ca/collections/collection_2011/rhdcc-hrsdc/HS64-11-2010-eng.pdf.

Good disability plans pay when you are unable to work at your regular job; poor disability plans pay only when you are unable to work at any job. A good disability plan will also make partial disability payments when you return to work on a part-time basis.

DISABILITY INSURANCE TRADE-OFFS

Following are some important trade-offs you should consider in purchasing disability income insurance.

WAITING OR ELIMINATION PERIOD Benefits don't begin on the first day you become disabled. Usually, there is a waiting or elimination period of between 30 and 90 days. Some waiting periods may be as long as 180 days. Generally, disability income policies with longer waiting periods have lower premiums. If you have substantial savings to cover three to six months of expenses, the reduced premiums of a policy with a long waiting period may be attractive. But if you need every paycheque to cover your bills, you are probably better off paying the higher premium for a short waiting period. Short waiting periods, however, are very expensive.

DURATION OF BENEFITS The maximum time a disability income policy will pay benefits may be a few years, to age 65, or for life. You should seek a policy that pays benefits for life. If you became permanently disabled, it would be financially disastrous if your benefits ended at age 55 or 65.

Did you know?

In 2012, roughly 8 out of every 10 Canadian adults aged 15 and over with disabilities used or needed technical aids or specialized equipment to help them perform one or more daily activities. Over 3.8 million Canadians (13.7 percent of the population) aged 15 and over reported being limited in their daily activities due to disability.

SOURCE: http://www.statcan.gc.ca/pub/89-654-x/89-654-x2013002-eng.htm.

AMOUNT OF BENEFITS You should aim for a benefit amount that, when added to your other income, will equal 60 to 70 percent of your gross pay. Of course, the greater the benefits, the greater the cost.

ACCIDENT AND SICKNESS COVERAGE Consider both accident and sickness coverage. Some disability income policies will pay only for accidents, but you want to be insured for illness, too.

GUARANTEED RENEWABILITY Ask for non-cancellable and guaranteed renewable coverage. Either coverage will protect you against your insurance company dropping you if your health becomes poor. The premium for these coverages is higher, but the coverages are well worth the extra cost. Furthermore, look for a disability income policy that waives premium payments while you are disabled.

SOURCES OF DISABILITY INCOME

Before you buy disability income insurance, remember that you may already have some form of such insurance. This coverage may come to you through your employer, government benefits, or workers' compensation. In addition, if you have credit disability insurance, the insuring company will make credit card and other loan payments on your behalf if you should become disabled. Use Exhibit 9–7 to determine how much income you will have available if you become disabled.

EMPLOYER Many, but not all, employers provide disability income protection for their employees through group insurance plans. Your employer may have some form of wage

Exhibit 9–7

Disability Income
Worksheet

How much income will you have available if you become disabled?

	Monthly Amount	After Waiting:	For a Period of:
Sick leave or short-term disability	_____	_____	_____
Group long-term disability	_____	_____	_____
Employment Insurance	_____	_____	_____
Other government programs	_____	_____	_____
Individual disability insurance	_____	_____	_____
Credit disability insurance	_____	_____	_____
Other income:	_____	_____	_____
Savings	_____	_____	_____
Spouse's income	_____	_____	_____
Total monthly income while disabled:	$_____		

Did you know?

In 2014, the average Canada Pension Plan disability benefit was $896.87 per month.

SOURCE: http://www.servicecanada.gc.ca/eng/services/pensions/cpp/payments/.

continuation policy that lasts a few months or an employee group disability plan that provides long-term protection. In most cases, your employer will pay part or all of the cost of this plan.

PRIVATE   Most medical insurance policies offered by insurance companies include coverage for disability. The exact details of coverage depend on the cost of your premium, the company, and your policy details.

PUBLIC   The provincial governments have established various social programs to provide some insurance against disability. The protection available varies from one province to another, and eligibility requirements might include your having previously contributed to the program or your having suffered your injury either at work or during military service. The major social supports available to the disabled in Canada are outlined briefly below.

Employment Insurance   This is a federal program that provides short-term benefits to those who have previously contributed. While helpful for short-term health issues, its benefits are limited by the relatively short term in which payments are made.

Canada and Quebec Pension Plans   Both these plans include a disability pension for contributors with a severe or prolonged disability. The funds can also be used in compensation for dependants and survivors. Again, the payments obtained from these plans are inadequate to maintain a decent standard of living. The Canada Pension Plan provides a disability pension of up to a maximum of $1,236.31 monthly to age 65 (rate as of April 2014), after which a regular pension is paid. Furthermore, the rules and restrictions regarding these plans are strict, and many disabilities do not qualify, particularly if they are only partial.

Workers' Compensation   These are provincial plans that provide medical, financial, and rehabilitative assistance to workers who suffer disability as a result of accidents or illness related to their work.

Short-Term or Long-Term Welfare Provided at a municipal and provincial level, these programs are geared toward those with extremely limited alternative financial resources.

Whatever the form of social support you receive, it is almost certain to be insufficient for your needs. At best, these government programs should be viewed as a supplement to your disability insurance coverage, rather than as a replacement.

DETERMINING YOUR DISABILITY INCOME INSURANCE REQUIREMENTS

When considering the amount of benefits available, several separate calculations should be made, depending on different levels of disability (severe to mild) and based on how long your current resources, all mentioned above (e.g., employer-provided sick leave, workers' compensation, non-salary income from investments) would last in the event that a disability occurred. If the sum of your disability benefits approaches your after-tax income, you can safely assume that should disability strike, you'll be in good shape to pay your day-to-day bills while recuperating.

You should know how long you would have to wait before the benefits begin (the waiting or elimination period) and how long they would be paid (the benefit period).

What if your disability benefits are not sufficient to support your family? In that case, you may want to consider buying disability income insurance to make up the difference.

Don't expect to insure yourself for your full salary. Most insurers limit benefits from all sources to no more than 70 to 80 percent of your take-home pay. For example, if you earn $800 a week, you could be eligible for disability insurance of about $560 to $640 a week. You will not need $800 because while you are disabled, your work-related expenses will be eliminated and your taxes will be far lower or may be even zero.

CRITICAL ILLNESS INSURANCE

Critical illness insurance is gaining recognition in Canada as a valuable insurance tool. Many people are coming to realize that the probability of being struck by a critical illness at some point is very high. As a result, the costs of insurance coverage to provide for the eventuality become much more viable.

Critical illness insurance pays a tax-free lump sum 30 days after you are diagnosed with such a serious illness or condition as cancer, heart disease, stroke, multiple sclerosis, blindness, organ transplant, kidney failure, and paralysis, but not usually HIV/AIDS. There are also specialty programs, such as one product dealing specifically with women's cancers.

One in two men and one in three women will be struck by cancer, heart attack, or stroke at some point in their lives. For the most part, that will engender potentially devastating financial costs along with the emotional and physical trauma.

With all the advancements in the field of medicine, many critical illnesses are not only treatable but also curable; however, the costs can be extremely high. Critical illness insurance helps pay for those costs. The money can also be used to pay off any other debts, such as your mortgage, or allow you to take time off from work during recovery without putting you in financial distress. Critical illness insurance is offered to those between the ages of 18 and 65. It can be bought as a stand-alone policy or bundled with another life insurance policy. Critical illness insurance offers different options that can be added on. One example is a waiver of premium—in the event of a disability resulting in an insufficient amount of income to pay for your premium, you are protected and will not lose your policy. Finally, in the unfortunate event of death, all premiums are refunded to the beneficiaries.

It is important to understand that while life insurance pays out when you die, critical illness does so while you are alive. It is a product you buy to protect yourself and your dependants, and it removes finances from the long list of concerns associated with critical illness.

Disability Income
Policy Checklist

Every disability income policy may have different features. The following checklist will help you compare policies you may be considering:

	Policy A	Policy B
1. How is disability defined?		
Inability to perform your own job?	____	____
Inability to perform any job?	____	____
2. Does the policy cover		
Accident?	____	____
Illness?	____	____
3. Are benefits available		
For total disability?	____	____
For partial disability?	____	____
Only after total disability?	____	____
Without a prior period of total disability?	____	____
4. Are full benefits paid, whether or not you are able to work, for loss of		
Sight?	____	____
Speech?	____	____
Hearing?	____	____
Use of limbs?	____	____

	Policy A	Policy B
5. What percentage of your income will the maximum benefit replace?	____	____
6. Is the policy noncancellable, guaranteed renewable, or conditionally renewable?	____	____
7. How long must you be disabled before premiums are waived?	____	____
8. Is there an option to buy additional coverage, without evidence of insurability, at a later date?	____	____
9. Does the policy offer an inflation adjustment feature?	____	____
If so, what is the rate of increase?	____	____
How often is it applied?	____	____
For how long?	____	____

	Policy A		Policy B	
	With Inflation Feature	**Without Inflation Feature**	**With Inflation Feature**	**Without Inflation Feature**
10. What does the policy cost?				
For a waiting period of ____ days and (30–180)	_____	_____	_____	_____
For a benefit period of ____? 1 yr.–lifetime	_____	_____	_____	_____
Total	_____	_____	_____	_____

SOURCE: Health Insurance Association of America, Washington DC.

CONCEPT CHECK 9–7

1. What is disability income insurance?
2. What are the three main sources of disability income?
3. How can you determine the amount of disability income insurance you need?

SUPPLEMENTAL HEALTH INSURANCE

After duly considering the health and disability coverage currently available to you from the government, your employer, and other policies, you may decide to seek further coverage. You can purchase insurance from a number of sources. You should consider a number of factors, including the cost of premiums, the precise coverage, and the amount of deductible that you may be required to pay on your claims. As with the auto insurance policies discussed in the previous chapter, the amount you agree to pay as a deductible on claims affects the cost of your premiums. The greater your deductible, the lower the cost of your premiums.

LO8
Understand the value of supplemental health insurance.

While claim limits, deductibles, premiums, and other details vary according to your specific policy, a basic supplemental health insurance plan should cover 40 to 80 percent of the following health-care needs: dental maintenance, vision care, health-care services not covered by your provincial plan, health coverage during travel, and accidental death or dismemberment.

DENTAL EXPENSE INSURANCE

Dental expense insurance provides reimbursement for the expenses of dental services and supplies and encourages preventive dental care. The coverage normally provides or partially provides for oral examinations (including X-rays and cleanings), fillings, extractions, inlays, bridgework, and dentures, as well as oral surgery, root canal therapy, and orthodontics.

VISION CARE INSURANCE

A recent development in health insurance coverage is *vision care insurance*. An increasing number of insurance companies and pre-payment plans offer this insurance, usually to groups.

Vision and eye health problems are prevalent chronic health-care concerns. Good vision care insurance should cover diagnosing and treating eye diseases (e.g., glaucoma), periodic eye examinations, eyeglasses, contact lenses, and eye surgery.

In considering vision and dental coverages, you should analyze their costs and benefits. Sometimes, these coverages cost more than they are worth.

HEALTH SERVICES INSURANCE

A basic supplemental health insurance plan should provide coverage for the following health-care services: prescription drugs not covered by your provincial plan; semi-private or private hospital accommodation; home care and nursing; prosthetic appliances; wheelchairs and other durable equipment; and specific paramedic or medical services from physiotherapists, chiropractors, podiatrists, psychologists, and other health professionals that are not covered by your government plan.

TRAVEL INSURANCE

Under most supplemental plans, hospital and medical expenses incurred outside Canada are covered for up to $1 million for trips lasting a maximum of 8 to 10 days. It is important to familiarize yourself with the extent of coverage provided by your supplemental health insurance plan. In some cases, you may have to pay first and then send in your claim. An emergency medical problem in the United States could set you back thousands of dollars and you may not be able to afford to pay for your medical expenses up front.

To fill the gaps in your supplemental plan or for longer trips, you may want to consider purchasing travel insurance. A travel insurance plan provides medical coverage and offers additional benefits such as baggage and personal effects insurance, flight and travel accident insurance, and trip interruption/after-departure insurance.

Advice from a Pro

Long-Term Care Insurance

Wendy Miller, head of benefits research at Merck & Company, laments that when offered LTC policies, Merck employees have been slow to purchase them. The company has offered LTC coverage since 1991, but fewer than 10 percent of its 18,500 eligible employees have signed on. "People think of it as old-age insurance," says Miller. "They tend to be over insured in life insurance, yet don't have key elements of income protection, such as long-term care."

The best LTC policies cover both home care and nursing-home stays. Policies offer a range of benefits, from $50 per day for a year or $200 per day for a lifetime. You may need an inflation protection option, especially if you buy when you are young.

long-term care (LTC)
Provides day-in, day-out care for long-term illness or disability.

ACCIDENTAL DEATH OR DISMEMBERMENT INSURANCE

Adults under 65 years of age are insured for up to $25,000 for accidental death or dismemberment. Adults over 65 and children have coverage up to $10,000 for death or dismemberment.

LONG-TERM CARE INSURANCE

Long-term care is day-in, day-out assistance that you might need if you ever have an illness or a disability that lasts a long time and leaves you unable to care for yourself. You may or may not need lengthy care in a nursing home, but you may need help at home with daily activities, such as dressing, bathing, and doing household chores. While in the United States there is a large and growing market for long-term care (LTC) insurance, Canadian consumers are generally unaware such insurance even exists.

Despite this, over the next 5 to 10 years it is expected that the giant baby boom generation will gravitate to LTC insurance as it faces the reality that its parents are coming into the long-term care years. For the moment, however, only a small percentage of the elderly are in assisted-living or LTC programs. The rest live by themselves or are supported by their families.

The families of people who receive LTC are well aware of the emotional cost of providing such care themselves and of the financial cost of hiring professionals. The insurance is not inexpensive, but should it prove necessary it is preferable to wiping out a family's assets or those of a future estate.

Long-term care can be expensive. Private Canadian nursing homes can cost from $3,000 to $6,000 a month, and even at $100 a day the cumulative costs of long-term care can quickly eat into savings. Government nursing homes can cost less but have long waiting lists. Even with government subsidies, ward coverage in Ontario can cost $1,700 a month. Home care may cost between $35 and $48 an hour for a private registered nurse, or $70 an hour for an occupational therapist or physiotherapist. Less skilled personal care to help with eating or light housework may cost $15 an hour. If you depend on government programs, they may provide only 60 hours a month, or two hours a day, for home care.

Clearly, anticipating the costs of long-term care by considering insurance is sound financial planning, but there are various factors to consider. The cost of LTC insurance itself can be prohibitive, depending on your age and policy options.

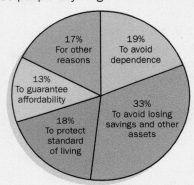

Did you know?

Why do people buy long-term-care insurance?

- 17% For other reasons
- 19% To avoid dependence
- 13% To guarantee affordability
- 33% To avoid losing savings and other assets
- 18% To protect standard of living

SOURCE: Based on data obtained from "Who Buys Long-Term Care Insurance? A 20-Year Study of Buyers and Non-Buyers 1990–2010," American Health Insurance Plans, April 2012, https://www.ahip.org/WhoBuysLTCInsurance2010-2011/.

The annual premium for LTC policies can range depending on your age and the choices you make. The older you are when you enrol, the higher your annual premium. Typically, individual insurance plans are sold to the 50-to-80 age group, pay benefits for a maximum of two to six years, and carry a dollar limit on the total benefits they will pay.

MAJOR PROVISIONS IN A HEALTH INSURANCE POLICY

An insurance company usually allows you a minimum of 10 days to review your health insurance policy, so be sure to check the major provisions that affect your coverage. All health insurance policies have certain provisions in common. Be sure you understand what your policy covers. Even the most comprehensive policy may be of little value if a provision in small print limits or denies benefits.

ELIGIBILITY   The eligibility provision defines who is entitled to benefits under the policy. Age, marital status, and dependency requirements are usually specified in this provision. For example, foster children usually are not automatically covered under the family contract, but stepchildren may be. Check with your insurance company to be sure.

ASSIGNED BENEFITS   When you assign benefits, you sign a paper allowing your insurance company to make payments to your hospital or doctor. Otherwise, the payments will be made to you when you turn in your bills and claim forms to the company.

INTERNAL LIMITS   A policy with internal limits will pay only a fixed amount for your hospital room no matter what the actual rate is. For example, if your policy has an internal limit of $200 per hospital day and you are in a $300-a-day hospital room, you will have to pay the difference.

CO-PAYMENT   Co-payment is a type of cost sharing. Most major medical plans define co-payment as the amount the patient must pay for medical services after the deductible has been met. You pay a flat dollar amount each time you receive a covered medical service. Co-payments for prescriptions are common. The amount of co-payment does not vary with the cost of service.

co-payment A provision under which the insured pays a flat dollar amount each time a covered medical service is received after the deductible has been met.

BENEFIT LIMITS   The benefit limits provision defines the maximum benefits possible, in terms of either a dollar amount or a number of days in the hospital. Many policies today have benefit limits.

EXCLUSIONS AND LIMITATIONS   The exclusions and limitations provision specifies the conditions or circumstances for which the policy does not provide benefits. For example, the policy may exclude coverage for pre-existing conditions or cosmetic surgery.

COORDINATION OF BENEFITS   As discussed earlier, the coordination of benefits provision prevents you from collecting benefits from two or more group policies that would in total exceed the actual charges. Under this provision, the benefits from your own and your spouse's policies are coordinated to allow up to 100 percent payment of your covered charges.

GUARANTEED RENEWABLE   With this policy provision, the insurance company cannot cancel a policy unless you fail to pay premiums when due. Also, it cannot raise premiums unless a rate increase occurs for all policyholders in that group.

CANCELLATION AND TERMINATION   This provision explains the circumstances under which the insurance company can terminate your health insurance policy. It also explains your right to convert a group contract into an individual contract.

HEALTH INSURANCE TRADE-OFFS

The benefits of health insurance policies differ, and the differences can have a significant impact on your premiums. Consider the following trade-offs:

REIMBURSEMENT VERSUS INDEMNITY   A reimbursement policy provides benefits based on the actual expenses you incur. An indemnity policy provides specified benefits, regardless of whether the actual expenses are greater or less than the benefits.

INTERNAL LIMITS VERSUS AGGREGATE LIMITS   A policy with internal limits stipulates maximum benefits for specific expenses, such as the maximum reimbursement for daily hospital room and board. Other policies may limit only the total amount of coverage, such as $1 million major expense benefits, or may have no limits.

DEDUCTIBLES AND CO-INSURANCE   The cost of a health insurance policy can be greatly affected by the size of the deductible (the amount you must pay toward medical expenses before the insurance company pays), the degree of co-insurance, and the share of medical expenses you must pay (e.g., 20 percent).

OUT-OF-POCKET LIMIT   A policy that limits the total of the co-insurance and deductibles you must pay (e.g., $2,000) limits or eliminates your financial risk, but it also increases the premium.

HEALTH-CARE EXPENDITURES IN CANADA

Canadians have been spending more on health care year after year since 1975 (see Exhibit 9–8). This steady increase has taken health-care expenditures from $12.2 billion in 1975 to $200.1 billion in 2011, more than doubling the per capita spending from 1975 to 2011, and in 2013, spending is forecasted to reach $211 billion, or $5,988 per person. Most of the costs increase has been covered by public funds. Total spending in 2011 was equivalent to 11.4 percent of the gross domestic product (GDP), and in 2013 was forecasted to be 11.2 percent of the GDP. These numbers were slightly above the average for Organisation for Economic Co-operation and Development (OECD)

Exhibit 9–8   Health Expenditure by Source of Finance, Canada, 1975–2013

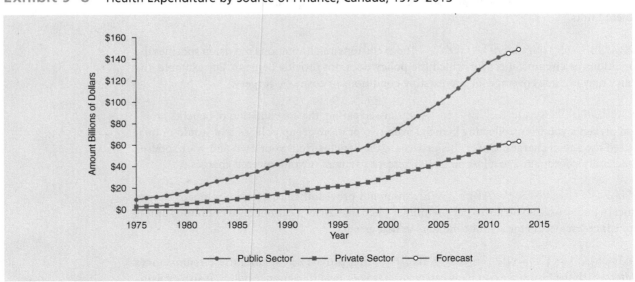

SOURCE: National Health Expenditure Database, Canadian Institute for Health Information.

countries, and below the $8,508 spent per capita on health care in the United States in 2011. Health expenditures are forecasted to be at 19 percent by 2031 at the rate they are increasing, stated David Dodge, former Governor of the Bank of Canada, and former central bank economist Richard Dion. This increase is due mainly to new technologies, an aging population, and rising demand and prices for health-related goods and services.

HEALTH INFORMATION ONLINE

Recent studies indicate that consumers are seeking information on health and health care online to supplement traditional medical counsel. Many legitimate providers of reliable health and medical information, including Health Canada, offer brochures and in-depth information on specific topics at their Web sites.

CONCEPT CHECK 9–8

1. What are several types of health insurance coverage available under group and individual policies?
2. What are the major provisions of a health insurance policy?
3. How do you decide which coverage to choose?
4. How can you analyze the costs and benefits of your health insurance policy?

SUMMARY OF LEARNING OBJECTIVES

LO1 Define *life insurance* and describe its purpose and principle.

Life insurance is a contract between an insurance company and a policyholder under which the company agrees to pay a specified sum to a beneficiary upon the insured's death. Most people buy life insurance to protect someone who depends on them from financial loss caused by their death. Fundamental to the life insurance principle is the predictable mortality experience of a large group of individuals.

LO2 Determine your life insurance needs.

In determining your life insurance needs, you must first determine your insurance objectives and then use the income replacement method or the family need method to calculate the amount of insurance needed. The family need method is recommended. You should consider a number of factors before you buy insurance, including your present and future sources of income, other savings and income protection, group life insurance, group annuities (or other pension benefits), and government benefits.

LO3 Distinguish between the two types of life insurance policies and analyze various types of life insurance.

The two types of life insurance policies are term life and permanent life. In general, term insurance provides protection against a specified financial risk for a finite period of time, often 10 or 20 years. Permanent life insurance is purchased to cover lifelong needs, such as funeral expenses and supplementing a survivor's income. Many variations of these two types of life insurance policies are available. Term life insurance is available with a renewability option, a conversion option, or a decreasing option. Permanent life insurance is available in the following forms: whole life, universal life, and variable insurance. There are many other options; therefore, you should check with your insurance company to determine which type offers the best policy for your particular needs at the lowest price.

As with other forms of insurance, price should not be your only consideration in choosing a life insurance policy. You should also consider the financial stability, reliability, and service the insurance company provides.

LO4 Select important provisions in life insurance contracts.

The naming of the beneficiary, the grace period, policy reinstatement, the non-forfeiture clause, the incontestability clause, the suicide clause, automatic premium loans, the misstatement of age provision, and the policy loan provision are important provisions in most life insurance policies. Common riders in life insurance policies are the waiver of premium disability benefit, the accidental death benefit, the guaranteed insurability option, critical illness benefits, and the joint, last to die benefit.

LO5 **Create a plan to buy life insurance.**

Before buying life insurance, consider your present and future sources of income, group life insurance, group annuities (or other pension benefits), and government benefits. Then compare the costs of several life insurance policies. Examine your policy before and after the purchase, and choose appropriate settlement options. The most common settlement options are lump-sum payment, limited instalment payment, life income option, and proceeds left with the company. Online services provide a wealth of information about all topics related to life insurance.

LO6 **Define** *health insurance* **and explain its importance in financial planning.**

Health insurance is protection that provides payment of benefits for a covered sickness or injury. Disability income insurance protects a person's most valuable asset: the ability to earn income. Critical illness insurance protects against the most common critical illnesses.

Health insurance, critical illness, and disability income insurance are three protections against economic losses due to illness, accident, or disability. These should be a part of your overall insurance program to safeguard your family's economic security.

Disability can cause even greater financial problems than death. In fact, disability is often called "the living death." Disabled persons lose their earning power while continuing to incur normal expenses. In addition, they often face huge expenses for the medical treatment and special care their disabilities require.

LO7 **Recognize the need for disability income insurance.**

Disability income insurance provides regular cash income lost by employees as the result of an accident or illness. Sources of disability income insurance include the employer, private policies, and government benefits and unions.

LO8 **Understand the value of supplemental health insurance.**

Supplemental health insurance is coverage that you can purchase in addition to the coverage available to you from the government, your employer, and other policies. Types of supplemental health insurance include dental expense insurance, vision care insurance, and long-term care insurance.

KEY TERMS

beneficiary 268	**incontestability clause** 269	**rider** 270
cash value 264	**interest-adjusted index** 272	**suicide clause** 269
co-payment 283	**level premiums** 264	**term insurance** 262
disability income insurance 276	**long-term care (LTC)** 282	**universal life** 266
double indemnity 270	**non-forfeiture clause** 268	**whole life policy** 264

FINANCIAL PLANNING PROBLEMS

McGraw Hill connect™ Practise and learn online with Connect.

1. *Illustrating the Principle of Life Insurance.* A group of 100,000 males, age 30, wish to contribute each year an amount to a common fund sufficient to pay $1,000 to the dependants of each group member who dies during the year. Use the mortality table in Exhibit 9–1 to determine the following: LO1
   a. How many members of the group can be expected to die during the year?
   b. What amount must each of the 100,000 members contribute at the beginning of the year to provide $1,000 for the dependants of those who die before the end of the year?

2. *Calculating the Amount of Life Insurance Needed Using the Income Replacement Method.* You are the wage earner in a "typical family," with $30,000 gross annual income. Use the income replacement method to determine how much life insurance you should carry. LO2

3. *Comparing the Methods of Determining Life Insurance Requirements.* Analyze the two methods of determining life insurance requirements. Which method is best, and why? LO2

4. *Estimating Life Insurance Needs Using the Family Need Method.* You and your spouse are in good health and have reasonably secure careers. You make about $35,000 annually and have opted for life insurance coverage of three times your salary through your employer. With your spouse's income, you are able to absorb ongoing living costs of $45,000 a year. You own a home with an $80,000 mortgage. Other debts include a $10,000 car loan, $5,000 student loan, and $3,000 charged to credit cards. In the event of your death, you wish to leave your family debt-free. One of your most important financial goals involves building an education fund of $50,000 to cover the cost of a three-year university program for your two-year-old child. To date, you have accumulated $15,000 toward this goal. Should you die, your beneficiaries would receive a $2,500 lump sum payment from the Canada Pension Plan and $10,000 from your corporate pension plan. Your other financial assets are as follows:

Bank accounts	$2,100
Term deposits (3 months)	3,000
Canada Savings Bonds	1,000
Stock investment account	2,500

Use the family need method to determine your life insurance needs. LO2

5. *Comparing the Costs of Life Insurance and Various Provisions in a Life Insurance Policy.* Obtain premium rates for $25,000 whole life, universal life, and term life policies from local insurance agents. Compare the costs and provisions of these policies. LO3

6. *Calculating Your Life Insurance Needs.* Use Exhibit 9–2 to calculate your life insurance needs. LO3

7. *Calculating the Amount of Disability Benefits.* Georgia Braxton, a widow, has take-home pay of $600 a week. Her disability insurance coverage replaces 70 percent of her earnings after a four-week waiting period. However, depending on who is making the premium payments, the replacement earnings may be taxable. What amount would she receive in disability benefits if an illness kept Georgia off work for 16 weeks? LO7

FINANCIAL PLANNING ACTIVITIES

1. *Assessing the Need for Life Insurance.* Interview relatives and friends to determine why they purchased life insurance. Prepare an essay summarizing your findings. LO1

2. *Comparing Premiums for Life Insurance Policies.* Choose one stock company and one mutual life insurance company. Obtain and compare premiums for:
   a. Term life insurance for $50,000.
   b. Whole life insurance for $50,000.
   c. Universal life insurance for $50,000.

   Prepare a summary table indicating which policy you would consider and why. LO3

3. *Reviewing an Employer's Health Benefit Package.* List the benefits included in your employee benefit package, such as health insurance, disability income insurance, and life insurance. Discuss the importance of such a benefit package to the consumer. LO6

4. *Comparing Major Provisions in a Health-Care Insurance Policy.* Obtain sample health insurance policies from insurance agents or brokers, and analyze the policies for definitions, coverages, exclusions, limitations on coverage, and amounts of coverage. In what ways are the policies similar? In what ways do they differ? LO7

CREATING A FINANCIAL PLAN

Comparing Health Insurance Plans

Changing programs and regulations influence your ability to be properly covered for health care and disability insurance coverage. Awareness of policy types, coverages, and limitations will help you plan this phase of your financial plan.

Web Sites for Life Insurance

- Find out more about the insurance industry by visiting the Canadian Life & Health Insurance Association at **clhia.ca.**

- Find out about the protection afforded to Canadian insurance product buyers at **assuris.ca**, the site for Assuris.

- Robert Barney has written a number of articles strongly in favour of term insurance over whole life and universal life insurance for *Canadian MoneySaver* magazine. You can view these articles as well as contributions by other authors at **canadianmoneysaver.ca.**

Web Sites for Health and Disability Insurance

- Visit the Health Canada site at **hc-sc.gc.ca/hcs-sss** to learn more about Medicare and the Canada Health Act.

- The Life and Health Insurance Foundation for Education (LIFE), at **lifehappens.org**, is an American non-profit organization that provides information and education on life, health, and disability insurance. They also have a "disability needs" calculator to help you establish how much disability insurance you may need. Much of the information is applicable to Canada.

- You can visit the Blue Cross's Canadian Web site at **bluecross.ca** to find out about the health and disability insurance products it offers.

(Note: Addresses and content of Web sites change, and new sites are created daily. Use search engines to update and locate Web sites for your current financial planning needs.)

Short-Term Financial Planning Activities

1. Analyze current health insurance coverage in relation to family and household needs.

2. Compare the cost of health insurance programs available from various sources.

Long-Term Financial Planning Activities

1. Develop a plan for reducing health care and disability insurance costs.

LIFE SITUATION CASE

How Much Is Enough?

Joanne and Glenn Kitsos recently had their second child and decided to change their life insurance. "We've got two kids now, and we have to start thinking about the future." Joanne said.

The Kitsos' and other new parents are among the people experts say ought to have life insurance. Anyone who has someone financially dependent on them or anyone whose death would cause someone to lose money should be insured.

"Term life insurance is extraordinarily cheap when people are in their 20s and 30s, so people with children should purchase a sufficient amount," says Elliot S. Lipson, a financial planner. "All too often, people buy expensive policies that offer savings or investment components but lack a basic benefit that is large enough to provide for their needs."

The amount you need isn't easy to determine because the total can be as little as five times and as much as 10 times your annual salary.

Jim Hunt, consultant to a major insurance group, says the total need for an average couple with two young children is close to six to eight times their salary. For example, the Kitsos' combined income is $100,000, so they probably need a minimum of $600,000 in insurance and maybe a little more if they have no group life insurance at work.

Here are a few questions to ask when figuring how much life insurance you need:

- How much income will your dependants need every year if you die?

- How much income will your dependants have from other sources, such as investments, pensions, or savings, if you die?

- How much income will your dependants have access to from sources such as your spouse's salary or government benefits?

Once you've come up with a total, you have to decide whether you want term, whole life, or some hybrid variation.

Your goal, Hunt says, is to buy as much insurance as you need. But because of the costs of whole life insurance, that often means term. While whole life costs more in the early years, it guarantees that you will pay the same premium 10, 15, or even 20 years down the road.

The Kitsos' started out with whole life insurance, but they decided to switch to term insurance that will last until their kids graduate from university. They want to have enough insurance to cover their funeral costs and the cost of their children's post-secondary educations. But rather than using their insurance as an investment, they plan to invest more in mutual funds.

Questions

1. What is the advantage of buying life insurance when you are younger, and what is a good reason for having it?

2. What is the total coverage needed for an average couple with two children and a combined income of $45,000?

3. What is one advantage of whole life insurance?

4. Is term insurance the right choice for the Kitsos'? Why, or why not?

SOURCES: Earl C. Gottschalk Jr., "Avoiding the Big Mistakes along Life's Path," *The Wall Street Journal*, May 27, 1997, p. C1; Candy McCampbell, "How Much Insurance to Carry Is a Question Not Easily Answered," *Gannett News Service*, July 9, 1997, p. S12.

CONTINUOUS CASE FOR PART 3

MANAGING RISKS FOR EFFECTIVE FINANCIAL PLANNING

Life Situation
Pamela, 36; Isaac, 38; three children, ages 9, 7, and 4

Financial Goals

- Evaluate property and liability insurance needs
- Assess the need for disability insurance
- Determine additional life insurance needs

Financial Data

Monthly income	$ 4,300
Living expenses	4,075
Assets	150,850
Liabilities	99,520

Both Pamela and Isaac Mortimer are comfortable. They now have three children, are happy with their home, and are more financially secure than they were six years ago. In fact, everything seems to be right on track. Yet the Mortimers still have financial needs they must address. Several changes have affected their financial planning:

- The value of their home has increased due to inflation and home improvements.
- They have purchased a used car to meet additional transportation needs.

- Isaac's current employer offers him only 30 days of sick leave.
- Pamela's life insurance policy is for only $2,000. Isaac has life insurance coverage equal to approximately eight times his annual salary.

Questions

1. How should the Mortimers determine whether they have enough insurance coverage for their home?

2. What factors should the Mortimers consider in deciding whether to purchase collision insurance coverage for their used car?

3. When considering disability income insurance, what length of waiting period and duration of benefits should the Mortimers consider?

4. Do you think Pamela and Isaac Mortimer have enough life insurance? If not, what changes would you recommend? Explain your answer.

part 4

Investing Your Financial Resources

The Pillaging of America: The Great Recession

Following the news of the U.S. Government passing the US$700 billion Bailout Bill in 2008, the financial markets headed into the doldrums, there were threats of bank runs across the globe, and liabilities in the trillions were the focus for every government, trumping all other issues. Those conditions prove that personal financial planning and management are more important than ever. Before moving into a discussion of investing your financial resources, we comment on the economic conditions at play in the world and how we arrived here.

CONSUMERS: BORROWING OUR WAY INTO DEBT

Historically, periods of technological revolution and tremendous growth are ideal conditions for speculative excess. In a deregulated environment—like the one existing for the past decade—financial markets are rife with speculation, imprudent practices are condoned, and all players, including governments, become habitual users of leverage.

The overvaluations during the dot-com bubble were a precursor to the economic crisis that lead to the Great Recession. Following the dramatic crash of equities in 2000, the bailout then took the form of cheap credit—especially to households investing in real estate. Believing that a house is a *real* and not a *paper* asset, households across the U.S. saw what they thought were genuine price increases in their homes and a real increase in their standards of living. Then, as house prices increased and access to credit became easier, households were encouraged to purchase homes worth more than their family income would prudently allow. They were assured that higher home prices were the best insurance for more debt and never considered—let alone prepared for—the consequences of a downturn in prices.

BUSINESS: PHANTASMIC GROWTH

Meanwhile, CEOs and officers of public corporations were indebting their companies to create growth from cheap money and extracting millions in salary, bonuses, options, and complex remuneration packages. Chapters 11, 12, and 13 discuss the various instruments public corporations offer to investors; look to these chapters to explain each investment type and the implications of downside risk.

The Enron scandal in the U.S. (discussed on page 345 of Chapter 11) and the Nortel fiasco in Canada were signs of systematic failures in governance in a climate of market illusions. Growth in reported profits was not all that real

but the debt obligations were very real. The basic principles of prudent valuation were ignored as oversight mechanisms evaporated. Meanwhile the financial industry grew to become the most leveraged in history.

For institutional investors who manage our pensions, insurance, and savings, a generation of new investment vehicles flooded the market. The products were essentially a complex array of repackaged "asset-backed" securities, approved by reputable rating agencies; they are now worthless because their prices were derived from overvalued assets.

GOING FORWARD: ASKING THE TOUGH QUESTIONS

If history repeats itself, we can foresee some immediate outcomes: fingers will be pointed and some of the actors involved will be vilified. There will be a call for more regulation, oversight, and transparency. But will the system find ways to self-correct? To do so will mean answering some of these tough questions: Will the pendulum swing away from a culture of "growth at all costs"? Will accounting practices recognize off-balance sheet liabilities? Will investors be able to identify organizational structures that conceal trails of unlimited leverage? Will the marketplace have access to reliable information to stress-test firms that are likely candidates for duress? Will management practices change?

But who will provide the answers? The principal players—governments, their central banks, their financial institutions, and some of the major corporations and their officers—created and benefited from this sick system and now are being asked to heal it. Ordinary taxpayers also are being asked to pay even as their distrust of the people who appear to be complicit in this economic downturn grows. There is a familiarity to these stories, reminiscent of the robber barons of the past. They were the models for those who began the pillaging of America in this century.

But the toughest question to answer is this: Will consumers' attitudes towards savings and spending change, especially if they are enticed again to participate in borrowing more to spend their way out of trouble? Under these circumstances, personal financial management is more important than ever before. The next few chapters, 10 to 13, will provide some information and tools to help you better understand the current economic situation and guide you in your own personal financial management.

SOURCE: Copyright October 8, 2008, Arshad Ahmad & Paul Dontigny Jr. Used with permission.

Fundamentals of Investing

THE MONEYSENSE PERSONAL FINANCE WEB SITE: HELP YOU CAN USE

Need some help establishing an investment program? Why not go to the Internet? That's what Jane and Brian Seward did.

One afternoon, Jane was helping one of the kids with a homework assignment to determine the effect of compounding on savings. After looking at a number of different sites, they found the MoneySense personal finance Web site. As they wandered around through the site, they soon forgot about the assignment. The site, beyond offering current rates and various types of calculators, was a gold mine of personal finance information. There were no "get rich quick" schemes, but instead some solid financial advice and analysis that would help the Seward family with their finances.

Today, more and more Canadians are using the Internet to help plan their financial future, evaluate investment alternatives, and monitor the value of their investments.

Although just one of many, the MoneySense site (money-sense.ca) is an excellent choice not only for beginning investors like Jane and Brian but also for more experienced investors. Within the site, the Sewards found information on credit, investing, tax planning, home mortgages, and a number of other important topics.

After reading the material on the site, both Jane and Brian decided it was time to take charge of their family's finances. They began by paying off some high-interest credit card bills and saving some money they could use for emergencies. Then, they started saving the money needed to finance an investment program. During this time, they also continued to learn. They studied additional material in the MoneySense site, visited other financial planning Web sites, and began to read personal finance magazines such as *MoneySaver*. They even began tracking some potential stock and mutual fund investments in anticipation of when they could purchase their first investments. According to Brian, their financial planning was not only rewarding but also fun. For the first time since they got married, they were getting their financial affairs in order.

Keep in mind that although the Internet is a useful tool when trying to create an investment program for yourself, consulting a professional before you go ahead with your chosen route is important and is highly recommended for sound financial decision making.

QUESTIONS

1. How important is an investment program for financial planning?
2. Jane and Brian Seward began their search for investment information by examining the MoneySense Web site. If you were seeking help to establish an investment program, where would you obtain the needed information?

PREPARING FOR AN INVESTMENT PROGRAM

LO1

Explain why you should establish an investment program.

There's an old saying, "I've been rich and I've been poor, but believe me, rich is better." While being rich doesn't guarantee happiness, the accumulation of money does provide financial security and is a worthy goal. Jane and Brian Seward, the couple in the opening case, began their financial planning and investment program by examining the material in the Moneysense Web site. Why not take a look and see the type of financial and investment information that it offers? View the material that the Sewards used to create their financial plan. Visit the Moneysense Web site, where you will find links to information on investments, stocks, and money management.

By studying the material contained in the site and following the basic investment principles presented in this chapter, along with the information on stocks, bonds, mutual funds, real estate, and other investments in the remaining chapters in Part 4, you can create an investment plan that is custom-made for you.

The decision to establish an investment plan is an important first step to accomplishing your long-term financial goals. Like other decisions, the decision to start an investment plan is one you must make for yourself. No one is going to make you save the money you need to fund an investment plan. These things won't be done unless you want to do them. In fact, the *specific* goals you want to accomplish must be the driving force behind your investment plan.

ESTABLISHING INVESTMENT GOALS

Some people say they want to be rich. Others say they want to be financially secure. But it takes more than just wishing. While it would be nice if you could magically accumulate wealth, it takes careful planning and discipline to achieve the financial freedom you desire. For most people, the first step is establishing investment goals. Without investment goals, you cannot know what you want to accomplish.

To be useful, investment goals must be specific and measurable. They must be tailored to your particular financial needs. Some financial planners suggest that investment goals be stated in terms of money. For example, "By December 31, 2028, I will have total assets of $600,000." Other financial planners believe investors are more motivated to work toward goals that are stated in terms of the particular things they desire; "By January 1, 2028, I will have accumulated enough money to purchase a second home in the mountains." The following questions will help you establish valid investment goals:

1. What will you use the money for?
2. How much money do you need to satisfy your investment goals?

3. How will you obtain the money?
4. How long will it take you to obtain the money?
5. How much risk are you willing to assume in an investment program?
6. What possible economic or personal conditions could alter your investment goals?
7. Considering your economic circumstances, are your investment goals reasonable?
8. Are you willing to make the sacrifices necessary to ensure that you meet your investment goals?
9. What will the consequences be if you don't reach your investment goals?

Your investment goals are always oriented toward the future. In Chapter 1, we classified goals as short term (less than two years), intermediate (two to five years), or long term (more than five years). These same classifications are also useful in planning your investment program. For example, you may establish a short-term goal of accumulating $5,000 in a savings account over the next 18 months. You may then use the $5,000 to purchase stocks or mutual funds to help you obtain your intermediate or long-term investment goals.

PERFORMING A FINANCIAL CHECKUP

Before beginning an investment program, your personal financial affairs should be in good shape. In this section, we examine several factors you should consider before making your first investment.

WORK AND LEARN TO SAVE TO BALANCE YOUR BUDGET
Most often, people must learn to live within their means before they begin investing. Many individuals regularly spend more than they make. They purchase items on credit and then must make monthly instalment payments and pay finance charges ranging between 0 and 28 percent or higher (some retail cards can charge up to 28.8 percent interest). With this situation, it makes no sense to start an investment program until credit card and instalment purchases, along with the accompanying finance charges, are reduced or eliminated. Therefore, you should limit credit purchases to only the necessities or to purchases required to meet emergencies. A good general rule is to limit instalment payments to 10 percent of your monthly pay after taxes. Eventually, the amount of cash remaining after the bills are paid will increase and can be used to start a savings program or finance investments. A word of caution: Corrective measures take time, and it is impossible to improve a bad situation overnight.

OBTAIN ADEQUATE INSURANCE PROTECTION
We discussed insurance in detail in Part 3 and will not cover that topic again here. However, it is essential that you consider insurance needs before beginning an investment program. The types of insurance and the amount of coverage varies from one person to the next. Before you start investing, examine the amount of your insurance coverage for life insurance, hospitalization, your home and other real estate holdings, automobiles, and any other assets that may need coverage.

START AN EMERGENCY FUND
Most financial planners suggest that an investment program should begin with the accumulation of an **emergency fund**. An emergency fund is an amount of money you can obtain quickly in case of immediate need. This money should be deposited in a savings account paying the highest available interest rate or in a money market mutual fund that provides immediate access to cash, if needed.

emergency fund An amount of money you can obtain quickly in case of immediate need.

The amount of money to be put away in the emergency fund varies from person to person. However, most financial planners agree that an amount equal to three to nine months' living expenses is reasonable. For example, Della Martinez earns $60,000 a year. Her monthly expenses total $3,200. Before Della can begin investing, she must save at least $9,600 ($3,200 × 3 months = $9,600) in a savings account or other near-cash investments to meet emergencies.

HAVE ACCESS TO OTHER SOURCES OF CASH FOR EMERGENCY NEEDS   You may also want to establish a line of credit, which is an arrangement between a financial institution (usually a bank) and a customer establishing a maximum loan balance that the bank will permit the borrower to maintain. The advantage of a line of credit compared to a regular loan is that you usually don't pay interest on the part of the loan that you don't use. Because the paperwork has already been completed and the loan has been pre-approved, you can later obtain the money as soon as you need it. The cash advance provision offered by major credit card companies can also be used in an emergency.

However, both lines of credit and credit cards have a ceiling, or maximum dollar amount, that limits the amount of available credit. If you have already exhausted both these sources of credit on everyday expenses, they will not be available in an emergency.

GETTING THE MONEY NEEDED TO START AN INVESTMENT PROGRAM

Once you have established your investment goals and completed your personal financial checkup, it's time to start investing—assuming you have enough money to finance your investments. Unfortunately, the money doesn't automatically appear. In today's world, you must work to accumulate the money you need to start any type of investment program.

Did you know?

While 56 percent of Canadians say they will contribute to an RRSP, TFSA, or both in 2014, a staggering 64 percent of those planning to contribute say they do not have enough money set aside for their planned contribution.

SOURCE: http://www.newswire.ca/en/story/ 1305189/cibc-poll-most-canadians-scrambling- to-find-the-money-to-make-their-planned- rrsp-contributions.

PRIORITY OF INVESTMENT GOALS   How badly do you want to achieve your investment goals? Are you willing to sacrifice some purchases to provide financing for your investments? The answers to both questions are extremely important. Take Rita Plouffe, a 32-year-old nurse in a large Vancouver hospital. As part of a divorce settlement in 2010, she received a cash payment of almost $95,000. At first, she was tempted to spend this money on a trip to Europe, a new BMW, and new furniture. But after some careful planning, she decided to save $75,000 in a Guaranteed Investment Certificate (GIC) and invest the remainder in a conservative mutual fund.

As pointed out earlier in this chapter, no one can make you save money to finance your investment program. You have to *want* to do it.

And *you* may be the most important part of a successful investment program. What is important to you? What do you value? Each of these questions affects your investment goals. At one extreme are people who save or invest as much of each paycheque as they can. Their savings and investment program and the satisfaction they get from attaining their intermediate and long-term financial goals are more important than the more immediate satisfaction of spending a large part of their paycheques on new clothes, a meal at an expensive restaurant, or a weekend getaway. At the other extreme are people who spend everything they make and run out of money before their next paycheque. Most people find either extreme unacceptable and take a more middle-of-the-road approach. These people often spend money on the items that make their life more enjoyable and still save enough to fund an investment program. As you will see later in this section, even a small amount of money saved or invested on a regular basis can amount to a large sum over a period of time.

Here are some suggestions to help you obtain the money you need.

1. *Pay yourself first.* Too often, people save or invest what is left over after they have paid everything else. As you might guess, nothing is left over in many cases, and the investment program is put on hold for another month. A second and much better approach is to (1) pay your monthly bills, (2) save a reasonable amount of money, and (3) use whatever money is left over for personal expenses, such as new clothes or entertainment.

2. *Participate in an elective savings program.* You can elect to have money withheld from your paycheque each payday and automatically deposited in a savings account. It is much easier to put money into the account than it is to get money out of it. You can also make investing easier by arranging with a mutual fund or brokerage firm to take a fixed sum from your bank account automatically every month and invest it. An elective savings program is an excellent way to fund a Registered Retirement Savings Plan (RRSP), Tax-free Savings Account (TFSA), or Registered Education Savings Plan (RESP) discussed in Chapters 3 and 14).

3. *Make a special savings effort one or two months each year.* Some financial planners recommend that you cut back to the basics for one or two months each year to obtain additional money for investment purposes.

4. *Take advantage of employer-sponsored retirement programs.* Many employers will match part or all of the contributions you make to a retirement program. Here's how a matching program works. For every dollar the employee contributes, the employer matches it with a specified amount such as 25 cents, 50 cents, or even $1. To make this option even more attractive, many matching programs are often part of an employer-sponsored retirement program that receives favourable tax treatment. (The tax benefits of different types of retirement programs are discussed in Chapter 14.)

5. *Take advantage of gifts, inheritances, and windfalls.* During your lifetime, you will likely receive gifts, inheritances, salary increases, year-end bonuses, or income tax refunds. Often, people opt to spend this extra money on something they could not afford under normal circumstances. A better approach is to use the money to fund your investment program.

THE VALUE OF LONG-TERM INVESTMENT PROGRAMS

Many people never start an investment program because they have only small sums of money. But even small sums grow over a long period of time. For instance, if you invest $2,000 each year for 40 years at a 6 percent annual rate of return, using the time value of money concepts in Chapter 1 and its Appendix 1B, your investment will grow to $309,520. The rate of return and the length of time your money is invested *do* make a difference. Exhibit 10–1 shows how much your investment portfolio will be worth at the end of selected time periods and with different rates of return.

Note that the value of your investments increases each year because of two factors. First, it is assumed you will invest another $2,000 each year. For example, at the end of 40 years, you will have invested a total of $80,000 ($2,000 × 40 years). Second, all investment earnings are allowed to accumulate and are added to your yearly deposits. Thus, the totals illustrated in Exhibit 10–1 are a result of continuous yearly deposits *plus* earnings on your investments.

Rate of Return	Balance at End of Year					
	1	5	10	20	30	40
4	2,000	10,833	24,012	59,556	112,170	190,050
5	2,000	11,051	25,156	66,132	132,878	241,600
6	2,000	11,274	26,362	73,572	158,116	309,520
7	2,000	11,502	27,632	81,990	188,922	399,280
8	2,000	11,734	28,974	91,524	226,560	518,120
9	2,000	11,970	30,386	102,320	272,620	675,780
10	2,000	12,210	31,874	114,550	328,980	885,180
11	2,000	12,456	33,444	128,406	398,040	1,163,660
12	2,000	12,706	35,098	144,104	482,660	1,534,180

Exhibit 10–1

Growth Rate for $2,000 Invested at the End of Each Year at Various Rates of Return for Different Time Periods

Financial Planning for Life's Situations

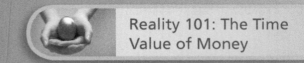

Reality 101: The Time Value of Money

Should college and university students worry about planning for retirement? You bet! There is no better time to begin an investment program than when you are young. The reason is quite simple: if you start an investment program when you're young, let the time value of money work for you, and make sound investments, you won't have to worry about finances when you reach retirement age. With these facts in mind, it's even possible for a person with an average salary to retire early.

Take Mary and Peter Anopoulos. Mary is a high school history teacher. Peter runs his own computer consulting business. Together, they earn about $120,000 a year and enjoy their careers. Both want to make sure they have enough money to retire on when Peter reaches age 65.

When the Anopouloses married just over 10 years ago, they established a long-term goal to accumulate a retirement nest egg of $1.5 million. They consulted with Gina Anastas, a financial planner whom a friend recommended. Anastas explained that if they chose quality investments that earned a 12 percent average annual return and invested just $2,000 each year, their investment portfolio would be worth $1,534,180 at the end of 40 years, when Peter reached age 65. She explained that most of this amount was the result of the time value of money, an investment concept that allows all interest, dividends, and the dollar appreciation that occurs when investments increase in value to accumulate over a long period of time.

According to Anastas, there is no better time to begin an investment program than right now. To drive this point home, she calculated that if the Anopouloses waited 10 years before starting their investment program and made the same investments for a 30-year period, their investment portfolio would be worth only $482,660. They would lose over $1 million! Needless to say, the Anopouloses realized they had to start their investment program immediately.

Today, after 10 years of investing in long-term stocks and mutual funds, the Anopouloses estimate that their investments are worth approximately $45,000. While the current value of their investment portfolio is a long way from $1.5 million, Gina Anastas forecasts that if they keep investing in the same types of investments, the time value of money will enable their portfolio to grow to more than $1.5 million by the time Peter reaches age 65.

The investment earnings illustrated in Exhibit 10–1 are taxable as ordinary income. To avoid or postpone taxation, you may want to invest your money in an RRSP, TFSA, RESP, or one of the tax-deferred investments described in Chapter 3. Further details concerning different types of retirement accounts are presented in Chapter 14. Although taxes are always a consideration, this complication does not reduce the importance of the time value of money. In fact, the time value of money is so important for a successful investment program that you may want to review this concept (see Chapter 1 and its Appendix 1B) before you begin to invest.

Also, note that if investments earn a higher rate of return, total portfolio values increase dramatically. For example, a $2,000 annual investment that earns 6 percent a year is worth $309,520 at the end of 40 years. But if the same $2,000 annual investment earns 12 percent each year, your investment portfolio value increases to $1,534,180 at the end of the same 40-year period. The search for higher returns is one reason many investors choose stocks and mutual funds that offer higher potential returns compared with GICs or savings accounts. You should know that to earn higher returns, you must take more chances. In fact, the material in the next section will help you determine if you should invest in these higher-risk investments.

CONCEPT CHECK 10–1

1. How can the Internet help you create a financial plan or establish an investment program?
2. Why should an investor develop specific investment goals?
3. What factors should you consider when performing a financial checkup?
4. How can an investor accumulate the money needed to fund an investment program?
5. Explain the time value of money concept and how it could affect your investment program.

FACTORS AFFECTING THE CHOICE OF INVESTMENTS

Millions of Canadians buy stocks, bonds, or mutual funds, purchase gold and silver, or make similar investments. And they all have reasons for investing their money. Some people want to supplement their retirement income when they reach age 65, while others want to become millionaires before age 40. Although each investor may have specific, individual goals for investing, all investors must consider a number of factors before choosing an investment alternative.

LO2
Describe how safety, risk, income, growth, and liquidity affect your investment decisions.

SAFETY AND RISK

The safety and risk factors are two sides of the same coin. You cannot evaluate any investment without assessing how safety relates to risk. Safety in an investment means minimal risk of loss. On the other hand, risk in an investment means a measure of uncertainty about the outcome. Investments range from very safe to very risky. At one end of the investment spectrum are very safe investments that attract conservative investors. Investments in this category include government savings bonds, savings accounts, term deposits, GICs, and certain negotiable government and corporate bonds. Investors pick such investments because they know there is little chance that investments of this kind will fluctuate in value or become worthless. Many investors choose conservative investments because of the individual life situations in which they find themselves. As people approach retirement, for example, they usually choose more conservative investments with less chance of losing a large part of the nest egg they have built up over the years. Today, one interesting change in investment philosophy is that most financial planners recommend that retirees still invest a small portion of their money in investments that will increase in value. The reason is simple: People are living longer, and they need more money for their retirement years. Some people choose to invest one-time windfalls or inheritances in a conservative investment because they know it may be impossible to replace the money if it is lost. Finally, some investors simply dislike taking chances.

At the other end of the investment spectrum are speculative investments. A **speculative investment** is a high-risk investment made in the hope of earning a relatively large profit in a short time. Such investments offer the possibility of a larger dollar return, but if they are unsuccessful you may lose most or all of your initial investment. Speculative stocks, certain bonds, real estate, derivatives, commodities, options, precious metals, precious stones, and collectibles are risk-oriented investments. Although many of these investments are discussed in detail in later chapters, they are often considered too risky for beginning investors.

speculative invest-ment A high-risk investment made in the hope of earning a relatively large profit in a short time.

By now, you probably realize that the safety and risk factors are more complex than the simple definitions just presented. From an investor's standpoint, one basic rule sums up the relationship between the factors of safety and risk: *The potential return on any investment should be directly related to the risk the investor assumes.* For example, Anne Landry was injured in a work-related accident three years ago. After a lengthy investigation, she received an insurance settlement totalling $420,000. As a result of the injury, she was no longer qualified to perform her old job as an assembler for an electronics manufacturer. When she thought about the future, she knew she needed to get a job but realized she would be forced to acquire new employment skills. She also realized she had received a great deal of money that could be invested to provide a steady source of income not only for the next two years while she obtained job training but also for the remainder of her life. Having never invested before, she quickly realized her tolerance for risk was minimal. She had to conserve her $420,000 settlement. Eventually, after much discussion with professionals and her own research, she chose to save about half her money in GICs. For the remaining half, she chose three stocks that offered a 4 percent average dividend, a potential for growth, and a high degree of safety because of the financial stability of the corporations that issued the stocks.

A more risk-oriented investor might have criticized Anne's decisions as too conservative. In fact, this second type of investor might have chosen to invest in more speculative stocks that offer a greater potential for growth and increase in market value even though the corporations issuing the stocks are not paying dividends at the present time. Often, beginning investors are afraid of the risk associated with many investments. But it helps to remember that without the risk, it is impossible to obtain the larger returns that really make an investment program grow. The key is to determine how much risk you are willing to assume and then choose quality investments that offer higher returns without an unacceptably high risk. The bottom line is this: What is right for one investor may not be right for another.

The problem of assessing safety and risk is further complicated by the large number of potential investments from which to choose. You must determine how much risk you are willing to assume. Once you have determined the amount of risk with which you are comfortable, you can choose different investments that hopefully will provide the expected return.

RISK TOLERANCE   Risk tolerance is the amount of psychological pain you're willing to suffer from your investments. There are risks associated with investing: you could lose part or all of your principal, the purchasing power of your investment can decrease, and you may not receive the returns you expected. In addition, unlike GICs, the money you invest in securities, mutual funds, and other similar investments is not insured by the Canada Deposit Insurance Corporation (CDIC). Therefore, it is important to determine your risk tolerance before you start investing your money. Since you have already determined your investment goals, you already have an idea of how much risk you can tolerate. For example, if you are saving for a short-term goal, you should choose a less risky investment because you need to guarantee that the cash will be available when you need it; you don't want to have to wait if the investment has decreased in value. Some financial advisers may tell you that regardless of age, you must always look toward long-term investing. This is false and is often used as an excuse by investment companies to cover up poor performance. To help you determine how much risk you are willing to assume, see the Advice from a Pro feature from Merrill Lynch on page 302.

COMPONENTS OF THE RISK FACTOR   The risk factor associated with a specific investment does change from time to time. For example, the stock of Computer-Tabulating-Recording Company was once considered a high-risk investment. Then, this company changed its name to IBM and eventually became a leader in the computer industry. By the early 1980s, many conservative investors were purchasing IBM stock because of its safety and earnings potential. But in the early 1990s, many of these same investors sold their IBM stock because changes in the computer industry had brought financial problems for IBM. IBM was once again considered too risky for many investors. Now, as a result of solving many of its financial problems, IBM is once again considered a good choice for many investors.

When choosing an investment, you must carefully evaluate changes in the risk factor. We can differentiate different types of risk according to their source, be it the company or its business sector, the economy as a whole, or international factors.

Business Risk   Business risk is associated with investments in common stock, preferred stock, and corporate bonds. With each of these investments, you face the possibility that bad management, unsuccessful products, competition, or a host of other factors will cause the business to be less profitable than originally anticipated. Lower profits usually mean lower dividends or no dividends at all. If the business continues to operate at a loss, even interest payments and repayment of bond principal may become difficult. The business may even fail and be forced to file for bankruptcy, in which case your investment may become totally worthless. Of course, the best way to protect yourself against such losses is to carefully evaluate the companies that issue the stocks and bonds you purchase. It also helps to purchase stock in more than one company and thus diversify your investments.

Inflation Risk   Your investments can provide a way to keep up with or stay ahead of inflation. While inflation rates have fallen sharply from the high levels of the early 1980s, the dollar is still shrinking over time. As defined in Chapter 1, inflation is a rise in the general level of prices.

During periods of high inflation, there is a risk that the financial return on an investment will not keep pace with the inflation rate. To see how inflation reduces your buying power, let's

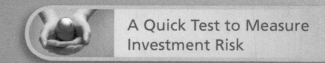

Financial Planning for Life's Situations

A Quick Test to Measure Investment Risk

The following quiz, adapted from one prepared by the T. Rowe Price group of mutual funds, can help you discover how comfortable you are with varying degrees of risk. Other things being equal, your risk tolerance score is a useful guide in deciding how heavily you should weight your portfolio toward safe investments versus more risk-oriented, speculative investments.

1. You're the winner on a TV game show. Which prize would you choose?
   - ☐ $2,000 in cash (1 point).
   - ☐ A 50-percent chance to win $4,000 (3 points).
   - ☐ A 20-percent chance to win $10,000 (5 points).
   - ☐ A 2-percent chance to win $100,000 (9 points).

2. You're down $500 in a poker game. How much more would you be willing to put up to win the $500 back?
   - ☐ More than $500 (8 points).
   - ☐ $500 (6 points).
   - ☐ $250 (4 points).
   - ☐ $100 (2 points).
   - ☐ Nothing—you'll cut your losses now (1 point).

3. A month after you invest in a stock, it suddenly goes up 15 percent. With no further information, what would you do?
   - ☐ Hold it, hoping for further gains (3 points).
   - ☐ Sell it and take your gains (1 point).
   - ☐ Buy more—it will probably go higher (4 points).

4. Your investment suddenly goes down 15 percent one month after you invest. Its fundamentals still look good. What would you do?
   - ☐ Buy more. If it looked good at the original price, it looks even better now (4 points).
   - ☐ Hold on and wait for it to come back (3 points).
   - ☐ Sell it to avoid losing even more (1 point).

5. You're a key employee in a startup company. You can choose one of two ways to take your year-end bonus. Which would you pick?
   - ☐ $1,500 in cash (1 point).
   - ☐ Company stock options that could bring you $15,000 next year if the company succeeds, but will be worthless if it fails (5 points).

Your total score: _____

SCORING

5–18 points You are a more conservative investor. You prefer to minimize financial risks. The lower your score, the more cautious you are. When you choose investments, look for high credit ratings, well-established records, and an orientation toward stability. In stocks, bonds, and real estate, look for a focus on income.

19–30 points You are a less conservative investor. You are willing to take more chances in pursuit of greater rewards. The higher your score, the bolder you are. When you invest, look for high overall returns. You may want to consider bonds with higher yields and lower credit ratings, the stocks of newer companies, and real estate investments that use mortgage debt.

---

assume you have deposited $10,000 in the bank at 4 percent interest. At the end of one year, your money will have earned $400 in interest ($10,000 × 4% = $400). Assuming an inflation rate of 6 percent, it will cost you an additional $600 ($10,000 × 6% = $600), or a total of $10,600, to purchase the same amount of goods you could have purchased for $10,000 a year earlier. Therefore, even though you earned $400, you lost $200 in purchasing power. And after paying taxes on the $400 interest, your loss of purchasing power is even greater.

The rate of return when adjusted for inflation varies from one investment to another. Before you rush out and invest in common stocks, realize that you should consider other factors when choosing an investment. On the other hand, rate of return is a major concern during periods of high inflation.

Interest Rate Risk The interest rate risk associated with a fixed-return investment in preferred stocks or government or corporate bonds is the result of changes in the interest rates in the economy. The value of preferred stocks, government bonds, or corporate bonds decreases when overall interest rates increase. In contrast, the value of these same investments rises when overall interest rates decrease. For example, suppose you purchase a $1,000 corporate bond

Your risk tolerance depends on many things, including:

Your goals and time frames. You most likely have several goals, such as your children's education, a vacation home, or an early retirement. You may be willing to take more risk with some goals than with others, depending on your time horizon for each goal.

Your income and asset base. The larger your income and asset base, the more risk you may be willing to take, again depending in part on your time frames. Some investors with a large asset base may choose a more conservative approach, knowing they don't need to take on additional risk to meet their goals.

Your personality. Be frank and honest with yourself. Some people are simply predisposed to take lesser or greater risk. Making the right determination of your personal feelings in this regard allows you to

maintain a proper investment course, even in market storms.

STAYING CURRENT: THE IMPORTANCE OF PERIODIC REVIEW

Over time, you may need to adjust your portfolio's investment mix, depending on your life circumstances, your investing time frames, and market performance. Your tolerance for risk is likely to change with your age as well as with major life changes, such as marriage, children, or retirement. Your financial advisor can help you evaluate your portfolio periodically in light of your goals and tolerance for risk and can help determine if you are on track to achieving your goals.

Did you know?

One dollar placed in a safety deposit box in early 1980 had a buying power of 34 cents in mid 2014.

SOURCE: Bank of Canada, http://www.bankofcanada.ca/rates/related/inflation-calculator/.

issued by RBC (Royal Bank of Canada), which matures in 2025 and pays 5 percent interest until maturity. This means RBC will pay $50 ($1,000 × 5% = $50) each year until the maturity date in 2018. If bond interest rates for comparable bonds increase to 7 percent, the market value of your 5 percent bond will decrease. No one will be willing to purchase your bond at the price you paid for it, since a comparable bond that pays 7 percent can be purchased for $1,000. As a result, you will have to sell your bond for less than $1,000 or hold it until maturity. If you decide to sell your RBC bond, the approximate dollar price you could sell it for is $714 ($50 ÷ 7% = $714). This price provides the purchaser with an 7 percent return, and your initial investment is reduced by $286 ($1,000 − $714 = $286) because you owned a bond with a fixed interest rate of 7 percent during a period when overall interest rates in the economy increased.

Of course, if overall interest rates declined, your bond would increase in value. Let's assume that interest rates on comparable corporate bonds declined to 3 percent. As a result, the value of your RBC bond that pays 5 percent would increase. The approximate price you could sell it for is $1,667 ($50 ÷ 3% = $1,667). This price provides the purchaser with a 3 percent return, and you earn an additional $667 ($1,667 − $1,000 = $667) because you owned a bond with a fixed interest rate of 5 percent during a period when overall interest rates in the economy declined.

Market Risk The prices of stocks, bonds, and mutual funds that invest in both types of securities may fluctuate because of changes in the economic environment. In the economic cycle, recurring periods of rapid growth are followed by periods of recession. Firms in different sectors of the economy perform better or worse given the stage of the cycle. For example, firms that are termed defensive offer products and services that are essential to consumers and businesses, such as electricity and other utilities. The demand for such staples is less responsive to changes in the economic cycle, and firms in defensive industries outperform during periods of recession. Other firms offer products that become more attractive as consumers' discretionary income rises during periods of rapid economic expansion. These firms perform well when the economy is in an upswing, but fare poorly when the economy is in a recession. These sectors are termed cyclical, and returns on firms operating in these sectors tend to follow the results of the market as a whole, as the performance of the majority of firms is cyclical in nature.

Global Investment Risk Today, more investors are investing in stocks and bonds issued by foreign firms and in global mutual funds. While we discuss these investments in more detail in the remainder of Part 4, you should know that investing in global securities creates additional risk. An investor can purchase stocks or bonds issued by individual foreign firms or, as most financial analysts recommend, purchase shares in a global mutual fund. For the small investor who has less than $200,000 to invest and is unaccustomed to the risks in foreign investments, global mutual funds offer more safety. Here are two factors to consider before taking the plunge.

First, *global investments must be evaluated just like domestic investments*. But evaluating foreign firms and global mutual funds may be difficult because reliable accounting information on foreign firms is often scarce. Of course, you can get an annual report, but you won't know whether the foreign firm uses the generally accepted accounting principles used by Canadian firms or follows its own national accounting rules.

Second, *changes in the currency exchange rate may affect the return on your investment*. The foreign currency exchange rate is applied whenever securities are bought and sold and whenever dividends are paid. For instance, if you want to purchase stock issued by a French firm, your Canadian currency must be converted into Euros. And the Euros you receive when you sell your shares in the foreign firm must be converted back to Canadian dollars. Your potential return is determined not only by how well your investment performed but also by whether the currency exchange rate became more or less favourable during the time you held the investment.

INVESTMENT INCOME

Investors sometimes purchase certain investments because they want a predictable source of income. The safest investments—passbook savings accounts, GICs, Canada Savings Bonds, and Canadian Treasury bills—are also the most predictable sources of income. With these investments, you know exactly what the interest rate is and how much income will be paid on a specific date.

If investment income is a primary objective, you can also choose government bonds, corporate bonds, preferred stocks, utility stocks, or rental real estate. When purchasing stocks or corporate bonds for potential income, most investors are concerned about the issuing corporation's overall profits, future earnings picture, and dividend policies. For example, some corporations are proud of their long record of consecutive dividend payments and will maintain that policy if at all possible.

Some Canadian corporations that trade on a Canadian stock exchange and have paid dividends consecutively for a period of five or more years include RBC, TD Bank, Fortis, Canadian Utilities, Canadian Western Bank, Thomson Reuters, Empire Company, Ensign Energy Services, Imperial Oil, Metro, and Canadian National Railway. For a list of American corporations with a long history of consecutive dividend payments, see Exhibit 10–2.

Other investments that may provide income potential are mutual funds and real estate rental property. Although the income from mutual funds is not guaranteed, you can choose funds whose primary objective is income. Income from rental property is not guaranteed because the possibility of either vacancies or unexpected repair bills always exists.

The more speculative investments, such as commodities, options, precious metals, gemstones, and collectibles, offer little, if any, potential for regular income.

INVESTMENT GROWTH

To investors, *growth* means their investments will increase in value. Often, the greatest opportunity for growth is an investment in common stock. During the 1990s, investors found that

Exhibit 10–2

Amercian Corporations with Consecutive Dividend Payments for at Least 100 Years

Corporation	Dividends Since	Type of Business
The York Water Company	1816	Utility
Exxon Mobil Corporation	1882	Oil and gas
Consolidated Edison, Inc.	1885	Utility
Procter & Gamble	1891	Consumer products
Coca-Cola Company	1893	Bottled beverages
Colgate-Palmolive Company	1895	Consumer products
General Mills, Inc.	1898	Food products
Norfolk Southern Corp.	1901	Railroad
Chevron Corporation	1912	Oil and gas

stocks issued by corporations in the electronics, technology, energy, and health-care industries provided the greatest growth potential. In fact, goods and services provided by companies in these industries promise to be in even greater demand in the 21st century, even though, recently, there has been a slight decrease in growth resulting from the recessionary environment.

When purchasing growth stocks, investors often sacrifice immediate cash dividends in return for greater dollar value in the future. Such companies as Facebook, Amazon, and other technology firms are considered to be growth companies and pay few or no dividends. For most growth companies, profits that would normally be paid to shareholders in the form of dividends are re-invested in the companies in the form of retained earnings. The money the companies keep can provide at least part of the financing they need for future growth and expansion and control the cost of borrowing money. As a result, they grow at an even faster pace. Growth financed by *retained earnings* normally increases the dollar value of a share of stock for the investor.

Government bonds, corporate bonds, mutual funds, and real estate may also offer growth possibilities. Precious metals, gemstones, and collectibles are more speculative investments that offer less predictable growth potential. Investments in commodities and options are more speculative investments that usually stress immediate returns as opposed to continued long-term growth.

INVESTMENT LIQUIDITY

liquidity The ability to buy or sell an investment quickly without substantially affecting the investment's value.

Liquidity is the ability to buy or sell an investment quickly without substantially affecting the investment's value. Investments range from near-cash investments to frozen investments, from which it is impossible to get your money. Chequing and savings accounts are very liquid because they can be quickly converted to cash. GICs impose penalties for withdrawing money before the maturity date.

With some investments, you may be able to sell quickly, but market conditions, economic conditions, or other factors may prevent you from regaining the amount you originally invested. For example, a real estate owner may have to lower the asking price to find a buyer. And it may be difficult to find a buyer for investments in collectibles, such as antiques and paintings.

CONCEPT CHECK 10–2

1. Why are safety and risk two sides of the same coin?
2. What are the five components of the risk factor?
3. How do income, growth, and liquidity affect the choice of an investment?

In Chapter 1 we discussed the life cycle approach to financial planning, in which our financial goals change as we go through the different stages of life. Similarly, according to life cycle investing theory, our investment goals and the risk we are willing to assume change as we go through the various stages of life. The theory suggests that certain types of investments and risk exposure are more suitable than others for the different stages of investors' lives.

In the early years, when net worth is small and liabilities often are large, the average investor is looking for long-term growth. Young investors are typically willing to take on more risk in hopes of receiving higher returns on investments. As time passes, investment income (such as dividends from stocks and interest from bonds) becomes more important. In the middle years and in middle age, investment income growth remains important but safety becomes an important consideration to protect the wealth that has accumulated. To this effect, investors will typically settle for investments that provide moderate returns at moderate risk.

Finally, in the retirement years safety is of prime concern. In this phase, low-risk investments that generate income are most suitable for the average investor.

SOURCE: Richard J. Maturi, "How to Tailor Your Investments to Your Life Stage," June 15, 2007, rediff.com/money/2007/jun/15invest.htm.

AN OVERVIEW OF INVESTMENT ALTERNATIVES

Once you consider the risks involved, establish your emergency fund, and have some money accumulated for investment purposes, it's time to consider the investment alternatives most people choose. You should begin by gathering as much information as possible about investment alternatives. Then you can decide whether purchasing stocks, bonds, real estate, or mutual funds is a better use of your money than putting it in the bank. The remainder of this section provides a brief overview of different investment alternatives. The remaining chapters of Part 4 provide more detailed information on stocks, bonds, mutual funds, segregated funds, real estate, and other investment alternatives.

LO3
Identify the major types of investment alternatives.

STOCK OR EQUITY FINANCING

Equity capital is money that a business obtains from its owners. If a business is a sole proprietorship or a partnership, it acquires equity capital when the owners invest their own money in the business. For a corporation, equity capital is provided by shareholders, who buy shares of its stock. In simplest terms, a stock is a certificate that shows the amount of the company that you own. Since all shareholders are owners, they share in the success of the corporation. This can make buying stock an attractive investment opportunity.

equity capital Money that a business obtains from its owners.

However, you should consider at least two factors before investing in stocks. First, a corporation is not required to repay the money obtained from the sale of stocks or to repurchase the stocks at a later date. Assume you purchased 100 shares of Google stock. Later, you decide to sell your Google stock. Your stocks are sold to another investor, not back to the company. In many cases, a shareholder sells his or her stocks because he or she thinks their price is going to decrease in value. The purchaser, on the other hand, buys those stocks because he or she thinks their price is going to increase. This creates a situation in which either the seller or the buyer earns a profit while the other party to the transaction experiences a loss.

Second, a corporation is under no legal obligation to pay dividends to shareholders. A **dividend** is a distribution of money, stocks, or other property that a corporation pays to shareholders. Dividends are paid out of earnings, but if a corporation that usually pays dividends has a bad year, its board of directors can vote to omit dividend payments to help pay necessary business expenses. Corporations may also retain earnings to make additional financing available for expansion, research and product development, or other business activities.

dividend A distribution of money, stocks, or other property that a corporation pays to shareholders.

There are two basic types of stocks: *common stocks* and *preferred stocks*. Both types have advantages and disadvantages that you should consider before deciding which to use for an investment program. A share of common stocks represents the most basic form of corporate ownership. People often purchase common stocks because this type of investment can provide (1) a source of income if the company pays dividends, (2) growth potential if the dollar value of the stocks increases, and (3) growth potential if the company splits its common stocks. And because it is a popular type of investment, most large corporations sell common stocks to satisfy a large part of their financing needs.

The most important priority an investor in preferred stocks enjoys is receiving cash dividends before common shareholders are paid any cash dividends. This factor is especially important when a corporation is experiencing financial problems and cannot pay cash dividends to both preferred and common shareholders. Other factors you should consider before purchasing both common or preferred stocks are discussed in Chapter 11.

CORPORATE AND GOVERNMENT BONDS

corporate bond
A corporation's written pledge to repay a specified amount of money, along with interest.

government bond
The written pledge of a government or a municipality to repay a specified sum of money, along with interest.

There are two types of bonds an investor should consider. A **corporate bond** is a corporation's written pledge to repay a specified amount of money, along with interest. A **government bond** is the written pledge of a government or a municipality to repay a specified sum of money, along with interest. Thus, when you buy a bond, you are lending a corporation or government entity money for a period of time. Regardless of who issues the bond, you need to consider two major questions before investing in bonds. First, will the bond be repaid at maturity? The maturity dates for most bonds range between one and 30 years. An investor who purchases a bond has two options: keep the bond until maturity and then redeem it, or sell the bond to another investor. In either case, the value of the bond is closely tied to the ability of the corporation or government agency to repay the bond at maturity. Second, will the corporation or government agency be able to maintain interest payments to bondholders? Bondholders normally receive interest payments every six months. Again, if a corporation or government agency cannot pay the interest on its bonds, the value of those bonds will decrease.

Receiving periodic interest payments until maturity is one method of making money on a bond investment. Investors also use two other methods that can provide more liberal returns on bond investments. Chapter 12 discusses each of these methods. Corporate bonds are a way for corporations to raise money for their endeavours and operation. This is also referred to as debt financing, since this is money that they borrow from the public, or whoever is buying the bonds. An alternative is equity capital, discussed above, which is essentially money invested in the company by individuals or entities that purchase stock in the corporation. The main difference between the two is that with debt financing, the corporation must pay the bond back with interest in a specified amount of time, whereas with equity capital, the corporation pays the investors back in terms of return on their investment. This is either in the form of dividends or capital gains.

MUTUAL FUNDS

mutual fund An investment alternative chosen by people who pool their money to buy stocks, bonds, and other securities selected by professional managers employed by an investment company.

A **mutual fund** is an investment alternative chosen by people who pool their money to buy specific quantities of stocks, bonds, and other securities selected by professional managers employed by an investment company. Professional management is an especially important factor for investors with little or no previous experience in financial matters. Another reason investors choose mutual funds is *diversification*. Since mutual funds invest in a number of different securities, an occasional loss in one security is often offset by gains in other securities. As a result, the diversification provided by a mutual fund reduces risk.

The goals of one investor often differ from those of another. Mutual fund managers realize this and tailor their funds to meet individual needs and objectives. Some invest in Canadian companies, while others invest in stocks and bonds issued by companies in foreign countries. As a result of all the different investment alternatives, mutual funds range from very conservative to extremely speculative investments.

Although investing money in a mutual fund provides professional management, even the best managers can make errors in judgment. The responsibility for choosing the right mutual fund is still based on the investor's evaluation of a mutual fund investment. Chapter 13 presents more information on the different types of mutual funds, the costs involved, and techniques for evaluating these investments.

SEGREGATED FUNDS

A **segregated fund** is a type of annuity that combines the growth and diversification potential of mutual funds with the security of insurance. These funds are sold only by life insurance companies, and have maturities of at least 10 years. It is like buying an insurance contract, using the money from each contract to invest in an underlying mutual fund. You don't actually own the mutual fund; however, your investment closely tracks its performance. Segregated funds are especially attractive because they come with guarantees designed to protect your money from market instability. Between 70 and 100 percent of your initial investment is guaranteed to be paid out at death or upon maturity of the contract, regardless of how markets perform. Once the annuity matures, the investor is entitled to 100 percent of the initial investment minus any withdrawals. Furthermore, upon maturity, the payment can be passed directly to any beneficiaries without any probate fees. Similar to mutual funds, segregated funds can be bought or sold at any time. If you sell prior to maturity, the fund is sold at market value, which may be less than the initial investment.

In addition, some segregated funds offer protection from potential creditors, in case the policyholder were to ever face a lawsuit or bankruptcy. This is called creditor protection. Certain conditions apply; for example, the absence of any creditor issues at the time of the investment. Creditor protection can be challenged by a creditor if there is evidence that the insurance was purchased as a means to avoid financial obligations. The policyholder must name an irrevocable beneficiary or a preferred beneficiary (spouse, child, parent, or grandchild) for the protection to apply at the time of his or her death. This aspect of a segregated fund also gives it an advantage over mutual funds, as the latter do not allow for this sort of protection.

segregated fund An investment alternative in the form of an annuity that is similar to a mutual fund but that is less risky as it provides a certain degree of insurance to the investor.

REAL ESTATE

As a rule, real estate increases in value and eventually sells at a profit, but there are no guarantees. Although many beginning investors believe real estate values increase by 10 or 15 percent a year, and while the Canadian real estate market has seen strong price increases over the past five to 10 years, in reality the nationwide long-term average annual increase is about 3 to 5 percent. This growth rate makes real estate a long-term investment and not a get-rich-quick scheme.

Success in real estate investments depends on how well you evaluate alternatives. Experts often tell would-be investors that the three most important factors when evaluating a potential real estate investment are *location, location,* and *location.* While location may be the most important factor, other factors may determine whether or not a piece of real estate is a good investment. For example, you should answer the following questions before making a decision to purchase any property:

1. Is the property priced competitively with similar properties?
2. What type of financing is available, if any? What are the current interest rates?
3. How much are the taxes?
4. What is the condition of the buildings and houses in the immediate area?
5. Why are the present owners selling the property?
6. Is there a chance that the property will decrease in value?
7. How will I maintain and care for the property?
8. Can I afford the mortgage payments if interest rates go up?

Any investment has disadvantages, and real estate is no exception. Many people were "taken" by unscrupulous promoters who sold inaccessible land in the Florida Everglades. Poor location can cause a piece of property to decrease in value. Also, to sell your property, you must find an interested buyer who is able to obtain enough money or financing to complete the transaction. Finding a buyer can be difficult if loan money is scarce, the real estate market is in a decline, or you overpaid for the property. If you are forced to hold your investment longer than you originally planned, you must also consider taxes and loan payments.

One way to invest in real estate but maintain high liquidity is to invest in a Real Estate Investment Trust (REIT). A REIT, like other *income trusts,* is issued in the stock market and is designed to pay out money generated from a business or a set of investments through cash disbursements to unitholders. They are popular because of their ability to produce constant funds for investors.

A REIT invests in real estate, either through properties or mortgages. Equity REITs own properties and their revenues typically come from their properties' rents. Mortgage REITs loan money to owners of real estate properties or purchase existing mortgages. Their revenues come from the interest earned on the mortgage loans. It is also possible to invest in hybrid REITs that invest in both properties and mortgages.

Under old tax laws, REITs and other income trusts, such as business/hybrid trusts and royalty/energy trusts, paid little or no corporate tax because almost all their cash flow was distributed to unitholders in the form of capital distributions and non-sheltered taxable income. Unitholders in turn had the option to defer the taxable portion of the distribution by holding it in an RRSP.

Legislative changes by the federal government implemented a new tax on distributions from income trusts, referred to as "specified investment flow-throughs" (SIFT). REITs are exempt from the new tax only if they meet the following conditions:

1. Property test—The property test generally requires that the fair market value of all "non-portfolio properties" that are "qualified REIT properties" held by the trust is at least 90 percent of the total fair market value at that time of all non-portfolio properties held by the trust.
2. Ninety percent passive revenue test—The passive revenue test requires the REIT to derive not less than 90 percent (down from 95 percent under the old rules) of the trust's "gross REIT revenue" for the taxation year from rent, interest, and other eligible sources.
3. Seventy-five percent real property revenue test—The real property revenue test requires that not less than 75 percent of the trust's gross REIT revenue for the taxation year be derived from: rent from real or immovable properties, interest or dispositions of properties.
4. Qualifying property value test—Under the qualifying property value test, at least 75 percent of the trust's "equity value" throughout the taxation year must be comprised of the total fair market value of a trust's real or immovable property, bankers' acceptance of a Canadian corporation, money, or certain government debt or deposits with a credit union.
5. Publicly traded test—The REIT must be publicly traded. (Source: https://www.kpmg.com/Ca/en/IssuesAndInsights/ArticlesPublications/TNF/Pages/tnfc1304.htm.)

These changes come at a time when global trends have been toward decreasing regulatory measures in order to increase the competitiveness of REITs. More information on income trusts and the proposed changes in the Income Tax Act can be found on the following Web sites: KPMG.ca, http://www.cra-arc.gc.ca/, and http://cpacanada.ca/.

SECURITIZED DEBT INSTRUMENTS

Securitization is the process in which debt is passed on to entities, that in turn break them into bonds and sell them. Some examples of securitized debt are credit card receivables, wholesale receivables, retail receivables, instalment receivables such as automobile and agriculture and commercial loans, amongst many others. Efforts are being made to develop structures to securitize other debts, such as real estate and commodities. The main advantage of securitizing debts is that it lowers interest rates and frees up capital to banks, but on the other hand, it does encourage lending for reasons other than long-term profit.

PROCESS

Securitized debt instruments are a result of original holder (like a bank) selling his or her debt obligation to a third party, called a Special Purpose Vehicle (SPV). The original lender receives a payment from the SPV equal to the balance of the debt sold, which gives the lender greater liquidity. The SPV then divides the debt into bonds, which will be sold on the open market.

These bonds are divided into "tranches," which denote varying degrees of risk and therefore different yields for the bondholder.*

OTHER INVESTMENT ALTERNATIVES

As defined earlier in this chapter, a speculative investment is a high-risk investment made in the hope of earning a relatively large profit in a short time. By its very nature, any investment may be speculative; that is, it may be quite risky. However, a true speculative investment is speculative because of the methods investors use to earn a quick profit. Typical speculative investments include:

- Call options
- Put options
- Derivatives
- Commodities
- Hedge funds
- Precious metals
- Gemstones
- Coins
- Stamps
- Antiques and collectibles

Without exception, investments of this kind are normally referred to as speculative for one reason or another. The gold market has many unscrupulous dealers who sell worthless gold-plated lead coins to unsuspecting, uninformed investors. Call and put options are a risky way to make money without investing too much of your own. The risk lies in the position you take as the buyer; for example, you need to decide whether you think the underlying stock price will fall or rise and, based on that, purchase an option. It is risky in that you are only speculating and, without insider information (which is illegal!), it is hard to ensure that your position will be the profitable choice. Derivatives are securities such as options, and forward and futures contracts, whose value depends on the performance of an underlying security. Hedge funds are considered derivative investments. The basic idea behind a hedge fund is to take two simultaneous positions in two different investments in order to reduce risk. An example is buying long/selling short, where managers buy securities they believe are under-priced and then sell them once they appreciate in price, thus making a profit for their clients. Concurrently, the manager sells securities that the fund does not own, from investment dealers, intending to buy them back once the price of the stock drops, then paying back the borrowed money to the broker and pocketing the difference. Since the market is guaranteed to go up or down, the position you hold can be considered hedged to a certain degree against risk. With any speculative investment, it is extremely important to deal with reputable dealers and recognized investment firms. It pays to be careful. While investments in this category can lead to large dollar gains, they should not be used by anyone who does not fully understand the risks involved. More information on investment alternatives can be found on investopedia.com. Chapter 11 presents more information on options.

SUMMARY OF FACTORS THAT AFFECT INVESTMENT CHOICES

Earlier in this chapter, we examined how safety, risk, income, growth, and liquidity affect your investment choices. In the preceding section, we looked at available investment alternatives. Now, let's compare the factors that affect the choice of investments with each alternative. Exhibit 10–3 ranks the alternatives in terms of safety, risk, income, growth, and liquidity.

It is now appropriate to introduce the topic of diversification. **Diversification** is the process of spreading your assets among several types of investments to lessen risk. In fact, diversification can reduce the risk associated with putting all your eggs in one basket—a common mistake made by investors. To avoid this mistake, many financial planners suggest that you think of your investment program as a pyramid consisting of four levels, as illustrated in Exhibit 10–4. This

diversification The process of spreading your assets among several types of investments to lessen risk.

---

*SOURCES: ehow.com/list_6739322_securitized-debt-instruments.html; stikeman.com/cps/rde/xchg/se-en/hs.xsl/1570.htm.

Exhibit 10–3

Factors Used to
Evaluate Typical
Investment
Alternatives

	Type of Investment	Factors to be Evaluated				
		Safety	Risk	Income	Growth	Liquidity
Traditional investments	Common stocks	Average	Average	Average	High	Average
	Preferred stocks	Average	Average	High	Average	Average
	Corporate bonds	Average	Average	High	Low	Average
	Government bonds	High	Low	Low	Low	High
	Real estate	Average	Average	Average	Average	Low
Speculative investments	Options	Low	High	N/A	Low	Average
	Derivatives	Low	High	N/A	Low	Average
	Commodities	Low	High	N/A	Low	Average
	Precious metals, gemstones, and collectibles	Low	High	N/A	Low	Low

N/A = Not applicable.

approach to investing can provide financial growth and protection, regardless of your age, marital status, income, or level of financial sophistication.

In Exhibit 10–4, the investments in level 1 provide the foundation for an investment program. After the foundation is established in level 1, most investors choose from the investment alternatives in level 2 and level 3. Be warned: Many investors may decide the investments in level 4 are too speculative for their investment programs. While investments at this level may provide spectacular dollar gains, they pose the risk that they will lose value or even become totally worthless.

Once you understand the risk factors associated with different investment alternatives and the principle of diversification, the next step is to develop a personal investment plan.

A PERSONAL INVESTMENT PLAN

To be a successful investor, you must develop a plan and then implement it. Most people use a series of steps like those listed in Exhibit 10–5 to develop their own personal plan for investing.

You begin investment planning by establishing realistic goals. Many factors affect your short-, medium-, and long-term investment goals, including your own expectations, risk tolerance, market volatility, and investment behaviour. A way to determine if the goals you are

Exhibit 10–4

Possible Investments
for Financial Security,
Safety and Income,
Growth, and
Speculation

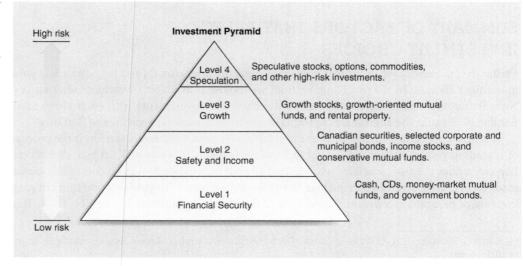

Advice from a Pro

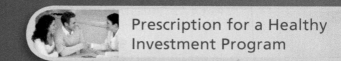

Prescription for a Healthy
Investment Program

According to the pros, life is not a dress rehearsal. This is all we've got! One host of a popular radio program on financial planning says that retiring means getting up in the morning and doing what *you* want to do. He often asks potential clients a basic question: what worthy goal would you pursue if money were no object? It is toward *this* goal that you start investing.

In addition to helping clients determine goals that are important, he also encourages clients to adopt the 15/15/70 rule. He recommends that you first give away 15 percent. You must learn that money is a servant, not a master. You must learn that it really is "more blessed to give than to receive." Then, give yourself 15 percent.

Most people say, they'll pay all the bills, then invest whatever is left. It won't happen; pay yourself off the top. Finally, live on the remaining 70 percent. Learn to discipline yourself in order to pay those bills.

Once a client has accumulated enough money to finance an investment program, he encourages the client and his radio listeners to choose long-term investments. For many beginning investors, he often suggests good mutual funds with a four-or five-star rating, excellent long-term performance, and good management. Above all, this pro believes that you should pick investments that are suitable for your risk comfort level.

setting for yourself are realistic is to look at past performance. For example, if you see that a certain investment has consistently returned 5 percent over the past five years, it may be unrealistic to set a goal anticipating a 10 percent return over the next year. You need to decide for yourself what combination of risk and return on investment is acceptable to you (without being unrealistically optimistic) and build your goals based on that. Your current situation (e.g., age, income, etc.) generally dictates the amount of risk you are willing to assume. For example, an elderly couple will be less willing to assume high levels of risk if they are investing their retirement money. Once you identify what you want, then you can identify how best to get it by allocating a percentage of your resources to different types of investments. The second step is to determine the amount of money you will obtain by a specific date. The total amount of money specified in step 2 should be based on your goals. The amount of money you now have available for investment purposes is specified in step 3. For most investors, the money currently available for investment purposes has accumulated over a period of time. For example, Sharon and Derek Timmons began saving $200 a month to finance a future investment program more than three years ago. They deposited the money in an interest-bearing savings account. Now, after three years, they have accumulated more than $8,000, which they can use to purchase different investments. In step 4, you list specific investment alternatives that you want to evaluate.

Because of the relationship between risks and returns for each investment, step 5 is divided into two components. In step 5(a), you examine the risk factor for each investment alternative.

1. Establish your investment goals.
2. Determine the amount of money you need to obtain your goals.
3. Specify the amount of money you currently have available to fund your investments.
4. List different investments that you want to evaluate.
5. Evaluate (a) the risk factor, and (b) the potential return for all investments.
6. Reduce possible investments to a reasonable number.
7. Choose at least two different investments.
8. Continue to evaluate your investment program.

Exhibit 10–5

Steps for Effective Investment Planning

311

In step 5(b), you examine the potential return associated with each alternative. The information needed to complete steps 5(a) and 5(b) should be based on your research of potential investments. At the very least, this requires some expert advice, careful study, and a commitment of your time. In step 6, you reduce potential investments to a reasonable number. In step 7, you make a final decision to choose at least two different investments. By choosing at least two alternatives, you build a certain amount of diversification into your investment program. As the total dollar value of your investments grows, you will probably want to continue to consider additional investments. After all, spreading potential risks among different investments is a key factor in diversifying your investment program.

Step 8 provides for continued evaluation of your investments. Investors' circumstances often change as they go through life. As a result, investors are often forced to adapt their planning to new situations. For example, if you accept a new job at a substantially higher salary, changes in investment goals may make your present personal plan of action obsolete. Also, different investments may become more or less attractive because of changes in economic and financial conditions. During the early 1980s, for example, many investors sold their common stocks and placed their money in GICs that paid high guaranteed interest. More recently, low interest rates have led investors to cash their bonds and GICs and purchase common stocks and mutual funds that offer more potential.

To illustrate the above planning process, let's use the case of Salomé Mari, who accepted a position in advertising after university. After two years, Salomé is earning $90,000 a year. Her net pay after deductions is $6,000 a month. Her living expenses are about $4,800 a month, which leaves a surplus of $1,200. After graduating from university, she immediately began saving a portion of each month's surplus. First, she established an emergency fund. Now, she has $42,000 available for investment purposes. After much thought, Salomé developed the personal plan of action illustrated in Exhibit 10–6.

Exhibit 10–6

A Personal Investment Plan for Salomé Mari

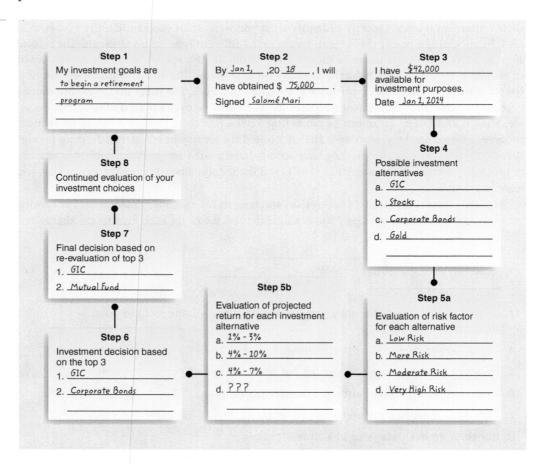

Your own plan may be quite different from Salomé's, but the principle is the same. Each person has different ideas and goals. Establish your investment goals first, and then follow through. Often, the follow-through is the most important component when it comes to developing a successful investment plan. Simply put: How important are your investment goals, and are you willing to work to attain them?

CONCEPT CHECK 10–3

1. Of all the investment alternatives presented in this chapter, which one do you think would help you obtain your investment goals? Why?

2. Why do investors purchase stocks?

3. What are two chief advantages of investing in mutual funds?

4. What factors should you consider before purchasing real estate for investment purposes?

5. How can the investment pyramid presented in Exhibit 10–4 help you build an investment program to reach your financial goals?

6. What are the steps required for a personal investment plan?

FACTORS THAT REDUCE INVESTMENT RISK

In this section, we examine the factors that can spell the difference between success and failure for an investor. We begin by reviewing the role of a financial planner. Then, we consider your role in the investment process.

LO4

Recognize the role of the professional financial planner and your role in a personal investment program.

THE ROLE OF A FINANCIAL PLANNER

To achieve their financial goals, many people seek professional help. In many cases, they turn to stockbrokers, lawyers, accountants, bankers, or insurance agents. However, these professionals are specialists in one specific field and may not be qualified to provide the type of advice required to develop a thorough financial plan.

While there is no such thing as a nationally designated "personal financial planner" in Canada, a number of organizations allow special designations after certain criteria have been met. The Financial Advisers Association of Canada (Advocis) requires that all Registered Financial Planners (RFP) achieve an academic or professional standing recognized by the Association. The member must be sponsored by other planners in the industry, be currently engaged in the profession, and have demonstrated competence in financial planning. A minimum of two years' experience in the practice of financial planning is required. Advocis members must abide by the Advocis/CLU Institute Code of Professional Conduct and make an ongoing commitment to maintaining professional standards through continuing education. The Financial Planning Standards Council (FPSC) believes that it is important that Canada participate in the international movement trying to globalize the financial planning profession, through the Certified Financial Planner (CFP) designation. There are four steps, similar to the RFP, which must be completed in order to be awarded the internationally recognized CFP designation. The Canadian Institute of Financial Planning (CIFP) requires the successful completion of four Web-based courses and a comprehensive program exam as part of its education requirement necessary for sitting the Certified Financial Planner Examination administered by the FPSC. Finally, the Canadian Securities Institute (CSI) and the Institute of Canadian Bankers (ICB) both offer a number of investment and personal finance courses.

In selecting financial advisers, you need to be aware of how they are paid as well as how this might influence the advice you are given. Salaried employees of such institutions as banks or trust companies are sometimes designated as financial planners, and provide advice either free

Why do many investors fall prey to irrational financial thinking? The usual explanation is simple: fear and greed. Glen Whyte, a professor at the Rotman School of Management at the University of Toronto, specializes in the study of risky decision making. "For most people," he says, "the motive to get into the market is a simple desire to generate a gain. But once they're in, most investors make critically important decisions in a half-baked way, without valid information."

Which human characteristic causes the most problems? Stubbornness. All too often, investors desperately hold on to a loser in the hope it will pay off. Experts in behavioural finance call this loss aversion: study after study shows that people are willing to run a greater risk to avoid a loss than to make a gain.

Another motive for hanging on too long is the so-called endowment effect—the belief that because we own something, it must be of superior value. Often, the price an investor pays for a stock becomes a kind of psychological line in the sand. If the owner is compelled to sell below that price, he or she experiences shame, denial, or regret. If, on the other hand, the market value is higher than the purchase price, the dominant emotions are pride, vindication, and satisfaction. Often, the real sting of investment losses is that we have no one to blame but ourselves. Investors tend to flock together when choosing their investments. Rather than basing their buy-and-sell decisions on their own research—in which case, they risk looking stupid as well as losing money—most people would rather tag along with the crowd. At least that way if they lose they can comfort themselves with the knowledge that everyone else was fooled, too. Yet another psychological tendency that gets in the way of profitable investing is cognitive bias. Our cognitive bias blinds us to potential dangers. When deciding where to put their money, most people consider the range of possible outcomes and decide which one they think is most likely. After arriving at that decision, however, they ignore all other possibilities.

One of the reasons people like to construct scenarios around their investments is that they are desperate to convince themselves that markets make sense. Human beings constantly seek meaning and patterns, and the markets don't offer much of either. In the absence of reliable information, investors become anxious and tend to rely on their emotions, which makes them vulnerable to rumours and hot tips.

How can investors stay out of trouble?

- Understand the extent to which your own personality can push you to make bad decisions.
- Follow a realistic investment plan that fits your needs and goals.
- Educate yourself. If your sense of self-efficiency is based on knowledge rather than ego, you're less likely to get carried away by your own success.
- Learn humility. A success rate of 60 to 70 percent in picking stocks is the best most people can expect to achieve.
- Finally, it is a good idea to develop a strong relationship with a trusted professional adviser or a group of fellow investors.

SOURCE: Vivian Smith, "Mind Games," *The Maclean's Guide to Personal Finance 2000*, p. 28.

of charge or for a nominal fee. Commission planners receive their compensation from the sellers of the services and products that they recommend. In general, it is a safe bet to assume that any advice you get from either of these types of planners is biased in some way.

More objective advice might be available from fee-based planners and fee-only or fee-for-service planners. Fee-based planners receive their compensation partly in the form of fees paid by you and partly in the form of commissions from the institutions. Fee-only or fee-for-service planners will charge you directly on an hourly basis (typically from $100 to $400 per hour), and that will be their sole source of income for the service that they provide to you.

YOUR ROLE IN THE INVESTMENT PROCESS

Successful investors continually evaluate their investments. They never sit back and let their investments manage themselves. Obviously, different types of investments require different methods of evaluation. Some factors to consider when choosing different investments are described next.

EVALUATE POTENTIAL INVESTMENTS   Let's assume you have $25,000 to invest. Also assume your investment will earn a 10 percent return the first year. At the end of one year, you will have earned $2,500 and your investment will be worth $27,500. Not a bad return on your original investment! Now ask yourself: How long would it take to earn $2,500 if I had to work for this amount of money at a job? For some people, it might take a month; for others, it might take longer. The point is that if you want this type of return, you should be willing to work for it, but the work takes a different form than a job. When choosing an investment, the work you invest is the time it takes to research different investments so that you can make an informed decision.

Some people invest large sums of money and never research the investments they purchase. Obviously, this is a flawed approach that can lead to large dollar losses. On the other hand, an informed investor has a much better chance of choosing the types of investments that will increase in value. In fact, much of the information in the remainder of Part 4 will help you learn how to evaluate different investment opportunities. But you have to be willing to work and learn if you want to be a successful investor. As you will see in the next section, evaluation doesn't stop once you make a decision to purchase an investment. It continues as long as you own the investment.

MONITOR THE VALUE OF YOUR INVESTMENTS   Would you believe that some people invest large sums of money and don't know what their investments are worth? They don't know if their investments have increased or decreased in value. They don't know if they should sell their investments or continue to hold them. A much better approach is to monitor the value of your investments. If you choose to invest in stocks, bonds, mutual funds, commodities, or options, you can determine the value of your holdings by looking at the price quotations reported on the Internet, on financial news television and radio programs, and in newspapers. Your real estate holdings may be compared with similar properties currently for sale in the surrounding area. Finally, you can determine the value of your precious metals, gemstones, and collectibles by checking with reputable dealers and investment firms. Regardless of which type of investment you choose, close surveillance will keep you informed of whether your investment increases or decreases in value. The Financial Planning Calculations box on page 316 presents further information on monitoring the value of your investments.

KEEP ACCURATE AND CURRENT RECORDS   Accurate record keeping helps you spot opportunities to maximize profits or reduce dollar losses when you sell your investments. Accurate record keeping also helps you decide whether you want to invest additional funds in a particular investment. At the very least, you should keep purchase records for each of your investments that include the actual dollar cost of the investment, plus any commissions or fees you paid. It is also useful to keep a list of the sources of information (Internet addresses, business periodicals, research publications, and so on), along with copies of the material you used to evaluate each investment. Then, when it is time to re-evaluate an existing investment, you will know where to begin your search for current information. As you will see in the next section, accurate record keeping is also necessary for tax purposes.

TAX CONSIDERATIONS

As discussed in Chapter 3, one aspect of a personal tax strategy is to build a tax-efficient portfolio. Dividends, interest, rental income, and capital gains are taxed in different ways by the Canada Revenue Agency (CRA) and provincial governments. Interest and rental income, net of expenses, is fully taxed. Dividends and capital gains receive more favourable tax treatment. Therefore, in order to ensure the most favourable tax treatment of your investment portfolio, it is best to hold interest-generating assets inside registered accounts, such as RRSPs, RESPs, and Tax Free Savings Account (TFSAs; covered in Chapter 3), and dividend and capital-gains-generating assets in non-registered accounts. Rental property is a real asset, not a financial asset, and therefore cannot be held in registered accounts.

As always in personal financial planning, it is important to realize all the consequences of your investment and tax decisions. Areas of concern for the former might include decisions about

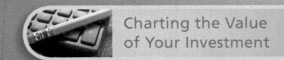
To monitor the value of their investments, many investors use a simple chart like the one illustrated here. To construct a chart like this one, place the original purchase price of your investment in the middle on the side of the chart. Then use price increments of a logical amount to show increases and decreases in dollar value.

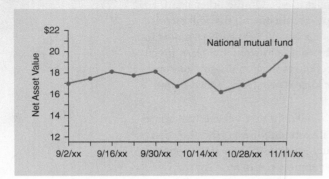

Place individual dates along the bottom of the chart. For stocks, bonds, mutual funds, and similar investments, you may want to graph every two weeks and chart current values on, say, a Friday. For longer-term investments, such as real estate, you can chart current values every six months.

A WORD OF CAUTION

If an investment is beginning to have a large increase or decrease in value, you should watch that investment more closely. You can still continue to chart at regular intervals, but you may want to check dollar values more frequently—in some cases, daily.

NOW IT'S YOUR TURN!

Using the dates and the dollar amounts below, construct a graph to illustrate the price movements for a share of stock issued by Chesapeake Manufacturing.

Date	Price
June 1	$19
June 15	$17
June 29	$18
July 13	$20
July 27	$22
August 10	$24
August 24	$22

dividends, interest, rental income, and capital gains and losses. As for taxes, it's important to keep in mind the tax effect of all your sources of income, as some income may be more advantageous.

DIVIDENDS, INTEREST INCOME, AND RENTAL INCOME   As defined earlier in this chapter, a dividend is a distribution of money, stocks, or other property that a corporation pays to shareholders. Dividends are taxed in a peculiar way that is designed to reflect that the corporation paying you a dividend has already paid taxes on its profits (which it is sharing with you in the form of dividend payments).

In 2006, the federal government implemented the enhanced dividends tax credit to reduce taxes on "eligible" dividends (generally, dividends paid to Canadian residents by Canadian public companies). Since 2006, these rules have been revised and adjusted. Currently, this means that if you receive $100 in eligible dividends you will report it "grossed-up" by 38 percent as $138 in income. You will then be taxed at your marginal rate minus a dividend tax credit of 15.0 percent. If the dividends you receive are not eligible, as of 2014, the amount you receive is grossed-up by 18 percent and you are then taxed at a marginal rate minus a dividend tax credit of 11 percent. Capital dividends, or dividends derived from a corporation's capital gains, are the exception to this rule and are not taxed. Exhibit 10–7 demonstrates how federal taxes are calculated on dividends income.

Each province and territory sets its own dividends tax credit rate. Some have followed the federal government's lead by increasing their own credit rate to stimulate investment in public corporations. Ontario, for example, went from a dividend tax credit rate of 5.13 percent in 2005 to 6.7 percent in 2007, reached 7.4 percent in 2009, was lowered to 6.4 percent for 2010 to 2013 but is expected to increase to 10.0 percent for 2014 once legislatively approved. The higher rate is for eligible dividends only. Non-eligible dividends continue to be taxed at the old rate. Exhibit 10–8 demonstrates how taxes on dividends income are calculated for an Ontarian in the highest tax bracket.

	Federal Tax Rates			
	15%	**22%**	**26%**	**29%**
Eligible dividends received	$1,000.00	$1,000.00	$1,000.00	$1,000.00
Gross-up (38 percent)	380.00	380.00	380.00	380.00
Grossed-up dividends	1,380.00	1,380.00	1,380.00	1,380.00
Federal tax	207.00	303.60	358.80	400.20
Less dividend tax credit (15% of grossed-up dividends)[1]	(207.00)	(207.00)	(207.00)	(207.00)
Net federal tax	(0)	96.60	151.80	193.20
Net federal tax rate (marginal rate)	0%	9.66%	15.18%	19.32%
Non-eligible dividends received	$1,000.00	$1,000.00	$1,000.00	$1,000.00
Gross-up (18 percent)	180.00	180.00	180.00	180.00
Grossed-up dividends	1,180.00	1,180.00	1,180.00	1,180.00
Federal tax	177.00	259.20	306.80	342.20
Less dividend tax credit (11.00% of grossed-up dividends)[2]	(129.80)	(129.80)	(129.80)	(129.80)
Net federal tax	47.20	129.40	177	212.40
Net federal tax rate (marginal rate)	4.72%	12.94%	17.70%	21.24%

Exhibit 10–7

Calculation of Federal Tax Rates on Dividend Income for Eligible and Non-eligible Dividends

Notes:
[1]This amount is equal to 20.7 percent of actual dividends received.
[2]This amount is equal to 13 percent of actual dividends received.

	Rate	Eligible Dividends	Rate	Non-eligible Dividends
Dividends received		$1,000.00		$1,000.00
Grossed-up	38%	1,380.00	18%	1,180.00
Federal tax	29%	400.20	29%	342.20
Less: Federal dividends tax credit (% actual dividends received)	15% 20.7%	(207.00)	11% 13.0%	(129.80)
Net Federal Tax	**19.32**	**193.20**	**21.24%**	**212.40**
Ontario tax	11.16%	154.01	11.16%	131.69
Less: Ontario dividend tax credit (% actual dividends received)	10.0% 13.8%	(138.00)	4.50% 5.31%	(53.10)
Net Ontario Tax		**16.01**		**78.59**
Add: Ontario surtax on net amount	20% 36%	3.20 15.65	20% 36%	15.72 28.29
Total Ontario Tax	**3.49%**	**34.86**	**12.26%**	**122.60**
Total Combined Tax	**22.81%**	**228.06**	**35%**	**335**

Exhibit 10–8

Calculation of Taxes on Dividend Income for Eligible and Non-eligible Dividends for an Ontarian in the Highest Tax Bracket

Financial Planning Calculations

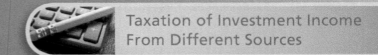

Taxation of Investment Income From Different Sources

An individual residing in Ontario who earns approximately $15,000 a year, wants to compare her after-tax income if she received $1,000 in the form of eligible dividends, capital gains, or interest. Her federal tax rate is 15 percent and the applicable provincial tax rate is 5.05 percent.

	Dividends	Capital Gains	Interest
Income	$1,000	$1,000	$1,000
Federal dividend gross-up	380	0	0
Less non-taxable gain	0	−500	0
Taxable income	1,380	500	1,000
Federal tax	207	75	150
Less dividend tax credit	−207	0	0
Basic federal tax (15%)	0	75	150
+ Provincial tax (5.05%)	0	25.25	50.50
= Total tax	0	100.25	200.50
Income after tax	1,000	899.75	799.50

Note: Users should be cautioned that the above scenario should not imply that in all cases, earning dividends would be more efficient from a tax point of view than other sources of income, such as capital gains. Typically, capital gains are the most tax-efficient source of income.

Interest from banks, credit unions, and savings and loan associations is subject to federal taxation. Interest that you receive from promissory notes, loans, bonds, and Canadian securities must also be reported as income. You must report the total of such income as ordinary income on your tax return.

Net income from rental property is also subject to federal taxation and is treated as ordinary income like wages or salaries. Generally, you must report all income and expenses on rental property.

CAPITAL GAINS AND CAPITAL LOSSES   Under current laws, profit resulting from the sale of stocks, mutual funds, bonds, land, and some personal property is considered a capital gain. For owners of certain small businesses and farm property, there is a $750,000 capital gains exemption. However, these two types of investments are defined very specifically, and you should check in advance to verify that your investment qualifies for the deduction. You will be taxed on 50 percent of all other capital gains you receive, minus any losses you may have incurred on non-depreciable assets, considered capital losses.

For example, assume Cody Shaw sold 100 shares of TD Bank stocks for a profit of $1,000. If he is in the 26 percent federal tax bracket, the total federal tax he will pay on his profit is $130 (26% × $500 = $130). Now suppose that he also incurred a capital loss of $200 upon selling 100 shares of BlackBerry. Now his total taxes will be $104 (26% × (500 − 100) = $104).

Under current taxation laws, an allowable capital loss is 50 percent of a capital loss; this amount can be used to offset taxable capital gains. However, if you do not have capital gains, you will not be allowed to use your capital loss to offset other income.

CONCEPT CHECK 10–4

1. What type of training does a qualified financial planner have?
2. What is your role in the investment process?
3. How do dividends, interest, and rental income differ from capital gains and losses?

SOURCES OF INVESTMENT INFORMATION

With most investments, more information is available than you can read and comprehend. Therefore, you must be selective in the type of information you use for evaluation purposes. With some investments, however, only a limited amount of information is available. For example, a wealth of information is available on individual stocks and mutual funds, whereas the amount of information on a metal, such as cobalt or manganese, may be limited to one source. Regardless of the number or availability of sources, always determine how reliable and accurate the information is. Following are sources of information you can use to evaluate present and future investments.

LO5
Use various sources of financial information that can reduce risks and increase investment returns.

THE INTERNET AND ONLINE COMPUTER SERVICES

While no one knows the exact number, experts estimate that there will be more than 3 billion Internet users worldwide by the end of 2014.* Today, more people have access to information provided by computers located in their homes or at libraries, universities, or businesses than ever before, and this number is growing. More importantly, a wealth of information is available on most personal finance topics and different investment alternatives. For example, you can obtain interest rates for GICs; current price information for stocks, bonds, and mutual funds; and brokers' recommendations to buy, hold, or sell a corporation's stocks. You can even trade securities online just by pushing the right button on your computer keyboard. You can also use computers and financial planning software to develop a personal financial plan.

To use your computer to generate information you really need, you must be selective. One of the best ways to access needed information is to use a search engine. Search engines, such as Yahoo Canada, Bing.com, Google.ca, and Canada.com, allow you to do a keyword search for the personal finance topic or investment alternative that you want to explore. Federal, provincial, and local governments, and most corporations also have Web sites where you can obtain valuable information.

Today, thousands of Internet service providers allow users to connect to the Internet and use search engines, newsgroups, mailing lists, blogs, and email. While it is impossible to list all of the Internet sites related to personal finance, those listed in Exhibit 10–9 will get you started. We will examine other specific Internet sites in the remaining chapters in Part 4. Also, read Appendix 1A at the end of Chapter 1 for information on how to use the Internet for personal financial planning.

NEWSPAPERS AND NEWS PROGRAMS

One of the most readily available sources of information for the average investor is the financial page of a national newspaper or the *Financial Post*. There you will find a summary of the day's trading on the TSX Venture Exchange, the Toronto Stock Exchange, and the two main American exchanges, the NASDAQ Stock Market and the New York Stock Exchange. In addition to stock coverage, most newspapers provide information on stocks traded in the over-the-counter markets, mutual funds, corporate and government bonds, commodities and options, and general economic news. Detailed information on how to read price quotations for stocks, bonds, mutual funds, and other investments is presented in the remaining chapters of Part 4.

It is also possible to obtain economic and investment information on radio or television. Many stations broadcast investment market summaries and economic information as part of their regular news programs. See Exhibit 10–10 on page 321 for publications and news programs used by successful investors.

---

*SOURCE: http://www.voanews.com/content/number-of-internet-users-worldwide-approaching-3-billion/1908968.html.

Exhibit 10–9

Useful Internet
Sites for Personal
Financial Planning

The following Internet sites provide information that you can use to establish a financial plan and begin an investment program.

Sponsor and Description	Web Address
Canoe.ca provides current financial material that can help both beginning and experienced investors sharpen their investment skills.	canoe.ca/money
Quicken provides information about investments, home mortgages, insurance, taxes, banking and credit, and different types of retirement programs.	quicken.intuit.ca
About Canada has an Investing: Canada link under its Business/Careers section. Click here to find a tremendous array of personal finance facts, advice, articles, and more. There's also an Investing for Beginners section.	financialplan.about.com
Globe Investor has a section on finance that offers everything from family finance to current business and finance news to information on borrowing, budgeting, and more.	http://www .theglobeandmail.com/ globe-investor/
The **Investor Learning Centre of Canada** makes learning about investing easier than it has ever been before. Whether you're an absolute beginner or a seasoned investor, you'll find what you need.	qtrade.ca/investor/en/ ilcsite/index.html
Investopedia provides an online investment dictionary, various articles, investing tutorials, stock ideas, simulators, as well as many different free tools to aid in investment decisions.	investopedia.com

BUSINESS PERIODICALS AND GOVERNMENT PUBLICATIONS

Most business periodicals are published weekly, twice a month, or monthly. *The Globe and Mail*'s *Report on Business, Business Week, Canadian Business, Fortune,* and similar business periodicals provide not only general news about the overall economy but also detailed financial information about individual corporations. Some business periodicals—for example, *Business 2.0* and *Canadian Banker*—focus on information about firms in a specific industry. In addition to business periodicals, more general magazines, such as *The Economist, Time,* and *Maclean's,* provide investment information as a regular feature. Finally, *Money, MoneySaver, Canadian MoneySaver,* and similar periodicals provide information and advice designed to improve your investment skills.

The Canadian government is an excellent source of information that is often free or offered at low cost. Statistics Canada provides information compiled both nationally and regionally. Industry Canada's Strategis is also an excellent resource for businesses and consumers alike.

CORPORATE REPORTS

The federal government requires corporations selling new issues of securities to disclose information about corporate earnings, assets and liabilities, products or services, and the

While individual investors have their favourite sources for investment information, it is quite likely that most successful investors use some of the following newspapers, periodicals, and news programs on a regular basis.

Exhibit 10–10

A Personal Reading List for Successful Investing

Newspapers
- Larger local newspapers
- *National Post*
- *The Globe and Mail*

Television
- CBC Business News, BNN (Business News Network), Business Television, CNN

Business Periodicals
- *The Globe and Mail's Report on Business* (ROB)
- *BusinessWeek*
- *Canadian Business*
- *Fortune*
- *The Economist*
- *Newsweek* (online only)

Personal Financial Publications
- *Canadian MoneySaver*
- *Money*
- *MoneySaver*
- *Maclean's Guide to Personal Finance*

qualifications of top management in a *prospectus* that they must give to investors. In addition to the prospectuses, all publicly owned corporations send their shareholders annual reports and quarterly reports that contain detailed financial data. Included in annual and quarterly corporate reports are statements of financial position, which describe changes in assets, liabilities, and owners' equity. Also included in these reports are income statements, which provide dollar amounts for sales, expenses, and profits or losses.

STATISTICAL AVERAGES

Investors often gauge the value of their investments by following one or more widely recognized statistical averages. Such an average is a statistical measure that indicates whether a broad investment category (stocks, bonds, mutual funds, and so on) is increasing or decreasing in value.

How much importance should you attach to statistical averages? These averages show trends and direction, but they do not pinpoint the actual value of a specific investment. The remaining chapters of Part 4 describe many of these averages.

INVESTOR SERVICES AND NEWSLETTERS

Many stockbrokers and financial planners mail a free monthly or quarterly newsletter to their clients. In addition, investors can subscribe to services that provide investment information. The fees for investor services generally range from $50 to $1,000 a year.

Four widely used services are available for investors who specialize in stocks, bonds, and mutual funds:

1. *SEDAR.* The System for Electronic Document Analysis and Retrieval (SEDAR) is used for electronically filing securities information in Canada. Since January 1, 1997, it has been mandatory for Canadian companies to file electronically. SEDAR, therefore, provides access to all Canadian public companies and mutual fund filings, including annual

reports, prospectuses, financial statements, press releases, and continuous disclosure documents. (See sedar.com.)

2. *Stockhouse Canada.* Located at stockhouse.ca, this site offers free access to a number of newsletters, as well as quotes, charts, chats, and news.

3. *The Fund Library.* The Fund Library, at fundlibrary.com, tracks more than 2,000 mutual funds and offers a number of tools and advice to help you compare them.

4. *Value Line.* This service provides reports supplying detailed information, such as earnings, dividends, sales, liabilities, and other financial data, about major corporations. While the focus is the U.S. market, more than 100 Canadian corporations are also examined. (See valueline.com.)

Other investment publications that may help you evaluate potential investments are the Canadian Bond Rating Service's (CBRS) *Guide to Conservative Fixed-Income Investing*; the *Blue Book of CBS Stock Reports*; the *Investor's Digest of Canada* from MPL Communications; and publications by the International Monetary Fund.

In addition to the preceding publications, each of the following securities exchanges provides information through printed materials and the Internet:

- Toronto Stock Exchange (tmx.com)
- TSX Venture Exchange (tmx.com)
- Montreal Exchange (tmx.ca)
- New York Stock Exchange (nyse.com)
- NASDAQ Stock Market (nasdaq.com)
- Federation of World Exchanges (world-exchanges.org)

Each of these Web sites provides basic information about the exchange, offers educational material and a glossary of important terms, and describes how investors can profit from transactions through the exchange.

The preceding discussion of investor services and newsletters is not exhaustive, but it gives you some idea of the amount and scope of information available to serious investors. Although most small investors find many of the services and newsletters described here too expensive for personal subscriptions, this information may be available from stockbrokers or financial planners. This type of information is also available at many public libraries.

DESKTOP INFORMATION SERVICES

Recently introduced into the financial services industry are desktop information services such as S&P Capital IQ, Bloomberg Professional service (about.bloomberg.com/), and Reuters (about.reuters.com/), which provide instantaneous access to real-time historical financial data, news, and many other services. These desktop information services have transformed the securities business and levelled the playing field between buyers and sellers.

CONCEPT CHECK 10–5

1. What do you think is the most readily available source of information for the average investor? Explain your answer.

2. What type of information can you obtain using the Internet?

3. Briefly describe the additional sources of information you can use to evaluate a potential investment and lessen risk.

SUMMARY OF LEARNING OBJECTIVES

LO1 **Explain why you should establish an investment program.**

Investment goals must be specific and measurable and should be classified as short-term, intermediate, and long-term. Before beginning an investment program, you must make sure your personal financial affairs are in order. This process begins with learning to live within your means and obtaining adequate insurance protection. The next step is the accumulation of an emergency fund equal to three to nine months' living expenses. Then, and only then, is it time to save the money needed to establish an investment program.

LO2 **Describe how safety, risk, income, growth, and liquidity affect your investment decisions.**

Although each investor may have specific, individual reasons for investing, all investors must consider the factors of safety, risk, income, growth, and liquidity. Especially important is the relationship between safety and risk. Basically, this concept can be summarized as follows: The potential return for any investment should be directly related to the risk the investor assumes. The risk factor can be broken down into five components: inflation risk, interest rate risk, business failure risk, market risk, and global investment risk.

LO3 **Identify the major types of investment alternatives.**

Investment alternatives include stocks, bonds, mutual funds, segregated funds, and real estate. More speculative investment alternatives include options, derivatives, commodities, precious metals, gemstones, and collectibles. Before choosing a specific investment, you should evaluate all potential investments on the basis of safety, risk, income, growth, and liquidity. You should also diversify your investments to lessen risk. With all of these factors in mind, the next step is to develop a specific, personal investment plan to help you accomplish your goals.

LO4 **Recognize the role of the professional financial planner and your role in a personal investment program.**

There are no hard and fast rules that define what a person must do in order to use the designation of Personal Financial Planner. In general, however, there are a number of reputable associations that regulate the use of related designations, such as Certified Financial Planner (CFP), Registered Financial Planner (RFP), and Financial Planner (FP). The associations generally insist on formal training of some kind as well as a minimum of experience and commitment. Financial planners can help people achieve their investment goals, but choosing a qualified planner is your responsibility. It is also your responsibility to evaluate and to monitor the value of your investments and to keep accurate and current records.

LO5 **Use various sources of financial information that can reduce risks and increase investment returns.**

Because more information on investments is available than most investors can read and comprehend, you must be selective in the type of information you use for evaluation purposes. Sources of information include the Internet, newspapers and news programs, business periodicals and government publications, corporate reports, statistical averages, investor services and newsletters, and desktop information services.

KEY TERMS

corporate bond 306

diversification 309

dividend 305

emergency fund 295

equity capital 305

government bond 306

liquidity 304

mutual fund 306

segregated fund 307

speculative investment 299

KEY FORMULAS

Page	Topic	Formula
302	Interest calculation for a corporate bond *Example:*	Dollar amount of annual interest = Issue price × Interest rate Dollar amount of interest = \$1,000 × 7% = \$1,000 × 0.07 = \$70

302   Approximate market price

$$\text{Approximate market price} = \frac{\text{Annual interest amount}}{\text{Comparable interest rate}}$$

Example:

$$\text{Approximate market price} = \frac{\$80}{9\%}$$

$$= \frac{\$80}{0.09}$$

$$= \$888.89$$

FINANCIAL PLANNING PROBLEMS

Mc Graw Hill connect™ Practise and learn online with Connect.

1. *Calculating the Amount for an Emergency Fund.* Beth-Anne and Martin Stewart have total take-home pay of $3,200 a month. Their monthly expenses total $2,800. Calculate the minimum amount this couple needs to establish an emergency fund. How did you calculate this amount? *LO1*

2. *Determining Interest and Approximate Bond Value.* Assume that three years ago, you purchased a 10-year corporate bond that pays 9.5 percent. The purchase price was $1,000. Also assume that three years after your bond investment, comparable bonds are paying 8 percent. *LO2*
   a. What is the annual dollar amount of interest that you receive from your bond investment?
   b. Assuming that comparable bonds are paying 8 percent, what is the approximate dollar price for which you could sell your bond?
   c. In your own words, explain why your bond increased or decreased in value.

3. *Analyzing Income and Growth Investments.*
   a. List three personal factors that might lead some investors to emphasize income rather than growth in their investment planning.
   b. List three personal factors that might lead some investors to emphasize growth rather than income. *LO2*

4. *Comparing Investment Alternatives.* Choose three of the investment alternatives presented in this chapter, then rank them from high to low on safety, risk, and liquidity. Assume that 3 is the highest score and 1 is the lowest score for each factor. On the basis of your ranking, which of the three

alternatives would you choose for your own investment program? Why? *LO3*

5. *Developing an Investment.* Assume you are single and have graduated from university. Your monthly take-home pay is $2,100, and your monthly expenses total $1,800, leaving you with a monthly surplus of $300. Develop a personal plan of action for investing like the one illustrated in Exhibit 10–6. *LO3*

6. *Monitoring an Investment's Financial Performance.* Based on the following information, construct a graph that illustrates price movement for a share of the First Canadian T-Bill Mutual Fund. (Note: You may want to review the material presented in the Financial Planning Calculations feature on page 316.) *LO4*

January	$18.70	July	$16.10
February	18.00	August	15.50
March	20.30	September	16.40
April	21.35	October	16.90
May	19.50	November	18.40
June	17.80	December	17.20

7. *Using Financial Information.* Suppose you just inherited 500 shares of General Motors of Canada stocks. List five sources of information you could use to evaluate your inheritance. Beside each source, briefly state how the information it contains could help in your evaluation. *LO5*

8. *Comparing Investment Income.* What is the main advantage of receiving dividend income vs. interest income? Explain. *LO3*

FINANCIAL PLANNING ACTIVITIES

1. *Using Investment Information.* Choose a current issue of *MoneySaver* or *Canadian MoneySaver* and summarize an article that provides suggestions on how you could use your money more effectively. *LO1*

2. *Planning for an Investment Program.* Assume you are 28 years old, your take-home pay is $2,200 a month, you have monthly living expenses that total $1,200, your

monthly car payment is $300, and your credit card debts total $4,900. Using the information presented in this chapter, develop a three-part plan to (a) reduce your monthly expenses, (b) establish an emergency fund, and (c) save $4,000 to establish an investment program. *LO1*

3. *Using the Internet to Obtain Information about Money Management.* As pointed out at the beginning of this chapter, it doesn't make sense to establish an investment program

until credit card and instalment purchases are reduced or eliminated. While most people are responsible and make payments when they're supposed to, some people get in trouble. To help avoid this problem, each of the following organizations has a site on the Internet:

- Credit Counselling Service of Sault Ste. Marie & District provides information on managing debt and credit, as well as a newsletter and other resources (soonet.ca).
- The National Foundation for Credit Counselling (NFCC) offers information about debt management, credit facts, and a budget calculator (nfcc.org).
- Equifax Canada is one of the two main credit bureaus in Canada (equifax.ca).

Choose one of the above organizations and visit its Web site. Then, prepare a report that summarizes the information provided by the organization. Finally, indicate if this information could help you manage your consumer debt. LO1

4. *Choosing Investment Alternatives.* From the investment alternatives described in this chapter, choose two specific investments you believe would help an individual who is 35 years old, divorced, and earns $20,000 a year. Assume this person has $30,000 to invest at this time. As part of your recommendation, compare each of your investment suggestions on safety, risk, income, growth, and liquidity. LO2

5. *Choosing Investment Alternatives.* Choose one of the investment alternatives presented in this chapter (stocks, bonds, mutual funds, real estate, or speculative investments) and prepare a two-page report describing why this investment would be appropriate for a woman who is 68 years old and has just lost her husband. Assume she is debt free and has inherited $175,000. LO3

6. *Explaining the Principle of Diversification.* Prepare a two-minute presentation describing why the principle of diversification is important when establishing an investment program. LO3

7. *Choosing a Financial Planner.* Many people call themselves financial planners. Describe the process you would use to choose one financial planner to help you develop an investment program. LO4

8. *Reporting Investment Income for Tax Purposes.* Choose four of the following sources of investment income. Then, describe how each type is taxed by the federal government. LO4
   a. Dividend income
   b. Interest income
   c. Rental income
   d. Capital gains
   e. Capital losses

9. *Using Investment Information.* Assume you have established an emergency fund and have saved an additional $12,000 to fund an investment in common stocks issued by Bell Canada. Using the sources of information discussed in this chapter, go to the library and obtain information about this company. Summarize your findings in a three-page report describing Bell's current operations and the firm's past and present financial performance. Finally, indicate if you would purchase Bell common stocks on the basis of the information in your report. LO5

10. *Using the Internet to Obtain Investment Information.* One of the most useful Internet search engines available is Canoe.ca. Visit the Canoe.ca Money site (money.canoe.ca). Then, describe in a two-page report the type of information available and how it could help you become a better investor. LO5

CREATING A FINANCIAL PLAN

Developing an Investment Plan

An investment program should consider safety, current income, growth potential, liquidity, and taxes. Your ability to set financial goals and select investment vehicles is crucial to long-term financial prosperity.

Web Sites for Investment Planning

- Online investing information at the Personal Finance link at **sympatico.msn.ca**, **canadianfinance.com**, and in the Money section of **about.com/money**.

- You can find investment articles from *Canadian MoneySaver* magazine at **canadianmoneysaver.ca**, and from *Canadian Business* at **canadianbusiness.com**.

- Market reports, corporate news and ratings, and various rates are all available online. Visit **fundlibrary.com**, **stockhouse.ca**, and **baystreet.com**.

- Online access to Canadian stock exchanges is at **tsx. com** for the Toronto Stock Exchange and for the TSX Venture

Exchange, and at **m-x.ca** for the Montreal Stock Exchange.

(NOTE: Addresses and content of Web sites change, and new sites are created daily. Use search engines to update and locate Web sites for your current financial planning needs.)

Long-Term Financial Planning Activities

1. Identify saving and investing decisions that would serve your changing life situations.

2. Develop a plan for revising investments as family and household situations change.

LIFE SITUATION CASE

First Budget, Then Invest for Success!

Jonathan and Meredith Faulk, married for 12 years, have an eight-year-old child. Six years ago, they purchased a home on which they owe about $110,000. They also owe $6,000 on their two-year-old automobile. All of their furniture is paid for, but they owe a total of $3,170 on two credit cards. Jonathan is employed as an engineer and makes $48,000 a year. Meredith works as a part-time computer analyst and earns about $18,000 a year. Their combined monthly income after deductions is $3,950.

About six months ago, the Faulks had what they now describe as a "financial meltdown." It all started one Monday afternoon when their air conditioner stopped cooling. Since their home was only six years old, they thought the repair ought to be a simple one—until the repair technician diagnosed their problem as a defective compressor. Unfortunately, the warranty on the compressor had run out about three months before the compressor broke down. According to the technician, it would cost more than $1,200 to replace the compressor. At the time, they had about $2,000 in their savings account, which they had been saving for their summer vacation, and now they had to use their vacation money to fix the air conditioner.

For the Faulks, the fact that they didn't have enough money to take a vacation was like a wake-up call. They realized they were now in their mid-30s and had serious cash problems. According to Jonathan, "We don't waste money, but there just never seems to be enough money to do the things we want to do." But according to Meredith, "The big problem is that we never have enough money to start an investment program that could pay for our daughter's post-secondary education or fund our retirement."

They decided to take a "big" first step in an attempt to solve their financial problems. They began by examining their monthly expenses for the past month. Here's what they found:

Income (cash inflow)

Jonathan's take-home salary	$2,800	
Meredith's take-home salary	1,150	
Total income		$3,950

Cash outflows

Monthly fixed expenses:
Home mortgage payment, including taxes and insurance	$1,190	
Automobile loan	315	
Automobile insurance	130	
Life insurance premium	50	
Total fixed expenses		$1,685

Monthly variable expenses:
Food and household necessities	$480	
Electricity	115	
Natural gas	50	
Telephone	55	
Family clothing allowance	130	
Gasoline and automobile repairs	120	
Personal and health care	100	
Recreation and entertainment	600	
Gifts and donations	300	
Minimum payment on credit cards	80	
Total variable expenses		$2,030
Total monthly expenses		**$3,715**
Surplus for savings or investments		**$ 235**

Once the Faulks realized they had a $235 surplus each month, they began to replace the $1,200 they had taken from their savings account to pay for repairing the air conditioner. Now it was time to take the next step.

Questions

1. How would you rate the Faulks' financial status before the air conditioner broke down?

2. The Faulks have a $235 surplus at the end of each month. Based on their current financial condition, what do you think they should do with this money?

3. The Faulks' take-home pay is almost $4,000 a month. Yet, after all expenses are paid, there is only a $235 surplus each month. Based on the information presented in this case, what expenses, if any, seem out of line and could be reduced to increase the surplus at the end of each month?

4. Given that both Jonathan and Meredith Faulk are in their mid-30s and want to retire when they reach age 65, what type of investment goals would be most appropriate for them?

5. How does the time value of money concept affect the types of long-term goals and the investments that a couple like the Faulks might use to build their financial nest egg?

6. Based on the different investments described in this chapter, what specific types of investments (stocks, mutual funds, real estate, and so on) would you recommend for the Faulks? Why?

Investing in Stocks

CAN YAHOO CANADA HELP YOU PICK WINNING STOCKS?

Can the Yahoo Canada Internet search engine help you pick stocks that will increase in value? The answer is a definite yes. Today, a wealth of information is available on the Internet, and the Yahoo Canada Finance Web site is an excellent place to start your search for a quality investment. That's what Jason Godwin did three years ago.

It all started when Jason, 26, moved to a small town in interior British Columbia. While he enjoyed the more relaxed lifestyle, he missed a lot of the conveniences he took for granted when he lived in the metropolitan Vancouver area. The convenience he missed the most was his trips to the public library. Ironically, he had never considered himself a bookworm, but he did enjoy researching different investments. Unfortunately, the local library in the nearest small town just didn't have the "stuff" that Jason used to make his investment decisions.

Jason had owned a computer for some time but had never really used the Internet except to download music and look up movie listings. A friend told him there was a

vast amount of investment information available online, a lot of it free. Knowing he had to have access to current information if he wanted to continue investing, Jason decided to give researching his investments online a try. He was pleasantly surprised to find that by accessing the Internet he could obtain more than enough information to evaluate stocks and other investments that caught his interest.

After five months of surfing the Net and examining different Web sites, Jason now uses the Yahoo Canada Finance site as a starting point when evaluating potential stock investments. By simply entering Yahoo Canada's address (ca.finance.yahoo.com/), typing in the name of a corporation or its stock symbol, and clicking his mouse, he can obtain information about management, new products and marketing activities, and financial data. Of particular interest to Jason are the recommendations made by brokers that follow a corporation's stock, the firm's earnings per share and earnings history, and access to research abstracts. And he can get current price information for a stock, along with graphs that show historical market values, current news about the firm, information submitted by the corporation to SEDAR, a profile of the company, and messages posted by investors. Now, Jason admits he has become a better investor than before he started using a computer. More importantly, his computer-based investment decisions have resulted in his investments increasing in value.

QUESTIONS

1. How important are evaluating a stock issue and the financial condition of a company when making a decision to buy or sell the company's stocks? Explain your answer.

2. If you needed to obtain financial data to make a decision to buy or sell a company's stocks, would you go to the library or the Internet? Why?

COMMON STOCKS

LO1

Identify the most important features of common stocks.

Many beginning investors face two concerns when they begin an investment program. First, they don't know where to get the information they need to evaluate potential investments. In reality, more information is available than most investors can read. And, as pointed out in the opening case, quality investment information is available not only in libraries but also on the Internet. Jason Godwin found more information than he needed to make informed investment decisions by accessing the Yahoo Canada Finance Web site.

Second, beginning investors sometimes worry that they won't know what the information means when they do find it. Yet, common sense goes a long way when evaluating potential investments. For example, positive indications are an increase in sales, an increase in profits, and a rise in earnings per share over time.

In fact, that's what this chapter is all about. We want you to learn how to evaluate a stock and to make money from your investment decisions. That's the way it's supposed to work.

HOW ARE THE MARKETS DOING?

index A statistical measure of the changes in a portfolio of stocks representing a portion of the overall market.

When people talk about "the market" they are actually referring to an **index**. With the growing importance of the stock market in our society, indexes, like the S&P/TSX Composite Index, DJIA, S&P 500, and NASDAQ Composite, have grown to become a part of our everyday vocabulary.

Investors use indexes to track the performance of the stock market because it would be too difficult to try to track every single security trading in the country. Therefore, they take a smaller sample of the market that is representative of the whole.

The following are some of the most popular indexes:

S&P/TSX COMPOSITE INDEX   With coverage of approximately 95 percent of the Canadian equities market, the S&P/TSX Composite Index is the primary gauge for Canadian-based, Toronto Stock Exchange listed companies. The size of the S&P/TSX Composite (C$1,839.57 billion in float market capitalization as of June 2014) and its broad economic sector coverage has made the S&P/TSX Composite the premier indicator of activity for equity markets in Canada since its launch on January 1, 1977. The constituents of this index are updated quarterly.

See Exhibit 11–1 for more information on the S&P/TSX Composite Portfolio Characteristics and Exhibit 11–2 for a graph of the index performance since 2009.

DOW JONES INDUSTRIAL AVERAGE   DJIA, often referred to as the Dow, is the best known and most widely reported indicator of the stock market's performance. The Dow tracks the price changes of 30 significant industrial stocks traded on the New York Stock Exchange.

NYSE COMPOSITE INDEX   An index that covers the price movements of all stocks listed on the New York Stock Exchange.

Index Characteristics	S&P/TSX Composite
Number of Constituents	244
Adjusted Market Capitalization (C$ billion)	1,839.57
Constituent Market Capitalization (Adjusted C$ billion):	
Average	7.54
Largest	108.42
Smallest	0.33
Median	2.61
% Weight Largest Constituent	5.84%
Top 10 Holdings (% Market Capitalization Share)	34.95%
Sector Breakdown	**S&P/TSX Composite**
Consumer Discretionary	5.45%
Consumer Staples	2.72%
Energy	27.07%
Financials	33.75%
Health Care	2.74%
Industrials	7.99%
Information Technology	1.74%
Materials	11.91%
Telecommunication Services	4.69%
Utilities	1.93%

Exhibit 11–1

S&P/TSX Composite Portfolio Characteristics as of June 2014

SOURCE: S&P/TSX Composite Equity Indices, www.tmxmoney.com, accessed June 14, 2014.

Exhibit 11–2   The S&P/TSX Composite Index 2009–2014

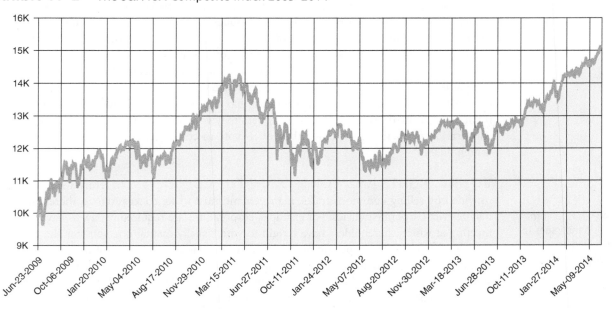

S&P/TSX Composite Index (^GSPTSE) - Index Value

Copyright CIQ 2014

SOURCE: Capital IQ, capitaliq.com/home.aspx.

NASDAQ COMPOSITE INDEX   An index that covers the price movements of all stocks traded on the NASDAQ stock market. The NASDAQ (pronounced "nazzdack") Composite is heavily weighted in technology and Internet stocks. As such, the companies listed in the composite are considered to have high growth potential.

STANDARD & POOR'S 500 STOCK INDEX   The S&P 500 is one of the best benchmarks in the world for large-cap stocks. By containing 500 companies it has great diversification, and is considered one of the best overall indicators of market performance.

WHY CORPORATIONS ISSUE COMMON STOCKS

As mentioned in Chapter 10, a stock represents your ownership portion in a company. The two basic stock types are common and preferred. Corporations issue common stocks to finance their business startup costs and to help pay for their ongoing business activities. Today, corporations are classified as either private corporations or public corporations. A *private corporation* is a corporation whose stocks are owned by relatively few people and not traded openly in stock markets. A *public corporation* is a corporation whose stocks are traded openly in stock markets and may be purchased by individuals. Public corporations may have thousands or even millions of shareholders. Corporate managers prefer selling common stocks as a method of financing for several reasons.

A FORM OF EQUITY   Corporations don't have to repay the money a shareholder pays for stocks. Generally, a shareholder in a public corporation may sell his or her stocks to another individual. The selling price is determined by how much a buyer is willing to pay for the stocks. Simply put, if the demand for a particular stock increases, the market value of the stock increases. If the demand for a particular stock decreases, the market value of the stock decreases. Demand for a stock changes when information about the firm or its future prospects is released to the general public. For example, information about expected sales revenues, earnings, expansions or mergers, or other important developments within the firm can increase or decrease the demand for, and ultimately the market value of, the firm's stocks.

DIVIDENDS NOT MANDATORY   Dividends are paid out of profits, and dividend payments must be approved by the corporation's board of directors. Dividend policies vary among corporations, but most firms distribute between 30 and 70 percent of their earnings to shareholders. However, some corporations follow a policy of smaller or no dividend distributions to shareholders. In general, these are rapidly growing firms, such as Amazon (online shopping), Facebook (social media), and Priceline.com (discount travel), that retain a large share of their earnings for research and development, expansion, or major projects. On the other hand, utility companies and other financially secure enterprises may distribute 80 to 90 percent of their earnings. Always remember that if a corporation has had a bad year, dividend payments may be reduced or omitted. Although board members may vote to continue paying dividends when a corporation is operating at a loss, they often vote to completely omit dividend payments to shareholders.

proxy A legal form that lists the issues to be decided at a shareholders' meeting and requests that shareholders transfer their voting rights to some individual or individuals.

VOTING RIGHTS AND CONTROL OF THE COMPANY   In return for the financing provided by selling common stocks, management must make concessions to shareholders that may restrict corporate policies. For example, corporations are required by law to have an annual meeting at which shareholders have a right to vote, usually casting one vote per share of stock. Shareholders may vote in person or by proxy. A **proxy** is a legal form that lists the issues to be decided at a shareholders' meeting and requests that shareholders transfer their voting rights to some individual or individuals. The common shareholders elect the board of directors and must approve major changes in corporate policies. Typical changes in corporate policy include (1) an amendment of the corporate charter, (2) the sale of certain assets, (3) possible mergers, (4) the issuance of preferred stocks or corporate bonds, and (5) changes in the amount of common stocks.

Legally, a corporation may include a provision for pre-emptive rights in its corporate charter. A **pre-emptive right** is the right of current shareholders to purchase any new stock the corporation issues before it is offered to the general public. By exercising their pre-emptive rights, shareholders are able to maintain their current proportion of corporate ownership. This may be important when the corporation is small and management control is a matter of concern to shareholders.

Finally, corporations are required by law to distribute annual and quarterly reports to shareholders. These reports contain details about sales, earnings, and other vital information.

pre-emptive right The right of current shareholders to purchase any new stocks the corporation issues before it is offered to the general public.

WHY INVESTORS PURCHASE COMMON STOCKS

How do you make money by buying common stocks? Basically, common stock investments can increase your wealth in two ways: income from dividends and dollar appreciation of stock value.

INCOME FROM DIVIDENDS   While the corporation's board members are under no legal obligation to pay dividends, most board members like to keep shareholders happy (and prosperous). Few things will unite shareholders into a powerful opposition force more rapidly than omitted or lowered dividends. Therefore, board members usually declare dividends if the corporation's after-tax profits are sufficient for them to do so. Since dividends are a distribution of profits, investors must be concerned about future after-tax profits. In short, how secure is the dividend?

Corporate dividends for common stocks may take the form of cash, additional stocks, or company products. However, the last type of dividend is extremely unusual. If the board of directors declares a cash dividend, each common shareholder receives an equal amount per share. Although dividend policies vary, most corporations pay dividends on a quarterly basis. Some corporations, particularly those experiencing large swings in earnings, declare special year-end or extra dividends in addition to their regular quarterly dividends.

Exhibit 11–3 shows that Computershare Inc. has declared a quarterly dividend of $0.05 per share to shareholders who owned the stock on the record date of June 27. The **record date** is the date on which a shareholder must be registered on the corporation's books in order to receive dividend payments. When a stock is traded around the record date, the company must determine whether the buyer or the seller is entitled to the dividend. To solve this problem, this rule is followed: *Dividends remain with the stock until two business days before the record date.* On the second day before the record date, the stock begins selling ex-dividend. The term **ex-dividend** describes a situation when a stock trades "without dividend," and the seller—not the buyer—is entitled to a declared dividend payment. An investor who purchases an ex-dividend stock is not entitled to receive dividends for that quarter, and the dividend is paid to the previous owner of the stock.

record date The date on which a shareholder must be registered on the corporation's books in order to receive dividend payments.

ex-dividend A stock trades without a dividend and the seller is entitled to the declared dividend payment.

For example, Computershare Inc. declared a quarterly dividend of $0.05 per share to shareholders who owned stocks on Friday, June 27. The stocks went ex-dividend on Wednesday, June 25, 2014, two *business* days before the June 27 date. A shareholder who purchased the stock on June 25 or after was not entitled to this quarterly dividend payment. Computershare Inc. made the actual dividend payment on July 17 to shareholders who owned stocks on the record date. Investors are generally conscious of the date on which a stock goes ex-dividend, and the dollar value of the stock may go down by the value of the quarterly dividend.

DIVIDENDS
Corporate dividends declared Wednesday (quarterly unless otherwise indicated):
Computershare Inc. : Common, $0.05. Payable July 17. Record June 27.

Exhibit 11–3

Typical Information on Corporation Dividends as Presented in *The Globe and Mail*

SOURCE: Adapted from *The Globe and Mail*, Thursday, June 13, 2014.

CHANGES IN STOCK VALUE   In most cases, you purchase stocks and then hold on to them for a period of time. If the market value of the stocks increases, you must decide whether to sell them at the higher price or continue to hold them. If you decide to sell, the dollar amount of difference between the purchase price and the selling price represents your profit. Of course, the market value of the stock can also decline, in which case the decision is the same—to sell and trigger a loss or continue to hold in the expectation that the stock price will rise.

Let's assume that on June 4, 2003, you purchased 100 shares of IMAX Corp. on the TSX at a cost of $13 a share. Your cost for the stocks was $1,300 plus $29 commission charges, for a total investment of $1,329. (Note: Commissions, covered later in this chapter, are charged when you purchase stocks *and* when you sell stocks.) Let's also assume you held your 100 shares until June 4, 2014, and then sold them for $38 a share. Each year of the three-year period you owned IMAX Corp., the company paid an annual dividend totalling $2.20 a share. Exhibit 11–4 shows your return on the investment. In this case, you made money because of quarterly dividend distributions and through an increase in stock value from $13 to $38 per share. Exhibit 11–4 shows the cash flows of your transaction. Of course, if the stock's value should decrease, or if the firm's board of directors reduces or votes to omit dividends, your return may be less than the original investment.

POSSIBILITY OF INCREASED VALUE FROM STOCK SPLITS   Investors potential profits may increase through a stock split. A **stock split** is a procedure in which the shares of stock owned by existing shareholders are divided into a larger number of shares. Although a stock split itself does not create profits, better share appreciation may occur as the price is brought back into trading range. In 2013 for example, TD Bank's board of directors approved a 2-for-1 stock split. After the stock split, a shareholder who had previously owned 100 shares now owned 200 shares. The most common stock splits are 2-for-1, 3-for-1, and 4-for-1.

Why do corporations split their stocks? In many cases, a firm's management has a theoretical ideal price range for the firm's stocks. If the market value of the stocks rises above the ideal range, a stock split brings the market value back in line. In the case of TD Bank, the 2-for-1 stock split reduced the price of a share to about one-half of the stock's previous price. The lower price for each share of stock was the result of dividing the dollar value of the company by a larger number of shares of common stocks. Also, a decision to split a company's stocks and the resulting lower price makes the stocks more attractive to the investing public. This attraction is based on the belief that most corporations split their stocks only when their financial future is improving and on the upswing. As a result, investors have an expectation of future financial growth. This expectation of future growth can mean increases in the firm's sales and

stock split A procedure in which the shares of common stocks owned by existing shareholders are divided into a larger number of shares.

Exhibit 11–4

Sample Stock Transaction for IMAX Corp.

Assumptions			
100 shares of common stocks purchased June 4, 2003, sold June 4, 2014; annual dividends of $2.20 per share for the 11-year period.			

Cost when purchased		Proceeds when sold	
100 shares @ $13 =	$1,300	100 shares @ $38 =	$3,800
Plus commission	29	Minus commission	−29
Total cost	$1,329	Net proceeds	$3,771

Transaction summary	
Net proceeds	$ 3,771
Minus total cost	−1,329
Profit from stock sale	$ 2,442
Total annual dividends	+2,420 ($2.20 per share per year × 100 shares × 11 years)

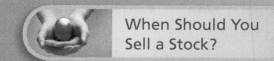
Assume that in May 2012, Marina Stahl purchased 100 shares of Facebook, one of the innovators in social media, for $38.23 a share. According to Marina, all the financial information about Facebook looked good. Two years later, when the value of Facebook had increased to $68.60 a share, Marina decided to sell the stocks for a profit. During that two-year period, she had thought about selling her stocks at least four times. But she just couldn't make the decision to sell.

According to financial experts, the value of a share of stock may go up or down, but investors like Marina Stahl always have trouble deciding when to sell. Generally, most investors have a reason for buying a stock, but when it is time to sell that same stock, they are often blinded by a sense of loyalty to "their" investments, whether deserved or not. Although no sure cures for this problem exist, the following suggestions may help:

1. *Follow your stock's value.* Too often, investors purchase a stock and then forget about it. They assume everything is okay and the stock will magically increase in value. A much better approach is to graph the dollar value of your stock on a weekly basis.
2. *Watch the company's financials.* Smart investors evaluate a stock investment before they make it. The smartest investors use all the available information to continuously evaluate their stocks. If the amounts reported or projected for sales,

profits, or other important financial measures are declining or are well below industry averages, it may be time to sell the stocks. If you would not buy the same investment today, it's time to sell it no matter how much you have gained or lost.

3. *Track the firm's product line.* Simply put, if the firm's products become obsolete and the company fails to introduce state-of-the-art new products, its sales—and ultimately profits—may take a nosedive. The failure to introduce new products may destroy the firm's ability to compete.
4. *Monitor economic developments.* An economic recession or an economic recovery may cause the value of a stock investment to increase or decrease. For example, most consumers who are unemployed don't buy new cars. Therefore, manufacturing firms, such as General Motors or Ford, may experience lower sales, lower profits, and lower stock values until the employment outlook brightens. Also, watch the inflation rate, interest rates, productivity rates, and similar economic indicators that may be a red flag.
5. *Be patient.* The secret of success for making money with stocks is time. As pointed out earlier in this chapter, stocks have returned over 10 percent before adjusting for inflation each year for over a 40-year period and, assuming you purchased good stocks, your investments will eventually increase in value.

profits *and* increases in the market value of the firm's stocks. *Be warned: There are no guarantees that a stock's market value will go up after a split.*

CONCEPT CHECK 11–1

1. If you needed information about a stock investment, would you go to the library or the Internet? Why?
2. Why do corporations issue common stocks?
3. What are the typical issues on which shareholders vote?
4. Describe two reasons shareholders purchase common stocks.

PREFERRED STOCKS

In addition to or instead of purchasing common stocks, you may purchase preferred stocks. The most important priority an investor in preferred stocks enjoys is receiving cash dividends before common shareholders are paid any cash dividends. This factor is especially important when a corporation is experiencing financial problems and cannot pay cash dividends to both preferred and common shareholders. Unlike the amount of the dividend on common stocks, the dollar

LO2

Discuss the most important features of preferred stocks.

amount of the dividend on preferred stocks is known before the stocks are purchased. The dividend amount is a stated amount of money for each share of preferred stock.

Preferred stocks are often referred to as "middle" investments because they represent an investment midway between common stocks (an ownership position) and corporate bonds (a creditor position). When compared with corporate bonds, the yield on preferred stocks is often smaller than the yield on bonds. When compared with common stocks, preferred stocks are safer investments that offer more secure dividends. They are often purchased by conservative investors wanting preferential tax treatment on the dividend and possible capital gains. They are also purchased by other corporations because corporations receive a tax break on the dividend income from preferred stocks.

While preferred stocks do not represent a legal debt that must be repaid, if the firm is dissolved or declares bankruptcy, preferred shareholders do have first claim to the corporation's assets after creditors (including bondholders).

callable preferred stocks Stocks that a corporation may exchange, at its option, for a specified amount of money.

Generally, preferred stocks are callable. **Callable preferred stocks** are stocks that a corporation may exchange, at its option, for a specified amount of money. To understand why a corporation would call in a preferred stock issue, you must first realize that dividend rates paid by similar investments increase and decrease. If dividends are decreasing and similar investments provide a smaller return than the corporation's preferred stock issue, management may decide to call in their existing preferred issue and substitute new preferred stocks that pay a lower dividend. Management may also decide to call in the preferred stocks and issue common stocks with no specified dividend. The dividend amount paid on a preferred issue can also affect the market value of the stock. For example, the preferred stock issue in the last example paid a 6 percent dividend. When the corporation issued preferred stocks, the 6 percent dividend was competitive with the dividends paid by corporations issuing preferred stocks at that time. If dividend rates on similar investments decrease, the market value of the 6 percent preferred stock issue increases due to its higher dividend. On the other hand, if dividends paid on similar investments increase, the market value of the 6 percent preferred stock issue falls due to its lower dividend rate.

When compared with corporations selling common stocks, preferred stocks are used less often and by only a few corporations, yet it is an alternative method of financing that may attract investors who do not wish to buy common stocks. Preferred stocks, like common stocks, are equity financing that does not have to be repaid. And dividends on preferred stocks, as on common stocks, may be omitted by action of the board of directors.

Many small investors consider preferred stocks to be as safe as corporate bonds. Generally, however, they are less safe because corporate bonds represent borrowed money that must be repaid. Bondholders are more likely to receive interest payments until maturity and eventual repayment of their initial investment than preferred shareholders are to continue receiving dividends or recover their initial investment in the stocks. To make preferred stock issues more attractive, some corporations may offer three additional features.

THE CUMULATIVE FEATURE OF PREFERRED STOCKS

cumulative preferred stocks Stocks with unpaid dividends that accumulate and must be paid before any cash dividend is paid to common shareholders.

If the corporation's board of directors believes that omitting dividends is justified, it can vote to omit both the dividends paid to common and preferred shareholders. One way preferred shareholders can protect themselves against omitted dividends is to purchase cumulative preferred stocks. **Cumulative preferred stocks** are stocks with unpaid dividends that accumulate and must be paid before any cash dividend is paid to the common shareholders. If a corporation does not pay dividends to the cumulative preferred shareholders during one dividend period, the amount of the missed dividends is added to the following period's preferred dividends. If you own non-cumulative preferred stocks, an omitted dividend will not be made up later.

THE PARTICIPATION FEATURE OF PREFERRED STOCKS

To make a preferred stock issue more attractive, corporations sometimes add a *participation feature*. This feature allows preferred shareholders to share with the common shareholders in the corporation's earnings. Participating preferred stocks are rare; this feature is used only when special measures are necessary to attract investors.

The participation feature of preferred stocks works like this: (1) The required dividend is paid to preferred shareholders; (2) a stated dividend, usually equal to the dividend amount paid to preferred shareholders, is paid to common shareholders; and (3) the remainder of the earnings available for distribution is shared by both preferred and common shareholders.

THE CONVERSION FEATURE OF PREFERRED STOCKS

Convertible preferred stocks can be exchanged, at the shareholder's option, for a specified number of shares of common stocks. The conversion feature provides the investor with the added safety of preferred stocks and the possibility of greater speculative gain through conversion to common stocks.

All the information relating to the number of shares of common stocks that may be obtained through conversion of preferred stocks is stated in the corporate records and is usually printed on the preferred stock certificate. For example, assume Martin & Martin Manufacturing Corporation has issued convertible preferred stocks. Each share of preferred stocks in this issue is convertible into two shares of common stocks. Assume the market price of Martin & Martin's convertible preferred stocks is $24 and the stocks pay an annual dividend of $1.60 a share. Also assume the market price of the company's common stocks is $9 and the common stock currently pays an annual dividend of $0.54 a share. Under these circumstances, you would keep the preferred stocks. If the market price of the common stocks increased to above $12 a share, however, you would have an incentive to exercise the conversion option.

The decision to convert preferred stocks to common stocks is complicated by three factors. First, the dividends paid on preferred stocks are more secure than the dividends paid on common stocks. Second, the amount of the dividend for preferred stocks is generally higher than the amount of the dividend for common stocks. Third, because of the conversion option, the market value of convertible preferred stocks usually increases as the market value of common stocks increases.

The next section discusses additional factors you should evaluate before purchasing either preferred stocks or common stocks.

CONCEPT CHECK 11–2

1. What is the most important priority a preferred shareholder has compared with common shareholders?
2. Why would a corporation call in preferred stocks?
3. Why do corporations issue preferred stocks?
4. Describe three features corporations can offer to make preferred stocks more attractive.

EVALUATION OF A STOCK ISSUE

Many investors expect to earn a 10 percent or higher return on their investments, yet they are unwilling to spend the time required to become a good investor. In fact, many people purchase investments without doing *any* research. They wouldn't buy a car without a test drive or purchase a home without comparing different houses, but for some unknown reason they invest without doing their homework. The truth is that there is no substitute for a few hours of detective work when choosing an investment. This section explains how to evaluate a potential stock investment.

LO3

Explain how to evaluate stock investments.

STOCK VALUATION

Before you become an active participant in the stock market, it is important to understand different approaches used by experts in analyzing stocks. There are at least two views that use different assumptions about how stock prices change: *fundamental analysis* and *technical analysis*.

fundamental analysis A way to value stocks by looking at micro and macro factors that might influence the economic value of the stock.

Fundamental analysis values stocks by looking at micro and macro factors that might influence the economic value of the stock. These factors include the firm's financial statements, the cash flows the firm is able to generate, management strategy, industry and competitive conditions, the state of the economy, and the like. The value of the stock in essence is derived from the present value of future cash it is going to generate. If the market is mispricing securities, the fundamental analyst recommends a buy, hold, or sell recommendation.

technical analysis The idea that changes in investor sentiment are responsible for changes in trends, and that the value of a stock can be predicted by extrapolating price from historical patterns.

Technical analysis maintains that changes in investor sentiment are responsible for changes in trends, and that the value of a stock can be predicted by extrapolating price from historical patterns. Thus, various charts are analyzed indicating peaks, troughs, and movements that suggest the momentum of price movements.

The **efficient market hypothesis** (EMH) contradicts technical analysis since it states that future prices cannot be predicted from past trends and patterns. Even if technical analysis were considered valid, the EMH would suggest that trades based on such patterns are already reflected in the existing price.

efficient market hypothesis States that future prices cannot be predicted from past trends and patterns.

The concept of market efficiency is the cornerstone of how academics believe prices are determined. Simply stated, an efficient market is one in which the prices of all assets (in particular financial assets like stocks and bonds) fully reflect all available information. Since price is determined by how investors react to information, the implication of an efficient market is that no investor can expect to earn more or less than a "fair" rate of return from trading assets. While securities and assets markets may not meet these conditions perfectly, years of empirical evidence suggest that they come very close. The assumptions of the EMH imply many buyers and sellers, cheap and accessible information, and low transaction costs.

For you the investor, EMH has several implications including:

1. Stock prices move randomly and therefore cannot be predicted from past trends in any consistent manner.
2. The current market price of a security reflects its "true" value. Therefore, it is difficult, if not impossible, to consistently find bargains.
3. Securities are priced and traded on their expected risk–return merits and not on their unique features. Prices incorporate new information almost instantly and excess returns are almost impossible to obtain based on historical information.
4. Market indices (such as the S&P/TSX Composite) and other aggregate market trends are usually leading indicators of future economic prospects and serve as benchmarks as to the price behaviour of the average stock.
5. The relationship between risk and return is positive and the average risk premium (risk − the risk-free return) is fairly constant over time.

Many studies support the EMH and many investors believe that experts who analyze and trade securities act rationally on the merits of economic information. It is worth remembering that the EMH does not imply portfolio managers and investors can never achieve superior returns, or that the market does not make sense because price changes are random. And, most importantly, the EMH does not absolve you, the investor, from doing a thorough evaluation of a company, the industry that it is in, and the returns you can realistically hope to achieve, before investing in its stock.

CLASSIFICATION OF STOCK INVESTMENTS

A wealth of information is available to stock investors. Information sources include newspapers, the Internet, business periodicals, corporate reports, and investor services. Most local newspapers carry several pages of business news. The *Financial Post* and *Canadian Business* are devoted almost entirely to financial and economic news. And more people are using the

Internet to evaluate or monitor the value of their investments. Obviously, different types of investments require different methods of evaluation, but a logical place to start the evaluation process for stock is with the classification of different types of stock investments. When evaluating a stock investment, stockbrokers, financial planners, and investors often classify stocks into different categories. We describe eight commonly used classifications.

A **blue-chip stock** is a safe investment that generally attracts conservative investors. Stocks of this kind are issued by the strongest and most respected companies, such as Bell Canada Enterprises, Royal Bank, and Suncor Energy. Characteristics to watch for when evaluating this type of stock include leadership in an industrial group, a history of stable earnings, and consistency in paying dividends.

An **income stock** pays higher-than-average dividends. To be able to pay above-average dividends, a corporation must have a steady, predictable source of income. Stocks issued by electric, gas, telephone, and other utility companies are generally classified as income stocks. Many investors seeking income may also include quality preferred stock issues in their portfolios.

A **growth stock** is issued by a corporation that has the potential to earn profits above the average profits of all firms in the economy. Key factors to evaluate when choosing a growth stock include an expanding product line of quality merchandise and an effective research and development department. Retail expansion, state-of-the-art manufacturing facilities, and expansion into international markets are also characteristic of growth stocks. In fact, most growth companies retain a large part of their earnings to pay for their research and development efforts. As a result, such companies generally pay out less than 30 percent of their earnings in dividends to their shareholders. Since 2010, typical growth stocks included Apple, Michael Kors, and Oracle.

A **cyclical stock** follows the business cycle of advances and declines in the economy. When the economy expands, the market value of a cyclical stock increases; when the economy declines, the market value decreases. Most cyclical stocks are in basic industries, such as automobiles, steel, paper, and heavy manufacturing. Investors try to buy cyclical stocks just before the economy expands and sell them just before it declines. Typical cyclical stocks include Ford Motor Company, Caterpillar Inc., and US Steel.

A **defensive stock** remains stable during declines in the economy. Generally, companies that issue such stocks have a history of stable earnings and are able to maintain dividend payments to shareholders during periods of economic decline. Many stocks that are classified as income stocks or blue-chip stocks are also classified as defensive stocks because of their stable earnings and consistent dividend policies. Stocks in this classification include Procter & Gamble, Kellogg, and stocks issued by utility companies.

Stocks may also be classified as large cap or small cap. A **large-cap stock** is issued by a large corporation that has a large number of stocks outstanding and a large amount of capitalization. In financial circles, **capitalization** is usually defined as the total amount of securities—stocks and bonds—issued by a corporation. Typically, the companies listed in the Dow Jones averages are considered large caps. Because many large-cap stocks are often considered much more secure than small-cap stocks, they may appeal to more conservative investors. A **small-cap stock** is generally defined as a stock issued by a company that has a capitalization of $150 million or less. Since these stocks are issued by smaller companies, they tend to be more speculative and are often purchased by investors hoping to make a quick profit.

A **penny stock** typically sells for less than $1 a share. These are stocks issued by new companies or companies with erratic sales and earnings. Therefore, penny stocks are more volatile than more conservative stocks. These stocks are classified as high-risk investments and are more difficult to research because information about them is hard to find. They are also more difficult to track, and dramatic increases and decreases in market value are common. Unfortunately, when the bubble bursts, these stocks can become worthless. As a result, penny stocks should be purchased only by investors who understand *all* the risks.

---

blue-chip stock A safe investment that generally attracts conservative investors.

income stock A stock that pays higher-than-average dividends.

growth stock A stock issued by a corporation that has the potential to earn profits above the average profits of all firms in the economy.

cyclical stock A stock that follows the business cycle of advances and declines in the economy.

defensive stock A stock that remains stable during declines in the economy.

large-cap stock A stock issued by a large corporation that has a large amount of stocks outstanding and a large amount of capitalization.

capitalization The total amount of securities—stocks and bonds—issued by a corporation.

small-cap stock A stock issued by a company that has a capitalization of $150 million or less.

penny stock A stock that typically sells for less than $1 per share.

Did you know?

Blue chips are named after the blue chip in poker, which is the chip that carries the highest value.

HOW TO READ THE FINANCIAL SECTION OF THE NEWSPAPER

Most metropolitan newspapers contain information about stocks listed on the Toronto Stock Exchange, the TSX Venture Exchange, and other major stock exchanges, and stocks of local interest. Although not all newspapers print exactly the same information, they usually provide the basic information. Stocks are listed alphabetically, so your first task is to move down the table to find the stocks in which you're interested. Then, to read the stock quotation, you simply read across the table. The first row in Exhibit 11–5 gives detailed information about Finning International Inc. (Each numbered entry in the list below the enlarged stock table refers to a column of the stock table.)

If a corporation has more than one stock issue, the common stock issues are always listed first. Then the preferred stock issues are listed and are indicated by the letters *pf* behind the firm's name.

Exhibit 11–5   Financial Information about Common Stock Given in the *Financial Post*

THE FINANCIAL POST, SATURDAY, JULY 1, 2000

52W high	52W low	Stock	Ticker	Div	Yield %	P/E	Friday Vol 00s	High /ask	Low /bid	Net chg	Earnings data fiscal	Interim EPS	12 mth EPS	Week Vol 00s	High	Low	Cls/ last	Net chg
15.40	11.50	Finning◆	FTT	0.20	1.6	14.9	413	12.75	12.50	−0.05	Ma 3M	0.17	0.84	8333	12.95	12.50	12.50	
n 10.50	8.00	FirmCap	FC	p0.67	7.3		nt	9.80	9.30					31	9.50	9.25	9.25	−0.25
5.95	4.20	1stAsia un	FAI	p0.52	10.2	14.7	26	5.20	5.10		Ma 3M	0.35	0.35	899	5.35	5.05	5.10	−0.10
9.90	7.10	1stAustPr	FAP	0.84	10.7	10.0	255	7.95	7.75	+0.05	Ja 3M	0.18	0.78	2065	8.00	7.75	7.85	−0.10
0.35	0.05	1stAust wt					z85	0.055	0.055					47	0.055	0.055	0.055	
2.70	0.35	1stCalg	FCP				648	0.85	0.82	−0.01	Ma 3M	d0.01	d0.22	13766	1.21	0.82	0.85	−0.13

1. Highest price paid for one share of Finning International during the past 52 weeks: $15.40

2. Lowest price paid for one share of Finning International in the past 52 weeks: $11.50

3. Name of the company: Finning International Inc.

4. Ticker symbol or letters that identify a stock for trading: FTT

5. Projected annual dividend for next year based on the amount of the firm's last dividend: $0.20

6. Yield percentage, or the percentage of return based on the dividend and current price of the stock: $0.20 ÷ $12.50 = 0.016 = 1.6%

7. Price–earnings (P/E) ratio—the price of a share of stock divided by the corporation's earnings per share of stock outstanding over the last 12 months: 12.50 ÷ 0.84 = 14.9

8. Number of shares of Finning International traded during the previous business day, expressed in hundreds of shares: 413

9. Highest price paid for one share of Finning International during the previous business day: $12.75

10. Lowest price paid for one share of Finning International during the previous business day: $12.50

11. Price paid for the last transaction of the day: $12.50

12. Difference between the price paid for the last share today and the price paid for the last share on the previous day: minus $0.05 (in Bay Street terms, Finning International "closed down 0.05" on this day)

13. Fiscal year-end for reporting earnings: March (3 months)

14. Interim earnings per share: $0.17

15. Annual earnings per share: $0.84

16. Number of shares traded during the week, expressed in hundreds: 8,333

17. Highest price paid for one share during the week: $12.95

18. Lowest price paid for one share during the week: $12.50

19. Price paid for last transaction for the week: $12.50

20. Difference between the price paid for the last trading day and the price paid one week ago: $0

SOURCE: Adapted from the *Financial Post,* "FP Investing," July 1, 2000.

THE INTERNET

Today, all major publicly traded corporations have a Web site, and the information these pages provide is especially useful. First, it is easily accessible. All you have to do is use a search engine to locate the corporation's site. Second, the information on the site may be more up to date than printed material obtained from the corporation or outside sources. Finally, this information may be more complete than that in the corporation's annual report, quarterly report, or other publications.

You can also use such Web sites as finance.yahoo.com and other search engines to obtain information about stock investments. Each site provides links to additional information, updates, and advice on specific types of investments, such as stocks, bonds, and mutual funds. At most sites, you can also obtain current stock quotes, track individually chosen securities, and receive updates on news releases and industry events. Exhibit 11-6 lists some of the popular sites used for evaluating the stocks of a corporation.

STOCK ADVISORY SERVICES

In addition to newspapers and the Internet, sources of information you can use to evaluate potential stock investments are the printed materials provided by stock advisory services. In choosing among the hundreds of stock advisory services that charge fees for their information, you must consider both the quality and the quantity of the information they provide. The information ranges from simple alphabetical listings to detailed financial reports.

SEDAR, Standard & Poor's reports, and Value Line are briefly described in Chapter 10. A useful online service is found at zacks.com. Here we examine a company report for BCE, Canada's largest communications company.

The report shown in Exhibit 11–7 is a document issued by Zacks Investment Research. The top section lists the company name and symbol on an exchange (here, the New York Stock Exchange) and identifies the industry that BCE participates in.

Web Site and Description	Web Address
Financial Post: Provides news, opinions, market and investment information, tools, and much more.	financialpost.com
Market Watch: Current price information, news, corporate profile, analyst estimates, industry analysis about individual corporate stock issues. Free, but registration may be required.	marketwatch.com
Tmx: Tmx Datalinx provides current, historical, and index data, along with news, corporate information, equities, fixed income, and foreign exchange statistics to help Canadian investors make investment decisions on the Canadian capital markets. Information is also available through tmxmoney.com.	tmx.com and tmxmoney.com
Standard & Poor's: Many experienced investors rely on S&P's stock reports to provide a snapshot of a corporation's activities, performance, and investment outlook. Individual reports are available for purchase.	www.standardandpoors.com
Value Line: Detailed research and software that can be used to sort, screen, graph, and report on individual common stocks, industry groups, or stock portfolios. Some information is available for free, but a subscription is required for more detailed information.	valueline.com

Exhibit 11–6

Web Sites That Help You Evaluate a Corporation's Stock

Below the market information, such as the most recent price, price–earnings ratio (P/E), and dividend and capitalization values, is a brief description of the company. This description displays the company's most prominent products and identifies its clientele.

BCE Inc. shares trading on the New York Stock Exchange have been bought or sold for a 52-week low of $38.72 and as high as $46.70. 459,941 shares are traded on average on a daily basis.

Exhibit 11–7   Zacks Investment Research Report for BCE Inc.

   **Jun 18, 2014**

BCE Inc.   (BCE-NYSE)

Current Recommendation	NEUTRAL
Prior Recommendation	Outperform
Date of Last Change	09/05/2010
Current Price (06/17/14)	$45.63
Target Price	**$48.00**

SUMMARY

We are maintaining our Neutral recommendation on BCE Inc. The successful execution of management's six strategic initiatives is expected to reap profits in the coming quarters. At the same time, acquisition costs from the Astral takeover might impede margin growth. Going forward, the company's wireless segment will benefit from solid subscriber additions within the post-paid segment along with increased data usage by smartphone users. On the wireline front, BCE is expected to benefit from growth in Fibe TV and Fibe Internet customers. However, continuous loss of large business customers in Network Access service will affect its wireline segment. Additionally, certain headwinds such as stiff competition, possible formation of another large carrier, loss of advertisement revenues and union issues prevent us from being too optimistic on the stock.

SUMMARY DATA

52-Week High	$46.70
52-Week Low	$38.72
One-Year Return (%)	10.03
Beta	0.58
Average Daily Volume (ADS)	459,941
ADS Outstanding (mil)	777
Market Capitalization ($mil)	$35,470
Short Interest Ratio (days)	10.31
Institutional Ownership (%)	42
Insider Ownership (%)	0
Annual Cash Dividend	$2.28
Dividend Yield (%)	4.9
5-Yr. Historical Growth Rates	
Sales (%)	4.5
Earnings Per ADS (%)	5.2
Dividend (%)	10.4
P/E using TTM EPADS	16.2
P/E using 2014 Estimate	16.0
P/E using 2015 Estimate	15.4
Zacks Rank *: Short Term 1 – 3 months outlook	3 - Hold

* Definition / Disclosure on last page

Risk Level *	Low,
Type of Stock	Large-Blend
Industry	Diversified Com
Zacks Industry Rank *	105 out of 267

ZACKS CONSENSUS ESTIMATES

Revenue Estimates
(In millions of $)

	Q1	Q2	Q3	Q4	Year
	(Mar)	(Jun)	(Sep)	(Dec)	(Dec)
2012	4,967 A	4,929 A	4,977 A	5,178 A	20,051 A
2013	4,911 A	4,806 A	4,883 A	4,860 A	19,460 A
2014	4,648 A	4,746 E	4,680 E	4,920 E	18,994 E
2015	4,810 E				19,402 E

Earnings Per ADS Estimates
(EPADS is operating earnings before non-recurring items, but including employee stock options expenses)

	Q1	Q2	Q3	Q4	Year
	(Mar)	(Jun)	(Sep)	(Dec)	(Dec)
2012	$0.80 A	$1.02 A	$0.76 A	$0.65 A	$3.23 A
2013	$0.77 A	$0.73 A	$0.72 A	$0.63 A	$2.85 A
2014	$0.73 A	$0.79 E	$0.69 E	$0.64 E	$2.85 E
2015	$0.76 E				$2.96 E

1 ADS= 1 Share
Projected EPADS Growth - Next 5 Years %   **4**

SOURCE: Zacks Investment Research Inc., Company Reports, June 2014.

Exhibit 11–8 presents the first page of a detailed report on BCE issued by Thomson Reuters. While other stock advisory services provide basically the same types of information as in Exhibits 11–7 and 11–8, it is the investor's job to interpret such information and decide whether or not the company's stocks are a good investment.

Exhibit 11–8   Thomson Reuters Stock Report for BCE

Company Overview

BCE INC.   (Toronto Stock Exchange: BCE)

1 CARREFOUR ALEXANDER-GRAHAM-BELL, VERDUN, QUEBEC H3E 3B3, CANADA		Sector (ICB)	Fixed Line Telecommunications	CUSIP	05534B760	SIC Code	4813	Employees	55,830
+1 514 786-3891	http://www.bce.ca	Subsector (ICB)	Fixed Line Telecommunications	SEDOL	B188TH2	Auditor	Deloitte LLP	Fiscal Year End :	12/31/13

Financial Summary

	Last Twelve Months as of 03/31/14	12/31/13 (A)	12/31/14 (E)	12/31/15 (E)
Sales (MM)	20,580	20,400	20,910	21,233
Growth	3.0	2.1	2.5	1.5
Gross Profit (MM)	11,188	11,112	-	-
Margin	54.4	54.5	-	-
EBITDA (MM)	7,601	7,527	8,320	8,502
Margin	36.9	36.9	39.8	40.0
EBIT (MM)	4,193	4,147	4,749	4,889
Margin	20.4	20.3	22.7	23.0
Net Income (MM)	2,155	1,975	2,530	2,598
Margin	10.5	9.7	12.1	12.2
EPS	2.61	2.55	3.16	3.24
Growth	(18.6)	(24.9)	24.0	2.7
Free Cash Flow	(212)	8	-	-

Currency: CAD   Source: Worldscope, IBES

Business Description

BCE Inc. is a communications company, providing residential, business and wholesale customers with a range of solutions to all their communications needs. During the fiscal year ended March 14, 2012, the Company operates in four segments: Bell Wireline, Bell Wireless, Bell Media and Bell Aliant. Bell Canada (Bell), which encompasses its core operations, is comprised of its Bell Wireline, Bell Wireless and Bell Media segments. Bell Media is multimedia company with assets in television, radio and digital media, including CTV Inc. (CTV), Canada's television network based on viewership. Bell was a wireless service provider in Canada to launch a Fourth Generation (4G) Long Term Evolution (LTE) network in the Greater Toronto Area (GTA) on September 14, 2011. In October 2012, the Company along with Ontario Teachers' Pension Plan, Providence Equity Partners and Madison Dearborn Partners LLC acquired Q9 Networks. Effective July 5, 2013, BCE Inc acquired the entire interest of Astral Media Inc.

Market Data

Price (04:01 PM*)	45.26	Change	▼ -0.28(-0.61%)
Volume	492,482	52 Wk Range	46.70 - 38.72
Consolidated Market Cap**	40,414 (MM)	Dividend Yield	5.00%
1 Year Total Return	16.32%	Beta (Historical)	0.56
Float as % of Shares Outstanding	100%		

*Time stamp based on security's exchange (US), USD   **Prices as of 06/20/14, CAD

Key Ratios

	Last Twelve Months as of 03/31/14 *	12/31/13 (A)	12/31/14 (E)	12/31/15 (E)
Enterprise Value/Sales	3.1	2.9	3.0	3.0
Enterprise Value/EBITDA	8.4	7.8	7.6	7.5
Enterprise Value/EBIT	15.1	14.2	13.4	13.0
Total Debt/Enterprise Value	0.3	0.3	-	-
Total Debt/EBITDA	2.5	2.5	2.3	2.3
EBITDA/Interest Expense	7.9	7.9	8.7	8.8
EBITDA-Capital Expenditures/Interest Expense	4.2	4.2	4.9	5.1
EBIT/Interest Expense	4.4	4.4	4.9	5.1
Price/Earnings	18.8	18.1	15.5	15.1
PEG	-	-	2.9	4.0
Price/Sales	1.9	1.7	1.8	1.8
Price/Cash Flow	7.2	6.5	3.2	5.9
Price/Book Value	3.3	3.1	2.7	2.6
Return On Assets	6.6	6.5	9.1	9.2
Return On Equity	19.5	17.9	16.6	17.8
Return On Invested Capital	8.5	8.5	-	-

*EV and Price Multiples calculated using price as of 06/20/14   Source: Worldscope, IBES

Price and Volume: 1 Year

Analyst Rating

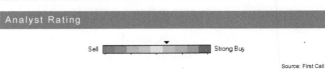

Source: First Call

Advice from a Pro

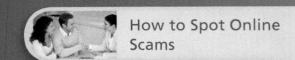

The development of the Internet has been among the most important technological innovations of the past twenty years. Millions of Canadians use the Web daily to get their news and to connect with their communities. But it has also provided fraudsters with new ways to defraud us with new online scams and online versions of schemes that have been around in other forms for decades.

Every year in March, over 100 private and public sector organizations support Fraud Prevention Month to remind Canadians to be on the alert and report incidents of fraud. The members of the Fraud Prevention Forum carry out this important work because, despite the diligent efforts of law enforcement, scammers continue to prey on Canadian citizens, robbing individuals and companies of their hard-earned dollars.

This year, the organization I head, the Competition Bureau, and its Fraud Prevention Forum partners are raising awareness of Internet fraud because it has become a primary vehicle for fraudsters. Online fraud now costs the economy millions of dollars each year and puts everyone at risk regardless of age, education, income or where we live. Indeed, the Canadian Anti-Fraud Centre (formerly PhoneBusters) has detected a dramatic rise in online scams in recent years—a 77-percent leap since 2005.

While Internet fraud is fairly new and provides us with certain novel challenges, our fight remains the same and we need your help. It is important that we all learn how to recognize the signs of fraud, protect ourselves, and know how and where to report it. With your assistance, law enforcement agencies and my colleagues at the Competition Bureau will be able to crackdown on fraud even more effectively.

Scammers routinely use online services to make offers to prospective victims or to draw individuals and businesses into fraudulent transactions. Online scams are designed to appear that they come from familiar and trusted places. The following scams are among those we are highlighting this year:

- **Job scams** that often promise high income for little effort, or ask you to send a cheque in order to pay for materials or information that allow you to work from home.

- **Health claim scams** often involve bogus products that make "breakthrough" health claims on the Internet or promise to cure illnesses, such as cancer or the H1N1 virus.
- **Business or investment opportunities** can appear to be lucrative but may, in reality, be illegal pyramid schemes.
- **Supply and merchandise scams** may involve buying products over the Internet–for business or consumer use—that are never sent, or receiving a bill for merchandise that was never ordered or received. For businesses, toner cartridge, paper and business directory scams are particularly common.
- **Identity theft** happens when someone tricks you into providing personal information to commit fraud.

Some of the following tips can help you avoid scams and better protect yourself online:

- Never provide details about your bank accounts or credit cards by e-mail, over the phone or by fax, **before doing background checks.**
- Always seek independent advice if an offer involves time pressure, providing personal information, or sending money, particularly if it is for a job or an investment opportunity. If the offer is legitimate, they can wait a day or two for a response.
- If you receive a cheque and are asked to return an "overpayment" portion using a money transfer company…**Beware!**

Catching these criminals is critical, and that's why Fraud Prevention Forum members urge you to **recognize it, report it, and help stop it.**

For more tips, or to report a scam, contact the Competition Bureau at competitionbureau.gc.ca/fraud or call 1-800-348-5358, or the Canadian Anti-Fraud Centre at antifraudcentre.ca or call 1-888-495-8501.

SOURCE: Melanie Aitken, Commissioner of Competition, Competition Bureau, "Online Scammers—Recognize It, Report It, and Help Stop It," May 18, 2010, competitionbureau.gc.ca/eic/site/cb-bc.nsf/eng/03233.html, accessed June 23, 2014. Reproduced with the permission of the Minister of Public Works and Government Services Canada, 2014.

CORPORATE NEWS

As mentioned in Chapter 10, the federal government requires corporations selling new issues of securities to disclose information about corporate earnings, assets and liabilities, products or services, and the qualifications of top management in a prospectus that they must give to

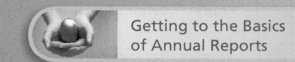
One of the best resources you can use to determine the soundness of a stock investment is a corporation's annual report. These reports are an excellent tool for learning about a company, its management, its past performance, and its goals. But while thumbing through these glossy publications, you must always keep in mind that corporations use this medium to "toot their own horns." The letter from the chair of the board, the upbeat, smiling faces of the employees, and the artistic layout and beautiful photographs are nice to look at, but it's the accounting statements and footnotes that give the true picture of the financial health of a corporation. Understanding the items presented on these pages tucked away in the back of the report is the real key to determining if a company is making a profit. Once you know the basics of reading annual reports, you will be in a better position to evaluate different investment opportunities.

Experts recommend that before investing, you review and compare the annual reports a corporation has published over the last three years. Read the shareholders' letters to see if they met their goals each year. Are any areas of concern mentioned? Are the facts presented in a straightforward manner, or do you have to struggle to interpret their meaning? Learn to read between the lines to separate the hype from the truth. And watch for words or phrases like *except for*, *challenges*, and *contingencies*.

Next, turn to the statement of financial position (sometimes called the balance sheet). This is where you can compare the corporation's financial position by noting changes in its current assets, current liabilities, inventories, total liabilities, and owners' equity. Information on the income statement will enable you to determine if the corporation earned a profit. Be sure to look at the amounts reported for sales, expenses, and profit or loss figures.

Finally, don't overlook the footnotes: they contain (and sometimes hide) important information.

investors. In addition to a prospectus, all publicly owned corporations send their shareholders an annual report and quarterly reports that contain detailed financial data. Even if you're not a shareholder, you can obtain an annual report from the corporation. For most corporations, all it takes is a call to a toll-free telephone number. A written request to the corporation's headquarters can also help you obtain an annual report.

In addition to corporate publications, many periodicals can help you evaluate a corporation and its stock issues. *Report on Business*, *Canadian Business*, and *BusinessWeek* provide not only general economic news but detailed financial information about individual corporations. Magazines, such as *MoneySense*, *MoneySaver*, and *Consumer Reports*, provide information to help you make informed investment decisions. Trade or industry publications, such as *Canadian Banker*, provide information about firms within a specific industry. Finally, news magazines, such as *The Economist* and *Maclean's,* feature financial news on a regular basis.

FACTORS THAT INFLUENCE THE PRICE OF A STOCK

A **bull market** occurs when investors are optimistic about the nation's economy and buy stocks. In a bull market, the fact that more investors are buying stocks causes the value of both individual stocks and the stock market as a whole to increase. A **bear market** occurs when investors are pessimistic about the nation's economy and sell their stocks. Because more investors are selling their stocks, the value of both individual stocks and the stock market as a whole declines.

How do you determine whether it is the right time to buy or sell a particular stock? Many factors affect the market value of a stock. Therefore, you must also consider potential sales revenues, profits or losses, cash flow, and other important fundamentals when determining whether a stock will increase or decrease in value. In the remainder of this section, we examine some numerical measures that indicate corporate performance and shareholder returns, psychological traps when investing, and analytical techniques that help us to overcome some common investing mistakes and determine whether a stock is priced correctly.

bull market Occurs when investors are optimistic about a nation's economy and buy stocks.

bear market Occurs when investors are pessimistic about a nation's economy and sell their stocks.

MEASURES OF CORPORATE RISK, PERFORMANCE, AND SHAREHOLDERS' RETURNS

Investors should track an investment's return over time to see if it is performing well. As mentioned earlier in the chapter, shareholders purchase stocks to earn dividend income and see the value of their investment increase over time, generating a capital gain.

Let's use the example of an investment in BCE Inc. to track an investor's return over the years of 2011 to 2013, given the information below that was taken from the company's 2013 Annual Report:

Year	2013	2012	2011
Dividends per share	$ 2.33	$ 2.17	$ 2.07
Market value at year-end	$47.40	$46.62	$40.18

The cost of acquiring BCE stock at the end of 2011 was $40.18. Over the year 2012, the investor would have earned a $2.17 dividend, and the value of the stock would have risen $6.44 ($46.62 − $40.18). In total, if the investor chose to sell the stock, then he or she would have made $2.17 + $6.44 = $8.61 on an investment of $40.18. The annual return would have been:

annual shareholder return A stock's annual dividend and increase in value divided by its beginning-of-year stock price.

$$\text{Annual shareholder return} = \frac{\text{Annual dividend } + \text{ Appreciation in value}}{\text{Initial stock investment}}$$

$$= \frac{\$2.17 + (\$46.62 - \$40.18)}{\$40.18}$$

$$= 0.21423 \text{ or } 21.4 \text{ percent}$$

This return can be broken down into two parts: the dividend yield and the capital gains yield. These two components of the total shareholder return are calculated as follows:

annual dividend yield A stock's annual dividend divided by its beginning-of-year stock price. If the dividend is divided by the end-of-year stock price, it is referred to as its trailing dividend yield.

$$\text{Annual dividend yield} = \frac{\text{Annual dividend}}{\text{Initial stock investment}}$$

$$= \frac{\$2.17}{\$40.18}$$

$$= 0.054000 \text{ or } 5.4 \text{ percent}$$

capital gains yield A stock's increase in value divided by its beginning-of-year stock price.

$$\text{Capital gains yield} = \frac{\text{Appreciation in value}}{\text{Initial stock investment}}$$

$$= \frac{(\$46.62 - \$40.18)}{\$40.18}$$

$$= 0.16028 \text{ or } 16 \text{ percent}$$

Investors looking for income will choose stocks that they expect will pay a high dividend. BCE's dividend yield in 2012 was over 5 percent, while that of the S&P/TSX Composite Index was about 2 percent. Investors looking for growth will choose stocks that are expected to appreciate in value.

If we perform the same calculations using the 2013 dividend and increase in stock value from the end of 2012 to the end of 2013, BCE's 2013 total return was 6.9 percent. An investor who purchased the stock at the end of 2011 and sold it at the end of 2013 (over a period of two years) would have earned an average annual compound return of:

$$\text{Annual average compound return} = [(1.212)(1.609)]^{1/2} - 1$$

$$= 0.141 \text{ or } 14.1 \text{ percent}$$

The deeper Enron scandal lies not in the nervous contacts with cabinet members when the giant corporation was sliding down the tube, but in its ability to manipulate a government awash in campaign contributions in the days when the company was flying high.

That President Bush called CEO Kenneth Lay "Kenny Boy" was not a scandal. What was a scandal was that Enron profited from a climate of regulatory laxity that it helped to dictate. Mr. Lay and other Enron executives met several times last year with Vice President Dick Cheney, who was heading the president's energy task force. Mr. Cheney is still stonewalling congressional efforts to find out what happened in those meetings.

But the task force recommendations for "reforming" the utility regulation law to provide "greater regulatory certainty" (read: deregulation) could have been written by Enron. Enron helped create what some called a regulatory "black hole."

The Bush White House was deeply penetrated by a company that became the nation's seventh-biggest corporation not by making energy but by making deals. Economic counsellor Lawrence Lindsey had been a paid adviser. Political strategist Karl Rove had been a big investor. Republican national chairman Mark Racicot had been a paid lobbyist. Lay himself had been on an early list of possible cabinet appointments.

So much influence did Enron wield with the Bush administration that Lay could tell Curtis Herbert Jr., chairman of the Federal Energy Regulatory Commission, that he would be reappointed if he changed his views on electricity regulation. Mr. Herbert didn't, and he wasn't.

Congress was not left untainted. More than two-thirds of the Senate and 40 percent of the House benefited—if that's the word—from Enron money, some of which is now being returned by embarrassed lawmakers of both parties.

The $5.8 million in campaign donations from Enron sources since 1989 appear to have been a good investment. The tax rebate provision of the House-passed economic stimulus package alone would give Enron $254 million.

The consequences of Enron's penetration of the United States government remain to be investigated by anyone left in government who doesn't have to recuse himself. Some day we may know whether Enron would have been able to bilk employees, investors, and a nation, were it not for that regulatory black hole that it bought for itself.

Enron is not unique in the annals of lobbyist interests prevailing over the public interest. From contracts for unneeded weapons to a banana trade war, the decisions tend to come out in favour of the big contributors. What makes the Enron story different is the drama of the huge implosion in full view of thousands of victimized employees and investors.

SOURCE: Daniel Schorr, "The Real Enron Scandal," *The Christian Science Monitor,* January 18, 2002; csmonitor.com/2002/0118/p11s03-cods.html, accessed June 23, 2014.

While it is easy to calculate historical returns where all the facts are known, we must be careful not to presume that historical returns indicate what will happen in the future. For example, the investor who purchased the stock at the end of 2011 could not be certain as to the level of the dividend or whether or not the stock would appreciate in value.

Earnings per share (EPS) are a corporation's after-tax earnings divided by the number of outstanding common shares. For example, BCE's 2013 and 2012 earnings per share were $2.54 and $3.17, respectively. Most shareholders consider the level of a firm's earnings per share to be an important measure of the company's profitability. No meaningful average for this measure exists, mainly because the number of common shares issued at any point in time may vary. As a general rule, an increase in earnings per share is a healthy sign for the corporation and its shareholders. However, potential investors should be aware of what specific factors have caused changes in a firm's EPS over time.

The **price–earnings (P/E) ratio** is calculated by dividing a company's year-end stock price by its earnings per share. (This ratio is referred to as the *trailing* P/E ratio because the earnings per share are taken from the year just ended.) Using the BCE example, its end-of-year 2013 P/E ratio was

earnings per share (EPS) A corporation's after-tax earnings divided by the number of outstanding shares of common stocks.

price–earnings (P/E) ratio The price of a share of stock divided by the corporation's earnings per share of stocks outstanding over the last 12 months.

345

Financial Planning Calculations

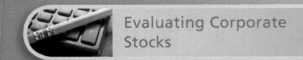

Evaluating Corporate Stocks

No checklist can serve as a foolproof guide for choosing common or preferred stocks. However, the following questions will help you evaluate a potential stock investment.

CATEGORY 1: THE BASICS

1. What is the corporation's name? _____
_____

2. What are the corporation's address and telephone number? _____
_____

3. Have you requested the latest annual and quarterly reports? ☐ Yes ☐ No

4. What information about the corporation is available on the Internet? _____

5. Where are the stocks traded? _____
_____

6. What types of products or services does this firm provide? _____
_____

7. Briefly describe the prospects for this company. (Include significant factors such as product development, expansion or merger plans, etc.)
_____
_____
_____

CATEGORY 2: DIVIDEND INCOME

8. Is the corporation currently paying dividends? If so, how much? _____

9. What is the current yield for this stock? _____

10. Has the dividend payout increased or decreased over the past seven years? _____

11. How does the yield for this investment compare with those for other potential investments?
_____

CATEGORY 3: FINANCIAL PERFORMANCE

12. Is the corporation profitable? What are the firm's earnings per share for the last three years? _____
_____

13. Have profits increased over the last seven years? ☐ Yes ☐ No

14. What is the 52-week high and low for these stocks? _____
What is the stock's current price?
_____

15. What is the firm's beta?

16. What is the firm's current P/E ratio?

17. How does the firm's P/E ratio compare with other firms in general? With other firms in the same industry? _____
_____
_____

18. Are this year's sales higher than last year's sales? ☐ Yes ☐ No

19. Have sales increased over the last seven years? ☐ Yes ☐ No

20. Briefly describe any other information that you obtained from SEDAR, Zacks, Standard & Poor's, or other stock advisory services. _____
_____
_____
_____

A WORD OF CAUTION

When you use a checklist, there is always a danger of overlooking important relevant information. This checklist is not all-inclusive, but it does provide some sound questions that you should answer before making a decision to invest in stocks. Quite simply, it is a place to start. If you need other information, *you* are responsible for obtaining it and for determining how it affects your potential investment.

18.66 ($47.40 ÷ $2.54) versus a ratio of 14.71 ($46.62 ÷ $3.17) in 2012. The P/E ratio tells us what investors are willing to pay for $1 of current earnings. It is useful to identify the trend in a company's P/E ratio over time or to compare it to the P/E ratios of other firms in the same industry or market in general. Ideally, investors should try to identify firms with relatively low P/E ratios that they expect will outperform in the future. They would expect the firm's share price to rise eventually, driving its P/E ratio up. Although P/E ratios vary by industry, they range between 5 and 35 for most corporations. In June 2014, the S&P/TSX Composite Index average P/E ratio was 33.33.

The **beta** is an index reported in many financial publications that compares the risk associated with a specific stock issue with the risk of the stock market in general. The beta for the stock market in general (or the "average" stock) is 1.0. Most stocks have betas between 0.5 and 2.0. Generally, conservative stocks have low betas and speculative stocks have high betas. In other

beta An index that compares the risk associated with a specific stock issue with the risk of the stock market in general.

words, if a stock's price movement is more volatile than the stock market as a whole, then the beta value is greater than 1. The opposite is true of stocks with less volatility compared to the entire market, and consequently the beta is less than 1.

Before completing this section, you may want to examine the Financial Planning Calculations box Evaluating Corporate Stocks above.

CONCEPT CHECK 11–3

1. What sources of information would you use to evaluate a stock issue?

2. How would you define (1) a blue-chip stock, (2) an income stock, (3) a growth stock, (4) a cyclical stock, (5) a defensive stock, (6) a penny stock, (7) a large-cap stock, and (8) a small-cap stock?

3. What do the terms *annual shareholder return*, *dividend yield*, *capital gains yield*, *earnings per share*, *price–earnings ratio*, and *beta* refer to?

BUYING AND SELLING STOCKS

To purchase a pair of Levi Strauss jeans, you simply walk into a store that sells Levi's, choose a pair, and pay for your purchase. To purchase common or preferred stocks, you generally have to work through a brokerage firm. In turn, your brokerage firm must buy the stocks in either the primary or secondary market. In the **primary market**, you purchase financial securities, via an investment bank or other representative, from the issuer of those securities. An **investment bank** is a financial firm that assists corporations in raising funds, usually by helping to sell new security issues.

New security issues sold through an investment bank can be issued by corporations that have sold stocks and bonds before and need to sell new issues to raise additional financing. The new securities can also be initial public offerings. An **initial public offering (IPO)** occurs when a corporation sells stocks to the general public for the first time. Highly visible companies that have sold stocks to raise capital include Research In Motion and Quebecor. Investors bought these stocks through brokerage firms acting as agents for an investment banking firm, and the money they paid for common stocks flowed to the corporations that issued the stocks. Because these companies used the financing obtained through IPOs wisely, they have grown and prospered, and investors have profited from their IPO investments. However, not all companies that use IPOs to raise capital are good investments.

Be warned: The promise of quick profits often lures investors to purchase IPOs. An IPO is generally classified as a high-risk investment—one made in the hope of earning a relatively large profit in a short time. Depending on the corporation selling the new security, IPOs are usually too risky for most people.

After a stock has been sold through the primary market, it is traded through the secondary market. The **secondary market** is a market for existing financial securities that are currently traded among investors. Once the stocks are sold in the primary market, they can be sold time and again in the secondary market. The fact that stocks can be sold in the secondary market improves the liquidity of stock investments because the money you pay for stocks goes to the seller of the stocks.

PRIMARY MARKETS FOR STOCKS

How would you sell $100 million worth of common stocks or preferred stocks? For a large corporation, the decision to sell stocks is often complicated, time consuming, and expensive. There are basically two methods.

First, a large corporation may use an investment bank to sell and distribute the new stocks issue. Most large corporations that need a lot of financing use this method. If this method is used, the investment bank's analysts examine the corporation's financial position to determine whether the new issue is financially sound and how difficult it will be to sell.

LO4
Describe how stocks are bought and sold.

primary market A market in which an investor purchases financial securities, via an investment bank or other representative, from the issuer of those securities.

investment bank A financial firm that assists corporations in raising funds, usually by helping to sell new security issues.

initial public offering (IPO) Occurs when a corporation sells stocks to the general public for the first time.

secondary market A market for existing financial securities that are currently traded among investors.

If the investment bank is satisfied that the new stocks are a good risk, it buys the stocks and then resells them to its customers—commercial banks, insurance companies, pension funds, mutual funds, and the general public. The investment bank's commission, or spread, ranges from less than 1 percent for a utility firm to as much as 25 percent for a small company selling stocks for the first time. The size of the spread depends on the quality and financial health of the issuing corporation. The commission allows the investment bank to make a profit while guaranteeing that the corporation will receive the financing it needs.

If the investment bank's analysts believe the new issue will be difficult to sell, the investment bank may agree to take the stocks on a best-efforts basis, without guaranteeing that the stocks will be sold. Because the corporation must take back any unsold stocks after a reasonable time, most large corporations are unwilling to accept this arrangement. If the stock issue is too large for one investment bank, a group of investment bankers may form an *underwriting syndicate*. Then, each member of the syndicate is responsible for selling only a part of the new issue.

The second method used by a corporation trying to obtain financing through the primary market is to sell directly to current shareholders. Usually, promotional materials describing the new stock issue are mailed to current shareholders. These shareholders may then purchase the stocks directly from the corporation.

You may ask, "Why would a corporation try to sell its own stocks?" The most obvious reason for doing so is to avoid the investment bank's commission. Of course, a corporation's ability to sell a new stock issue without the aid of an investment bank is tied directly to investors' perception of the corporation's financial health. Another reason is that the corporation wants to help its current shareholders maintain their percentage of holding of the firm. This is done through a rights offering, whereby current shareholders are given the "right" to be the first to purchase any new shares being issued by the corporation, usually below market price.

SECONDARY MARKETS FOR STOCKS

How do you buy or sell stocks in the secondary market? To purchase common or preferred stocks, you usually have to work with an employee of a brokerage firm who buys or sells for you in a securities marketplace, at a securities exchange or through the over-the-counter market.

securities exchange A marketplace where member brokers who represent investors meet to buy and sell securities.

A **securities exchange** is a marketplace where member brokers who represent investors meet to buy and sell securities. The securities sold at a particular exchange must first be listed, or accepted for trading, at that exchange. In Canada, the national stock exchanges are owned and operated by TMX Group. Large-cap firms can list their shares for trading on the Toronto Stock Exchange, while emerging firms can list on the TSX Venture Exchange. Derivative securities, such as options and futures, are traded on the Montreal Exchange. The securities of large corporations may be traded at more than one exchange. Canadian firms that do business abroad may also be listed on foreign securities exchanges—in Tokyo, New York, London, or Paris, for example.

over-the-counter (OTC) market A network of dealers who buy and sell the stocks of corporations that are not listed on a securities exchange.

Not all securities are traded on organized exchanges. Stocks issued by several thousand companies are traded in the over-the-counter market. The **over-the-counter (OTC) market** is a network of dealers who buy and sell the stocks of corporations that are not listed on a securities exchange. Today, these stocks are not really traded over the counter. The term was coined more than 100 years ago when securities were sold "over the counter" in stores and banks.

NASDAQ An electronic marketplace for over 2,800 stocks.

Most over-the-counter securities are traded through **NASDAQ**. NASDAQ is an electronic marketplace for more than 2,800 different stocks. In addition to providing price information, this computerized system allows investors to buy and sell shares of companies listed on NASDAQ. When you want to buy or sell shares of a company that trades on NASDAQ—say, Facebook—your account executive sends your order into the NASDAQ computer system, where it shows up on the screen with all the other orders from people who want to buy or sell Facebook stocks. Then, a NASDAQ dealer (sometimes referred to as a *market maker*) sitting at a computer terminal matches buy and sell orders for Facebook. Once a match is found, your order is completed.

Begun in 1971 and regulated by the National Association of Securities Dealers, NASDAQ is the third-largest securities market in the world in terms of volume, trailing only the NYSE and

Tokyo Stock Exchange. It is known for its innovative, forward-looking growth companies. Although many securities are issued by smaller companies, some large firms, including Intel, Microsoft, Facebook, Apple, and Cisco, also trade on NASDAQ. NASDAQ Canada was launched in 2000 and encompasses firms in a broad cross-section of industries.

BROKERAGE FIRMS AND ACCOUNT EXECUTIVES

An **account executive**, or *stockbroker*, is a licensed individual who buys or sells securities for his or her clients. Actually, *account executive* is the more descriptive title because such individuals handle all types of securities, not just stocks. While all account executives can buy or sell stocks for clients, most investors expect more from their account executives. Ideally, an account executive should provide information and advice to be used in evaluating potential investments. Many investors begin their search for an account executive by asking friends or business associates for recommendations. This is a logical starting point, but remember that some account executives are conservative, while others are more risk oriented.

Before choosing an account executive, you should have already determined your short-term and long-term financial objectives. Then, you must be careful to communicate those objectives to the account executive so that he or she can do a better job of advising you. Needless to say, account executives may err in their investment recommendations. To help avoid a situation in which your account executive's recommendations are automatically implemented, you should be *actively* involved in the decisions of your investment program and you should never allow your account executive to use his or her discretion without your approval. Watch your account for signs of churning. **Churning** is excessive buying and selling of securities to generate commissions. From a total-dollar-return standpoint, this practice usually leaves the client worse off or at least no better off. Churning is illegal under the rules established by the provincial securities exchange commissions; however, it may be difficult to prove. Finally, keep in mind that account executives generally are not liable for client losses that result from their recommendations. In fact, most brokerage firms require new clients to sign a statement in which they promise to submit any complaints to an arbitration board. This arbitration clause generally prevents a client from suing an account executive or a brokerage firm. Above all, remember you are investing *your* money and you should make the final decisions with the help of your account executive.

SHOULD YOU USE A FULL-SERVICE OR A DISCOUNT BROKERAGE FIRM?

Today, a healthy competition exists between full-service brokerage firms and discount brokerage firms. While the most obvious difference between full-service and discount firms is the amount of the commissions they charge when you buy or sell stocks and other securities, there are at least three other factors to consider. First, consider how much research information is available and how much it costs. Both types of brokerage firms offer excellent research materials, but you are more likely to pay extra for information if you choose a discount brokerage firm. While most discount brokerage firms don't charge a lot of money for research reports, the fees can mount up over time and can offset the lower commissions they charge to buy or sell stocks.

Second, consider how much help you need when making an investment decision. Many full-service brokerage firms argue that you need a professional to help you make important investment decisions. While this may be true for some investors, most account executives employed by full-service brokerage firms are too busy to spend unlimited time with you on a one-on-one basis, especially if you are investing a small amount. Still, the full-service account executive is there to answer questions and make investment recommendations. On the other side, many discount brokerage firms argue that you alone are responsible for making your investment decisions. They are quick to point out that the most successful investors are the ones involved in their investment programs. And they argue that they have both personnel and materials dedicated to helping you learn how to become a better investor.

account executive A licensed individual who buys or sells securities for clients; also called a *stockbroker.*

churning The excessive buying and selling of securities to generate commissions.

Third, consider how easy it is to buy and sell stocks and other securities when using either a full-service or discount brokerage firm. Questions to ask include:

1. Can I buy or sell stocks over the phone?
2. Can I trade stocks online?
3. Where is your nearest office located?
4. Do you have a toll-free telephone number for customer use?
5. How often do I get statements?
6. Is there a charge for statements, research reports, and other financial reports?
7. Are there any fees in addition to the commissions I pay when I buy or sell stocks?

While many people still prefer to use telephone orders to buy and sell stocks, a growing number are using computers to complete security transactions. To meet this need, online, discount, and many full-service brokerage firms allow investors to trade online. As a rule of thumb, the more active the investor is, the more sense it makes to use computers to trade online.

Although there are exceptions, the following information may help you decide whether to use a full-service, discount, or online brokerage firm.

Service Type	Investor Type
• Full-service	Beginning investors with little or no experience. Individuals who are uncomfortable making investment decisions.
• Discount	People who understand the "how to" of researching stocks and prefer making their own decisions. Individuals who are uncomfortable trading stocks online.
• Online	People who understand the "how to" of researching stocks and prefer making their own decisions. Individuals who are comfortable trading stocks online.

TYPES OF STOCK ORDERS

Once you and your account executive decide on a particular transaction, it is time to execute an order to buy or sell. Today, most investors either call their account executives or use the Internet and trade online. Let's begin by examining three types of orders used to trade stocks.

A **market order** is a request to buy or sell stocks at the current market value. Since the stock exchange is an auction market, the account executive's representative tries to get the best price available and the transaction is completed as soon as possible.

A **limit order** is a request to buy or sell a stock at a specified price. When you purchase stocks, a limit order ensures that you buy at the best possible price, but not above a specified dollar amount. When you sell stocks, a limit order ensures that you sell at the best possible price, but not below a specified dollar amount. For example, assume you place a limit order to buy BMO common stocks for $60 a share. The stocks are not purchased until the price drops to $60 a share or lower. Likewise, if your limit order is to sell BMO for $60 a share, the stocks are not sold until the price rises to $60 a share or higher. *Be warned:* Limit orders are executed if and when the specified price or better is reached and *all* other previously received orders have been fulfilled. Let's assume you enter a limit order to purchase Metro stocks at $55. If the stocks drop to $55, all purchase orders are filled in the sequence in which they were received. If the price of Metro begins to increase before your order can be filled, you may miss an investment opportunity because you were unable to buy the stocks at the specified price.

Many shareholders are certain they want to sell their stocks if they reach a specified price. A limit order does not guarantee this will be done. With a limit order, orders by other investors may be placed ahead of your order. If you want to guarantee that your order is executed, you place a special type of limit order known as a stop order. A **stop order** (sometimes called a

market order A request to buy or sell stocks at the current market value.

limit order A request to buy or sell stock at a specified price.

stop order An order to sell a particular stock at the next available opportunity after its market price reaches a specified amount.

stop-loss order) is an order to sell a particular stock at the next available opportunity after its market price reaches a specified amount. This type of order is used to protect an investor against a sharp drop in price and, thus, stop the dollar loss on a stock investment. For example, assume you purchase a software company's common stocks at $35 a share. Two weeks after making your investment, the company faces multiple product liability lawsuits. Fearing that the market value of your stocks will decrease, you enter a stop order to sell your stocks at $30. This means that if the price of the stock decreases to $30 or lower, the account executive will sell your stocks. While a stop order does not guarantee that your stocks will be sold at the price you specified, it does guarantee that they will be sold at the next available opportunity. Both limit and stop orders may be good for one day, one week, one month, or good till cancelled (GTC).

You can also choose to place a discretionary order. A **discretionary order** is an order to buy or sell a security that lets the account executive decide when to execute the transaction and at what price. Financial planners advise against using a discretionary order for two reasons. First, a discretionary order gives the account executive a great deal of authority. If the account executive makes a mistake, it is the investor who suffers the loss. Second, financial planners argue that only investors (with the help of their account executives) should make investment decisions.

discretionary order An order to buy or sell a security that lets the account executive decide when to execute the transaction and at what price.

COMPUTERIZED TRANSACTIONS

While some people still prefer to use telephone orders to buy and sell stocks, most use computers or smartphones to complete security transactions. To meet this need, discount brokerage firms and most full-service brokerage firms allow investors to trade online.

A good investment software package can help you evaluate potential investments, monitor the value of your investments, and place buy and sell orders online. As a general rule, the more active the investor is, the more sense it makes to use computers to trade online. Other reasons that justify using a computer include:

1. The size of your investment portfolio.
2. The ability to manage your investments closely.
3. The capability of your computer and the software package.

While computers can make the investment process easier and faster, you should realize that *you* are still responsible for analyzing the information and making the final decision to buy or sell a security. All the computer does is provide more information and, in most cases, complete transactions more quickly and economically.

COMMISSION CHARGES

Most brokerage firms have a minimum commission ranging from $25 to $55 for buying and selling stocks. Additional commission charges are based on the number of shares and the value of stock bought and sold. On the trading floor of a stock exchange, stocks are traded in round lots or odd lots. A **round lot** is 100 shares or multiples of 100 shares of a particular stock. An **odd lot** is fewer than 100 shares of a particular stock.

round lot One hundred shares or multiples of 100 shares of a particular stock.

Exhibit 11–9 shows typical charges and services provided by online brokerage firms. Note that many of the online brokerage firms illustrated in Exhibit 11–9 charge for research information and other investor services. You should also realize that when you choose an online brokerage firm, you have to make your own decisions.

odd lot Fewer than 100 shares of a particular stock.

Generally, full-service and discount brokerage firms charge higher commissions than those charged by online brokerage firms. As a general rule, full-service brokers may charge as much as 1.5 to 2 percent of the transaction amount. For example, if you use a full-service brokerage firm such as BMO Nesbitt Burns or Caldwell Securities to purchase Home Depot stocks valued at $10,000, and the brokerage firm charges 1.5 percent, you will pay commissions totalling $150 ($10,000 $\times$ 0.015 = $150). In return for charging higher commissions, full-service brokers usually spend more time with each client, help make investment decisions, and provide free research information. For the same transaction, most discount brokerage firms would charge

Exhibit 11–9   Typical Commission Charges and Services Provided by Online Brokerage Firms

Firm	Basic Flat Fees*	Additional Services
RBC Direct from the Royal Bank of Canada rbcdirectinvesting.com	$9.95 for all equity trades	Education centre, monthly data, statements for tax reporting, links
Scotia iTrade scotiabank.com /iTrade	$4.99 to $9.99 per trade, depending on volume and account balance	Margin interest, quarterly statements, analyst reports, tax statements, research
Questrade questrade.com	$4.95 to $9.95 per trade, depending on volume and account balance	Market analyses, online service demonstration, portfolio management tools
Investorline from the Bank of Montreal bmoinvestorline.com	$9.95 for all equity trades	Online services demonstration, glossary of products
TD Direct Investing from TD Bank http://www.tdwaterhouse.ca/ products-services/investing/ td-direct-investing/index.jsp	$7.00 to $9.95 per trade, depending on volume and account balance	Real-time quotes, research, news, charts, statistics
An independent online brokerage qtrade.ca	$7.00 to $9.95, depending on volume	Online tools and research available, as well as information and tutorials on many investment options; low commission rates.

Note: Prices for market orders only.
*Visit the Web sites for up-to-date information.

commissions ranging between $55 and $85. Today, discount brokerage firms are popular with many investors who have yet to venture into online trading, want to talk to an employee of the brokerage firm, and prefer to place their transaction orders over the telephone.

While full-service brokerage firms usually charge higher commissions, on some occasions a discount brokerage firm may charge higher commissions. This generally occurs when the transaction is small, involving a total dollar amount of less than $1,000, and the investor is charged the discount brokerage firm's minimum commission charge.

SECURITIES REGULATION

Though there is no federal regulatory body for the securities industry in Canada, extensive legislation and regulations are in place to protect the investor. This protection flows from self-regulatory organizations (SROs) such as the Investment Industry Regulatory Organization of Canada (IIROC) and the stock exchanges, as well as the provincial securities regulators and administrators (e.g., the Ontario Securities Commission). The general principle underlying the legislation is not to evaluate the investment merits of any given security but rather to ensure that full, true, and plain disclosure of all relevant facts is made by sellers of securities to the public.

PROVINCIAL REGULATION   In general, the provincial acts legislating the securities industry include three methods to protect investors: registration, disclosure, and enforcement. In the first method, provincial administrators protect investors by requiring those who sell securities or advise investors to register with an exchange or IIROC, who impose strict requirements regarding experience and training prior to registration. Disclosure, the second protective measure, ensures that investors have the necessary information to make informed decisions and analyze risk. Finally, enforcement of the laws and policies ensures proper adherence to the law.

SELF-REGULATORY ORGANIZATIONS (SROS)   IIROC and the various Canadian exchanges are directly responsible for industry conformity with securities legislation. They have powers to establish and enforce industry regulations to protect investors and to maintain fair, equitable, and ethical practices. Typical policies include a "Know Your Client" rule that clients are served according to their needs, a "Confirmation" rule that all transactions are written up in full detail and the record is sent promptly to clients, and an ethical trading and conduct rule to prevent such things as hidden interests, insider trading, and stock manipulation.

CONCEPT CHECK 11–4

1. What is the difference between the primary market and the secondary market?

2. Describe how stocks are bought or sold in the secondary market.

3. Assume you want to purchase stocks. Would you use a full-service broker or a discount broker? Would you ever trade stocks online?

LONG-TERM AND SHORT-TERM INVESTMENT STRATEGIES

Once you purchase stocks, the investment may be classified as either long term or short term. Generally, individuals who hold an investment for a long period of time are referred to as *investors*. Typically, long-term investors hold their investments for at least a year or longer. Individuals who routinely buy and then sell stocks within a short period of time are called *speculators* or *traders*.

LO5
Explain the trading techniques used by long-term investors and short-term speculators.

LONG-TERM TECHNIQUES

In this section, we discuss the long-term investment techniques of diversification, buy and hold, dollar cost averaging, direct investment programs, and dividend reinvestment programs.

DIVERSIFICATION   In the section on investment analysis, we pointed out that if financial markets are efficient, then an investor's best investment strategy involves the correct choice of asset allocation, combined with broad **diversification** of assets within each asset class. An investor's asset allocation is determined by two factors: his or her level of risk tolerance and the expected rate of return in each asset class—liquid investments, fixed income, and equity (stock) investments. Most financial institutions offer easy-to-understand risk tolerance assessments that link results to model portfolios. For example, the suggested asset allocation for a conservative investor might be 20 percent in liquid investments, 50 percent in fixed income securities, and 30 percent in equities or stocks. A more risk tolerant investor may have 10 percent in liquid investments, 40 percent in fixed income securities, and 50 percent in equities. This *strategic* asset allocation should be revisited and potentially modified at least once a year to incorporate changes in the individual's risk tolerance or expected performance of the market.

diversification Investment technique that involves combining many assets in a portfolio to reduce its risk.

When choosing which stocks to purchase, investors should keep in mind that diversification reduces risk. If you look back at Exhibit 11–1 you will see that there are many sectors in the Canadian stock market. If you concentrate your stock investments in only one or two sectors, you may be adversely affected if these sectors do not perform well. Therefore, it's best to build a stock portfolio that includes investments in many sectors, rather than too few. If you are just starting out and do not have a large amount of money to invest, it is still easy to obtain broad diversification by purchasing Canadian equity mutual funds or exchange-traded funds, discussed in Chapter 12.

BUY-AND-HOLD TECHNIQUE   Many long-term investors purchase stocks and hold on to them for a number of years. When they do this, their investment can increase in value in three ways. First, they are entitled to dividends if the board of directors approves dividend payments to shareholders. Second, the price of the stocks may go up. Third, if they combine this approach with a dividend reinvestment plan (discussed below), the value of their stock investment will grow over time.

dollar cost averaging
A long-term technique used by investors who purchase an equal dollar amount of the same stocks at equal intervals.

DOLLAR COST AVERAGING   **Dollar cost averaging** is a long-term technique used by investors who purchase an equal dollar amount of the same stocks at equal intervals. Assume you invest $2,000 in Phoenix International's common stocks each year for a period of three years. The results of your investment program are illustrated in Exhibit 11–10. Note that when the price of the stocks increased in 2013, you purchased fewer shares. When the price decreased in 2014, you purchased more shares. The average cost for a share, determined by dividing the total investment ($6,000) by the total number of shares, is $57.64 ($6,000 ÷ 104.1 = $57.64). Other applications of dollar cost averaging occur when employees purchase their company's stocks through a payroll deduction plan or as part of an employer-sponsored retirement plan over an extended period of time.

Investors use dollar cost averaging to avoid the common pitfall of buying high and selling low. In the situation shown in Exhibit 11–10, you would lose money only if you sold your stocks at less than the average cost of $57.64. With dollar cost averaging, you can make money if the stocks are sold at a price higher than the average purchase price.

direct investment plan   A plan that allows shareholders to purchase stocks directly from a corporation without having to use an account executive or a brokerage firm.

dividend reinvestment plan   A plan that allows current shareholders the option to reinvest or use their cash dividends to purchase stocks of the corporation.

DIRECT INVESTMENT AND DIVIDEND REINVESTMENT PLANS   Today, a large number of corporations offer direct investment plans. A **direct investment plan** allows you to purchase stocks directly from a corporation without having to use an account executive or a brokerage firm. Similarly, a **dividend reinvestment plan** allows you the option to reinvest your cash dividends to purchase the corporation's stocks. For shareholders, the chief advantage of both plans is that they enable shareholders to purchase stocks without paying a commission charge to a brokerage firm. (Note: A few companies may charge a small fee for dividend reinvestment, but it is less than what most brokerage firms charge.) As an added incentive, some corporations offer their stocks at a small discount to encourage the use of their direct investment and dividend reinvestment plans. Also, with the dividend reinvestment plan, you can take advantage of dollar cost averaging, discussed in the previous section. For corporations, the chief advantage of both plans is that they provide an additional source of capital. As an added bonus, the corporations provide a service to their shareholders.

PRIVATE EQUITY

Private equity is an asset class consisting of equity securities in companies that are not publicly traded in a stock exchange. Investments in private equity generally involve either injecting capital into or acquiring a company. Typically, institutional investors provide capital for private equity. For the most part, investment strategies in private equity include leveraged buyouts, venture capital, growth capital, distressed investments, and mezzanine capital. In a classic leveraged buyout transaction, an existing or mature firm's majority control is purchased by the private equity firm. This differs significantly from a venture capital or growth capital investment, in which the private equity firm rarely obtains majority control, but instead invests in an emerging company.*

Exhibit 11–10

Dollar Cost Averaging

Year	Investment	Stock Price	Shares Purchased
2012	$2,000	$50	40.0
2013	2,000	65	30.8
2014	2,000	60	33.3
Total	$6,000		104.1

*SOURCE: en.wikipedia.org/wiki/Private_equity.

SHORT-TERM TECHNIQUES

In addition to the long-term techniques presented in the preceding section, investors sometimes use more speculative, short-term techniques. In this section, we discuss buying stock on margin, selling short, and trading in options. *Be warned:* The methods presented in this section are risky; do not use them unless you fully understand the underlying risks. Also, you should not use them until you experience success using the more traditional long-term techniques described above.

BUYING STOCK ON MARGIN   When buying stocks on **margin**, you borrow part of the money needed to buy a particular stock. The margin requirements are set by the exchanges and are subject to periodic change. Although margin rules are regulated by the exchanges, margin requirements and the interest charged on the loans used to fund margin transactions may vary among brokers and dealers. Usually, the brokerage firm either lends the money or arranges the loan with another financial institution. Investors buy on margin because doing so offers them the potential for greater profits. Exhibit 11–11 gives an example of buying stocks on margin.

margin A speculative technique whereby an investor borrows part of the money needed to buy a particular stock.

As Exhibit 11–11 shows, it is more profitable to use margin. In effect, the financial leverage (often defined as the use of borrowed funds to increase the return on an investment) allowed William Oliver, who is single and 32 years old, to purchase a larger number of stocks. Since the dollar value of each share increased, William obtained a larger profit by buying the stocks on margin.

In this example, William's stocks did exactly what they were supposed to do: They increased in market value. His stocks increased $4 per share, and he made $4,000 because he owned 1,000 shares. His actual profit would be reduced by commissions and the amount of interest his broker

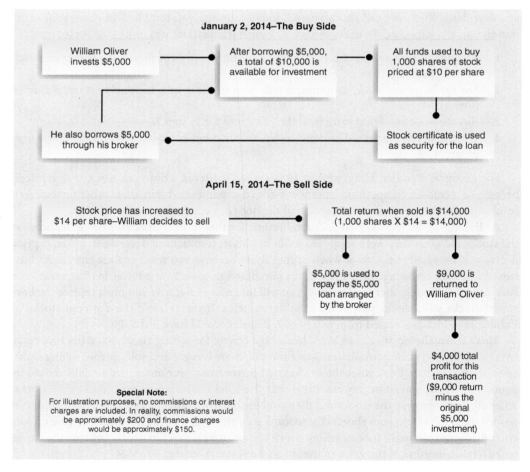

Exhibit 11–11

A Typical Margin Transaction

charges for the margin transaction. Had the value of the stocks gone down, buying on margin would have increased his loss. For example, William would have lost $3,000 if the price of the stocks had dropped from $10 a share (the original purchase price) to $7 a share.

If the market value of a margined stock decreases to approximately one-half of the original price, you will receive a *margin call* from the brokerage firm. After the margin call, you must pledge additional cash or securities to serve as collateral for the loan. If you don't have acceptable collateral or cash, the margined stocks are sold and the proceeds are used to repay the loan. The exact price at which the brokerage firm issues the margin call is determined by the amount of money you borrowed when you purchased the stocks. Generally, the more money you borrow, the sooner you will receive a margin call if the market value of the margined stocks drops.

In addition to facing the possibility of larger dollar losses, you must pay interest on the money borrowed to purchase stocks on margin. Most brokerage firms charge 1 to 3 percent above the prime rate. Normally, economists define the prime rate as the interest rate that the best business customers pay. Interest charges can absorb the potential profits if the value of margined stocks does not increase rapidly enough and the margined stocks must be held for long periods of time.

SELLING SHORT   Your ability to make money by buying and selling securities is related to how well you can predict whether a certain stock will increase or decrease in market value. Normally, you buy stocks and assume they will increase in value, a procedure referred to as buying long. But not all stocks increase in value. In fact, the value of a stock may decrease for many reasons, including lower sales, lower profits, reduced dividends, product failures, increased competition, and product liability lawsuits. With this fact in mind, you may use a procedure called selling short to make money when the value of a stock is expected to decrease in value. **Selling short** is selling stock that has been borrowed from a brokerage firm and must be replaced at a later date. When you sell short, you sell today, knowing you must buy or cover your short transaction at a later date. To make money in a short transaction, you must take these steps:

selling short Selling stocks that have been borrowed from a brokerage firm and must be replaced at a later date.

1. Arrange to *borrow a stock certificate* for a certain number of shares of a particular stock from a brokerage firm.
2. *Sell the borrowed stock*, assuming it will drop in value in a reasonably short period of time.
3. *Buy the stock at a lower price* than the price sold for in step 2.
4. Use the stocks purchased in step 3 to *replace the stocks borrowed from the brokerage firm* in step 1.

For example, Beatrice Maly, who is 28 years old, believes a dot-com stock is overpriced because of increased competition among dot-com companies and numerous other factors. As a result, she decides to sell short 100 shares of the dot-com company (Exhibit 11–12).

As Exhibit 11–12 shows, Beatrice's total return for this short transaction was $700 because the stocks did what they were supposed to do in a short transaction: decrease in value. A price decrease is especially important when selling short because you must replace the stocks borrowed from the brokerage firm with stocks purchased (hopefully at a lower market value) at a later date. If the stocks increase in value, you will lose money because you must replace the borrowed stocks with stocks purchased at a higher price. If the price of the dot-com stocks in Exhibit 11–12 had increased from $90 to $97, Beatrice would have lost $700.

There is usually no special or extra brokerage charge for selling short, since the brokerage firm receives its regular commission when the stocks are bought and sold. Before selling short, consider two factors. First, since the stocks you borrow from your broker are actually owned by another investor, you must pay any dividends the stocks earn before you replace the stocks. After all, you borrowed the stocks and then sold the borrowed stocks. Eventually, dividends can absorb the profits from your short transaction if the price of the stocks does not decrease rapidly enough. Second, to make money selling short, you must be correct in predicting that the stocks will decrease in value. If the value of the stocks increases, you lose.

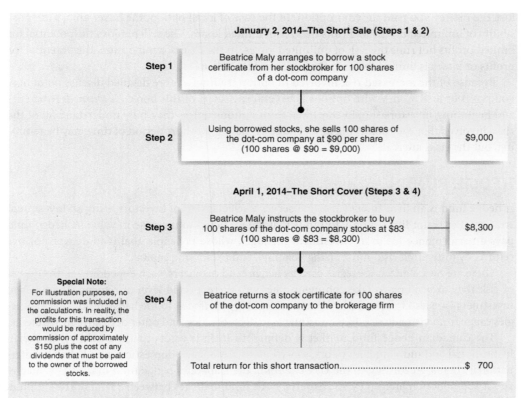

Exhibit 11–12

An Example of
Selling Short

January 2, 2014–The Short Sale (Steps 1 & 2)

Step 1 — Beatrice Maly arranges to borrow a stock certificate from her stockbroker for 100 shares of a dot-com company

Step 2 — Using borrowed stocks, she sells 100 shares of the dot-com company at $90 per share (100 shares @ $90 = $9,000) —— $9,000

April 1, 2014–The Short Cover (Steps 3 & 4)

Step 3 — Beatrice Maly instructs the stockbroker to buy 100 shares of the dot-com company stocks at $83 (100 shares @ $83 = $8,300) —— $8,300

Special Note:
For illustration purposes, no commission was included in the calculations. In reality, the profits for this transaction would be reduced by commission of approximately $150 plus the cost of any dividends that must be paid to the owner of the borrowed stocks.

Step 4 — Beatrice returns a stock certificate for 100 shares of the dot-com company to the brokerage firm

Total return for this short transaction...$ 700

TRADING IN OPTIONS   An **option** gives you the right to buy or sell stocks at a predetermined price during a specified period of time. Options are usually available for three-, six-, or nine-month periods. If you think the market price of a stock will increase during a short period of time, you may decide to purchase a call option. A *call option* is sold by a shareholder and gives the purchaser the right to *buy* 100 shares at a guaranteed price before a specified expiration date.

It is also possible to purchase a put option. A *put option* is the right to *sell* 100 shares at a guaranteed price before a specified expiration date. With both call and put options (see Exhibit 11–13), you are betting that the price of the stocks will increase or decrease in value before the expiration date. If this price movement does not occur before the expiration date, you

option The right to buy or sell stocks at a predetermined price during a specified period of time.

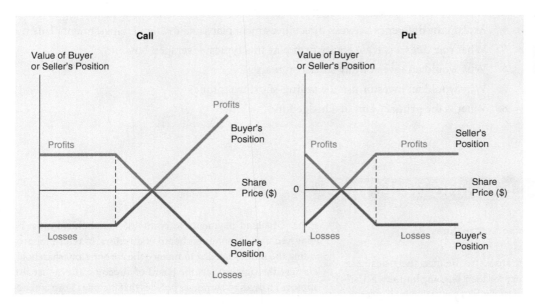

Exhibit 11–13

Payoff for Call and
Put Options

lose the money you paid for your option. In the case of a call option, the buyer enjoys the possibility of unlimited profits and runs the risk of limited losses. The seller enjoys the potential for limited profits but runs the risk of unlimited losses. In the case of a put option, the potential for profits or losses is limited for both the buyer and the seller.

Because of the increased risk involved in option trading, a more detailed discussion of how you profit or lose money with options is beyond the scope of this book. *Be warned:* Amateurs and beginning investors should stay away from options unless they fully understand all of the risks involved. For the rookie, the lure of large profits over a short period of time may be tempting, but the risks are real.

HEDGE FUNDS

A hedge fund is an investment fund that serves a select group of investors using an investment strategy that is not limited only to funds that are expected to increase in value. A hedge fund pays a performance fee to its investment manager, whose principle goal is to deliver positive returns by mitigating risk, minimizing volatility, and preserving capital.

There are over a dozen strategies used by hedge fund managers, each depending on the degree of risk they are willing to take commensurate with the expected level of returns. The types of investments are also influenced by investment strategy particular to the hedge fund. These strategies range from virtually risk-free investments to debt, equities, and other derivative instruments.

The Canadian hedge fund market is defined to include assets that are held by Canadian institutional and individual investors, as well as ones managed domestically on behalf of international clients. According to the *Globe & Mail*, the Canadian hedge fund market is valued at about $35 billion, managed by 150 experts. Each fund manages between $50 and $100 million. When compared with the American market, where the five largest hedge funds manage more than $100 billion, Canada is a small player in huge industry.*

---

*SOURCES: theglobeandmail.com/globe-investor/investment-ideas/streetwise/petite-potatoes-canadas-hedge-fund-industry/article1715574/; en.wikipedia.org/wiki/Hedge_fund.

CONCEPT CHECK 11–5

1. Why is it better for investors to diversify their stock portfolios?
2. How can an investor make money using the buy-and-hold technique?
3. What is the advantage of using dollar cost averaging?
4. Explain the difference between direct investment plans and dividend reinvestment plans.
5. What role does a private equity firm play in a typical leveraged buyout?
6. Why would an investor buy stocks on margin?
7. Why would an investor use the selling-short technique?
8. What is the primary aim of a hedge fund?

SUMMARY OF LEARNING OBJECTIVES

LO1 Identify the most important features of common stocks.

Corporations sell common stocks to finance their business startup costs and to help to pay for their ongoing business activities. People invest in common stocks because of dividend income, appreciation of value, and the possibility of gain through stock splits. Dividend payments to common shareholders must be approved by a corporation's board of directors. In return for providing the money needed to finance the corporation, shareholders have the right to elect the board of directors. They must also approve changes to corporate policies that include (1) an amendment to the corporate charter, (2) the sale of certain assets,

(3) possible mergers, (4) the issuance of preferred stocks or corporate bonds, and (5) changes in the amount of common stocks.

LO2 Discuss the most important features of preferred stocks.

The most important priority an investor in preferred stocks enjoys is receiving cash dividends before any cash dividends are paid to common shareholders. Still, dividend distributions to both preferred and common shareholders must be approved by the board of directors. To make preferred stock issues more attractive, corporations may add a cumulative feature, a participation feature, and/or a conversion feature to these issues.

LO3 Explain how to evaluate stock investments.

A number of factors can make a stock share increase or decrease in value. When evaluating a particular stock issue, most investors begin with the information contained in daily newspapers or on the Internet. Prospective investors should become familiar with various measures of corporate and investment performance, typical psychological biases, the two different analytical techniques used in stock selection, and the theory of efficient markets that supports a diversified approach to investing.

LO4 Describe how stocks are bought and sold.

A corporation may sell a new stock issue through an investment bank or directly to current shareholders. Once the stock has been sold in the primary market, it can be sold time and again in the secondary market. In the secondary market, investors purchase stocks listed on a securities exchange or traded in the over-the-counter market. Most securities transactions are made through an account executive who works for a brokerage firm. A growing number of investors are completing security transactions online. In fact, a good investment software package can help you evaluate potential investments, monitor the value of your investments, and place buy and sell orders online. Most brokerage firms charge a minimum commission for buying or selling stocks. Additional commission charges are based on the number and value of the shares bought or sold and whether you use a full-service or discount broker or trade online. There are a number of regulations in place to protect investors.

LO5 Explain the trading techniques used by long-term investors and short-term speculators.

Purchased stocks may be classified as either a long-term investment or a speculative investment. Long-term investors typically hold their investments for at least a year or longer; speculators (sometimes referred to as *traders*) usually sell their investments within a shorter time period. Traditional trading techniques long-term investors use include building a diversified portfolio, the buy-and-hold technique, dollar cost averaging, and direct investment and dividend reinvestment plans. More speculative techniques include buying on margin, selling short, and trading in options.

KEY TERMS

KEY FORMULAS

Page	Topic	Formula
344	Annual shareholder return	Annual shareholder return $= \dfrac{\text{Annual dividend} + \text{Appreciation in value}}{\text{Initial stock investment}}$
	Example:	$= \dfrac{\$0.73 + (\$29.00 - \$25.13)}{\$25.13}$
		$= 0.18304$ or 18.3 percent
344	Annual dividend yield	Annual dividend yield $= \dfrac{\text{Annual dividend}}{\text{Initial stock investment}}$
	Example:	$= \dfrac{\$0.73}{\$25.13}$
		$= 0.02904$ or 2.9 percent
344	Capital gains yield	Capital gains yield $= \dfrac{\text{Appreciation in value}}{\text{Initial stock investment}}$
	Example:	$= \dfrac{(\$29.00 = \$25.13)}{\$25.13}$
		$= 0.15999$ or 16 percent
344	Annual average compound return	Annual average compound return $= [(1 + R_1)(1 + R_2).....(1 + R_n)]^{1/n} - 1$ where R is the annual shareholder return for each consecutive year of ownership
	Example:	$= [(1.174)(1.309)]^{1/2} - 1 = 0.24$ or 24 percent
345	Earnings per share	Earnings per share $= \dfrac{\text{After-tax earnings}}{\text{Number of outstanding shares of common stocks}}$
	Example:	Earnings per share $= \dfrac{3{,}926\,\text{million}}{804.8\,\text{million}}$
		$= \$4.88$ per share
345	Price–earnings (P/E) ratio	(P/E) ratio $= \dfrac{\text{Price per share}}{\text{Earnings per share of stocks outstanding over the last 12 months}}$
	Example:	Price–earnings ratio $= \dfrac{\$39.65}{\$4.88}$
		$= 8.13$

FINANCIAL PLANNING PROBLEMS

 Practise and learn online with Connect.

1. *Calculating Dividend Amounts.* Jennifer and Jeff Cooke own 220 shares of Petro-Canada common stocks. Assume that Petro-Canada's quarterly dividend is $10 per share. What is the amount of the dividend cheque the Cooke couple will receive for this quarter? *LO1*

2. *Calculating Annual Shareholder Return.* Tamara June purchased 100 shares of All-Canadian Manufacturing

Company at $29.50 a share. One year later, she sold the stock for $38 a share. She paid her broker a $34 commission when she purchased the stocks and a $42 commission when she sold them. During the 12 months she owned the stocks, she received $184 in dividends. *LO1, LO2*

a. Calculate Tamara's annual shareholder return.

b. Break this total return into its components: dividend yield and capital gains yield.

3. *Calculating Annual Rate of Return.* You bought 100 shares of stock at $25 each. At the end of year 1 you received $400 in dividends and at the end of year 2, you received $100 in dividends and your stock was worth $2,700. What annual rate of return did you earn from your investment? *LO3*

4. *Annual Average Compound Return.* Marie and Brian Hume purchased 100 shares of a Canadian utility stock in January 2008. They calculated annual shareholder return to be 5 percent, −3 percent, and 7 percent for the years 2008, 2009, and 2011, respectively. What was the annual average compound return of their investment to the end of 2011? *LO1*

5. *Determining a Preferred Dividend Amount.* Thom Hayes owns Gaz Métropolitain preferred stocks. If this preferred stock issue pays 6.25 percent based on a par value of $25, what is the dollar amount of the dividend for one share of Gaz Métropolitain? *LO2*

6. *Calculating the Dividend for a Cumulative Preferred Stock Issue.* A sports equipment company issued a $3 cumulative preferred stock issue. In 2010, the firm's board of directors voted to omit dividends for both the company's common stock and its preferred stock issues. Also, the corporation's board of directors voted to pay dividends in 2011. *LO2*
   a. How much did the preferred shareholders receive in 2010?
   b. How much did the common shareholders receive in 2010?
   c. How much did the preferred shareholders receive in 2011?

7. *Calculating Annual Shareholder Return and Annual Average Compound Return.* Two years ago, you purchased 100 shares of a cola company. Your purchase price was $50 a share, plus a commission of $5 per share, for a total cost of $55 per share. After one year, the stock's market value had risen to $58. At the end of two years, you sold your cola company stocks for $68 a share, less a per-share commission of $2. During the two years you held the stock, you received dividends of $0.56 per share for the first year and $0.68 per share for the second year. *LO3*
   a. Calculate your annual shareholder return for each of the two years you owned the stock.
   b. Calculate your annual average compound return.

8. *Calculating Earnings per Share and Price–Earnings Ratio.* As a shareholder of an oil company, you receive its annual report. In the financial statements, the firm reported assets of $9 million, liabilities of $5 million, after-tax earnings of $2 million, and 750,000 outstanding shares of common stock. *LO3*
   a. Calculate the earnings per share of this oil company's common stock.
   b. Assuming a share of this oil company's common stock has a market value of $40, what is the firm's price–earnings ratio?

9. *Using Dollar Cost Averaging.* For four years, Marie St. Louis invested $3,000 each year in a bank's stocks. The stock sold for $34 in 2008, $48 in 2009, $37 in 2010, and $52 in 2011. *LO5*
   a. What is Marie's total investment in this bank?
   b. After four years, how many shares does Marie own?
   c. What is the average cost per share of Marie's investment?

10. *Using Margin.* Brian Campbell invested $4,000 and borrowed $4,000 to purchase shares in a large retailing company. At the time of his investment, the stocks were selling for $45 a share. *LO5*
    a. If Brian paid a $70 commission, how many shares could he buy if he used only his own money and did not use margin?
    b. If Brian paid a $100 commission, how many shares could he buy if he used his $4,000 and borrowed $4,000 on margin to buy these stocks?
    c. Assuming Brian did use margin, paid a $250 total commission to buy and sell his stocks, and sold his stocks for $53 a share, how much profit did he make on this investment?

11. *Selling Short.* After researching a software company's common stocks, Sarah Jackson is convinced the stocks are overpriced. She contacts her account executive and arranges to short sell 200 shares. At the time of the sale, a share of common stock had a value of $35. Six months later, the stocks were selling for $23 a share, and Sarah instructed her broker to cover her short transaction. Total commissions to buy and sell the stocks were $120. What is her profit for this short transaction? *LO5*

FINANCIAL PLANNING ACTIVITIES

1. *Surveying Investors.* Survey investors who own stocks. Then explain, in a short paragraph, their reasons for owning stocks. *LO1*

2. *Interviewing an Account Executive.* Interview an account executive about the cumulative feature, participation feature, and conversion feature of a preferred stock. What do these features mean to preferred shareholders? *LO2*

3. *Using Research Information.* Divide a sheet of paper into three columns. In the first column, list sources of information you can use to evaluate stock investments. In the second column, state where you would find each of these sources. In the third column, describe the types of information each source would provide. *LO3*

4. *Using Stock Advisory Services.* Pick a stock that interests you and research the company at the library by examining the information contained in reports published by Moody's, Standard & Poor's, Zacks, or business periodicals such as *Canadian Business*, *MoneySense*, or *BusinessWeek*. Then write a one- or two-page summary of your findings. Based on your research, would you still want to invest in these stocks? Why, or why not? *LO3*

5. *Using the Internet.* Choose a stock that you think would be a good investment. Then research the stock using the Internet. *LO3*
   a. Based on the information contained on the corporation's Web site, would you still want to invest in the stock? Explain your answer.
   b. What other investment information would you need to evaluate the stock? Where would you obtain this information?

6. *Conducting Library Research.* Conduct library research on the fundamental theory, the technical theory, and the efficient market theory described in this chapter. How do these theories explain the movements of a stock traded on the TSE or over-the-counter market? *LO3*

7. *Exploring Career Opportunities.* Prepare a list of questions you could use to interview an account executive about career opportunities in the field of finance. *LO4*

8. *Using Long-Term Investment Techniques.* Interview people who have used the long-term investment techniques of buy and hold, dollar cost averaging, direct investment plan, or dividend reinvestment plan. Describe your findings. *LO5*

9. *Analyzing Short-Term Investments.* Prepare a chart that describes the similarities and differences among buying stocks on margin, selling short, and trading in options. *LO5*

CREATING A FINANCIAL PLAN

Investing in Stocks

For many investors, selection of stocks for their portfolios is an important element that helps achieve various investment goals.

Web Sites for Investing in Stocks

- Stock market and corporate information at **stockhouse.ca**, SEDAR, at **sedar.com**, the U.S. Securities Exchange Commission at **sec.gov**, and investment research from Zacks at **zacks.com**.
- Stock charts from BigCharts at **bigcharts.com**.
- Stock analysis and chat groups from Raging Bull at **ragingbull.com**, from TheStreet.com at **thestreet.com**, from Big Charts at **bigcharts.com**, and from Whisper Number at **whispernumber.com**.
- Initial Public Offering (IPO) information from IPO Central at **ipocentral.com** and IPO.com at **ipo.com**.
- Information about investing at **canoe.ca/money**, **canadianfinance.com**, **globeinvestor.com**.

(Note: Addresses and content of Web sites change, and new sites are created daily. Use search engines to update and locate Web sites for your current financial planning needs.)

Short-Term Financial Planning Activities

1. Identify investment goals that might be appropriate for investing in stocks for your life situation.

2. Research potential stocks based on your various financial goals. Consider risk, potential growth, income, and recent market performance.

3. Monitor current economic conditions that may affect the value of individual stocks as well as the stock market as a whole.

4. Compare the cost of various investment broker services.

Long-Term Financial Planning Activities

1. Identify stock investing decisions that might be used for achieving long-term financial goals.

2. Develop a plan for investing in stocks as family and household situations change.

LIFE SITUATION CASE

Research Information Available from Zacks and Standard & Poor's

This chapter stressed the importance of evaluating potential investments. Now, it's your turn to try your skill at evaluating a potential investment in BCE. Assume you could invest $10,000 in the company's common stocks. To help you evaluate this potential investment, carefully examine Exhibits 11–7 and 11–8, which reproduce the research reports on BCE from Zacks and Standard & Poor's, respectively.

Questions

1. Based on the research provided by Zacks and Standard & Poor's, would you buy BCE stock? Justify your answer.

2. What other investment information would you need to evaluate BCE common stocks? Where would you obtain this information?

3. At year-end 2013, BCE common stocks were selling for $47.40 a share. Using a newspaper, determine the current price for a share of BCE common stocks. Based on this information, would your BCE investment have been profitable if you had purchased the common stocks for $47.40 a share?

Investing in Bonds

LEARNING OBJECTIVES

LO1 Describe the characteristics of corporate bonds.

LO2 Discuss why corporations issue bonds.

LO3 Explain why investors purchase corporate bonds.

LO4 Discuss why federal, provincial, and municipal governments issue bonds and why investors purchase government bonds.

LO5 Evaluate bonds when making an investment.

FOR ONE INVESTOR, TELECOM BONDS ARE THE RIGHT CALL

Before reading this chapter, answer these two questions: (1) Are you discouraged by the low interest rates offered by banks, trust companies, and credit unions on Guaranteed Investment Certificates? (2) Are you afraid of investing in stocks because of the increased risk?

If you answered yes to both questions, you may want to consider investing in bonds. That's what Bethan Jackson, 27, did in 2014. The low returns offered on Guaranteed Investment Certificates have forced many investors like Jackson to evaluate other investments that offer higher returns.

Jackson considered investing in stocks and mutual funds but was afraid of losing her $22,000 nest egg. She wanted an investment that was more secure and offered a predictable source of income. That's when she purchased 12 corporate bonds issued by a Canadian telecommunications utility. Although the utility used many different bond issues to finance its operations, Jackson chose a

bond issue with a 4.5 percent interest rate and a maturity date in 2024.

Jackson began her search for an investment by thinking about the products she used daily. Since the utility was the company that provided her wireless phone service and since she was using her wireless phone more and more, she assumed it must be rolling in profits. Not content with just a "feeling that the company must be profitable," she researched the company on the Internet. At the company's Web site, she examined the company's financial statements and learned that it was, indeed, profitable. Also, the company had a reasonable amount of long-term debt compared with its total assets.

Still not quite sure, Jackson went to the library and found that the Dominion Bond Rating Service (DBRS) rated the utility's debentures with an AA. According to the DBRS rating definitions, securities rated A are considered to be of superior quality and to have favourable long-term investment characteristics. Companies with this rating have maintained a history of adequate asset and earnings protection. Continued interest payments and eventual repayment of the principal are assured for bonds with these ratings.

Based on her research, Bethan Jackson decided to purchase 12 of the company's bonds at $1,000 each. Each year until 2024, the utility will pay investors who own bonds in this issue $45 per bond in interest payments. And after receiving her first interest cheque, Jackson believes she made the right decision. In fact, she is looking forward to more interest cheques until the bond's maturity in 2024, when the company will repay bondholders $1,000 for each bond they own. (By the way, Jackson also decided to place the remainder of her $22,000 nest egg in a six-month Guaranteed Investment Certificate that paid 1.25 percent.)

QUESTIONS

1. What might make a particular investment, such as utility bonds, a good investment for one person and a poor one for another person?
2. Bethan Jackson divided her $22,000 nest egg between bonds and a Guaranteed Investment Certificate. Would you have made the same decision?
3. Based on what you've learned thus far, would you buy bonds issued by a utility such as this one? Explain your answer.

Opportunity costs! Bethan Jackson, the woman in the opening case, took a chance when she purchased 12 corporate bonds issued by a utility company. Her investment, which cost more than $12,000, could decrease in value. But because she took the time to evaluate the investment using reliable sources, she could be reasonably certain she would receive interest payments each year and eventual repayment when this bond issue reaches maturity in 2024.

The company that issued the bond also took advantage of the concept of opportunity costs when it sold bonds. It agreed to pay bondholders 4.5 percent interest until the bonds mature in 2024. It also agreed to repay Jackson's original investment when the bonds mature. In return, the company obtained the money it needed to provide telecommunications services to its customers, provide more jobs, and ultimately earn larger profits.

We begin this chapter by describing the basic characteristics of corporate bonds that define the relationship between investors, like Bethan Jackson, and corporations that sell bonds to obtain financing.

CHARACTERISTICS OF CORPORATE BONDS

LO1

Describe the characteristics of corporate bonds.

corporate bond A corporation's written pledge to repay a specified amount of money, along with interest.

face value The dollar amount the bondholder will receive at the bond's maturity.

A **corporate bond** is a corporation's written pledge to repay a specified amount of money with interest. Exhibit 12–1 shows a typical corporate bond. Note that it states the dollar amount of the bond, the interest rate, and the maturity date. The **face value** is the dollar amount the bondholder will receive at the bond's maturity. The usual face value of a corporate bond is $1,000, but the face value of some corporate bonds may be as high as $50,000. The total face value of all the bonds in an issue usually runs into millions of dollars (see Exhibit 12–2). Between the time of purchase and the maturity date, the corporation pays interest to the bondholder, usually every six months, at the stated interest rate (referred to as the coupon rate of the bond). For example, assume you purchase the bond shown in Exhibit 12–1, and the coupon rate for this bond is 8.5 percent. Using the following formula, you can calculate the annual interest amount for this bond:

$$\text{Dollar amount of annual interest} = \text{Face value} \times \text{Interest rate}$$
$$= \$1,000 \times 8.5 \text{ percent}$$
$$= \$1,000 \times 0.085$$
$$= \$85$$

Exhibit 12–1
A Typical Corporate Bond

In this situation, you receive interest of $85 a year from the corporation. The interest is paid semi-annually, or every six months, in $42.50 ($85 ÷ 2 = $42.50) instalments until the bond matures.

The **maturity date** of a corporate bond is the last date on which the corporation is to repay the borrowed money. At the maturity date, the bondholder returns the bond to the corporation and receives cash equal to the bond's face value. Maturity dates for bonds generally range from 1 to 30 years after the date of issue. Maturities for corporate bonds may also be classified as short term (under 5 years), intermediate term (5 to 15 years), and long term (over 15 years).

maturity date For a corporate bond, the date on which the corporation is to repay the borrowed money.

Exhibit 12–2
Advertisement for a 7½ Percent Convertible Debenture Issued by Meditrust (Meditrust was renamed La Quinta in 2001)

bond indenture A legal document that details all the conditions relating to a bond issue.

The actual legal conditions for a corporate bond are described in a bond indenture. A **bond indenture** is a legal document that details all of the conditions relating to a bond issue. Often containing over 100 pages of complicated legal wording, the bond indenture remains in effect until the bonds reach maturity or are redeemed by the corporation.

trustee A financially independent firm that acts as the bondholders' representative.

Since corporate bond indentures are difficult for the average person to read and understand, a corporation issuing bonds appoints a trustee. The **trustee** is a financially independent firm that acts as the bondholders' representative. Usually, the trustee is a bank or some other financial institution. The corporation must report to the trustee periodically regarding its ability to make interest payments and eventually redeem the bonds. In turn, the trustee transmits this information to the bondholders along with its own evaluation of the corporation's ability to pay. If the corporation fails to live up to all the provisions in the indenture agreement, the trustee may bring legal action to protect the bondholders' interests. In cases of bankruptcy, certain bondholders are paid before others depending upon the class or type of bond; they are always paid after Canada Revenue Agency and the employee payroll.

CONCEPT CHECK 12–1

1. If you needed information about a bond issue, would you go to the library or use the Internet?
2. What is the usual face value for a corporate bond?
3. What is the annual interest amount for a $1,000 bond issued by Power Corporation of Canada that pays 6.5 percent interest?
4. In your own words, define *maturity date* and *bond indenture*.
5. How does a trustee evaluate the provisions contained in a bond indenture?

WHY CORPORATIONS SELL CORPORATE BONDS

LO2

Discuss why corporations issue bonds.

Let's begin this section with some basics of why corporations sell bonds. Corporations, such as Meditrust (see Exhibit 12–2), borrow when they don't have enough money to pay for major purchases—much as individuals do. Bonds can also be used to finance a corporation's ongoing business activities. In addition, corporations often sell bonds when it is difficult or impossible to sell stocks. Selling bonds can also improve a corporation's financial leverage—using borrowed funds to increase the corporation's return on investment. Finally, the interest paid to bond owners is a tax-deductible expense and can be used to reduce the taxes the corporation must pay to the federal and provincial governments.

While a corporation may use both bonds and stocks to finance its activities, there are important distinctions between the two. Issuing corporate bonds is a form of *debt financing*, whereas issuing stocks is a form of *equity financing*. Bond owners must be repaid at a future date; shareholders do not have to be repaid. Interest payments on bonds are required; dividends are paid to shareholders at the discretion of the board of directors. Finally, in the event of bankruptcy, bondholders have a claim to the corporation assets prior to that of shareholders.

Before issuing bonds, a corporation must decide what type of bond to issue and how the bond issue will be repaid.

TYPES OF BONDS

debenture A bond that is backed only by the reputation of the issuing corporation.

Most corporate bonds are debentures. A **debenture** is a bond that is backed only by the reputation of the issuing corporation. If the corporation fails to make either interest payments or repayment at maturity, debenture bondholders become general creditors, much like the firm's suppliers. In the event of corporate bankruptcy, general creditors, including debenture bondholders, can claim any asset not specifically used as collateral for a loan or other financial obligations.

To make a bond issue more appealing to conservative investors, a corporation may issue a mortgage bond. A **mortgage bond** is a corporate bond secured by various assets of the firm. This type of bond pledges land, buildings, or equipment as security for the loan and entitles the trustee to take ownership of these assets on behalf of bondholders if interest and principal payments are defaulted. A first mortgage bond is the most secure that a corporation can offer and is considered foremost of all obligations a company may have. Often, this type of mortgage will apply against both current and future assets. A general mortgage bond is secured by all the fixed assets of the firm that have not been pledged as collateral for other financial obligations. A *collateral trust bond* is secured by a pledge of securities and is often issued by companies that do not own many fixed assets but do own other securities.

A secured bond is safer than a debenture because it is secured by the issuing company's pledge of a specific asset or the income stream from the project that the bond was used to finance. In the event of default, the issuing company transfers the ownership of the asset or the money that has been set aside to the bondholders. A **subordinated debenture** is an unsecured bond that gives bondholders a claim secondary to that of other designated bondholders with respect to interest payments, repayment, and assets. Investors who purchase subordinated debentures usually enjoy higher interest rates than other bondholders because of the increased risk associated with this type of bond.

mortgage bond A corporate bond secured by various assets of the issuing firm.

subordinated debenture An unsecured bond that gives bondholders a claim secondary to that of other designated bondholders with respect to both interest payments and assets.

CONVERTIBLE BONDS AND BONDS WITH WARRANTS

A special type of bond a corporation may issue is a convertible bond. A **convertible bond** can be exchanged, at the owner's option, for a specified number of shares of the corporation's common stock. This conversion feature allows investors to enjoy the lower risk of a corporate bond but also take advantage of the speculative nature of common stock. For example, assume ABC Inc.'s $1,000 bond issue with a 2018 maturity date is convertible. Each bond can be converted to 28.9 shares of the company's common stocks. This means you could convert the bond to common stocks whenever the price of the company's common stocks is $34.60 ($1,000 ÷ 28.9 = $34.60) or higher.

In reality, there is no guarantee that ABC bondholders will convert to common stocks even if the market value of the common stocks does increase to $34.60 or higher. The reason for choosing not to exercise the conversion feature in this example is quite simple. As the market value of the common stocks increases, the market value of the convertible bond also increases. By not converting to common stocks, bondholders enjoy the added safety of the bond and interest income in addition to the increased market value of the bond caused by the price movement of the common stocks.

The corporation gains three advantages by issuing convertible bonds. First, the interest rate on a convertible bond is often 1 to 2 percent lower than that on traditional bonds. Second, the conversion feature attracts investors who are interested in the possible gain that conversion to common stocks may provide. Third, if the bondholder converts to common stocks, the corporation no longer has to redeem the bond at maturity.

Some bonds are issued with warrants. A *warrant* is an option that is detachable from the associated bond that gives the holder the right to purchase the firm's common shares at a set price for a pre-determined period, usually a number of years. Warrants are attached to newly issued bonds to make them more attractive to potential investors. They can usually be detached from the bonds they were issued with and traded separately.

convertible bond A bond that can be exchanged, at the owner's option, for a specified number of shares of the corporation's common stocks.

PROVISIONS FOR REPAYMENT

Today, most corporate bonds are callable. A **call feature** allows the corporation to call in or buy outstanding bonds from current bondholders before the maturity date. In the 1990s, investors saw a large number of bonds called because corporations could replace high-interest bond issues with new bond issues that have lower interest rates. The money needed to call a bond may come from the firm's profits, the sale of additional stocks, or the sale of a new bond issue that has a lower interest rate.

call feature A feature that allows the corporation to call in or buy outstanding bonds from current bondholders before the maturity date.

In most cases, corporations issuing callable bonds agree not to call them for the first 5 to 10 years after the bonds have been issued. When a call feature is used, the corporation may have to pay the bondholders a *premium*, an additional amount above the face value of the bond. The amount of the premium is specified in the bond indenture; a $10 to $50 premium over the bond's face value is common.

A corporation may use one of two methods to ensure that it has sufficient funds available to redeem a bond issue. First, the corporation may establish a sinking fund. A **sinking fund** is a fund to which annual or semi-annual deposits are made for the purpose of redeeming a bond issue. The fund is invested and administered by a trustee who is outside of the corporation. To retire a $100-million bond issue that matures in 2032, a Canadian corporation agreed to make annual sinking fund payments of $5 million on April 15 of each year beginning in 2014 and continuing through 2031. Note that the corporation will have made sinking fund payments totalling $90 million ($5 million $\times$ 18 years = $90 million) over the 18-year period. From a financial management standpoint, each annual sinking fund payment of $5 million can be invested and is an example of the time value of money (increases in an amount of money as a result of interest earned), a concept stressed throughout this text. At maturity, the $90 million contributed by the corporation *plus* the investment earnings will enable the corporation to pay off this $100 million bond issue.

sinking fund A fund to which annual or semi-annual deposits are made for the purpose of redeeming a bond issue.

A sinking fund provision in the bond indenture is generally advantageous to bondholders. Such a provision forces the corporation to make arrangements for bond repayment before the maturity date. If the terms of the provision are not met, the trustee or bondholders may take legal action against the company.

serial bonds Bonds of a single issue that mature on different dates.

Second, a corporation may issue serial bonds. **Serial bonds** are bonds of a single issue that mature on different dates. For example, Seaside Productions used a 20-year, $100 million bond issue to finance its expansion. None of the bonds mature during the first 10 years. Thereafter, 10 percent of the bonds mature each year until all the bonds are retired at the end of the 20-year period.

Detailed information about provisions for repayment, along with other vital information (including maturity date, interest rate, bond rating, call provisions, trustee, and details about collateral), is available from DBRS, Standard & Poor's Corporation, Moody's Investors Service, and other financial service companies.

OTHER TYPES OF BONDS

DOMESTIC, FOREIGN, AND EUROBONDS   Domestic bonds are issued in the country and currency of the issuer. Foreign bonds are, quite simply, bonds issued primarily in a currency and country other than the issuer's, allowing issuers access to huge sources of capital in other countries. Eurobonds differ from foreign bonds in that they are bonds issued on the international bond market in any currency. For example, a bond issued by an American corporation in the U.K., denominated in U.S. dollars, would be referred to as a Eurobond. The international bond market is regulated by the International Securities Market Association (ISMA).

UNITS   Units are packages of two or more corporate securities bundled by an investment dealer and sold at an overall price. In the past, the traditional bundle usually included a bond or debenture bundled with a number of common shares.

STRIP BONDS   This type of bond, also called a zero-coupon bond, first appeared in Canada in 1982. It is the result of an investment dealer buying a block of existing high-quality bonds and then separating the individual interest coupons from the bonds.

The coupons and bonds are then sold separately at significant discounts to their face values. You earn money by paying a discounted price and then redeeming them at the maturity date.

CONCEPT CHECK 12–2

1. Why do corporations sell bonds?
2. What are the differences between a debenture, a mortgage bond, and a subordinated debenture?
3. Why would investors be attracted to bonds issued with warrants attached?
4. Why would an investor purchase a convertible bond?
5. Describe three reasons a corporation would sell convertible bonds.
6. Explain the methods corporations can use to repay a bond issue.

WHY INVESTORS PURCHASE CORPORATE BONDS

In Chapters 10 and 11, we compared the historical returns provided by stocks and bonds. Stocks have had higher returns than most bonds and Treasury bills (T-bills). With this fact in mind, you may be wondering why you should consider bonds as an investment alternative. Why not just choose stocks because they provide the highest possible return of the three investment alternatives?

LO3

Explain why investors purchase corporate bonds.

STOCKS ALWAYS BEAT BONDS: MYTH OR FACT?

Even if stocks do not always beat bonds, the financial industry will tell you otherwise because most brokerage firm profits come from investment banking commissions on stocks. Commissions are skewed heavily towards equities (2.5 percent) as compared to bonds (1.5 percent) and money market funds (0.5 percent).

In efficient markets, shareholders expect to earn superior returns to bondholders because they bear more risks and are consequently rewarded in the end. This positive risk/return premium was the mantra of financial advice to entice investors to own shares.

However, there have been many long periods when bonds or T-bills have outperformed stocks. Using the Canadian Long-Term Bond total return index and the TSE Index (now the S&P/TSX), the period from 1970 to 2005 shows the bond index outperforming stocks. During the 1980s, T-bills were the best asset class in the U.S., followed by bonds and then equities.

Be wary of mantras, as stocks do not always beat bonds. Learn more about investing in bonds.

Some investors use corporate and government bonds to diversify their investment portfolios through a method called *asset allocation*. This is a fancy way of saying that you need to avoid the mistake of putting all of your eggs in one basket—a common mistake made by many investors. The fact is that many corporate and government bonds are safer investments and are often considered a "safe harbour" in troubled economic times. For example, many stock investors lost money during the last part of 2007 and throughout 2008 because of the economic downturn and the crisis in the mortgage lending, housing, and automobile industries in the U.S. For example, Susan and Brandon Davidson had an investment portfolio valued at more than $270,000. Not bad for a couple in their early 40s. Yet they lost almost $100,000 during the economic crisis. If their investment portfolio had been diversified, using asset allocation and investing some of their money in bonds, they would have reduced their losses or even made some money, depending on the amounts they invested in different investment alternatives. Basically, investors purchase corporate bonds for three reasons: (1) interest income, (2) possible increase in value, and (3) repayment at maturity.

INTEREST INCOME

As mentioned earlier in this chapter, bondholders normally receive interest payments every six months. As we saw, the dollar amount of interest is determined by multiplying the interest rate by the face value of the bond. In fact, because interest income is so important to bond investors, let's review this calculation. If Canadian Tire issues a 5.65 percent bond with a face value of $1,000, the investor receives $56.50 ($1,000 × 5.65% = $56.50) a year, paid in instalments of $28.25 at the end of each six-month period.

The method used to pay bondholders their interest depends on whether they own registered bonds, registered coupon bonds, bearer bonds, or zero-coupon bonds. A **registered bond** is registered in the owner's name by the issuing company. Interest cheques for registered bonds are mailed directly to the bondholder of record. A variation of a registered bond is the registered coupon bond. A **registered coupon bond** is registered for principal only, not for interest. To collect interest payments on a registered coupon bond, the owner must present one of the detachable coupons to the issuing corporation or the paying agent.

A third type of bond is a **bearer bond**, which is not registered in the investor's name. As with a registered coupon bond, the owner of a bearer bond must detach a coupon and present it to the issuing corporation or the paying agent to collect interest payments. *Be warned:* If you own a bearer bond, you can be out of luck if it is lost or stolen. Anyone—the rightful owner or a thief—can collect interest payments and the face value at maturity if he or she has physical possession of the bearer bond or its detachable coupons. While some bearer bonds are still in circulation, corporations no longer issue them.

A zero-coupon or strip bond is sold at a price far below its face value, makes no annual or semi-annual interest payments, and is redeemed for its face value at maturity. With a zero-coupon bond, the buyer receives a return based on the bond's increased market value as its maturity date approaches. For example, assume you purchased a Loblaw's Inc. zero-coupon bond for $350 in 2012 and Loblaw's Inc. will pay you $1,000 when the bond matures in 2029. For holding the bond for 18 years, you will receive interest of $650 ($1,000 face value − $350 purchase price = $650 interest) at maturity.

Before investing in **zero-coupon bonds**, you should consider at least two factors. First, even though all of the interest on these bonds is paid at maturity, the government requires you to report interest each year—that is, as you earn it, not when you actually receive it. Second, zero-coupon bonds are more volatile than other types of bonds. When evaluating such bonds, as in evaluating other types of bonds, the most important criterion is the quality of the issuer. It pays to be careful.

registered bond A bond that is registered in the owner's name by the issuing company.

registered coupon bond A bond that is registered for principal only, and not for interest.

bearer bond A bond that is not registered in the investor's name.

zero-coupon bond A bond that is sold at a price far below its face value, makes no annual or semi-annual interest payments, and is redeemed for its face value at maturity.

CHANGES IN BOND VALUE

Most beginning investors think that a $1,000 bond is always worth $1,000. In reality, the price of a corporate bond may fluctuate until the maturity date. Changes in overall interest rates in the economy are the primary cause of most bond price fluctuations. Changing bond prices that result from changes in overall interest rates in the economy are an example of interest rate risk, discussed in Chapter 10. In fact, there is an inverse relationship between a bond's market value and overall interest rates in the economy. When Canadian Tire issued the bond mentioned earlier, the 5.65 percent interest rate was competitive with the interest rates offered by other corporations issuing bonds at that time. If overall interest rates fall, the Canadian Tire bond will go up in market value due to its higher 5.65 percent interest rate. On the other hand, if overall interest rates rise, the market value of the Canadian Tire bond will fall due to its lower 5.65 percent interest rate.

When a bond is selling for less than its face value, it is said to be selling at a *discount*. When a bond is selling for more than its face value, it is said to be selling at a *premium*. A more detailed explanation on the relationship between market interest rates and bond pricing is provided in Appendix 12. Generally, investors consult the *Financial Post*, *Report on Business*, the Internet, or a newspaper to determine the price of a bond. Information on how to read bond quotations is provided later in this chapter.

It is also possible to approximate a bond's market value using the following formula:

$$\text{Approximate market value} = \frac{\text{Dollar amount of annual interest}}{\text{Comparable interest rate}}$$

For example, assume you purchase a corporate bond that pays 4⅞ percent interest based on a face value of $1,000. Also, assume that new corporate bond issues of comparable quality are currently paying 7 percent. The approximate market value is $696, as follows:

$$\text{Dollar amount of annual interest} = \$1,000 \times 4\tfrac{7}{8} \text{ percent}$$
$$= \$1,000 \times 4.875 \text{ percent}$$
$$= \$48.75$$

$$\text{Approximate market value} = \frac{\text{Dollar amount of annual interest}}{\text{Comparable interest rate}} = \frac{\$48.75}{7\%}$$

$$= \$696$$

The market value of a bond may also be affected by the financial condition of the company or government unit issuing the bond, the factors of supply and demand, an upturn or downturn in the economy, and the proximity of the bond's maturity date.

BOND REPAYMENT AT MATURITY

Corporate bonds are repaid at maturity. After you purchase a bond, you have two options: you may keep the bond until maturity and then redeem it, or you may sell the bond at any time to another investor. In either case, the value of your bond is closely tied to the corporation's ability to repay its bond indebtedness. For example, when the telecommunication firm Nortel filed for reorganization under the provisions of the Bankruptcy Act. As a result, the bonds issued by Nortel immediately dropped in value due to questions concerning the prospects for bond repayment at maturity. On the other hand, if a corporation establishes a reputation as an aggressive firm with excellent and innovative products, experienced and capable managers, and increasing sales and profits, the value of your bond may increase depending on the interest rate of the bond and the stability of the issuer. Simply put, other investors will pay more money to get a quality bond that has excellent prospects of repayment at maturity.

COMPARING BONDS TO GICS

Bonds are included in a portfolio to generate steady income, stabilize overall return, and provide the investor with some security. Bonds are debt instruments much like Guaranteed Investment Certificates (GICs). When you invest in a GIC, you are lending your money to a bank, and in return it pays you interest. In contrast, when you invest in a bond, you are lending your money to a corporation or to a government (whoever issued the bond) for which it also pays you interest. Both guarantee that the loan value will be repaid upon maturity. However, a GIC offers better protection against uncertainty, as its value is guaranteed by a bank and insured by the Canada Deposit Insurance Corporation (CDIC). For bonds, there is no such protection. The value of the bond is only as good as the issuer. There is always the risk that the issuing company may default prior to maturity and will no longer be able to make the stated interest payments. The risk associated with bonds is what accounts for the higher interest that is paid in comparison to GICs. For bonds, the amount of interest paid is generally attached to the bond rating the company has been given. The higher the possibility that the company may default, the higher the interest paid must be in order to incite investors to buy them. Bonds also tend to have longer maturities (5 to 30 years) than GICs (1 to 10 years). Furthermore, a bond is a marketable security, which means that it can be sold in the bond market at any time before it matures. This allows investors to take advantage of market fluctuations to pay less than the face value for the bond; however, at the same time, the value of the bond may increase beyond the face value.

A TYPICAL BOND TRANSACTION

Assume that on October 8, 1999, you purchased an 8.375 percent corporate bond issued by Telus. Your cost for the bond was $680. You held the bond until October 8, 2013, when you sold it at its current market value of $1,256. Exhibit 12–3 shows the return on your investment.

Since commissions for bonds, strip coupons, GICs, T-bills, and other fixed income securities are already included in the quoted price, you experienced a capital gain of $576 because the market value of the bond increased from $680 to $1,256. The increase in the value of the bond resulted because overall interest rates in the economy declined during the 11-year period in which you owned the bond. Also, Telus established a reputation for efficiency and productivity during this period. Increased efficiency and productivity help ensure that Telus will be able to repay bondholders when the bond reaches maturity in 2027.

You also made money on your Telus bond because of interest payments. For each of the 11 years you owned the bond, Telus paid you $83.75 ($1,000 × 8.375% = $83.75) interest. The average annual compound return you earned each year during the period that you held the bond is calculated as:

2ND		CLRTVM	
680+/−		PV	
1,030		FV	
83.75		PMT	
11		N	
COMP	I/Y		14.49%

This calculation assumes that you reinvested the $83.75 of interest received every year at the average annual compound rate of 14.49 percent. If the reinvestment rate of the bond's coupons had been lower or higher, then the calculation of the average annual compound return would have to be adjusted. Refer to Problem 9 under Financial Planning Problems on page 388 for an example of the required adjustment.

Exhibit 12–3

Sample Corporate Bond Transaction for Telus

Assumptions			
Interest, 9.2 percent; maturity date, 2027; purchased March October 8, 1999; sold October 7, 2013.			

Costs when Purchased		**Return when Sold**	
1 bond @ $680		1 bond @ $1256	
Total investment	$680	Dollar return	$1,256

Transaction Summary	
Dollar return	$1,256.00
Minus total investment	− 680.00
Profit from bond sale	+ 576.00
Plus interest ($83.75 for 11 years)	+ 921.25
Total return on the transaction	$1,497.25

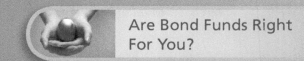
Simply put, bond funds are an indirect way of owning bonds, debt instruments, and IOUs issued by the Canadian treasury, corporations, or province, city, and local school districts. Many financial experts recommend bond funds for small investors because these investments offer diversification and professional management. Diversification spells safety because an occasional loss incurred with one bond issue is usually offset by gains from other bond issues in the fund. Also, professional managers should be able to do a better job of picking bonds than individual investors. But before investing, consider two factors. First, even the best managers make mistakes. Second, it may cost more to purchase bond funds than individual bonds. As with most investments, the key to making money with funds is evaluation.

EVALUATING BOND FUNDS

Marie Hamel, a working mother with one child, received $44,000 following the death of her grandmother. After some careful planning, she decided to invest $34,000 in two high-quality corporate bond funds. She used the remaining $10,000 to pay off some credit card debts and establish an emergency fund. During the next two years, she earned more than 8 percent on her bond investments each year—not bad during a period when GICs were paying between 1 and 3 percent.

Marie's 8 percent return wasn't just luck. She began by establishing an investment goal: Find a safe investment with minimal risk. After establishing her goal, she talked with an account executive at Yorkton Securities and asked for five suggestions that would enable her to attain her goal. Of the five original suggestions, three were conservative bond funds.

Next, Marie took a crucial step that many investors don't: She decided to do her own research and not just rely on the account executive's suggestions. She contacted the firms that managed each of the three bond funds and asked them to mail her a prospectus and an annual report. After receiving the information, she was able to (1) determine each fund's investment objective, (2) identify the investments each fund contained, and (3) calculate the approximate fees and expenses charged by each fund.

Then, she made a trip to the library, where she analyzed the performance of each of the three bond funds in the special mutual fund editions of *Maclean's* and *Canadian Business*. Each publication ranked the three bond funds according to the total return for the previous 12 months, three years, and five years. Although past performance is no guarantee of future performance, it may be one of the best predictors available. Based on the account executive's suggestions and her own research, she chose the "top" two bond funds.

Marie admits that she spent almost 30 hours researching her investments but believes the time was well spent. When you consider the amount of money she made on her bond fund investments during the first two years—more than $5,400—she made almost $180 an hour.

Before investing in bonds, you should remember that the price of a corporate bond can decrease and that interest payments and eventual repayment may be a problem for a corporation that encounters financial difficulties or enters bankruptcy. In addition to purchasing individual bonds, some investors prefer to purchase bond funds.

THE MECHANICS OF A BOND TRANSACTION

Most bonds are sold through full-service brokerage firms, discount brokerage firms, or the Internet. If you use a brokerage firm, your account executive should provide both information and advice about bond investments. Many experts urge you to remember one basic rule: It is always *your* money, and *you* should be the one who makes the final decision to buy or sell a bond. Your account executive's role is to make suggestions and provide information that may enable you to make a more informed decision. As with stock investments, the chief advantage of using a discount brokerage firm or trading online is lower commissions, but you must do your own research and make the decision to buy or sell a bond issue. As you will see later in this chapter, many sources of information can be used to evaluate bond investments.

The bond market is referred to as an "over-the-counter" (OTC) exchange. Unlike stock markets, there is no centralized floor. Rather, the market is decentralized and transactions are made via telephone or computer, among buyers and sellers who might be continents apart or next door to one another. Trading volumes are enormous and may average more than 20 times the volume of the stock markets.

Buyers and sellers trade bonds through bond or investment dealers, who are paid through a fee that is already represented in the price that buyers pay. There are about 190 dealers and a smaller number of banks and trust companies involved in this market, and all of the dealers are linked together by five inter-dealer bond brokers that are regulated by the Investment Dealers Association (IDA).

CONCEPT CHECK 12–3

1. Describe the three reasons investors purchase bonds.
2. What are the differences among a registered bond, a registered coupon bond, a bearer bond, and a zero-coupon bond?
3. In what ways can interest rates in the economy affect the price of a corporate bond?
4. Why is the value of a bond closely tied to the issuing corporation's ability to repay its bond indebtedness?
5. How are corporate bonds bought and sold?

GOVERNMENT BONDS AND DEBT SECURITIES

LO4

Discuss why federal, provincial, and municipal governments issue bonds and why investors purchase government bonds.

In addition to corporations, the federal, provincial, and local governments issue bonds to obtain financing. In this section, we discuss bonds issued by these three levels of government and look at why investors purchase these bonds.

The federal government sells bonds and securities to finance both the national debt and the government's ongoing activities. The main reason investors choose Canadian government securities is that most investors consider them risk free. In fact, some financial planners refer to them as the ultimate safe investment because their quality is considered to be higher than that of any other investment. Because they are backed by the full faith and credit of the Canadian government and carry a decreased risk of default, they offer lower interest rates than corporate bonds.

TYPES OF BONDS

GOVERNMENT OF CANADA SECURITIES

The government of Canada issues three main types of securities: marketable bonds, T-bills, and Canada Savings Bonds (CSBs). It is also the largest single issuer in the Canadian bond market, having direct marketable debt in the hundreds of billions of dollars. Government of Canada bonds are also classified as debentures for the simple reason that they do not have any assets pledged to them; they are backed only by the government's reputation (which generally is good enough).

Did you know?

Canadian Government Bond Yields

10-year bond data from 2003–2014 represent 10-year yield

SOURCE: Chart from Capital IQ.

MARKETABLE BONDS   These issues are referred to as marketable bonds because in addition to having a specific maturity date and interest rate, they are also transferable and, as a result, can be traded in the bond market. They are generally non-callable, which means that the government does not have the option of calling them in to be redeemed before maturity. Government of Canada Real Return Bonds have all the benefits of regular Government of Canada Bonds, but in addition guarantee a rate of return that is adjusted for inflation. With this type of bond, the maturity value is calculated by multiplying the original face value of the bond times the total inflation since the date of issue.

TREASURY BILLS   A Treasury bill, sometimes called a *T-bill*, is sold in a minimum unit of $1,000 with additional increments of $1,000 above the minimum. T-bills with terms to maturity of 91, 186, or 364 days are currently auctioned on a bi-weekly basis, generally on Tuesday for delivery on Thursday. See Exhibit 12–4 for an example of a T-bill.

T-bills are discounted securities, and the actual purchase price you pay is less than the maturity value of the T-bill. Let's assume you purchased a 91-day T-bill with a purchase price of $990.13 and a face value of $1,000. This means that the discounted amount is $9.87 ($1,000 − $990.13). The convention in Canada is to quote T-bills in yield terms. In this example, you receive $9.87 on a $990.13 investment which produces an annualized rate of return equal to 4 percent, computed as follows:

$$Y = [(F - P) \div P] \times (365 \div T)$$

where

Y = Current yield for a T-bill $Y = [(\$1,000 - \$990.13) \div \$990.13] \times [365 \div 91]$
F = Face value of the T-bill $Y = [\$9.87 \div \$990.13] \times 4$
P = Purchase price $Y = 0.03987$ or approximately 4 percent
T = Term

The price of the T-bill can be determined by rearranging the above equation and solving for $(F - P) \div P$ and then, given F, solving for P.

Exhibit 12–4

A Canadian Treasury Bill

SOURCE: Bank of Canada and Federal Reserve.

CANADA SAVINGS BONDS   These bonds first went on sale in the fall of 1946 and were developed from Victory bonds, which were issued between 1940 and 1944 to help Canada fight in World War II. Over the past half century or so, they have played an important role in the federal government's borrowing, though less so in recent times. The year 2013 marked the issue of Series 131. See Exhibit 12–5 for a sample CSB.

Since 1977, CSBs have been available as either a regular interest bond or a compound interest bond. The *regular interest bond* pays annual interest either by cheque or direct deposit to the holder's bank account on November 1 of each year. It is available in denominations of $300, $500, $1,000, $5,000, and $10,000, with a maximum of five each of the $300 and $500 bonds per registered owner. Interest is paid only on bonds held longer than three months from the date of issue. Should you choose to do so, you may also exchange your regular interest bond for a compound interest bond of the same series up to August 31 of the year following the issue.

The *compound interest bond* allows you to forfeit receipt of annual interest to allow the unpaid interest to compound annually and earn interest on the accumulated interest. This bond is available in denominations of $100, $300, $500, $1,000, $5,000, and $10,000, with a limit of five each of the $100, $300, and $500 bonds per registered owner. You may also exchange your compound interest bond for a regular interest bond of the same series at any time until maturity.

A consideration in buying this type of bond is that you must report compound interest as taxable income each year that you hold the bond, despite the fact that you will not actually receive those funds until you choose to redeem the bond. In planning your personal finance

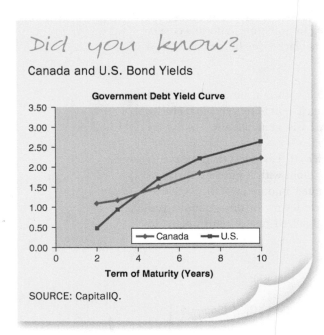

Did you know?

Canada and U.S. Bond Yields

SOURCE: CapitalIQ.

Exhibit 12–5

A Canada Savings Bond

SOURCE: csb.gc.ca/eng/.

portfolio, this might be an important consideration if you anticipate investing a portion of your savings this way. Another thing to take into consideration before purchasing this type of bond is that the government is at liberty to adjust the interest rate at any time.

The convenience, safety, and liquidity of CSBs make them an attractive alternative to simple savings accounts. Additionally, you can purchase these bonds as part of a payroll savings plan. This allows a type of "forced saving" that obeys the personal finance principle of "pay yourself first."

CANADA SAVINGS BONDS PAYROLL PROGRAM   For more than 55 years, the Payroll Savings Program has been Canada's easiest and safest way to save. The Payroll Savings Program allows you to save effortlessly through regular payroll deductions. The minimum you can deduct is $2 per weekly pay period (or $8 per monthly pay period). The Payroll Savings Program offers daily interest, competitive rates, one-time sign-up, easy changes, RRSP option, easy redemptions, instant portability, and bond owner receipt. For more information, see the Canada Savings Bonds Web site at csb.gc.ca.

REAL RETURN BONDS   Real Return Bonds (RRBs) are Government of Canada bonds that pay you a rate of return that is adjusted for inflation. Unlike regular bonds or bonds that pay nominal interest, this feature maintains purchasing power regardless of the future rate of inflation. RRBs pay interest semi-annually based on an inflation-adjusted principal, and at maturity they repay the principal in inflation-adjusted dollars. You can buy these bonds for as low as $1,000 through most securities dealers.

One advantage of RRBs is providing investors with a predetermined, real return. This feature reduces volatility with purchasing power safeguarded to a large extent. Moreover, RRBs have low correlation with other asset classes making it an obvious choice for diversifying an asset portfolio.

On the other hand, RRBs can be difficult to follow because of the ongoing inflation adjustments to their interest payments and market price, and due to tax implications for the bondholder.*

CANADA PREMIUM BONDS   According to the Canada Savings Bonds official Web site "The Canada Premium Bond (CPB), introduced in 1998 by the Government of Canada, offers the same general features as Canada Savings Bonds, but has a higher rate of interest at the time of issue than a CSB on sale at the same time, and can be redeemed each year on the anniversary of the issue date and during the 30 days thereafter. While the Canada Premium Bond has a ten-year term to maturity, interest rates are often announced for a shorter period and remain in effect for that announced period. At the end of the period, new rates will be announced by the Minister of Finance based on the prevailing market conditions." For more details, see csb.gc.ca/about/our-products/.

PROVINCIAL GOVERNMENT SECURITIES AND GUARANTEES

Typically, a provincial bond or debenture issue is used to provide funds to the province for program spending and fund deficits, and all of the provinces have statutes covering how the raised funds are used. Virtually all provinces have bonds available in a wide range of denominations, with the most popular being $500, $1,000, $5,000, $10,000, and $25,000. The term usually depends on the uses to which the proceeds from the bond sale will be put and the availability of investment funds.

Did you know?

Over one million Canadians buy Canada Savings Bonds through payroll deductions each year.

SOURCE: csb.gc.ca.

*SOURCE: bylo.org/rrbs.html.

Riddle me this: If a 7-Eleven is open 24 hours a day, seven days a week, 365 days a year, then *why* do the doors have locks? No answer?

Next question: If stocks have historically outperformed bonds, then why bother making bonds a part of your portfolio? Simple answer: *diversity*.

Buying bonds or other fixed-income investment diversifies a portfolio. By venturing outside the stock market, bond investors are purchasing securities that offer safety and stability. Corporate bonds, bank GICs, and Canadian treasury securities pay investors interest income. These interest payments can drastically boost your return, especially when the stock market sags. In addition to interest, the price of bonds itself fluctuates with interest rates. When not held to "maturity," it is quite possible to make money investing in individual bonds.

Generally, you need serious cash to purchase a diversified portfolio of individual bonds, so those looking for fixed-income exposure might want to use bond mutual funds. These funds, which are not federally insured, are offered in a variety of risk profiles.

Thinking safety? In lieu of putting cash under your mattress, try a money market fund. Available through every major fund company, these investments function as really short-term bond funds and are perfect surrogates for the savings account.

MUNICIPAL BONDS/INSTALMENT DEBENTURES

The market-capital-raising instrument most often used by municipalities is the instalment debenture, or serial bond. With this type of bond issue, often called "munis," a part will mature every year for its term. As an example, a debenture issue of $100,000 would be arranged so that $10,000 becomes due each year for 10 years. In general, instalment debentures are non-callable, such that the buyer of these bonds knows how long he or she can hold the investment.

HIGH-YIELD BONDS

As of 2008, credit spreads on high-yield bonds, also known as junk bonds, attained new heights. Although the market for them in Canada is still small relative to the U.S. (the U.S. is about 300-times larger), it has been picking up steam.

According to Bloomberg Businessweek, sales of junk bonds in Canada set a record in 2010 when issuance went from $800 million in 2009 to $3.5 billion in 2010. The returns on these bonds beat the returns on the rest of the world's high-yield debt market in 2010.

Investors snatch up junk bonds, lured in by Canada's low debt-to-output ratio. More companies are realizing that they can come to the market, and an increasing number are looking to make their debut in the Canadian high-yield debt market.*

CONCEPT CHECK 12–4

1. What are the maturities for different government securities?
2. How is the interest for Canada Savings Bonds calculated?
3. What risks are involved when investing in municipal bonds?

---

*SOURCE: businessweek.com/news/2011-01-06/junk-bonds-lure-first-time-issures-as-yields-fall-canada-credit.html.

THE DECISION TO BUY OR SELL BONDS

One basic principle we stress throughout this text is the need to evaluate any potential investment. Certainly, corporate *and* government bonds are no exception. Only after you complete your evaluation should you purchase bonds. Of course, a decision to sell bonds also requires evaluation. In fact, evaluation may be even more critical for bond investments because there are fewer bonds from which to choose. Although the *Financial Post* lists pages and pages of information on stocks, it provides less than a page for federal, provincial, and corporate bonds (see Exhibit 12–6). In bond quotations, prices are given as a percentage of the face value, which is typically $1,000. For example, Enbridge (listed in Exhibit 12–6) had a bid price of $106.23, which means a market price of 10 × $106.23 = $1,062.30. As this bond is selling at a premium, the yield on Enbridge must be less than the fixed coupon interest rate that it offers. This can be confirmed by comparing the last column Yield (1.82%) with the first column Coupon (1.82%). Note that the opposite is true for bonds selling at a discount. These relationships are further explained under the heading Bond Yield Calculations on page 382. Also note, column two indicates that Enbridge will mature on May 19, 2016. For the remainder of this section, we examine methods you can use to evaluate bond investments.

LO5

Evaluate bonds when making an investment.

Exhibit 12–6

Financial Information about Corporate Bonds, Available in the *Financial Post*

Canadian Bonds on 2014.06.23 Federal				
	Coupon	Maturity Date	Bid $	Yield %
Government of Canada	1.500	09/01/2017	100.46	1.35
Government of Canada	4.250	06/01/2018	110.56	1.48
Government of Canada	3.750	06/01/2019	109.82	1.67
Government of Canada	3.500	06/01/2020	109.51	1.80
Government of Canada	10.500	03/15/2021	154.13	1.89
Government of Canada	3.250	06/01/2021	108.46	1.94
Government of Canada	9.750	06/01/2021	150.85	1.89
Government of Canada	2.750	06/01/2022	104.77	2.10
Government of Canada	9.250	06/01/2022	152.64	2.03
Government of Canada	3.800	06/15/2021	109.39	2.33

Provincial				
	Coupon	Maturity Date	Bid $	Yield %
Province of British Columbia	4.700	06/18/2037	116.74	3.62
Hydro - Quebec	6.500	02/15/2035	137.74	3.84
Hydro - Quebec	6.000	02/15/2040	134.39	3.87
Hydro - Quebec	5.000	02/15/2045	120.67	3.85
Province of Nova Scotia	6.600	06/01/2027	133.49	3.38
Province of Ontario	5.600	06/02/2035	126.68	3.75
Province of Ontario	4.700	06/02/2037	114.00	3.78
Province of Quebec	5.500	12/01/2014	101.91	1.04
Province of Quebec	5.000	12/01/2015	105.39	1.19
Province of Quebec	5.000	12/01/2041	118.92	3.87

Corporate				
	Coupon	Maturity Date	Bid $	Yield %
Bell Canada	4.850	06/30/2014	100.04	3.02
Bank of Montreal	4.870	04/22/2015	102.66	1.62
Bank of Nova Scotia	3.430	07/16/2014	100.13	1.34
Canadian Imperial Bank of Commerce	3.150	11/02/2015	101.95	1.69
Canadian Tire Corp Ltd.	4.950	06/01/2015	103.11	1.59
Enbridge Inc.	5.170	05/19/2016	106.23	1.82
Encana Corp	5.800	01/18/2018	112.11	2.24
GE Capital Canada Funding Co.	4.650	02/11/2015	102.05	1.36
Great-West Life Co.	4.650	08/13/2020	110.13	2.84
HSBC Bank Canada	4.800	04/10/2017	107.04	2.19
Hydro One Inc.	4.890	03/13/2037	110.58	4.17

1. The first line of the first column shows information for a Government of Canada bond issue bearing a coupon value of 1.5 percent of the face value. It pays $1,000 × 0.015 = $15 per year and matures on September 1, 2017.
2. The current yield, or return, based on today's price is 1.35%.
3. The current bid to purchase a bond from this issue is for $100.46.

SOURCE: Material reprinted with the express permission of National Post Inc.

ANNUAL REPORTS

As pointed out earlier in this chapter, bondholders must be concerned about the financial health of the corporation or government unit that issues bonds. To understand how important financial information is when evaluating a bond issue, consider the following two questions:

- Will the bond be repaid at maturity?
- Will you receive interest payments until maturity?

While it may be difficult to answer these questions with 100 percent accuracy, the information contained in a firm's annual report is the logical starting point. Today, there are three ways to obtain a corporation's annual report. First, you can either write or telephone the corporation and request an annual report. (Hint: Many corporations have toll-free telephone numbers for your use.) Second, as mentioned previously, all major corporations maintain a Web site that contains detailed information about their financial performance. Third, you can also obtain information that corporations have reported to the System for Electronic Document Analysis and Retrieval (SEDAR) by accessing the SEDAR Web site (sedar.com).

Regardless of how you obtain an annual report, you should look for signs of financial strength or weakness. Is the firm profitable? Are sales revenues increasing? Are the firm's long-term liabilities increasing? In fact, there are many questions you should ask before making a decision to buy a bond. To help you determine the right questions to ask when evaluating a bond issue, examine the Financial Planning Calculations feature on page 381. Also, you may want to examine the bond's rating and perform the calculations described on pp. 382–384 before investing your money.

THE INTERNET

Just as you can use the Internet to evaluate a stock investment, you can use much of the same financial information to evaluate a bond investment. By accessing a corporation's Web site and locating the topics "financial information," "annual report," or "investor relations," you can find many of the answers to the questions discussed in the last section. As an added bonus, corporations almost always provide more than one year's annual report on their Web sites, so you can compare one year to another.

When investing in bonds, you can use the Internet in three other ways. First, you can obtain price information on specific bond issues to track your investments. Especially if you live in an area without access to newspapers that provide bond coverage, the Internet can be a welcome source of current bond prices. Second, it is possible to trade bonds online and pay lower commissions than you would pay a full-service or discount brokerage firm. Third, you can get research about a corporation and its bond issues (including recommendations to buy or sell) by accessing specific bond Web sites. *Be warned:* Bond Web sites are not as numerous as Web sites that provide information on stocks, mutual funds, or personal financial planning. And many of the better bond Web sites charge a fee for their research and recommendations. Each of the following Web sites provides information and educational materials designed to make you a better bond investor:

bondsonline.com   canoe.ca/money
moodys.com   investinginbonds.com
dbrs.com   standardandpoors.com

BOND RATINGS

To determine the quality and risk associated with bond issues, investors rely on the bond ratings provided by the DBRS and Standard & Poor's. Both companies rank thousands of corporate and municipal bonds.

Did you know?

Government of Canada Long-term Credit Ratings

	Domestic Debt Trend	Foreign Debt Trend
Standard & Poor's Current	AAA Stable	AA1 Stable
Moody's Investors Service Current	Aaa Stable	AA1 Stable
Canadian Bond Rating Service Current	AA1 Stable	AA1 Stable
Dominion Bond Rating Service Current	AAA Stable	AA (high) Stable

SOURCE: Canada Savings Bonds Web site, csb.gc.ca.

Financial Planning Calculations

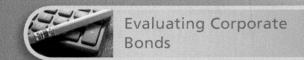

Evaluating Corporate Bonds

No checklist can serve as a foolproof guide for choosing a corporate or government bond. However, the following questions will help you evaluate a potential bond investment. (Usual sources of information include Moody's and DBRS.)

CATEGORY 1: INFORMATION ABOUT THE CORPORATION

1. What is the corporation's name? _____
2. What are the corporation's address and telephone number? _____
_____
3. What type of products or services does this firm provide? _____
_____
4. Briefly describe the prospects for this company. (Include significant factors, such as product development, expansion or merger plans, etc.)
_____
_____
_____

CATEGORY 2: BOND BASICS

5. What type of bond is this? _____
6. What is the face value for this bond? _____
7. What is the interest rate for this bond? _____
8. What is the annual interest amount for this bond? _____
9. When are interest payments made to bondholders? _____
10. Is the corporation currently paying interest as scheduled? ☐ Yes ☐ No
11. What is the maturity date for this bond? _____
12. What is the Moody's rating for this bond? _____
13. What is the DBRS rating for this bond? _____
14. What do these ratings mean? _____
_____
_____
_____

15. What was the original issue date? _____
16. Who is the trustee for this bond issue? _____
_____
17. Is the bond callable? If so, when? _____
_____
18. Is the bond secured with collateral? If so, what?
☐ Yes ☐ No
19. How did the corporation use the money from this bond issue?
_____

CATEGORY 3: FINANCIAL PERFORMANCE

20. Has the firm's total debt increased over the last three years? ☐ Yes ☐ No
21. Is the corporation profitable? If so, how profitable? ☐ Yes ☐ No $ _____
22. Have profits increased over the last seven years?
☐ Yes ☐ No
23. Are this year's sales higher than last year's sales?
☐ Yes ☐ No
24. Have sales increased over the last seven years?
☐ Yes ☐ No
25. Briefly describe any other information that you obtained from Moody's, Standard & Poor's, or other advisory services. _____
_____
_____
_____
_____

A WORD OF CAUTION

When you use a checklist, there is always a danger of overlooking important relevant information. The above checklist is not a cure-all, but it does provide some very sound questions that you should answer before making a decision to invest in bonds. Quite simply, it is a place to start. If you need other information, *you* are responsible for obtaining it and for determining how it affects your potential investment.

As Exhibit 12–7 illustrates, bond ratings generally range from AAA (the highest) to D (the lowest). The first four categories represent investment-grade securities. Investment-grade securities are suitable for conservative investors who want a safe investment that provides a predictable source of income. Bonds in the next two categories are considered speculative in nature. Finally, the C and D categories are used to rank bonds that may be in default due to poor prospects of repayment or even continued payment of interest. Bonds that fall in those categories can be termed **junk bonds**, which offer a high return but with an unreasonable amount of risk, thus making them undesirable to the average investor. Although

junk bond A type of bond that offers a very high return but is very risky as the bond is nearing or currently in default.

Exhibit 12–7   Description of Bond Ratings Provided by the Dominion Bond Rating Service

Quality	Rating by DBRS	Description
Highest credit quality	AAA	The capacity for the payment of financial obligations is exceptionally high and unlikely to be adversely affected by future events.
Superior credit quality	AA	The capacity for the payment of financial obligations is considered high. Credit quality differs from AAA only to a small degree. Unlikely to be significantly vulnerable to future events.
Good credit quality	A	The capacity for the payment of financial obligations is substantial, but of lesser credit quality than AA. May be vulnerable to future events, but qualifying negative factors are considered manageable.
Adequate credit quality	BBB	The capacity for the payment of financial obligations is considered acceptable. May be vulnerable to future events.
Speculative, non-investment grade credit quality	BB	The capacity for the payment of financial obligations is uncertain. Vulnerable to future events.
Highly speculative credit quality	B	There is a high level of uncertainty as to the capacity to meet financial obligations.
Very highly speculative credit quality	CCC CC C	In danger of defaulting on financial obligations. There is little difference between these three categories, although CC and C ratings are normally applied to obligations that are seen as highly likely to default, or subordinated to obligations rated in the CCC to B range. Obligations in respect of which default has not technically taken place but is considered inevitable may be rated in the C category.
	D	When the issuer has filed under any applicable bankruptcy, insolvency, or winding up statute or there is a failure to satisfy an obligation after the exhaustion of grace periods, a downgrade to D may occur. DBRS may also use SD (Selective Default) in cases where only some securities are impacted, such as the case of a "distressed exchange."

SOURCE: DBRS Limited.

bond ratings may be flawed or inaccurate, most investors regard the work of the DBRS as highly reliable.

Generally, government securities are not graded because they are risk-free for practical purposes. The rating of long-term municipal bonds is similar to that of corporate bonds.

BOND YIELD CALCULATIONS

yield The rate of return earned by an investor who holds a bond for a stated period of time.

For a bond investment, the **yield** is the rate of return earned by an investor who holds a bond for a stated period of time. In the section A Typical Bond Transaction (on page 372), we discussed the calculation to determine the average annual compound return from holding a bond investment when all the cash flows from the investment are known with certainty. Two additional methods are used to measure the expected yield on a bond investment when the cash flows are not known for certain, but anticipated: current yield and yield to maturity.

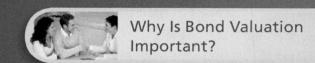
Problem: How do I know if a bond is overvalued or undervalued before I invest my money?

Solution: Use software or financial calculators to determine the true value of bonds before investing your money.

Although software can help you determine a bond's value, you must first identify potential bonds that you would consider purchasing before you can use the software. Below are some ideas that will help you get started.

1. *Start the search with an Internet bond screener.* Today, there are more than 50,000 corporations and government entities that issue bonds. To help narrow the field of potential investments, many investors begin their search for a bond investment with a bond screener. For example the Yahoo! bond site (finance.yahoo.com/bonds) has one of the best bond screeners available on the Internet. By entering information about the type of bond you want (Treasury, corporate, or municipal) and different criteria for acceptable interest rates, years to maturity, current yields, and other factors, the Yahoo! screener displays bonds that match your criteria.

2. *Dig deeper to find important information about the issuer.* Many of the sources of bond information discussed in this chapter can be used to gather important financial information about the issuer and a specific bond issue, including the number of years to maturity, the interest (or coupon) rate, face value, and yield to maturity. To help guide your search and organize the information, use the Financial Planning Calculations box, "Evaluating Corporate Bonds" on page 381.

3. *Use a financial calculator to perform bond valuation calculations.* After you identify a potential bond investment and dig out financial information about the issuer, it's time to determine the value of the bond. While there are formulas that can be used to determine whether a bond is overvalued or undervalued, it may be easier to use a financial calculator available on the Internet. For example, the bond calculator at calculator .com/calcs/bondcalc.html is an excellent tool. All you have to do is enter the number of years to maturity, coupon rate, face value, and yield to maturity, and it calculates the bond's value for you.

The **current yield** is determined by dividing the dollar amount of annual interest from an investment by its current market value. For bonds, the following formula may help you complete this calculation:

$$\text{Current yield for a corporate bond} = \frac{\text{Dollar amount of annual interest}}{\text{Current market value}}$$

current yield Determined by dividing the dollar amount of annual interest from an investment by its current market value.

For example, assume you own a Rogers Communications corporate bond that pays 5.5 percent interest on an annual basis. This means that each year you will receive $55 ($1,000 × 5.5% = $55). Also assume the current market price of the Rogers Communications bond is $960. Because the current market value is less than the bond's face value, the current yield increases to 5.7 percent, as follows:

$$\text{Current yield} = \frac{\$55}{\$960}$$

$$= 0.057, \text{ or } 5.7 \text{ percent}$$

This calculation allows you to compare the yield on a bond investment with the yields of other investment alternatives, which include GICs, common stocks, preferred stocks, and mutual funds. Naturally, the higher the current yield, the better it is! A current yield of 7 percent is better than a current yield of 5.7 percent.

The **yield to maturity** takes into account the relationships among a bond's maturity value, the time to maturity, the current price, and the dollar amount of interest. A formula for calculating the approximate yield to maturity is as follows:

yield to maturity A yield calculation that takes into account the relationships among a bond's maturity value, the time to maturity, the current price, and the dollar amount of interest.

$$\text{Yield to maturity} = \frac{\text{Dollar amount of annual interest} + \dfrac{\text{Face value} - \text{Market value}}{\text{Number of periods}}}{\dfrac{\text{Market value} + \text{Face value}}{2}}$$

For example, assume that on January 1, 2005, you purchased a corporate bond with a $1,000 face value issued by Nike, at the current market price of $830. The bond pays 7 percent annual interest, and its maturity date is 2021. The yield to maturity is 8.7 percent, as follows:

$$\text{Yield to maturity} = \frac{\$70 + \dfrac{\$1,000 - \$830}{17}}{\dfrac{\$830 + \$1,000}{2}}$$

$$= \frac{\$80}{\$915}$$

$$= 0.087, \text{ or } 8.7 \text{ percent}$$

In this situation, the yield to maturity takes into account two types of return on the bond. First, you will receive interest income from the purchase date until the maturity date. Second, at maturity you will receive a payment for the face value of the bond. If you purchased the bond at a price below the face value, the yield to maturity will be greater than the stated interest rate. If you purchased the bond at a price above the face value, the yield to maturity will be less than the stated interest rate. (Remember, the actual price you pay for a bond may be higher or lower than the face value because of many factors, including changes in the economy, increases or decreases in comparable interest rates on other investments, and the financial condition of the company.) The precise yield to maturity (YTM) can be calculated using the time value of money concepts from Chapter 1, where the bond price is equated to the present value of coupon plus principal payments discounted at the YTM.

CALCULATOR

2ND		CLRTVM
830+/−		PV
1,000		FV
70		PMT
17		N
COMP	I/Y	8.98%

The yield to maturity is the annual yield an investor expects when purchasing a bond. However, it is based on two assumptions. First, it assumes that the bondholder will hold the bond to its maturity and receive the face value of $1,000. Second, it assumes that the interest received on an annual or semi-annual basis will be reinvested at the bond's yield to maturity. If either of these assumptions does not hold, then the investment's average annual compound return may be more or less than the expected yield to maturity.

One additional calculation, times interest earned, is described in the Financial Planning Calculations box on page 385.

OTHER SOURCES OF INFORMATION

Investors can use additional sources of information to evaluate potential bond investments. Business periodicals provide information about the economy and interest rates, and detailed financial information about a corporation or government entity that issues bonds. You can locate many of these periodicals at your school or public library or on the Internet.

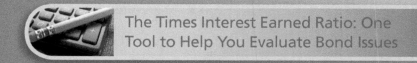
After evaluating a Canadian telecommunications utility, Bethan Jackson, the investor in the opening case, wanted to purchase the firm's corporate debentures. But she was concerned about the corporation's ability to make future interest payments. To determine the utility's ability to pay interest, she used the *times interest earned* ratio formula, illustrated below:

Times interest earned = $\dfrac{\text{Operating income before interest and taxes}}{\text{Interest expense}}$

Assume that the utility had interest expense of $837 million and operating income before interest and taxes of $6,588 million in 2014. The times interest earned ratio for the utility is 7.87 to 1, as follows:

$$\text{Times interest earned} = \frac{\$6,588 \text{ million}}{\$837 \text{ million}}$$
$$= 7.87 \text{ to } 1$$

Although the average for the times interest earned ratio varies from industry to industry, a higher number is better than a lower number. The utility is earning slightly over 7.87 times the amount required to pay the annual interest on its long-term notes, bonds, and other financial obligations. With a times interest earned ratio of 7.87 to 1, the utility could experience a "significant" drop in earnings and still meet its financial obligations.

A number of federal agencies provide information that may be useful to bond investors in either printed form or on the Internet. Reports and research published by the Bank of Canada and the Department of Finance may be used to assess the nation's economy. As noted previously, you can also obtain information that corporations have reported by accessing the SEDAR Web site (sedar.com). Finally, provincial and municipal governments provide information about specific provincial and municipal bond issues.

CONCEPT CHECK 12–5

1. What is the market value for a bond with a face value of $1,000 and a newspaper quotation of 77.25?
2. What type of information is contained in a corporation's annual report? On a corporation's Web site? How could this information be used to evaluate a bond issue?
3. How important are bond ratings when evaluating a bond issue?
4. Why should you calculate the current yield and yield to maturity on a bond investment?
5. How can business periodicals and government publications help you evaluate a bond issue?

SUMMARY OF LEARNING OBJECTIVES

LO1 Describe the characteristics of corporate bonds.

A corporate bond is a corporation's written pledge to repay a specified amount of money with interest. All of the details about a bond (face value, interest rate, maturity date, repayment, etc.) are contained in the bond indenture. The trustee is the bondholder's representative.

LO2 Discuss why corporations issue bonds.

Corporations issue bonds and other securities to help finance their ongoing activities. Bonds may be debentures, mortgage bonds, subordinated debentures, or convertible bonds. Most bonds are callable. To ensure that the money will be available when needed to repay bonds, most corporations establish a sinking fund. Corporations can also issue serial bonds that mature on different dates.

LO3   **Explain why investors purchase corporate bonds.**

Investors purchase corporate bonds for three reasons: (1) interest income, (2) possible increase in value, and (3) repayment at maturity. The method used to pay bondholders their interest depends on whether they own registered bonds, registered coupon bonds, bearer bonds, or zero-coupon bonds. Because bonds can increase or decrease in value, it is possible to purchase a bond at a discount and hold the bond until it appreciates in value. Changes in overall interest rates in the economy are the primary causes of most bond price fluctuations. If you pay too much for a bond or it decreases in value, you can lose money on your investment. You can also choose to hold the bond until maturity and the corporation will repay the bond's face value. Corporate bonds can be bought or sold through account executives who represent brokerage firms.

LO4   **Discuss why federal, provincial, and municipal governments issue bonds and why investors purchase government bonds.**

Bonds issued by the Canadian government are used to finance the national debt and the ongoing activities of the federal government. The Canadian government issues three principal types of bonds: marketable bonds, T-bills, and Canada Savings Bonds. Provincial and local governments issue bonds to finance their ongoing activities and special projects, such as schools, roads, and toll bridges. Canadian government bonds can be purchased through banks, trust companies, and other financial institutions. Municipal bonds are generally sold through the government entity that issued them or through account executives.

LO5   **Evaluate bonds when making an investment.**

Some local newspapers, the *National Post*, and *The Globe and Mail* provide bond investors with information they need to evaluate a bond issue. Detailed financial information can be obtained by requesting a printed copy of the corporation's annual report or accessing its Web site. It is also possible to trade bonds online and obtain research information via the Internet. To determine the quality of a bond issue, most investors study the ratings provided by the DBRS. Investors can also calculate a current yield and a yield to maturity to evaluate bond issues.

The current yield is determined by dividing the dollar amount of annual interest of the bond by its current market value. The yield to maturity takes into account the relationship among a bond's maturity value, the time to maturity, the current price, and the dollar amount of interest.

KEY TERMS

bearer bond 370

bond indenture 366

call feature 367

convertible bond 367

corporate bond 364

current yield 383

debenture 366

face value 364

junk bond 381

maturity date 365

mortgage bond 367

registered bond 370

registered coupon bond 370

serial bonds 368

sinking fund 368

subordinated debenture 367

trustee 366

yield 382

yield to maturity 383

zero-coupon bond 370

KEY FORMULAS

Page	Topic	Formula
364	Annual interest	Dollar amount of annual interest = Face value × Interest rate
	Example:	Dollar amount of annual interest = $1,000 × 6.75 percent
		= $1,000 × 0.0675
		= $67.50
371	Approximate market value	Approximate market value = $\dfrac{\text{Dollar amount of annual interest}}{\text{Comparable interest rate}}$
	Example:	Approximate market value = $\dfrac{\$80}{0.095}$
		= $842.11

375	Current yield for a T-bill	$\text{Current yield} = \dfrac{\text{Face value} - \text{Purchase price}}{\text{Purchase price}} \times \dfrac{365}{T}$
	Example:	$\text{Current yield} = \dfrac{\$5}{\$995} \times \dfrac{365}{91}$
		$= 0.0202 = 2.02 \text{ percent}$

383	Current yield for a corporate bond	$\text{Current yield} = \dfrac{\text{Dollar amount of annual interest}}{\text{Current market value}}$
	Example:	$\text{Current yield} = \dfrac{\$75}{\$800}$
		$= 0.094 = 9.4 \text{ percent}$

384	Yield to maturity	$\text{Yield to maturity} = \dfrac{\text{Dollar amount of annual interest} + \dfrac{\text{Face value} - \text{Market value}}{\text{Number of periods}}}{\dfrac{\text{Market value} + \text{Face value}}{2}}$
	Example:	$\text{Yield to maturity} = \dfrac{\$60 + \dfrac{\$1,000 - \$900}{10}}{\dfrac{\$900 + \$1,000}{2}}$
		$= 0.074 \text{ or } 7.4 \text{ percent}$

Calculator:

2ND	CLRTVM
1,000	FV
930+/−	PV
60	PMT
10	N
COMP I/Y	7.45%

YTM = 7.45%

FINANCIAL PLANNING PROBLEMS

Mc Graw Hill connect™ Practise and learn online with Connect.

1. *Calculating Interest.* What is the annual interest amount for a $1,000 bond that pays 7.75 percent interest? *LO1*

2. *Explaining Different Types of Corporate Bonds.* Dorothy Martin wants to invest $10,000 in corporate bonds. Her account executive suggested that she consider debentures, mortgage bonds, and convertible bonds. Since she has never invested in bonds, she is not sure how these types of bonds differ. How would you explain their differences to her? *LO2*

3. *Evaluating Zero-Coupon Bonds.* List the reasons investors might want to buy zero-coupon bonds. Then, list the reasons investors might want to avoid zero-coupon bonds. Based on

these lists, do you consider zero-coupon bonds a good alternative for your investment program? Why, or why not? *LO2*

4. *Analyzing Why Investors Purchase Bonds.* In your own words, explain how each of the following factors is a reason to invest in bonds: *LO3*
   a. Interest income.
   b. Possible increase in value.
   c. Repayment at maturity.

5. *Explaining Different Types of Government Securities.* Complete the following table: LO4

	Minimum Amount	Maturity Range	How Interest Is Paid
T-bill	_____	_____	_____
Canada Savings Bond	_____	_____	_____

6. *Using the Newspaper.* Use the information provided by a newspaper (for example, *The Globe and Mail*) to answer questions about the following bond issues: Manulife Financial and Power Corporation. LO4
   a. What is the ticker symbol for each bond issue?
   b. Determine the current bond yield for each issue. What does the current yield calculation measure?
   c. Determine the yield to maturity for each issue. What does the yield to maturity mean?
   d. Based on your answers to the previous questions, which bond would you select for your investment program? Briefly explain.
   e. Using the information on the Standard & Poor's Web site, determine the current yield for each bond issue. What does the current yield calculation measure?
   f. Using the information on the Standard & Poor's Web site, determine the yield to maturity for each bond issue. What does the yield to maturity calculation measure?
   g. What are the Standard & Poor's ratings for each bond? What do these ratings mean?
   h. Based on your answers to the previous questions, which bond would you choose for your investment portfolio? Explain your answer.

FINANCIAL PLANNING ACTIVITIES

1. *Explaining the Purpose of a Bond Indenture.* Prepare a one-minute oral presentation that describes the type of information contained in a bond indenture. LO1

2. *Investigating a New Bond Issue.* Locate an advertisement for a new bond issue in *The Globe and Mail*, the *Financial Post*, or a local newspaper. Then, go to the library or use the Internet to research the corporation or government entity that is issuing the bonds. Based on your research, prepare a two-page report on the issuer. Be sure to describe its financial condition and how it will use the money raised by selling the bonds. LO2

3. *Interviewing an Account Executive.* Talk to an account executive or a banker about the differences among debentures, mortgage bonds, and subordinated debentures. Describe your findings. LO2

4. *Making Investment Decisions.* Assume you just inherited 10 Westcoast Energy Inc. bonds and each bond is

7. *Evaluating a Corporate Bond Issue.* Choose a corporate bond listed in the *Financial Post*, and use your online resources to answer the following questions about this bond issue: LO5
   a. What is the Standard & Poor's rating for the issue?
   b. What is the purpose of the issue?
   c. Does the issue have a call provision?
   d. Who is the trustee for the issue?
   e. What collateral, if any, has been pledged as security for the issue?
   f. Based on the information you obtained, is the bond a good investment for you? Why, or why not?

8. *Calculating Yields.* Assume you purchased a corporate bond at its current market price of $850 on January 1, 2005. It pays 9 percent interest and will mature on December 31, 2014, at which time the corporation will pay you the face value of $1,000. LO5
   a. Determine the current yield on your bond investment at the time of purchase.
   b. Determine the yield to maturity on your bond investment at time of purchase.

9. *More on Calculating Yields.* Referring to the bond described in Problem 8, assume that the bond's interest payments were reinvested at a rate of 5 percent per annum. LO5
   a. What is the future value of the reinvested coupons (there are 10 years of coupons received between 2005 and 2014)?
   b. Given the purchase price of $850, the maturity value of $1,000 added to the future value of the reinvested coupons, what was the bond's average annual compound return?
   c. Repeat this calculation assuming bond interest was reinvested at 15 percent per annum. What was the bond's average annual compound return?
   d. What do you conclude from these two calculations?

convertible to 64.5 shares of the corporation's common stocks. LO2
   a. What type of information do you need to help you decide whether to convert your bonds to common stocks?
   b. Where would you obtain this information?
   c. Under what conditions would you convert your bonds to common stocks?
   d. Under what conditions would you keep the bonds?

5. *Analyzing Why Investors Purchase Bonds.* Survey at least two investors who own either corporate or government bonds. Then answer the following questions: LO3
   a. Why did these investors purchase the bonds?
   b. How long have they invested in bonds?
   c. Do they consider their bond issues to be conservative or speculative investments?
   d. Why did they decide to purchase bonds instead of other investments, such as GICs, stocks, mutual funds, or real estate?

6. *Reading Financial Information in the Newspaper.* Using information from the local newspaper or the *Financial Post*, answer the following questions on the following bond issues: ⌐O5

Newspaper _____ Date _____

	Current Yield	Volume	Close Price
AirCa 6.750l	_____	_____	_____
BCE 6.2	_____	_____	_____
Molson 5.4	_____	_____	_____

7. *Analyzing Yields.* In your own words, describe what affects the current yield and the yield to maturity for a bond. ⌐O5

8. *Evaluating a Bond Transaction.* Choose a corporate bond that you would consider purchasing. Then, using information obtained in the library or on the Internet, answer the questions on the evaluation form presented in the Financial Planning Calculations feature on page 381. Based on your research, would you still purchase this bond? Explain your answer. ⌐O5

CREATING A FINANCIAL PLAN

Investing in Bonds

Including bonds in an investment portfolio can be useful for achieving various financial goals when certain life situations, business conditions, and economic trends arise.

Web Sites for Investing in Bonds

- **money.canoe.ca**
- **standardandpoors.com**
- **dbrs.com**
- **fin.gc.ca**
- **csb.gc.ca**
- **myfinancialsite.com**

(Note: Addresses and content of Web sites change, and new sites are created daily. Use search engines to update and locate Web sites for your current financial planning needs.)

Short-Term Financial Planning Activities

1. Assess various types of bond investments that might be appropriate for your various financial goals and life situation.

2. Compare the recent performance of various corporate bonds that could be appropriate investments for you.

3. Research the recent performance of federal government and municipal bonds. Determine how these might be used in your investment portfolio.

Long-Term Financial Planning Activities

1. Identify bond investing situations that could help minimize risk.

2. Develop a plan for selecting bond investments in the future.

LIFE SITUATION CASE

A Lesson from the Past

Back in 1990, Mary Goldberg, a 34-year-old divorcee, got a telephone call from a Bay Street account executive who said that one of his other clients had given him her name. Then, he told her his brokerage firm was selling a new corporate bond issue in New World Explorations, a company heavily engaged in oil exploration in western Canada. The bonds in this issue paid investors 13.2 percent a year. He then said that the minimum investment was $10,000 and that if she wanted to take advantage of this "once in a lifetime" opportunity, she had to move fast. To Mary, it was an opportunity that was too good to pass up, and she bit hook, line, and sinker. She sent the account executive a cheque—and never heard from him again. When she went to the library to research her bond investment, she found there was no such company as New World Explorations. She lost her $10,000 and quickly vowed she would never invest in bonds again. From now on, she would put her money in the bank, where it was guaranteed.

Over the years, she continued to deposit money in the bank and accumulated more than $90,000. Things seemed to be pretty much on track until one of her GICs matured. When she went to renew the GIC, the bank officer told her interest rates had fallen and current GIC interest rates ranged between 1.33 and 4.5 percent. To make matters worse, the banker told Mary that only the bank's three-year GIC offered the 4.5 percent interest rate. GICs with shorter maturities paid lower interest rates.

Faced with the prospects of lower interest rates, Mary decided to shop around for higher rates. She called several local

banks and got pretty much the same answer. Then, a friend suggested that she talk to Peter, an account executive for TD Waterhouse. Peter told her there were conservative corporate bonds and quality stock issues that offered higher returns. But, he warned her, these investments were *not* guaranteed. If she wanted higher returns, she would have to take some risks.

While Mary wanted higher returns, she also remembered how she had lost $10,000 investing in corporate bonds. When she told Peter about her bond investment in the fictitious New World Exploration, he pointed out that she had made some pretty serious mistakes. For starters, she bought the bonds over the phone from someone she didn't know, and she bought them without doing any research. He assured her that the bonds and stocks he would recommend would be issued by real companies, and she would be able to find a lot of information on each of his recommendations at the library.

Questions

1. According to Mary Goldberg, the chance to invest in New World Explorations was "too good to pass up." Unfortunately, it was too good to be true, and she lost $10,000. Why do you think so many people are taken in by get-rich-quick schemes?

2. During the last part of the 1990s, investors were forced to look for ways to squeeze additional income from their investment portfolios. Do you think investing in corporate bonds or quality stocks is the best way to increase income? Give reasons for your answer.

Market Interest Rates and Bond Pricing

appendix 12

Here we use the example of a 10-year, ABC Inc., 8 percent bond issued at par with semi-annual interest payments of $40 to demonstrate the effect of changing markets rates on bond prices.

At par, the discount rate (or yield to maturity) equals the coupon rate, which is 4 percent (8 percent ÷ 2) for a total of 20 periods (10 years × 2).

Using a financial calculator (BA II Plus Texas Instruments):

2ND	CLRTVM	
20	N	(10 years × 2 periods per year)
4	I/Y	(I/Y = 8% ÷ 2 periods)
1,000	FV	
40	PMT	
CPT	PV	

The solution $1,000 displays.

As the market interest rate (discount rate) falls, the present value of the coupon payments and the present value of the face value rise, thereby increasing the price of the bond. We confirm this by calculating the new bond price if the market interest rates fall to 6 percent.

Using a financial calculator:

2ND	CLRTVM	
20	N	(10 years × 2 periods per year)
4	I/Y	(I/Y = 6% ÷ 2 periods)
1,000	FV	
40	PMT	
CPT	PV	

The solution $1,148.77 displays.

In effect, the bond is now selling at a premium to compensate for the fact that it is paying a higher interest rate than other comparable bonds currently in the market.

In the opposite situation, if the market interest rate (discount rate) rises, the present value of the coupon payments and the present value of the face value fall, thereby decreasing the price of the bond. We confirm this by calculating the new bond price if the market interest rates rise to 10 percent.

Using a financial calculator:

2ND	CLRTVM	
20	N	(10 years × 2 periods per year)
4	I/Y	(I/Y = 10% ÷ 2 periods)
1,000	FV	
40	PMT	
CPT	PV	

The solution $875.38 displays.

In effect, the bond is now selling at a discount to compensate for the fact that it is paying a lower interest rate than other comparable bonds currently in the market

Bond prices and market interest rates are, therefore, inversely related. If market interest rates go up, bond prices go down. If market rates go down, bond prices go up.

chapter 13

Investing in Mutual Funds

LEARNING OBJECTIVES

LO1   Describe the characteristics of mutual fund investments.

LO2   Classify mutual funds by investment objective.

LO3   Evaluate mutual funds for investment purposes.

LO4   Describe how and why mutual funds are bought and sold.

A NOVICE TO MUTUAL FUNDS

At the beginning of 2014, 25-year-old Sally Pitt inherited $5,000 when her grandmother passed away. As she had already established an emergency fund the year before, she felt this would be a good opportunity to invest in stocks. She had only one small problem—she did not know much about the stock market.

A few weeks later, she met her uncle David at a family gathering and found out that he had invested in mutual funds with Mackenzie Investments some years back and had done quite well with his investment. According to her uncle, "investing in mutual funds was a safe way for me as a novice to invest in stocks." That night, Sally went on the Mackenzie Web site and conducted some research.

Sally wanted a fund that invested in Canadian companies with good prospects. She did not want to invest in anything too risky and she wanted "reasonable" returns on her investment. After comparing fund objectives, past performance, and equity content, she decided to invest her money in Mackenzie Canadian Growth Fund, which had a moderate risk tolerance. She felt the fund's compound annual return of 9.5 percent since inception in 1976 gave it credibility. Sally was especially pleased

to read that some of the major equity holdings included well-known Canadian companies, such as Telus Corporation, Imax Corporation, and Toronto-Dominion Bank.

Mackenzie Canadian Growth Fund

Compound Returns as at May 31, 2014

3 Mo	1 Year	2 Year	3 Year	5 Year	10 Year	20 Year
3.3%	20.8%	15.9%	7.6%	8.6%	5.8%	6.3%

Calendar Year Returns			
2004	16.2%	2005	8.4%
2006	11.4%	2007	6.5%
2008	−20.7%	2009	19.9%
2010	3%	2011	−9.2%
2012	10.4%	2013	21.2%
2014 YTD	6%		

SOURCE: mackenzieinvestments.com.

 Practise and learn online with Connect.

QUESTIONS

1. Based on the information provided, do you think Sally made a good choice? Was her research adequate?
2. What other factors should she have taken into consideration before making her investment?

mutual fund An investment chosen by people who pool their money to buy stocks, bonds, and other financial securities selected by professional managers who work for an investment company.

If you ever thought about buying stocks or bonds but decided not to, your reasons were probably like most other people's: You didn't know enough to make a good decision, and you lacked enough money to diversify your investments among several choices. These same two reasons explain why people invest in mutual funds. By pooling your money with money from other investors, a mutual fund can do for you what you can't do on your own. Specifically, a **mutual fund** is an investment chosen by people who pool their money to buy stocks, bonds, and other financial securities selected by professional managers who work for investment companies. Every person who invests in a mutual fund has the right to his or her proportional share of the assets of the fund and any income that the fund earns. Mutual funds are an excellent choice for many individuals. In many cases, they can also be used for retirement accounts.

Sally Pitt, the investor in the opening case, did her homework before purchasing shares in the Mackenzie Universal Canadian Growth mutual fund. It is equally important that she continue to monitor the value of her investment after her initial purchase. Make no mistake about this: *Good investors evaluate an investment before purchase. The best investors continue to evaluate their investments after the purchase.*

An investment in mutual funds is based on the concept of opportunity costs, which we discuss throughout this text. Simply put, you have to be willing to take some chances if you want to get larger returns on your investments. Before deciding whether mutual funds are the right investment for you, read the material presented in the next section.

WHY INVESTORS PURCHASE MUTUAL FUNDS

LO1

Describe the characteristics of mutual fund investments.

Investors like—no, love—their mutual fund investments. The following statistics illustrate how important mutual fund investments are to both individuals and the nation's economy:

1. Although the mutual fund concept originated in Europe and then spread to North America in the late 1800s, mutual funds didn't gain real popularity until the last 30 years.
2. As of May 2014, the Investment Funds Institute of Canada (IFIC), the national trade association for the Canadian mutual fund industry, had a membership of roughly 150 mutual fund managers, dealers, and professional and business services firms that support the investment funds industry.
3. The value of assets under management in the industry has increased from $3.5 billion in 1981 to nearly $1.1 trillion—making mutual funds the fastest-growing sector of the Canadian financial services industry.

No doubt about it, the mutual fund industry is big business. And yet, you may be wondering why so many people invest in mutual funds.

The major reasons investors purchase mutual funds are *professional management* and *diversification*. Most investment companies do everything possible to convince you that they can do a better job of picking securities than you can. Sometimes these claims are true, and sometimes they are just so much hot air. Still, investment companies do have professional fund managers with years of experience who devote large amounts of time to picking just the "right" securities for their funds' portfolios. *Be warned:* Even the best portfolio managers make mistakes. So you, the investor, must be careful!

The diversification mutual funds offer spells safety because an occasional loss incurred with one investment contained in a mutual fund is usually offset by gains from other investments in the fund. With a mutual fund, you can diversify your holdings in two ways: (1) by buying a mutual fund that owns stock in hundreds of different companies, or (2) across asset classes by buying a mutual fund that owns stocks and bonds, as well as other securities. For example, consider the diversification provided in the portfolio of the RBC Canadian Equity Fund, shown in Exhibit 13–1. With more than $4.5 billion in assets, this fund contains 117 different stock investments spread over eight different industrial areas. (For more up-to-date information on the composition of investments within the fund or other information about the fund, visit the RBC Asset Management Web site at funds.rbcgam.com.)

Regardless of professional management and diversification, investing in mutual funds does have its risks, which should not be overlooked. The risks presented by mutual funds are based on the investments they hold. For example, a bond fund faces interest rate risk and income risk. Bond values are inversely related to interest rates. If interest rates go up, bond values go down and vice versa. Similarly, a sector stock fund (which invests in a single industry, such as oil) may surrender to industry risk, where its price declines due to new developments within its industry. A stock fund that invests across many industries is better protected from this risk, although it may succumb to other forms of risk, such as market risk, which affects the market as a whole and cannot be diversified away.

> ### Did you know?
>
> According to the Investment Funds Institute of Canada (ific.ca), total mutual fund assets at the end of 2013 amounted to almost $1 trillion—almost 18 percent more than the previous year ($849.7 billion in December 2012). This large internal pool of capital has grown dramatically since the 1990s and has served a large concentration of Canadian investors.
>
> SOURCE: ific.ca.

CHARACTERISTICS OF MUTUAL FUNDS

An **investment company** is a firm that, for a management fee, invests the pooled funds of small investors in securities appropriate to its stated investment objectives. Today, mutual funds sponsored by investment companies may be classified as either closed-end or open-end mutual funds.

investment company A firm that, for a management fee, invests the pooled funds of small investors in securities appropriate to its stated investment objectives.

CLOSED-END MUTUAL FUNDS   A **closed-end fund** is a fund of finite size. Its shares are issued by an investment company only when the fund is set up. Once that's done, the fund size remains more or less static. The fund neither issues nor redeems shares. Since a closed-end fund does not ever have to buy back shares from investors like an open-end mutual fund, it does not have to maintain a percentage of its assets in cash; therefore, 100 percent of the fund's assets can be invested at all times. After all the shares originally issued are sold, an investor can purchase shares only from another investor who is willing to sell. Shares of closed-end funds are traded on the floors of stock exchanges or in the over-the-counter market. Like the prices of stocks, the prices of shares for closed-end funds are determined by the factors of supply and demand, by the value of stocks and other investments contained in the fund's portfolio, and by investor expectations.

closed-end fund A mutual fund whose shares are issued by an investment company only when the fund is originally set up.

OPEN-END MUTUAL FUNDS   An **open-end fund** is a mutual fund whose shares are issued and redeemed by the investment company at the request of investors. Investors are free to buy and sell shares at the net asset value. The **net asset value (NAV)** per share is equal to the current market value of securities contained in the mutual fund's portfolio minus the mutual fund's liabilities divided by the number of shares outstanding:

open-end fund A mutual fund whose shares are issued and redeemed by the investment company at the request of investors.

$$\text{Net asset value per share} = \frac{\text{Current market value of the fund's portfolio} - \text{Liabilities}}{\text{Number of shares outstanding}}$$

For example, assume the portfolio of all investments contained in the Scotia Canadian Income Fund has a current market value of $124 million. The fund also has liabilities

net asset value (NAV) The current market value of the securities contained in the mutual fund's portfolio minus the mutual fund's liabilities divided by the number of shares outstanding.

Exhibit 13–1   Types of Securities Included in the RBC Canadian Equity Fund Portfolio

**RBC Global
Asset Management**

FUND FACTS

RBC Canadian Equity Fund - Series A
February 27, 2014

This document contains key information you should know about RBC Canadian Equity Fund (Series A). You can find more details in the fund's simplified prospectus. Ask your representative for a copy, contact RBC Global Asset Management Inc. (RBC GAM) at 1-800-463-FUND (3863), funds.investments@rbc.com, or visit www.rbcgam.com/investorinfo.

Before you invest in any fund, you should consider how it would work with your other investments and your tolerance for risk.

Quick facts

Fund code:	RBF269	**Fund manager:**	RBC Global Asset Management Inc.
Date series started (Series A):	April 17, 1967	**Portfolio manager:**	RBC Global Asset Management Inc.
Total value of the fund on December 31, 2013:	$4,502.2 Million	**Distributions:**	Annually in December
Management expense ratio (MER):	2.07%	**Minimum investment:**	$500 initial, $25 additional investment

What does the fund invest in?

The fund invests primarily in equity securities of major Canadian companies. The fund may invest no more than 25% of its assets in foreign securities.

The charts below give you a snapshot of the fund's investments on December 31, 2013. The fund's investments will change.

Top 10 investments (December 31, 2013)

1.	RBC Canadian Small & Mid-Cap Resources Fund	6.9%
2.	Royal Bank of Canada	6.4%
3.	Toronto-Dominion Bank	5.9%
4.	Bank of Nova Scotia	4.8%
5.	Suncor Energy Inc.	3.8%
6.	Canadian National Railway Co.	3.5%
7.	Canadian Natural Resources Ltd.	3.0%
8.	Cash & Cash Equivalents	2.7%
9.	Manulife Financial Corporation	2.6%
10.	Bank of Montreal	2.4%

The top 10 investments make up 42% of the fund.

Total Investments: 117

Investment mix (December 31, 2013)

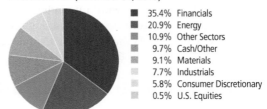

- 35.4% Financials
- 20.9% Energy
- 10.9% Other Sectors
- 9.7% Cash/Other
- 9.1% Materials
- 7.7% Industrials
- 5.8% Consumer Discretionary
- 0.5% U.S. Equities

How risky is it?

The value of the fund can go down as well as up. You could lose money.

One way to gauge risk is to look at how much a fund's returns change over time. This is called "volatility".

In general, funds with higher volatility will have returns that change more over time. They typically have a greater chance of losing money and may have a greater chance of higher returns. Funds with lower volatility tend to have returns that change less over time. They typically have lower returns and may have a lower chance of losing money.

Risk rating

RBC GAM has rated the volatility of this fund as **medium**.

This rating is based on how much the fund's returns have changed from year to year. It doesn't tell you how volatile the fund will be in the future. The rating can change over time. A fund with a low risk rating can still lose money.

Low	Low to Medium	**Medium**	Medium to High	High

For more information about the risk rating and specific risks that can affect the fund's returns, see the sections entitled "What are the risks of investing in the fund?" and "Who should invest in this fund?" in the fund's simplified prospectus.

No guarantees

Like most mutual funds, this fund doesn't have any guarantees. You may not get back the amount of money you invest.

How has the fund performed?

This section tells you how Series A units of the fund have performed over the past ten years. Returns are after expenses have been deducted. These expenses reduce the fund's returns.

totalling $4 million. If this mutual fund has 6 million shares outstanding, the net asset value per share is $20:

$$\text{Net asset value} = \frac{\text{Current market value of the fund's portfolio} - \text{Liabilities}}{\text{Number of shares outstanding}}$$

$$= \frac{\$124 \text{ million} - \$4 \text{ million}}{6 \text{ million shares}}$$

$$= \$20 \text{ per share}$$

For most mutual funds, the net asset value is calculated at the close of trading each day. In addition to buying and selling shares on request, most open-end funds provide their investors with a wide variety of services, including payroll deduction programs, automatic reinvestment programs, automatic withdrawal programs, and the option to change shares in one fund to another fund within the same fund family—all topics discussed later in this chapter.

Two funds have gained popularity in the marketplace: **index funds** and **exchange-traded funds (ETFs)**. Both funds allow investors an affordable way to invest in a diversified basket of securities. The index fund is constructed to track the components of a market index such as the S&P 500 or the S&P/TSX Composite. The main advantage is that this passive form of management results in lower management expense ratios. Also, index funds can outperform most mutual funds, as most mutual funds fail to beat the market. Index funds are bought at end-of-day prices, and mainly through big banks.

The main advantage of an ETF over a mutual fund is that it trades throughout the day on a stock exchange at changing market prices. ETFs provide you with the diversification of an index fund but with the flexibility of a stock. You can buy an ETF through your broker by paying a commission. You can also buy them on margin or **short sell** them (the practice of selling a borrowed stock in the hope you will be able to cover the sale by buying it at a lower price later). Like index funds, ETFs are passively managed. As a result, ETFs have lower management expenses than their conventional mutual fund cousins. It is important to note that while ETFs attempt to replicate the return on market indexes, there is no guarantee they will do so exactly. Today there are many different types of ETFs available that attempt to track all kinds of indexes that include mid- and small-cap stocks, fixed income securities, stocks issued by companies in specific industries, stocks issued by corporations in different countries, and commodities.

In most cases, ETFs are more tax-efficient than mutual funds. Gains and dividends realized by a mutual fund are passed along to its shareholders. Investors who sell ETF shares pay taxes on their own profits, and the remaining shareholders do not suffer any unexpected capital gains. In a mutual fund, when an investor sells his or her shares, the manager has to sell shares to pay the investor. This could potentially trigger capital gains for the remaining investors. ETF shareholders are further insulated from unexpected capital gains because although investors buy and sell shares through a broker, the manner in which the authorized participant (usually a bank) and the ETF buy and sell shares is simply viewed as two companies exchanging shares. This enables the fund to avoid potential capital gains.

The major disadvantage of ETFs is the cost of buying and selling shares. Because they are traded like stocks, investors must pay commissions when they buy *and* sell shares. EFTs are increasing in popularity, as of May, 2014, more than 400 ETFs were started since 2010.

T-SERIES MUTUAL FUNDS   T-series mutual funds are designed for investors who are looking for a tax-efficient income stream without trading in capital gains. The "T" stands for tax, and alludes to the fact that they are tax efficient, mostly because T-series funds distribute return of capital (ROC) that is not immediately taxable.

When mutual funds make interest, dividend, or capital gains payouts, the monies are taxed in the same year they are paid. However, distributions from T-series funds are not taxed until your investment capital is depleted, which means they are only taxed when the adjusted cost base (ACB) reaches zero, or until the units are sold. This tax deferral is a key reason why T-series

index fund An affordable way for investors to invest in a diversified basket of securities; constructed to track the components of a market index such as the S&P 500 or the S&P/TSX Composite.

exchange-traded funds (ETFs) An affordable way for investors to invest in a diversified basket of securities; provides the diversification of an index fund with the flexibility of a stock.

short sell The practice of selling a borrowed stock in the hope of covering the sale by buying it at a lower price later.

funds are considered tax-efficient. Another reason is that when the distributions are taxed, it is at the same rate as capital gains tax, which is lower than the tax rate for interest income.

The ability to defer taxes on income earned from a fund is a significant advantage to an investor. You benefit from a greater after-tax income and the compounding effects of a larger investment. Moreover, you may also be able to decrease the amount of tax you pay in the future, due to lower marginal tax rates or lower capital gains inclusion rates.

When considering T-series funds, verify the payout rates as they are different. Also look for T-series funds that make investment sense: Poor returns result in smaller monthly distributions. Certain funds are designed so that the ROC distribution takes up all or most of the expected return, giving you the opportunity to preserve your original investment in the fund.

As a bonus, T-series funds that are part of a corporate class structure allow you to switch between asset classes without triggering a capital gain.*

LOAD FUNDS AND NO-LOAD FUNDS　　Before investing in mutual funds, you should compare the cost of this type of investment with the cost of other investment alternatives, such as stocks or bonds. Regarding cost, mutual funds are classified as load funds or no-load funds. A **load fund** is a mutual fund in which investors pay a commission every time they buy (front-end load) or sell (back-end load) shares. The commission charge, sometimes referred to as the sales fee, may be as high as 8.5 percent of the price for investments under $10,000. (Typically, this fee declines for investments over $10,000.)

load fund A mutual fund in which investors pay a commission (as high as 8.5 percent) every time they purchase or sell shares.

While many exceptions exist, the average load charge for mutual funds is between 3 and 5 percent. Let's assume you invest $10,000 in the Standard Life Growth Equity Fund. This fund charges a sales load of 5 percent that you must pay when you purchase shares. The dollar amount of the sales charge on your $10,000 investment is $500 ($10,000 × 5% = $500). After paying the $500, the amount available for investment is reduced to $9,500 ($10,000 − $500 = $9,500). The "stated" advantage of a load fund is that the fund's sales force (account executives, financial planners, or brokerage divisions of banks and other financial institutions) explains the mutual fund to investors and offers advice as to when fund shares should be bought or sold.

> ## Did you know?
>
> Recent independent research confirms that, to meet their financial goals, Canadians have greater confidence in mutual funds (81 percent) than other financial products such as GICs (65 percent), bonds (57 percent), and stocks (61 percent).
>
> As of July 2010, 34.4 percent (4.6 million) of Canadian households held mutual funds.
>
> Mutual funds account for 26 percent of Canadians' financial wealth.
>
> Mutual fund assets have increased by an average of 15 percent per year over the last 20 years.
>
> SOURCE: ific.ca.

Instead of charging investors a fee when they purchase shares in a mutual fund, some mutual funds charge a **contingent deferred sales load** (sometimes referred to as a *back-end load*). These fees range from 1 to 6 percent, depending on how long you own the mutual fund before making a withdrawal. For example, assume you withdraw $5,000 from shares that you own in the Greenline Balanced Growth mutual fund within a year of your original purchase date. You must pay a 5 percent contingent deferred sales fee. Your fee is $250 ($5,000 × 5% = $250). After the

contingent deferred sales load A charge of 1 to 6 percent that shareholders pay when they withdraw their investment from a mutual fund.

fee is deducted from your $5,000 withdrawal, you will receive $4,750 ($5,000 − $250 = $4,750). Generally, the deferred charge declines until there is no withdrawal charge if you own the shares in the fund for more than five to seven years. Unlike a front-end load, your entire $5,000 goes to work for you immediately. There is no deduction when you purchase. Choosing the back-end load allows all of your investment dollars to go to work for you immediately. Keep in mind, however, that although you don't pay a fee directly to your sales representative at the time of purchase, the mutual fund company does. This, of course, increases its costs. As a result, you

*SOURCE: gpcapital.com/00002345.aspx.

may be paying a higher management expense ratio (MER; see discussion below). In addition, if the fund does not perform as well as expected, due to a change in management or other circumstances, you may be reluctant to switch because of the high penalty. If all other factors are equal, a fund that doesn't charge a contingent deferral sales load is superior to a fund that does.

A **no-load fund** is a mutual fund in which the individual investor pays no sales charge. No-load funds don't charge commissions when you buy or sell shares because they have no salespeople. If you want to buy shares of a no-load fund, you must deal directly with the investment company. The usual means of contact is by telephone or the Internet. You can also purchase shares in a no-load fund from many discount brokers, such as Scotia iTrade.

As an investor, you must decide whether to invest in a load fund or a no-load fund. Some investment salespeople claim that load funds outperform no-load funds. But many financial analysts suggest there is no significant difference between mutual funds that charge commissions and those that do not. *Since no-load funds offer the same investment opportunities load funds offer, you should investigate them further before deciding which type of mutual fund is best for you.* Although the sales commission should not be the decisive factor, the possibility of saving an 8.5 percent load charge is a factor to consider. For example, suppose Marianne Lowen invests $10,000 in a mutual fund that charges an 8.5 percent sales fee. Since this fee is deducted in advance, her initial $10,000 investment is reduced by $850. Simply put, she now has $9,150 that she can use to buy shares in this load fund. By comparison, Jane Edwards decides to invest $10,000 in a no-load mutual fund. Since there is no sales fee, she can use the entire $10,000 to purchase shares in this no-load fund. Depending on the load fund's performance, it may take Marianne a year or more to "catch up" and cover the cost of the sales fee.

no-load fund A mutual fund in which the individual investor pays no sales charge.

MANAGEMENT FEES AND OTHER CHARGES

In evaluating a specific mutual fund, you should consider management fees and other charges. The investment companies that sponsor mutual funds charge management fees. This fee, which is disclosed in the fund's prospectus, is a fixed percentage of the fund's asset value. Today, annual management fees range between 0.5 and 5 percent of the fund's asset value. While fees vary considerably, the average is between 2 and 3 percent of the fund's assets. A 2013 Morningstar report noted that mutual fund fees in Canada are amongst the highest in the world.

Generally, all mutual funds have management expenses that are deducted from the fund. The management fee pays for such things as the mutual fund company's investment management and marketing and administrative costs. Each fund also pays its own operating costs, such as brokerage fees on securities trading, audit fees, and unitholder communications.

MANAGEMENT EXPENSE RATIO

The fund reports the management fee and direct costs it pays each year as a management expense ratio (MER) that relates those costs to the fund's value. If a $100 million fund has $2 million in costs, its MER is 2 percent. The costs are deducted before the fund's performance returns are calculated. If your fund made 13 percent and the MER was 2 percent, the reported return for the year is 11 percent.

SPECIAL FEES

Unlike management expenses, which apply to all unitholders, special fees apply to individual situations. You pay them directly or through specific deductions. Some examples include:

- Annual RRSP, RRIF, or RESP trustee fee—this covers the plan operating cost.
- Account setup fee—some dealers levy a one-time charge for new clients.
- Short-term trading fee—mutual fund companies are allowed to deduct an amount, generally 2 percent, from any redemption that occurs within 90 days of purchase; however, many don't.

Exhibit 13–2   Sample Fund Profile on the BMO Canadian Equity Class Fund

 | **Mutual Funds**

FUND FACTS
BMO Canadian Equity Fund
Series A
(formerly BMO Equity Fund)
April 3, 2014
Manager: BMO Investments Inc.

This document contains key information you should know about BMO Canadian Equity Fund. You can find more detailed information in the fund's simplified prospectus. Ask your representative for a copy, contact BMO Investments Inc. at 1-800-665-7700 or mutualfunds@bmo.com or visit www.bmo.com/mutualfunds.
Before you invest in any fund, you should consider how it would work with your other investments and your tolerance for risk.

Quick facts

Date series started:	August 3, 1993	**Fund manager:**	BMO Investments Inc.
Total value of fund on March 6, 2014:	$2.2 billion	**Portfolio manager(s):**	BMO Asset Management Inc.
Management expense ratio (MER):	2.39%	**Distributions:**	Annually in December (any net income and any net capital gains)
		Minimum investment:	$500 initial, $50 additional

What does the fund invest in?

This fund's objective is to increase the value of your investment over the long term by investing in equities of well-established Canadian companies. The fund may invest up to 30% of the purchase cost of the fund's assets in foreign securities.

The charts below give you a snapshot of the fund's investments on March 6, 2014. The fund's investments will change.

Top 10 investments (March 6, 2014)

1. Toronto-Dominion Bank, The,   8.2%
2. Bank of Nova Scotia   6.1%
3. Canadian National Railway Company   5.0%
4. Canadian Natural Resources Limited   4.3%
5. TELUS Corporation   4.3%
6. Manulife Financial Corporation   3.9%
7. Royal Bank of Canada   3.8%
8. Tourmaline Oil Corp.   2.9%
9. CGI Group Inc., Class A   2.8%
10. Cenovus Energy Inc.   2.6%
Top 10 investments: 43.9% of the fund

Total investments: 57

Investment mix (March 6, 2014)

Portfolio Allocation
- 33.7% Financials
- 23.9% Energy
- 9.5% Consumer Discretionary
- 9.4% Information Technology
- 7.9% Industrials
- 5.3% Materials
- 4.3% Telecommunication Services
- 2.3% Health Care
- 2.2% Consumer Staples
- 1.8% Money Market Investments
- -0.3% Cash/Receivables /Payables

How risky is it?

The value of the fund can go down as well as up. You could lose money.

One way to gauge risk is to look at how much a fund's returns change over time. This is called "volatility".

In general, funds with higher volatility will have returns that change more over time. They typically have a greater chance of losing money and may have a greater chance of higher returns. Funds with lower volatility tend to have returns that change less over time. They typically have lower returns and may have a lower chance of losing money.

Risk rating
BMO Investments Inc. has rated the volatility of this fund as **Medium**.

This rating is based on how much the fund's returns have changed from year to year. It doesn't tell you how volatile the fund will be in the future. The rating can change over time. A fund with a low risk rating can still lose money.

For more information about the risk rating and specific risks that can affect the fund's returns, see the "What are the risks of investing in a mutual fund" section of the fund's simplified prospectus.

No guarantees
Like most mutual funds, this fund doesn't have any guarantees. You may not get back the amount of money you invest.

SOURCE: BMO Mutual Funds, http://fundfacts.bmo.com/RetailEnglish/BMO_Canadian_Equity_Fund-EN-Series_A.pdf, accessed June 23, 2014. Used by permission of BMO Canada.

- Transfer fee—at the discretion of the individual adviser, dealers can levy a charge of up to 2 percent when you switch among funds in the same family.
- Processing fees—your fund company may levy a fee if you require transactions that require special processing.

SERVICE FEES   Also called *trailers*, these are ongoing commissions to pay advisers and dealers for ongoing service. The adviser or dealer gets a yearly amount that equals a certain percentage of your account's value. That's often about 1 percent on front-load accounts and 0.5 percent on deferred sales load accounts. No-load companies may also pay trailers to dealers. You do not pay service fees directly. They're paid by the mutual fund company—in most cases, from its management fee. As with commissions, funds that carry low trailers or none at all may or may not have lower management expense ratios.

There are no easy answers, but your professional financial adviser or broker can help you determine which particular mutual fund best suits your financial needs. You can also do your own research to determine which fund is right for you. Factors to consider include whether you want to invest in a load fund or no-load fund, as well as the fund's management fees and expense ratios. As you will see later in this chapter, a number of sources of information can help you make your investment decisions.

The investment company's prospectus must provide all details relating to management fees, contingent deferred sales fees, and other expenses. Exhibit 13–2 shows a fund profile for the BMO Canadian Equity Class Fund. Here, you'll see a reported MER of 2.39 percent and the objectives of the mutual fund.

Exhibit 13–3 summarizes load charges and no-load charges. In addition, it reports management fees, contingent deferred sales loads, and other charges.

> **Did you know?**
>
> Say, for example, you invest $1,000 in a fund with an MER of 2.5 percent. After 15 years, you would lose 32 percent of your contribution to fees and, after 25 years, you would lose 47 percent. But compare with a low MER of 0.5 percent. After 15 years, the fee costs you only 7 percent of your contribution. After 25 years, the amount is 12 percent.
>
> SOURCE: "In Tough Times, Fees Matter More" by Carolyn Leitch, for *The Globe and Mail*, February 7, 2002, Section M.

Type of Fee or Charge	Definition and Rate
Load fund	Either a front-end or back-end sales charge
No-load fund	No sales charge
Front-end load	A sales fee charged with each purchase; reduces the funds actually invested. Most fund companies have lowered the maximum front-end load on their funds to around 6 percent.
Back-end load	Also referred to as a contingent deferred sales load. One to six percent of withdrawals on a sliding scale decreasing with time held, then zero if selling after a set number of years.
Management fee	Expressed as a fixed percentage of the fund's total value, called the Management Expense Ratio (MER). Ranges from 0.25 percent (rare) to 4 percent, to cover investment company's costs. Fee is up to 0.5 percent higher for back-end load funds.

Exhibit 13–3

Typical Fees Associated with Mutual Fund Investments

1. What type of information about a mutual fund can be found on the Internet?
2. What are two major reasons investors purchase mutual funds?
3. How do a closed-end fund and an open-end fund differ?
4. What are the typical fees charged for a load and no-load mutual fund?
5. What are the typical management fees, and front and back load fees?

CLASSIFICATIONS OF MUTUAL FUNDS

LO2

Classify mutual funds by investment objective.

Mutual fund managers tailor their investment portfolios to their customers' investment objectives. Usually, a fund's objectives are plainly disclosed in its prospectus. For example, the objectives of the Royal Balanced Growth Fund are as follows:

> The Royal Balanced Growth Fund is considered a "one-decision" fund, for growth-oriented investors investing in a diversified portfolio of Canadian, U.S., and International equities, and Canadian bonds, and short-term debt securities. The fund employs a more aggressive asset allocation strategy and invests in a more focused list of securities than the Royal Balanced Fund, in order to achieve the highest possible total return consistent with a moderate level of risk. The percentage of assets held in each asset class will vary according to the outlook for the economy and financial markets, and the fund intends to maximize its foreign content. The fund may also invest in derivative instruments.

While it may be helpful to categorize the 1,400-plus mutual funds into different categories, note that different sources of investment information may use different categories for the same mutual fund. In most cases, the name of the category gives a pretty good clue as to the types of investments included within the category. The *major* fund categories are described as follows:

- *Money market funds* seek to achieve a high level of income and liquidity through investment in short-term money market instruments, such as T-bills, commercial paper, and short-term government bonds. These are relatively low risk.
- *Mortgage funds* aim for income and safety. Investors in mortgage funds hold a group of mortgages, rather than a single property title. These have a lower risk than bond funds.
- *Bond funds* aim for safety of principal and income but are subject to capital gains and losses, which have tax implications. Bond funds are generally invested in good quality, high-yielding government and corporate debt securities. The risk here is related to changes in interest rates.
- *Dividend funds* aim for tax-advantaged income with some possibility of capital growth, and invest in preferred shares as well as high quality common shares that have a history of consistently paying dividends.
- *Balanced* and *asset allocation funds* are similar in that they both aim to provide a mixture of safety, income, and capital appreciation. Where they differ is in the fact that only balanced funds need respect a stated minimum investment in given classes of aggressive or defensive types of investments.
- *Equity* or *common stock funds* aim for capital gains and, as such, are invested almost entirely in common shares. These tend to fluctuate in price much more than any of the previously listed funds.
- *Specialty funds* sacrifice diversification in an effort to build capital gains. They concentrate portfolio holdings on shares of a group of companies in one industry, geographical area, or segment of the capital market. They can be susceptible to fluctuations within industries, as well as currency value fluctuations.
- *International* or *global funds* are often considered a subset of specialty funds in that they are focused investments, with portfolios holding investments in the markets that offer the best prospects, regardless of location.

- *Real estate funds* aim for long-term growth through capital appreciation and the reinvestment of income by investing in income-producing real property. These are generally the least liquid of all the types of mutual funds.
- *Ethical funds* seek to make investment decisions that are guided by moral criteria that can vary from fund to fund. Each investment made is examined from the perspective of obeying certain requirements.
- *Segregated funds* are offered by insurance companies as an alternative to conventional mutual funds and offer a range of investment objectives and categories of securities. They are unique in that they guarantee that a portion (usually 75 percent or more) of your principal will be returned to you at maturity, regardless of the fund performance. The insurance offered with segregated funds is at the cost of higher management fees than that of regular mutual funds.

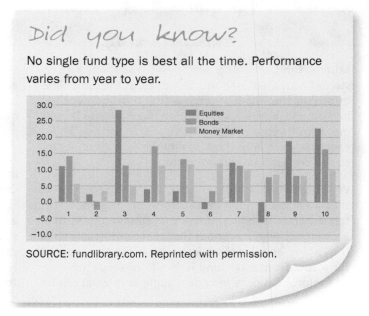

Did you know?

No single fund type is best all the time. Performance varies from year to year.

SOURCE: fundlibrary.com. Reprinted with permission.

- *Labour-sponsored venture capital corporations (LSVCCs)* are sponsored by labour organizations, and their specific mandate is to invest in small to medium-sized businesses. LSVCCs have the advantage of being eligible for generous federal and provincial tax credits but entail significantly higher risks. LSVCC funds invest in firms that are new, not listed on a stock exchange, and cannot qualify for conventional bank financing. While these companies have the potential for substantial growth, the risks are extremely high because these firms are often small with unproven track records.

A **family of funds** exists when one investment company manages a group of mutual funds. Each fund within the family has a different financial objective. For instance, one fund may be a government bond fund and another a growth fund. Most investment companies offer exchange privileges that enable shareholders to switch among the mutual funds in a fund family. For example, if you own shares in the Desjardins growth fund, you may switch to the Desjardins ethical income fund. Generally, investors may give instructions to switch from one fund to another within the same family either in writing, over the telephone, or via the Internet. The family-of-funds concept makes it convenient for shareholders to switch their investments among funds as different funds offer more potential, financial reward, or security. Charges for exchanges, if any, generally are small for each transaction. For funds that do charge, the fee may be as low as $5 per transaction. **Managed Asset Programs (MAP)** are becoming more and more prevalent amongst mutual fund investors. These programs are designed for investors who want to invest in a selection of mutual funds rather than in just one. Each portfolio consists of several, separate mutual funds packaged together. This allows you to have several individual, skilled fund managers managing your assets. MAPs attempt to optimize asset allocation, through the selection of several different funds, as well as to adequately diversify the portfolio for the investor based on their time horizon and tolerance for risk.

Many financial analysts suggest that the true mark of a quality mutual fund investment is the fund's ability to increase the investor's return during good times and maintain that return during bad times. To help accomplish this task, a large number of investors have turned to market timers. A **market timer** is an individual who helps investors decide when to switch their investments from one fund to another fund, usually within the same family of funds. Market timers usually charge an annual fee of 1.5 to 3 percent of the dollar value of the funds they manage. When evaluating market timers, keep in mind that the services they offer are a relatively recent innovation. Thus, it may be hard to judge their long-term track record accurately.

family of funds A group of mutual funds managed by one investment company.

Managed Asset Program (MAP) A program allowing individuals to invest in portfolios grouping together many different mutual funds.

market timer An individual who helps investors decide when to switch their investments from one fund to another fund, usually within the same family of funds.

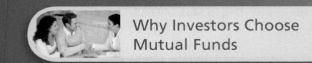
Mutual fund investing provides a good way to get started with small amounts of money, at the same time affording the investor professional management. By investing in mutual funds you can diversify your investments to fit your personal goals and objectives. However, the most important advantage is still the ability to get professional management.

When choosing a mutual fund, the pros recommend that investors rely on research. Research gives investors an understanding of the kind of investment they are making, whether or not they feel comfortable with the choice, and lets them know what the track record for a specific mutual fund is. While research may not be foolproof, it does provide a guide as to what can be

expected of a particular fund in the future. Only after an investor has researched a potential investment is it possible to find a mutual fund that fits the investor's needs, had good management, and has a successful long-term track record.

According to a pro, many investors are always changing funds and chasing funds that were hot last year. Consequently, they incur more fees, sales charges, and so on. This can make mutual fund investing more expensive, and in most cases, investors end up with smaller total returns. This is not to say that changes cannot be made in the mutual funds an investor owns. However, it is best to give a well-managed fund time to work.

Early research indicates that market timers must be evaluated on their individual investment philosophy and their past performance, and it is impossible to pass judgment on *all* market timers as a group.

CONCEPT CHECK 13–2

1. How important is the investment objective as stated in a fund's prospectus?
2. Why do you think fund managers offer so many different kinds of funds?
3. What is a family of funds? How is it related to shareholder exchanges?
4. How does a market timer help people manage their mutual fund investments?

HOW TO MAKE A DECISION TO BUY OR SELL MUTUAL FUNDS

LO3

Evaluate mutual funds for investment purposes.

Often, the decision to buy or sell shares in mutual funds is "too easy" because investors assume they do not need to evaluate these investments. Why question what the professional portfolio managers decide to do? Yet, professionals do make mistakes. The responsibility for choosing the right mutual fund rests with *you*. After all, you are the only one who knows how much risk you are willing to assume and how a particular mutual fund can help you achieve your goals.

If you think there are mutual funds designed to meet just about any conceivable investment objective, you are probably right. Hundreds of mutual funds trade daily under the headings "aggressive growth," "small-cap," and "growth-income." Fortunately, a lot of information is available to help you evaluate a specific mutual fund. Unfortunately, you can get lost in all the facts and figures and forget your ultimate goal—to choose a mutual fund that will help you achieve your financial goals. To help you sort out all the research, statistics, and information about mutual funds and give you some direction as to what to do first, we have provided the checklist in Exhibit 13–4. Don't forget, when evaluating the funds, that past performance may not necessarily be indicative of future returns. The remainder of this section explains the types of information you can obtain from each source listed in the exhibit.

Exhibit 13–4

Common Steps
Used by Investors
to Evaluate Mutual
Funds

☐ **Step 1: Perform a financial checkup to make sure you are ready to invest.**
For more information, review the material presented in Chapter 10.

☐ **Step 2: Obtain the money you need to purchase mutual funds.**
Although the amount varies, $250 to $10,000 is usually required to open an
account with a brokerage firm or an investment company.

☐ **Step 3: Determine your investment objectives.**
For more information, review the material presented in Chapter 10.

☐ **Step 4: Find a fund with an objective that matches your objective.**
The *Financial Post* and *The Globe and Mail's Report on Business* may help you
identify funds with objectives that match your investment objectives. Also, you can
contact the investment company and ask for a prospectus and an annual report for
a specific mutual fund. Finally, you can use the Internet to screen mutual funds
that are compatible with your investment objectives.

☐ **Step 5: Evaluate, evaluate, and evaluate any mutual fund before buying or selling.**
Complete the Evaluation of a Mutual Fund form on p. 411 before making a
decision to buy or sell a mutual fund. Possible sources of information include
newspapers, the fund's prospectus, the fund's annual report, financial publications,
the Internet, and professional advisory services—all sources described in this
chapter. Be sure to evaluate the fund manager's background and how long the
manager has been managing the fund.

HOW TO READ THE MUTUAL FUNDS SECTION OF THE NEWSPAPER

The *Financial Post* and *The Globe and Mail* provide information about mutual funds. Exhibit 13–5 is a guide to reading mutual fund tables. Various newspapers have similar reporting schemes, and in general all provide the fund name, family, and current price. In addition, the 52-week highest and lowest paid prices will be shown, as well as the net asset value per share (NAVPS) and the percentage change in price. Much of this same information is also available on the Internet.

FINANCIAL OBJECTIVES—AGAIN

In Chapter 10, we talked about establishing investment goals and objectives. In this chapter, we have looked at the investment objectives of mutual funds. Here, our aim is to point out the relationship between the two. In establishing your own investment goals and objectives, you must evaluate the personal factors of age, family situation, risk tolerance, income, and future earning power. Only then can you establish short-term, intermediate, and long-term objectives. Now, you must find a mutual fund whose investment objectives match your own.

You may want to look at the *Financial Post*, which spotlights a different fund investment category, along with the top performers in each category, every week. You can also use the mutual fund filter on the Fund Library Web site (fundlibrary.com) to identify funds whose objective matches your objective. Finally, as mentioned earlier in this chapter, a mutual fund's prospectus provides a detailed description of the fund's investment objective. *Be warned:* Many mutual funds have developed objectives that sound good but don't really describe the investment philosophy. While the fund's objective is a place to start, you still need to gather as much information as possible about the fund and the investment company that sponsors it.

Exhibit 13–5

Obtaining Mutual Fund Information From a Newspaper

The newspaper coverage described in this section is a good means of monitoring the value of your mutual fund investments. However, online sources of information provide a more complete and timely basis for evaluating mutual fund investments. Information on mutual funds is available free of charge from globefund.com.

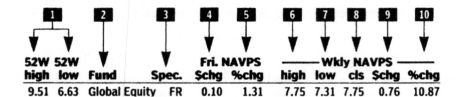

How to read the mutual fund tables

Mutual fund rate of return figures appear in the Financial Post Mutual Funds Monthly Report, which runs the third Saturday of each month.

52W high	52W low	Fund	Spec.	Fri. NAVPS $chg	%chg	Wkly NAVPS high	low	cls	$chg	%chg
9.51	6.63	Global Equity	FR	0.10	1.31	7.75	7.31	7.75	0.76	10.87

1. 52-week high/low: Highest and lowest price reached in the previous 52 weeks

2. Fund: name

3. Specifics: footnotes: ♦ – denotes segregated fund Y – delayed NAVPS or yield U – US$ * – RRSP eligible (funds without * may generally be held in RRSPs as foreign property) X – trading ex-dividend Z – not available to general public N – no load fund F – front-end load or fee D – deferred declining redemption fee based on original capital invested R – deferred declining redemption fee based on market value FD – For D at buyer's option FR – For R at buyer's option B – both front- and back-end fee ... – data not available

Friday NAVPS data:
4. Dollar change: from previous day
5. % Change: from previous day
Friday NAVPS data:
6. High on week
7. Low on week
8. Close on week
9. $ Change from previous week
10 % Change from previous week

Money Market Funds
Data for money market funds and segregated money market funds reflect current yields, not NAVPS. For example, under "dollar change" the figures would indicate the change in a fund's current yield in terms of percentage points. Pricing and yield data supplied by Fundata Canada Inc. is for information purposes only. Confirmation of price should be obtained from the fund sponsor.

- The letters beside the name of a specific fund can be very informative. You can find out what they mean by looking at the footnotes that accompany the mutual fund quotations. Generally, "N" means no-load, "U" means U.S. currency, "F" is front load or fee, and "B" signifies both front- and back-end fees.

- In many cases, the search for a no-load fund starts with a quotation as seen in Figure 13-5. Therefore, the N footnote is especially important. As pointed out earlier, no-load mutual funds do not charge sales fees. Since no-load funds offer the same investment opportunities that load funds do, financial experts often recommend these funds.

- The Net Asset Value Per Share (NAVPS) column lists information on the close of the preceding business day. Each mutual fund calculates its NAVPS every business day by dividing the market value of its total assets, less liabilities, by the number of shares outstanding. The High, Low, and Change data give a sense of the variability of the fund.

- The newspaper or similar Internet coverage described in this section is a starting point to monitor the value of your mutual fund investments. However, other sources of information (see sections below) provide a more complete basis for evaluating mutual fund investments.

SOURCE: *The Financial Post* (as part of the *National Post*), July 1, 2000, p. C7.

MUTUAL FUND PROSPECTUS

An investment company sponsoring a mutual fund must give potential investors a prospectus. According to financial experts, the prospectus is usually the first piece of information investors receive, and they should read it completely before investing. Although it may look intimidating, a common-sense approach to reading a fund's prospectus can provide valuable insights. In fact, most investors find that a fund's prospectus can provide a wealth of information. As pointed out earlier, the prospectus summarizes the fund's objective. Also, the fee table provides a summary of the fees a fund charges. In addition to information about objectives and fees, the prospectus should provide the following:

- A statement describing the risk factor associated with the fund.
- A description of the fund's past performance.
- A statement describing the type of investments contained in the fund's portfolio.

- Information about dividends, distributions, and taxes.
- Information about the fund's management.
- Information on limitations or requirements the fund must honour when choosing investments.
- The process investors can use to buy or sell shares in the fund.
- A description of services provided to investors and fees for services, if any.
- Information about how often the fund's investment portfolio changes (sometimes referred to as its *turnover ratio*).

Finally, the prospectus provides information about how to open a mutual fund account with the investment company.

MUTUAL FUND ANNUAL REPORT

If you are a prospective investor, you can request an annual report through the mail, a toll-free telephone number, or the Internet. Once you are a shareholder, the investment company will send you an annual report. A fund's annual report contains a letter from the president of the investment company, from the fund manager, or both. *Caution: Don't forget the role of the fund manager in determining a fund's success.* One important question is, how long has the present fund manager been managing the fund? If a fund has performed well under its present manager over a five-year, 10-year, or even longer period, there is a strong likelihood that it will continue to perform well under that manager in the future.

The annual report also contains detailed financial information about the fund's assets and liabilities, statement of operations, and statement of changes in net assets. Next, the annual report includes a schedule of investments. (Take a second look at the schedule of investments for the RBC Canadian Equity Fund in Exhibit 13–1.) Finally, the fund's annual report should include a letter from the fund's independent auditors that provides an opinion as to the accuracy of the fund's financial statements.

FINANCIAL PUBLICATIONS

Investment-oriented magazines, such as *Canadian Business* and *Report on Business*, are another source of information about mutual funds. Each of these publications provides an annual survey of mutual funds and ranks them on a number of important investment criteria.

In addition, a number of mutual fund guidebooks are available at your local bookstore or online for download. Some of the more popular publications are:

1. Gordon Williamson, *The 100 Best Mutual Funds You Can Buy, 2014*
2. Stephen Makee, *Grow your investments with the best mutual funds and EFTs*
3. Russel Kinnel, *Fund Spy*
4. Stephen Gadsen, *The Canadian Mutual Funds Handbook*
5. Eric Kirzner, Gordon Pape, *Gordon Pape's 2013 Buyer's Guide to Mutual Funds*
6. David Swansen, *Common Sense on Mutual Funds*

A great deal of information is also available online. Updated information on mutual funds can also be accessed through a subscription to Gordon Pape's Web site, buildingwealth.ca. A sample of the information provided on the Fund Library Web site for the BMO Dividend Fund is illustrated in Exhibit 13–6.

THE INTERNET

Many investors have found a wealth of information about mutual fund investments on the Internet. Basically, there are three ways to access information. First, you can obtain current market values for mutual funds by using one of the Internet search engines, such as google.ca; the finance page (finance.yahoo.ca) has a box where you can enter the symbol of the mutual

Exhibit 13–6

Online FundCARD
for All-Canadian
Capital Fund

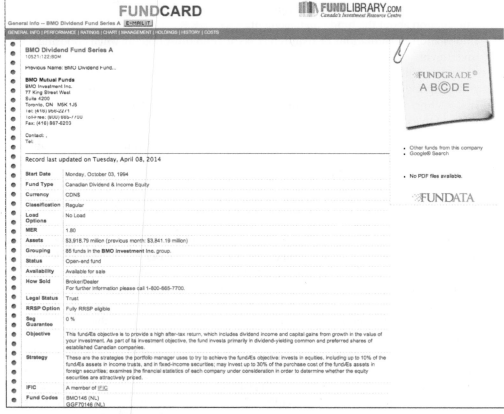

FUNDCARD   **FUNDLIBRARY**.COM
                                                       Canada's Investment Resource Centre

General Info -- BMO Dividend Fund Series A E-MAIL IT

GENERAL INFO | PERFORMANCE | RATINGS | CHART | MANAGEMENT | HOLDINGS | HISTORY | COSTS

BMO Dividend Fund Series A
10521:122:BOM

Previous Name: BMO Dividend Fund...

BMO Mutual Funds
BMO Investment Inc.
77 King Street West
Suite 4200
Toronto, ON M5K 1J5
Tel: (416) 956-2271
Toll-Free: (800) 665-7700
Fax: (416) 867-6203

Contact: ,
Tel:

FUNDGRADE®
A B©D E

- Other funds from this company
- Google® Search

- No PDF files available.

FUNDATA

Record last updated on Tuesday, April 08, 2014

Start Date	Monday, October 03, 1994
Fund Type	Canadian Dividend & Income Equity
Currency	CDN$
Classification	Regular
Load Options	No Load
MER	1.80
Assets	$3,918.79 million (previous month: $3,841.19 million)
Grouping	85 funds in the **BMO Investment Inc.** group.
Status	Open-end fund
Availability	Available for sale
How Sold	Broker/Dealer For further information please call 1-800-665-7700.
Legal Status	Trust
RRSP Option	Fully RRSP eligible
Seg Guarantee	0 %
Objective	This fundÆs objective is to provide a high after-tax return, which includes dividend income and capital gains from growth in the value of your investment. As part of its investment objective, the fund invests primarily in dividend-yielding common and preferred shares of established Canadian companies.
Strategy	These are the strategies the portfolio manager uses to try to achieve the fundÆs objective: invests in equities, including up to 10% of the fundÆs assets in income trusts, and in fixed-income securities; may invest up to 30% of the purchase cost of the fundÆs assets in foreign securities; examines the financial statistics of each company under consideration in order to determine whether the equity securities are attractively priced.
IFIC	A member of IFIC
Fund Codes	BMO146 (NL) GGF70146 (NL)

SOURCE: fundlibrary.com. Reprinted with permission.

fund you want to research. In addition to current market values, you can obtain a price history for a mutual fund and a profile that includes specific holdings the fund owns.

Secondly, all investment companies that sponsor mutual funds have Web pages. To obtain information, all you have to do is access one of the Internet search engines and type in the name of the fund. Before reading on, take a look at Exhibit 13–7, the opening page for the American

Exhibit 13–7

Homepage of the
AGF Web site

Growth Fund (AGF; formerly Acuity Funds Ltd.). Generally, statistical information about individual funds, procedures for opening an account, available literature (including a prospectus and an annual report), and different investor services are provided. *Be warned:* Investment companies want you to become a shareholder. As a result, the Web sites for *some* investment companies read like a sales pitch. Read between the glowing descriptions and look at the facts before investing your money.

Note that information about the fund symbol, current NAV, adviser and portfolio manager, and minimum investment amounts is provided. It is also possible to obtain a current quote, chart, and information on returns, risk, holdings, and news by clicking on the appropriate button of the Web site.

For more information on the evaluation process, study the checklist provided in the Financial Planning Calculations feature on page 411.

CONCEPT CHECK 13–3

1. Many financial experts say that purchasing a mutual fund is "too easy." Do you think this statement is true or false? Explain.

2. How can the following help you evaluate a mutual fund?
   a. Newspapers
   b. The fund's objective
   c. The prospectus
   d. The annual report
   e. Financial publications
   f. The Internet

THE MECHANICS OF A MUTUAL FUND TRANSACTION

For many investors, mutual funds have become the investment of choice. In fact, you probably either own shares or know someone who owns shares in a mutual fund—they're that popular! They may be part of a retirement savings plan or owned outright by purchasing shares through a brokerage firm or an investment company that sponsors a mutual fund. As you will see later in this section, it's easy to purchase shares in a mutual fund. For $250 to $2,500, you can open an account and begin investing. And there are other advantages that encourage investors to purchase shares in funds. Unfortunately, there are also disadvantages. Exhibit 13–8 summarizes the advantages and disadvantages of mutual fund investments.

One advantage of any investment is the opportunity to make money on it. In the next section, we examine how you can make money by investing in closed-end funds or open-end funds. We consider how taxes affect your mutual fund investments. Then, we look at the options used to purchase shares in a mutual fund. Finally, we examine the options used to withdraw money from a mutual fund.

LO4
Describe how and why mutual funds are bought and sold.

RETURN ON INVESTMENT

As with other investments, the purpose of investing in a closed-end fund or an open-end fund is to earn a financial return. Shareholders in such funds can receive a return in one of three ways. First, both types of funds pay income dividends. **Income dividends** are the earnings a fund pays to shareholders after it has deducted expenses from its dividend and interest income. Mutual fund dividends are usually paid once or twice a year. Second, investors may receive capital gain distributions. **Capital gain distributions** are the payments made to a fund's shareholders that result from the sale of securities in the fund's portfolio. These amounts generally are paid once a year. Third, as with stock and bond investments, you can buy shares in both types of funds at a low price and then sell them after the price has increased. For example, assume you purchased

income dividends
The earnings a fund pays to shareholders after it has deducted expenses from its dividend and interest income.

capital gain distributions The payments made to a fund's shareholders that result from the sale of securities in the fund's portfolio.

Exhibit 13–8

Advantages and
Disadvantages of
Investing in Mutual
Funds

Advantages

- Diversification
- Professional management
- Ease of buying and selling shares
- Smaller amount of money often required to open a mutual fund account
- Multiple withdrawal options
- Distribution or reinvestment of income and capital gains
- Switching privileges within the same fund family
- Services that include toll-free telephone numbers, complete records of all transactions, and savings and chequing accounts

Disadvantages

- Purchase/withdrawal costs
- Ongoing management fees
- Poor performance that does not match the TSE 300 Stock Index or some other index
- Inability to control when capital gain distributions occur and complicated tax-reporting issues
- Potential market risk associated with all investments
- Some sales personnel are aggressive

shares in the Royal Dividend Mutual Fund at $22.50 per share and sold your shares two years later at $25 per share. In this case, you made $2.50 ($25 selling price minus $22.50 purchase price) per share. With this financial information and dollar amounts for income dividends and capital gain distributions, you can calculate a total return for your mutual fund investment.

When shares in a mutual fund are sold, the profit that results from an increase in value is referred to as a *capital gain*. Note the difference between a capital gain distribution and a capital gain. A capital gain distribution occurs when *the fund* distributes profits that result from *the fund* selling securities in the portfolio at a profit. On the other hand, a capital gain is the profit that results when *you* sell your shares in the mutual fund for more than you paid for them. Of course, if the price of a fund's shares goes down between the time of your purchase and the time of sale, you incur a loss.

TAXES AND MUTUAL FUNDS

Income dividends, capital gain distributions, and financial gains and losses from the sale of closed-end or open-end funds are subject to taxation. At the end of each year, investment companies are required to send each shareholder a statement specifying how much he or she received in dividends and capital gain distributions. Investment companies may provide this information as part of their year-end statement.

Income passed through a mutual fund to its shareholders retains its nature; in other words, it retains its character as interest, foreign or Canadian dividends, or capital gains. As discussed in Chapter 3, Planning Your Tax Strategy, interest and foreign dividend income are 100 percent taxable at the investor's marginal tax rate, while Canadian dividends are grossed-up by 38 percent and offset by a dividend tax credit that is equal to 20.73 percent of the actual dollar dividend received. Fifty percent of capital gains are taxable.

Three specific problems develop with taxation of mutual funds. First, almost all investment companies allow you to reinvest income distributions and capital gain distributions from the fund in additional shares instead of receiving cash. Even though you didn't receive cash because you chose to reinvest such distributions, they are still taxable and must be reported on your federal and provincial tax returns as current income. Second, when you purchase shares of stock, corporate bonds, or other investments and use the buy-and-hold technique described in Chapter 11, you

Financial Planning Calculations

Evaluation of a Mutual Fund

No checklist can serve as a foolproof guide for choosing a mutual fund. However, the following questions will help you evaluate a potential investment in such a fund.

CATEGORY 1: FUND CHARACTERISTICS

1. What is the value of the assets of this fund?
_____
2. What is this fund's DBRS rating? _____
3. What is the minimum investment? _____
4. Does the fund allow telephone exchanges?
   ☐ Yes ☐ No
5. Is there a fee for telephone exchanges?
   ☐ Yes ☐ No

CATEGORY 2: COSTS

6. Is there a front-end load charge? If so, how much is it? _____
7. Is there a redemption fee? If so, how much is it?
_____
8. How much is the annual management fee?
_____
9. What is the fund's expense ratio? _____

CATEGORY 3: DIVERSIFICATION

10. What is the fund's objective? _____
11. What types of securities does the fund's portfolio include? _____
12. How many securities does the fund's portfolio include? _____
13. How many types of industries does the fund's portfolio include? _____

CATEGORY 4: FUND PERFORMANCE

14. How long has the fund manager been with the fund? _____
15. How would you describe the fund's performance over the past 12 months? _____
_____
16. How would you describe the fund's performance over the past five years? _____
_____
17. How would you describe the fund's performance over the past 10 years? _____
_____

CATEGORY 5: CONCLUSION

18. Based on the above information, do you think an investment in this fund will help you achieve your investment goals?
    ☐ Yes ☐ No
19. Explain your answer to question 18.
_____
_____
_____

A WORD OF CAUTION

When you use a checklist, there is always a danger of overlooking important relevant information. The above checklist is not a cure-all, but it does provide some sound questions that you should answer before making a mutual fund investment decision. Quite simply, it is a place to start. If you need other information, *you* are responsible for obtaining it and for determining how it affects your potential investment.

decide when you sell. Therefore, you can pick the tax year when you pay tax on capital gains or deduct capital losses. Mutual funds, on the other hand, buy and sell securities within the fund's portfolio on a regular basis during any 12-month period. At the end of the year, profits that result from the mutual fund's buying and selling activities are paid to shareholders in the form of capital gain distributions. Unlike with investments that you manage, you have no control over when the mutual fund sells securities and when you will be taxed on capital gain distributions. Finally, if you purchase a mutual fund toward the end of the year, but before distributions are paid, you will be subject to tax on the entire distribution as if you had owned the mutual fund for the entire year. This may result in an unfair tax burden, when a successful mutual fund sells stocks at year-end that have grown throughout the year.

To ensure having all of the documentation you need for tax reporting purposes, it is essential that *you* keep accurate records. For example, additional shares of a mutual fund can be purchased by reinvesting interest, dividends, and capital gains distributions. However, these distributions have already been reported by you for tax purposes and you do not want to be taxed on the same

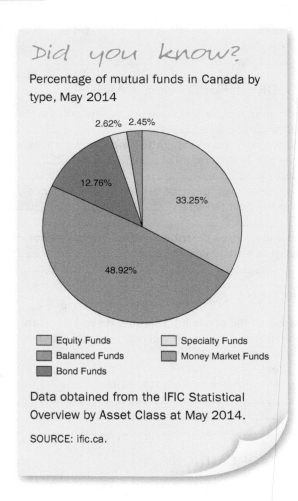

Did you know?

Percentage of mutual funds in Canada by type, May 2014

2.62% 2.45%

12.76%

33.25%

48.92%

☐ Equity Funds   ☐ Specialty Funds
☐ Balanced Funds   ☐ Money Market Funds
☐ Bond Funds

Data obtained from the IFIC Statistical Overview by Asset Class at May 2014.

SOURCE: ific.ca.

amount twice. Therefore, it's up to you to keep track of their adjusted cost base, which is equal to the amounts reinvested. When these shares are eventually redeemed, their adjusted cost base is subtracted from their net redemption value to determine the capital gain (or loss). The same records help you monitor the value of your mutual fund investments and make more intelligent decisions with regard to buying and selling these investments.

PURCHASE OPTIONS

You can buy shares of a closed-end fund through various stock exchanges or in the over-the-counter market. You can purchase shares of an open-end, no-load fund by contacting the investment company that sponsors the fund. You can purchase shares of an open-end, load fund through a salesperson who is authorized to sell them, through an account executive of a brokerage firm, or directly from the investment company that sponsors the fund.

You can also purchase both no-load and load funds from mutual fund supermarkets, available through discount brokerage firms. A mutual fund supermarket offers at least two advantages. First, instead of dealing with numerous investment companies that sponsor mutual funds, you can make one toll-free phone call to obtain information, purchase shares, and sell shares in a large number of mutual funds. Second, you receive one statement from the discount brokerage firm instead of receiving a statement from each investment company you deal with. One statement can be a real plus because it provides the information you need to monitor the value of your investments in one place and in the same format.

Because of the unique nature of open-end fund transactions, we will examine how investors buy and sell shares in this type of mutual fund from an investment company.

To purchase shares in an open-end mutual fund from an investment company, you may use four options: regular account transactions, voluntary savings plans (pre-authorized contribution [PAC]), contractual savings plans, and reinvestment plans. The most popular and least complicated method of purchasing shares in an open-end fund is through a regular account transaction. When you use a regular account transaction, you decide how much money you want to invest, when you want to invest, and simply buy as many shares as possible.

The chief advantage of the voluntary savings plan is that it allows you to make smaller purchases than the minimum purchases required by the regular account method described above. At the time of the initial purchase, you declare an intent to make regular minimum purchases of the fund's shares. Although there is no penalty for not making purchases, most investors feel an "obligation" to make purchases on a periodic basis, and, as noted throughout this text, small monthly investments are a great way to save for long-term objectives. For most voluntary savings plans, the minimum purchase ranges from $25 to $100 for each purchase after the initial investment. Funds try to make investing as easy as possible. Most offer payroll deduction plans, and many will deduct, upon proper shareholder authorization, a specified amount from a shareholder's bank account. Also, many investors can choose mutual funds as a vehicle to invest money that is contributed to an RRSP account. Chapter 14 provides more information on the tax advantages of different types of retirement accounts.

Contractual savings plans require you to make regular purchases over a specified period of time, usually 10 to 15 years. These plans are sometimes referred to as *front-end load funds* because almost all of the commissions are paid in the first few years of the contract period. You will incur penalties if you do not fulfill the purchase requirements. For example, if you drop out of a contractual savings plan before completing the purchase requirements, you sacrifice the prepaid commissions. Many financial experts and government regulatory agencies are critical of contractual savings plans.

You may also purchase shares in an open-end fund by using the fund's reinvestment plan. A **reinvestment plan** is a service provided by an investment company in which income dividends and capital gain distributions are automatically reinvested to purchase additional shares of the fund. Most reinvestment plans allow shareholders to use reinvested money to purchase shares without having to pay additional sales charges or commissions. *Reminder:* When your dividends or capital gain distributions are reinvested, you must still report these transactions as taxable income.

All four purchase options allow you to buy shares over a long period of time. As a result, you can use the principle of *dollar cost averaging*, which was introduced in Chapter 11. Dollar cost averaging allows you to average many individual purchase prices over a long period of time. This method helps you avoid the problem of buying high and selling low. With dollar cost averaging, you can make money if you sell your mutual fund shares at a price higher than their *average* purchase price.

reinvestment plan
A service provided by an investment company in which shareholder income dividends and capital gain distributions are automatically reinvested to purchase additional shares of the fund.

WITHDRAWAL OPTIONS

Because closed-end funds are listed on securities exchanges or traded in the over-the-counter market, it is possible to sell shares in such a fund to another investor. Shares in an open-end fund can be sold on any business day to the investment company that sponsors the fund. In this case, the shares are redeemed at their net asset value. All you have to do is give proper notification, and the fund will send you a cheque. With some funds, you can even write cheques to withdraw money from the fund.

In addition, most funds have provisions that allow investors with shares that have a minimum net asset value of at least $5,000 to use four options to systematically withdraw money. First, you may withdraw a specified, fixed dollar amount each investment period until your fund has been exhausted. Normally, an investment period is three months, and most funds require investors to withdraw a minimum amount, usually $50, each investment period.

A second option allows you to liquidate or "sell off" a certain number of shares each investment period. Since the net asset value of shares in a fund varies from one period to the next, the amount of money you receive will also vary. Once the specified number of shares has been sold, a cheque is mailed directly to you.

A third option allows you to withdraw a fixed percentage of asset growth. For example, assume you arrange to receive 60 percent of the asset growth of your investment, and the asset growth of your investment amounts to $800 in a particular investment period. For that period, you will receive a cheque for $480 ($800 × 60% = $480). If no asset growth occurs, no payment is made to you. Under this option, your principal remains untouched.

A final option allows you to withdraw all asset growth that results from income dividends and capital gains earned by the fund during an investment period. Under this option, your principal remains untouched.

CONCEPT CHECK 13–4

1. How can you make money when investing in mutual funds?
2. What is the difference among income dividends, capital gain distributions, and capital gains?
3. How are income dividends, capital gain distributions, and capital gains reported on your federal tax return?
4. Whom would you contact to purchase a closed-end fund? An open-end fund?
5. What options can you use to purchase shares in a mutual fund from an investment company?
6. What options can you use to withdraw money from a mutual fund?

SUMMARY OF LEARNING OBJECTIVES

LO1 Describe the characteristics of mutual fund investments.

The major reasons investors choose mutual funds are professional management and diversification. Mutual funds are also a convenient way to invest money. There are two types of mutual funds. A closed-end fund is a mutual fund whose shares are issued only when the fund is originally set up. An open-end fund is a mutual fund whose shares are sold and redeemed by the investment company at the net asset value (NAV) at the request of investors. Mutual funds are also classified as load or no-load funds. A load fund charges a commission every time you purchase shares. No commission is charged to purchase shares in a no-load fund. Mutual funds can also be front-end load or back-end load. Other possible fees include management fees and contingent deferred sales loads.

LO2 Classify mutual funds by investment objective.

The managers of mutual funds tailor their investment portfolios to the investment objectives of their customers. The major fund categories include money market funds, mortgage funds, bond funds, dividend funds, balanced and asset allocation funds, equity or common stock funds, specialty funds, international or global funds, real estate funds, ethical funds, segregated funds, and labour-sponsored venture capital corporations (LSVCCs). Today, many investment companies use a family of funds concept, which allows shareholders to switch their investments among funds as different funds offer more potential, financial reward, or security.

LO3 Evaluate mutual funds for investment purposes.

The responsibility for choosing the "right" mutual fund rests with you, the investor. The information in newspapers, the financial objectives of the fund, the information in the prospectus and annual reports, financial publications, professional advisory services, and the Internet can all help you evaluate a mutual fund.

LO4 Describe how and why mutual funds are bought and sold.

The advantages and disadvantages of mutual funds have made mutual funds the investment of choice for many investors. For $250 to $2,500, you can open an account and begin investing. The shares of a closed-end fund are bought and sold on organized stock exchanges. The shares of an open-end fund may be purchased through a salesperson who is authorized to sell them, through an account executive of a brokerage firm, from a mutual fund supermarket, or from the investment company that sponsors the fund. The shares in an open-end fund can be sold to the investment company that sponsors the fund. Shareholders in mutual funds can receive a return in one of three ways: income dividends, capital gain distributions when the fund buys and sells securities in the fund's portfolio at a profit, and capital gains when shares in the mutual fund are sold at a higher price than the price paid. A number of purchase and withdrawal options are available.

KEY TERMS

capital gain distributions 409

closed-end fund 395

contingent deferred sales load 398

exchange-traded funds (ETFs) 397

family of funds 403

income dividends 409

index fund 397

investment company 395

load fund 398

Managed Asset Program
   (MAP) 403

market timer 403

mutual fund 394

net asset value (NAV) 395

no-load fund 399

open-end fund 395

reinvestment plan 413

short sell 397

KEY FORMULAS

Page	Topic	Formula
397	Net asset value	$\text{Net asset value} = \dfrac{\text{Current market value of a fund's portfolio} - \text{Liabilities}}{\text{Number of shares outstanding}}$
	Example:	$\text{Net asset value} = \dfrac{\$24,500,000 - \$2,000,000}{1,800,000}$
		$= \$12.50 \text{ per share}$

FINANCIAL PLANNING PROBLEMS

Mc Graw Hill connect™   Practise and learn online with Connect.

1. *Calculating Net Asset Value.* Given the following information, calculate the net asset value for the Altamira Bond mutual fund. LO1

Total assets	$225,000,000
Total liabilities	$ 5,000,000
Total number of shares	4,400,000

2. *Calculating Net Asset Value.* Given the following information, calculate the net asset value for the New Empire small-cap mutual fund. LO1

Total assets	$350,000,000
Total liabilities	$ 10,000,000
Total number of shares	17,000,000

3. *Calculating Sales Fees.* Jane Tong invested $15,000 in the ADA Diversified Futures Mutual Fund. The fund charges a 5.5 percent commission when shares are purchased. Calculate the amount of commission Jane must pay. LO1

4. *Calculating Sales Fees.* Tony Matteo invested $9,800 in the CI Harbour Growth growth and income fund. The fund charges a 5.3 percent commission when shares are purchased. Calculate the amount of commission Tony must pay. LO1

5. *Determining Management Fees.* Chris Lavigne invested a total of $8,500 in the AIC Diversified Canada Mutual Fund. The management fee for this particular fund is 2.38 percent of the total investment amount. Calculate the management fee Chris must pay this year. LO1

6. *Calculating Contingent Deferred Sales Loads.* Mary Canfield purchased the All-Canadian Compound bond fund. While this fund doesn't charge a front-end load, it does charge a contingent deferred sales load of 4 percent for any withdrawals in the first five years. If Mary withdraws $6,000 during the second year, how much is the contingent deferred sales load? LO1

7. *Matching Mutual Funds with Investor Needs.* This chapter classified mutual funds into different categories based on the

nature of their investments. Using the following information, pick a mutual fund category that you consider suitable for each investor described and justify your choice. LO2

a. A 25-year-old single investor with a new job that pays $30,000 a year.
   Mutual fund category _____
   Why? _____

b. A single parent with two children who has just received a $100,000 divorce settlement, has no job, and has not worked outside the home for the past five years.
   Mutual fund category _____
   Why? _____

c. A husband and wife who are both in their early 60s and retired.
   Mutual fund category _____
   Why? _____

8. *Using Dollar Cost Averaging.* Over a four-year period, Matt Ewing purchased shares in the Barreau du Quebec Canadian Equity Fund. Using the information below, answer the questions that follow. You may want to review the concept of dollar cost averaging in Chapter 11 before completing this problem. LO4

Year	Investment Amount	Price per Share
2010	$3,000	$40 per share
2011	$3,000	$50 per share
2012	$3,000	$60 per share
2013	$3,000	$45 per share

a. At the end of four years, what is the total amount invested?

b. At the end of four years, what is the total number of mutual fund shares purchased?

c. At the end of four years, what is the average cost for each mutual fund share?

FINANCIAL PLANNING ACTIVITIES

1. *Deciding If Mutual Funds Are Right for You.* Assume you are 35, are divorced, and have just received a $120,000 legal settlement. Prepare a two-page report on the major reasons you want to invest in mutual funds. LO1

2. *Applying Terms to Mutual Fund Investments.* Using recent newspapers, magazines, mutual fund reports, or the Internet, find examples of the following concepts: LO1
   a. The net asset value for a mutual fund.
   b. An example of a load fund
   c. An example of a no-load fund.

d. The management fee for a specific mutual fund.
e. A fund that charges a contingent deferred sales load.

3. *Understanding Fees Associated with Mutual Fund Investments.* Assume you are single, are 28 years old, and have decided to invest $8,000 in mutual funds. LO1
   a. Prepare a chart that shows the typical charges for load funds, no-load funds, and management fees.
   b. Calculate the following fees for your $8,000 mutual fund investment: (1) a 5 percent load charge, and (2) an annual 0.50 percent management fee.

4. *Matching Mutual Funds with Investor Needs.* This chapter explored a number of different classifications of mutual funds. $LO2$

    a. Based on your age and current financial situation, which type of mutual fund seems appropriate for your investment needs? Explain your answer.

    b. As people get closer to retirement, their investment goals often change. Assume you are now 45 years old and have accumulated $110,000 in a retirement account. In this situation, what type of mutual fund would you choose? Why?

    c. Assume you are now 60 years old and have accumulated $400,000 in a retirement account. Also, assume you would like to retire when you are 65. What type of mutual funds would you choose to help you reach your investment goals? Why?

5. *Using Information to Evaluate Mutual Funds.* Obtain specific information on either the Fidelity Disciplined Equity Class mutual fund or the Fidelity Canadian Short Term Bond-A fund. Then, describe how each of the following sources of information can help you evaluate one of these mutual funds: $LO3$

    a. Newspapers.
    b. The fund's investment objective.
    c. The fund's prospectus.
    d. The fund's annual report.
    e. Financial publications.
    f. The Internet.

    After researching one of the Fidelity funds, would you invest in the fund? Why or why not?

6. *Evaluating Mutual Funds.* Choose one of the following mutual funds and use information from newspapers, magazines, mutual fund reports, or the Internet to complete the mutual fund evaluation form presented in the Financial Planning Calculations feature on page 411. Then, answer the following questions: $LO3$

Name of Fund	Type of Fund
AIM Canadian Premier	Large-cap equity
Altamira Health Sciences	Specialty
Dynamic APEX Balances	Balanced
BMO Emerging Markets	Emerging markets
AIC Diversified Canada	Canadian equity

    a. Which fund did you choose?
    b. Why did you choose that fund?
    c. Do you think that fund can help you achieve your investment objectives? Explain your answer.

7. *Applying the Concept of Dollar Cost Averaging.* In a one-page report, explain how the concept of dollar cost averaging applies to the options used to purchase mutual funds. $LO4$

8. *Reading a Prospectus.* Obtain a mutual fund prospectus to determine the options you can use to purchase and redeem shares. Then, prepare a chart that illustrates which options can be used to purchase and redeem shares in the fund, and answer the following questions: $LO4$

    a. Which purchase option appeals to you?
    b. Assuming you are now of retirement age, which withdrawal option appeals to you?

CREATING A FINANCIAL PLAN

Investing in Mutual Funds

Diversification through the use of mutual funds provides investors with convenience and professional management. The variety of mutual funds contributes to your ability to achieve various financial goals.

Web Sites for Mutual Funds

- The Fund Library at **fundlibrary.com**
- Canoe Money mutual funds at **canoe.ca/money**
- Fundata Canada Inc. at **fundata.com**
- GLOBEfund at **globefund.com**
- The Investment Funds Institute of Canada at **ific.ca**
- Investcom at **investcom.com**
- SEDAR at **sedar.com**

- Morningstar Canada at **morningstar.ca**
- The Canadian Financial Network at **canadianfinance .com**
- Yahoo Mutual Funds Center at **finance.yahoo.com/ funds**
- Mutual Fund Education Alliance at **mfea.com**

(Note: Addresses and content of Web sites change, and new sites are created daily. Use search engines to update and locate Web sites for your current financial planning needs.)

Short-Term Financial Planning Activities

1. Identify types of mutual funds that might be appropriate for your various financial goals and life situations.

2. Research the recent performance records and costs of various mutual funds that could be appropriate investments for you.

Long-Term Financial Planning Activities

1. Identify types of mutual funds that you might use for your long-term financial goals.

2. Develop a plan for selecting and monitoring your mutual fund portfolio.

LIFE SITUATION CASE

The Wrong Mutual Fund?

According to Mike and Lorraine Racine, an Edmonton couple in their mid-30s, mutual funds were one of the biggest disappointments in their lives. In 2005, they invested $11,500 in the All-Canadian Resources mutual fund. Three years later, their original investment had lost over 20 percent, or about $2,500, during a period when most mutual funds were posting huge profits. What went wrong?

Three years after their investment, the Racines admitted they had invested money without researching the All-Canadian fund. They made their investment choice because Mike had heard a "high-powered" financial planner on a radio talk show raving about gold as the "ultimate" safe investment. Over the next two days, Mike had convinced Lorraine that gold was an investment that could be trusted. The Racines would have purchased the gold coins the talk show host was selling, but Mike lost the phone number. For lack of some other way to invest in gold, they decided to purchase shares in the All-Canadian Resources mutual fund. Besides, they reasoned, shares in a mutual fund would be a better investment than purchasing individual coins because mutual funds provided diversification and professional management. Both thought they were choosing the right investment. What could be better than a mutual fund that "specialized" in gold? Their investment would be a safe choice even if other investments went down in value.

The Racines also thought that since everybody was investing in mutual funds, they had to be the perfect investment. After all, there were thousands of different funds to choose from. Indeed, it seemed almost fashionable to invest in mutual funds. Because of professional management and diversification, there was no need to evaluate a mutual fund. Certainly, the fund manager knew more about picking the investments contained in the fund's portfolio than they did. It seemed mutual funds were almost guaranteed to increase in value. But after losing over 20 percent in three years, they realized that "almost guaranteed" was not the same thing as "guaranteed."

At the time of their investment, both had heard good things about All-Canadian mutual funds. A number of their friends had opened accounts with All-Canadian and had done well. And All-Canadian made it so easy! Just fill out an application, send the money, and let the professional managers make all the decisions. In fact, the Racines didn't realize that All-Canadian, the nation's largest mutual fund family, offered funds ranging from very conservative to very speculative investments. Simply put, they chose the wrong All-Canadian mutual fund.

Questions

1. Often, investors indicate that diversification and professional management are the two main reasons they choose mutual fund investments. How important do you consider these two factors? Why?

2. According to the Racines, everybody was investing in mutual funds—indeed, it seemed almost fashionable to invest in mutual funds. In your own words, what did the Racines do wrong?

3. Obtain information about a reputable mutual fund at the library or via the Internet. Then, complete a mutual fund evaluation form (see the Financial Planning Calculations feature on page 411) for this fund and answer the following questions:
   a. What sources of information did you use to evaluate the fund?
   b. What fees must investors pay to invest in the fund?
   c. What is the investment objective for the fund?
   d. How would you describe the fund's financial performance over the past 12 months? The past three years? The past five years?
   e. How would you rate the risk associated with the fund?
   f. Would you invest your money in this fund? Justify your answer.

CONTINUOUS CASE FOR PART 4

BUILDING AN INVESTMENT PROGRAM

Life Situation
Pamela, 43; Isaac, 45; three children, ages 16, 14, and 11

Financial Goals

• Evaluate current financial condition

• Build an investment portfolio that considers various risk factors

Financial Data

Monthly income	$ 4,900
Living expenses	4,450
Assets	262,700
Liabilities	84,600
Emergency fund	5,000

With approximately 20 years to retirement, Pamela and Isaac Mortimer want to establish a more aggressive investment program to accumulate funds for their long-term financial needs. Isaac does have a retirement program at work. This money, about $110,000, is invested in various conservative mutual funds. The Mortimers also established their own investment program about four years ago, and today, they have about $36,000 invested in conservative stocks and mutual funds.

In addition to their investment program, the Mortimers have accumulated $11,000 to help pay for the children's education. Also, they have $5,000 tucked away in a savings account that serves as the family's emergency fund. Finally,

both will qualify for the Canada Pension Plan when they reach retirement age.

Questions

1. How would you rate the Mortimers' financial condition at this stage in their lives?

2. Given the fact that Pamela is 43 and Isaac is 45 and they have three children who will soon begin their post-secondary education, what investment goals would be most appropriate for this middle-aged couple?

3. According to Pamela, "We both know we should have started our investment program sooner, but we always seemed to have 'emergencies' that took what extra money we had." Many investors feel the same way and, to compensate for a late start, often invest in highly speculative investments that promise large returns. Would you recommend such investments to a couple like the Mortimers? Explain your answer.

4. Describe the investment portfolio you would recommend for the Mortimers. Be sure to include *specific* types of investments (stocks, bonds, mutual funds, and so on), as well as information about the risk factor(s) associated with each investment alternative.

part **5**

Controlling Your Financial Future

chapter 14

Retirement Planning

LEARNING OBJECTIVES

LO1   Recognize the importance of retirement planning.

LO2   Analyze your current assets and liabilities for retirement.

LO3   Estimate your retirement spending needs.

LO4   Identify your retirement housing needs.

LO5   Determine your planned retirement income.

LO6   Develop a balanced budget based on your retirement income.

SCOPE OUT YOUR SOCIAL SECURITY BENEFITS

When Meg Hansen and her husband, Andrew Belanger, checked their CPP retirement benefits four years ago, they confirmed a nagging suspicion: They would have to play catchup to have a comfortable retirement. As a result, they closed their home renovation business in Red Deer, Alberta, and switched to careers that would provide steadier incomes. Hansen became a certified massage therapist, and Belanger returned to his previous occupation as a social worker.

The document that supplied the couple's wake-up call was the Canada Pension Plan (CPP) statement of contributions. This document provides you with a tally of your CPP contributions as well as estimates of the benefits you are eligible to receive. "When I got the statement, I realized I would get only about $300 a month in CPP benefits unless I did something about it," says Hansen, now 54. Belanger, now 65, would have been entitled to about $600,

but his career switch enabled him to draw $763 each month when he began collecting his CPP benefits.

When making retirement plans for clients, Marilyn, a personal finance adviser in Alberta, starts with the CPP personal contributor statement. She suggests that clients look at the benefit level and see if they can live on it. Often, they say they can't. "That serves as a motivator to make sure savings are moving in the right direction," she says.

The amount of the benefits you will receive is based on your earnings and your contributions to the plan. CPP covers virtually all working Canadians, except those who live in Quebec; Quebec workers come under the Quebec Pension Plan (QPP). These two plans are closely coordinated so that you are protected wherever you live in Canada. Whether in Canada or abroad at the time of retirement, you will receive your benefits in Canadian dollars.

By going to the Service Canada Web site, you can view a statement of your CPP contributions along with an estimate of the monthly benefit you can expect to receive when you retire at age 65. You may also apply for your personal statement of contributions by mail by submitting a written request.

It is important to check that the personal information that appears on your statement is accurate and complete. All CPP benefits you may be eligible for in the future are based on this information. If your name, birthdate, social insurance number, or earnings and contributions information is incorrect or missing you should ask to have it corrected.

Next, you need to determine whether you can live on your benefits. Keep in mind that the CPP was designed to replace only 25 percent of the salary from which you made your CPP contributions. There are also restrictions regarding when you actually retire. From 2012 to 2016, the Government of Canada is gradually changing the early pension reduction from 0.5 percent to 0.6 percent for each month you receive it before age 65. This means that by 2016, an individual who starts receiving their CPP retirement pension at the age of 60 will receive 36 percent less than if they had taken it at 65.

The CPP statement of contributions is an important personal finance tool. Make sure you carefully consider how the information it holds may affect your retirement plans and goals. It could be a real eye-opener.

QUESTIONS

1. What were Meg Hansen's and Andrew Belanger's concerns about retirement income?
2. Why did they close their home renovation business?
3. What document served as the couple's wake-up call?
4. How can the Internet assist you in retirement planning?

WHY RETIREMENT PLANNING?

Retirement can be a rewarding phase of your life. However, a successful, happy retirement doesn't just happen; it takes planning and continual evaluation. Thinking about retirement in advance can help you anticipate coming changes and gain a sense of control over the future.

Recognize the importance of retirement planning.

The ground rules for retirement planning are changing rapidly. Re-examine your retirement plans if you hold any of these misconceptions:

- My expenses will drop when I retire.
- My retirement will last only 15 years.
- I can depend on the government and my company pension to pay for my basic living expenses.
- My pension benefits will increase to keep pace with inflation.
- My employer's health insurance plan and Medicare will cover my medical expenses.
- There's plenty of time for me to start saving for retirement.
- Saving just a little bit won't help.

It is vital to engage in basic retirement planning activities throughout your working years and to update your retirement plans periodically. While it is never too late to begin sound financial planning, you can avoid many unnecessary and serious difficulties by starting this planning early. Saving now for the future requires tackling the trade-offs between spending and saving, thus taking advantage of the time value of money.

TACKLING THE TRADE-OFFS

Although exceptions exist, the old adage "You can't have your cake and eat it too" is particularly true in planning for retirement. For example, if you buy state-of-the-art home entertainment systems, drive expensive cars, and take extravagant vacations now, don't expect to retire with plenty of money.

Only by saving now and curtailing current spending can you ensure a comfortable retirement later. Yet, saving money doesn't come naturally to many young people. Ironically, although the time to begin saving is when you are young, the people who are in the best position to save are middle-aged.

THE IMPORTANCE OF STARTING EARLY

Consider this: If from age 25 to 65 you invest $300 per month and earn an average of 9 percent interest a year, you'll have $1.4 million in your retirement fund. Waiting just 10 years until age 35 to begin your $300-a-month investing will yield about $550,000, while if you wait 20 years to begin this investment, you will have only $201,000 at age 65. Exhibit 14–1 shows how even a $2,000 annual investment earning just 4 percent will grow.

For 40 years, your life, and probably your family's life, revolves around your job. One day, you retire, and practically every aspect of your life changes. There's less money, more time, and no daily structure.

You can expect to spend about 16 to 30 years in retirement—too many years to be bored, lonely, and broke. You want your retirement years to be rewarding, active, and rich in new experiences. It's never too early to begin planning for retirement; some experts even suggest starting while you are in school. Be certain you don't let your 35th birthday roll by without a comprehensive retirement plan. Remember, the longer you wait, the less you will be able to shape your life in retirement.

Exhibit 14–1

It's Never Too Late to Start Planning for Retirement

Start young. A look at the performance of $2,000 per year of retirement plan investments over time even at 4 percent shows the value of starting early.

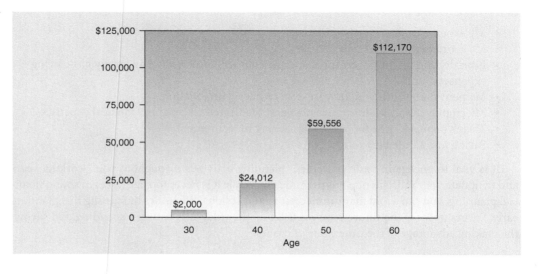

Retirement planning has both emotional and financial components. Emotional planning for retirement involves identifying your personal goals and setting out to meet them. Financial planning for retirement involves assessing your post-retirement needs and income and plugging any gaps you find. Financial planning for retirement is critical for several reasons:

1. You can expect to live in retirement for up to 20 years. At age 65, the average life expectancy is 19 more years for a man and 22 for a woman.
2. Government benefits and a private pension, if you have one, are most often insufficient to cover the cost of living.
3. Inflation may diminish the purchasing power of your retirement savings. Even a 2 percent rate of inflation will cause prices to double every 36 years.

You should anticipate your retirement years by analyzing your long-range goals. What does retirement mean to you? Does it mean an opportunity to stop work and relax, or does it mean time to travel, develop a hobby, or start a second career? Where and how do you want to live during your retirement? Once you consider your retirement goals, you are ready to evaluate their cost and assess whether you can afford them.

THE BASICS OF RETIREMENT PLANNING

Before you decide where you want to be financially, you have to find out where you are. Therefore, your first step is to analyze your current assets and liabilities. Then estimate your spending needs and adjust them for inflation. Next, evaluate your planned retirement income. Finally, increase your income by working part-time, if necessary. Recent articles and other retirement information may be accessed through online computer services. Exhibit 14–2 shows some good online sources for retirement planning using a personal computer.

CONCEPT CHECK 14–1

1. Why is retirement planning important?
2. What are the four basic steps in retirement planning?

CONDUCTING A FINANCIAL ANALYSIS

As you learned in Chapter 2, your assets include everything you own that has value: cash on hand and in chequing and savings accounts; the current value of your stocks, bonds, and other investments; the current value of your house, car, jewellery, and furnishings; and the current value of your life insurance and pensions. Your liabilities are everything you owe: your

LO2

Analyze your current assets and liabilities for retirement.

Exhibit 14–2

Using a Personal Computer for Retirement Planning

General Web Sites
Canadian Bankers Association (cba.ca; see Consumer Information, Saving and Investing)
Globeinvestor (globeinvestor.ca)
Canoe Money (canoe.ca/money)
Service Canada (servicecanada.gc.ca)
CARP, Canada's Association for the Fifty-Plus (carp.ca)
Software Packages
Quicken Cash Manager (http://quicken.intuit.ca/personal-finance-software/index.jsp)
RRIFmetic, Personal Use Edition, by Fimetrics (fimetrics.com)
RetireWare (retireware.com)

mortgage, car payments, credit card balances, taxes due, and so forth. The difference between the two totals is your *net worth*, a figure you should increase each year as you move toward retirement. Use Exhibit 14–3 to calculate your net worth now and at retirement.

REVIEW YOUR ASSETS

Reviewing your assets to ensure they are sufficient for retirement is a sound idea. Make any necessary adjustments in your investments and holdings to fit your circumstances. In reviewing your assets, consider the following factors:

HOUSING   If you own your house, it is probably your biggest single asset. However, the amount tied up in your house may be out of line with your retirement income. You might consider selling your house and buying a less expensive one. The selection of a smaller, more easily maintained house can also decrease your maintenance costs. The difference saved can be put into a savings account, Guaranteed Investment Certificates (GICs), or other income-producing investments.

If you wish to remain in your existing home, programs are available to assist homeowners with significant home equity but a need for cash. In 1986, the Canada Home Income Plan (CHIP) created Canada's first lifetime reverse mortgage. A reverse mortgage is designed exclusively for homeowners age 55 and older. It provides the homeowner with a tax-free income in the form of a loan that is paid back (with interest) when the home is sold or the homeowner dies. You can receive up to 50 percent of the appraised value of your home. The specific amount is based on your age (and that of your spouse), the location and type of housing you own, and the current appraised value of the home. To find out how much you might get, go to chip.ca and request an estimate.

Exhibit 14–3

Review Your Assets, Liabilities, and Net Worth

Net worth: Assets of $108,800 minus liabilities of $16,300 equals $92,500.

	Sample Figures	Your Figures
Assets: What We Own		
Cash:		
Chequing account	$ 800	_____
Savings account	4,500	_____
Investments:		
Canada Savings Bonds (current cash-in value)	5,000	_____
Stocks, mutual funds	4,500	_____
Life insurance:		
Cash value, accumulated dividends	10,000	_____
Company pension rights:		
Accrued pension benefit	20,000	_____
Property:		
House (resale value)	50,000	_____
Furniture and appliances	8,000	_____
Collections and jewellery	2,000	_____
Vehicle	3,000	_____
Other:		
Loan to brother	1,000	_____
Gross assets	$108,800	_____
Liabilities: What We Owe		
Current unpaid bills	600	_____
Home mortgage (remaining balance)	9,700	_____
Vehicle loan	1,200	_____
Property taxes	1,100	_____
Home improvement loan	3,700	_____
Total liabilities	$ 16,300	_____

The money is received tax-free. It is not added to your taxable income and does not affect Old Age Security (OAS) and Guaranteed Income Supplement (GIS) payments you may be entitled to receive. With a CHIP Home Income Plan you can choose how you want to receive the money. You can receive a lump sum advance or a monthly income based on the current market value of the home, the loan's interest rate, and its term. At the end of the term, the loan and accrued interest must be repaid from the homeowner's estate, or by selling the house if the homeowner is still living.

It is possible that the money lost to compound interest could be greater than the "disposable" cash received by the homeowner, given a situation where the person lives for many years. This is something that must be given the proper consideration before opting for a reverse mortgage.

Reverse annuity mortgages (RAM) are used to buy a life annuity from an insurance company that pays out a given sum of money on a regular basis for as long as the homeowner lives. When the homeowner dies or the house is sold, the mortgage and accrued interest must be repaid. The amount you can borrow increases as you grow older, usually in the range of 15 to 45 percent of the equity in your home.

With a reverse annuity mortgage the lender holds a mortgage on your house, but as the owner you are not required to either move or sell the house. Another advantage is that this revenue is not taxed since the income you receive is generated from the equity in your home. Also, you are protected against a decline in real estate values because if the value of your home falls beneath the mortgage amount, you are accountable only for the actual value of the home.

There are two disadvantages to this arrangement, though both are essentially the same. First, a reverse annuity mortgage is essentially a choice to *spend your equity*. You are choosing to reduce your net worth. Second—the other side of the same coin—is that the remainder owing on your mortgage at the time of your death will be paid by your estate, thereby reducing the amount of inheritance available to your family.

> **reverse annuity mortgage (RAM)** A loan based on the equity in a home that provides elderly homeowners with tax-free income and is paid back with interest when the home is sold or the homeowner dies.

LIFE INSURANCE   You may have set up your life insurance to provide support and education for your children. Now you may want to convert some of this asset into cash or income (an annuity). Another possibility is to reduce premium payments by decreasing the face value of your insurance. This will give you extra money to spend on living expenses or invest for additional income.

OTHER INVESTMENTS   Evaluate any other investments you have. When you chose them, you may have been more interested in making your money grow than in getting an early return. Has the time come to take the income from your investments? You may now want to take dividends rather than reinvest them.

After thoroughly reviewing your assets, estimate your spending needs during your retirement years.

CONCEPT CHECK 14–2

1. How can you calculate your net worth today and at retirement?

RETIREMENT LIVING EXPENSES

The exact amount of money you will need in retirement is impossible to predict. However, you can estimate the amount you will need by considering the changes you anticipate in your spending patterns, and in where and how you live.

Your spending patterns will probably change. Although no two families adjust their spending patterns to changes in the life cycle in the same manner, the tabulation in Exhibit 14–4 can guide you in anticipating your own future spending patterns.

> *LO3*
> Estimate your retirement spending needs.

Exhibit 14–4

Average Household
Expenditures,
Canada 2012

	Average Expenditure per Household $	Household Reporting Expenditures %
Total Expenditures	**75,443**	**100%**
Total current consumption	56,279	75%
Food expenditures	7,739	10%
Shelter	15,811	21%
Principal accommodation	14,373	19%
Other accommodation	1,438	2%
Household operation	4,111	5%
Household furnishings and equipment	2,183	3%
Clothing and accessories	3,461	5%
Transportation	11,216	15%
Health care	2,285	3%
Personal care	1,194	2%
Recreation	3,373	5%
Education	1,386	2%
Reading materials and other printed matter	214	0%
Tobacco products and alcoholic beverages	1,274	2%
Games of chance	202	0%
Miscellaneous expenditures	1,430	2%
Income taxes	13,060	17%
Personal insurance payments and pension contributions	4,272	6%
Gifts of money, alimony, and contributions to charity	1,831	2%

SOURCE: Adapted from Statistics Canada's Summary Tables, "Average Household Expenditures, by Province and Territory," http://www.statcan.gc.ca/tables-tableaux/sum-som/l01/cst01/famil130a-eng.htm, accessed June 23, 2014.

The following expenses may be lowered or eliminated:

- *Work expenses.* You will no longer make payments into your retirement fund. You will not be buying gas and oil for the drive back and forth to work, or paying for train or bus fares. You may be buying fewer lunches away from home.

- *Clothing expenses.* You will probably need fewer clothes after you retire, and your dress may be more casual.
- *Housing expenses.* If you have paid off your house mortgage by the time you retire, your cost of housing may decrease (although increases in property taxes and insurance may offset this gain).
- *Federal income taxes.* Your federal income taxes will probably be lower. No federal tax has to be paid on some forms of income, such as GIS benefits, trading down on your home, or getting a reverse mortgage. You will probably pay taxes at a lower rate because your taxable income will be lower.

You can also estimate which of the following expenses may increase:

- *Insurance.* The loss of your employer's contribution to health and life insurance will increase your own payments.
- *Medical expenses.* Although medical expenses vary from one person to the next, they tend to increase with age.

Did you know?

THE EFFECTS OF INFLATION OVER TIME

This chart shows you what $10,000 will be worth in 10, 20, and 30 years assuming a 2 percent rate of inflation.

$8,203.48 — in 10 years
$6,729.71 — in 20 years
$5,520.71 — in 30 years

Retirement? Ah, yes: *retirement*. Better to save now and avoid the deprivation later. You know the spiel: government pensions, a joke; corporate pensions, another joke; job security, gone; the 30-minute-pizza guarantee, not any more! With such an uncertain future, it's best to be prepared.

There are monetary returns, although the pros contend that the psychological feeling of safety that regular investing provides trumps all. While the boomers freak about not having saved enough for retirement, young people have time to spare. With a long-term horizon, investing is safe, easy, and relatively hassle free. Mutual funds have made retirement investing more convenient than sleeping through that 9 a.m. class. Automatic investment plans can deduct as little as $25 a month from bank accounts or paycheques. Even pocket cash can get things rockin': Take that double tall latte ($4.00) and raisin cinnamon scone ($2.25) you snag each morning and put it in an index fund. You'll have over $20,000 before your first mid-life crisis. Keep it up until your second, and you'll have accumulated over $110,000—more than enough to pay for intensive therapy and a week in Boca. Systematic investing is the fiscal equivalent of a tetanus shot: a regular bummer that doesn't hurt as bad as you might think.

If you're frightened of investing, worried that a crash or prolonged bear market will turn your retirement into an episode of "Good Times," *you've gotta chill!* Don't waste the Xanax worrying about the market because the fact is that over a long period of time, stocks go up. Over a two-year time horizon, the market's *worst* performance has been about 2 percent. While it might seem you can't afford to invest, the unfortunate reality is that you can't afford not to. With inflation humming along, common stocks are the only asset class that will consistently keep you ahead, the pros advise.

RRSPs, RPPs, pension plans—stock 'em full of quality mutual funds and chill. "Home runs" look great on the cover of *Money* magazine, but real wealth happens over time. Compound interest, or the titillating phenomenon of earning interest on interest, provides hefty gains to patient investors. This "get-rich-slowly" scheme won't get your picture in *Barron's*, but it will provide for an adequate retirement.

- *Expenses for leisure activities.* With more free time, many retirees spend more money on leisure activities. You may want to put aside extra money for a retirement trip or other large recreational expenses.
- *Gifts and contributions.* Many retirees who continue to spend the same amount of money on gifts and contributions find their spending in this area takes a larger share of their smaller income. Therefore, you may want to re-evaluate such spending.

Using the worksheet in Exhibit 14–5 on page 429, list your present expenses and estimate what these expenses would be if you were retired. To make a realistic comparison, list your major spending categories, starting with fixed expenses, such as rent or mortgage payments, utilities, insurance premiums, and taxes. Then, list variable expenses—food, clothing, transportation, and so on, as well as miscellaneous expenditures, such as medical expenses, entertainment, vacations, gifts, contributions, and unforeseen expenses.

Be sure you have an emergency fund for unforeseen expenses. Even when you live a tranquil life, unexpected events can occur.

Did you know?

Many financial planners say that you will need about 80 percent of your current (pre-tax) earnings to maintain your standard of living in retirement. For example, if you earn $80,000 now, you might aim for $64,000 of income in retirement. However, this is only a general rule. You'll need to look at your own circumstances to decide what level of income is right for you.

SOURCE: http://www.investopedia.com/university/retirement/retirement2.asp.

Financial Planning Calculations

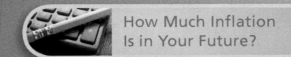

How Much Inflation Is in Your Future?

Years to Retirement	Estimated Annual Rate of Inflation Between Now and Retirement									
	3%	4%	5%	6%	7%	8%	9%	10%	11%	12%
5	1.2	1.2	1.3	1.3	1.4	1.5	1.5	1.6	1.7	1.8
8	1.3	1.4	1.5	1.6	1.7	1.8	2.0	2.1	2.3	2.5
10	1.4	1.5	1.6	1.8	2.0	2.2	2.4	2.6	2.8	3.1
12	1.5	1.6	1.8	2.0	2.3	2.5	2.8	3.1	3.5	3.9
15	1.6	1.8	2.1	2.4	2.8	3.2	3.6	4.2	4.8	5.5
18	1.8	2.0	2.4	2.8	3.4	4.0	4.7	5.6	6.5	7.7
20	2.0	2.2	2.7	3.2	3.9	4.7	5.6	6.7	8.1	9.6
25	2.1	2.7	3.4	4.3	5.4	6.8	8.6	10.8	13.6	17.0

1. Choose from the first column the approximate number of years until your retirement.
2. Choose an estimated annual rate of inflation. The rate of inflation cannot be predicted accurately and varies from year to year.
3. Find the inflation factor corresponding to the number of years until your retirement and the estimated annual inflation rate. (Example: 10 years to retirement combined with a 4 percent estimated annual inflation rate yields a 1.5 inflation factor.)
4. Multiply the inflation factor by your estimated retirement income and your estimated retirement expenses. (Example: $6,000 × 1.5 = $9,000.)

Total annual inflated retirement income: $_____.

Total annual inflated retirement expenses: $_____.

SOURCES: These figures are from a compound interest table showing the effective yield of lump-sum investments after inflation that appeared in Charles D. Hodgman, ed., *Mathematical Tables from the Handbook of Chemistry and Physics* (Cleveland: Chemical Rubber Publishing, 1959); *Citicorp Consumer Views*, July 1985, pp. 2–3, © Citicorp, 1985; *Financial Planning Tables*, A. G. Edwards, August 1991.

ADJUST YOUR EXPENSES FOR INFLATION

You now have a list of your likely monthly (and annual) expenses if you were to retire today. With inflation, however, those expenses will not be fixed. The potential loss of buying power due to inflation is what makes planning ahead so important. Since 1991, inflation in Canada has ranged between 1 and 3 percent.

To help you plan for this likely increase in your expenses, use the inflation factor table in the Financial Planning Calculations feature above.

CONCEPT CHECK 14–3

1. How can you estimate the amount of money you will need during retirement?
2. What expenses are likely to increase or decrease during retirement?
3. How might you adjust your expenses for inflation?

Monthly Expenses		
Item	**Present**	**Retirement**
Fixed expenses:		
Rent or mortgage payment	$_____	$_____
Taxes	_____	_____
Insurance	_____	_____
Savings	_____	_____
Debt payment	_____	_____
Other	_____	_____
Total fixed expenses	_____	_____
Variable expenses:		
Food and beverages	_____	_____
Household operation and maintenance	_____	_____
Furnishings and equipment	_____	_____
Clothing	_____	_____
Personal	_____	_____
Transportation	_____	_____
Medical expenses	_____	_____
Recreation and education	_____	_____
Gifts and contributions	_____	_____
Other	_____	_____
Total variable expenses	_____	_____
Total expenses	_____	_____

Exhibit 14–5

Your Present Monthly Expenses and Your Estimated Monthly Retirement Expenses

PLANNING YOUR RETIREMENT HOUSING

Think about where you will want to live. If you think you will want to live in another city, it's a good idea to plan vacations now in areas you might enjoy later. When you find one that appeals to you, visit that area during various times of the year to experience the year-round climate. Meet the people. Check into available activities, transportation, and taxes. Be realistic about what you will have to give up and what you will gain.

LO4 Identify your retirement housing needs.

Where you live in retirement can influence your financial needs. You must make some important decisions about whether to stay in your present community and in your current home. Everyone has unique needs and preferences; only *you* can determine the location and housing that are best for you.

Consider what moving involves. Moving is expensive, and if you are not satisfied with your new location, returning to your former home may be impossible. Consider the social aspects of moving. Will you want to be near your children, other relatives, and good friends? Are you prepared for new circumstances?

TYPE OF HOUSING

Housing needs often change as people grow older. The ease and cost of maintenance, and proximity to public transportation, shopping, church/synagogue, and entertainment often become more important to people when they retire.

Many housing alternatives exist, several of which were discussed in Chapter 7. Staying in their present homes, whether a single-family dwelling, a condominium, or an apartment, is the alternative preferred by most people approaching retirement. That's what Mike and Abby Wootton decided to do after Mike took early retirement at age 47 from his job as a service manager of a Saskatoon Ford dealership in 2013. Even though the couple had already paid off the mortgage on their small, three-bedroom ranch house and could have moved into a bigger or fancier place, all Mike wanted to do was tinker in the garage and dabble in the stock market.

Diane Forrest of Grenville, Ontario, has seen the future, and she wants to be prepared. Diane, 69, has osteoporosis, just as her mother did. Although she's not having difficulty now, she knows the debilitating bone condition eventually could make it difficult, if not impossible, to navigate steep stairs, cramped bathrooms, and narrow doorways. So, two years ago, she and her husband Carl, a 72-year-old retired sales executive, moved into a novel type of home, one that can comfortably accommodate them no matter what disabilities old age may bring. Called a "universal design home," their residence is on the cutting edge of an architectural concept that an aging population may well embrace. The only house of its kind in the neighbourhood, it has wide doors, pull-out cabinet shelves, easy-to-reach electrical switches, and dozens of other features useful for elderly persons or those with disabilities. Yet, these features are incorporated into the design unobtrusively.

This new setup suits the Forrests just fine. Unlike their peers who are moving into continuing-care communities, they want to stay where they have always lived, near their three children and around people of all ages. They now have a home that can accommodate a wheelchair and even has a room for a nurse, if the need arises. "We hope to be able to live here for the rest of our lives," says Diane—in comfort and with all the touches they need to ease their daily tasks.

For seniors who wish to continue living in their own homes, the Canada Mortgage and Housing Corporation (CMHC) offers the following programs:

1. **Home Adaptations for Seniors' Independence Program:** Helps homeowners pay for minor modifications, such as adding handrails and grab bars.
2. **Emergency Repair Program:** Helps low-income homeowners in rural or remote areas make emergency repairs to keep their homes safe.
3. **Residential Rehabilitation Assistance Program:** Helps low-income homeowners, or landlords who own units occupied by low-income tenants, pay for repairs to bring their properties up to minimum health and safety standards. This program also helps owners modify their homes to make them accessible to those who are disabled.

For more information about these programs, visit cmhc.ca.

For seniors who no longer wish to live in their homes, other housing alternatives are available. The most common ones are *adult lifestyle/retirement communities*, *life lease housing*, and *retirement homes*.

Adult lifestyle/retirement communities provide independent living residences for retirees or semi-retirees in a community of healthy seniors. Residences can be bungalows, townhouses, or smaller homes. Amenities may include 24-hour security, social interaction with peers, and other recreational activities.

Life lease housing is a form of housing tenure. A tenant is given the right to live in a dwelling unit in return for an upfront payment and monthly maintenance fees. Typically, life lease housing is operated by non-profit organizations such as charities.

Retirement homes are private businesses that provide seniors various combinations of accommodation, support services, and personal care. Retirement homes are typically run by for-profit organizations. Care and support services provided are not regulated by provincial governments.

Whatever retirement housing alternative you choose, make sure you know what you are signing and understand what you are buying.

AVOIDING RETIREMENT HOUSING TRAPS

Too many people make the move without doing enough research, and invariably it's a mistake. How can retirees avoid being surprised by hidden tax and financial traps when they move? Here are some tips from retirement specialists on how to uncover hidden taxes and other costs of a retirement area before moving:

- E mail, write or call the local chamber of commerce to get an economic profile and details on area property taxes.
- Contact the province's tax department to find out provincial income, sales, and inheritance taxes and special exemptions for retirees. If your pension will be taxed by the province you're leaving, check whether the new province will give you credit for those taxes.

adult lifestyle/ retirement communities Independent living residences (bungalows, townhouses, or smaller homes) for retirees or semi-retirees in a community of healthy seniors.

life lease housing A form of housing tenure where a tenant is given the right to live in a dwelling unit in return for an upfront payment and monthly maintenance fees.

retirement homes Private businesses that provide seniors various combinations of accommodation, support services, and personal care.

- Subscribe to the weekend edition of a local newspaper.
- Call a local accountant to find out which taxes are rising.
- Check with local utilities to estimate your energy costs. Visit the area in as many seasons as possible. Talk to retirees and other local residents about costs of health care, auto insurance, food, and clothing.
- Rent for a while instead of buying immediately.

CONCEPT CHECK 14–4

1. What are some housing options for retirees?
2. How can retirees avoid retirement housing traps?

PLANNING YOUR RETIREMENT INCOME

Once you determine your approximate future expenses, you must evaluate the sources and amounts of your retirement income. Possible sources of income for many retirees are public pension plans, employer pension plans, and personal retirement plans (see Exhibit 14–6).

LO5
Determine your planned retirement income.

PUBLIC PENSIONS

Public pensions have existed since 1927 and were initially paid only to those over the age of 70. Federal programs are the major source of public retirement pensions, but most provinces and the territories also provide income supplements for residents in financial need.

Canada's retirement income system has three levels. The Old Age Security (OAS) provides the first level, or foundation. If you meet certain residence requirements, you'll be entitled to a modest monthly pension once you reach the age of 65 (or, starting in 2013, at the age of 67). The Canada Pension Plan (CPP), or Quebec Pension Plan (QPP), is the second level of the system. It provides you with a monthly retirement pension as early as 60, if you have paid into it. Also available are the Guaranteed Income Supplement (GIS) and Spouse's Allowance (SPA). Public pensions are not intended to meet all your financial needs in retirement. Rather, they provide a modest base for you to build upon with additional, private savings. The third level of the retirement income system consists of private pensions and savings.

The various types of public pensions were and are tied to either residency requirements or income requirements, and could be contributory or non-contributory.

CANADA/QUEBEC PENSION PLAN (CPP/QPP)   The CPP dates to 1966, when the federal government started the program as a mandatory defined benefit indexed pension plan for all Canadians (besides residents of Quebec, who have a similar plan called the Quebec Pension Plan [QPP]). There are three kinds of Canada Pension Plan benefits: disability benefits (which include pensions for disabled contributors and benefits for their dependent children), a

Pensions	Non-Pension Savings
Old Age Security (OAS)	Registered Retirement Savings Plan (RRSP)
Guaranteed Income Supplement (GIS)	Deferred Profit Sharing Plan (DPSP)
Canada Pension Plan (CPP)	House (if you trade down)
Employer's Registered Pension Plan (RPP)	Vacation property (if you will sell)
	Tax shelters
	Reverse mortgage
	Unsheltered savings
	Locked-in funds

Exhibit 14–6

Sources of Retirement Income

SOURCE: Ho & Robinson, *Personal Financial Planning,* Third Edition (Captus Press, 2000, page 383).

retirement pension, and survivor benefits (which include the death benefit, the surviving spouse's pension, and the children's benefit).

CPP CONTRIBUTIONS   According to the official Service Canada Web site (servicecanada.gc.ca), the amount you pay is based on your salary. If you are self-employed, your contribution is based on your net business income, after expenses. You do not contribute on any other source of income, such as investment earnings. If, during a year, you contributed too much or earned less than a set minimum amount, you will receive a refund of contributions when you complete your income tax return.

You only pay contributions on your annual earnings between set minimum and maximum levels, which are called your "pensionable" earnings. The minimum level is frozen at $3,500. The maximum level is adjusted each January, based on increases in the average wage.

Depending on whether you earn (1) less than the minimum level of pensionable earnings; (2) between the minimum and maximum; or (3) more than the maximum level of pensionable earnings in a given year, you can use the tables and the three examples provided on the Service Canada Web site to calculate your contribution or determine whether or not you will receive a refund. For more information, visit servicecanada.gc.ca/eng/isp/ cpp/contribrates.shtml.

BENEFITS   Both CPP and QPP benefits are payable at age 65, whether you continue to work or not. You can also start to receive your benefits as early as age 60 or as late as age 70. The amount of your pension will depend on how much and for how long you *have contributed to the CPP* and on your age when you want your pension to start. If you take it before age 65, your pension will be reduced, by up to 32.4 percent at age 60. If you take it after age 65, your pension may be larger, by up to 42 percent at age 70. The full CPP benefit is based on 25 percent of your average monthly pensionable earnings, adjusted for increases in each year's maximum pensionable earnings.

There are two clauses in the CPP/QPP regulations that favour a better benefit for you. The *dropout clause* allows you to leave the lowest 15 percent of your monthly contributions during your working years out of your calculations of contribution rates. The *child-rearing clause* allows up to seven years per child of not contributing. The overall objective of these clauses is to minimize the effect on your CPP benefits of financially adverse life events.

Review Exhibit 14–7 for the types of benefits available through the CPP, the average monthly benefit in 2014, and the maximum monthly benefit for 2014. You should also note that a portion of your CPP benefits can be assigned to your spouse or common-law partner, provided that he or she is at least 60 years old. This may give your family a tax advantage if your spouse is not in a position to receive CPP benefits.

According to the Canada Revenue Agency:

Pension Adjustment (PA)   "The RRSP/PA system has a single maximum for tax assisted retirement savings of 18% of earned income (up to a yearly dollar limit) that applies to total contributions and benefits earned under all registered retirement plans. Pension adjustment (PA) ensures that all employees at comparable income levels will have access to comparable tax assistance, regardless of what type of registered pension plan, DPSP or RRSP they belong to."

Pension Adjustment Reversal (PAR)   "The RRSP/PA system has a comprehensive limit for tax assisted retirement savings of 18% of earned income up to a dollar limit (i.e., money

Type of Benefit	Average Monthly Benefit (January 2014)	Maximum Monthly Benefit (2014)
Retirement (at age 65)	$633.46	$1,038.33
Disability	$896.87	$1,236.35
Survivor—younger than 65	$401.53	$567.91
Survivor—65 and older	$302.28	$623.00
Children of disabled contributors	$230.72	$230.72
Children of deceased contributors	$230.72	$230.72
Death (maximum one-time payment)	$2,285.48	$2,500.00
Combined benefits—survivor/retirement (retirement at 65)	$799.79	$1,038.33
Combined benefits—survivor/disability	$1,029.05	$1,236.35

Exhibit 14–7

Canada Pension Plan Payment Rates January–December 2014

Canada Pension Plan rates are adjusted every January if there are increases in the cost of living as measured by the Consumer Price Index.

SOURCE: "Canada Pension Plan—Payment Rates: January–December 2014," http://www.servicecanada .gc.ca/eng/services/pensions/cpp/payments/. Accessed June 23, 2014. Reproduced with the permission of the Minister of Public Works and Government Services Canada, 2014.

purchase limit) that applies to total contributions under registered retirement savings plans (RRSPs), money purchase provisions (MP provisions) of registered pension plans and deferred profit sharing plans (DPSPs) and benefits accrued under defined benefit provisions (DB provisions) of registered pension plans (RPP). . . . The PA is the total of all pension credits for the year in respect of the individual and the employer. An individual receives a pension credit for each DPSP or benefit provision of a registered pension plan (RPP) in which they participate during the year. In most cases the employee participates in only one provision; therefore, their pension credit will also be their PA.

PAR is used to restore an individual's RRSP room when a member terminates their membership in a benefit provision of a registered pension plan or deferred profit sharing plan (DPSP)."

Past Service Pension Adjustments (PSPAs)   These "ensure that benefit upgrades and past service purchases to defined benefit pension plans are charged against the 18% limit."

For more information on PA, PAR, and PSPA, see the Canada Revenue Agency Web site at cra-arc.gc.ca/tx/rgstrd/papspapar-fefespfer/menu-eng.html.*

OLD AGE SECURITY (OAS)   This public pension benefit was introduced in the Old Age Security Act, which came into effect in 1952. It is indexed to inflation on a quarterly basis. If you are over the age of 65 and have been a resident of Canada for at least 40 years since age 18, you qualify for full OAS benefits. With a minimum of 10 years of residency, you receive 1/40 of the full benefit for each year you were a resident of Canada between the ages of 18 and 65. Note that beginning in 2023, the minimum age to qualify to OAS will be 67.

This benefit is taxed and is *clawed back* at a rate of 15 cents for each dollar once your net income (as of 2008) exceeds $64,718. By the time your net income is $104,903, the entire OAS received must be repaid to the federal government.

GUARANTEED INCOME SUPPLEMENT (GIS)   Also introduced in the OAS Act of 1952, this pension is payable to low-income OAS recipients who are 65 and older. The amount you receive depends on your marital status as well as your income. As of 2014, the maximum monthly supplement for single individuals with no income was $747.86. For each $24 of annual

*SOURCE: cra-arc.gc.ca.

income reported by the individual, the monthly benefit is reduced by $1 ($12 per year). Thus, earned income essentially reduces benefits by 50 percent. This is not a tax, but rather an adjustment to benefits reported upon filing taxes. OAS benefits are not included as income for determining reductions to the GIS benefits. This benefit is not taxed. For a single individual, the GIS stops being paid completely if your income is $16,228 or higher.

SURVIVOR ALLOWANCE   Yet another pension introduced in the OAS Act of 1952 was the spouse's allowance, newly termed the *survivor allowance*. These benefits are payable to widows, widowers, and the spouses of OAS beneficiaries who are between 60 and 65 years old.

EMPLOYER PENSION PLANS

Another possible source of retirement income is the pension plan your company offers. With employer plans, your employer contributes to your retirement benefits, and sometimes you contribute, too. These plans are called either *contributory* or *non-contributory*. Pension plans administered by employers on behalf of their employees are formally called a *Registered Pension Plan*, or RPP. An employer pension plan that includes employee contributions enables employees to defer current taxation on a portion of their salary.

Since private pension plans vary, you should find out (1) when you become eligible for pension benefits, and (2) to what benefits you will be entitled. Most employer plans are defined contribution or defined benefit plans.

defined benefit pension plan A plan that specifies the benefits the employee will receive at the normal retirement age.

DEFINED BENEFIT PENSION PLAN   In a **defined benefit pension plan**, the plan document specifies the dollar value of benefits payable to the employee at his or her normal retirement age. The plan itself does not specify how much money the employer must contribute annually. The plan's actuary determines the annual employer contribution required so that the plan will have sufficient funds to pay out the promised benefits as each participant retires. If the fund is inadequate, the employer must make additional contributions. Because of their actuarial aspects, defined benefit plans tend to be more complicated and more expensive to administer than defined contribution plans. It is generally the employer's responsibility to ensure that sufficient funds are available to pay your pension when you retire. The employer assumes the risk of investing all contributions wisely to guarantee the future value of your pension. Since the value of a defined benefit pension plan increases exponentially with seniority, the cost to the employee of terminating his employment late in his career but prior to his normal retirement age is high, posing a problem in this age of increased career and job mobility.

This is one reason why many companies are transitioning their retirement plans from defined benefit to defined contribution plans. "Paternalistic employers are dying fast—if they're not already dead," says an actuary with an international consulting firm. The result is that "the shift to defined contributions has forced employees to take more responsibility for retirement, since they have discretion over how to invest their money and must make substantive decisions about their own financial futures."*

defined contribution pension plan Also called a *money purchase pension plan*, this plan specifies the contributions from both the employee and/or employer, but it does not guarantee the specific pension benefit that the employee will receive.

DEFINED CONTRIBUTION PENSION PLAN   Over the last three decades, the prevalence of defined contribution pension plans has continued to grow rapidly. A **defined contribution pension plan** involves an individual account for each employee; therefore, these plans are sometimes called *money purchase pension plans*. The plan document describes the respective amounts that the employee and/or employer must contribute, but it does not promise any specific dollar benefit. When a plan participant retires, the benefit is the total amount in his or her account, including all past investment earnings on amounts deposited into the employee's account. Exhibit 14–8 compares defined benefit plans to defined contribution plans.

---

*SOURCE: Carol Kleinman, "Firms Shifting Retirement Planning, Risk to Workers," *Chicago Tribune*, January 19, 1992, sec. 8, p. 1.

Exhibit 14–8   Comparison of Defined Benefit and Defined Contribution Plans

	Defined Benefit	**Defined Contribution**
Determined in advance	Benefit after retirement	Contributions while working
Payment in retirement	Determined by employer	Depends on investment returns
Vesting period	Usually five years	Usually 0–2 years
When accrued	Greatest wealth accrues at end of career	Evenly, throughout career
Funding	Employer	Employees; some employer matching
Portability (changing employers)	Difficult to transfer assets	Easy to transfer assets
Control of assets	Employer manages investments	Employees manage investments; choices designated by employer
Investment risk	Employer bears investment risk	Employees bear investment risk
Administrative costs	Large administrative costs when employee turnover is high	Less costly for firms to administer with an increasingly mobile workforce

Defined contribution plans include the following:

1. *Money-purchase pension plans.* Your employer promises to set aside a certain amount for you each year, generally a percentage of your earnings.
2. *Employee Stock Ownership Plan (ESOP).* Your employer's contribution consists in buying stock in the company for you. The stock is usually held in trust until you retire, at which time you can receive your shares or sell them at their fair market value.
3. *Profit-sharing plans.* Your employer's contribution depends on the company's profits.

An Example: How Funds Accumulate   All earnings in a tax-sheltered annuity (TSA) grow and are not currently taxed. Dollars saved on a pre-tax basis while your earnings grow will enhance the growth of your funds.

The disadvantage of a defined contribution plan is that retirement income is not guaranteed, since it depends on market conditions. On the positive side, if the investment portfolio is managed well you could end up with a better income than you expected (see Exhibit 14–9).

	Without a TSA	**With a TSA**
Your income	$28,000	$28,000
TSA contribution (18%)	0	−5,040
Taxable income	$28,000	$22,960
Estimated federal income tax (15%)	−4,200	−3,444
Gross take-home pay	$23,800	$19,516
After-tax savings contributions	−5,040	0
Net take-home pay	$18,760	$19,516
Increase in take-home pay with a TSA		$ 756

Exhibit 14–9

Accumulating Funds With or Without a TSA

SOURCES: canadianfundwatch.com/modules.php?name=News&file=article&sid=28; cra-arc.gc.ca/tx/ndvdls/fq/txrts-eng.html.

vesting An employee's right to keep at least a portion of the benefits accrued under an employer pension plan, even if the employee leaves the company before retiring.

What happens to your benefits under an employer pension plan if you change jobs? One of the most important aspects of such plans is vesting. **Vesting** is your right to at least a portion of the benefits accrued from the employer's contributions to the pension plan in the event that you leave the company before you retire. Typically, you become vested after completing two years of continuous service with the participating employer. If your employment terminates before your benefits are vested, you are entitled to a refund of your own contributions plus interest earned.

DEFERRED PROFIT SHARING PLAN (DPSP)

Although not a registered pension plan governed by federal pension legislation, a DPSP can be considered another form of a company pension plan. A DPSP is a form of retirement saving set up for contributions from the employer only; these contributions are tax-deductible for the company. The contribution is based on the company's net income according to an agreed-upon formula, and you are not taxed on the DPSP holdings until you withdraw them.

One issue to consider with registered pension plans and DPSPs is that all contributions made to a defined contribution plan and deferred profit sharing plan, or deemed to have been made in the case of a defined benefit plan, reduce your personal RRSP contribution room. Furthermore, while your portion of the contribution to registered pension plans of both types (DCPP and DBPP) generates a non-refundable tax credit, the employer's contribution to a DPSP does not. This is because the contributions that you receive are placed in a trust account until your retirement or termination of employment. These contributions and the interest accrued in the trust fund are not considered payable until they are actually distributed to you. Upon withdrawal, they are taxed as income or they can be further tax-sheltered by purchasing an annuity or transferring them to an individual RRSP.

GROUP REGISTERED RETIREMENT SAVINGS PLAN

This type of plan is an RRSP set up for a particular company's employees. The advantage this plan may have over a regular RPP relates to liquidity. Group RRSPs are the property of the employees, so they can take money out if they are in financial need (despite disincentives set up by the company to discourage this). Additionally, participation in a group RRSP by an employee may lower payroll tax withholding. The principal disadvantage to a group RRSP is that it may provide a smaller return than would a company pension plan.

PLAN PORTABILITY

At one time, employees who changed jobs could not take their pension credits with them. Recent legislation enforcing *pension portability*, the right to transfer pension credits from one employer to another, changed that. Now, workers with vesting rights have three different options when they change jobs. They can leave their pension credits with their former employer and receive a pension on retirement, transfer their credits to their new employer if that firm's policy permits it, or transfer their benefits to a locked-in RRSP. In cases where the employee has not met the criteria allowing them vesting rights, changing companies will signify a total loss of their pension credits.

Use the checklist in Exhibit 14–10 to help you determine what your pension plan provides and requires.

PERSONAL RETIREMENT PLANS

In addition to the retirement plans offered by public pension plans and employer pension plans, many individuals have set up personal retirement plans. The most popular personal retirement plan is an RRSP.

Registered Retirement Savings Plan (RRSP) An investment vehicle that allows you to shelter your savings from income taxes.

WHAT IS AN RRSP?

An **RRSP** is an investment vehicle that allows you to shelter your savings from income taxes. Despite the common misconceptions, it is not a specific type of investment but a way to shelter your money in one or more of a variety of investment vehicles.

Exhibit 14–10   Know Your Pension Plan Checklist

A. Plan Type Checklist

My plan is a:
☐ *Defined-benefit plan*
☐ *Defined-contribution plan*

B. Contributions Checklist

My pension plan is financed by:
☐ Employer contributions only.
☐ Employer and employee contributions.
☐ Union dues and assessments.
I contribute to my pension plan at the rate of
$ _____ per I month/I week/I hour, or
_____ percent of my compensation.

C. Vesting Checklist

My plan provides vesting after _____ years.
I need _____ more years of service to be fully vested.

D. Credited Service Checklist

I will have a year of service under my pension plan:
☐ If I work _____ hours in a 12-consecutive-month period.
☐ If I meet other requirements (specify).
The plan year (12-month period for which plan records are kept) ends on _____ of each year.
I will be credited for work performed:
☐ Before I became a participant in the plan.
☐ After the plan's normal retirement age.
As of now, _____ [date],
I have earned _____ years of service toward my pension.

E. Retirement Benefit Checklist

I may begin to receive full normal retirement benefits at age _____.
Working beyond the normal retirement age ☐ will
☐ will not increase the pension paid to me when I retire.
I may retire at age _____ if I have completed _____ years of service. Apart from the age requirement, I need _____ more years of service to be eligible for early retirement benefits.
The amount of my normal retirement benefit is computed as follows:
The amount of my early retirement benefit is computed as follows:
My retirement benefit will be:
☐ Paid monthly for life.
☐ Paid to me in a lump sum.
☐ Adjusted to the cost of living.
☐ Paid to my survivor in the event of my death (see "Survivors' Benefit Checklist" below).

F. Disability Benefit Checklist

My plan ☐ does ☐ does not provide disability benefits.
My plan defines the term *disability* as follows: _____
_____
To be eligible for disability retirement benefits, I must be _____ years old and must have _____ years of service.
A determination as to whether my condition meets my plan's definition of disability is made by:
☐ A doctor chosen by me.
☐ A doctor designated by the plan administrator.
☐ Other.
I must send my application for disability retirement benefits to _____ within _____ months after I stop working.
If I qualify for disability benefits, I will continue to receive benefits:
☐ For life, if I remain disabled.
☐ Until I return to my former job.
☐ Other.

G. Survivors' Benefit Checklist

My pension plan ☐ provides ☐ does not provide a joint and survivor option or a similar provision for death benefits.
My spouse and I ☐ have ☐ have not rejected in writing the joint and survivor option.
Electing the joint and survivor option will reduce my pension benefit to _____.
My survivor will receive _____ per month for life if the following conditions are met (specify):
_____
_____.

H. Plan Termination Checklist

My benefits ☐ are ☐ are not insured.

I. Benefit Application Checklist

My employer ☐ will ☐ will not automatically submit my pension application for me.
I must apply for my pension benefits ☐ on a special form that I get from _____ within _____ months ☐ before ☐ after ☐ I retire.
My application for pension benefits should be sent to
_____.
I must furnish the following documents when applying for my pension benefits: _____.
If my application for pension benefits is denied, I may appeal in writing to _____ within _____ days.

J. Suspension of Benefits Checklist

☐ I am covered by a single-employer plan or by a plan involving more than one employer.
☐ I am covered by a multi-employer plan.

SOURCE: Based on *Know Your Pension Plan* (Washington, DC: U.S. Department of Labor, 1992), pp. 5–10.

Legally, an RRSP is a trust, an arrangement in which certain property is given by a settlor to a trustee, an independent third party who holds the property on behalf of the beneficiary (or beneficiaries) who will receive income and/or capital from the trust. As contributor to the plan you are the settlor, and more often than not the trustee is a bank, though it can also be a trust company, a brokerage firm, or a life insurance company. You are the beneficiary, unless you have designated the plan as a spousal RRSP, in which case your spouse is the beneficiary.

Perhaps the result of aggressive promotion in the personal finance industry, another common misconception about RRSPs is that everyone should have one. This is not correct. The principal motive behind RRSPs should be to allow you to defer taxation. The idea is to defer your income taxes to a time when your marginal rate of taxation will be less. Exhibit 14–11 shows the power of tax-deferred compounding of earnings. If your financial circumstances are already such that you pay little or no income tax, you likely don't need an RRSP or its restrictions—Canada's federal *Income Tax Act* allows you to register only certain specified investments as RRSPs. Other restrictions include contribution limits and early withdrawal penalties. These are discussed below.

Eligible Investments   You can choose to register a number of investments, in combination or individually. Qualified investments include savings accounts, cash, Canada Savings Bonds (CSBs) and treasury bills (T-bills), term deposits and GICs, corporate bonds (including stripped bonds), stocks, eligible mutual funds, and real estate. Qualified investments can be divided into three categories.

The first of the categories is *guaranteed funds*, such as savings accounts, term deposits, and GICs. These funds ensure the return of your principal plus a guaranteed rate of return, and are available from most financial institutions.

A second category of RRSP investments is *mutual funds*. These have no guarantee regarding rate of return or safety of your principal and are available from most financial institutions including investment dealers and life insurance companies. Mutual fund investments include equity funds, bond funds, balanced funds, and money market funds.

Finally, *life insurance and life annuity products*, sold by life insurance companies, may also qualify as RRSP investments. Be aware, however, that tying your life insurance to your RRSP may not be a sound financial plan, as doing so might require fixed annual payments that limit your annual contribution and your freedom to move your funds within the RRSP.

Types of RRSPs   The most commonly held RRSP, known as a regular RRSP, is the type that most Canadians have. A regular RRSP draws on the two first categories of investments only. They are a popular choice because fees are minimal and your investments require minimal management by you, but the return on investment is lower, given that your funds are invested in principally low-risk, low-return investments.

The second main type of RRSP, a *self-directed* RRSP, allows you greater scope and permits you to invest in all categories. Available from most financial institutions, including investment dealers, this type of RRSP allows you to invest in cash, T-bills, bonds (including CSBs), mortgages, mutual funds, and stocks. The fees are higher than for regular RRSPs, and you need to pay closer attention, but many people find that the investment return and other advantages outweigh the disadvantages engendered by price and effort.

Another type of registered pension plan is a *spousal* RRSP, which is also available to common-law couples and same-sex couples. With this plan, you contribute to an RRSP in which your spouse is named as the beneficiary. This can be especially useful in cases where one spouse does not participate in the labour market, such as when young children must be cared for. Note that your contribution reduces your allowable contribution to your own plan, and you may not transfer funds from your own RRSP to your spouse's except in conditions where one spouse dies or under court order following a break-up. Further, if your spouse withdraws the funds sooner than two years plus the amount of time remaining in the year you make your contribution, the full amount of the funds will be taxed as though it were in your hands.

Exhibit 14–11   Tackling the Trade-offs (Saving Now versus Saving Later)

	Saver: Abe				Saver: Ben		
Age	Years	Contributions	Year-End Value	Age	Years	Contributions	Year-End Value
25	1	$2,000	$ 2,188	25	1	$ 0	$ 0
26	2	2,000	4,580	26	2	0	0
27	3	2,000	7,198	27	3	0	0
28	4	2,000	10,061	28	4	0	0
29	5	2,000	13,192	29	5	0	0
30	6	2,000	16,617	30	6	0	0
31	7	2,000	20,363	31	7	0	0
32	8	2,000	24,461	32	8	0	0
33	9	2,000	28,944	33	9	0	0
34	10	2,000	33,846	34	10	0	0
35	11	0	40,494	35	11	2,000	2,188
36	12	0	37,021	36	12	2,000	4,580
37	13	0	44,293	37	13	2,000	7,198
38	14	0	48,448	38	14	2,000	10,061
39	15	0	52,992	39	15	2,000	13,192
40	16	0	57,963	40	16	2,000	16,617
41	17	0	63,401	41	17	2,000	20,363
42	18	0	69,348	42	18	2,000	24,461
43	19	0	75,854	43	19	2,000	28,944
44	20	0	82,969	44	20	2,000	33,846
45	21	0	90,752	45	21	2,000	39,209
46	22	0	99,265	46	22	2,000	45,075
47	23	0	108,577	47	23	2,000	51,490
48	24	0	118,763	48	24	2,000	58,508
49	25	0	129,903	49	25	2,000	66,184
50	26	0	142,089	50	26	2,000	74,580
51	27	0	155,418	51	27	2,000	83,764
52	28	0	169,997	52	28	2,000	93,809
53	29	0	185,944	53	29	2,000	104,797
54	30	0	203,387	54	30	2,000	116,815
55	31	0	222,466	55	31	2,000	129,961
56	32	0	243,335	56	32	2,000	144,340
57	33	0	266,162	57	33	2,000	160,068
58	34	0	291,129	58	34	2,000	177,271
59	35	0	318,439	59	35	2,000	196,088
60	36	0	348,311	60	36	2,000	216,670
61	37	0	380,985	61	37	2,000	239,182
62	38	0	416,724	62	38	2,000	263,807
63	39	0	455,816	63	39	2,000	290,741
64	40	0	498,574	64	40	2,000	320,202
65	41	0	545,344	65	41	2,000	352,427
		$20,000				$62,000	

Value at retirement*	$545,344		Value at retirement*	$352,427
Less total contributions	$ 20,000		Less total contributions	$ 62,000
Net earnings	$525,344		Net earnings	$290,427

*The table assumes a 9-percent fixed rate of return, compounded monthly, and no fluctuation of the principal. Distributions from an RRSP are subject to ordinary income taxes when withdrawn and may be subject to other limitations under RRSP rules.
SOURCE: *The Franklin Investor* (San Mateo, CA: Franklin Distributors, Inc., January 1989).

RRSP funds can also be used for a down payment on your first home under the Home Buyers' Plan. If you qualify as a first-time buyer you are allowed to withdraw up to $25,000 as a loan from your RRSP to buy or build a home, without counting the withdrawal as income. You must then repay the loan, without interest, over the next 15 years. Generally, you will have to repay an amount to your RRSPs each year until you have repaid the entire amount you withdrew. If you do not repay the amount due for a year, it will be included in your income for that year.

RRSP funds can also be used to finance full-time training or education for you or your spouse or common-law partner under the Lifelong Learning Plan (LLP). LLP lets you withdraw up to $10,000 a year (to a maximum of $20,000). You have to repay these withdrawals to your RRSPs over a period of no more than 10 years. Any amount that you do not repay when it is due will be included in your income for the year it was due.

Contribution Limits   If you have earned income (salary, wages, royalties, business income, rental income, or alimony) in a given year, you can contribute to your RRSP, but the amount allowable is subject to a maximum set by the government.

The amount of your maximum annual contribution depends on whether you also participate in an RPP, which has the effect of reducing your allowable contribution by a pension adjustment calculated by your employer and by the Canada Revenue Agency. The result of that calculation is sent to you late in each year and will differ for defined benefit plans and defined contribution plans.

If you don't participate in an RPP, you can contribute up to 18 percent of your earned income or the stated maximum, whichever is less. The maximum is $24,270 in 2014, and $24,930 in 2015. Having invested the maximum, your earnings must have been $134,833 in 2014 and $138,500 in 2015.

There are also other rules to consider. You are allowed to exceed your limit by $2,000 without incurring a penalty, but beyond this amount, you will be fined 1 percent per month. Further, in the event that you are unable to make your full contribution to the plan, you are allowed to "carry forward" the full amount of unpaid contribution to a later year. This means that if you for any reason have a year in which savings are minimal, you will be able to make up for your contribution shortfall by investing more in a year when you can put more aside.

OPTIONS WHEN YOU DEREGISTER AN RRSP   Your RRSP must be deregistered by the end of the year of your 71st birthday. At that point, you will have six choices as to what to do with your funds. The options available are: (1) withdraw the funds and pay the income tax; (2) purchase a single-payment life annuity; (3) purchase a fixed-term annuity; (4) set up a Registered Retirement Income Fund (RRIF); (5) set up a Life Income Fund (LIF); or (6) set up a segregated fund. Each option is discussed below.

Full Withdrawal   The least favourable option when you deregister your RRSP is to simply withdraw the funds and pay the income tax on them, as doing this negates the purpose of using this tax minimization tool. It is likely that your accumulated funds will be large enough to draw the highest marginal tax rate if you accept them as a lump sum. At the time of withdrawal, the financial institution is required to apply a withholding tax calculated as a percentage of the sum withdrawn. For example, withdraw less than $5,000 and there is a 10 percent withholding tax (outside Quebec); withdraw $5,001 to $15,000 and there is a 20 percent withholding tax; withdraw $15,001 or more and there is a 30 percent withholding tax. The full withdrawal must be added to your taxable income and the withholding tax is entered as the tax already paid. Any additional taxes due are determined the following April when you file your income tax return. If, by chance, the withholding tax exceeds the tax bill generated by the withdrawal, you will receive a tax refund when you file your annual return.

Annuities   Annuities are an investment that usually pays a fixed level of payments on a regular basis (usually monthly or annually) for either a specified amount of time or until the death of the holder. They are meant to provide retirement income in much the same way as a salary provides regular income. If the annuity is bought with funds from a registered plan, then the purchase of the annuity is tax free, but the entire amount of each annuity payment is taxed. There are two main types of annuities: life annuities and fixed-term period annuities.

Following is a list of advantages and disadvantages that annuities have over other retirement income options:

Advantages
- Payment can continue until death, if it is a life annuity
- Level payments may suit your income needs better
- Simplicity—not having to worry about investments or withdrawals
- No heavy record keeping requirements
- A legitimate tax shelter
- No investment limits
- Tax-free transfers between annuity companies

Disadvantages
- Less control over investments
- Less control over payout of income
- No protection from inflation, unless it is indexed
- No opportunity for retirement income to grow
- No opportunity for tax deferral
- Can't take out a lump sum for major purchases, unless cashable
- No protection for spouse, unless joint or a guaranteed minimum payout is specified
- No estate planning benefits, unless joint or a guaranteed minimum payout is specified

Make sure you take into consideration such fees as commission, underwriting, fund management, and penalties when choosing your annuity provider.

Life Annuities If you purchase a single-payment life annuity, then the full amount of your RRSP funds are transferred directly to the life insurance company from which you bought the annuity. The company converts those funds into a lifetime income payable to you, and your marginal rate of taxation is based on your annual income rather than the whole of your funds. At any time, you have the option to cancel the annuity and take the commuted value of the remaining payments. Having done so, you can then either remove the funds from the tax shelter and pay the tax, or you can roll the funds over into an RRIF, discussed below. It must be noted that when the holder dies, there is no payment to the beneficiary or estate if the guaranteed minimum number of payments has been made.

Fixed-Term Annuities Fixed-term annuities are available from both life insurance companies and trust companies. As with life annuities, this method allows you to convert your RRSP funds into income. The principal difference is that the benefit paid and cost of this type of annuity is not based upon your life expectancy, or on the pooling of your funds with those of others. Instead, your funds are simply converted into an income stream to be paid out for a fixed term. In the event that you die prior to the end of the term, the remaining unpaid funds are paid to your estate or beneficiary, and your monthly income is based on the amount of your purchase, the term, and the current interest rates. As with the life annuity, you have the option to cancel at any time and either pay the taxes on the commuted value or roll it over to an RRIF.

Registered Retirement Income Funds (RRIFs) An RRIF is similar to a self-directed RRSP in that you can make your own investment decisions if you choose. Alternatively, you may set one up so that little management is required. In either case, the Canada Revenue Agency requires that you withdraw a minimum amount from the plan until you reach the age of 71. The minimum withdrawal amount starts at 4.76 percent of the total value of the RRIF at age 69 and increases incrementally to 20 percent by age 94. You can adjust the amount and the frequency of the payments you receive. Monthly, quarterly, semi-annual, or annual payments are all options, as are lump-sum withdrawals. For example, if you have an RRIF worth $250,000 and are aged 65 on January 1, in that year you must withdraw at least $11,900 (4.76 percent of $250,000) and will be accordingly taxed on that amount. Exhibit 14–12 shows minimum RRIF withdrawal amounts.

Life Income Funds (LIFs)   Upon terminating your membership in your company RPP, or when you transfer funds from a locked-in RRSP, you may elect to purchase an LIF. This income fund is available in all provinces, and the minimum deposit you must make to start one is $10,000. Similar to an RRIF, with an LIF you must withdraw a minimum amount every year, and the tax treatment is the same, but with this plan you are also subject to a maximum annual withdrawal amount based on interest rates and available investment returns. The balance of the funds in your LIF must be used to purchase a life annuity before December 31 of the year you turn 80. If you die before the end of the LIF term, the amount remaining in the fund will go to your designated beneficiary.

Segregated Funds   Similar to mutual funds, but sold exclusively through life insurance companies, a segregated fund is essentially the purchase of units representing a share in a pool of assets supervised by a fund manager. The term "segregated" refers to the fact that the money in these funds is kept separate from the company's other assets. The principal advantages that segregated funds have over mutual funds are that (1) when you die, your fund's assets go directly to your beneficiary rather than to your estate, and (2) a percentage of your capital is guaranteed no matter how poorly the fund performs. The percentage is generally around 75 percent but can go as high as 100 percent, in which case your only concern is the depreciation of your money due to inflation. Furthermore, segregated funds are eligible for coverage by Assuris. This provides policyholders with protection (within limits) from loss of benefits in the event the fund management company becomes insolvent.

Exhibit 14–12

RRIF Minimum Withdrawal Amounts

Age	Percentage*		Age	Percentage
69	4.76		81	8.99
70	5.00		82	9.27
71	7.38		83	9.58
72	7.48		84	9.93
73	7.59		85	10.33
74	7.71		86	10.79
75	7.85		87	11.33
76	7.99		88	11.96
77	8.15		89	12.71
78	8.33		90	13.62
79	8.53		91	14.73
80	8.75		92	16.12
			93	17.92
			94+	20.00

*For RRIFs opened after 1992.
SOURCE: tdcanadatrust.com.

WILL YOU HAVE ENOUGH MONEY DURING RETIREMENT?

Now that you have reviewed all the possible sources of your retirement income, estimate what your annual retirement income will be. Don't forget to inflate incomes or investments that increase with the cost of living (such as CPP benefits) to what they will be when you retire. (Use the inflation factor table in the Financial Planning Calculations box on page 428.) Remember, inflation is a major uncontrollable variable for retirees.

Now, compare your total estimated retirement income with your total inflated retirement expenses. If your estimated income exceeds your estimated expenses and a large portion of your planned income will automatically increase with the cost of living during your retirement, you are in good shape. (You should evaluate your plans every few years between now and retirement to be sure your planned income is still adequate to meet your planned expenses.)

If, however, your planned retirement income is less than your estimated retirement expenses, now is the time to take action to increase your retirement income. Also, if a large portion of your retirement income is fixed and will not increase with inflation, you should make plans for a much larger retirement income to meet your rising expenses during retirement.

CONCEPT CHECK 14–5

1. What are possible sources of income for retirees?
2. How do defined contribution plans differ from defined benefit plans?
3. What options do you have for deregistering your retirement investments?

LIVING ON YOUR RETIREMENT INCOME

As you planned retirement, you estimated a budget or spending plan, but you may find your actual expenses at retirement are higher than anticipated.

LO6
Develop a balanced budget based on your retirement income.

The first step in stretching your retirement income is to make sure you are receiving all of the income to which you are entitled. Examine the possible sources of retirement income mentioned earlier to see whether you could qualify for more programs or additional benefits. What assets or valuables could you use as a cash or income source?

To stay within your income, you may also need to make some changes in your spending plans. For example, you can use your skills and time instead of your money. There are probably many things you can do yourself instead of paying someone else to do them. Take advantage of free and low-cost recreation, such as walks, picnics, public parks, lectures, museums, libraries, art galleries, art fairs, gardening, and church and club programs.

TAX ADVANTAGES

Be sure to take full advantage of all the tax savings and benefits available to retirees. For more information, contact Service Canada (servicecanada.gc.ca). Service Canada provides a number of guides and publications to help you understand your available options.

WORKING DURING RETIREMENT

You may want to work part-time or start a new part-time career after you retire. Work can provide you with a greater sense of usefulness, involvement, and self-worth, and may be the ideal way to add to your retirement income. You may want to pursue a personal interest or hobby, or you can contact your provincial or local agency on aging for information about employment opportunities for retirees.

Over 50 percent of recent retirees want to continue working part-time or even full-time after retirement, and only a small percentage are worried about outliving their financial resources. There is a rich talent pool of Canadians in the 55–75 age range, over 50 percent of whom are retired—and many of them are interested in continued employment. These individuals, with their proven skills and abilities, provide a flexible, cost-effective resource that can sustain our productivity gains and economic growth. What drives many of them is the desire to remain productively engaged in life.

If you decide to work part-time after you retire, you should be aware of how your earnings will affect your public pension income. As long as you do not earn more than the annually exempt amount, your payments will not be affected. But if you earn more than the annual exempt amount, your payments will be reduced. Check with your Service Canada office for the latest information.

INVESTING FOR RETIREMENT

The guaranteed-income part of your retirement fund consists of money paid into lower-yield, safe investments. To offset inflation, your retirement assets must earn enough to keep up with, and even exceed, the rate of inflation.

DIPPING INTO YOUR NEST EGG

When should you draw on your savings? The answer depends on your financial circumstances, your age, and how much you want to leave to your heirs. Your savings may be large enough to allow you to live comfortably on the interest alone. Or you may need to make regular withdrawals to help finance your retirement. Dipping into savings isn't wrong, but you must do so with caution.

How long would your savings last if you withdrew monthly income? If you have $10,000 in savings that earns 5.5 percent interest, compounded quarterly, you could take out $68 every month for 20 years before reducing this nest egg to zero. If you have $40,000, you could collect $224 every month for 30 years before exhausting your nest egg. For different possibilities, see Exhibit 14–13.

Exhibit 14–13   Dipping Into Your Nest Egg

Starting Amount of Nest Egg	You Can Reduce Your Nest Egg to Zero by Withdrawing This Much Each Month for the Stated Number of Years...					Or You Can Withdraw This Much Each Month and Leave Your Nest Egg Intact
	10 Years	**15 Years**	**20 Years**	**25 Years**	**30 Years**	
$ 10,000	$ 107	$ 81	$ 68	$ 61	$ 56	$ 46
15,000	161	121	102	91	84	69
20,000	215	162	136	121	112	92
25,000	269	202	170	152	140	115
30,000	322	243	204	182	168	138
40,000	430	323	272	243	224	184
50,000	537	404	340	304	281	230
60,000	645	485	408	364	337	276
80,000	859	647	544	486	449	368
100,000	1,074	808	680	607	561	460

Note: Based on an interest rate of 5.5 percent per year, compounded quarterly.
SOURCE: Select Committee on Aging, U.S. House of Representatives.

Exhibit 14–14   Major Sources of Retirement Income: Advantages and Disadvantages

Source	Advantages	Disadvantages
Public Pension Plans		
In planning	Forced savings Portable from job to job Cost shared with employer	Increasing economic pressure on the system as population ages
At retirement	Inflation-adjusted survivorship rights	Minimum retirement age specified Earned income may partially offset benefits
Employee Pension Plans		
In planning	Forced savings Cost shared or fully covered by employer	May not be portable No control over how funds are managed
At retirement	Survivorship rights	Cost-of-living increases may not be provided on a regular basis
Individual Saving and Investing (including housing, LIF, and RRSP plans)		
In planning	Current tax savings (e.g., RRSPs) Easily incorporated into family (i.e., housing) Portable Control over management of funds	Current needs compete with future needs Penalty for early withdrawal (RRSPs and LIF)
At retirement	Inflation resistant Can usually use as much of the funds as you wish, when you wish (within certain requirements)	Some sources taxable Mandatory minimum withdrawal restrictions (RRIF and LIF)
Post-retirement Employment		
In planning	Special earning skills can be used as they are developed	Technology and skills needed to keep up may change rapidly
At retirement	Inflation resistant	Ill health can mean loss of this income source

Exhibit 14–14 summarizes major sources of retirement income and their advantages and disadvantages.

CONCEPT CHECK 14–6

1. What is the first step in stretching your retirement income?
2. How should you invest to obtain retirement income?

SUMMARY OF LEARNING OBJECTIVES

LO1 Recognize the importance of retirement planning.
Retirement planning is important because you will probably spend many years in retirement. Public pensions and a private pension may be insufficient to cover the cost of living, and inflation may erode the purchasing power of your retirement savings. Many young people are reluctant to think about retirement, but they should start retirement planning before they reach age 40.

LO2 Analyze your current assets and liabilities for retirement.
Analyze your current assets (everything you own) and your current liabilities (everything you owe). The difference between your assets and your liabilities is your net worth. Review your assets to ensure they are sufficient for retirement.

LO3 Estimate your retirement spending needs.
Since the spending patterns of retirees change, it is impossible to predict the exact amount of money you will need in retirement. However, you can estimate your expenses. Some of those expenses will increase while others will decrease. The expenses that are likely to be lower or eliminated are work-related expenses, clothing, housing expenses, federal income taxes, and commuting expenses.

LO4 Identify your retirement housing needs.
Where you live in retirement can influence your financial needs. You are the only one who can determine the location and housing that are best for you. Would you like to live in your present home or move to a new location? Consider the social aspects of moving.

LO5 Determine your planned retirement income.
Estimate your retirement expenses and adjust those expenses for inflation using the appropriate inflation factor. Your possible sources of income during retirement include the CPP, other public pension plans, employer pension plans, and personal retirement plans.

LO6 Develop a balanced budget based on your retirement income.
Compare your total estimated retirement income with your total inflated retirement expenses. If your income approximates your expenses, you are in good shape; if not, determine additional income needs and sources.

KEY TERMS

adult lifestyle/retirement community 430
defined benefit pension plan 434
defined contribution pension plan 434

life lease housing 430
Registered Retirement Savings Plan (RRSP) 436
retirement homes 430

reverse annuity mortgage (RAM) 425
vesting 436

FINANCIAL PLANNING PROBLEMS

connect Practise and learn online with Connect.

1. *Preparing a Net Worth Statement.* Prepare your net worth statement using the guidelines presented in Exhibit 14–3. LO2

2. *Comparing Spending Patterns During Retirement.* How will your spending patterns change during your retirement years? Compare your spending patterns with those shown in Exhibit 14–4. LO3

3. *Calculating Maximum Contributions.* Jean and Dan Sladek both work. Each earns a salary of $30,000, but only Jean is a member of a registered pension plan. Both she and her employer contribute 2 percent of her gross salary to a defined contribution pension plan. Dan has $15,000 of unused contribution room carried forward since 1991. Calculate the maximum RRSP contribution that each can make. LO5

4. *Calculating Net Pay and Spendable Income.* Assume your gross pay per pay period is $2,000 and you are in the 26 percent tax bracket (ignore provincial tax). Calculate your net pay and spendable income in the following situations: LO5

a. You save $200 per pay period after paying income tax on $2,000.
b. You save $200 per pay period in an RPP.

5. *Planning for Deregistering RRSPs.* Your grandfather is turning 71 and he must deregister his remaining RRSP funds of $200,000 this year. Both your grandparents are in good health and they have enough income from your grandfather's current monthly RRIF payments to meet their expenses. He would like to minimize the tax burden of this withdrawal, and enjoy some growth potential while keeping the principal safe. He would also like to have some liquidity in the event of an emergency. He knows you are taking a personal finance course and asks for your advice. How would you advise him? Explain your rationale. LO5

6. *Calculating Monthly Withdrawals.* You have $50,000 in your retirement fund that is earning 5.5 percent per year, compounded quarterly. How many dollars in withdrawals per month would reduce this nest egg to zero in 20 years? How many dollars per month can you withdraw for as long as you live and still leave this nest egg intact? LO6

FINANCIAL PLANNING ACTIVITIES

1. *Conducting Interviews.* Survey friends, relatives, and other people to get their views on retirement planning. Prepare a written report of your findings. LO1

2. *Obtaining Information about Reverse Mortgages.* Obtain consumer information about reverse mortgages in the Royal Bank's *Your Money Matters*, available in all Royal Bank branches or online at royalbank.com. Evaluate the information. How might a reverse mortgage help you or a member of your family? LO2

3. *Determining Expenses During Retirement.* Read newspaper or magazine articles to determine what expenses are likely to increase and decrease during retirement. How might this information affect your retirement-planning decisions? LO3

4. *Evaluating Retirement Housing Options.* Which type of housing will best meet your retirement needs? Is such housing available in your community? Make a checklist of the advantages and disadvantages of your housing choice. LO4

5. *Balancing a Retirement Budget.* Outline the steps you must take to live on your retirement income and balance your retirement budget. LO6

CREATING A FINANCIAL PLAN

Planning for Retirement

Long-term financial security is a common goal of most people. Retirement planning should consider both personal decisions (location, housing, activities) and financial factors (investments, pensions, living expenses).

Web Sites for Retirement Planning

- Canada Revenue Agency, at **cra-arc.gc.ca**, provides important tax-related retirement information through its Forms and Publications link.

- CARP, at **carp.ca**, is a non-profit organization dedicated to 50+ lifestyles.

- Cannex, at **cannex.com**, is an online financial rate site providing up-to-date rates for annuities, GICs, RRSPs, mortgages, and other financial products. It is a great site to get information on the current market.

- Benefits Canada, at **benefitscanada.com**, is a magazine that claims to provide the most current pension and investment information available in Canada.

- Seniors Canada On-line, at **seniors.gc.ca**, provides single-window access to Web-based information and services that are relevant to seniors 55+, their families, caregivers, and supporting service organizations.

- Service Canada-Services for Seniors, at **servicecanada.gc.ca/eng/audiences/seniors/index.shtml**, provides detailed information for seniors on retirement issues.

(Note: Addresses and content of Web sites change, and new sites are created daily. Use search engines to update and locate Web sites for your current financial planning needs.)

Short-Term Financial Planning Activities

1. Identify personal and financial retirement needs for various stages of your life.
2. Compare the benefits and costs of an RRSP, an RPP, and other pension plans.

Long-Term Financial Planning Activities

1. Research costs and benefits of various housing alternatives.
2. Estimate future retirement income needs and identify appropriate investments to meet those needs.
3. Develop a plan for expanding personal interests and increasing contributions to retirement accounts.

LIFE SITUATION CASE

To Be Young, Thrifty, and in the Black: The Importance of Starting Early

Ann Farrell, a 28-year-old hydrogeologist, is one of the lucky ones. As a 4th-year university student in 2008, Farrell attended a seminar on investing early for retirement. "I remembered the figures if you started saving when you were young," she says. Indeed, the payoff is huge. Through compounding, 25-year-olds who invest $2,000 a year and stop at 34 will earn $142,000 more by the time they are 65 than someone who begins investing $2,000 at 35 and contributes $2,000 each year for the next 30 years.

Farrell already has $22,000 in her RRSP. That's a nice start compared with most of her peers. Research has found that nearly 70 percent of adults ages 22 to 32 have saved less than $10,000 for retirement.

When Farrell was a new employee in 2008 at an environmental consulting firm, she was barred for a year from the company's pension plan. Once eligible, she committed 8 percent of her paycheque in the two most aggressive stock funds offered (retirement growth and asset manager). The company matched 50 percent of her pre-tax contributions, up to 5 percent of her $48,000 salary.

Of course, it helped that her expenses were low. After graduation, Farrell—with only $500 to her name—moved back in with her parents, who charged her $400 a month for rent. She also travelled three out of every four weeks on work. "There is nowhere to spend money on the road," she claims. Still, she had to repay a $20,000 school loan and a $8,000 car loan. She also wanted to build an emergency fund. Once she began making headway on these goals, Farrell moved to her own place and gradually increased her pre-tax contribution to 10 percent. Last year, she upped it to 13 percent. The government allows

employees to make a pre-tax contribution of up to $24,270 in 2014. Farrell is currently chipping in about $5,000 a year.

Oddly, the lack of growth in environmental consulting has worked to Farrell's benefit. While most Gen-Xers find themselves changing jobs every two years or so to get ahead, Farrell stayed put because there wasn't much movement in her industry. So, she will become fully vested in her RPP this October, after five years in the plan.

Farrell has done a lot right, but she has a long road ahead of her. When she makes her next move—she may leave her company and go to business school—she needs to recognize the potholes that exist when protecting her retirement assets. For instance, if she decides to roll over her RPP, she'll have to examine all of the investment options and rollover requirements. If she doesn't, she could lose her head start on retirement savings.

Questions

1. What did Ann Farrell learn when she attended a seminar on retirement?

2. How much money did Farrell originally commit to her company pension plan? In what funds did she invest her money?

3. What is the maximum contribution Farrell can make to her RRSP?

4. After how long and when did Farrell become fully vested in her RPP?

SOURCE: Adapted from Toddi Guttner, "To Be Young, Thrifty, and in the Black," *BusinessWeek*, July 21, 1997, p. 76.

chapter 15

Estate Planning

LEARNING OBJECTIVES

LO1   Analyze the personal aspects of estate planning.

LO2   Assess the legal aspects of estate planning.

LO3   Distinguish among will formats.

LO4   Appraise various types of trusts and estates.

A PLAN FOR THE ENDGAME

Harry Frank talked to his lawyer about drafting a living will, but never completed one. Then, in 2009, he suffered severe brain damage in an automobile accident and spent three years in a persistent vegetative state. Last year, after his wife moved him to a nursing home to be close to his parents, she requested that his feeding tube be removed. Other family members objected. The device eventually was withdrawn, and Frank died—but only after an agonizing legal battle that tore his family apart.

Imagine suffering a stroke or being left in a coma as a result of an auto accident. Would you want to be kept on life support, fed through a tube, or given pain-controlling drugs, even if they hastened your death? You have the right to make these choices. You'll need two documents, called *advanced directives:* a living will that tells doctors and hospitals how you want to be cared for should you become terminally ill, and a health-care proxy that designates an advocate who can make sure your wishes are honoured.

Living wills do not give a hospital the right to "pull the plug" without consent of a patient's legal representative. If you want doctors to exhaust every effort to keep you alive,

no matter what, you can also request that in a living will. You can say "I don't want anything done," or you can say "I want absolutely everything." Lawyers say it is important to be as specific as possible. If you want morphine or other pain medication in your last days, even if it is addictive or makes you drowsy, say so. If you want life support turned off if you are near death, write that down, too. Whatever its contents, a living will is one legal document that should not be kept in your safety deposit box. Give copies to your lawyer, your doctor, your parents, and your adult children, and take one to the hospital on your next visit.

However, putting your wishes in writing does not guarantee that a hospital will honour them. To make sure it does, you need to appoint a legal representative, usually a relative or friend, who can handle your health-care decisions if you cannot. You make this choice by executing a designation of health-care proxy, health-care surrogate, or medical power of attorney. You might want to make your spouse your representative. But think about giving backup power to an adult child if you are not sure your spouse could handle such difficult decisions at a time of great stress.

QUESTIONS

1. How can you protect your wishes and your peace of mind with a living will?
2. Would you want to be kept on life support? Why, or why not?
3. In your opinion, who should have the right to make life-and-death decisions?
4. Should you keep your living will in a safety deposit box? Why, or why not?

WHY ESTATE PLANNING?

LO1

Analyze the personal aspects of estate planning.

estate Everything you own.

Your **estate** consists of everything you own. While you work, your objective is to accumulate funds for your future and for your dependants. As you grow older, your point of view will change. The emphasis in your financial planning will shift from accumulating assets to distributing them wisely. Your hard-earned wealth should go to those whom you wish to support and not to the various taxation agencies.

Contrary to widely held notions, estate planning, which includes wills and trusts, is useful not just to rich and elderly people. Trusts can be used for purposes other than tax advantages, such as choosing a guardian for children and avoiding family fights over personal belongings. Furthermore, most people can afford the expense of using trusts.

This chapter discusses a subject most people would rather avoid: death—your own or that of your spouse. Many people give little or no thought to setting their personal and financial affairs in order.

As you learned in Chapter 14, most people today live longer than those of previous generations and have ample time to think about and plan for the future. Yet, a large percentage of people do little or nothing to provide for those who will survive them.

Planning for your family's financial security in the event of your death or the death of your spouse is not easy. Therefore, the objective of this chapter is to help you initiate discussions about questions you should ask before that happens. Does your spouse, for instance, know what all of the family's resources and debts are? Does your family have enough insurance protection?

The question of whether your family can cope financially without your or your spouse's income and support is a difficult one. This chapter can't provide all of the answers, but it supplies a basis for sound estate planning for you and your family.

WHAT IS ESTATE PLANNING?

estate planning A definite plan for the administration and disposition of one's property during one's lifetime and at one's death.

Estate planning is a definite plan for the administration and disposition of one's property during one's lifetime and at one's death. Thus, it involves both handling your property while you are alive and dealing with what happens to that property after your death.

Estate planning is an essential part of retirement planning and an integral part of financial planning. It has two components. The first consists of building your estate through savings, investments, and insurance. The second involves transferring your estate, at your death, in the manner you specify. As this chapter explains, an estate plan is usually implemented by a will and one or more trust agreements.

Nearly every adult engages in financial decision making and must keep important records. Whatever your status—single or married, male or female, taxi driver or corporate executive—you must make financial decisions that are important to you. Those decisions may be even more important to others in your family. Knowledge in certain areas and good record keeping can simplify those decisions.

At first, planning for financial security and estate planning may seem complicated. Although many money matters require legal and technical advice, if you and your spouse learn the necessary skills, you will find yourselves managing your money affairs more efficiently and wisely.

PROVINCIAL FAMILY LAW

Provincial family law can have a significant impact on your estate planning. For example, getting married will usually void a will made prior to the wedding. Equally, divorce and separation might also affect the validity of part or all of a will.

Provincial family law might also impact your capacity to order the disposition of your estate. In effect, you must provide for the support of your spouse, dependent children, and other family members who can prove personal financial needs that have normally been met by you. If inadequate provisions are made, your will can be contested and declared invalid. The court will order the estate to provide for dependants according to the law of the province. Family law also stipulates similar support in the event of a marital breakdown. Notice, however, that these laws do not oblige the deceased to provide for family members who were not being financially supported at the time of death.

The particular nature and scope of the laws vary from province to province, although the motive behind these laws is always the same. The idea is to protect those who have traditionally depended on you and to ensure a just distribution of your estate. While provincial family law differs significantly across Canada and can be complex, in the event that a marriage terminates through death or divorce, most legislation provides for the equal division between spouses of *family assets* acquired during the marriage. Exceptions are often made for gifts, inheritances, lottery winnings, and insurance settlements received during the marriage, and any property brought into the marriage with the exception of the matrimonial home. Even the definition of family assets that may be subject to division can differ from province to province. For example, Quebec has a much more restrictive definition than other provinces, covering only the family's residences, furnishings, motor vehicles, and pension benefits acquired during the course of the marriage.

Did you know?

56 percent of adult Canadians do not have a will.

SOURCES: retirehappy.ca.

Regardless of your familial situation, you should take the necessary steps to ensure that you clearly make your desires known regarding your estate. While these instructions might be constrained somewhat by your provincial laws, the alternative is to have your will declared invalid, die *intestate* (without a will), and have the whole of your estate distributed through an insensitive and not always apt legal system. It should be noted that most provinces do not yet recognize common-law unions for purposes of determining matrimonial rights; British Columbia and Ontario do. British Columbia considers a common-law spouse of two years to be a spouse for the purpose of distributing an intestate estate. Ontario's Succession Law Reform Act's definition of a dependant includes a married spouse or common-law or same-sex partner who has lived with you for at least three years (or less if you were the natural or adoptive parents of a child). If you are unsure about the family or succession (estate) laws in your own province, see a legal adviser.

THE OPPORTUNITY COST OF RATIONALIZING

Daily living often gets in the way of thinking about death. You mean to organize things that others need to know in case you die, but you haven't done this yet. One of your rationalizations may be that you are not sure what information you need to provide.

Think about the outcome of your delay. Your beneficiary will meet people who offer specific types of assistance—morticians, clergy, lawyers, insurance agents, clerks of federal government agencies, and so on. These people will probably be strangers—sympathetic, courteous, and helpful, but disinterested. Also, your bereaved beneficiary may find it difficult to reveal confidences to them. Today, the information survivors need is as close as the Internet.

The moral is to plan your estate while you are in good health and think through the provisions carefully. Last-minute "death-bed" estate planning may fail to carry out your wishes. Many

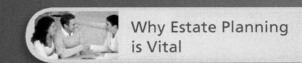
Two men were lifelong friends and similar in many ways. Both were affluent, mid-fifties, healthy, with several children and grandchildren. Life was good.

Then tragedy struck. Returning home from a golf weekend together, their car was involved in a serious auto accident. Neither of them survived. Both families were devastated. But one was far more devastated than the other.

Because although these two men were so similar in their lifetimes, they left remarkably different legacies for their families in their deaths. One had an estate plan. Everything from funeral arrangements to the trusts for his grandchildren had been pre-planned. Right down to who got his beloved sailboat. His spouse and family were able to properly mourn his passing with love and the comforting knowledge that he had planned so carefully for their welfare. His friend had always thought it was bad luck to talk about his death. So not only did he not have an estate plan, he didn't even have a Will. Perhaps if he had just thought about the consequences for his family, things may have been different.

His grief-stricken spouse was left to arrange for his funeral, burial and all the legal and financial requirements. And all of it with no Will to guide her in making decisions. The stress of dealing with all this added to her emotional strain was nearly more than she could bear. To make matters worse, the arguing and bickering among family members over the estate delayed a settlement and cost a fortune in legal fees. The end result was a severely depleted estate and bitterness in the family that will probably last for years. Every year, too many families go through unnecessary nightmares simply because someone didn't believe in estate planning. Fortunately, more and more people are realizing that estate planning is an essential part of financial planning and is one of the most important things you will ever do for yourself and your family.

SOURCE: "Welcome to estate planning—Wealth preservation for you and your heirs," Royal Bank of Canada, August 18, 2014, http://www.rbcfinancial-planning.com/estate-planning.html.

Canadians are considering pre-planned funeral arrangements as part of their estate plan. Pre-planned funeral arrangements allow for family input, minimize the chances of additional costs, and ensure that your wishes are followed without burdening family members.

CONCEPT CHECK 15–1

1. If you needed information about estate planning, would you go to the library or the Internet? Why?
2. Why is estate planning an important component of financial planning?
3. Why is estate planning important for single as well as married individuals?

LEGAL ASPECTS OF ESTATE PLANNING

LO2

Assess the legal aspects of estate planning.

When death occurs, proof of claims must be produced or the claims will not be processed. If no thought was given to gathering the necessary documents beforehand (with a sufficient number of copies), a period of financial hardship may follow until proof is obtained. If needed documentation cannot be located, irretrievable loss of funds may occur. Your heirs may experience emotionally painful delays until their rights have been established.

Important papers include the following:

1. Birth certificates—yours, your spouse's, and your children's.
2. Marriage certificates—always important, but especially important if you or your spouse were married previously—and divorce papers.

3. Legal name changes—judgment of court documents pertaining to any legal changes in the names that appear on birth certificates (especially important to protect the adopted children of a previous marriage or children who have been adopted through adoption agencies).
4. Military service records—or any other official statement of your military service details, if appropriate.

Here is a list of additional important documents:

- Government benefit documents.
- Veteran documents.
- Insurance policies.
- Transfer records of joint bank accounts.
- Safety deposit box records.
- Registration of automobiles.
- Title to stock and bond certificates.

You should have several copies of certain documents, because when you submit a claim the accompanying proof often becomes a permanent part of the claim file and is not returned. Remember too that in some circumstances, children may be required to furnish proof of their parents' birth, marriage, or divorce.

WILLS

One of the most vital documents every adult should have is a written will. A **will** is the legal declaration of a person's mind as to the disposition of his or her property after death. Thus, a will is a way to transfer your property according to your wishes after you die (see Exhibit 15–1).

Whether you prepare a will before you die or neglect to take that sensible step, you still have a will. If you fail to prepare your own will, the province in which you legally reside steps in and controls the distribution of your estate without regard for wishes you may have had but failed to define in legal form. Thus, if you die **intestate**—without a valid will—the province's law of descent and distribution becomes your copy of the will. An individual recognized as a "spouse" according to the family and/or succession laws of a province is entitled to an amount set by the province called a "preferential share," and to a share of the balance of the estate called a "distributive share." The size of the distributive share depends on the number of surviving children or grandchildren. See Exhibit 15–2 on page 455 for the distribution of property in Ontario when a person dies intestate.

will The legal declaration of a person's mind as to the disposition of his or her property after death.

intestate Without a valid will.

THE EFFECT OF MARRIAGE OR DIVORCE ON YOUR WILL   As previously mentioned, changes to your marital status can affect the validity of your will. Or, you may personally wish to make changes related to the changing role of a partner in your life. In the case of divorce, for example, the issue of ownership of familial debts and assets is often heatedly debated, and you should ensure that your will respects whatever agreement you come to.

If you marry after you have made a will, the will is revoked automatically (except in Quebec) unless certain conditions are met. For example, marriage does not revoke a will if:

- The will indicates an intent that it not be revoked by a subsequent marriage.
- The will was drafted under circumstances indicating that it was in contemplation of marriage.

Because your existing will's legal status may be uncertain, you are better off drawing a new will to fit your new circumstances.

COST OF A WILL   Legal fees for drafting a will vary with the complexities of your estate and family situation. A standard will costs $300 and up, not including a living will or power of

Exhibit 15–1   What's in a Will

A will requires careful planning to ensure all aspects are covered. The chart below outlining the contents of a basic will clearly demonstrates this point.

Common Clause	Purpose of the Clause
Identification and Revocation Clause	Identifies you and your residence. Declares that this is your last will, which revokes all prior wills.
Appointment of Executor(s)	Designates the individual or institution you appoint as your executor. May also designate alternative and successor executors if your original executor cannot act. The clause may provide for the payment of compensation to the executor for their services.
Payment of Debts	Directs your executor to pay all debts, such as mortgages, loans, and funeral and estate administration expenses.
Payment of Taxes and Fees	Authorizes your executor to pay income tax or probate fees that may be due.
Specific Bequests	Outlines the distribution of specific personal property, such as furniture, jewellery, cars. May also refer to your RRSPs, RRIFs, and pensions.
Legacies	Directs specific cash amounts to be paid.
Residual Estates	Outlines the distribution of your remaining property after all the specific bequests have been made.
Trusts	Sets out the terms of any trust created by your will.
Power Clauses	Enables your executor to exercise various powers in the management of your estate without the approval of the court.
Life Interest Clause	Used when you want to leave someone the income or the enjoyment of the asset, rather than the asset itself. Upon the life tenant's death, the asset would pass on to another beneficiary.
Encroachment Clause	Used in a trust when you want the trustee to be able to give the life tenant or a capital beneficiary additional funds for special circumstances or needs.
Common Disaster Clause	Outlines the distribution of your assets if an intended beneficiary dies at the same time as you.
Survival Clause	States that a beneficiary must survive you for a set period of time (often 30 days) before he or she can benefit from your estate.
Guardian Appointment	Names the individual(s) who would be appointed guardian of your minor children.
Testimonium and Attestation Clauses	These clauses are found at the end of your will. They ensure the legal requirements for a validly executed will are met.

SOURCE: Ho and Robinson, *Personal Financial Planning,* Third Edition (Captus Press, 2000, page 426).

attorney. The price varies from place to place, but generally the cost of writing a will is less than that for writing a living trust (to be discussed later in the chapter). Look for an attorney experienced in drafting wills and in estate planning.

You can also write your own will with the help of an online will writing service, such as Canadian Legal Wills (legalwills.ca) or MakeYourWill.com (canada.makeyourwill.com), where you can create your own will in minutes for as little as $15. You can even access a sample will at no cost from taxtips.ca. However, note that a do-it-yourself will may not be appropriate in all

Dies Leaving	Distribution
Spouse and no children	All to spouse
Children only	All to children, per *stirpes**
Spouse and one child	$200,000 to spouse, rest split equally, *per stirpes*
Spouse and children	First $200,000 to spouse; 1/3 remainder to spouse, and 2/3 to children, *per stirpes*
Spouse and relatives	All to spouse
No spouse or child	Closest next of kin according to table of consanguinity

per stirpes means that if the entitled person is deceased, his or her share of the inheritances will go to his or her children, equally.
SOURCE: Ontario Estate Planning by Marni Whitaker from Lang Michener LLP, langmichener.ca/uploads/content/LMOntarioEstatePlanning0505.pdf.

Exhibit 15–2

Distribution of Property When a Person Dies Intestate (without a will) in Ontario

situations. Be sure the will you choose is legally recognized in the province of your residence. In Quebec, for example, a will must be notarized to be valid. Although it is more expensive, it is a good idea to have a legal professional review your will to ensure it conforms to current provincial laws. A sample will is provided in Exhibit 15–3.

CONCEPT CHECK 15–2

1. What are the legal aspects of estate planning?
2. What is a will? Why is it an important estate planning tool?
3. How does marriage or divorce affect a will?

TYPES AND FORMATS OF WILLS

There are three types of legal wills. A **holographic will** is a handwritten will that you prepare yourself. It should be written, dated, and signed entirely in your handwriting; no printed or typed information should be on its pages. Some provinces may not recognize a holographic will.

A **formal will** is usually prepared with an attorney's assistance. It may be either typed or on a pre-printed form. You must sign the will and acknowledge it as your will in the presence of two witnesses, neither of whom is a **beneficiary** (a person you have named to receive property under the will). The witnesses must then sign the will in your presence.

A **notarial will**, available only in Quebec, is typed and signed in the presence of the notary and at least one witness. The notary keeps the original will and can issue a certified copy to the heirs once proof of death has been established. A notarized will is considered a legal deed and, as such, the will does not need to be probated (see later discussion).

WRITING YOUR WILL

The way to transfer your property according to your wishes is to write a will specifying those wishes. Joint ownership is no substitute for a will. Although jointly owned property passes directly to the joint owner and may be appropriate for some assets, such as your home, only a will allows you to distribute your property as a whole exactly as you wish. Select a person who will follow your instructions (your *executor*). By naming your own executor, you eliminate the need for a court-appointed administrator, prevent unnecessary delay in the distribution of your property, and minimize settlement costs.

LO3
Distinguish among will formats.

holographic will A handwritten will.

formal will A will that is usually prepared with an attorney's assistance.

beneficiary A person who has been named to receive property under a will.

notarial will A will made in the presence of a notary and at least one witness, and that does not require probate. Available only in Quebec.

Exhibit 15–3   Sample of a Last Will and Testament

Last Will And Testament

THIS IS THE LAST WILL AND TESTAMENT of me, Jane Dobbs, florist, of 2250 Elm Street, in the City of Toronto, in the Province of Ontario.

I HEREBY REVOKE all former Wills and other Testamentary dispositions by me at any time heretofore made and DECLARE this to be and contain my Last Will and Testament.

I NOMINATE, CONSTITUTE AND APPOINT my husband, Peter Dobbs, 2250 Elm Street, in the City of Toronto, Ontario, to be the sole Executor and Trustee of this my Last Will and Testament, and I herein after refer to him as my 'Trustee'. IN THE EVENT that Peter Dobbs shall be unable or unwilling for any reason whatsoever to act or continue acting as my Executor and Trustee, I then appoint my daughter, Janet Smith, of 3150 Baker Street, in the City of Toronto, Ontario, Executor and Trustee of this my Last Will and Testament (hereinafter referred to as 'my Trustee').

I GIVE, DEVISE AND BEQUEATH all my estate, both real and personal, of every nature and kind and wheresoever situate, including any property over which I may have a general power of appointment, to my husband, Peter Dobbs, if he survives me for a period of thirty (30) days, for his own use absolutely.

IF MY SAID husband should predecease me, or die within a period of thirty (30) days following my death, I GIVE, DEVISE AND BEQUEATH all my estate, both real and personal, of **every** nature and kind and wheresoever situate, including any property over which I may have a general power of appointment, to my Trustees to hold upon the following trusts:

a)   To use their discretion in the realization of my estate, with power to my Trustee to sell, call in and convert into money any part of my estate not consisting of money at such time or times, in such manner and upon such terms, and either for cash or credit or for part cash and part credit, as my said Trustee in their uncontrolled discretion may decide upon, or to postpone such conversion of my estate or any part or parts thereof for such length of time as they may think best and I HEREBY DECLARE that my said Trustee may retain any portion of my estate in the form in which it may be at my death (notwithstanding that it may not be in the form of an investment in which Trustee are authorized to invest funds and whether or not there is a liability attached to any such portion of my estate) for such length of time as my said Trustee may in their discretion deem advisable, and my Trustee shall not be held responsible for any loss that may happen to my estate by reason of their so doing.

b)   To pay out of the capital of my general estate my just debts, funeral and testamentary expenses and all succession duties and inheritance and death taxes, whether imposed by or pursuant to the law of this or any province, state, country or jurisdiction whatsoever, that may be payable in connection with an insurance on my life or any gift or benefit given by me either in my lifetime or by survivorship or by this my Will or any Codicil thereto.

c)   To divide the rest and residue of my estate into equal shares, to be transferred and distributed equally among the following persons:

   1.   Peter Dobbs, husband
   2.   Janet Smith, daughter

IF one of my above-named beneficiaries shall predecease me, then the equal share set apart for that deceased beneficiary shall instead be distributed to his or her descendants, equally share and share alike. If one of my above-named beneficiaries shall predecease me leaving no descendants surviving, then the equal share set apart for that deceased beneficiary shall be distributed to my other beneficiary, or if my other beneficiary has predeceased me, then to his or her descendants, equally share and share alike.

IN WITNESS WHEREOF I have hereunto set my hand to this and the preceding page at Toronto, in the Province of Ontario, this 1st day of April, AD 2014.

Jane Dobbs
_____

Jane Dobbs

SIGNED, PUBLISHED AND DECLARED

by the above named Testator, Jane Dobbs,

as and for her last will and Testament,

in our presence, who at her request and in her

presence, have hereunto subscribed our names as

witnesses:

_____	_____
SIGNATURE	SIGNATURE
Witness _____	Witness _____
Address	Address
City, Province	City, Province
Phone # .	Phone #

SOURCE: Created using a sample will from taxtips.ca.

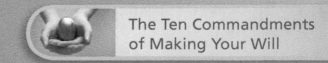
1. Work closely with your spouse as you prepare your will. Seek professional help so that your family objectives can be met, regardless of who dies first.

2. Write your will to conform with your current wishes. When your circumstances change (for example, when you retire or move to another province), review your will and, if appropriate, write a new one.

3. Do not choose a beneficiary as a witness. If such a person is called on to validate your will, he or she may not be able to collect an inheritance.

4. If you remarry, consider signing a pre-nuptial agreement to protect your children. If you sign such an agreement before the wedding, you and your intended spouse can legally agree that neither of you will make any claim on the other's estate. The agreement can be revoked later, if you both agree.

5. Consider using percentages, rather than dollar amounts, when you divide your estate. For example, if you leave $15,000 to a friend and the rest to your spouse, your spouse will suffer if your estate shrinks to $17,000.

6. Both you and your spouse should have a will, and those wills should be separate documents.

7. Be flexible. Don't insist that your heirs keep stock or run a cattle ranch. If you do so, they may suffer if economic conditions change.

8. Sign the original copy of your will and keep it in a safe place; keep an unsigned copy at home for reference.

9. Alter your will by preparing a new will or adding a codicil. Don't change beneficiaries by writing on the will itself; this may invalidate the will.

10. Select an executor who is both willing and able to carry out the complicated tasks associated with the job.

An executor has many important tasks—one of these is to obtain probate from court. **Probate** is the legal procedure of proving a valid or invalid will. It is the process by which an executor manages and distributes your property after you die, according to your will's provisions. A probate court generally validates wills and makes sure debts are paid. You should avoid probate because it is expensive, lengthy, and public. As you'll read later, a living trust avoids probate and is less expensive, quicker, and more private.

probate The legal procedure of proving a valid or invalid will.

SELECTING AN EXECUTOR   Select an executor, referred to as a liquidator in Quebec and a trustee in Ontario, who is both willing and able to carry out the complicated tasks associated with executing a will. These tasks are preparing an inventory of assets, collecting any money due, paying off any debts, preparing and filing all income and estate tax returns, liquidating and reinvesting other assets to pay off debts and provide income for your family while the estate is being administered, distributing the estate, and making a final accounting to your beneficiaries and to the probate court.

Your executor can be a family member, a friend, an attorney, an accountant, or the trust department of a bank. Exhibit 15–4 summarizes typical duties of an executor.

SELECTING A GUARDIAN   In addition to disposing of your estate, your will should name a guardian and/or trustee to care for minor children if both parents die at the same time, such as in an automobile accident or a plane crash. A **guardian** is a person who assumes the responsibilities of providing the children with personal care and of managing the estate for them. A **trustee**, on the other hand, is a person or an institution that holds or generally manages property for the benefit of someone else under a trust agreement.

guardian A person who assumes responsibility for providing children with personal care and managing the deceased's estate for them.

You should take great care in selecting a guardian for your children. You want a guardian whose philosophy on raising children is similar to yours and who is willing to accept the responsibility.

Through your will, you may want to provide funds to raise your children. You could, for instance, leave a lump sum for an addition to the guardian's house and establish monthly payments to cover your children's living expenses.

trustee A person or an institution that holds or manages property for the benefit of someone else under a trust agreement.

The guardian of the minor's estate manages the property you leave behind for your children. This guardian can be a person or the trust department of a financial institution, such as a bank.

Exhibit 15–4

Major Responsibilities of an Executor

The complexity of the estate determines the duties to be performed and the sequence. Certain provincial statutes may vary these duties.

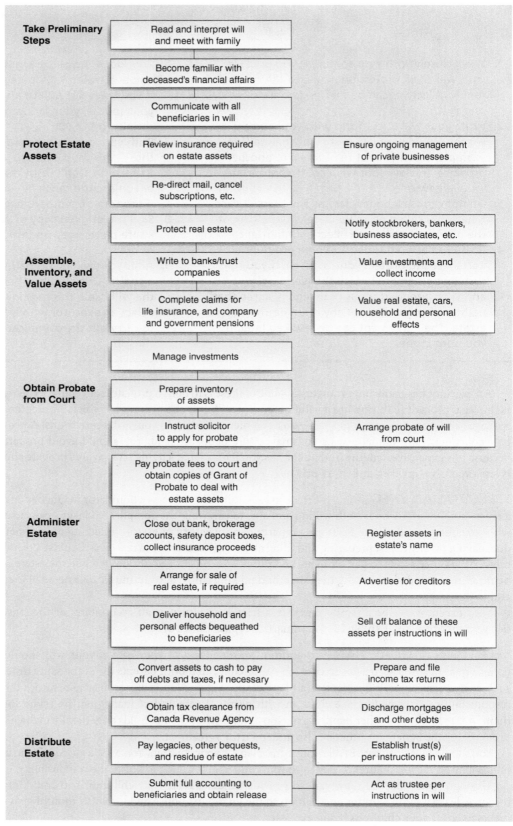

Take Preliminary Steps
- Read and interpret will and meet with family
- Become familiar with deceased's financial affairs
- Communicate with all beneficiaries in will

Protect Estate Assets
- Review insurance required on estate assets — Ensure ongoing management of private businesses
- Re-direct mail, cancel subscriptions, etc.
- Protect real estate — Notify stockbrokers, bankers, business associates, etc.

Assemble, Inventory, and Value Assets
- Write to banks/trust companies — Value investments and collect income
- Complete claims for life insurance, and company and government pensions — Value real estate, cars, household and personal effects
- Manage investments

Obtain Probate from Court
- Prepare inventory of assets
- Instruct solicitor to apply for probate — Arrange probate of will from court
- Pay probate fees to court and obtain copies of Grant of Probate to deal with estate assets

Administer Estate
- Close out bank, brokerage accounts, safety deposit boxes, collect insurance proceeds — Register assets in estate's name
- Arrange for sale of real estate, if required — Advertise for creditors
- Deliver household and personal effects bequeathed to beneficiaries — Sell off balance of these assets per instructions in will
- Convert assets to cash to pay off debts and taxes, if necessary — Prepare and file income tax returns
- Obtain tax clearance from Canada Revenue Agency — Discharge mortgages and other debts

Distribute Estate
- Pay legacies, other bequests, and residue of estate — Establish trust(s) per instructions in will
- Submit full accounting to beneficiaries and obtain release — Act as trustee per instructions in will

SOURCE: Adapted from Ho and Robinson, *Personal Financial Planning,* Third Edition (Captus Press, 2000, pp. 431–432).

Property that you place in trust for your children can be managed by the trustee, rather than by the guardian of the minor's estate.

SPECIFIC REQUIREMENTS FOR A WILL

Any person over the age of majority and of sound mind can draft his or her own will, with or without an attorney's help, although legal counsel is recommended especially to those who have expensive homes and valuable possessions or a hefty sum of money to bequeath. Additional requirements may vary, depending on the jurisdiction, but generally include the following:

- You must clearly state your full name and where you reside in Canada. You must also declare that you are of sound mind and that this will be your last will and testament. Once you have done this, you must date the legal document.
- Normally, a new will renders any former will(s) inapplicable; however, this is typically when the earlier will is altogether inconsistent with the new one. When a subsequent will is not completely inconsistent with a previous will, the previous will may be subject to debate or scrutiny. Therefore, it is best that you state that you revoke all other wills and testaments.
- Name all of your living relatives, and write each person's full name along with his or her address. This includes spouse, children, parents, and siblings. Once done with this, list the names of all your relatives who died before you. To conclude, mention any beneficiaries that are not related to you, such as friends, charities, or business associates.
- Make a list of all assets, valuables, and property that you would like to leave to people. You should also note the approximate worth of each asset and to whom it will go.
- You must appoint an executor for your will, who will ensure that your wishes are carried out. Typically, you should list alternative executors in case the person you appoint is no longer alive at the time the will has to be carried out. In Canada, the executor can be a member of your family.
- Your signature must be placed at the end of the will, in the presence of two witnesses. If the witnesses aren't present when you sign the will, you must acknowledge their signatures to validate their role as witnesses. There must be at least three signatures at the end of the will, along with the date.
- Keep the will in a secure place that is not accessible to other people. However, do ensure that the executor knows where it is. It is not inadvisable to keep a copy in your house for reference or in case the original is misplaced.*

codicil A document that modifies provisions in an existing will.

ALTERING OR REWRITING YOUR WILL

You should review your will if: you move to a different province; you sell property mentioned in the will; the size and composition of your estate change; you marry, divorce, or remarry; or potential heirs have died or been born.

Don't make any changes on the face of your will. Additions, deletions, or erasures on a will that has been signed and witnessed can invalidate the will.

If only a few changes are needed in your will, adding a codicil may be the best choice. A **codicil** is a document that explains, adds, or deletes provisions in your existing will. It identifies the will being amended and confirms the unchanged sections of the will. To be valid, it must conform to the legal requirements for a will.

If you wish to make major changes in your will or if you have already added a codicil, preparing a new will is preferable to adding a new codicil. In the new will, include a clause revoking all earlier wills and codicils.

Did you know?

Only certain provinces—Alberta, British Columbia, Manitoba, Newfoundland, Ontario, Prince Edward Island, and Saskatchewan—have laws making health-care directives binding. Quebec and Nova Scotia permit health-care proxies, but not living wills or advance health-care directives. However, court decisions suggest that living wills may be legally enforceable even in those provinces that do not have legislation authorizing them.

SOURCE: professionalreferrals.ca/article-113.html.

*SOURCES: en.wikipedia.org/wiki/Will_%28law%29; http://www.ehow.com/how_5173466_write-canada.html.

pre-nuptial agreement A documentary agreement between spouses before marriage.

If you are rewriting a will because of a remarriage, consider drafting a **pre-nuptial agreement**. This is a documentary agreement between spouses before marriage. In such agreements, one or both parties often waive a right to receive property under the other's will or under provincial law. Be sure to consult an attorney in drafting a pre-nuptial agreement.

Wills have existed for thousands of years; the oldest known will was written by the Egyptian pharaoh Uah in 2448 B.C. Recently, a new type of will, called a *living will*, has emerged.

A LIVING WILL

living will Describes the legal directives each province sanctions with respect to your medical care wishes, should you become unable to communicate them.

A **living will** provides for your wishes to be followed if you become so physically or mentally disabled that you are unable to act on your own behalf. A living will is not a substitute for a traditional will. The term "living will" is not a legal term in Canada. However, it is used to describe the legal directives each province sanctions with respect to your medical care wishes, should you become unable to communicate your wishes. Exhibit 15–5 is an example of a typical living will.*

To ensure the effectiveness of a living will, discuss your intention of preparing such a will with the people closest to you. You should also discuss this with your family doctor. Sign and date your document before two witnesses. Witnessing shows that you signed of your own free will.

*SOURCE: cbc.ca/news/background/wills/.

Exhibit 15–5

Example of a Living Will

Living Will Declaration

Declaration made this _____ day of _____ (month, year)

I, _____, being of sound mind, willfully and voluntarily make known my desire that my dying shall not be artificially prolonged under the circumstances set forth below, do hereby declare

If at any time I should have an incurable injury, disease, or illness regarded as a terminal condition by my physician and if my physician has determined that the application of life-sustaining procedures would serve only to artificially prolong the dying process and that my death will occur whether or not life-sustaining procedures are utilized, I direct that such procedures be withheld or withdrawn and that I be permitted to die with only the administration of medication or the performance of any medical procedure deemed necessary to provide me with comfort care.

In the absence of my ability to give directions regarding the use of such life-sustaining procedures, it is my intention that this declaration shall be honoured by my family and physician as the final expression of my legal right to refuse medical or surgical treatment and accept the consequences from such refusal.

I understand the full import of this declaration, and I am emotionally and mentally competent to make this declaration.

Signed _____

City and Province of Residence _____

The declarant has been personally known to me, and I believe him or her to be of sound mind.

Witness _____

Witness _____

SOURCE: *Don't Wait until Tomorrow* (Hartford, CT: Aetna Life and Casualty Company, n.d.), p. 11.

Give copies of your living will to those closest to you, and have your family doctor place a copy in your medical file. Keep the original document readily accessible, and look it over periodically—preferably once a year—to be sure your wishes have remained unchanged. To verify your intent, re-date and initial each subsequent endorsement.

Working through end-of-life issues is difficult, but it can help avoid forcing your family to make a decision in a hospital waiting room—or worse, having your last wishes ignored.

A living will can become a problem. A once-healthy person may have a change of heart and prefer to remain alive even as death seems imminent. Living wills call for careful thought, but they do provide you with a choice as to the manner of your death.

ETHICAL WILL

Since the September 11, 2001 terrorist attacks in the U.S., interest in another type of will has re-emerged. An **ethical will** is a way to impart your values and beliefs to your heirs. It is not a legally binding document, however, ethical wills can help with estate planning.

An excerpt from Dundee Wealth Senior Investment Advisor Kevin Hegedus's newsletter *Money Sense* gives us a brief look at the dynamics of such a will, and what it could do for your family.

> Before taking a trip to California shortly after September 11, 2001, Kim Payfrock, 42, wrote letters to her two sons and two stepsons, ages 11 to 17. The letters expressed her love for them as well as her joys and regrets in life. "I was nervous about flying and wanted them to open the letters if anything happened to me," says Payfrock, who is an activity coordinator at an assisted-living community in Minneapolis. "This was a way to leave them my thoughts, to give them a part of myself."
>
> Payfrock didn't know it at the time, but she had written each of her children an ethical will. Whereas legal wills bequeath material wealth, ethical wills dispense emotional and spiritual wealth. "It's a way to pass on your values, share lessons learned, express love, and address any regrets," says Barry Baines, the medical director of a hospice in Minneapolis and author of *Ethical Will: Putting Your Values on Paper*. Preparing such a document is not easy, since it requires earnest self-examination. But writers and recipients of ethical wills say the result is an invaluable legacy.*

ethical will A document that dispenses emotional and spiritual wealth to heirs.

Related to the concept of a living will is a **power of attorney**. A power of attorney is a legal document authorizing someone to act on your behalf. At some point in your life, you may become ill or incapacitated. You may then wish to have someone attend to your needs and your personal affairs. You can assign a power of attorney to anyone you choose. Power of attorney varies across Canada; refer to your provincial or territorial government or law society Web site(s) for more information.

power of attorney A legal document authorizing someone to act on one's behalf.

The person you name can be given limited power or a great deal of power. The power given can be special (to carry out certain acts or transactions), or it can be general (to act completely for you). A conventional power of attorney is automatically revoked in a case of legal incapacity.

LETTER OF LAST INSTRUCTION

In addition to your will, you should prepare a *letter of last instruction*. This document, though not legally enforceable, can provide your heirs with important information. It should contain the details of your funeral arrangements. It should also contain the names of the people who are to be notified of your death and the locations of your bank accounts, safety deposit box, and other important items.

---

*SOURCE: "Money Sense," a newsletter from the office of Kevin Hegedus, Dundee Wealth, 2nd Quarter 2011; dundeewealth.com/adv/khegedus-newsletter-2ndquarter2011.pdf, retrieved November 17, 2011. Disclaimer: This newsletter is solely the work of Kevin Hegedus for the private information of his clients. Although the author is a registered Senior Investment Advisor with DWM Securities Inc., a Dundee Wealth Inc. Company, this is not an official publication of DWM Securities Inc. The views (including any recommendations) expressed in this newsletter are those of the author alone, and they have not been approved by, and are not necessarily those of DWM Securities Inc.

> ## CONCEPT CHECK 15–3
>
> 1. What are the three formats of wills?
> 2. What are the steps in writing your will?
> 3. What is a power of attorney?
> 4. What is a letter of last instruction?

TYPES OF TRUSTS AND ESTATES

LO4

Appraise various types of trusts and estates.

settlor The creator of a trust; also called the grantor.

trust A legal arrangement through which one's assets are held by a trustee.

living trust A trust that is created and provides benefits during the settlor's lifetime.

A trust is a property arrangement in which the **settlor** sets up a trust by gifting property (the *subject* of the trust) that is legally owned and managed by a *trustee* according to the terms of the trust deed for the benefit of someone else, referred to as the *beneficiary*.

It is a good idea to discuss with your attorney the possibility of establishing a trust as a means of managing your estate. Basically, a **trust** is a legal arrangement through which a trustee holds your assets for your benefit or that of your beneficiaries. "Trusts today are used for everything from protecting assets from creditors to managing property for young children or disabled elders,"* according to one tax attorney.

TYPES OF TRUSTS

There are two types of personal trusts: a living, or *inter vivos*, trust and a testamentary trust. A trust established for the sole benefit of your spouse is referred to as a spousal trust. It can take either of the two forms just mentioned.

LIVING OR INTER VIVOS TRUST

A **living trust**, or inter vivos trust, is a property management arrangement set up during the settlor's lifetime. Assets are deemed to be transferred to the trust at their fair market value unless the trust is for the sole benefit of the spouse, in which case they are deemed to have been transferred at the settlor's adjusted cost base.

Living trusts can provide many advantages.

1. The settlor can retain control of how assets transferred to the trust are to be managed, and how the income and capital of the trust are to be distributed to the beneficiaries.
2. Assets transferred to the trust no longer form part of the settlor's estate and so are not subject to probate; nor are they deemed to have been sold upon the settlor's death.
3. If the trust is *irrevocable*, the assets transferred to the trust cannot be seized by the settlor's creditors.
4. A trust can be established to manage property for the benefit of disabled individuals, seniors, or minors. If the trust is established for a disabled individual, the *preferred beneficiary election* may permit income earned and held in trust for the beneficiary to be taxed at the beneficiary's lower rate.

Most of the disadvantages of a living trust centre around their tax treatment. Unless the trust is established for the sole benefit of a spouse, assets are deemed to be transferred to the trust at their fair market value, an assumption that may trigger an immediate taxable capital gain. Any income not distributed by the trust is taxed at the highest personal marginal tax rate, and income distributed from the trust to minors or a spouse remains subject to the attribution rules discussed in Chapter 3. Capital losses incurred through the disposition of assets held in trust cannot be allocated to beneficiary, but must be used to offset capital gains generated within the trust. Finally, the assets of non-spousal *inter vivos* trusts are deemed to be sold every 21 years, likely triggering a capital gain.

---

*SOURCE: Lynn Asinof, "Trust Funds Are Just for the Rich? Think Again," *The Wall Street Journal,* January 9, 1995, pp. C1, C10.

Waiting too long can be very costly, say the pros. Too often people either don't want to think about death and incompetency or they do not have enough information to make informed decisions. Then a problem occurs, and by then many valuable planning opportunities have been lost. Anyone with a home, savings, or minor children should consult an experienced estate planning attorney.

The term *estate planning* generally refers to the legal issues involved in planning for death, incompetency, and reducing or avoiding estate taxes. The process for settling a deceased person's affairs is called *probate*. Probate is a court process with two primary goals: (1) to make sure all debts are paid, and (2) to distribute property to the proper recipients. A will is a set of your instructions to a probate court judge for settling your affairs. A will allows you to avoid some of the more expensive aspects of probate. If you have minor children, a will is an absolute necessity for naming guardians, who will raise your children if you and your spouse are deceased. If you don't have a will, your province will give you a will by statute. This is called *intestate probate*. Intestate probate usually takes much longer and is more expensive. Everyone should at least have a will or risk leaving the families with a lot of unnecessary cost and aggravation.

Planning for incompetency may be even more important than planning for death. What happens if, because of age or illness, you cannot make decisions for yourself? Everyone should have durable powers of attorney for health care and property management. A *durable power of attorney* is a document that authorizes the person you choose to make decisions for you if you cannot make decisions for yourself. A *living will* is a statement of intent that you do not want your life to be artificially prolonged by a life support system.

A *living trust* is a modern approach to solving many of the problems of basic estate planning. A properly established living trust avoids probate and guardianship, and may reduce or eliminate estate taxes. When you create a living trust, you establish a new legal "person" that becomes the owner of your property. You do not give up any control of your affairs. Typically, you are the trustee (the manager of your property) and the beneficiary (the person entitled to the property). During your lifetime, there will be no effect on your day-to-day affairs. However, upon your death, because your trust—not you—is the legal owner of your property, there is no need for probate. Your designated successor trustee, typically your spouse or children, takes control of the trust and distributes your property according to your wishes without the cost and time of probate. If you become incompetent, a trust empowers your successor trustees to manage your affairs for you without the need for guardianship. A living trust can also be an invaluable tool to reduce or avoid estate taxes.

TESTAMENTARY TRUST A **testamentary trust** is established by your will and becomes effective upon your death. Such a trust can be valuable if your beneficiaries are inexperienced in financial matters and it might be beneficial to limit access to assets until a later date. A testamentary trust also provides the benefits of asset management and financial bookkeeping. Additional benefits include the following:

testamentary trust
A trust established by the creator's will that becomes effective upon his or her death.

1. Assets are protected from the beneficiary's creditors.
2. Inheritances are not subject to division upon the breakdown of a marriage unless one spouse has chosen to share, or commingle, them with the other. A testamentary trust can prevent the beneficiary from commingling assets with a spouse.
3. Income earned in a testamentary trust is taxed at progressive tax rates, although the trust does not benefit from personal tax credits. As long as income is payable to the beneficiaries, the executor of the trust can file an election to have the income taxed in the hands of the trust at the lower personal tax rates. This can significantly reduce the tax burden if beneficiaries are in the highest marginal tax bracket.

SPOUSAL TRUST Subject to certain conditions, you can create a trust for your spouse (or common-law spouse). The principal conditions are that (1) all of the income of the trust must be paid to the spouse during the spouse's lifetime, and (2) that none of the capital can be distributed to anyone else during your spouse's lifetime. This trust can actually be classified as either an inter vivos trust or a testamentary trust. The condition that the surviving spouse cannot remarry would nullify the trust. Assets can be transferred to a spousal trust at their adjusted cost base, thus avoiding capital gains. However, unlike non-spousal trusts, the assets are deemed to have been disposed of at their fair market value once the beneficiary spouse dies. Non-spousal trusts can transfer assets from the trust to the beneficiaries at their adjusted cost base, thus deferring any capital gain until the beneficiary sells the asset. Spousal trusts are not subject to the 21-year disposition rule and can be used if:

1. The beneficiary spouse needs guidance in financial management.
2. The deceased wishes to provide for the surviving spouse in a second marriage, but wishes to pass assets to children from a first marriage.
3. The deceased wishes to avoid double probate of assets (once in the hands of the deceased, and a second time upon the death of the surviving spouse who has received the assets outright).

PROS AND CONS OF A TRUST

PROS

- Typically, a will has to be probated, which can be a lengthy process especially if it is a large estate or a complicated case (e.g., a family business). A family trust renders the need to probate redundant as the assets in the living trust are transferred by a trustee according to the terms of the trust. Essentially this means that the assets are distributed without going through probate.
- Generally, when a will undergoes probate, its contents become a public record and are available for anyone to read. Establishing a living trust usually keeps the matter private, and may also be a saving grace if there are people who might file lawsuits as a result of a will being exposed.
- It is easier to change the terms of a living trust as circumstances change than to change the contents of a will, since the latter requires more formality and procedures. Generally, a will should be rewritten when changes are necessary.
- Having assigned a trustee while setting up the living trust, you can rest assured that this person has the authority to manage your assets in event that you become disabled, without having to go through guardianship proceedings to determine who can act for you.

CONS

- The trust must be properly funded. Your assets must be formally transferred to the trust for the creation of the trust to be a useful exercise. If you do not adequately fund your trust, then the advantages above do not apply. This transfer takes time and has some expense. In addition, transferring real estate can pose a problem if any financial obligations on the property need to be modified (e.g., getting a new mortgage).
- The cost of having an attorney set up a trust is generally greater than the cost of writing a will. This cost is in addition to the expenses of funding the living trust.*

ESTATES

Your *estate* is everything you own. It includes all of your property—tangible and intangible, however acquired or owned, whether inside or outside the country. It may include jointly owned property, life insurance, and employee benefits. Thus, an important step in estate planning is taking inventory of everything you own, such as:

1. Cash, chequing accounts, savings accounts, GICs, and money market funds.
2. Stocks, bonds (including provincial and Canada Savings Bonds), mutual funds, commodity futures, and tax shelters.

---

*SOURCE: retirementinvestigator.com/living-trust-pros-and-cons.html.

3.   Life insurance, employee benefits, and annuities.
4.   Your home and any other real estate, land and buildings, furniture, and fixtures.
5.   Farms, grain, livestock, machinery, and equipment.
6.   Proprietorship, partnership, and close corporation interests.
7.   Notes, accounts, and claims receivable.
8.   Interests in trusts and powers of appointment.
9.   Antiques, works of art, collectibles, cars, boats, planes, personal effects, and everything else.

ESTATE ASSETS NOT DISTRIBUTED BY A WILL

By law, there are two situations in which your assets will go directly to a beneficiary, independently of your will. The first is one in which your assets, such as life insurance, annuities, and RRSPs, already have a named beneficiary. Unless your beneficiary has pre-deceased you, these assets are transferred directly without being subject to the process or expense of probate. In cases where the beneficiary has pre-deceased you, then the values are transferred to your estate.

The second situation occurs when you have assets held in *joint tenancy*, which confers the right of survivorship. Note that this is not the same as *tenancy in common*, where the assets are owned in undivided shares. For example, if a couple owns a home in joint tenancy, then the ownership of that home passes in its entirety to the spouse upon death of the other spouse. However, if the same couple owns their home as *tenants in common*, where the tenants have the right to dispose of their interest in the joint property at death, there is no automatic right of survivorship and one-half of the value of the home will count into the deceased spouse's estate.

LIFE INSURANCE AND EMPLOYEE BENEFITS   Life insurance proceeds are free of income tax and excluded from probate. Assigning ownership to your beneficiary or a trust removes a life insurance policy from your estate. Death benefits from qualified pension plans are excluded from your estate, unless they are payable to it.

Did you know?

"Without a will, your estate would be distributed according to the laws of the province you lived in. The legislation applies a set formula to divide the estate among your spouse, children and relatives, and the results could be very different from what you really want…".

SOURCE: http://www.tdwaterhouse.ca/products-services/investing/private-client-services/wande-planning.jsp.

CHARITABLE DONATIONS   You can structure charitable gifts both during your lifetime and in your will to further your estate planning goals and make the most of available tax credits. There are a number of ways in which gifts of capital or property can be made with significant tax benefits. One example of this is if you elect to make a charitable gift through your will. In this case, your taxable income in the year of your death is reduced by the tax credit for charitable donations. The gift could be up to 100 percent of your net income in the year of death, and excess can be carried back to the preceding year. If a similar gift was made during your lifetime, the gift could not exceed a maximum of 75 percent of your net income, and any excess would have to be carried forward for up to five years.

If you sit down with a qualified adviser and carefully map out a gifting strategy for your estate, it is possible to both fulfill your philanthropic desires and have your estate receive favourable tax treatment.

SETTLING YOUR ESTATE

If you have had a will drawn, you are *testate* in the eyes of the law, and an executor (named in your will) will carry out your wishes in due time. If you have not named an executor, the probate court (the court that supervises the distribution of estates) will appoint an administrator to carry out the instructions in your will.

PROBATE AND ADMINISTRATION COSTS   Your estate administration costs includes fees for attorneys, accountants, appraisers, executors or administrators and trustees, court costs,

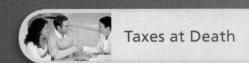

The old saying that "there are only two certainties in life—death and taxes" holds true even at death. There is no escaping it, but there are ways to lessen the burden of this unanticipated beneficiary, called the government. While there are no true "estate taxes" in Canada, three potential taxes or pseudo-taxes may be incurred at death:

- Income tax due to the deemed disposition rules
- Provincial probate taxes
- U.S. Estate Tax on your U.S. assets

DEEMED DISPOSITION

In the year of death, a final (terminal) tax return must be filed by the estate's executor/liquidator that includes all income earned by the deceased up to the date of death. Also, included in income at death is the net capital gain recognized under the deemed disposition rules. The deemed disposition rules of the Income Tax Act treat all capital property owned by the deceased as if it was sold immediately prior to death. Thus, all unrecognized capital gains and losses are triggered at that point with the net capital gain (gains less losses) included in income. The Income Tax Act does contain provisions to defer the tax owing under the deemed disposition rules if the asset is left to a surviving spouse or to a special trust for a spouse (spousal trust) created by the deceased's will. This provision allows the spouse or the spousal trust to take ownership of the asset at the deceased's original cost. Hence, no tax is payable until either the spouse or the spousal trust sells the asset or until the surviving spouse dies. The tax is then payable based on the asset's increase in value at that time.

RRSPs AND RRIFs

In addition to the potentially significant tax liability from recognized capital gains, it is also necessary to deregister (i.e., collapse) any registered assets, such as RRSPs or RRIFs, at the point of death. The full value of the RRSP or RRIF must be included on the deceased's final (terminal) tax return. There are exceptions to this deregistration requirement if the RRSP or RRIF is left to the surviving spouse, a common-law spouse, and, in some cases, to a surviving child or grandchild. An RRSP or RRIF can be transferred tax free to a surviving spouse's plan. Similar treatment is accorded the transfer of RRSP or RRIF assets to a mentally or physically infirm child or grandchild. If the RRSP or RRIF is left to a dependent child or grandchild under the age of 18, the registered funds must be used to purchase a term certain annuity with a term not exceeding the child's eighteenth year. This choice is available even if there is a surviving spouse.

PROBATE TAXES

Upon death, the executor of your estate is typically required to file for probate with the provincial court. The estate's executor must submit to the court the original will and an inventory of your assets. Upon acceptance of these documents by the court, letters (called "certificate of appointment of estate trustee with a will" in Ontario) are issued. The letters serve to verify that the submitted will is a valid document and confirms the appointment of your executor. With the executor's submission to the court, he or she must also pay a probate tax. This tax is based on the total value of the assets that flow through the will. The rate charged varies between provinces, with some provinces having a maximum fee. In situations where the estate is simple and does not require any involvement with a third party, such as a financial institution, the will may not need to be probated. As well, probate taxes can be reduced by using previously discussed strategies, such as naming beneficiaries, joint Tenancy with Right of Survivorship agreements, and using living trusts.

U.S. ESTATE TAX

In addition to the taxes payable in Canada, your estate may also be subject to a tax bill from the U.S. Government. Canadians who own American-sourced assets, such as real estate, corporate stocks and certain bonds, and government debt are required to pay U.S. Estate Tax based on the market value of their American assets at the time of death. For more information on U.S. Estate Tax, the Royal Bank of Canada offers a publication entitled, *Tax Implications of Investing in the United States*.

SOURCE: RBC Investments—Education Centre, rbcfinancialplanning.com/estate-planning.html.

bonding and surety costs, and miscellaneous expenses. These administration costs may run to 3 to 5 percent of your estate, depending on its size and complexity. While the percentage usually decreases as the size of the estate increases, it may be increased by additional complicating factors, such as handling a business interest. Inversely to administration costs, probate costs tend to rise with the size of the estate. The exact costs, payable to the court, are paid out of the proceeds of your estate and are set by the court.

If you don't have a will, you become *intestate* at your death. In that case, your estate is put under the control of a court-appointed administrator for distribution according to the laws of the province in which you reside.

Although the process of estate planning is a trying one because it forces you to think about emotionally charged issues, such as what you leave behind and to whom, a will may be its most important feature. Remember the old adage that the act of not deciding is a decision in itself.

As we discuss earlier in this chapter, if you don't make a will or use some other legal method to transfer your property when you die, provincial law will determine what happens to your property. This process is called "intestate succession." Your property will be distributed to your spouse and children or, if you have neither, to the closest next of kin according to a statutory formula (usually in this order: parents; if neither is surviving, siblings; if none, nieces/nephews; if none, other next of kin). If no relatives can be found to inherit your property, it all goes to the government.

CONCEPT CHECK 15–4

1. Differentiate among the types of trusts.
2. What is included in an estate?
3. What are the two types of joint ownership?

SUMMARY OF LEARNING OBJECTIVES

LO1 Analyze the personal aspects of estate planning.
Estate planning is an essential part of retirement planning and an integral part of financial planning. The first part of estate planning consists of building your estate; the second part consists of transferring your estate, at your death, in the manner you have specified. The personal aspects of estate planning depend on whether you are single or married. If you are married, your estate planning involves the interests of at least two people, and more if there are children. Never having been married does not eliminate the need to organize your financial affairs.

LO2 Assess the legal aspects of estate planning.
In the event of death, proof of claims must be produced or the claims will not be processed. Among the papers needed are birth certificates, marriage certificates, legal name changes, and military service records. Every adult should have a written will, which is the legal declaration of a person's wishes as to the disposition of his or her property after death. A will is a way to transfer your property according to your wishes after you die.

LO3 Distinguish among will formats.
The three formats for wills are holographic, formal, and notarial. A holographic will is handwritten and requires no witness but is a poor choice for most people and some provinces will not recognize it. A formal will is a typed document signed by you and witnessed by two individuals who must not be beneficiaries or the spouses of beneficiaries. A lawyer is usually employed to draft a formal will. A notarial will, available only in Quebec, is typed and signed in the presence of the notary and at least one witness. The notary keeps the original will and can issue a certified copy to the heirs once proof of death has been established.

LO4 Appraise various types of trusts and estates.
Establishing a trust can be an excellent way to manage your estate. Popular forms of trusts include living trusts, testamentary trusts, and spousal trusts. An attorney's help is needed to establish a trust.

KEY TERMS

beneficiary 455	**holographic will** 455	**probate** 457
codicil 459	**intestate** 453	**settlor** 462
estate 450	**living trust** 462	**testamentary trust** 463
estate planning 450	**living will** 460	**trust** 462
ethical will 461	**notarial will** 455	**trustee** 457
formal will 455	**power of attorney** 461	**will** 453
guardian 457	**pre-nuptial agreement** 460	

FINANCIAL PLANNING ACTIVITIES

 Practise and learn online with Connect.

1. *Preparing a Written Record of Personal Information.* Prepare a written record of personal information that would be helpful to you and your heirs. Make sure to include the location of family records, your military service file, and other important papers; medical records; bank accounts; charge accounts; the location of your safety deposit box; Canada Savings Bonds; stocks, bonds, and other securities; property owned; life insurance; annuities; and government benefits information. LO1

2. *Developing Long-Term Estate Planning Goals.* Develop a list of specific long-term estate planning goals with your family. Discuss how those goals could be achieved even if you or your spouse died unexpectedly. LO1

3. *Drafting a Simple Will.* Draft your will, using Exhibit 15–1 as a guideline. Whom will you appoint as a trustee or guardian for your minor children? Why? LO2

4. *Comparing Costs of Preparing a Will.* Contact several lawyers in your area to find out how much they would charge to prepare your simple will. Are their fees about the same? LO3

5. *Using the Internet to Obtain Information about Wills.* Visit Metropolitan Life Insurance Company's Web page at lifeadvice.com. Using this information, prepare a report on the following: (a) Who needs a will? (b) What are the elements of a will (naming a guardian, naming an executor, preparing a will, updating a will, estate taxes, where to keep your will, living will, etc.)? (c) How is this report helpful in preparing your own will? LO3

6. *Preparing the Letter of Last Instructions.* Prepare your own letter of last instructions. LO3

7. *Determining Criteria in Choosing a Guardian.* Make a list of the criteria you will use in deciding who will be the guardian of your minor children if you and your spouse die at the same time. LO3

8. *Establishing a Trust.* Discuss with your attorney the possibility of establishing a trust as a means of managing your estate. LO4

CREATING A FINANCIAL PLAN

Developing an Estate Plan

Most people do not think they have enough assets to do estate planning. However, the planned transfer of resources by using a will, trusts, and other legal vehicles is a necessary phase of your total financial plan.

Web Sites for Estate Planning

- Learn what's involved in developing an estate plan and how to take advantage of all your options at the TD Canada Trust site, **tdcanadatrust.com/planning/life-events/index.jsp.**

- The Royal Bank, at **royalbank.com**, has information on estate planning as part of its *Your Money Matters* series of guides.

- The Law Society of Upper Canada, at **lsuc.on.ca**, offers a guide for Ontario residents with regard to probating a will.

(Note: Addresses and content of Web sites change, and new sites are created daily. Use search engines to update and locate Web sites for your current financial planning needs.)

Short-Term Financial Planning Activities

1. Investigate the cost of a will. Decide on the type of will and provisions appropriate for your life situation.

2. Using the Canada Revenue Agency and other Web sites, identify recent estate tax law changes that may affect your financial planning decisions.

3. Compare the benefits and costs of different trusts that might be appropriate for your life situation.

Long-Term Financial Planning Activities

1. Develop a plan for actions to be taken related to estate planning.

2. Identify saving and investing decisions that would minimize future estate taxes.

LIFE SITUATION CASE

Don't Let Your Windfall Blow Away

Warren, a married entrepreneur who owns a successful promotions business, doesn't yet have kids, but he is already making plans. Last December, Warren received an unexpected inheritance of $1.4 million, after taxes, from his late grandfather. Instead of buying a Porsche or a new home, he did the right thing by his family-to-be and invested it all. "Warren is extremely fastidious," says Lesley Sommers, his financial planner.

Warren did what smart people do with sudden wealth: They decide not to blow it. A 1997 survey found that 59 percent of 1,000 respondents who received cash payouts of $20,000 or more had sought professional advice. An equal number had invested every dime. When Warren got his windfall, Sommers invested all but $100,000. Warren says, "She taught me that this

[windfall] should not change where I eat or go on vacation." So, if you win the lottery, don't blow it on houses, cars, vacations, and luxury items. Instead, pay off high-interest credit card and other debts that offer no tax deductions. Then, find a financial adviser. This professional can help you find a competent estate planner and create an investment plan.

Questions

1. What did Warren do with his $1.4 million inheritance?

2. What do smart people do with sudden wealth?

SOURCE: Adapted from Joan Oleck, "Don't Let Your Windfall Blow Away," *BusinessWeek On-line*, December 1999, p. 116. Reprinted from the March 1, 1999 issue of *BusinessWeek* by special permission. © 1999 McGraw-Hill Companies, Inc.

CONTINUOUS CASE FOR PART 5

PLANNING FOR TOMORROW

Life Situation
Pamela, 48; Isaac, 50; children, ages 21, 19, and 16

Financial Goals

- Replenish savings and investments used for college/university costs

- Plan for retirement in about 15 years

- Consider estate planning activities

Financial Data

Monthly income	$ 5,700
Living expenses	4,600
Assets	242,500
Liabilities	69,100

With two children in college, the Mortimers once again find their life situation changing. Compared with five years ago, their total assets have decreased from $262,700 to $242,500 due to college expenses. The Mortimers' oldest child will graduate next year, but the youngest will enter university in a couple of years. Therefore, the drain on the family's finances will continue.

The family's finances are adequate, but both Pamela and Isaac are beginning to worry about retirement. Over the years, Isaac has taken advantage of different career opportunities. Today, his annual salary, $68,400, is higher than it has ever been. But his employment changes have resulted in a smaller pension fund than would be available had he remained with the same organization. The current value of his pension plan is just over $115,000. The investment program he and Pamela started almost 10 years ago is growing and is now worth about $62,000. But they still worry whether they will have enough money to finance their retirement dreams when Isaac retires in 15 years. According to Isaac, "If I retired today, we couldn't maintain our current lifestyle. In fact, we couldn't even exist."

Questions

1. How would you rate the Mortimers' financial condition at this stage in their lives?

2. Given that Pamela is 48 and Isaac is 50, what should be their major priorities as they continue planning for retirement?

3. What types of estate planning, if any, should the Mortimers consider at this time?

Glossary

accident benefits Automobile insurance that covers medical expenses for people injured in one's car. 247

account executive A licensed individual who buys or sells securities for clients; also called a *stockbroker*. 348

actual cash value (ACV) A claim settlement method in which the insured receives payment based on the current replacement cost of a damaged or lost item, less depreciation. 244

adjusted balance method The assessment of finance charges after payments made during the billing period have been subtracted. 185

adult life cycle The stages in the family situation and financial needs of an adult. 10

adult lifestyle/retirement community Independent living residences (bungalows, townhouses, or smaller homes) for retirees or semi-retirees in a community of healthy seniors. 430

all risk A policy in which any event that causes loss or damage to the insured property is covered unless it is specifically excluded. 241

amortization The reduction of a loan balance through payments made over a period of time. 216

annual dividend yield A stock's annual dividend divided by its beginning-of-year stock price. If the dividend is divided by the end-of-year stock price, it is referred to as its *trailing* dividend yield. 344

annual percentage rate (APR) The yearly interest rate quoted by a financial institution on a loan. The APR may be compounded more frequently than once a year, in which case the effective annual rate on the loan will be higher than the APR. 180

annual shareholder return A stock's annual dividend and increase in value divided by its beginning-of-year stock price. 344

annuity A series of equal amounts (deposits or withdrawals) made at regular time intervals. 19

appraisal An estimate of the current value of a property. 223

assets Cash and other property with a monetary value. 51

automated teller machine (ATM) A computer terminal used to conduct banking transactions. 119

average daily balance method A method of computing finance charges that uses a weighted average of the account balance throughout the current billing period. 185

average tax rate Total tax due divided by total income. 78

bankruptcy A set of federal laws that allow you to either restructure your debts or remove certain debts. 23

bear market Occurs when investors are pessimistic about a nation's economy and sell their stocks. 343

bearer bond A bond that is not registered in the investor's name. 370

beneficiary (1) A person designated to receive something, such as life insurance proceeds, from the insured. 268; (2) A person who has been named to receive property under a will. 455

beta An index that compares the risk associated with a specific stock issue with the risk of the stock market in general. 345

blue-chip stock A safe investment that generally attracts conservative investors. 337

bodily injury liability Coverage for the risk of financial loss due to legal expenses, medical costs, lost wages, and other expenses associated with injuries caused by an automobile accident for which the insured was responsible. 247

bond indenture A legal document that details all the conditions relating to a bond issue. 366

budget A specific plan for spending income. 58

budget deficit The amount by which actual spending exceeds planned spending. 62

budget surplus The amount by which actual spending is less than planned spending. 62

budget variance The difference between the amount budgeted and the actual amount received or spent. 62

bull market Occurs when investors are optimistic about a nation's economy and buy stocks. 343

call feature A feature that allows the corporation to call in or buy outstanding bonds from current bondholders before the maturity date. 367

callable preferred stocks Stocks that a corporation may exchange, at its option, for a specified amount of money. 334

capacity The borrower's financial ability to meet credit obligations. 166

capital The borrower's assets or net worth. 166

capital gain distributions The payments made to a fund's shareholders that result from the sale of securities in the fund's portfolio. 410

capital gains yield A stock's increase in value divided by its beginning-of-year stock price. 344

capitalization The total amount of securities—stocks and bonds—issued by a corporation. 337

cash flow The actual inflow and outflow of cash during a given time period. 53

cash flow statement A financial statement that summarizes cash receipts and payments for a given period. 53

cash value The amount received after giving up a life insurance policy. 264

character The borrower's attitude toward credit obligations. 166

chartered bank A financial institution that offers a full range of financial services to individuals, businesses, and government agencies. 123

churning The excessive buying and selling of securities to generate commissions. 349

closed-end fund A mutual fund whose shares are issued by an investment company only when the fund is originally set up. 395

closing costs Fees and charges paid when a real estate transaction is completed; also called *settlement costs*. 220

codicil A document that modifies provisions in an existing will. 459

co-insurance clause A policy provision that requires a homeowner to pay for part of the losses if the property is not insured for the specified percentage of the replacement value. 243

collateral A valuable asset that is pledged to ensure loan payments. 166

collision Automobile insurance that pays for damage to the insured's car when it is involved in an accident. 248

compounding A process that calculates interest based on previously earned interest. 18

comprehensive physical damage Automobile insurance that covers financial loss from damage to a vehicle caused by a risk other than a collision, such as fire, theft, glass breakage, hail, or vandalism. 248

conditions The general economic conditions that can affect a borrower's ability to repay a loan. 166

condominium An individually owned housing unit in a building with several such units. 209

consumer credit The use of credit for personal needs (except a home mortgage). 144

consumer loan One-time loans that the borrower pays back in a specified period of time with a pre-determined payment schedule. 147

consumer proposal A maximum five-year plan for paying creditors all or a portion of a debt owed. 192

contingent deferred sales load A 1- to 6-percent charge that shareholders pay when they withdraw their investment from a mutual fund. 398

convertible bond A bond that can be exchanged, at the owner's option, for a specified number of shares of the corporation's common stocks. 367

co-operative housing A type of subsidized housing in which half the units have geared-to-income rental prices. 209

co-payment A provision under which the insured pays a flat dollar amount each time a covered medical service is received after the deductible has been met. 283

corporate bond A corporation's written pledge to repay a specified amount of money, along with interest. 306, 364

credit An arrangement to receive cash, goods, or services now and pay for them in the future. 144

credit bureau A reporting agency that assembles credit and other information about consumers. 160

credit insurance Any type of insurance that ensures repayment of a loan in the event the borrower is unable to repay it. 187

credit limit The dollar amount, which may or may not be borrowed, that a lender makes available to a borrower. 147

credit reporting legislation 162
Fair Credit Reporting Act—Applicable in British Columbia, Ontario, Nova Scotia, and Prince Edward Island
Credit Reporting Agencies Act—Applicable in Saskatchewan and Newfoundland and Labrador
Personal Investigations Act—Applicable in Manitoba
Consumer Protection Act—Applicable in Quebec

credit union/caisse populaire A user-owned, non-profit co-operative financial institution that is organized for the benefit of its members. 123

cumulative preferred stocks Stocks with unpaid dividends that accumulate and must be paid before any cash dividend is paid to common shareholders. 334

current liabilities Debts that must be paid within a short time, usually less than a year. 52

current yield Determined by dividing the dollar amount of annual interest from an investment by its current market value. 383

cyclical stock A stock that follows the business cycle of advances and declines in the economy. 337

debenture A bond that is backed only by the reputation of the issuing corporation. 366

deductions Expenses that can be deducted from total income, such as child care expenses, union dues, disability support payments, investment counselling fees, and certain employment-related expenses. 76

deed (or title) A document that transfers ownership of property from one party to another. 220

defensive stock A stock that remains stable during declines in the economy. 337

defined benefit pension plan A plan that specifies the benefits the employee will receive at the normal retirement age. 434

defined contribution pension plan Also called a *money purchase pension plan*, this plan specifies the contribution from the employee and/or employer but does not guarantee the pension benefit you will receive. 434

depreciated value A reduction in the value of an object, based upon its age and the percentage it has decreased each year. 238

direct investment plan A plan that allows shareholders to purchase stocks directly from a corporation without having to use an account executive or a brokerage firm. 354

disability income insurance Provides payments to replace income when an insured person is unable to work. 276

discretionary income Money left over after paying for housing, food, and other necessities. 55

discretionary order An order to buy or sell a security that lets the account executive decide when to execute the transaction and at what price. 351

diversification (1) The process of spreading your assets among several types of investments to lessen risk. 309; (2) Investment technique that involves combining many assets in a portfolio to reduce its risk. 353

dividend A distribution of money, stocks, or other property that a corporation pays to shareholders. 305

dividend reinvestment plan A plan that allows current shareholders the option to reinvest or use their cash dividends to purchase stocks of the corporation. 354

dollar cost averaging A long-term technique used by investors who purchase an equal dollar amount of the same stocks at equal intervals. 354

double indemnity A benefit under which the company pays twice the face value of the policy if the insured's death results from an accident. 270

driver classification A category based on the driver's age, gender, marital status, driving record, and driving habits; used to determine automobile insurance rates. 250

earnings per share (EPS) A corporation's after-tax earnings divided by the number of outstanding shares of common stocks. 345

economics The study of how wealth is created and distributed. 13

effective annual rate (EAR) A formula that calculates the effective return, taking compounding into account. 130

$$EAR = \left[1 + \frac{k}{m}\right]^m - 1$$

m = number of compounding periods in a year

k = rate of return quoted for a year

efficient market hypothesis States that future prices cannot be predicted from past trends and patterns. 336

emergency fund An amount of money you can obtain quickly in case of immediate need. 295

employment income Remuneration received for personal effort. 74

equity capital Money that a business obtains from its owners. 305

escrow account Money, usually deposited with the lending institution, for the payment of property taxes and homeowner's insurance. 220

estate Everything one owns. 450

estate planning A definite plan for the administration and disposition of one's property during one's lifetime and at one's death. 450

ethical will A document that dispenses emotional and spiritual wealth to heirs. 461

exchange-traded fund (ETFs) An affordable way for investors to invest in a diversified basket of securities; provides the diversification of an index fund with the flexibility of a stock. 397

excise tax A tax imposed on specific goods and services, such as gasoline, cigarettes, alcoholic beverages, tires, and air travel. 72

ex-dividend A stock trades without a dividend and the seller is entitled to the declared dividend payment. 331

face value The dollar amount the bondholder will receive at the bond's maturity. 364

family of funds A group of mutual funds managed by one investment company. 403

financial plan A formalized report that summarizes your current financial situation, analyzes your financial needs, and recommends future financial activities. 26

formal will A will that is usually prepared with an attorney's assistance. 455

for-profit co-operative housing Rental housing for which members own shares although they do not own the units in which they live. 209

fundamental analysis A way to value stocks by looking at micro and macro factors that might influence the economic value of the stock. 336

future value The amount to which current savings will increase based on a certain interest rate and a certain time period; typically involves compounding. 18

government bond The written pledge of a government or a municipality to repay a specified sum of money, along with interest. 306

gross debt service (GDS) ratio Your monthly shelter costs as a percentage of your gross monthly income; a ratio used to determine the maximum affordable mortgage payment, mortgage amount, and home purchase price. 210

growth stock A stock issued by a corporation that has the potential to earn profits above the average profits of all firms in the economy. 337

Guaranteed Investment Certificates (GICs) Term deposits made for a longer period, usually from one to five years. 129

guardian A person who assumes responsibility for providing children with personal care and managing the deceased's estate for them. 457

hazard A factor that increases the likelihood of loss through some peril. 231

high-risk pool Consists of people who are unable to obtain automobile insurance due to poor driving or accident records and must obtain coverage at high rates. 251

holographic will A handwritten will. 455

home equity line of credit A personal line of credit based on the current market value of your home less the amount still owed on the mortgage. 153

homeowner's insurance Coverage for a place of residence and its associated financial risks. 237

household inventory A list or other documentation of personal belongings, with purchase dates and cost information. 238

income Inflow of cash to an individual or a household. 54

income dividends The earnings a fund pays to shareholders after it has deducted expenses from its dividend and interest income. 409

income stock A stock that pays higher-than-average dividends. 337

incontestability clause A provision stating that the insurer cannot dispute the validity of a policy after a specified period. 269

index A statistical measure of the changes in a portfolio of stocks representing a portion of the overall market. 328

index fund An affordable way for investors to invest in a diversified basket of securities; constructed to track the components of a market index such as the S&P 500 or the S&P/TSX Composite. 397

inflation A rise in the general level of prices. 14

initial public offering (IPO) Occurs when a corporation sells stock to the general public for the first time. 347

insolvency The inability to pay debts when they are due because liabilities far exceed the value of assets. 53

insurance Protection against possible financial loss. 231

insurance company A risk-sharing firm that assumes financial responsibility for losses that may result from an insured risk. 231

insured A person covered by an insurance policy. 231

insurer An insurance company. 231

interest A periodic charge for the use of credit. 147

interest-adjusted index A method of evaluating the cost of life insurance by taking into account the time value of money. 272

intestate Without a valid will. 453

investment bank A financial firm that assists corporations in raising funds, usually by helping to sell new security issues. 347

investment company A firm that, for a management fee, invests the pooled funds of small investors in securities appropriate to its stated investment objectives. 395

investment income Income from property, including income in the form of interest, dividends, and rents net of expenses. 74

junk bond A type of bond that offers a very high return but is very risky as the bond is nearing or currently in default. 381

large-cap stock A stock issued by a large corporation that has a large amount of stocks outstanding and a large amount of capitalization. 337

lease A legal document that defines the conditions of a rental agreement. 205

level premiums Insurance premiums that remain the same over the lifetime of a policy. 263

liabilities Amounts owed to others. 52

liability Legal responsibility for the financial cost of another person's losses or injuries. 236

life cycle approach The idea that the average person goes through four basic stages in personal financial management. 10

life lease housing A form of housing tenure where a tenant is given the right to live in a dwelling unit in return for an upfront payment and monthly maintenance fees. 430

limit order A request to buy or sell stock at a specified price. 350

liquid assets Cash and items of value that can easily be converted to cash. 51

liquidity (1) The ability to readily convert financial resources into cash without a loss in value. 23; (2) The ability to buy or sell an investment quickly without substantially affecting the investment's value. 304

living trust A trust that is created and provides benefits during the settlor's lifetime. 462

living will A document that enables an individual, while well, to express the intention that life be allowed to end (i.e., no extraordinary medical measures or life support equipment be used) if he or she becomes terminally ill. 460

load fund A mutual fund in which investors pay a commission (as high as 8.5 percent) every time they purchase or sell shares. 398

long-term care (LTC) Provides day-in, day-out care for long-term illness or disability. 282

long-term liabilities Debts that are not required to be paid in full until more than a year from now. 53

Managed Asset Program (MAP) A program allowing an investor to invest in portfolios grouping together many different mutual funds. 403

manufactured home A housing unit that is fully or partially assembled in a factory before being moved to the living site. 208

margin A speculative technique whereby an investor borrows part of the money needed to buy a particular stock. 355

marginal tax rate The rate of tax paid on the next dollar of taxable income. 78

market order A request to buy or sell stocks at the current market value. 350

market timer An individual who helps investors decide when to switch their investments from one fund to another fund, usually within the same family of funds. 403

maturity date For a corporate bond, the date on which the corporation is to repay the borrowed money. 365

money management Day-to-day financial activities necessary to manage current personal economic resources while working toward long-term financial security. 48

money market fund A savings investment plan offered by investment companies, with earnings based on investments in various short-term financial instruments. 123

mortgage A personal loan used to purchase a property. 210

mortgage bond A corporate bond secured by various assets of the issuing firm. 367

mutual fund An investment alternative chosen by people who pool their money to buy stocks, bonds, and other securities selected by professional managers employed by an investment company. 306, 394

named perils A policy in which only those perils that are specifically listed will be covered should a loss occur. 241

NASDAQ (pronounced "nazzdack") An electronic marketplace for over 6,000 stocks. 348

negligence Failure to take ordinary or reasonable care in a situation. 236

net asset value (NAV) The current market value of the securities contained in the mutual fund's portfolio minus the mutual fund's liabilities divided by the number of shares outstanding. 395

net business income Net income from an activity that is carried out for profit, after expenses have been deducted. 74

net income Total income reduced by certain deductions, such as contributions to an RRSP or RPP. 76

net worth The difference between total assets and total liabilities. 53

no-fault insurance An automobile insurance program in which drivers involved in accidents collect medical expenses, lost wages, and related injury costs from their own insurance companies. 246

no-load fund A mutual fund in which the individual investor pays no sales charge. 399

non-forfeiture clause A provision that allows the insured not to forfeit all accrued benefits. 268

non-profit co-operative housing Rental housing owned by a community group, religious group, or non-profit organization to provide affordable housing. 209

notarial will A will made in the presence of a notary and at least one witness, and that does not require probate. Available only in Quebec. 455

odd lot Fewer than 100 shares of a particular stock. 351

open-end fund A mutual fund whose shares are issued and redeemed by the investment company at the request of investors. 395

opportunity cost What a person gives up by making a choice. 5

option The right to buy or sell stocks at a predetermined price during a specified period of time. 357

overdraft protection An automatic loan made to chequing account customers to cover the amount of cheques written in excess of the available balance in the account. 134

over-the-counter (OTC) market A network of dealers who buy and sell the stocks of corporations that are not listed on a securities exchange. 348

penny stock A stock that typically sells for less than $1 per share. 337

peril The cause of a possible loss. 231

personal articles endorsement Additional property insurance to cover the damage or loss of a specific item of high value. 238

personal balance sheet A financial statement that reports what an individual or a family owns and owes; also called a *net worth statement.* 51

personal financial planning The process of managing your money to achieve personal economic satisfaction. 3

personal line of credit A prearranged loan from a bank for a maximum specified amount. 148

policy A written contract for insurance. 231

policyholder A person who owns an insurance policy. 231

power of attorney A legal document authorizing someone to act on one's behalf. 461

pre-emptive right The right of current shareholders to purchase any new stocks the corporation issues before it is offered to the general public. 331

premium The amount of money a policyholder is charged for an insurance policy. 231

pre-nuptial agreement A documentary agreement between spouses before marriage. 460

prepayment penalty A charge imposed by the lender if the borrower pays off the loan early. 219

present value The current value for a future amount based on a certain interest rate and a certain time period; also referred to as *discounting.* 20

previous balance method A method of computing finance charges that gives no credit for payments made during the billing period. 185

price–earnings (P/E) ratio The price of a share of stock divided by the corporation's earnings per share of stocks outstanding over the last 12 months. 345

primary market A market in which an investor purchases financial securities, via an investment bank or other representative, from the issuer of those securities. 347

probate The legal procedure of proving a valid or invalid will. 457

property damage Insurance that covers damage to another's property, as by an automobile accident. 248

proxy A legal form that lists the issues to be decided at a shareholders' meeting and requests that shareholders transfer their voting rights to some individual or individuals. 330

pure risk A risk in which there is only a chance of loss; also called *insurable risk.* 232

rate cap A limit on the increases and decreases in the interest rate charged on an adjustable-rate mortgage. 218

rate of return The percentage of increase in the value of savings as a result of interest earned; also called *yield.* 130

rating territory The place of residence used to determine a person's automobile insurance premium. 250

record date The date on which a shareholder must be registered on the corporation's books in order to receive dividend payments. 331

refinancing The process of obtaining a new mortgage on a home to get a lower interest rate. 219

registered bond A bond that is registered in the owner's name by the issuing company. 370

registered coupon bond A bond that is registered for principal only, and not for interest. 370

Registered Retirement Savings Plan (RRSP) An investment vehicle that allows you to shelter your savings from income taxes. 436

reinvestment plan A service provided by an investment company in which shareholder income dividends and capital gain distributions are automatically reinvested to purchase additional shares of the fund. 413

replacement value A claim settlement method in which the insured receives the full cost of repairing or replacing a damaged or lost item. 244

retirement homes Private businesses that provide seniors various combinations of accommodation, support services, and personal care. 430

reverse annuity mortgage (RAM) A loan based on the equity in a home that provides elderly homeowners with tax-free income and is paid back with interest when the home is sold or the homeowner dies. 425

revolving credit A line of credit in which loans are made on a continuous basis and the borrower is billed periodically for at least partial payment. 147

rider (1) An addition of coverage to a standard insurance policy. 240; (2) A document attached to a policy that modifies its coverage. 270

risk Chance or uncertainty of loss; may also mean "the insured." 231

round lot One hundred shares or multiples of 100 shares of a particular stock. 351

safety deposit box A private storage area at a financial institution with maximum security for valuables. 49

secondary market A market for existing financial securities that are currently traded among investors. 347

securities exchange A marketplace where member brokers who represent investors meet to buy and sell securities. 348

segregated fund An investment alternative in the form of an annuity that is similar to a mutual fund but that is less risky as it provides a certain degree of insurance to the investor. 307

self-insurance The process of establishing a monetary fund to cover the cost of a loss. 232

selling short Selling stocks that have been borrowed from a brokerage firm and must be replaced at a later date. 356

serial bonds Bonds of a single issue that mature on different dates. 368

settlor The creator of a trust; also called the *grantor.* 462

short sell The practice of selling a borrowed stock in the hope of covering the sale by buying it at a lower price later. 397

simple interest Interest computed on the principal, excluding previously earned interest. 17

sinking fund A fund to which annual or semi-annual deposits are made for the purpose of redeeming a bond issue. 368

small-cap stock A stock issued by a company that has a capitalization of $150 million or less. 337

speculative investment A high-risk investment made in the hope of earning a relatively large profit in a short time. 299

speculative risk A risk in which there is a chance of either loss or gain. 232

stock split A procedure in which the shares of common stocks owned by existing shareholders are divided into a larger number of shares. 332

stop order An order to sell a particular stock at the next available opportunity after its market price reaches a specified amount. 350

strict liability A situation in which a person is held responsible for intentional or unintentional actions. 236

subordinated debenture An unsecured bond that gives bondholders a claim secondary to that of other designated bondholders with respect to both interest payments and assets. 367

suicide clause A provision stating that if the insured dies by suicide during the first two years the policy is in force, the death benefit will equal the amount of the premium paid. 269

take-home pay Earnings after deductions for taxes and other items; also called *disposable income.* 55

tax audit A detailed examination of your tax return by the Canada Revenue Agency. 103

tax credit An amount subtracted directly from the amount of taxes owing. 78

tax evasion The use of illegal actions to reduce one's taxes. 91

tax planning The use of legitimate methods to reduce one's taxes. 91

taxable capital gains Net gains from the sale of capital assets such as stocks, bonds, and real estate. One-half of net capital gains are taxable. 74

taxable income The net amount of income, after allowable deductions, on which income tax is computed. 74

technical analysis The idea that changes in investor sentiment are responsible for changes in trends, and that the value of a stock can be predicted by extrapolating price from historical patterns. 336

term deposit A deposit that is made for a specified term in exchange for a higher rate of return. Can be redeemed before maturity by earning a reduced rate of interest (paying a penalty). 129

term insurance Life insurance protection for a specified period of time; sometimes called *temporary life insurance.* 263

testamentary trust A trust established by the creator's will that becomes effective upon his or her death. 463

time value of money Increases in an amount of money as a result of interest earned. 6

title insurance Insurance that, during the mortgage term, protects the owner or the lender against financial loss resulting from future defects in the title and from other unforeseen property claims not excluded by the policy. 220

total debt service (TDS) ratio Your monthly shelter costs plus any outstanding debt payments and obligations as a percentage of your gross monthly income; a ratio used to determine the maximum affordable mortgage payment, mortgage amount, and home purchase price. 210

trust (1) A legal agreement that provides for the management and control of assets by one party for the benefit of another. 118; (2) A legal arrangement through which one's assets are held by a trustee. 462

trustee (1) A financially independent firm that acts as the bondholders' representative. 366; (2) A person or an institution that holds or manages property for the benefit of someone else under a trust agreement. 457

umbrella policy Supplementary personal liability coverage; also called a *personal catastrophe policy.* 240

uninsured motorist coverage Automobile insurance coverage for the cost of injuries to a person and members of his or her family caused by a driver with inadequate insurance or by a hit-and-run driver. 248

universal life A permanent life insurance policy that combines term insurance and investment elements. 264

values Ideas and principles that a person considers correct, desirable, and important. 4

variable-rate mortgage (VRM) A home loan with an interest rate that can change during the mortgage term due to changes in market interest rates; also called a *flexible-rate mortgage.* 218

vesting An employee's right to at least a portion of the benefits accrued under an employer pension plan, even if the employee leaves the company before retiring. 436

vicarious liability A situation in which a person is held legally responsible for the actions of another person. 236

voluntary medical payments Home insurance that pays the cost of minor accidental injuries on one's property. 240

whole life policy An insurance plan in which the policyholder pays a specified premium each year for as long as he or she lives; also called a *straight life policy,* a *cash-value life policy,* or an *ordinary life policy.* 264

will The legal declaration of a person's mind as to the disposition of his or her property after death. 456

yield The rate of return earned by an investor who holds a bond for a stated period of time. 382

yield to maturity A yield calculation that takes into account the relationships among a bond's maturity value, the time to maturity, the current price, and the dollar amount of interest. 383

zero-coupon bond A bond that is sold at a price far below its face value, makes no annual or semi-annual interest payments, and is redeemed for its face value at maturity. 370

zoning laws Restrictions on how the property in an area can be used. 213

Index